BASICS OF LEAN

Operations Management Principles

WITH APPLICATIONS FROM MANUFACTURING, SERVICE, & HEALTHCARE INDUSTRIES

Nesa L'abbé Wu, Joann Parrinder, Brandon Yu

Cover image © Shutterstock, Inc.

Kendall Hunt
publishing company

www.kendallhunt.com
Send all inquiries to:
4050 Westmark Drive
Dubuque, IA 52004-1840

Copyright © 2014 by Nesa L'abbé Wu, Joann Parrinder, Brandon Yu

ISBN 978-1-4652-8602-4

Kendall Hunt Publishing Company has the exclusive rights to reproduce this work, to prepare derivative works from this work, to publicly distribute this work, to publicly perform this work and to publicly display this work.

All rights reserved. No part of this publication may be reproduced, stored in a retrieval system, or transmitted, in any form or by any means, electronic, mechanical, photocopying, recording, or otherwise, without the prior written permission of the copyright owner.

Printed in the United States of America
10 9 8 7 6 5 4 3 2 1

Table of Contents

Chapter 4 Process Planning

Chapter 5 Workplace Organization and Standardized Work Procedures

Chapter 6 Work Design and Measurement

Chapter 7 Logistics of Location Analysis

Chapter 8 Facilities Planning – Layout and Capacity Planning

Chapter 13 Quality Management

Preface

Using the approach of the idea development lifecycle process, as explained in Chapter 2, this text covers the basics of lean operations management principles. In each chapter emphasis is placed on the concepts and tools of lean management as follows:

- In Chapter 3, the product/service design chapter, you learn about lean product development tools such as quality function deployment, computer aided design, rapid prototyping, group technology, and simultaneous or concurrent engineering.
- In Chapter 4, the process planning chapter, you are introduced to the spaghetti chart or diagram and value stream mapping, a tool that is used to efficiently re-engineer ineffective processes. Real life examples both from the manufacturing industry and the service industry (insurance company, health care industry, and hospitality industry) are detailed and worked out.
- In Chapter 5, the workplace organization and standardized work procedures chapter, you learn how to successfully implement the 5Ss of workplace organization and change management. These implementation concepts are illustrated with real life examples.
- In Chapter 6, the work design and measurement chapter, you study how to set standards for both direct and indirect work, the basis for any lean implementation plan: if you cannot measure results, you cannot claim improvement. Here you learn that the focus of setting standards and measuring work is not to encourage maximizing output of operations without regard for its effect on the total system. Rather, you learn that setting standards and developing lean standard work methods are necessary to balance the workload for each operation to the actual demand rate or takt time.
- In Chapter 7, the logistics of location analysis chapter, you are introduced to some of the sound techniques for choosing the best location for the firm in order to minimize both tangible and intangible costs.
- In Chapter 8, the layout and capacity planning chapter, you will covervarious layout expansion techniques, including the lean spine expansion design, together with various types of layouts. Emphasis is placed on what makes a layout lean, as GT or cellular layouts are discussed and the principles of a lean warehouse are explained.
- In Chapter 9, the forecasting chapter, you learn about the sales forecasting system that requires, for a forecast to be useful, that it be available on time, so it can be reviewed and finalized by the operations manager. Here you are also exposed to some simple, yet powerful forecasting techniques like the moving averages, exponential smoothing, and regression analysis.
- In Chapter 10, the production planning and control systems chapter, you are taught how to plan and control the flow of materials into, through, and out of the production system in such a manner that an optimal amount of value is added through the transformation process of the system. Here you learn about aggregate planning, master production scheduling, material requirement planning, and manufacturing resource planning.
- In Chapter 11, the inventory management chapter, you learn how one of the eight major wastes we find in our systems, namely inventories, can be managed and controlled through sound inventory systems and lean inventory control management techniques.
- In Chapter 12, the daily job scheduling and control chapter, you are introduced to the daily routine of scheduling jobs, including job sequencing rules, queuing management, and lean shop floor control using the theory of constraints of optimized production technology (OPT) and the just-in-time (JIT) Japanese system. This chapter ends with a discussion of visual controls, another lean technique to schedule and monitor the timely and quality execution of jobs.
- In Chapter 13, the quality management chapter, we finish with the study of quality management of the total system from design to product delivery. Here you learn about company-wide quality management, quality control techniques, the Japanese system of quality management, and the various tools to study and correct quality problems. Finally we go beyond lean with a discussion of lean Six Sigma and designing for Six Sigma.

No operations management text is suitable for business students unless it covers the whole gamut of industries that use lean operations management principles and techniques: the manufacturing industry and the service industry (the banking, hospitality, insurance, health care industries, to name a few).

In health care a system known as "pay-for-performance" or "P4P" is critical to improving the quality of patient care. This Act represents attempts by the U.S. government and private enterprise to require healthcare institutions to meet certain criteria that will increase the quality of care, while at the same time reducing health care costs. Under this Act, hospitals and health care systems are eligible to receive higher Medicare and medical reimbursements if they can demonstrate certain types of operational efficiencies and productivity improvements. Increased operational efficiency and healthcare productivity gains can be achieved through focusing on health care enterprise integration, pursuing a more integrated approach to the healthcare supply chain system for managing activities along the entire chain, and adapting operations management techniques to the health care industry.

Applying production/operations management techniques to the healthcare industry is not a new trend. It dates back to the early years of scientific management when, in 1912, Frank Gilbreth observed that healthcare posed a unique challenge to industrial engineers. From the Purdue University Library's archives we have learned that Frank Gilbreth addressed the audience at an annual convention of nursing school superintendents. In his speech he said that he had always thought of hospitals as a "Happiness Factory" and asked the audience whether standardization could help them to become more efficient. Now, more than a century later, this pioneer's words are even more relevant as efficiency and cost control have become major players in the health care delivery system because of the P4P Act. Health care must be optimized for the benefit of the providers as well as the patients.

Because there is a need for adapting operations management techniques to the health care industry and because we see continuous efforts in health care to improve their processes using lean operations management techniques, the authors have committed themselves to address and illustrate examples of this industry in the text. Experts in the field have contributed significantly by bringing forward real life applications of health care system improvements. We wish to thank the following contributors for their efforts:

Dr. Anita S. Craig, DO, contributed section 8.3 of Chapter 4, "Improving Health Care Processes via Value Stream Mapping."

Mrs. Mayble E. Craig, MS, RN, contributed two sections in the text: section 5.3 of chapter 5, "Hospital: to reduce time spent on documentation", and section 3.5 of chapter 12, "The Case of Improving the Patient Flow in the Emergency Department".

A significant contribution was received from Mr. Ron Crabtree, president of MetaOps, who provided the data for section 8.2 of Chapter 4, "Improving the Process of Preparing Insurance Claims." We wish to thank him too.

The authors are dedicating this textbook to their families, from whom they received support and encouragement throughout its development.

Nesa L'abbé Wu, PhD

Joann Parrinder, MSIE

Brandon Yu

Chapter 1

INTRODUCTION

1. THE PRODUCTIVE SYSTEM

Just as your life is a journey, so is your idea for a product or service. It is conceived and born, well-developed and matured to be produced, retired, and, of course, dies at its end-of-life. This journey involves a transformation from a dream to a prototype to an approved productive output output—called a ***product*** or ***service***. The **productive system** (Figure 1.1) is a man-made system, a *process,* a set of procedures, activities, tasks, or operations that transform inputs—**resources**—into desired, valuable outputs—**products or services**. We are going to discuss what makes up the productive system and how one manages and controls its performance, namely, **Production Operations Management.**

1.1 System's Input

The productive system's inputs consist of people, equipment, facilities, materials and supplies, energy, capital, information, and time.

Human resources or **people** include hourly workers, supervisors, managers, directors, staff personnel, executives, and professionals. Everyone involved in the transformation system performs a task that is necessary to increase the value of other inputs, while generating valuable products or services. As more technology is introduced in our productive systems, the labor force composition changes, such as in the manufacturing industry, where machines and automation have taken over much of the production and assembly processes , thus shrinking the labor needed in an area requiring manual labor, but freeing people to solve problems in other areas.

As a result of mechanization and automation in the manufacturing industry, more people shift from the manufacturing sector of the productive system to the service sector of that system where manual operations have traditionally dominated. However, mechanization and automation have also gradually taken place in the expanding service sector. While human resources have been replaced by machines and new technology in some industries, new industries are continuously developing a greater variety of new products and services that are becoming available to our society.

Equipment in a productive system includes machines, material handling systems, storage systems, computing and communication systems, and vehicles.

Facilities are structures and land. Production facilities and equipment provide the material means to the transformation processes and their type determines the level of technology.

Materials input in the manufacturing industry form the basis for the conversion process from raw materials to finished goods. Many service industries also require a certain type of materials input, such as foodstuffs in restaurants, medication in hospitals, lubricants and spare parts in automotive garages, and postage stamps in post offices.

Supplies are not usually part of the final product, but are needed to carry out the transformation process, such as office supplies, toilet paper, and packing material.

Energy input commonly includes electricity, fuel, gas and some less widely used forms such as solar energy, ocean wave energy, wind energy, thermo-nuclear energy, geo-thermal energy, and hydraulic energy. Energy input may be consumed directly or indirectly during the transformation process. In a hydro-electric power plant, the hydraulic energy is directly consumed during the transformation process to produce its output: electric energy. In aluminum production the electrical energy is directly consumed by the transformation process to produce aluminum alloy. But in most transformation processes, energy input is consumed indirectly in such tasks as driving the equipment and machinery, lighting the factory, or providing or reducing heat in the working areas.

Information input is important for a productive system. It facilitates the coordination of the production/operations processes and provides the bases for making management decisions. In the information-service related industries, such as newspaper and magazine publishing companies, TV and radio stations, wire services, or detective services, the information input is directly consumed by the transformation process as the productive system generates its desired output.

If inputs are not provided on **time,** then the transformation system will not generate goods and services on time to compete in world markets. Thus the company will not survive.

1.2 Transformation Process

The transformation process is the heart of any productive system. During this process, the less valuable and often disorganized input resources are transformed, or converted, into a more desirable and valuable output—products or services. The Productive System consists of several transformation processes, such as: product planning, process planning and control, work design and human resource management, capacity planning, facilities planning, maintenance control, production scheduling, materials management, inventory control, and quality control. A transformation process can be judged by its **capacity, efficiency, effectiveness, and flexibility.**

The ***capacity*** of the system is determined by how large a facility, how much equipment, labor, capital, and energy is available, and how it is all utilized to generate the desired kind and amount of output. Of major concern is whether the capacity is satisfactory for the objectives set forward by management and whether these capacities are properly distributed or assigned to generate desired products and services on an ongoing daily basis.

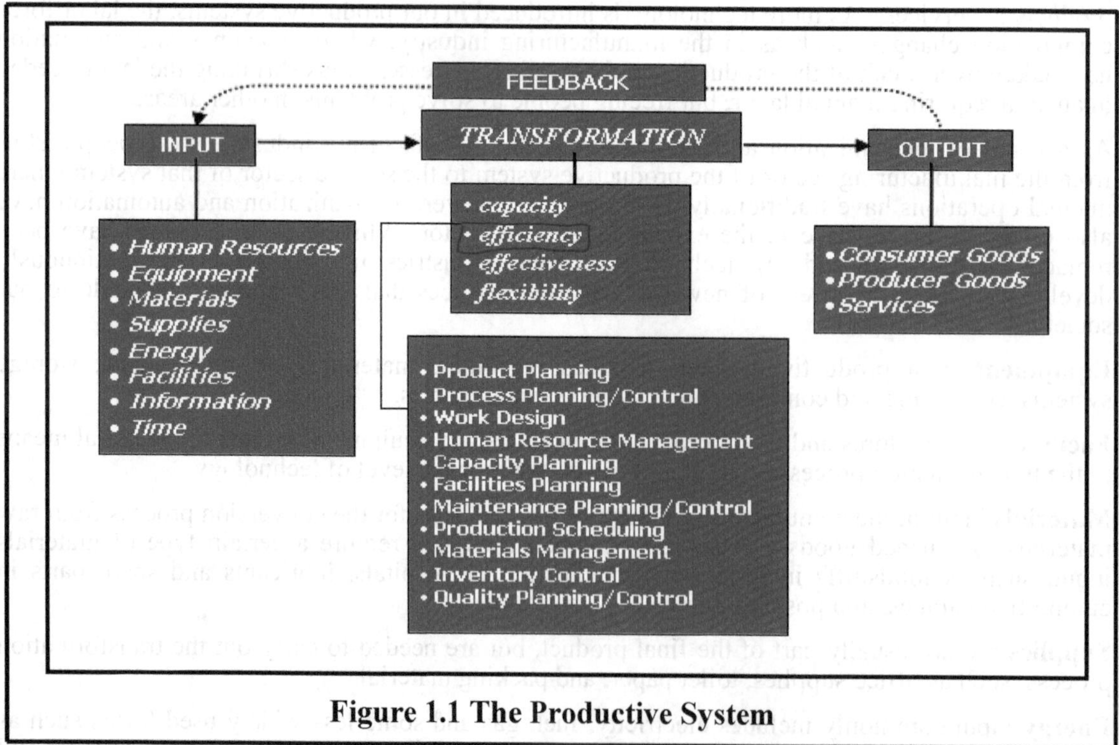

Figure 1.1 The Productive System

The ***efficiency*** of the transformation process can be measured by its output per unit of input. In this sense, efficiency is synonymous with productivity. A productive system must strive to utilize all its inputs, such as labor, materials and supplies, capital, and energy, in the most productive way. This can be accomplished through proper product and service design, process planning, work design and human resource management, capacity planning, facilities planning, production and maintenance scheduling, materials management, inventory planning and control, product and process quality management, and the efficient management of the supply chain as a whole. These activities will be discussed in detail in this text, but for introductory purposes, they should be defined.

The **product (or service) design planning** function is concerned with the conversion of the general specifications of a product into its technical specifications in an optimal way. Later, we will discuss the many ways to improve productivity of the product design function through computer aided design (CAD) and group technology (GT).

The function of **process planning** is to select and to design the right tools, the right methods, and the right sequence for the production processes, consistent with technical specifications generated by the product design function.

Work design and human resource management are concerned with determining the best way to integrate labor in the production/operations system. The work design function includes work study and measurement for determining manpower requirements, for evaluating plant or department efficiency, or for calculating productivity indexes. This function is also concerned with the man-machine interface, workplace layout and environmental conditions.

Capacity planning determines the size of the facility, equipment, and labor force, while **facilities planning** is concerned with the most efficient location and layout of the production facilities, warehouses, distribution, and service centers.

Production scheduling dictates when production and service activities will take place. However, to maintain the production system, the **maintenance planning and control function** is necessary to keep the existing equipment and facilities functioning as originally designed in terms of quality and quantity.

The correct amounts of materials, supplies, in-process inventory, and finished goods to be located at specific places and at specific times are determined by the **materials management and inventory planning and control function.**

The ***effectiveness*** of the transformation process is concerned with doing the right thing, producing the right set of outputs, and achieving the objectives of the organization in a timely fashion.

The ***flexibility*** is the most recently developed characteristic for judging a transformation system. Can the system easily and quickly be changed to produce other outputs, or quickly adjust to increases or decreases in demand? Recent changes in layout, machinery, and equipment (from specialized to general purpose equipment, e.g. robots, and flexible manufacturing systems) have increased the flexibility of many transformation systems.

1.3 System's Output

The transformation process of a productive system may generate products, services, or both. Our manufacturing industry produces consumer and producer goods. **Consumer goods**, such as food products, clothing, cars, personal computers, cell phones, books, and toys, are intended for direct consumption. When designing and producing such goods, companies are concerned about their functional needs, the aesthetic needs, and in some case the need for maintenance service to maintain these products. **Producer goods**—such as machines, material handling systems, computers, and robots—are concerned with their functional characteristics, such as safety, output rate, reliability, flexibility, maintainability, etc. Besides products, consumers and producers need a variety of **services**, such as transportation, health services, child care services, entertainment, safety and protective services, insurance, financial services, and consulting services.

1.4 Examples of Productive Systems

A **manufacturing plant** is a productive system that transforms such inputs as labor, raw materials, supplies, and energy into valuable finished goods through a variety of processes. The transformation takes place through the use of facilities, equipment, tools, labor, materials, goods, and knowledge.

The inputs of a **health care system** consist of doctors, nurses, staff, facilities, medical equipment, supplies, and materials. It is a service business that renders health care and provides needed services to its patients.

The **banking industry** provides financial services such as deposits, checking accounts, loans, and safekeeping. Its inputs consist of tellers, accountants, computers, data transmission and communication equipment, facilities, energy, supplies, notes, and cash. For this industry, examples of "transformation" are cash into investments and investments into cash, among others.

An **engineering or management consulting firm** provides professional consulting service to its clients. Its output can be oral consultation and/or written reports. The skills and knowledge of its consultants are the major inputs to a consulting service firm. Thus, in these types of firms knowledge and skills are transformed into professional consulting services. Other service systems are restaurants, universities, insurance companies, theaters, retail stores, child care centers, and government agencies.

2. ROLE OF PRODUCTION/OPERATIONS MANAGEMENT

The top management of an organization (see Figure 1.2) sets long-term objectives for the company, called the **corporate strategies**. These strategies are driven by the corporate mission and are based on capacity and resources available to management. They are influenced by economic, social, political, technological, and market forecasting by the level of technology, labor skills, customer needs, and by various business opportunities. Best-in-class companies' strategies are driven by value, quality, customer satisfaction, integrity, honesty, and character. In the global market place corporate strategies must include global strategies that are based on political risk, currency risk, social cost factors, brand fit, and others.

The long-term objectives of an organization are normally accomplished through the cooperation of three basic functions: the marketing function, the finance function, and the production/operations function. The **marketing function** is responsible for meeting or filling a demand for the products or service of the productive system. The **finance function** is concerned with the generation and control of short- and long-term capital for the acquisition of the inputs and the distribution of the outputs of the productive system. The **production/operations function** is concerned with the efficient design, planning, and control of the productive system. The role of production/operations management is to manage the production/operations function of the organization in conjunction with the marketing and the finance functions.

Production/Operations management deals with the long term **systems planning and design function** (2 to 10 years planning horizon), the medium term **aggregate planning** function (6 to 24 months period), the shorter term **master production scheduling** and **materials requirement planning** and **control function** (1 to 5 weeks), and the daily **shop floor control** (scheduling and sequencing).

The technical performance and operational characteristics of the transformation system directly result from long-term decisions made when designing and planning the system. The **systems planning and design** function includes product design, process design, work design and measurement, capacity planning, facilities layout, maintenance planning, and the design of management information systems.

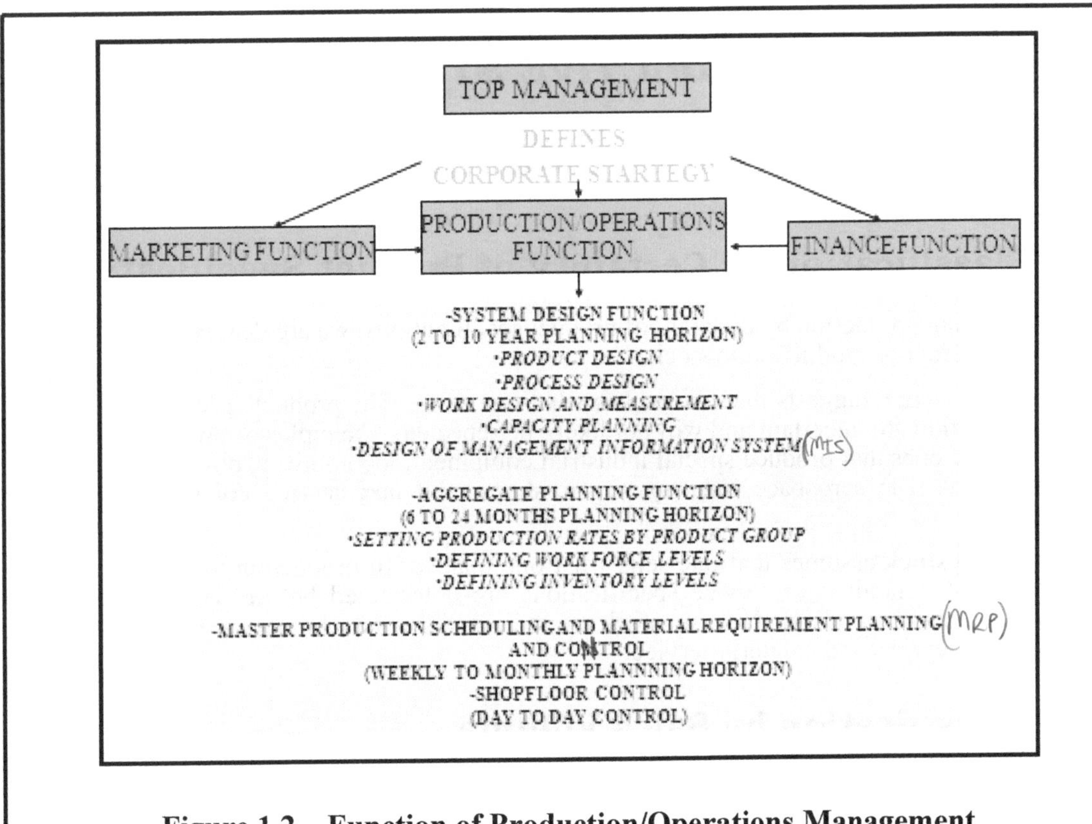

Figure 1.2 Function of Production/Operations Management

Aggregate planning sets production rates for each product group or for various broad categories of products for the intermediate term of 6 to 24 months. Here production/operations management is concerned with specifying the optimal combination of production rates and workforce and inventory levels. Inputs to the aggregate plan are forecasts, customer orders, and service needs.

Finally, the **master production scheduling** and the **materials requirement planning** and **control** functions deal with the weekly to monthly operation of the transformation system. Actual orders are now assigned to production centers, production is being scheduled, and materials are assigned and released to various work centers. This short-term scheduling system is constrained by process sequencing, available short-term capacity, available inventory and materials, and required maintenance.

Products and goods are not only managed within one company, but also need to be managed throughout the supply chain. **Supply Chain Management** (SCM) integrates the management of goods and services, from supply to demand management, within and across all companies involved. It deals with supplier relationships, manufacturers of goods and supplies, distribution centers, warehousing, supply/demand planning, transportation management, customer and supplier loyalty, and others. Because all companies deal with suppliers and customers, all companies, big or small, deal with supply chain management. Supply chain management (SCM) is the driving force behind the efficient and effective management of all global business interactions.

3. *TYPES OF PRODUCTIVE SYSTEMS*

Productive systems, regardless of whether they are service or manufacturing systems, can be classified by the **certainty of product specifications**, the **sales volume**, and the **make-up of the product**.

3.1 Classification by Certainty of Product Specifications

When classifying production by certainty of product specifications, we are dealing with either production to order or production to stock.

Production to order suggests that one makes what one sells. The product specifications of this type of production are uncertain and will not likely be repeated. Examples of production to order systems are the ones that produce special industrial equipment, locomotives, power generators, or dental products. The aerospace industry, repair shops, and taxi service companies are other examples.

Production to stock assumes that one sells what one makes. In production to stock industries, the details of the product or service specifications are determined before receiving customer orders. Examples of goods produced to stock are radio and TV sets, home appliances, hardware, scheduled bus service, and cafeteria service.

3.2 Classification by Sales Volume

By sales volume, production either falls under continuous flow production, intermittent production, or discontinuous production.

Continuous flow production is synonymous with production line, flow shop, or mass production and exhibits the following characteristics:

1. Large volume and small variety of products
2. Production lines are used
3. Production equipment capacities tend to be more balanced
4. Special purpose machines are used
5. Jobs are highly simplified and standardized
6. Direct/indirect labor ratio is low
7. Inventory level is low
8. Preventive maintenance is essential
9. Space utilization is high
10. The production cycle time is short

Examples of continuous flow production are paper mills, the food processing industry, most watchmakers, TV, radio and home appliances manufacturing companies, many automobile assembly plants, refineries, and institutional feeding systems (prisons, armed forces, etc.).

Intermittent production is synonymous with batch production. Some job shops produce a seemingly endless succession of different small-scale parts that many companies assemble into machines and other products. These are the job shops that typically manufacture auto parts and machine parts.

The following characteristics typify intermittent production:

1. Most parts are made in small lots
2. Similar equipment is grouped
3. Workloads in different departments or machine centers are unbalanced
4. General purpose machines are usually used
5. Production lot sizes are essential in controlling production cost

Examples of job shops are auto parts production centers, machine parts production centers, bakeries, and general education centers.

Discontinuous production includes jobbing, slow-movers, or projects. These types of productive systems are designed to produce only a few units of each product or only a limited number of small jobs. Discontinuous production differs from intermittent production essentially in the size and the scope of the job it can handle. Examples are missile or spaceship construction, the building of a bridge, motion-picture production, tutoring, and special education systems.

3.3 Classification by Make-up of the Product.

Discrete-part production and process production fall under the classification of the productive system by the make-up of the product.

Discrete-part production generates end products that are made up of discrete components. We normally deal with parts production that goes into sub-assemblies, which in turn become parts of a major product assembly. This type of production requires sophisticated control techniques and a high level of human participation. Here we usually find many alternatives of production processes and more choices of inputs for discrete-part production.

Most of the manufacturing goods are produced by discrete-part production systems, including the production of home appliances and automobiles.

Process production generates end products that cannot be disassembled and identified by components. There are no or very few alternate production processes and inputs for these processes. Examples are refineries, paper mills, and food processing.

4. HISTORICAL NOTES

Operations management techniques and quantitative techniques have been used since ancient times. The Egyptians used them in the construction of the pyramids. Fifteenth century Venetians used an assembly line type of operation in assembling ships. Simulation, a very popular quantitative technique, has been used in war games since 3,000 BC. Based upon Von Reisswitz' book of rules for military strategy models, war gaming was used as a training aid by nineteenth century Russian and German armies. Today, the U.S. Navy uses sophisticated models called simulators. Many quantitative methods and procedures, however, have their roots and applications in the field of production. Important pioneers and developments that led to the present status of production/operations management (POM) in business and industry are chronicled below.

4.1 Industrial Revolution

Even though POM techniques have been used since ancient times by the Egyptians, the Venetians, and many others, the systematic development and use of POM principles did not begin until the Industrial Revolution. This period is characterized by the birth of the factory system and James Watt's invention of the steam engine (1764) to power these factories. This was the age of mechanization with the substitution of handwork by machines that resulted in the replacement of the in-house manufacturing systems by the mechanized factory systems.

.Adam Smith (1776) -Division of Labor-

In his book *The Wealth of Nations*, Smith points out the effects of division of labor. It increases production output and worker dexterity, prevents loss of time in handling, and encourages the invention of machinery to facilitate individual tasks. His teaching and philosophy laid the foundation for the future developments in work simplification, process planning, and work measurement.

.Eli Whitney (1798) -Interchangeable Parts-

At his musket factory, Eli Whitney introduced the use of interchangeable parts rather than tailoring ammunition and parts to each individual musket. This paved the way for fast assembly of multi-component products.

.The Soho Engineering Foundry (1800s)

According to Professor Claude George, this English-based foundry was more than a century ahead of its time. In this foundry, sophisticated production/operations management techniques were used. Some of these were standardization of parts design, production planning, work study and work incentives, employee training and welfare programs, plant location and layout analysis, and cost control and cost accounting practices.

4.2 Scientific Management

.Charles Babbage (1832) -Different Pay Scales-

In his book *On the Economy of Machines and Manufactures*, Charles Babbage promoted the use of scientific methods to analyze business problems. He suggested time study, research and development activities, economic analysis, and other operations management techniques. Many of Babbage's principles were put into practice within 75 years after his book was published. He agreed with Smith that specialization yields higher productivity and carried the notion one step further. Based on an analysis of pin manufacturing he suggested different basic pay scales for different types of labor.

.Frederick Taylor (1910—1914) -Father of Scientific Management-

Unlike Smith and Babbage, Frederick Taylor worked through the ranks from laborer to management. He was a keen observer who put scientific management to work, and he is often referred to as the father of scientific management. Taylor proposed and applied the following four principles and duties of management:

1. Management must determine and employ the scientific method to do any type of work
2. Management must scientifically select, train, and help in the development of workers
3. Management is responsible for developing team spirit and hearty cooperation between workers and management
4. Management must ensure the division of work between workers and management

As a result of these principles of production management, Taylor was largely responsible for a number of new professions, including methods engineering, work measurement, experimental psychology, personnel, industrial relations, and planning and control.

Contemporaries of Taylor are Frank and Lillian Gilbreth and Henry L. Gantt.

.Frank Gilbreth (1911) -Motion Study-

Frank Gilbreth, who was mainly interested in improving work methods, stressed the application of the principles of motion economy to the minutest details of tasks. Regarded by many as the father of motion study, he established the original list of micro motions called therbligs (Gilbreth spelled backwards), but was never interested in establishing any manual or universal standard data. However, a number of people and groups of people have used his pioneering work to set such standards, including Western Electric, Westinghouse, DuPont, and General Motors, among others.

.Lillian Gilbreth (1911) -Industrial Psychology-

In her book *The Psychology of Management*, Lillian Gilbreth is concerned about the human factor in business organizations. She is well known for her pioneering work in industrial psychology and human relations and thus gained the well-deserved title of the "first lady of management."

.Henry L. Gantt (1913) -Job Scheduling-

Like Lillian Gilbreth, Henry Gantt (who initially worked for Taylor) placed considerable emphasis on the human element in management's attitude towards labor. He embraced the concept of the personnel department as a necessary entity of scientific management. He is now more known for his job scheduling techniques and the invention of the Gantt chart used in project management.

.Henry Ford (1913) -Moving Assembly Line in the Automotive Industry-

The first known assembly line was used by the Venetians in the fifteenth century in the assembling of ships. Oliver Evans in 1783 used an assembly line in a flour mill. The first modern assembly line was used in the United States around the 1870's in the packing houses of Cincinnati. Hogs were hoisted at a 24-inch interval onto an overhead moving rail. The first stations of operators were the executioners, followed by the scalding station before the scrapers and shavers took over. After the disemboweling station, the carcass was moved for final cleaning.

Standardization of parts, interchangeable parts, and specialization of labor were a necessity when Henry Ford introduced his moving automobile assembly line in 1913. Instead of spending over 12 hours on the assembly of an auto chassis, the work now was done in one minute and a half. This significant technological breakthrough, together with the improvement in labor productivity, fueled consumerism in the U.S. economy.

4.3 Quantitative Techniques to Plan and Control Production

Throughout the early 1900s, but especially during and after World War II, operations research techniques and quantitative methods developed at a rapid pace. Many of these techniques found use in production/operations management (Figure 1.3) and many functional areas of business to plan and control production and the distribution of goods and services. Some of these important developments follow.

.P.O. Johannsen and A.K. Erlang (1907) -Waiting Line Analysis-

Queuing problems have been researched actively since 1907. The first paper on the subject was published that year by P.O. Johannsen, entitled "Waiting Times and Number of Calls," in the *P.O. Electrical Engineers Journal*. In 1909, Erlang developed and applied queuing theory to problems encountered by the Copenhagen Telephone Company. His first paper on congestion in telephone exchanges appeared the same year, and during the next 20 years, Erlang published a series of articles on queuing theory. Erlang is credited with developing the theory of Poisson and exponential distributions, both bases for the early development of queuing theory and models used in industry.

.Frederick W. Lanchester (1914) -Operations Research-

Lanchester, an Englishman, approached military problems quantitatively in an attempt to predict the outcome of a battle as a function of the numerical strength of the warriors and their firepower. He tested his model against Admiral Nelson's battle plan of Trafalgar.

Thus he proceeded as an operations researcher by first designing a model and then testing it against a known real-world situation in order to validate it.

.F.W. Harris (1915—1927) -Inventory Model-

The economic order quantity (EOQ) model, suggested and derived by F.W. Harris in 1915, was the first inventory model. R.H. Wilson made the EOQ model popular in the 1920s when, as a consultant, he applied it to inventories of many companies. Other early contributors to the field of inventory control are H.S. Owen (1925), B. Cooper (1926), and W.A. Mueller (1927).

.Walter Shewhart (1924—1931) -Quality Control-

Walter Shewhart introduced sampling techniques and statistical tables for quality control. His co-workers were H.F. Dodge and H.G. Romig, who developed the now much-used Dodge and Romig Sampling Tables.

.W.Leontieff (1930's-depression period) -Input/Output Control-

W.Leontieff, a Harvard professor, developed the first linear model (called an input/output model) that represented the entire United States economy.

.L.H.C. Tippett (1935) -Work sampling-

Tippett introduced statistical work sampling theory. His work provided industry with a means of setting standards for work time and idle time of indirect work activities.

.L.V. Kantorovich, F.L. Hitchcock, T.C. Koopmans (1939, 1940s) -Transportation Model-

In 1939, L.V. Kantorovich identified a host of problems closely related to the transportation problem. Proposals made by this Russian professor were neglected during the next two decades. In 1941 F.L. Hitchcock was the first to formulate the standard form of the transportation problem in his paper "Optimum Utilization of the Transportation System." The classical transportation problem, often called the Hitchcock-Koopmans transportation problem, finds many applications in facilities planning and the distribution of goods and services.

.George B. Dantzig (1947) -Simplex Method-

After World War II, the U.S. military developed a model that would define optimal coordination of the nation's energy resources in the event of total war. This large-scale model could be solved only by using a scientific programming technique. In the summer of 1947 Dantzig developed the simplex method to derive the optimal feasible solution to that model. Since then, the simplex method of linear programming has been used widely by manufacturing and service industries to solve a variety of resource allocation problems.

.Booz, Allen and Hamilton (late 1950s) -Project Management-

In 1958, the Navy's Special Project Office, with the aid of the Booz, Allen and Hamilton consulting firm and the Lockheed Missile System Division, developed the project evaluation and review technique (PERT). PERT methodology shortened by two years the time estimated for completion of the engineering and development phases of the Polaris project. In 1956, the Integrated Engineering Control group of DuPont de Nemours and Company developed the management planning technique called the critical path method (CPM). This network model scheduled the activities of their engineering design and construction. Though both techniques were developed independently, they are very similar in what they are capable of doing in terms of scheduling and control of large projects.

.A. Charnes and W.W. Cooper (1961—1968) -Goal Programming-

A. Charnes and W.W. Cooper introduced one of the latest operations research techniques, goal programming (1961), and Y. Ijiri brought it into a usable form. In 1968 Contini considered goal programming under conditions of uncertainty, while in that same year I. Jaaskelainen applied it to aggregate production planning.

4.4 Computerization and Systems Approach in the Productive System

With the advent of faster and more powerful computers, the use of simulation techniques, introduced in the late 1950's for the analysis of complex business systems, has become almost routine. Instead of simplifying complex business systems and solving them with known optimal analytical techniques, systems are described as exactly as possible and then analyzed by the use of computer simulation.

.Scheduling and Inventory Management -the 1970s-

When computers were introduced to aid in production/operations management in the early 1970s, most of the applications were directed towards production scheduling and inventory control. Joseph Orlicky of IBM and production control consultant Oliver Wight pioneered the development of computer-based materials management systems, called MRP (material requirement planning) systems. The computer is essential in the planning and ordering of materials for assembled production because of the massive amount of data that needs to be managed in a timely manner in order to ensure the meeting of a specific end-item schedule.

MRP has not proven to be as momentous a leap forward as was scientific management (SM), but there are some similarities: both SM and MRP are strictly American innovations and, despite vastly improved worldwide communications networks, MRP has been slow to cross the oceans. The United States is most proficient in job-lot-manufacturing management because MRP was invented and nurtured here. Japan is most proficient in repetitive manufacturing management because the just-in-time (JIT) system was developed there. The European industry employs little Material Requirement Planning or Just-In-Time techniques.

The 1970s were characterized by a tremendous development of various computer software packages, such as production scheduling, job shop scheduling, project management, maintenance scheduling, layout planning, and forecasting.

.Modern Systems Approach

The last four decades have been characterized by a systems approach to solving real management problems, rather than the computation of narrowly defined mathematical problems. The systems approach in the enterprise suggests that a decision made by one function of the organization has an immediate effect on all other functions of that organization. Enterprise resource planning (ERP) systems integrate decision support programs of various functional areas, using a common data base. With ERP systems, e-commerce, internets, and extranets companies can now transfer information anywhere in the world to make marketing, financial, and operational decisions using common data and information.

Many of the computerized planning, scheduling, and controlling procedures, including the systems approach to management decision making, are now also being applied in the service industry and public and non-profit organizations.

4.5 Automation and the Factory of the Future

Automation has penetrated not only the production industry, but also the service industry. In manufacturing companies, automation is found in the form of fixed automation and programmable automation. Automation of office and clerical procedures has been made possible by widely adopted data processing systems.

Computer integrated manufacturing (CIM) is the key to the "factory of the future," in which everything from design to inventory, to assembly, to delivery is controlled by a central computerized "brain." Computer integrated manufacturing includes **computer aided design** (CAD) and **computer aided manufacturing** (CAM), and has **flexible automation** and **robots** for manufacturing and assembly purposes. It includes **machine vision**, **machine intelligence** and a common language to allow programmable tools to communicate with each other, to regulate the speed of assembly and processing, and to signal the need for repair. **Automated guided vehicles** (AGV), or driverless remote-controlled wheeled vehicles, are used to transport components in the factory of the future. These AGVs are guided by radio signals or electric paths in the floor and can be as small as a wheelbarrow or as large as a forklift.

Computer aided design (CAD) employs the computer in the design and drawing of new parts and products via the use of an electronic drafting table, a computer monitor, a keyboard, function buttons, and a computer. **Computer aided manufacturing** (CAM) is the process of converting a computer generated design to the manufacturing stage with machine tools directed by a computer.

Programmable factory machinery that can be adapted to numerous related tasks is called **flexible automation**, as opposed to "fixed automation," in which one tool performs the same task over and over. A flexible machining center, for instance, can be controlled by a computer to perform dozens of metal forming or grinding tasks with automatic tool changes.

A multi-functional re-programmable device used for a variety of manufacturing and assembly operations is called a **robot**. The robots being developed today approximate the physical movements of a person, and when sight and intelligence are added, a robot is able to perform most of the tedious, repetitive, and dangerous jobs now done by human workers. A robot can be programmed from a remote computer command center to do an endless array of tasks.

Machine intelligence is sophisticated computer software that allows a machine to choose among various options. A so-called "smart" machine, for instance, is able to diagnose an automobile or any other product's service problem and recommend a repair method.

Using cameras and other **machine vision systems**, robots and other "smart" machines are able to distinguish between different parts, to inspect and reject flawed components, and "see" if a person or vehicle is in the way. An AGV with machine vision may for example be the repair cart of the future. As such it will use its "sight" to guide it to a broken machine, identify the faulty part, and repair it from a self-contained spare parts bin.

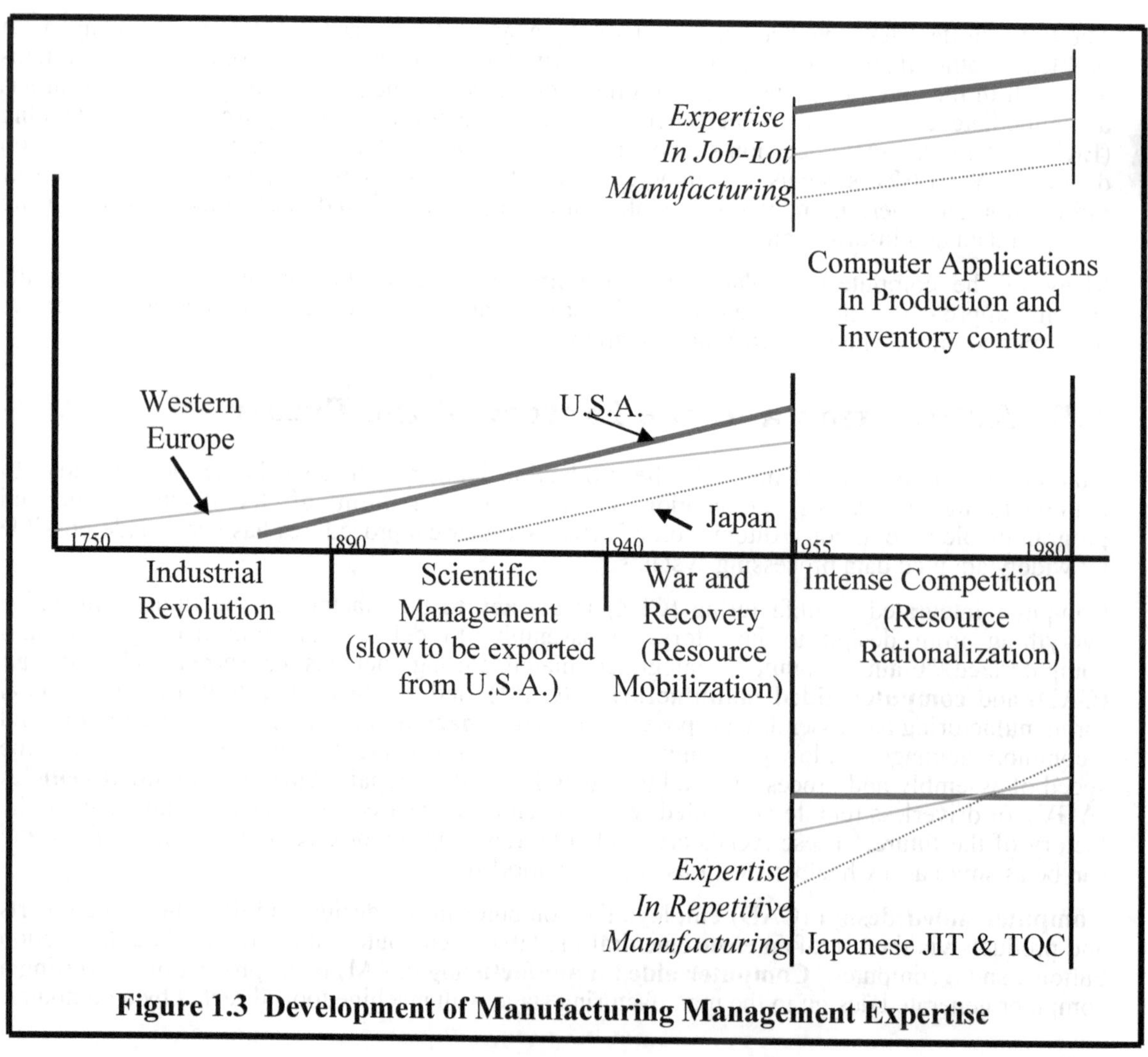

Figure 1.3 Development of Manufacturing Management Expertise

4.6 Lean and Agile Operations – The Last Three Decades

Lean management is the newest approach to managing operations and is based on the principles of elimination of waste, while maximizing quality and flexibility. Its fundamental objective is to provide perfect value to the customer through a perfect value creation from order entry to final shipment.

Operating in a lean way is a business philosophy that starts with the voice of the customer and focuses on the elimination of waste throughout all aspects of a business. By using certain principles, waste is identified and then through lean practices these wastes are eliminated or reduced on an on-going basis. Lean practices strive towards continuous improvement in all areas of a business organization: product development, the workplace, and all functions of the organization, including the shop floor.

The journey to "lean" started in the early 1980s with the Toyota production system (TPS) and the Toyota just-in-time (JIT) system. According to the president of Toyota Motors, Taiichi Ohno, TPS is a total management system in which people are expected to fully utilize the facilities and machines to satisfy customer requirements while working towards absolute elimination of waste.

Thus Toyota manufacturing initiated lean philosophies in their Toyota production system. The principles of the Toyota production system have become the foundation of today's lean philosophy. The essence of lean operations is to compress time from the receipt of an order all the way through to the receipt of payment for such order. The results of this time compression are greater productivity, shorter delivery times, lower cost, improved quality, and increased customer satisfaction.

Other elements that lead to lean thinking include total quality management (TQM), flexible manufacturing systems (FMS), optimal production technology (OPT), the theory of constraints (TOC), quality function deployment (QFD), and Six Sigma.

The just-in-time system (JIT) integrates and controls all processes and operations. The system specifies when, what, and how much should be stored, moved, and operated on. It strives towards continuously improving processes and attempts to eliminate all sorts of wastes. The initial and most popular system is the Kanban system.

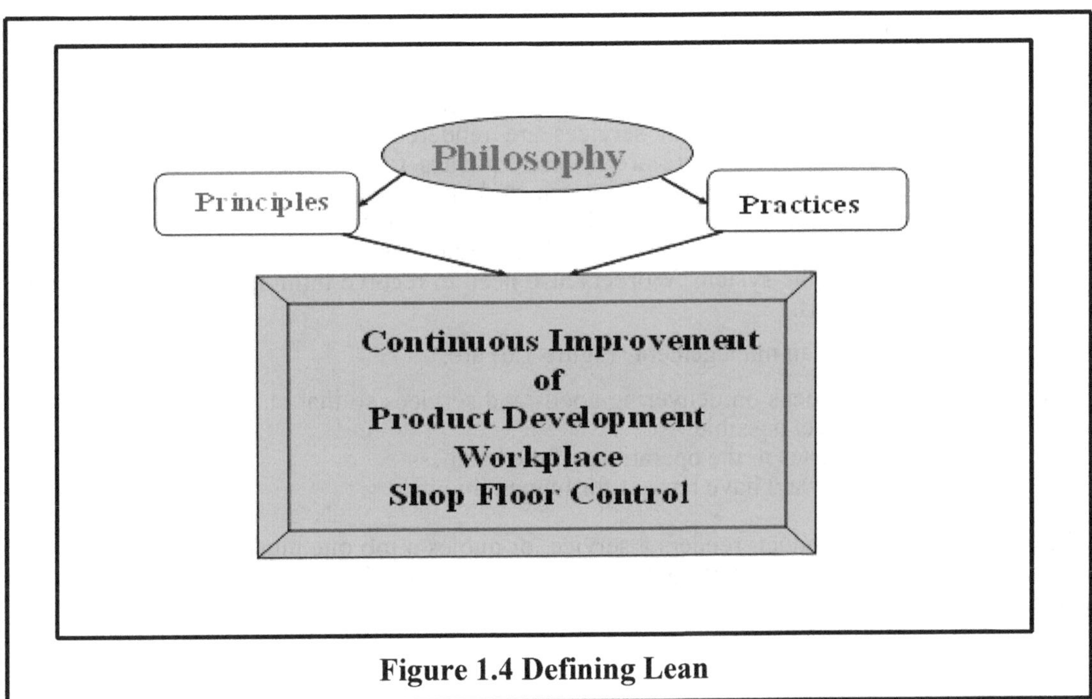

Figure 1.4 Defining Lean

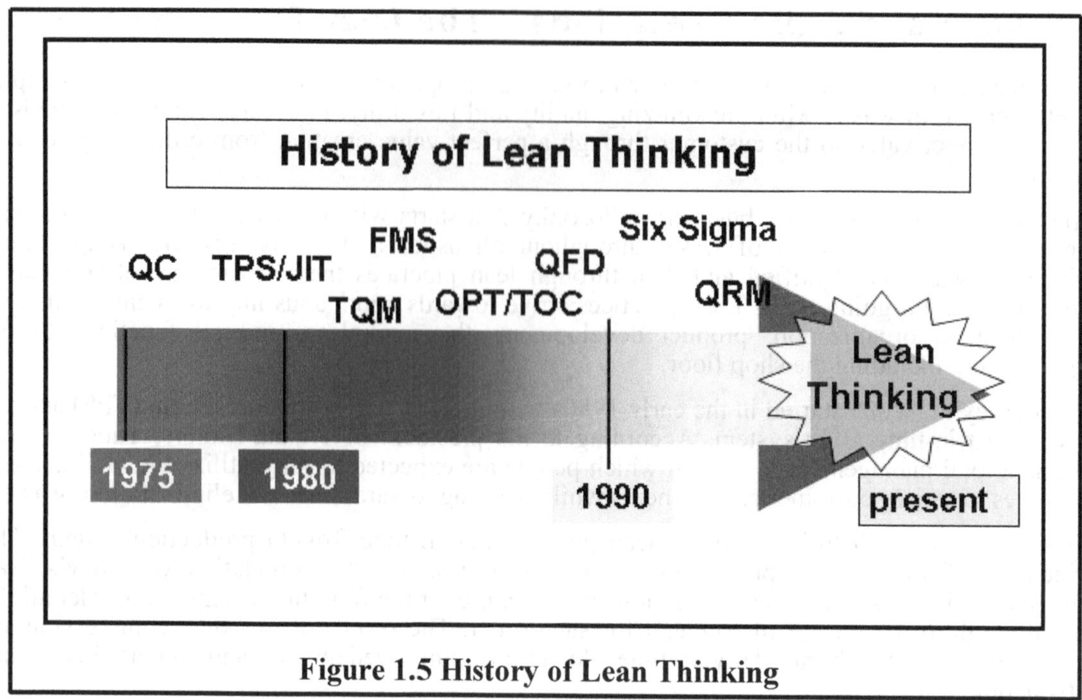

Figure 1.5 History of Lean Thinking

Total quality management and Six Sigma are business processes that drastically improve the bottom line of a business by designing every day's business activities in ways that result in minimizing waste and resources, while increasing quality and customer satisfaction. Optimal production technology and the theory of constraints control the shop floor by identifying bottleneck operations and maximizing production throughput in the most optimal way. Quality function deployment optimizes the design function through a methodology that ensures that all functions of the organization work together to provide the customers with exactly what they want.

Operating lean is a management system, a way of thinking, and a culture where all employees are continuously looking for ways to improve processes. It is a philosophy of eliminating all non-value-added activities in manufacturing and non-manufacturing environments.

The principles used to support lean operations can be used by anyone. The size of a company, the types of products produced, or what services are rendered do not make a difference to the application of these principles. There are no prerequisites for implementing lean principles. A company's dedication and willingness to learn and implement the principles are all that is required. Imperative to the success of implementing lean manufacturing is the support of top management. With the approval of the top of the organization, the company can begin with eliminating the waste in the system. Workers also need to receive training in lean manufacturing and learn to work in teams.

The three objectives of lean management (Figure 1.6) are:

1. Ensure that we focus on delivering goods and services so that our customers are satisfied at the highest level possible
2. Eliminate all wastes in the operations of the business
3. Empower people and have respect for human dignity

Whether one makes a product, renders a service, or quotes a job one must take action in order to accomplish our goal or task. These actions can be a combination of value-added or non-value-added activities.

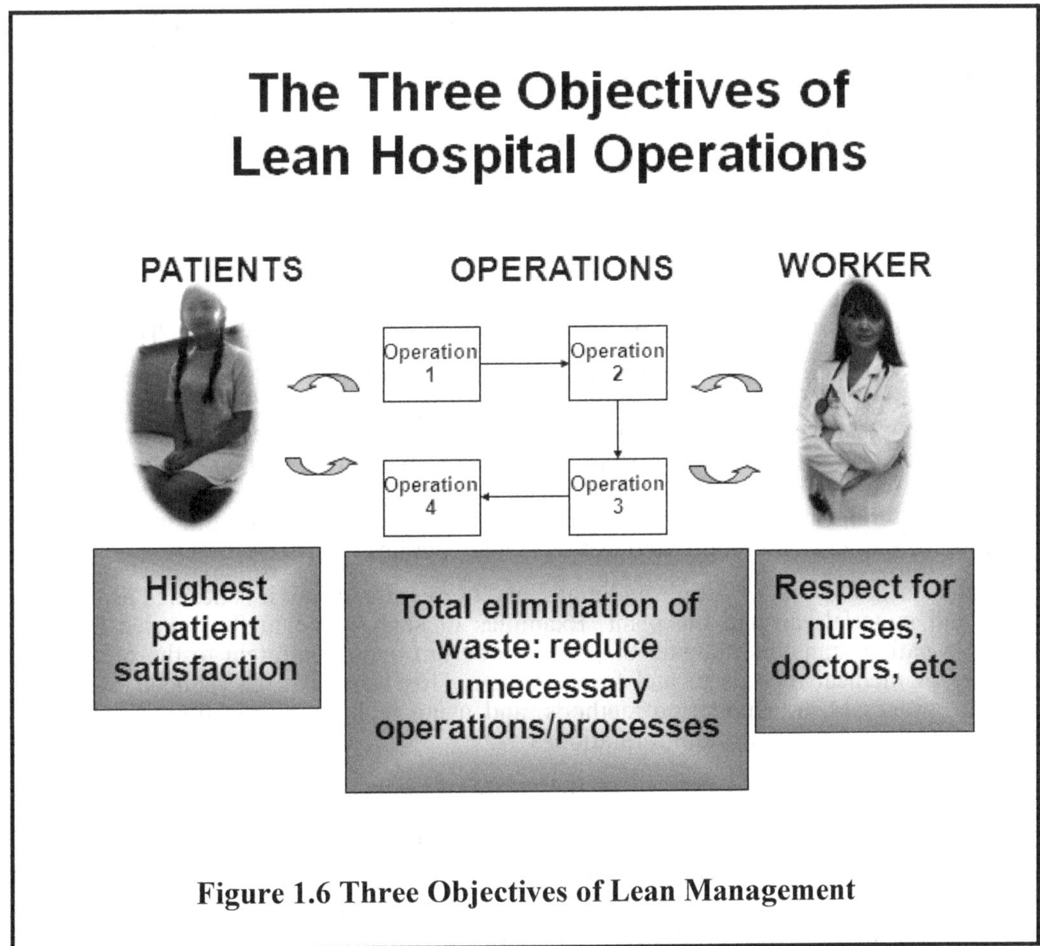

Figure 1.6 Three Objectives of Lean Management

A **value-added activity** is an activity that increases the market, form, or function of the product or service. In other words, these are activities the customer is willing to pay for. A **non-value-added activity** is any activity that does not add market, form, or function or is not necessary. These are the activities that the customer is not willing to pay for. These activities must therefore be eliminated, simplified, reduced, or integrated.

The Eight Types of Waste – DOWITHME

Lean operations management breaks waste into eight non-value-added activities: defects, overproduction, waiting waste, inventory excess, transportation excess, human talent waste, motion waste, and excess processing, or **DOWITHME**, as in now that you have excess and waste, "*What are you going to* ***do with me***?" Let us examine some of these wastes in various industries!

- **Defects** are defined as items that require inspection, repair, and corrective action. Improving the quality at the source can eliminate defects. In order to eliminate or significantly reduce defects a company must introduce total quality management (TQM) and Six Sigma. In a manufacturing environment we can expose quality problems that are caused through poor maintenance and introduce total productive maintenance (TPM). Examples of defects are: parts that do not fit, damaged materials, medication errors in a pharmacy, incomplete requisition forms, incorrect order entry, performing the wrong procedure on a patient, blood re-draws in labs, misdirected results on patient care, and incorrect billing.

- **Over-production** is defined as making more, sooner, or faster than required by the next process. It also includes inappropriate production. Over-production in a manufacturing environment can be resolved by thinking of the next process as being the customer. In other words, if the next process does not need it, then do not produce it. Examples of over-production from the service industry are unused printed results or reports, unnecessary lab procedures, or not needed office visits.
- **Waiting** is defined as idle time created when waiting for an activity or operation to be completed. It includes people, machine, and information idle time. Resolving or minimizing this idle time requires that we learn to balance work. Examples of excess waiting are a machine operator waiting for parts to work on, patients who arrived on time in a doctor's office who are waiting to be seen by a nurse or doctor, and delayed lab results.
- **Inventory Excess** of people, machines, information, or materials in queue or stock. In manufacturing it is defined as any supply in excess of a one-piece flow through the process. This requires that we produce in much smaller lots than we are used to. It also requires that we introduce some sort of a pull system to move the inventory based on customer orders. But first the company must get rid of all obsolete items. Examples of inventory excess are obsolete materials, in-process inventory of materials, customers waiting in lines to be served, patients waiting in exam rooms, and excess stored supplies in offices.
- **Transportation Waste** of people and materials. In manufacturing it is defined as transporting parts and materials around the plant. Examples of such waste in the service industry are multiple patient transfers, transfer of paperwork from one department to the other, physical transfer of medical records to and from storage. This waste can be reduced by improving layouts, processes, transportation methods, and using technology to eliminate the physical transfer of forms, records, and information.
- **Human Talent Unused** is defined as the waste of people's mental, creative, and physical abilities. It is important to train people, to empower them, and to make them part of the solution. Understand the capabilities of the people you employ, so that you do not underutilize their abilities. Examples of such waste are not allowing people to be part of the solution to problems in their work areas, nurses ordering prescription refills or making appointments, medical doctors doing simple patient education, and graduate assistants doing secretarial work
- **Motion Waste** is defined as any movement of people or machines that does not add value to the product or service. It includes travel, searching, and walking that can be eliminated. This requires that we minimize distances, eliminate "pick" and "place," and many other motions that will be discussed later on. Eliminating this waste may require significant improvements in the work place and the use of technology. Examples of such waste are walking to and from the copying machine, searching for misplaced forms, equipment, charts, people, and patients; and long clinic hallways
- **Excess Processing** is defined as efforts that add no value to the product or service from the customer's viewpoint. It includes redundant and unnecessary processing. It can be corrected through improved tooling, automation, changes in design, and the removal of all non-value added paper work. Examples are repeat collection of data, reentry of patient information, writing a prescription and then entering it into the computer, and doctors taking notes on paper so they can later enter them into the computer.

Eliminating these wastes will improve labor productivity, material productivity, capital productivity, and energy productivity.

The Benefits of Lean

The benefits of lean implementations can be seen in significant reduction in production lead time, productivity increase in all areas of company inputs (labor, materials, capital, and energy), reduction in work in process, quality improvement, and better utilization of space. Some companies have experienced the percentage improvements as shown in Figure 1.7.

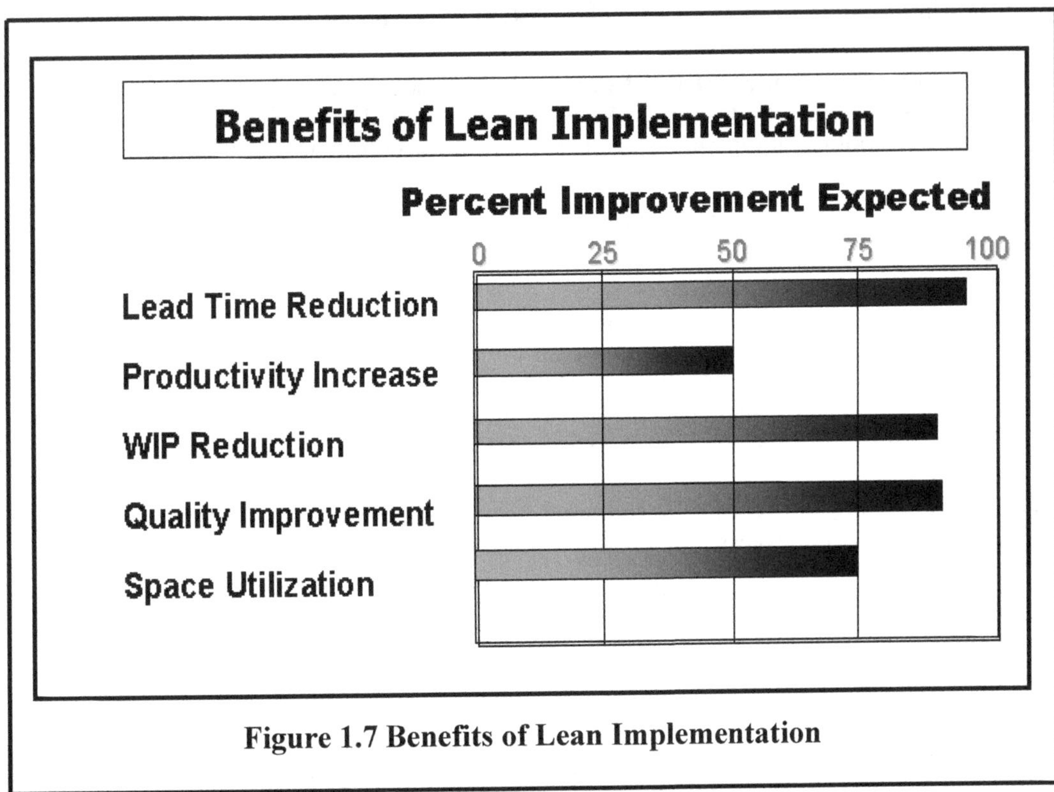

Figure 1.7 Benefits of Lean Implementation

5. *REPORTING ON WASTE IN OUR SYSTEMS*

In The New York Times, on January 17, 2013, Al Baker reports in an article, "At Root of Strike, Years of Unaddressed Waste in City's School Bus System" - on the waste in the New York City bus system.

> New York City's school bus system's last strike was over 34 years ago. The present strike idled over half of the city's yellow school busses, leaving the parents of over 113,000 children looking for alternate ways to get their kids to school.
>
> It was said that this strike was instigated by union workers over a fight of union jobs. However, its true purpose was to reform one of the most inefficient transportation systems in this country; a system that costs New York City almost $7,000 a year for each student passenger it brings to school. How is this possible? Well, consider the following observations:
>
> - The day before the strike it was observed that three students were dropped off at Public School #282 in Park Slope, Brooklyn. Though this bus had dropped off some of the kids at another school, it was estimated that this bus only transported a total of 10 students.
> - Seventeen (17) students were delivered at the same location in another large bus.
> - A modern, new bus that could carry 66 students only transported five (5) students.
> - The city's deputy schools chancellor, Kathleen Grimm, has been quoted that in some cases there is only one child on a bus.
>
> Following comparable statistics were presented in the article for the largest four school districts: New York City spends about $7,000 per child, whereas Los Angeles spends about $3,200, Chicago about $5,000, and Miami, $1,000.

6. GLOSSARY AND SUMMARY OF METHODS

Automation and the Factory of the Future - It includes computer integrated manufacturing (CIM), computer aided design (CAD), computer aided manufacturing (CAM), flexible automation, robotics, automated assembly, machine vision, machine intelligence, automated guided vehicles (AGV), etc.

Capacity - The capacity of the system is determined by how large a facility, how much equipment, labor, capital, and energy is available and how it is utilized to generate the desired kind and amount of output.

Computerization and Systems Approach in the Productive System - Joseph Orlicky and Oliver Wight (1970s - material requirement planning for scheduling and inventory control), Japan's just-in-time manufacturing systems, software packages (1970s - for production scheduling, job shop scheduling, project management, maintenance scheduling, layout planning, and forecasting), and the system's approach to decision making (enterprise resource planning).

DOWITHME - The eight types of waste are defects, over production, waiting waste, inventory excess, transportation excess, human talent waste, motion waste, and excess processing.

Effectiveness - The effectiveness of the transformation process is concerned with doing the right thing, producing the right set of outputs, and achieving the objectives of the organization in a timely fashion.

Efficiency - The efficiency of a system is measured by its output per unit input.

Finance Function - The finance function is responsible for generating and controlling short- and long-term capital for the acquisition of the inputs and the distribution of the outputs of the productive system.

Flexibility - Flexibility relates to how easily and quickly the system can be changed to produce other outputs.

Industrial Revolution - Adam Smith (1776 - division of labor), Eli Whitney (1798 - interchangeable parts), The Soho Engineering Foundry (1800s).

Judging the Transformation Process - The transformation process can be judged by its capacity, efficiency, effectiveness, and flexibility.

Just-in-Time System (JIT) - JIT integrates and controls all processes and operations. The system specifies when, what and how much should be stored, moved, and operated on. It strives towards continuously improving processes and attempts to eliminate all sorts of wastes.

Lean Manufacturing – Lean manufacturing is based on the principles of elimination of waste while maximizing quality and flexibility. The following elements lead to lean manufacturing: the Toyota production system, total quality management, optimized production technology and the theory of constraints, quality function deployment, and Six Sigma.

Marketing Function - The marketing function is responsible for generating a demand for the products and the services.

Optimal Production Technology (OPT) and the Theory of Constraints (TOC) - OPT and TOC control the shop floor by identifying bottle neck operations and maximizing production throughput in the most optimal way.

Production/Operations Function - The production/operations functions deals with the efficient design, planning, and control of the productive system.

Productive System - The productive system is a man-made system that provides the means of transforming inputs—resources—into desired valuable outputs—goods or services—with added value.

Quality Function Deployment (QFD) - QFD optimizes the design function through a methodology that ensures that all functions of the organization work together to provide the customers with exactly what they want.

Quantitative Techniques to Plan and Control Production - P. O. Johannsen and A. K. Erlang (1907 - waiting line analysis), Frederick W. Lanchester (1914 - operations research techniques), F. W. Harris (1915—1927 - EOQ inventory model), Walter Shewhart (1924—1931 - quality control), W. Leontieff (1930's - input/output control), L. H. C. Tippett (1935 - work sampling), L. V. Kantorovich, F. L. Hitchcock, T. C. Koopmans (1939 - transportation model), George B. Dantzig (1947 - simplex method), Booz, Allen and Hamilton (late 1950s - project management), A. Charnes and W. W. Cooper (1961—1968 - goal programming).

Scientific Management - Charles Babbage (1832 - different pay scales), Frederick Taylor (1910—1914 - father of scientific management), Frank Gilbreth (1911 - motion study), Lillian Gilbreth (1911 - industrial psychology), Henry L. Gantt (1913 - job scheduling), Henry Ford (1913 - moving assembly line in automotive company).

Supply Chain Management - Supply chain management (SCM) integrates the management of goods and services, from supply to demand management, within and across all companies involved.

Total Quality Management (TQM) and Six Sigma - These are business processes that drastically improve the bottom line of a business by designing every day's business activities in ways that result in minimizing waste and resources, while increasing quality and customer satisfaction.

7. ACRONYMS

AGV Automated Guided Vehicle
CAD Computer Aided Design
CAM Computer Aided Manufacturing
CIM Computer Integrated Manufacturing
CPM Critical Path Method
EOQ Economic Order Quantity
ERP Enterprise Resource Planning
FMS Flexible Manufacturing System
JIT Just-In-Time
MRP Material Requirement Planning
OPT/TOC Optimized Production Technology and the Theory of Constraints
PERT Project Evaluation and Review Technique
POM Production/Operations Management
QFD Quality Function Deployment
SCM Supply Chain Management
SM Scientific Management
TPS Toyota Production System
TQM Total Quality Management
TPM Total Productive Maintenance
DOWITHME Now that you have excess and waste, "What are you going to do with me"? It represents **D**efects, **O**verproduction, **W**aiting, **I**nventory, **T**ransportation, **H**uman talent unused, **M**otion, and **E**xcess processing.

8. REFERENCES

Babbage, Charles. *On the Economy of Machinery and Manufacturers*. 4th ed. London: Charles Knight, 1835.

Berger, P. and A. Gerstenfeld. "Decision Analysis for Increased Highway Safety." *Sloan Management Review* (Spring 1971): 11-22.

Bierman, H. and W. Hausman. "The Credit Granting Decision." *Management Science* 16 (April 1970): B519-B532.

Delbridge, R. *Life on the Line in Contemporary Manufacturing: The Workplace Experience of Lean Production and the Japanese Model*. Oxford: Oxford University Press, 2000.

Fulton, M. "New Factors in Plant Location." *Harvard Business Review* (May-June 1971): 4-17.

Hespos, R. and P.A. Strassmann. "Stochastic Decision Trees for the Analysis of Investment Decisions." *Management Science* 11 (August 1965): 244-59.

Hopkins, F. G. W. *The Symphony of Manufacturing: Integrating Lean Production in America.* Oakland Consulting Group, July 1999.

McNamee, Peter and John Celona. *Decision Analysis with Supertree*. San Francisco: The Scientific Press, 1990.

Magee, J. "How to Use Decision Trees in Capital Investment." *Harvard Business Review* (September-October 1964): 79-96.

Newendorp, P. "Use of Decision Trees Can Help Simplify Complex Problems." The Oil and Gas Journal (October 25, 1976): 98-102.

Newendorp, P. "Risk Evaluation Helps Make Better Decisions." *The Oil and Gas Journal* (October 18, 1976): 55-58.

Standard, C. and D. Davis. *Running Today's Factory: A Proven Strategy for Lean Manufacturing,* Cincinnati: Hanser-Gardner Publications, August 1999.

Sullivan, W. G. and W. Claycombe. "The Use of Decision Trees in Planning Plant Expansion." *S.A.M. Advanced Management Journal* (Winter 1975): 29-39.

Taylor, Frederick Winslow. *The Principles of Scientific Management*. New York: Harper & Bros., 1911.

Wu, N. L. and C. Walker. "Philosophy, Principles and Productivity of Lean Manufacturing." *Productivity Quarterly Journal* (Oct-Dec 2004).

9. REVIEW QUESTIONS

1. What is a productive system?
2. What are the four foremost concepts by which one must judge the transformation that takes place in the production/operations system? Approximately when did they become important?
3. What function is concerned with generating the inputs for an organization? Which function is concerned with the transformation system of an organization?
4. What is the difference between operations management and supply chain management?

5. What are the four principles of scientific management? Different fields evolved out of Taylor's work. Name one new field for each of the four new management duties/principles.

6. What are some of the elements of automated factories?

7. What is meant by systems approach to solve business problems?

8. Who (names) introduced the following production/operations management principles for the first time?

    a) Motion study
    b) Industrial quality control
    c) Division of labor for simplification and increased productivity.
    d) First inventory control model
    e) Work sampling
    f) Industrial psychology
    g) Project management
    h) Material requirement planning
    i) Different base pay scales for different types of labor
    j) Scientific management
    k) Job scheduling
    l) Moving assembly line in the automotive industry
    m) Project management

9. Historically, what elements lead to lean thinking?

10. What is meant by operating in a lean way?

11. What are the three objectives of lean operations?

12. What are the eight non-value-added wastes?

13. Give examples of these wastes.

14. How can we eliminate or reduce these wastes?

Chapter 2

PRODUCTIVITY MANAGEMENT and DEVELOPMENT LIFECYCLE

1. PRODUCTIVITY CONCEPT

The overall barometer of the health of a productive system is its productivity. Productivity measures the efficiency and effectiveness of a productive system in utilizing its scarce resources over time. A firm's productivity depends on the efficiency of labor, the effectiveness of management, and the level of technology. The efficiency of labor is often expressed as the amount of output per hour of labor expended. The effectiveness of management is often measured by the system's actual output against the planned output. The level of technology is measured against industry standards that frequently change as new technology becomes available. The desired productivity is the highest performance possible with the least consumption of resources. While there are always ways to improve the efficiency of labor and the effectiveness of management, long-run productivity gains often result from new technology. While production managers spend most of their time improving labor performance and management methods, production managers should always be sensitive to new technology. The ultimate and enduring objective of production and operations management is to improve productivity.

For many years, profit has been the most popular measure in the assessment of a firm. While profit is easy to measure and to understand, it does not always indicate the true health of a firm or does not indicate it over time. The profit picture is easily distorted by inflation and by cost accounting practices. Thus many of our firms have been misled by their bright, short-term profit picture and find out too late that their systems have long been obsolete.

While the United States is still the leader in labor productivity, other free-world countries, especially West Germany and Japan, are catching up rapidly. If the current trend of productivity improvement continues, these countries will soon surpass the United States' productivity level. From 1966 until 1979, the U.S. private sector's annual productivity growth rate experienced a decline. Labor statistics show that the average annual productivity growth rate, which had been 3.2% during 1947—1966, dropped to 2.1% for the period of 1966—1973 and to a meager 0.8% for the period of 1973—1979. In 1979, American industry actually experienced a negative productivity growth and, during the 1980—1982 period, the average productivity gain was only 0.5%. For the ten-year period between 1983 and 1993, the average productivity gain was approximately 1%. From 1994 until the turn of the century our economy was very good, exhibiting productivity gains of over 2% yearly. Since the turn of the century we have been struggling to maintain a healthy productivity gain.

During the seventies, our nation was concerned about its meager performance since low productivity triggered inflation in our country. Since inflation is one of the major causes of recession and unemployment, unless our productivity increased, one had to anticipate a spiral effect of inflation and recession. Our industrial sector was well aware of this problem. Strong action got under way to battle inflation by working towards increasing our productivity. Some improvement in labor productivity in this country was already apparent during the last quarter of 1982 when the average annual rate of productivity growth in the business sector of the economy rose to 2%. This awareness and action helped us to regain the productivity leadership in the world which we once enjoyed. This effort was reflected in the activities of various productivity and industrial engineering-oriented departments of our major industrial and non-industrial corporations. Typical titles given to people in productivity-oriented departments are: Productivity Coordinator, Productivity Analyst, Director of Productivity or Director of Productivity Service. The following titles are quite common in industrial engineering oriented departments: Industrial

Engineer, Manager of Industrial Engineering, Industrial Engineering Supervisor, Senior Industrial Engineer, Methods and Standards Engineer, Junior and Senior Methods Analyst, Work Measurement Analyst, Productivity and Cost Control Manager, etc.

2. PRODUCTIVITY MEASUREMENT

In its most general terms, productivity measurement relates tangible output to tangible input as shown in Figure 2.1.

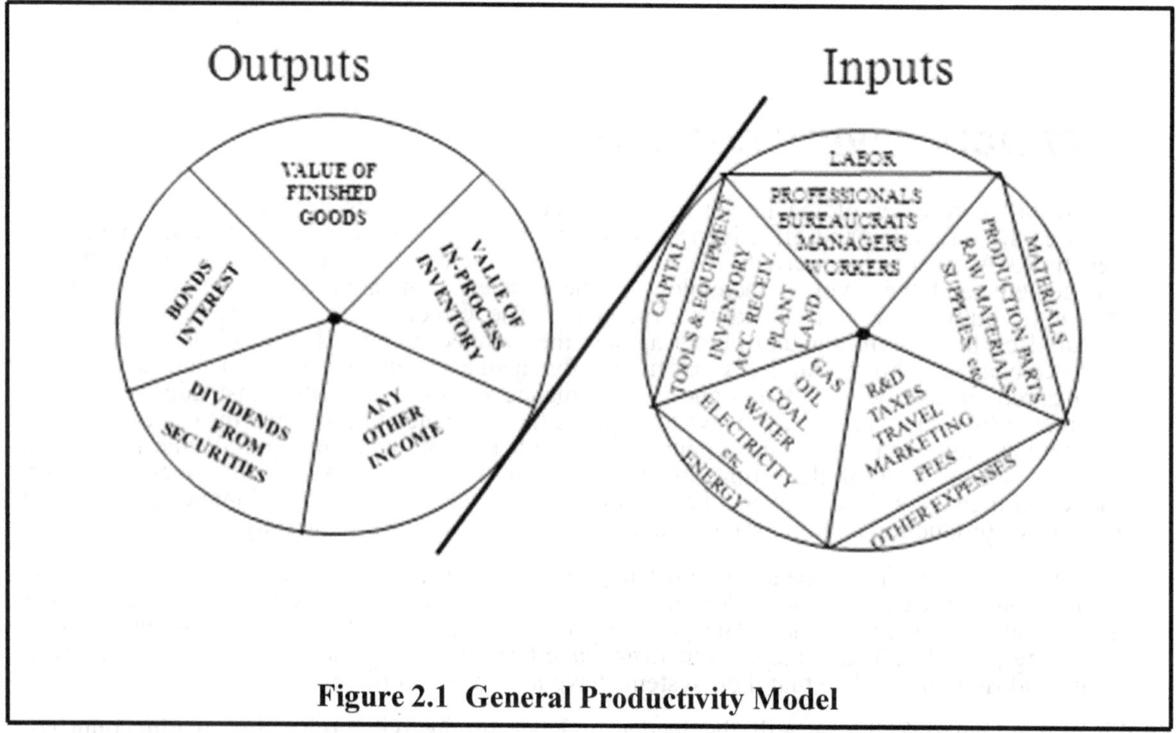

Figure 2.1 General Productivity Model

There are four basic output groups: finished goods, in-process inventory, dividends from securities, and interest on bonds. When evaluating the value of finished goods, one must consider all goods produced as opposed to goods sold. The per unit base period selling price is multiplied by the actual volume produced to come up with the value of finished goods. The value of in-process inventory is established by multiplying the volume of in- process inventory by the percent completion factor and the per unit base period selling price. Since dividends from securities and interest on bonds are the result of human and capital inputs, they too need to be included in evaluating the output value. However, if we wish to eliminate those elements which do not greatly influence the efficient use of resources at the operating level, then both income from bonds and dividends from securities can be ignored. Our productivity model will still be a good approximation.

There are four basic input groups: labor, capital, materials, and energy. All human resources that contribute to the output of the firm must be included in the labor input factor of the model. Human resources include the professionals, clerical and staff personnel (or the bureaucrats), managers, and all other workers. Man hours and average wage rates for all members of the firm are used to calculate the monetary value of the labor input factor. Both fixed and working capital need be considered in figuring the capital input factor. Depreciation methods should not be used to value the consumption of fixed capital. A popular method, however, for measuring the consumption of fixed capital is the labor input equivalent method whereby capital is valued based on the services it can render under a lease agreement. This method is considered to be most accurate. By **fixed capital** is meant land, facilities, warehouses, equipment, and tools. **Working capital** includes cash needed for inventory, accounts receivable, and notes receivable.

Under the energy input factor we consider only the energy that is actually consumed while producing the outputs. Since solar energy is freely available, no energy cost is attached to it. However, the solar panels necessary to tap this free energy will be considered in the fixed capital factor. Inputs and outputs must be evaluated at base period prices in order to eliminate the effect of inflation on prices. The **productivity factor** for period t is therefore:

$$P_t = \frac{FG_t + IPI_t + BI_t + SD_t + OI_t - IPI_{t-1}}{L_t + M_t + C_t + E_t + OE_t}$$

Where:

P_t = total productivity factor for period t
FG_t = base value of finished goods produced during period t
IPI_t = base value of in-process inventory at the end of period t
IPI_{t-1} = base value of in-process inventory at the end of period $t-1$
BI_t = base value of bond interest earned during period t
SD_t = base value of security dividends earned during period t
OI_t = base value of all other income earned during period t
L_t = base value of all human input for period t
M_t = base value of all material input for period t
C_t = base value of all capital input for period t
E_t = base value of all energy input for period t
OE_t = base value of all other expenditures made during period t

Even though the productivity factor seems to be a very simplistic ratio of outputs versus inputs, it is not always easy to define all input and output values that go into the model. Outputs can be hard to define when they come from many sectors of the organization, or groups, or even different lines and disciplines. In the service industry, in particular, we are dealing not only with tangible outputs, but intangible outputs need to be assessed as well. Likewise, inputs are often equally complex and hard to define and to evaluate.

When the productivity factors for the base period and period t are known, the productivity index is calculated as follows:

$$I_t = \frac{P_t}{P_0}$$

Where:

I_t = productivity index for period t
P_t = productivity factor for period t
P_o = productivity factor for base period 0

If I_t is larger than 1, the productivity in period t increased. For example, there is a 7% growth in productivity for period t if $I_t = 1.07$.

The Sumanth/Einspruch survey on productivity awareness in the U.S. shows that since the early eighties 75% of responding industrial companies and over 82% of the non-industrial companies already had a formal productivity measurement program. Productivity measurement in industrial companies is mainly at the plant/division level, whereas in non-industrial companies, productivity measurement is principally at the corporate level. Since most day-to-day management decisions are product oriented, more and more efforts are under way to calculate product productivity.

3. CLASSICAL PRODUCTIVITY MEASURES

Industry and business use three types of productivity measures: partial productivity, total-factor productivity, and total productivity.

Partial Productivity is the ratio of gross or net output to one type of input. Labor hours are often selected as input in such types of productivity measurement. The productivity of the U.S.A., as reported by the Bureau of Labor Statistics, is such a partial productivity ratio since it measures the value of goods and services produced per hour of labor expended. Here the output is the dollar gross domestic product (including goods and services) produced during a fixed time period, while the input consists of employee wages/salaries, social security contributions, and private benefit plans.

Labor is not always a valid measure of productivity, especially when other input factors contribute significantly to the end product. In an industry that is very energy intensive—such as smelting, chemical manufacturing, or refining—a partial productivity measurement with energy as its sole input factor is more appropriate than labor or material indicators. Companies where raw material contributes largely to the production cost may prefer to calculate material productivity over any other partial productivity factor. Among industrial and non-industrial corporations, partial productivity measurement is widely used on all levels: at the corporate, plant/division, department, and product level. Partial productivity seems to be the most popular productivity measure of our industry.

Total-Factor Productivity is the ratio of net output (gross output minus material value) to the sum of labor and capital. Total-factor productivity makes sense when the firm does not have much control over materials and material cost. A relatively small percentage of our industry calculates total-factor productivity.

Total Productivity is the ratio of the gross output of the firm to all its inputs, including labor, material, capital, energy, and other expenses. This productivity measure is calculated at the corporate, the plant/division, or department level. Furthermore, this productivity measurement is also calculated at the product level.

Because many companies have encountered problems in calculating the above types of productivity ratios, they have resorted to substitute productivity measures in an attempt to evaluate the firm's productivity. Some of these measures are "energy ratios" (units produced/energy used), "material ratios" (material in final product/total supplied material), "quality ratios" (cost for quality assurance/total product cost), and "capital intensity" (dollar value of capital equipment/number of workers).

Even though no one substitute ratio is all-inclusive since each one neglects some relevant input or output, it is generally agreed that they help in evaluating the productivity of the firm. Any improvement or growth of such substitute productivity ratios normally contributes to the overall productivity improvement of the firm. In this sense they are valuable general measurements for the company's overall productivity status. Industrial surveys show that productivity measurements in many companies are mostly being performed on a corporate or plant/division level. Yet, it is necessary to manage the productivity of each sub-function of the organization if one is going to get actively involved in improving the company's overall productivity level. In particular, one must manage the productivity of the production design function, the process planning function, the plant planning function, the material handling function, the production function, the inventory function, the maintenance function, and the quality control function.

Productivity management, as it relates to a sub-function of the organization, consists of five basic interlocking activities:

1. Measurement
2. Evaluation
3. Improvement
4. Planning
5. Dissemination

After appropriate productivity ratios for the sub-functions are defined, one must collect input and output data. Some of that data may be found in existing databases of the firm, while other data will have to be collected. Because productivity management must become an ongoing activity of the company, and because several sub-functions may share similar input/output data in calculating productivity ratios, new databases will emerge. All existing data must clearly be defined before new measurements and data collection are undertaken, since data gathering is a tedious and often expensive proposition.

After evaluating the productivity of the sub-functions, one must identify how productivity can be improved. In order to manage and improve the productivity of various sub-functions, one must think in terms of technology-based strategies, procedure based strategies, maintenance, capital investment, management by objectives, team committees, brainstorming, employment involvement, human factors, cost control, strategic planning, work measurement, zero-based budgeting, annual goal setting, and coordinating lean based activities. Most important factors in improving productivity in an organization depend on lean planning, more effective management, improved job procedures, effective human effort and personnel policies, better communications, new technology, better maintenance policies and procedures, more reliable tools and maintenance parts.

When changes need to be made in the operation of various sub-functions, careful planning of such changes is necessary. The need for such changes must be thoroughly explained to all people who will be affected by them. It is imperative that their full cooperation is sought. People must be motivated to welcome the changes and must become involved to see those changes through. Their motivation and work ethics with which changes are accomplished have a significant impact on work performance and therefore the function's overall productivity.

Finally, dissemination of data and improvements from one sub-system to another is necessary so that the whole organization can benefit from productivity management. Dissemination is best accomplished when reference data are in computer format. This reference data must be validated, updated, and controlled on a regular, ongoing basis in order to maintain its accuracy and integrity. This control function of data and information is enhanced by techniques used to validate and maintain the information in the form of a non-redundant, up-to-date, accessible collection of data items called a database. Special generalized computer programs, called database management packages, can be designed to organize, maintain, and summarize data elements for the purpose of productivity analysis and its dissemination amongst the functions of the organization.

4. CALCULATION OF TOTAL AND PARTIAL PRODUCTIVITY - AN EXAMPLE

Sanchez Corporation, a Mexico-based parts manufacturer, started its business two years ago (this starting year will be called the base year in our example and is designated as period 0). The company manufactures two products for which it uses three types of raw materials and purchases subassemblies. In an effort to increase productivity the company hired the services of Wu/Wu Creative Enterprises, a productivity consultancy firm. It took a full year to improve productivity and productivity data has been collected. The value of the company's output and input for the base year and this last year (designated as period 1) is shown and calculated in Tables 2.1 and 2.2.

4.1 Calculations for Table 2.1, the Output of the Company

The output of the company consists of the two products (product #1 and product #2), in process inventory of these two products (in-process inventory of product #1 is 40% completed by the end of period 0 and period 1; whereas in-process inventory of product #2 is 55% completed by the end of period 0 and period 1), dividends from securities, and interest from bonds. Their amounts are shown in columns two and three. Because base rates must be used to value all output produced during the base year and during this last year these rates are shown in column four of the table. The dividends and the interest the company earned in period 1 will be deflated to the base period by an appropriate index. This index shows the change in dividend and interest rate obtained in period 1 as compared to period 0. These indexes are found in column five of the table.

1	Table 2.1: Output Value Computation						
2	OUTPUT	AMOUNTS		BASE	INDEX	VALUES ($)	
3	FACTORS	Period 0	Period 1	RATE		Period 0	Period 1
4	Finished Goods						
5	Product #1	1,200	1.720	$14		16,800	24,080
6	Product #2	750	1,320	$17		12,750	22,440
7						29,550	46,520
8	In Process						
9	Product #1	550	400	$14		3,080	2,240
10	Product #2	400	340	$17		3,740	3,179
11						6,820	5,419
12							
13	Dividends	$4,000	$4,600		1.1	4,000	4,182
14							
15	Interest	$1,500	$1,700		1.1	1,500	1,545
16							
17				Total Output Value:		41,870	50,846

Sample Excel Formulas used:

= C5 x D5

= C9xD9x40%

= C13 / E13

= G7+G11+G13+G15 –F11

Since all units produced must be valued at base rates the value of finished goods for period 0 and period 1 is obtained by multiplying the units produced with their respective base rates:

Period 0	**Period 1**
1,200 units x $14/unit = $16,800	1,720 units x $14/unit = $24,080
750 units x $17/unit = $12,750	1,320 units x $17/unit = $22,440
Total: $29,550	**Total: $46,520**

Both the base rate (per unit selling price in the base period) and the percent completion must be considered in calculating the value of in-process inventory as follows:

Period 0	**Period 1**
550 units x $14/unit x 40% = $3,080	400 units x $14/unit x 40% = $2,240
400 units x $17/unit x 55% = $3,740	340 units x $17/unit x 55% = $3,179
Total: $6,820	**Total: $5,419**

Dividends and interest obtained during the last period (period 1) must be evaluated at base period values. This can be done by dividing these earnings by their respective index values:

Period 0	**Period 1**
Dividends as shown in table: **$4,000**	$4,600/1.10 = **$4,182**
Interest as shown in table: **$1,500**	$1,700/1.10 = **$1,545**

The total output value for period 0 is: $29,550 + $6,820 + $4,000 + $1,500 = **$41,870** (there was no in-process inventory to subtract because the company did not have any such inventory when it started up in the base year).

Because the in-process inventory value at the end of the base year is $6,820, the total output value for period 1 is: $46,520 + $5,419 + $4,182 + $1,545 - $6,820 = $50,846.

All the above values are shown in the last two columns of Table 2.1.

4.2 Calculations for Table 2.2, the Inputs of the Company

The inputs of the company consist of labor (workers, managers, professionals, and bureaucrats), three types of raw materials and purchased parts, fixed and working capital, energy (oil, gas, electricity, and water), and other inputs such as taxes, travel, and professional fees.

	A	B	C	D	E	F	G
1	Table 2.2: Input Value Computation						
2	Input Factors	Amounts		Base	Index	Value	
3		Period 0	Period 1	Rate		Period 0	Period 1
4	LABOR						
5	Workers (hrs)	180	190	5		900	950
6	Managers (hrs)						
7	Type 1	14	15	16		224	240
8	Type 2	15	17	20		300	340
9	Professionals (hrs)						
10	Type 1	30	32	12		360	384
11	Type 2	45	48	16		720	768
12	Bureaucrats (hrs)	50	56	7		350	392
13						2,854	3,074
14	MATERIALS						
15	Raw Materials						
16	Type 1 (tons)	3	3.7	60		180	222
17	Type 2 (gals)	1,200	1,300	1.2		1,440	1,560
18	Type 3 (cases)	1,300	1,400	0.4		520	560
19	Purchased Parts (units)	3,500	3,900	0.3		1,050	1,170
20						3,190	3,512
21	CAPITAL						
22	Fixed Capital						
23	Land ($)	1,500	1,500		1.15	1,500	1,304
24	Building ($)	4,000	4,700		1.2	4,000	3,917
25	Equipment/Tools ($)	2,000	2,400		1.16	2,000	2,069
26	Machines ($)	3,700	4,000		1.16	3,700	3,448
27	Working						
28	Inventory ($)	4,000	4,600	0.08	1.15	320	320
29	Cash ($)	10,000	12,000	0.08	1.2	800	800
30	Amounts Rec. ($)	3,000	3,500	0.08	1.18	240	237
31						12,560	12,096
32	ENERGY						
33	Oil (gallons)	700	900	1.35		945	1,215
34	Gas (cf.)	1,200	1,400	0.65		780	910
35	Electricity (Kw Hrs)	2,700	3,200	0.25		675	800
36	Water (gallons)	1,500	2,000	0.15		225	300
37						2,625	3,225
38	OTHERS						
39	Taxes($)	600	840		1.03	600	816
40	Travel ($)	800	450		1.08	800	417
41	Professional Fees ($)	4,700	8,500		1.07	4,700	7,944
42						6,100	9,176
43							
44			Total Input Value:			27,329	31,083

Sample Excel Formulas used:

= C8 x D8

= C25/E25

= C30*D30/E30

= C39/E39

All four categories of labor are considered in calculating the total labor value for period 0 and period 1. Their man hours are multiplied by their average hourly base salary/wages to obtain the labor values shown in Table 2.2.

The total value of materials is the sum of the values of all raw materials used and parts purchased. Again, the rates of the base period are used to calculate these values, regardless of a price increase or decrease in period 1.

The capital value consists of the value of fixed capital and the value of working capital. The depreciation method is not a good method to value fixed capital. Fixed capital could best be valued at their rental value to calculate the amount of fixed capital used in period 0 and period 1. The index values are used to properly deflate the fixed capital values of period 1 to base period values. As compared to the base year, these respective indexes for period 1 reflect the average increase in rental values of land (an increase of 15%), of buildings (an increase of 20%), of equipment/tools (an increase of 16%), and of machinery (an increase of 16%).

For example, the rental value of equipment for period 1 is calculated as follows:

$$\frac{\$\, Amount\ of\ Equipment\ and\ Tools}{Index\ of\ Equipment\ and\ Tools} = \frac{\$2{,}400}{1.16} = \$2{,}068.97$$

The base rate of working capital is the cost of capital after tax, or what is foregone for not having this working capital generating income through investment. The data in Table 2.2 show that this is 8% or 0.08. It is obtained by evaluating the firm's weighted average cost after tax of its current liabilities, long and short-term loans, common stock, etc. Thus the value of, for example, accounts receivable (Accounts Rec.) is calculated as follows:

$$Period\ 0:\quad \$\, Value\ Accounts\ Receivable * Base\ Rate = \$3{,}000 * 0.08 = \$240$$

$$Period\ 1:\quad \frac{\$\, Value\ Accounts\ Receivable * Base\ Rate}{Index\ Accounts\ Receivable} = \frac{\$3{,}500 * 0.08}{1.18} = \$237$$

Note that the "value for accounts receivable" for period 1 is the average book value of such accounts receivable and needs to be deflated to the base period value by the index. The index reflects the change in unit price (due to inflation or other price changes) of the goods for which these accounts receivable were created.

Input of the four energy factors are calculated by multiplying the units consumed by their base rates.

To value the two input items in the last section of the table, the values for period 1 must be deflated by the index to bring them back to base period values.

Finally, the total input value is the sum of the calculated values of all five input categories:

$$Period\ 0:\ I_0 = L_0+M_0+C_0+E_0+O_0 = \$2{,}854 + \$3{,}190 + \$12{,}560 + \$2{,}625 + \$6{,}100 = \$27{,}329$$

$$Period\ 1:\ I_1 = L_1+M_1+C_1+E_1+O_1 = \$3{,}074 + \$3{,}512 + \$12{,}095 + \$3{,}225 + \$9{,}177 = \$31{,}083$$

	A	B	C
1	Table 2.3: Total and Partial Productivities		
2	Description	Period 0	Period 1
3	Gross Output Value ($)	41,870	50,846
4	Total Input Value ($)	27,329	31,083
5	Total Productivity	1.532	1.636
6	Productivity Index		1.068
7			
8	Input Value of Labor ($)	2,854	3,074
9	Labor Productivity	14.671	16.541
10	Labor Index		1.127
11			
12	Input Value of Materials ($)	3,190	3,512
13	Material Productivity	13.125	14.478
14	Material Index		1.103
15			
16	Input Value of Capital ($)	12,560	12,095
17	Capital Productivity	3.334	4.204
18	Capital Index		1.261
19			
20	Input Value of Energy ($)	2,625	3,225
21	Energy Productivity	15.950	15.766
22	Energy Index		0.988
23			
24	Input Value of Others ($)	6,100	9,177
25	Other Productivity	6.864	5.541
26	Other Index		0.807

	A	B	C
1	Table 2.3: Total and Partial Productivities		
2	Description	Period 0	Period 1
3	Gross Output Value ($)	41870	50846
4	Total Input Value ($)	27329	31083
5	Total Productivity	=B3/B4	=C3/C4
6	Productivity Index		=C5/B5
7			
8	Input Value of Labor ($)	2854	3074
9	Labor Productivity	=B3/B8	=C3/C8
10	Labor Index		=C9/B9
11			
12	Input Value of Materials ($)	3190	3512
13	Material Productivity	=B3/B12	=C3/C12
14	Material Index		=C13/B13
15			
16	Input Value of Capital ($)	12560	12095
17	Capital Productivity	=B3/B16	=C3/C16
18	Capital Index		=C17/B17
19			
20	Input Value of Energy ($)	2625	3225
21	Energy Productivity	=B3/B20	=C3/C20
22	Energy Index		=C21/B21
23			
24	Input Value of Others ($)	6100	9177
25	Other Productivity	=B3/B24	=C3/C24
26	Other Index		=C25/B25

4.3 Analysis of Company's Productivities and Indexes

Table 2.3 summarizes total and partial productivities and productivity indexes of the company. Mr. Sanchez can now evaluate the efforts of the young productivity consultant he hired and identify which areas have been improved and why, and which areas need further improvement.

The total productivity has increased from $1.532 of output for each dollar of input to $1.636 deflated output for each deflated dollar of input. This represents a 6.8% increase in productivity as shown by the productivity index of 1.068. The partial productivities and their indexes show three areas where significant improvements occurred. These are labor, material, and capital. The consultant has paid a great deal of attention to improving these areas by introducing work incentives, by reassigning workers, through better process planning, by decreasing materials waste, by decreasing inventories, and by better utilizing plant space and equipment. As a result of these efforts, the partial productivity indexes were boosted to a very healthy level. Increases in partial productivities are as follows:

Labor Productivity Index: 16.541/14.671 = 1.127 or a 12.7% increase

Material Productivity Index: 14.478/13.125 = 1.103 or a 10.3% increase

Capital Productivity Index: 4.204/3.334 = 1.261 or a 26.1% increase

However, energy productivity has decreased slightly by 1.2% (0.988). Because Mr. Sanchez is concerned about a possible increase in energy cost that is eating into his profits, he wishes to start an energy conservation plan, starting with an energy audit. It is hoped that this effort will save energy and increase the energy productivity index too.

Because of the extra consulting fees Mr. Sanchez had to pay the consultant, it is understandable that the partial productivity of the "other" category has declined by 19.3% (0.807).

5. THE IDEA DEVELOPMENT LIFECYCLE PROCESS

It happens, you are inspired! You have a thought, an idea for something new. Slowly, it transforms itself into a vision in your mind; something very specific takes shape. It may be a product or service. It may be a delightful tune, a fragrant smell, a loan approval process, or a simpler way to do something. It is a product or service that you or your company can provide, sell or market, and it is hoped, make a profit, or save money. This transformation from idea to a real product, service, improvement, method, or whatever its final form may be, has a systematic development lifecycle to ensure final quality.

However, producing this idea as a product or service on a daily basis does not magically happen. Figure 2.2 depicts the **idea development lifecycle process** of any product or service. Once initiated, an idea is developed, it goes through many stages: concept requirements, design, build, integrate and test, make or implement, verify for customer approval to launch or release into production where it remains until it retires at its End-of-Life (EOL).

Each stage has its own process to develop the idea further and is displayed in Figure 2.2 as a blue line with an arrow to indicate the direction it goes toward. The two circular arrows indicate that it is repeated as necessary to ensure completeness. These processes are: gather requirements, design product or service, build prototypes of the product or manually perform the steps of the service, test the final version of the product or service, establish or implement all the necessary processes to consistently produce this product or provide this service in production and, finally, verify these necessary processes and document the analysis' results in a report as proof that they are working properly. Each process has at least two key milestones: its start and finish dates.

Developing a product or service is a one-time (temporary) **project,** composed of a set of activities to accomplish a specific deliverable, with start and end dates. Each stage can be considered a project because of the number of tasks or activities that are needed to complete its deliverable (e.g., the baseline requirements document for the concept stage). From the big picture perspective, these "stage" projects make up a larger project, called a **program,** where its deliverable is the final approved product or service which begins the production stage. Each stage's key milestones are scheduled, tracked, and controlled to ensure that all the deliverables are completed by their due dates.

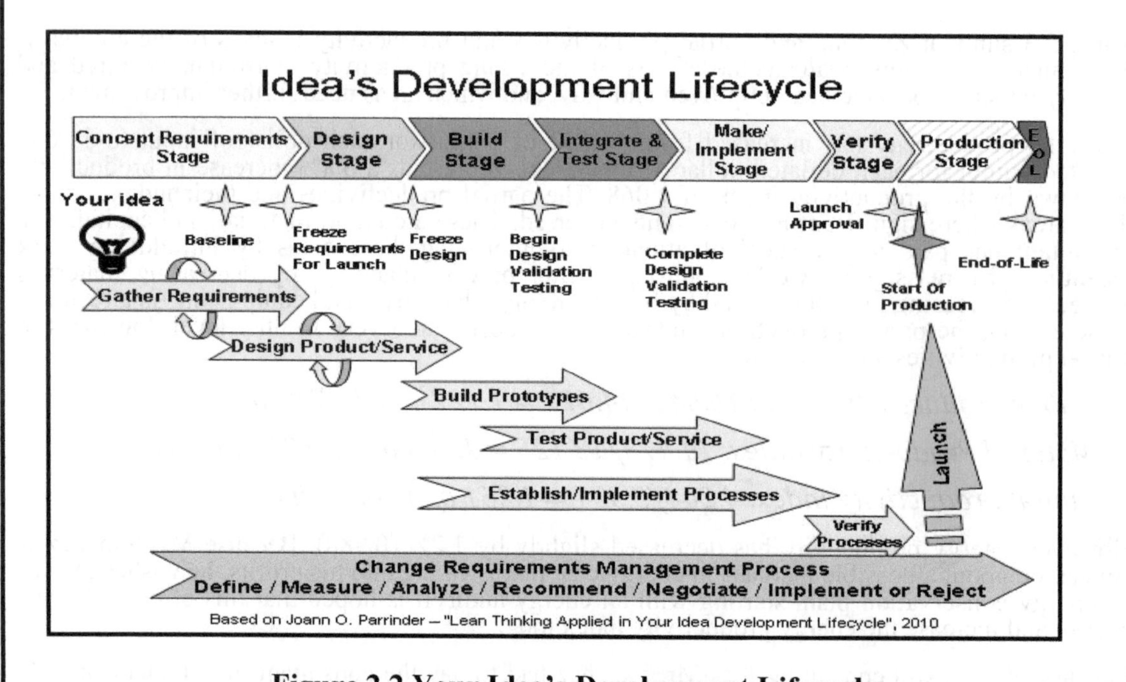

Figure 2.2 Your Idea's Development Lifecycle

The program manager oversees this lifecycle to ensure that the program stays within budget and meets all the deliverables including the final quality product or service to satisfy the customer.

The last process of Figure 2.2 depicts the change requirements management process. Throughout the idea's development lifecycle, changes do occur. Even as the idea is being organized, discussed, and documented, changes happen as it is reviewed and revised into its final form, the baseline requirements document. From this baseline, all the accepted additions, revisions, and deletions are integrated using the change requirements management process's phases: define, measure, analyze, recommend, negotiate, and implement or reject. Establishing such a process before beginning the development of any idea allows all the stakeholders, the ones invested in the program, including the engineering and manufacturing teams, to have clear guidelines on how to proceed when a change arises.

5.1 The Concept Requirements Stage

You begin the concept requirements stage by sorting out and communicating your idea to those who might be interested. One way to sort out your idea is to distinguish between "needs" and "nice-to-haves." What is a "need" versus a "nice-to-have"?

A "need" could be a product with basic features or functionality. For example, if the product is a remote key to open the driver side door of your car at the press of a specific button, then this remote key's basic function is a critical function that defines the product's basic purpose. If the need is a service, it could be like having your resume critiqued and professionally re-written for a position for which you are qualified and want to apply.

A "nice-to-have" includes those things that, while not necessary to the basic task or purpose at hand, would still add value to your experience. To illustrate this, consider your remote key to open the driver side of your car. Adding a remote start button on the electronic key would definitely be a "nice-to-have", but is not critical to the key's function of locking or unlocking doors and trunks. For the resume service (Figure 2.3), re-writing your resume for three different job positions is a "nice-to-have" in case you do not get the primary job for which you intend to apply, but is not critical for the task at hand: winning the project manager job you so desire. The "needs vs. nice-to-haves" chart allows you to sort out your idea's junk and eliminate waste. It is a format for later discussions on what process or product designs best fit the intended purpose.

An Example of a Resume Service Requirements or Options

Needs	Nice-To-Haves
• Critique current resume • Collect work experiences with start and finish dates, company, tasks, accomplishments • Write new resume for one position, e.g. project manager, that best uses the collection of work experiences • Write a cover letter that supports the project manager resume	• Re-write resume for a second position, e.g. IT project manager, using the work experiences that demonstrate this position • Write a cover letter that supports the IT project manager resume • Re-write resume for a third position, e.g. lean consultant, using the work experiences that demonstrate this position • Write a third cover letter that supports the lean consultant resume

Figure 2.3 Needs versus Nice-to-Haves

As your idea matures through the development timeline, each stage has start and end dates and key milestones that signal stage completion. Unless you communicate the concept of your idea in sufficient detail, however, it will remain a figment of your imagination. Therefore you must set up and organize your idea's concept and document it by using the **gather requirements process**.

You may start with a sketch, a list of features, a flow diagram, a value stream, or a one-page visual of your idea. Each sentence represents and describes a feature, in detail, possibly a length of time to perform a service, a condition when something should happen or not happen and so forth. The purpose of this stage is to set out a list of requirements necessary to see your idea all the way through to actual production.

Through your conversations, presentations, and discussions, you communicate in sufficient detail what this product or service is, so everyone will share the "vision" —the essence of your idea. This communication will be with your team, your management, your supplier and your customer or sponsor. When it is effective, they, too, will have the same vision for your idea. You have now developed a team that can help you take your idea from concept to reality.

Now you and your team must begin scrubbing and formalizing your idea by writing it down and creating the **requirements** or **specifications document**. This set of written requirements provides a permanent means to describe, explain, and communicate your idea to others. This gather requirements process allows you to scrub your idea, clean it up, and refine it with the help of experts, novices, owners, and anyone else who is a part of your team or interested in your idea. The value your idea brings to these people will also be written in the form of features, definitions of quality, operating instructions, test cases, and implementation procedures, to name a few. The requirements document will go through several iterations as you develop and refine the description of your idea into its final form.

Other questions to ask when scrubbing and documenting your idea are:

When is the product or service needed?

When are additional units or services necessary?

What kinds of testing must be done to ensure the consistent delivery of a quality product or service?

How much is the customer willing and financially able to spend?

What is the timetable for payment?

All are key components to aligning your customer needs and expectations with what your company can provide. The answers will help you successfully design and deliver the most suitable and flexible solution possible that will not only satisfy, but also surpass, the expectations of your customer.

Once all of the requirements are documented and scrubbed for accuracy, it is then called a **baseline requirements** or **specifications document**. This document is labeled "Version 1.0." This key milestone is noted by all stakeholders or their representatives through signed approval, signaling their agreement to proceed with materializing your idea through the production phase.

If your idea is to be provided by a supplier, the baseline requirements document is sent out in a Request-for-Quote (RFQ). The suppliers' responses are then evaluated for final selection. If your idea is to be created internally, such as assembly of a new product, a process improvement, or a new service, the baseline requirements document is distributed and your idea is presented and proposed to senior management for approval and funding. Whether it is supplier selection or funding approval, each step is a key milestone signaling that the concept_stage is completed, and you are ready to start the design stage in the development lifecycle process.

Throughout the idea lifecycle, it is important to recognize that changes do occur. Therefore, it is necessary to establish a **change management process** very early in your idea development lifecycle. Even as your idea is being organized, communicated, and written down, changes occur as it is refined into its final form, the baseline. This baseline requirements document is considered the "standard" in which to sustain your idea and all analyses for changes are compared to it. So all accepted additions, revisions, and deletions are integrated into this standard by using these change management process stages: define, measure, analyze, recommend, negotiate, and implement or reject each and every change that is considered.

Just as you did for your idea in the beginning, each change must be defined and written down: what it is, its purpose, and its benefit to the baseline. Once established, the change can be measured and analyzed with respect to how it would be integrated into your idea without causing the idea to lose its essence. Other considerations include how to do it in a timely manner and maintain cost effectiveness. The recommended integration and its cost must be negotiated to determine whether the change will be accepted or rejected. If accepted, the change, as part of the negotiation, must have an approved date to implement—a key milestone for the release of any approved change.

This release date may either be the original Start-Of-Production (SOP) date, or some date after the SOP date and released as an enhancement. Usually, the main roadblock to scheduling any change release is the length of time necessary to adequately develop and integrate the approved change into the overall solution to make it ready for release. When this happens, it usually means the release date falls after the SOP date.

Stakeholders must be careful to ensure that at some point a key milestone is put in place wherein all baseline changes must stop so that your idea can materialize on time and with quality. Ignoring this will jeopardize the SOP date and will prove costly. After all changes are made to the baseline specification, the document is updated as Version 1.1 and represents what will be launched at the start-of-production. Now the design can be fully developed and reviewed for accuracy with respect to the requirements.

5.2 The Design Stage

As the concept stage approaches completion with a baseline requirements document, your idea transitions to the next stage: design. In this stage, the baseline requirements begin to take shape, giving life to your idea and bringing it one step closer to the final outcome. This means there is sufficient detail to start laying it out, grouping the features perhaps, and establishing a sequence of drawings. For a product, it means the design engineer can start on the schematics and/or mechanical drawings. For a computer program, the programmer can begin to create technical designs, algorithms, flowcharts, and such. For a service, it means laying out what steps are needed, what skills are required to provide the service, and what length of time defines a service unit.

To sustain your idea through the design stage, it may be necessary to refine the requirements by utilizing your change management process. Once the design is approved by the engineering team, the design is frozen meaning no more changes are permitted and it is ready to move on to the build stage. Just as you did for your baseline requirements document, you label your final design specification drawings as version 1.0. Any approved changes to them would then require recognition with a change in this version number (e.g., 1.1, 1.2, etc.) to control changes. Now your idea can proceed to the next stage, the build stage.

5.3 The Build Stage

The build stage is when you begin to see the construction of the first units of your idea. For a product, you can see, touch, and operate it. For a service, you can begin to see the definition of the skills needed and the steps and procedures involved in executing the service. You can also plan for training, designate or hire employees to perform the service, and create a timetable for accomplishing the processes that make up your service. All these steps in the build stage transform your idea into its final form, which must not lose its essence. Everyone involved must study the design and ensure that there is enough detail to mentally construct it to completion or to ensure that it is built accurately.

For example, the program manager mentally constructs the idea to better understand any delays that may come up because of engineering issues. It also helps her to anticipate potential risks. Constant monitoring and controlling the schedule, budget, and scope comes from mentally constructing the idea into its final form. Having the mental image helps people grasp what the final form is and what it takes to keep the idea maturing through the development lifecycle process.

Just as you did in the previous stages of concept and design, if an issue or concern arises when building the product or performing the service, it may be necessary to revise (change) the requirements documented in the baseline requirements document. To protect and sustain the essence of your idea through the build stage, remember to use the change management process and define the change, analyze it for integration, and recommend or reject it. If this change involves additional funding or changes the requirement as it is in the baseline requirements document, then it will require customer approval to include the change and to increase the price to the customer. Sometimes the customer will approve the inclusion of the change, but will not approve the additional price, so you and your company may have to pay for the change. So it is important to get any and all changes as early as the concept stage because it becomes more expensive in later stages, like the build stage.

5.4 The Integrate and Test Stage

In the integrate and test stage, the first completed prototype product units or the first service set of procedures are tested. This may also require integrating or system testing them with other products or upstream or downstream processes to make sure they work as intended. If an electronics product (e.g., a cell phone, a radio, a microwave oven) requires software to operate, then its software must be loaded into the computer chip and perhaps integrated (e.g., parameters initiated) with other products or systems. Consequently, this integration must be tested so that all interactions work correctly to ensure expectations are met. For a service, you must execute scenarios or examples in which this service will be executed to test performance quality and to time the execution of each step. All defects, mistakes, or glitches —major or minor —are addressed. They must be documented, prioritized, and resolved in line with the baseline essence of the product or service.

If there is any issue or concern during this integrate and test stage, it may possibly affect the baseline requirements document. Just as you did in the previous stages, remember to use your change requirements management process to address and analyze all changes for acceptance or rejection while sustaining your idea through this integrate and test stage.

Finally, when the design validation tests and the process verification tests are completed with positive results, they are submitted to the customer to gain approval for launch into production. The customer acknowledges its approval by issuing a contract—invoice for quantities of the product or to establish the service on some frequency basis.

5.5 The Make or Implement Stage

In the make or implement stage, the product assembly operations or services provisioning processes established in the build stage are reviewed and refined where necessary to reduce operations time. In this stage, the manufacturing engineers are making sure that the processes are repeatable to make lots of quality products, and that there are sufficient resources and consistent quality expert services available. For a product, this establishes the production operations management processes—complete with proper and sufficient equipment, templates, operators, operator instructions, and the like—to build a quality product. The processes of making or implementing the idea as a product /service must be reviewed and approved to ensure that they will be done each and every time in a consistent manner. That way, the idea will be repeatable, sustainable, and quality-assured.

While it is less likely, should a change be necessary that would affect the baseline requirements document, remember to use your change requirements management process. This will allow your team to address any change and accept or reject it as you did with all previous changes to ensure that the essence of your idea is sustained. However, any change to the baseline requirements will be costly and most likely delay your launch into production, as defined by your original Start-Of-Production (SOP) date.

5.6 The Verify Stage

Once your operations management processes are established, they must be verified for approval to go into production. The verify stage is where everything is checked and traced back to the acceptance criteria requirements with measurements or data collected and evaluated against these criteria. The customer physically visits the plant and reviews the processes and results for acceptance or rejection. If rejected, all defects or mistakes identified and prioritized as "show-stoppers" must be resolved and re-verified to gain customer approval. Once approval is attained, the product, service, or process improvement—namely your idea—can be launched or released into production. At this point, your program typically is considered completed and the project closure phase begins while your idea transitions into production mode.

5.7 The Production Stage and End-of-Life

While in the production stage or, simply, in production, the change requirements management process continues to address all changes, enhancements, or improvements for acceptance or rejection. All accepted requirement changes must be added to the baseline document and its revision number updated. The changes themselves will be processed as projects with scheduled implementation release dates. This sustains the standard product or service documented in the latest version of the baseline requirements document.

Like most things, there comes a time to retire a product or service because there are no more orders for it or perhaps it has been replaced with a newer, better version. All version-controlled documentation must be kept for a determined period of time in a warehouse or archived records system in case it is needed while the product is still being used or while the outcome of the service is still under warranty. This time period could be as much as twenty years or more. For a product, some units may be required as spare parts; whereas for a service, expertise may be retained as part of the warranty period. Sometimes the design may be sold to aftermarket suppliers to provide these spare parts and/or services.

6. THE DEVELOPMENT LIFECYCLE KEY MILESTONES

As is mentioned above, each stage in the idea development lifecycle process has at least two key milestones: its start and finish dates. These key milestones are scheduled due dates when a stage should start by or finish by, or when a deliverable, such as a document, a prototype, or a report is due, in order to stay on track to launch the final product or service into production mode. Below is a summary of all of the major key milestones in the idea development lifecycle process.

6.1 Concept Requirement Stage

The key milestones (key due dates or delivery due dates) of the Concept Requirements Stage are:

- **Initiate the Concept** – when it all begins, that is, when an idea for a product or service is first discussed with key stakeholders, which include senior management of both the developers and potential customers.
- **Baseline the Requirements** – when an agreed-to set of requirements is completed so that the first look at the design of the product or service can begin; the first look at the finances as to what it will cost to construct the product or service is defined; and the first look from a marketing perspective including possible pricing, potential key clients and their volumes, and net profit is established.
- **Signing of the Development Contract** – when the development team has the authorization and the funding to begin developing the idea into a product/service to its completion with the approval to launch into production.
- **Kick-off Meeting** – when the first meeting takes place with the development team and key stakeholders to "kick off" the program and begin designing.
- **Freeze Requirements for Launch Date** – when no more approved changes can be done for this version of the product/service. From this date forward, any newly recommended and approved change must be released in a future version of the product/service. If this freeze date is not adhered to, then the product/service will not make the scheduled production launch date.
- **Start-Of-Production (SOP).**

6.2 Design Stage

The key milestones in the Design Stage are:

- **Freeze Design** – when the design of the product/service is the standard design completed so that the first prototypes are scheduled, built, and the testing to validate the design to the requirements begins to demonstrate that each requirement has been implemented in the design.

- **Freeze Final Design** – when the design of the product/service is completed (can sustain no more changes if it is to meet SOP) so that contracts with suppliers for specific components or subassemblies can be signed. Otherwise if the design is not frozen and changes are allowed, then the supplier cannot guarantee that he can deliver the correct quantity of the correct parts in time to begin production building at SOP, as well as the price, especially if a discount is included.

6.3 Build Stage

The key milestones of the Build Stage are:

- **Start Build (Prototypes) Date** – when the first prototypes are to begin construction and assembly. To ensure this date can happen, the material and component parts are needed a few days before, and a place or facility to assemble them must be identified if this build event is not going to happen in the company's plant.
- **Complete Prototype Build and Begin Design Validation (DV) Testing Date** – when the first prototypes are completely built so that testing can begin to validate the design to the requirements. Sometimes these two events happen on the same date.
- **Start the Process Verification Testing** – when data collection is started for the operations to assemble the product or to provide the service to determine if correct data is being captured and correct operations are being monitored to ensure consistency. It may take several trials to determine what to continue long term and what more is needed for design validation testing.

6.4 Integrate and Test Stage

The key milestones of the Integrate and Test Stage are:

- **Begin Design Validation Testing Date** – when the first prototypes are completely built or the date the first service procedures are completed so that testing can begin to validate the design to the requirements.

- **Complete Design Validation Testing Date** – when all of the prototypes or service pilots have satisfactorily completed all the DV testing and cases are used as planned to proof that the design is to spec, having met all the requirements.

6.5 Make or Implement Stage

The key milestones of the Make or Implement Stage are:

- **Start the Process Verification Testing** – when the testing starts—usually with the first prototype built—the activities are monitored and data collected on the process's key elements. These statistics act as proof that the process to build, to assemble the final product, or to provide the final service is according to the requirements that are repeatable and consistent. The analyzed documented data and its conclusions must show that the process is ready for approval, so one can begin producing products or services for the customers.

- **Complete Process Verification Testing** – when this testing is completed with "pass" results (no failures). These results must act as proof that the process to build and assemble the final product or provide the final service are according to the requirements that are repeatable and consistent.

6.6 Verify Stage

The key milestone for the Verify Stage is:

- **Gain Customer Approval to Launch and Receive Production Contract** – when the customer reviews all the reports, the processes, the production-ready prototypes, and compares them to the requirements for completeness and satisfaction. When the customer has completed this review, he/she decides that all is in order and grants the written approval for production to start by initiating the production contract via invoices for scheduled deliveries.

6.7 Production Stage

The key milestones for the Production Stage are:

- **Start of Production (SOP)** – when the first products or services are delivered and this process continues to make and deliver more products or provide more services to fill present and future customer orders.
- **End of Production or the End-of-Life (EOF)** – the last day when the final product is produced or the service is provided.

7. LOOKING AHEAD

All of these stages that we have briefly discussed here will be discussed in more detail in the coming chapters. However, the detail in these chapters will only be skimming the surface of what is necessary to take a product or service into production. We hope this text can provide you with a glimpse into how each stage may be accomplished. Each stage is performed by personnel of various levels of experience who have been educated by a degree program, such as a bachelor's degree program, or perhaps a certification program like one provided by a professional organization like APICS, the operations and supply chain management organization, or possibly your company will provide some form of company training in order for you and your co-workers to be able to do your jobs. So if the material presented in this book seems dauntingly complicated or difficult at times, it is, at first. But as you read, learn, and become more involved in the business operations processes of the company that you work for or will work for, you will become experienced enough to be able to perform them adequately and consistently as expected by your management and leaders.

8. GLOSSARY AND SUMMARY OF METHODS

Baseline Requirements or Specifications Document – The baseline requirements or specification document is established during the concepts requirement stage of the idea development lifecycle. This document reflects all requirements and is scrubbed for accuracy. At that point the document is labeled "Version 1.0."

Change Requirements Management Process – Change requirements management process is an established process defined before beginning the development of any idea, so that all the stakeholders have clear guidelines on how to proceed when change arises. The phases of the process consist of define, measure, analyze, recommend, negotiate, and implement or reject.

Gather Requirement Process – The gather requirement process is a process whereby you set up and organize your idea's concept in sufficient detail. You develop a list of requirements that are necessary to see your idea all the way through to actual production. It can include a sketch, a list of features, a flow diagram, a value stream, or a one-page visual of your idea.

Idea Development Lifecycle Process – The idea development lifecycle process is a systematic development lifecycle that moves an idea into the final product or service. The process moves the idea through seven stages. These stages are: the concept requirement stage, the design stage, the build stage, the integrate and test stage, the make or implement stage, the verify stage, and the final production stage.

Partial Productivity – The partial productivity is the ratio of gross or net output to one type of input.

Productivity Index – The productivity index is the ratio of two productivity factors.

Productivity Management – Productivity management relates to all functions of an organization and includes: measurement, evaluation, improvement, planning, and dissemination.

Productivity Measurement – Productivity measurement relates tangible output to tangible input.

Program – A program consists of various projects. The various projects, one for each stage, of the idea development lifecycle constitute a program with the final approved product or service as its deliverable.

Project – A project is a set of activities to accomplish a specific deliverable. Each activity has specific start and end dates. Each stage of the idea development lifecycle can be considered a project.

Requirements or Specifications Document – The requirements or specifications document is a permanent document to describe, explain, and communicate an idea to others.

Total Factor Productivity – The total factor productivity is the ratio of net output (gross output minus material value) to the sum of labor and capital.

Total Productivity – Total productivity is the ratio of all outputs versus all inputs.

9. ACRONYMS

EOR End-Of-Life
RFQ Request-For-Quote
SOP Start-Of-Production

10. REFERENCES

Aft, Lawrence S. *Productivity, Measurement and Improvement.* Reston, VA: Reston Publishing Company, 1983.

Ahmadian, A., Afifi, R. and W. D. Chandler. *Readings in Production and Operations Management - A Productivity Perspective.* Boston: Allyn and Bacon, 1990.

Dessler, Gary. *Improving Productivity at Work.* Reston, VA: Reston Publishing Company, Inc., 1983.

Ferdows, K. and A. De Meyer. "Manufacturing Futures Surveys, Europe." *Operations Management Review.* (Winter 1985).

Parrinder, Joann O. "Lean Thinking Applied to Your Idea Development Lifecycle." *Driving Operational Excellence: Successful Lean Six Sigma Secrets to Improve the Bottom Line.* Ron Crabtree, editor. MetaOps Publishing LLC, 2010, pp. 237–250.

Peters, T. J. and R.H. Waterman, Jr. *In Search of Excellence -Lessons from America's Best-Run Companies.* New York: Harper & Row Publishers, 1982.

Schermerhorn, J.R. Jr. *Management for Productivity.* New York: John Wiley & Sons, 1984.

Steele, Lowell W. *Managing Technology - The Strategic View.* McGraw Hill, 1989.

Sumath, J. and N. G. Einspruch N. G. "Productivity Awareness in the US: A Survey of some Major Corporations." *Journal of Industrial Engineering.* (October 1980): pp. 84–90.

11. REVIEW QUESTIONS

1. What is total productivity and the productivity index?
2. What is total factor productivity?
3. What is partial productivity and partial productivity index?
   Give some examples of partial productivity measures and explain how they are defined.
4. List all five productivity management activities and explain how they aid in improving productivity.
5. What are the stages of the idea's development lifecycle process?
6. Briefly explain each of these stages.
7. Why is it important to establish a change requirements management process at the beginning of the idea's development lifecycle process?
8. What is the baseline requirements or specifications document?
9. Can the baseline requirements or specification document change during the idea's development lifecycle process? Explain the process.
10. What is meant by "project" and "program"? Give examples.
11. Name some key milestones for each stage of the development lifecycle.

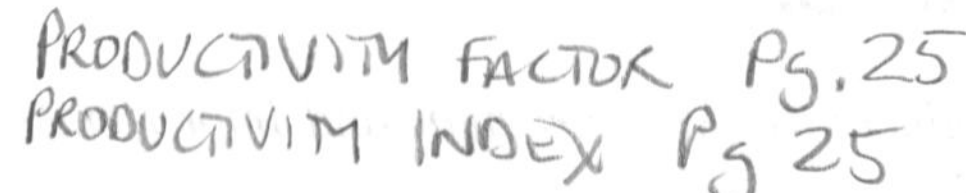

12. PROBLEMS

Problem #1 (EXCEL)

A company is solely involved in the manufacturing of 4 products. Their deflated output values (1985 is base year) for the last 5 years are as follows:

Year	Product #1	Product #2	Product #3	Product #4
1985	40,000	40,000	40,000	40,000
1986	53,000	53,000	53,000	53,000
1987	62,000	62,000	62,000	62,000
1988	53,500	62,000	62,000	62,000
1989	54,000	61,500	67,500	67,500

The deflated input values of the resources used to generate these products are as follows:

Year	Labor	Materials	Capital	Others
1985	60,000	24,000	30,000	6,000
1986	60,000	54,000	30,000	6,000
1987	66,000	59,000	33,000	6,600
1988	66,000	59,000	33,000	6,600
1989	66,000	59,000	41,500	6,600

a) Use the above data to calculate total productivity and partial productivity (labor, materials, capital, and others) for the years 1985 through 1989.

b) Also calculate total productivity indexes and partial productivity indexes (labor, materials, capital, and others) for the years 1986 through 1989.

c) Analyze these (total and partial) indexes and discuss how productive the company has been during the past four years.

Problem #2 (EXCEL)

Consider the following tables to answer all questions.

Table 1. Computation of the value of the output factors of ABC Company		
OUTPUT FACTORS	**Value Base Year**	**Value Last Year**
Finished goods In-process inventory Dividends Interest	\$24,570 \$ 4,980 \$2,900 \$1,100	\$33,960 \$ 3,960 \$ 3,050 \$ 1,130
at the beginning of the base year the in-process inventory value was \$3,000		

Table 2. Computation of the values of the input factors of ABC Company		
INPUT FACTORS	**Value Base Year**	**Value Last Year**
Labor	$2,233	$2,458
Materials	$2,230	$2,460
Capital-		
Fixed	$7,840	$7,517
Working	$952	$950
Energy	$1,838	$2,258
Other	$4,270	$6,424

a) Calculate the total productivity index.

b) What are the partial productivities of energy, labor, materials, total capital, and other?

c) What are their partial productivity indexes?

Problem #3 (EXCEL)

Consider the following data supplied by a Michigan-based utility company. This data does not include materials cost, because the company believes that it has no control over the utilization of all its materials.

	AMOUNT Base Month	AMOUNT Last Month	BASE RATE	INDEX
INPUT				
1. Labor	4,900 hours	5,100 hours	$12.70/hour	1.05
2. Short-Term Capital	$90,840	$102,560	12%	1.06
3. Rent/Supplies	$3,260	$3,800		1.04
OUTPUT				
Net Output	$100,000	$140,000*		
* There was a $20,000 rate hike made by the company last month.				

a) Calculate the values for the base month and last month for all inputs and outputs. (Warning: the table may have information that is not needed!)

b) Calculate the total factor productivity for the base month and the last month.

c) What is the total factor productivity index?

d) Calculate the labor productivity and the labor productivity index.

Chapter 3

PRODUCT/SERVICE DESIGN

1. FUNCTION OF PRODUCT DESIGN

The basic function of product design is to convert the general specifications of a product into its technical specifications. The requirements or general specifications of a product or service describe its functional requirements (i.e., its intended use), its performance quality, its reliability, its maintainability, as well as its market image. Put simply, the general specifications address the following questions about a product:

1. What can the product do?
2. How well can the product do what it is supposed to do?
3. How dependable is the product when it is doing what it is supposed to do?
4. How easy is it to repair or recondition the product when it fails?
5. How well do the customers think the product addresses the above questions?

The general specifications are based on information supplied by the marketing function. A well-defined general specification should accurately reflect the users' needs and the market requirements. The general specifications do not necessarily reflect the actual production capability of the system through which the product is made or through which the service is rendered.

The technical specifications of a product define the production requirements that will satisfy the product's general specifications and that can be achieved at a minimum cost under specific production conditions. Cost and productivity are the major concerns when converting the general specifications of a product into its technical specifications. The technical specifications may be expressed under different forms, including engineering drawings, engineering bills of materials, engineering databases, service contracts, insurance policies, course curricula, restaurant menus, or physician's medical prescriptions.

Technically and economically, it is not always possible to satisfy all the general specifications desired by the market. The product design decisions usually result from a rational trade-off among marketing requirements, engineering concepts, and production capabilities. Therefore, the product design does not necessarily meet all of the general specifications without some modification. The technical specifications, as determined by the product design function, dictate most of the productive activities of a firm, including manufacturing processes, facility layout, material handling, production control, inventory control, quality control, as well as transportation. In fact, the product design decisions set the basic tone for the entire organization.

2. TYPES OF PRODUCT DESIGN ACTIVITIES

To maintain an ageless vigor and a solid market position, a productive system must continuously search for new products and improve the existing products. For most of the manufacturing firms and an increasing number of service firms, product design is an on-going activity carried out under different forms. Generally, there are three different types of product design activities:

1. New product design projects
2. Major revisions in the design of existing products
3. Minor improvements in the design of current products

A new product design project involves a great number of activities. It usually starts with a product idea conceived by the marketing and product research function and approved by top management. The design activities often cycle through several stages: preliminary design, prototype testing, functional design, form design, and production design. At each stage, the new product design may not necessarily be accepted. In those cases, the design procedure will cycle back from where it failed. This procedure is not only required for the new product as a whole, but is also required for each and every part and component used in this new product. The relationship among all parts and components must also be thoroughly tested. When hundreds and thousands of parts are involved in some modern product, the coordination of a new product design project becomes one of the major concerns of the new product design function. Some of the better-managed firms use project management techniques to schedule and control the progress of their new product projects.

A major revision in the design of current products is often caused by the availability of new technology, new materials, new styles, new government regulations, or the discovery of some malfunction in the existing product design. Major revisions can be quite an expensive undertaking. However, revision is often necessary to revitalize an eroding market position or to take advantage of new technology and new materials, which may, in the long run, reduce the total cost through economical production. Such a revision is normally decided on by higher-level management and is often carried through the research and development stages before it reaches the production design function.

Minor improvements in the design of current products may be necessitated by a number of internal and external factors. The major source of minor improvements comes from a productivity improvement program and value analysis and value engineering (VAVE) activities. Those changes involve only the product design function and the directly affected areas. Normally, only a cost justification is required to initiate a minor improvement request. Value analysis and value engineering activities relate available alternatives and their costs to the purpose of the existing product and result in minor product improvements and reduction in product cost. In other words, VAVE is the result of analyzing the current design's value in dollars and re-engineering this design to one that costs less to produce the parts. An approved VAVE effort is a project which is funded using the savings that would be generated by using this less expensive design. These net savings must take into consideration the time spent to perform this VAVE effort as well as the time needed in re-doing the current design to the less-expensive design, building prototypes and testing them to demonstrate that they meet all quality criteria that the current design provides, and procuring any tools or manufacturing changes that are needed to put this newly designed part into production.

3. *MARKET FACTORS IN PRODUCT DESIGN*

To maintain a strong and lasting market appeal, the product design must satisfy the following basic requirements:

1. Sound in functional design
2. Attractive in appearance
3. Convenient in maintenance
4. Competitive in pricing

3.1 Functional Design

A new product, or the improvement of an existing product, should satisfactorily perform its intended functions under a set of given conditions. The functional design takes into consideration how the product is to be consumed or used, how it is put together, the physical and chemical characteristics, the quality and longevity of the product, as well as the materials that go into it. Thus, a sound functional design is able to ensure that the design will work and accomplish its intended purposes under the conditions of its intended users. However, a functional design may serve its intended purpose well, but it may not take into consideration its sales appeal and ease of maintenance and manufacturing. It is not uncommon to find a product with a functionally sound design that is failing miserably because of poor appearance, poor maintenance records, or noncompetitive pricing.

3.2 Appearance

With high competitiveness in the modern market and strong influence of the mass media, a superior visual appearance of a product often commands a decisive lead over similar products in the market. The appearance of a product may also create an initial, sometimes false, impression on a buyer about the functional performance of the product as well. The chrome finish or the white external paint may suggest cleanliness of hospital equipment; the streamlined body shape may suggest high performance of a car, etc.

The importance of appearance to sales is not only true for manufactured products; it is even more critical in the service industry. The outdoor decor may suggest the type of food served in a restaurant. The height of a building may suggest the financial strength of an insurance company. The way goods are packaged may suggest the quality of the merchandise carried by a retail store. However, the product that has an attractive appearance without a sound functional design may lose all of its initial gains shortly after its introduction. It may even create a bad reputation for the company that made that product and subsequently hurt the sales of other products of the same company. It may take a little longer for the customer to react to poor maintainability of the product. But the net result will be the same unless the company does not intend to stay in business for a long time.

3.3 Maintainability

Except for disposable goods, most products require some sort of periodic maintenance or repair to ensure or to reinstall their performance quality. Maintenance and repair for the user of the product results in loss of time, added expense, and temporary inconvenience while the item is being serviced. With skyrocketing service charges, more and more consumers perform their own maintenance at home. Therefore, ease of maintainability of a product becomes increasingly important to a buyer in selecting a product. The modular design of TV sets reduces the need for house-calls and service time. Machine-washable garments are more popular than those that need dry-cleaning. A machine with a centralized lubrication system is much more preferred over the ones with numerous lubricating points. The longevity or durability of a product is closely related to its maintainability. Therefore, the cost for providing product maintainability must be weighed against its replacement cost. Modern mass production and international manufacturing often reduce production cost to such a level that any maintenance work can become economically unreasonable, such as electronic watches and clocks, electronic calculators, black and white TV sets, portable radios, vacuum cleaners, toys, and numerous disposable goods.

3.4 Price

The price structure of a product must reflect its conceived value in the marketplace. It is the buyer or the customer who has to decide if he/she is willing to pay the price for the product. Pricing is essentially a marketing function. But the product designer must be sensitive to the value judgment of the market for the product or service under consideration. He should not over-design a product to such an extent that not one or very few buyers are willing to pay the extra price for it. Nor should he under-design a product so that it does not meet the expectation of the market. A good product design should strive for a high value product image at a minimum possible unit production cost.

During the introductory stage of a new product, the price tag may actually be below the current production cost. However, the marketing function must have reasons to believe that the sales volume will build up and the production function must have reasons to believe that the unit cost will drop below its selling price. In our economic system, competition is the major driving force that strives continuously for better and more goods at a minimal cost. The product design function is compelled to continuously search for ways to improve its designs. The ever-changing design or redesign are unavoidable. But we also should remember that any design change after the product has been released for production is likely to be much more expensive to make.

4. COST FACTORS IN PRODUCT DESIGN

The market factors reflect the demand side of constraints on the product design. The cost factors, in turn, are the supply side of the constraints. The final decision of a product design is often based on its cost effectiveness, that is, the dollar amount spent on a product versus the amount of dollars it generates through sales. Product design by itself does not determine the product cost. However, it sets the basic constraints for the production function in controlling the cost of the product.

Generally, one may break down the cost elements of a product as follows:

- Development cost
- Material cost
- Operating/manufacturing cost
- Marketing cost
- Capital cost (or opportunity cost)
- Overhead cost

Product design decisions have a direct impact on the material cost and the operating/manufacturing cost.

The types and the amount of material required to build a product are basically determined through product design. Product designers must constantly be aware of new material developments and material supply in the market in order to take advantage of newer, better, and/or cheaper materials and to avoid selecting the materials that are in short supply.

Manufacturing and operating costs consist of labor cost, facility cost, utility cost, and energy cost. The complexity of the shape, the accuracy of the dimensions, and the stringency of the performance requirements, as specified through product design, determine the manufacturing cost of the product. Product designers must be familiar with the production facilities of the firm and manufacturing methods of the trade. A product design may have perfect functional design with excellent sales appeal on the drawing board; yet, it cannot be made under the existing production conditions at a reasonable cost. This product design would not have any value to the organization and should never get into the production stage. Therefore, all product designs are normally carried out in two stages (i.e., the functional design and the design for production).

5. MAJOR PRINCIPLES IN PRODUCT DESIGN

In order to produce a large variety of low-cost, high quality products for mass consumption, modern production organizations often follow a series of design principles in their product design.

The four most important principles in modern product design are the following:

- Standardization
- Interchangeability
- Modularization
- Designing for production

5.1 Standardization

Standardization is one of the most important principles in all branches of modern industry. It establishes the mandatory or recommended norms to which different design attributes (i.e., dimensions, shapes, weights, and colors) of a product should conform. It reduces design repetitions and production changes. In other words, standardization is a design concept for ease of design itself. Depending on the type of the product and its attributes, the product standards may be set up for a shop, a plant, a firm, a trade, a state, an entire country, or a group of trading nations.

When a standard is set only for a firm, a plant or a shop, it is considered as an internal standard and its only purpose is to reduce production cost. If standards are set for an entire industry, then it would also improve the serviceability and reduce the maintenance cost of the product. For discrete parts manufacturers, production functions become manageable only through standardization. This is especially true, for example, for machine builders, where a very large variety of parts are used. The objectives of standardization on the production system are:

- To reduce a large number of different types of parts and to reduce dimensions of similar parts to a manageable number. With the smaller variety and larger quantity, it is possible to reduce production time and to avoid design repetition.
- To enable the perfection of the design, testing, and manufacturing of the standardized product. This results in improved quality and reliability of the product.
- To simplify the production changeover and to reduce the number of redesigns and retooling.
- To simplify the maintenance of the product, since replacement parts may be readily available.

The benefits of standardization in the service industry are also evident. For example, the food-service industry traditionally has little standardization. As a result, it exhibits low productivity. Data show that when standardization concepts are adopted by the fast food industry, its productivity improves drastically.

5.2 Interchangeability

Interchangeability relates closely to standardization. However, the two terms do not mean exactly the same thing. Interchangeability is a design concept for ease of manufacturing. It restricts variation amongst the fitting parts. Thus, parts coming from different production runs can perform identical functions as specified by the product design. Interchangeability is a prerequisite of mass production because it makes random part selection during assembly possible. For example, light bulbs and most bolts and nuts are interchangeable, whereas same-size ball bearings of different applications are not necessarily interchangeable.

Note that two standardized parts may not necessarily be interchangeable, but two interchangeable parts must be standardized.

5.3 Modularization

Modularization is a design concept for ease of maintenance of the product. Modularized product design suggests that a complicated product be subdivided into different building blocks that can be produced individually and replaced quickly. For example, filters in furnaces, cartridges in printers, fuses in electrical boxes, light bulbs, and batteries are all replaceable parts that can be purchased at local hardware-like retail stores. Modularization may also be used as an extension of standardization in product design. In the latter application, the designer creates several different models of the same product through substitution of one or more modules. Therefore, the production lot size can be increased and model change disturbances in the shops can be reduced or minimized.

5.4 Designing for Production

A perfect functional design of a product does not necessarily guarantee the success of the product in the marketplace if it is too expensive to make. The product design decisions are not only concerned with the functional utility and sales appeal of a product, but they are also concerned with the selection of materials, of manufacturing methods, of production processes, and of production equipment.

Designing for production is concerned with the design of a sound product for economical manufacturing. It is also concerned with the design and selection of tools, equipment, methods, and technology for its production. Designing for production is an inter-disciplinary function which is involved with both product and process design. It provides an important linkage between the product concept and the production reality. Since the primary concern of the product designer is the performance and appearance of a product, the designer often tends to over-design a product at the expense of productivity and production cost. In other instances, cost control and cost reduction have dominated management thinking. The design quality of the product may suffer and result in an inferior product. To keep check and balance among the different factors, design for production function integrates and takes all the design and production factors into consideration. Therefore, design for production is an essential step in product design. More on this subject will be discussed in the next chapter.

6. PRODUCT DESIGN PROCEDURE

Product or service design generally starts with ideas coming from individuals or consumers. When such ideas are brought to the company, a product management team is put together. This team may consist of representatives from various functions of the organization such as sales, manufacturing, engineering, marketing, costing, and others. It is their role to help navigate the concept from idea to manufacturing. The design engineer will evaluate the technical characteristics of the idea. This may be followed with a paper drawing or sketch, before the real design process takes place. A product is normally designed using modern tools such as computer aided design software. Depending on the complexity of a product, suppliers get involved as soon as possible to minimize delay.

Product design in the U.S. normally consists of the following six steps:

Step 1: Recognizing the market needs for either a new product or a modification of an existing product based on customer or market information.

Step 2: Defining the general specifications that may satisfy the market needs.

Step 3: Synthesizing all relevant information and conceptualizing the overall system and the individual elements of the product in order to come up with a preliminary design.

Step 4: Analyzing the feasibility of the preliminary design. In this step, one determines whether any improvement or adjustment needs to be made, whether the preliminary design is acceptable or should be rejected. Unless the preliminary design is acceptable, the design must be returned to Step 3.

Step 5: Evaluating the design against its general specifications and production requirements by the use of scale models, prototype models, or computer simulation models.

Step 6: Documenting and presenting the design to the shop floor and other production supporting functions. The commonly used product design documents include engineering drawings, electrical and electronic circuit diagrams, bills of materials, engineering and material specifications, design data bases, and so on.

The synthesis and analysis (steps 3 and 4) in product design are often iterative procedures that consume a great amount of engineering time. These two steps may generate a series of preliminary designs through trial and error, during which sophisticated engineering calculations are performed for each iteration. These two activities are traditionally considered to be highly creative and are manually performed using computer aided design (CAD) equipment and software by well-paid design engineers.

The documentation and presentation step of the final product design often consumes a great amount of time in drafting, tabulating, and checking of standards. This final step is not as demanding in creativity and engineering education as steps 3 and 4 are. Nevertheless, it requires extensive training and experience.

Product design goes beyond the six steps described above. Documents presented to the shop floor contain prints that specify materials and dimensions critical to safety performance and reliability. Selection of exact fasteners or non-critical parts may await negotiation with suppliers. Details of the fit of non-critical parts may not be determined until plant production starts. Often a new model start-up takes place with design engineers living in the plant and working out the changes. Several pilot production runs may be necessary to work out necessary changes. In many auto manufacturing companies, for example, several thousand minor design changes may occur during the start-up of a completely redesigned model.

7. LEAN PRODUCT DEVELOPMENT

Lean product development aims at reducing waste during the development process of a product or service. Waste of the product development activity occurs when time is wasted because of poor development procedures: when customers' desires are poorly understood resulting in products that require major redesigns over their product lifecycle, or when products are either over- or under-designed. Quality function deployment aims at making the product development function more lean and more in tune with the customers' desires. It is a methodology that ensures that all functions of the organization work together to provide the customers with exactly what they want.

Lean product development also aims at companies quickly responding to the changing needs and tastes of the customers. Successful companies increase value when they reduce or make more reliable the time-to-market lead time. The time-to-market lead time is the total time that a firm takes to conceive, design, test, or redesign products for the market. This requires the use of tools that accelerate product development. Some of these tools are:

- Quality function deployment (QFD)
- Computer aided design (CAD)
- Computer aided engineering analysis (e.g., determining reliability of the components, or performing computer simulation)
- Rapid prototyping, perhaps using stereo lithography apparatus (SLA), 3-D printer, or vacuum casting for rapid tooling
- Group technology principles found in your product data management software
- Simultaneous or concurrent engineering

Companies that have significantly decreased their time-to-market lead time are: Honda (cars from 5 years to 2 years), Navistar (trucks from 5 years to 2 years), AT&T (phones from 2 years to 1 year and even less), and Hewlett Packard (printers from 4.5 years to less than 1 year).

Why is it more important now than it was in the past to speed up the product development cycle and the prototype process? The most important reason is to increase sales. If a product is introduced quickly, then it is more probable that the competition will be taken off guard. The initial product in a given market obviously enjoys complete market share, which can translate into larger market share in the future. Higher profit margins can also be expected for those who are the market pioneers as competitive pricing pressure is initially nonexistent. If a competitor establishes a new market, it is even more critical to have a fast new product cycle so that the competition can be matched quickly before the pioneer can get too strong of a foothold on the market. Responsiveness and flexibility to meet quickly changing customer markets, styles, needs, and tastes have also become more important over time. Companies that are regarded as leaders in their industries usually rely on a steady stream of innovative new products. In those cases, fast new product development is considered one of their main strengths. Customers' needs and tastes are changing at an increasing rate and it is critical that companies respond to these changing needs quickly in order to remain successful in the future.

7.1 Quality Function Deployment (QFD)

Quality function deployment is a methodology that ensures that all functions of the organization work together to provide the customers with exactly what they want. It provides the company with a road map showing how each function, from design to delivery, must interact to fulfill all customers' requirements.

Quality function deployment enables the organization to:

1. Identify the qualities a customer desires to have in products/services
2. Identify the functions the products/services serve and what functions must be engaged to provide the customers with the desired products/services
3. Identify what available resources best provide the customers with their desired products/services
4. Translate broad general specifications or problems into specific technical specifications through a series of matrices

The QFD methodology consists of four phases. They are the ***design phase***, the ***detail phase***, the ***process phase***, and the ***production phase***. At each phase data are placed in a matrix-like diagram, called the ***house of quality***. The house of quality is a diagram that resembles a house. For example in the first QFD phase, the design phase, the customer requirements are broken down into attributes, the ***Whats***, and ranked for importance. Each attribute is then compared relatively speaking to the engineering designs, the ***Hows***, as to how well each design fulfills each requirement attribute. In this house, each attribute is also competitively analyzed, the ***Whys***, as to why it should be in the product because other competitors have it. Along with each attribute's engineering design, current performance level is considered against target performance levels. For the second QFD phase, the detail phase, a new house of quality diagram is created. This time, the engineering designs are the ***Whats***, and compared relatively speaking to, for example, the various suppliers' component parts that might fulfill the engineering design being evaluated, along with the current levels versus target levels of performance criteria. This process is repeated for the remaining two QFD phases, each with their own house of quality diagram.

An Example: Creating a More Powerful Cordless Drill

As a power tool manufacturer, your company finds out that your customers wish to have more powerful cordless drills.

Phase 1, The Design Phase: The customer's information of "*more power*" becomes the *What* on the matrix. This specification can be achieved with a larger motor, a different motor technology, or a different winding configuration. These three means become the *Hows*. After creating the correlation matrix and computing the values in the relationship matrix, the design team decides that the best solution is a *larger motor*. A *larger motor* becomes a *What* in the second phase.

Phase 2, The Detail Phase: When considering design specifications for a larger motor, through technical assessment and the relationship matrix, the company decides that maintaining the present shaft size will save redesign cost. *Present motor shaft size* is therefore entered in the matrix as a *How* and transfers to the next phase as the *What*.

Phase 3, The Process Phase: In this phase, ways are evaluated to improve the shaft's ability to manage a larger torque that will be generated by a larger motor. This can be achieved with different materials or heat-treating the present materials. The *Hows* are therefore different materials and heat-treating the present materials. These *Hows* are analyzed and it is decided that the best solution is *heat-treating the present materials* which becomes the *What* of the next phase.

Phase 4, The Production Phase: How to best make the shaft and assemble the motor are now determined. These can be done by either modifying the present equipment or by purchasing a new machine. Customers' requirements are best satisfied with a *new machine*.

7.2 Computer Aided Design (CAD)

Commonly referred to as CAD, computer aided design is performed by a computerized graphical system that involves a human (the designer), a machine (the computer hardware), and their interface (the software). The earliest application of the CAD system was for the preparation of engineering drawings. That is why the term CAD was once referred to as computer aided drafting. In this application, the system converts the digital information of some geometric forms or network relationships into graphics or drawings through an electronic x-y plotter.

The x-y plotter is essentially a numerically controlled machine that includes a large drawing board and one or more writing pens or pencils—for different color presentations. The writing heads can move along the y-axis of the coordinate system on a bridge which, in turn, can move along the x-axis. Here, information is inputted either through a keyboard, or a computer monitor display in the form of digital data. Using computers only for the preparation of engineering drawings does not take full advantage of the modern computer capabilities and often proves to be uneconomical. Modern trends in CAD tend to eliminate engineering drawings all together. The entire design information can be efficiently stored in digital form that can be conveniently retrieved, manipulated, and integrated with other production information.

A modern CAD system is a human-computer interactive system. The computer communicates with its user through a computer monitor, and the user (designer) sends data and commands through a keyboard, function buttons, and a light pen. The keyboard is used to enter design data, users' programs, and/or program commands. The function buttons are used to select hard-wired machine functions for creating, scaling, rotating, erasing, or reversing graphical images based on stored geometric information. The light pen provides a very convenient means for the designer to interact directly with the computer or the image displayed by the computer on the computer monitor.

The high speed and high storage capacity of the modern computer, together with a powerful CAD software package, make it possible for modern CAD systems to perform an enormous number of detailed computations with extreme accuracy within an incredibly short period of time. The computer is able to generate a series of design alternatives and the designer is able to manipulate these alternate designs on the computer monitor in search of an optimal solution. The computer is also able to check and reveal all the visual or conceptual errors at each iterative stage. Thus, the synergistic effect of the CAD system may immensely improve the productivity of the product design function. Designers are not only able to accomplish their work much faster, with much fewer design errors, but are also able to extend design capability to many tasks which previously were impossible. Clever capabilities, such as multiple views, or spatial relationships among parts in an assembly, or moving objects, are continuously expanding as more and more new CAD software becomes available.

In addition to generating geometric relationships in product design, the CAD system may also get involved with such engineering analyses as stress and strain analysis on a machine member, thermometer distributions, heat-transfer calculations, and dynamic system behavior simulation.

To take fully advantage of the synergistic effect, it is important to understand the relative strength between the human and the computer during the system and job design function. While the computer gradually takes over all of the memory and calculation tasks of the design process, the creative aspect of the design will remain in the human domain for the foreseeable future.

Much computer aided design effort today is broken into two parts, the engineering design concept developed by the engineer and documented as instructions to the computer aided design technician who performs the actual physical electronic design drawings much like the draftsmen did before the use of computers. With the internet and technology today, in some cases, the CAD technician's work can be done as contract work by a firm in another country.

7.3 Rapid Prototyping

First, it is important to establish the role that prototyping plays in the new product development cycle. What are prototypes used for and how are they critical in the new product development? Prototyping can be used for customer feedback and learning. Form, fit, and functionality of products/parts can be better visualized and concepts can be studied so that choices can be made relative to the remaining work on the concept. Prototypes also can help to bridge new concept communication and information gaps between parties from various backgrounds, experiences, and interests. Prototypes can be used to describe concerns and issues among the parties and can help in the decision making process. Prototypes can also be used to prove degrees of success to management, the customer, and financial institutions. Great enthusiasm about a product's future can be generated through the use of prototypes because the concepts become more "realistic" and believable to the outside world.

Stereo lithography apparatus (SLA) and 3-D printing are versatile, rapid prototyping tools that can not only turn concept into realism; but can also be combined with a vacuum casting process to turn out many functional test parts in less than a day. SLA for rapid prototyping was first put into practice in 1987. This new technique was the first commercially available cumulative layer process that utilized CAD data to generate a 3-dimensional prototype part quickly. The SLA process requires CAD input that is translated into stereo lithography format, and SLA equipment and hardware to generate the prototype. SLA parts are now approaching the accuracy of computer numerically controlled (CNC) machined parts. This means that prototype parts can be not only made rapidly, they can be made accurately as well. Part sizes can be as small as fractions of an inch cubed up to many feet cubed depending on the equipment used. Multiple parts (similar or different) may also be made in the same build batch using SLA.

The total time required to produce functional prototypes is an accumulation of the functions, as shown in Table 3.1. Until recently, prototyping could take up to several weeks or even months to make. Skilled trades were often required to manually manufacture parts. Although the total time to produce rapid prototype parts is currently very short compared to just ten years ago, it is certain that the goal of the rapid prototyping/tooling/parts industry will be to target the reduction of time required to complete the new product development cycle. More specifically, the SLA manufacturers will continually try to improve the time that it takes to fabricate a prototype part. Direct SLA parts that are fully functional are the ultimate in advancement. Once fully functional SLA parts are producible directly from CAD software, the focus will shift to delivering the fully functional part at increasing speed, using software that is easy to use. These advances will allow businesses that are committed to flexibility and speed to market for new products to adapt to the changing needs of the customer more efficiently. Those businesses that do not utilize these advances may fall by the wayside.

Table 3.1: Time Required for Rapid SLA Prototyping, Molds, and Parts

Rapid Prototype Step	Time to Complete Step (Estimated Hours – typical)	Cumulative Time (Estimated Hours – typical)
CAD design	Completely Variable	Completely Variable
Manipulation of 3-D STL file	1 to 3	1 to 3
Definition/processing of SLI(ce) file	1	2 to 4
Part fabrication using SLA(pparatus)	4 to 20	6 to 24
Post curing of parts	1 to 4	7 to 28
Rapid Tool Manufacturing	5 to 8	12 to 36
Rapid Part Manufacturing	1 (each)	13 to 36

7.4 Group Technology (GT)

In the U.S.A., Germany, Japan, Russia, the U.K, and other countries, group technology (GT) is a system with many names and definitions: part family manufacturing, family planning, family grouping, and many others.

Group technology is a manufacturing philosophy whereby similar parts are identified and grouped together to take advantage of their similarities in manufacturing and design. When GT is applied, the parts used by a manufacturing firm are classified and coded based on their geometric shapes, sizes, and/or manufacturing processes. Based on the code assigned to each part, similar parts can be quickly identified and grouped together as a part family.

In the U.S.A., the general concept and approach of GT has been practiced for a long time under different names in various forms of industrial engineering functions for more efficient, scientific, optimum manufacturing operations. However, it is only since the early eighties that GT has received formal recognition and has been practiced as a systematic scientific technology applied to small lot production, which is most common to small and medium industries. Although there have been many application examples of GT in various forms and degrees in the U.S., there are considerably fewer published studies, data, or case histories available to the public compared to European countries and Japan.

Before the use of GT, General Dynamics' Pomona Division, for example, came across a case where a virtually identical nut and coupling unit had been designed on five different occasions by five design engineers and then drawn by five draftsmen. These parts were purchased from five suppliers at prices ranging from $.22 to $7.50 each. The company also investigated 2,891 parts with different part numbers and discovered that the number of distinct shapes leveled out fairly quickly to comprise a population of only 541 shapes.

Such design proliferation occurs because, without the existence of a system such as GT the designer finds creating a new part easier than being patient in finding or looking up similar previously designed parts. Each time a new part is created, a new part number must be assigned to it, a new process plan made up for it, and new tools designed.

GT coding of parts is useful for the efficient retrieval of previous designs, as well as for design standardization. These features help speed up the design process and curb design proliferation. During the preliminary design stage, the designer can determine the appropriate code number for each new part required. Consequently, he can easily identify the new part with its family. The designer now can retrieve an existing part design within this part family that meets the specifications and requirements of the new part. If no exact match can be found within the part family, the designer needs only to make some alterations from the existing design to create the new part. Thus, the design effort is reduced significantly. For a typical new product design, reports show that about 40% of the parts already exist, another 40% need only some modifications, and only about 20% need new design.

Though GT is not a computer-dependent technology, the combination of GT and CAD can further increase the productivity of product design. The retrieval and alteration process as required by GT can be accomplished easily at the CAD terminals within a small fraction of the time required by traditional design methods. The application of GT can also facilitate standardization. Without special effort, the superior design features will be easily retained with family part design. Therefore, design quality can also be improved.

7.5 Simultaneous or Concurrent Engineering

The basic functions that are involved in bringing a new product to the market are: the marketing function to define the market requirements; the product planning function that helps in defining the general specifications of the product; the design function that translates the general specifications into technical specifications; the process planning function that deals with preparing the product for manufacturing; the manufacturing function; and the field services function. In a lean enterprise these functions are no longer done sequentially, one after the other, but are done simultaneously. This is often referred to as simultaneous engineering or concurrent engineering. In this way all functional groups have a global perspective on the entire project and problems are recognized early and resolved by all functions involved. The overlapping execution of the various functions makes the product suitable for manufacturing without further delays (designing for production) and shortens the birth process of the product significantly.

8. PRODUCT OR SYSTEM RELIABILITY

Basically there are two types of probability that are important for assessing reliability. First, there is the probability that the product or system will function on any given trial and, secondly, there is the probability that the product or system will function for a given length of time.

8.1 Fixed Time Reliability

The first type of probability focuses on one point in time and is used when a system or product must operate for one of a few numbers of times.

The probability that a product or system will perform at a given time is a function of the reliability of its component parts and how these parts are interrelated. The system reliability is equal to the product of the reliability of its component parts. Let us imagine a system that is composed of two components, A and B. Both components must work for the system to work. If the reliability of component A is .95 and if component B has a reliability of .90 then the system has a reliability of 0.855 (see Example 1).

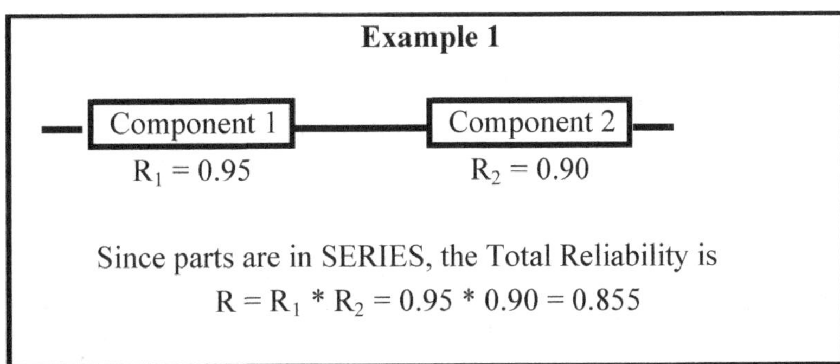

Example 1
Component 1
$R_1 = 0.95$
Component 2
$R_2 = 0.90$
Since parts are in SERIES, the Total Reliability is
$R = R_1 * R_2 = 0.95 * 0.90 = 0.855$

Similarly, if five components with reliability of 0.9, 0.9, 0.9, 0.8, and 0.8 must all work, the system or product has a reliability of 0.46656 (see Example 2).

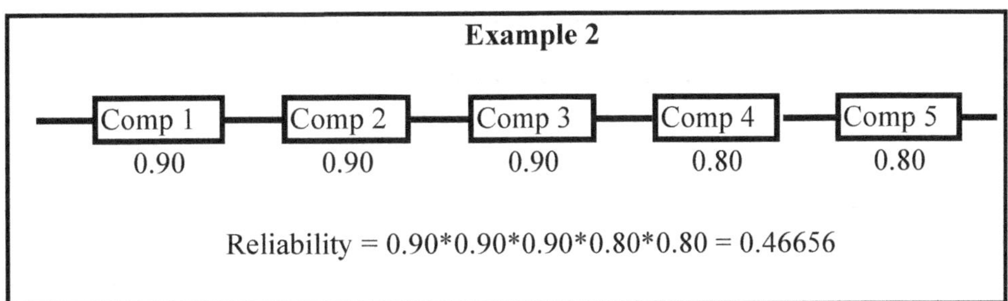

As you can see, even though the individual components of a system or product may have high reliability, the system or product as a whole will have considerably less reliability because all of the components that make up the system or product must function. In addition, as the number of components increases, the system reliability decreases unless the individual component reliability is 100% or 1.00. As an example, a system or product made up of twelve components, each with a reliability of 0.99, has a reliability of only $(0.99)^{12} = 0.8863845$.

Many products and systems have large numbers of component parts that must all operate for the system to be a success; thus some method to increase overall reliability is needed. One of the most common approaches used is redundancy or a backup in the design. This technique provides backup parts for some of the items of the system or product. Let us look at an example of a component with a reliability of 0.9 with a backup having a reliability of 0.8 that automatically switches on if the original component fails. As stated, the probability of the original part functioning is 0.9. Of the 10 % of parts that fail (1 – 0.9), 80% will be saved by the backup. Thus, the resulting reliability of this pair of components is 0.9 + 0.8(0.1) = 0.98 (see Example 3).

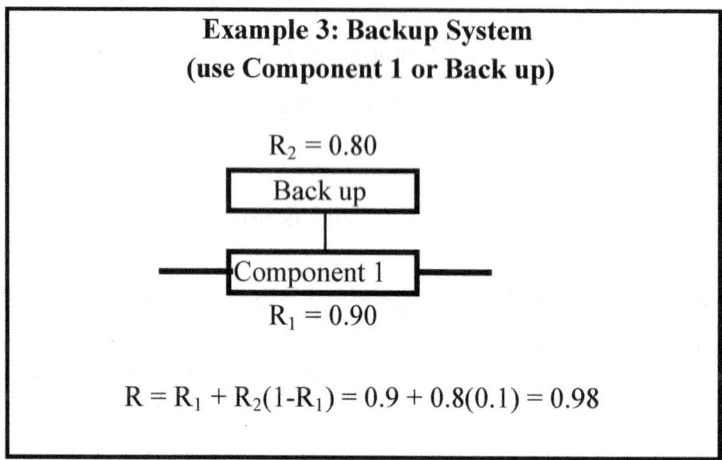

Consider the following example that shows a system that consists of two components (component #1 and component #2). Both components must work for the system to work. However, in order to increase the reliability of this system, the first component has two backups and the second component has one backup. The reliability data is as shown in Example 4. Component #1 has a reliability of 0.8 (R_1); its first backup has a reliability of 0.7 (R_2), and its second backup has a reliability of 0.6 (R_3). Component #2 has a reliability of 0.9 (R_4) and its backup has a reliability of 0.8 (R_5).

The first backup of component #1 will be engaged when component #1 fails, or 20% of the time ($1 - R_1 = 1 - 0.80$). The second backup of component #1 will be engaged when component #1 fails, or 20% of the time ($1 - R_1 = 1 - 0.80$) and when its first backup component fails, or 30% of the time ($1 - R_2 = 1 - 0.70$). Thus, they will both fail 6% of the time [$(1 - R_1)(1 - R_2) = 0.20 * 0.30 = 0.06$].

The backup of component #2 will be engaged when component #2 fails, or 10% of the time: ($1 - R_4 = 1 - 0.90 = 0.10$).

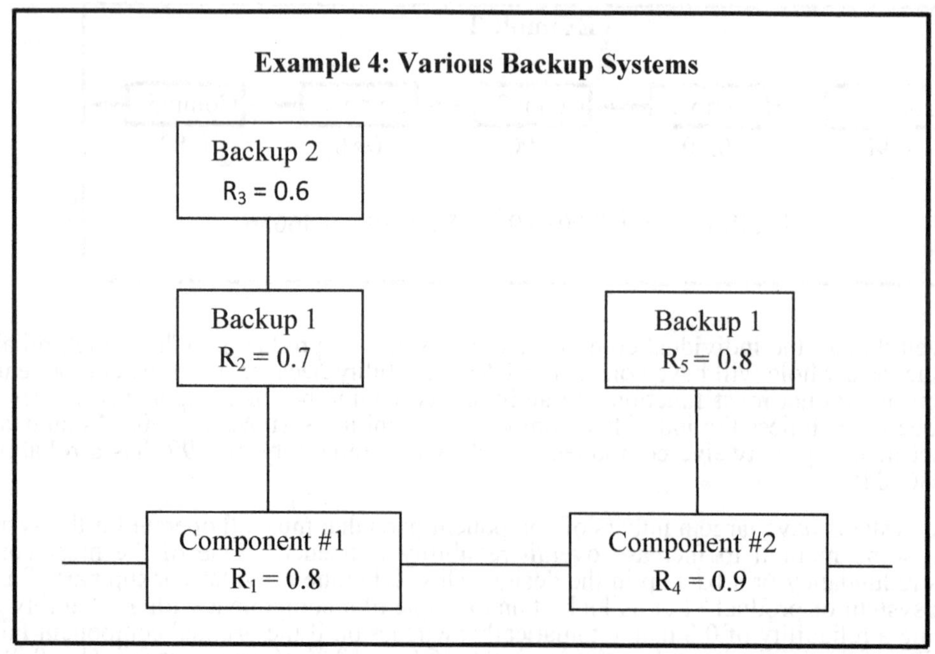

The reliability calculations are then as follows:

$$R = [R_1 + R_2(1 - R_1) + R_3(1 - R_1)(1 - R_2)] * [R_4 + R_5(1 - R_4)]$$

$$R = [0.8 + 0.7(1 - 0.8) + 0.6(1 - 0.8)(1 - 0.7)] * [0.9 + 0.8(1 - 0.9)]$$

$$= [0.8 + (0.7*0.2) + (0.6*0.2*0.3)] * [0.9 + (0.8*0.1)]$$

$$= [0.8 + 0.14 + 0.036] * [0.9 + 0.08]$$

$$= [0.976] * [0.98]$$

$$R = 0.95648$$

8.2 Reliability over Given Length of Time

The second way of looking at reliability involves the incorporation of a time dimension. These probabilities are figured relative to a specific length of time. This technique is applicable to product warranties. Figure 3.1 represents a normal profile of failure rate over time.

Due to its shape, this curve is referred to as a bathtub curve. Frequently, a large number of items fail soon after they have been put into service. This is not due to units wearing out but due to a defect they had to begin with. The rate of failure decreases rapidly as defective items are removed from service. In the middle phase, few failures are experienced due to the weeding out of defective units and it being too early to experience failures due to units wearing out. Failures that are due to wear out increase over time, causing a radical failure rate increase during the last phase.

Calculations relative to the distribution and duration of each phase of the failure rate curve require the collection and analysis of historical data.

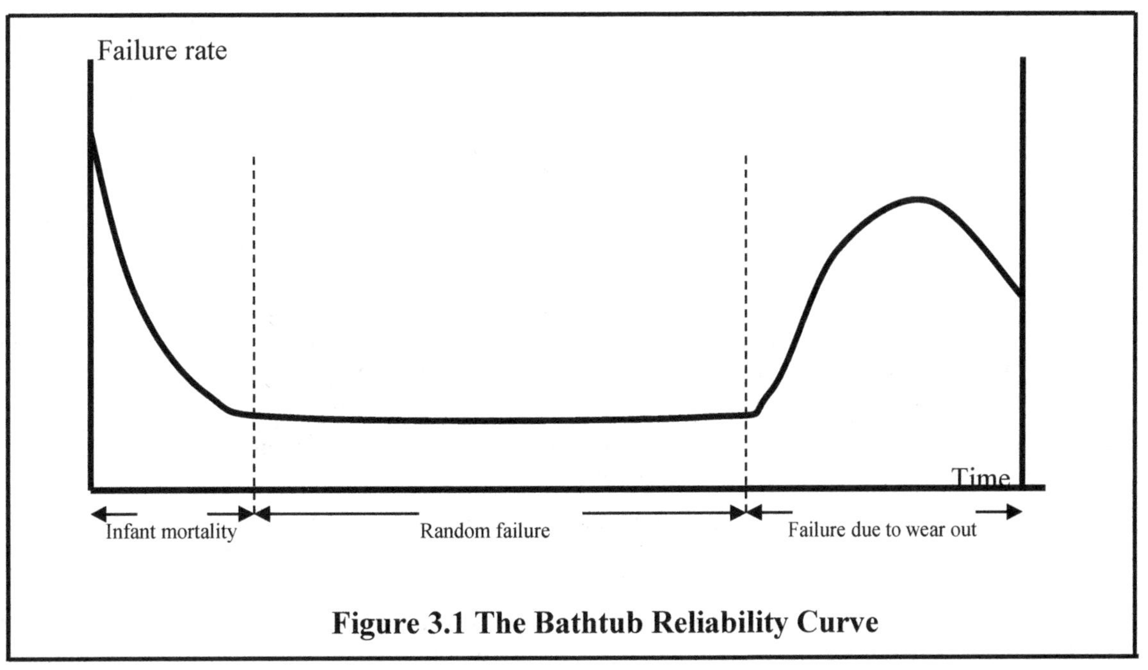

Figure 3.1 The Bathtub Reliability Curve

9. THE TRAMWAY OF PALM SPRINGS, CA

The tramway of Palm Springs is a marvel of design and reliability. In 1935, a young electrical engineer, Francis Crocker, dreamed of a tramway up the cliffs of the Chino Canyon to the top of the San Jacinto Mountains. His vision became a reality in 1950 when technicians actively moved to the design of the tram, overcoming numerous problems. Finally, $8.5 million in private revenue bonds started the construction of the tramway. This successful construction venture, labeled the "eighth wonder of the world," was completed in 1963. In 1998 a modernization program was embarked on that brought the largest rotating tram cars to the valley in September of 2000.

How reliable is this marvelous tramway? Aside from two known accidents in 1984 (in June, a bolt from a shock absorber snapped and sent a 30-pound piece of metal through the Plexiglas of the cabin, fatally injuring a passenger, and in September, during a routine maintenance, an auxiliary cable snapped, but fortunately wrapped itself around the main cable track, preventing two workers from plummeting down the mountain), its operating system is quite reliable with two backup systems in case the initial main system fails. The main 110-horsepower motor provides the input to the main drive gear box and coupling to the main drive wheel. If this main drive motor fails, the system can switch to its Cummins six-cylinder 190-horsepower hydrostatic drive. Finally, if both of them fail, the "Rescue Drive Counterweight System" can provide a way to lower the cars to the valley station with the use of gravity alone.

10. GLOSSARY AND SUMMARY OF METHODS

Computer Aided Design (CAD) – Computer aided design is performed by a computerized system that involves a human (the designer), a machine (the computer hardware), and their interface (the software).

Cost Factors in Product Design – The product cost elements are: development cost, material cost, operating/manufacturing cost, marketing cost, capital cost (or opportunity cost), and overhead cost.

Design Requirements – The product must meet the following design requirements: 1) sound in functional design, 2) attractive in appearance, 3) convenient in maintenance, and 4) competitive in pricing.

Group Technology (GT) – Group technology is a manufacturing philosophy whereby similar parts are identified and grouped together to take advantage of their similarities in manufacturing and design. When GT is applied, the parts used by a manufacturing firm are classified and coded based on their geometric shapes, sizes, and/or manufacturing processes.

Interchangeability – Interchangeability is a design concept for ease of manufacturing. It restricts variation amongst fitting parts. It is a prerequisite to mass production and assembly.

Lean Product Development – Includes QFD and tools to reduce the time-to-market lead time (CAD, computer aided analysis and simulation, product data management software and data bases using GT, rapid prototyping, and concurrent engineering).

Modularization – Modularization is a design concept for ease of maintenance. Modularized product design suggests that a complicated product be subdivided into different building blocks that can be produced individually and replaced quickly.

Principles in Modern Product Design – The four principles in modern product design are: 1) standardization, 2) interchangeability, 3) modularization, and 4) designing for production.

Product Design – The basic function of product design is to convert the general specifications of a product into its technical specifications.

Product Design Activities – The three product design activities are: 1) new product design, 2) major revisions in the design of existing products, and 3) minor improvements in the design of current products.

Product/System Reliability – Product/system reliability is the probability that the product or system will function on any given trial or the probability that the product or system will function for a given length of time.

Quality Function Deployment (QFD) – QFD is a methodology that ensures that all functions of the organization work together to provide the customers with exactly what they want, and it provides the company with a road map showing how each function, from design to delivery, must interact to fulfill all customers' requirements.

Rapid Prototyping – Rapid prototyping is accomplished through stereo lithography (STL) apparatus (SLA). The prototype consists of layers of laser-cured resin.

Standardization – Standardization establishes the mandatory or recommended norms to which different design attributes (i.e., dimensions, shapes, weights, and colors) of a product should conform. It is a design concept for ease of design.

Value Analysis and Value Engineering – Value analysis and value engineering refer to relating available alternatives and their costs to the purpose of the product at hand, thus resulting in minor product improvement changes and reduction in product cost.

11. ACRONYMS

CAD Computer Aided Design
CAE Computer Aided Engineering
CAM Computer Aided Manufacturing
CNC Computer Numeric Control
GT Group Technology
PFA Production Flow Analysis
QFD Quality Function Deployment
SLA Stereo Lithography Apparatus
VAVE Value Analysis and Value Engineering

12. REFERENCES

Boothroyd, G. "Design for Assembly - The Key to Design for Manufacturing."*International Journal of Advanced Manufacturing Technology* (1987): pp. 3–11.

Burt, D. N., and W. R. Soukup. "Purchasing's Role in New Product Development." *Harvard Business Review* (September-October 1985): 90–97.

Clark, K. B. and Takahiro Fujimoto. *Product Development Performance - Strategy, Organization and Management in the WorldAuto Industry*. Boston: Harvard Business School Press, 1991.

Cohen, L. *Quality Function Deployment: How to Make QFD Work for You*. Reading, MA: Addison-Wesley Publishing Company, 1995.

Finkin, E. F. "Developing and Managing New Products." *Journal of Business Strategy* (Spring 1983): 834–846.

Jacobs, Paul F. *Stereo Lithography and Other RP&M Technologies*. New York: ASME Press, 1996.

Guinta, L. R. and N. C. Praizler. *The QFD Book*. New York: American Management Association, 1993.

Gunn, Thomas G. "The Mechanization of Design and Manufacturing." *Scientific American*. (September 1982): 114–130.

Heany, D. F. "Degrees of Product Innovation." *Journal of Business Strategy*. (Spring 1983): 3–14.

McIntyre, S. H., and M. Statman. "Managing the Risk of New Product Development." *Business Horizons*. (May–June 1982): 51–55.

Niebel, B. W., and A. B. Draper. *Product Design and Process Engineering*. New York: McGraw-Hill, 1974.

Nussbaum, Bruce and Otis Port. "Smart Design." *Business Week*. (April 11, 1988): 102–107.

Shostack, G. Lynn. "How to Design a Service." *European Journal of Marketing*. (Vol.16, No.1, 1982): 49–63.

Smith, Preston G., and Donald G. Reinertsen. *Developing Products in Half the Time*. New York: John Wiley & Sons, Inc, 1998.

Stark, John. *Managing CAD/CAM - Implementation, Organization, and Integration*. New York: McGraw-Hill, 1988.

American Society of Tool and Manufacturing Engineers. *Value Engineering in Manufacturing*. Englewood Cliffs, NJ: Prentice -Hall, 1967.

Wheelwright, Steven C., and Kim B. Clark. *Revolutionizing Product Development*. New York: The Free Press, 1992.

13. REVIEW QUESTIONS

1. Differentiate between the concepts of standardization and interchangeability.
2. What are the four major principles in product design? Briefly explain what they are concerned with.
3. Give some examples of general specifications of a job, product, or service.
4. Briefly explain the three different types of product design activities.
5. Give some examples of technical specifications.
6. What is meant by functional design of a product? What does it take into consideration?
7. What are the four market requirements that need be considered when designing a product? Briefly explain these requirements.
8. What are the cost elements of a product?
9. What is meant by "designing for production"?
10. Why is it important to reduce the product development cycle?
11. What is being done to reduce the product development cycle?
12. How is computer aided design performed?
13. What is meant by rapid prototyping?
14. What role does group technology play in computer aided design?
15. What is group technology?
16. What does QFD stand for? What is it?
17. What are the four phases of QFD?
18. What design principles and tools lead to product development?
19. What is meant by product/system reliability?
20. Differentiate between fixed time reliability and reliability over a given length of time.
21. How can one increase the reliability of a component?
22. Describe the bathtub reliability curve.
23. What is lean product development?
24. Why is it important to speed up the product development cycle?

25. Enumerate some of the tools of lean product development.
26. What is meant by concurrent engineering?

14. PROBLEMS

Problem #1

A component has a reliability of 0.80. Two backup components, each with a reliability of 0.70, are placed into the system.

What is the reliability of this system?

Problem #2

A product consists of three components: A, B, and C. Components A and B are parallel components and they are in series with component C. (In other words the backup component of A is component B). Their reliabilities are as follows: R(A) = 0.95, R(B) = 0.90, and R(C) = 0.90.

What is the reliability of this product?

Problem #3

A product consists of two major components. In order to increase their reliability, these components are backed up with other components as follows:

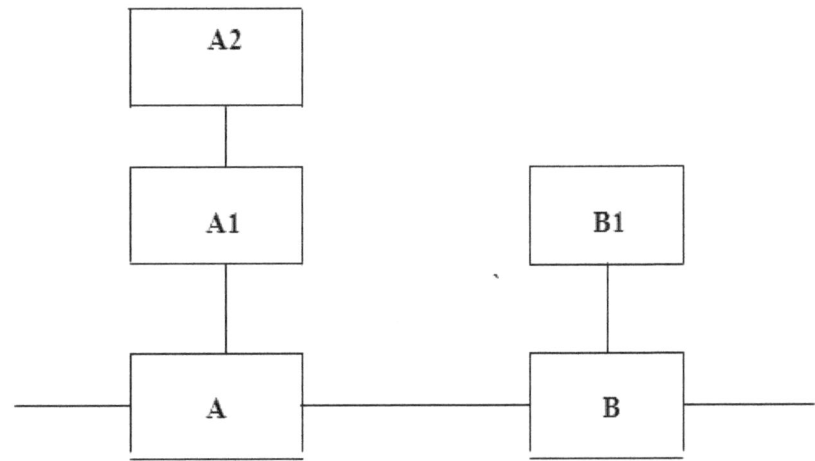

Consider the following reliabilities:

R(A) = 0.80, R(A1) = 0.70, R(A2) = 0.90

R(B) = 0.90, R(B1) = 0.80

a) What is the overall reliability of this system?
b) By how much is the reliability of the system increased because of all of the backup components?

Problem #4

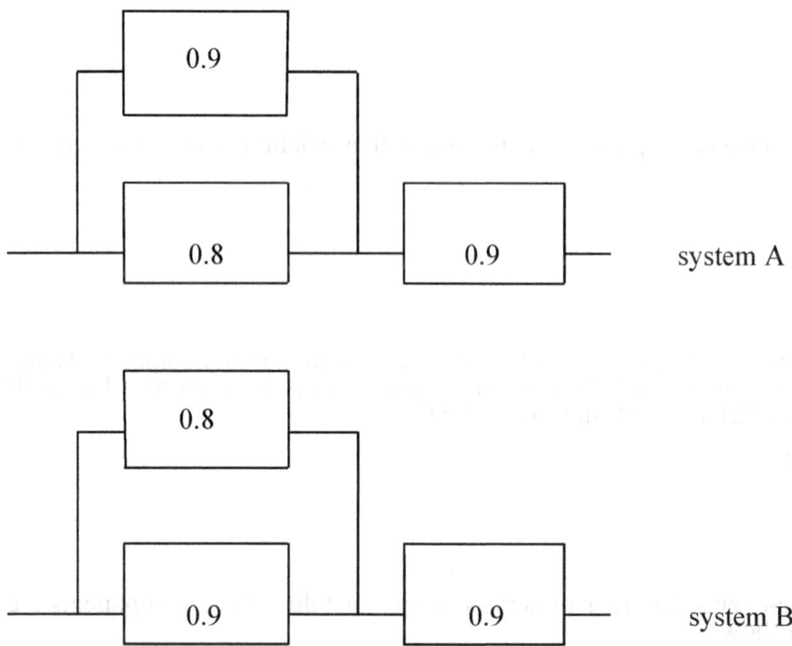

Which system has higher reliability? (show work)

Chapter 4

PROCESS PLANNING

1. FUNCTION OF PROCESS PLANNING

The function of process planning is to select and to design the right tools, the right methods, and the right sequence for the production processes consistent with technical specifications from the product design. Process planning determines 1) how a product should be made or operations carried out, 2) the service that should be performed to produce the required product/service, and 3) how to provide the service desired. A production/service process may consist of a series of operations that converts inputs into outputs through physical or, in some rare cases, non-physical changes. These changes may involve shape, size, appearance, location, chemical properties, mental condition, information, or knowledge.

These operations are performed by people, machines, or both. Machines are normally more productive, but require greater capital investment and result in somewhat lower flexibility. Only the mass market can justify the extensive use of machines. The manufacturing firms are traditionally more capital-intensive and the service industries are more people-intensive. However, the distinction is getting less clear as the service industries are catching up in using machines (including computers) to improve their productivity. Examples can be found throughout the service industries: in such diverse companies as banks, airlines, hotels, hospitals, insurance companies, telephone companies, fast food restaurants, grocery stores, and many others.

Once process decisions are made and implemented, the entire productive system and its decision processes will evolve around the process plans through which the production/operations function is physically carried out. Even future decisions concerned with operations and product planning will be greatly influenced by past process decisions, especially for capital-intensive industries. While production/operations design and capacity planning superimpose constraints upon the process planning, the latter subscribes to the basic characteristics of the productive system and its related management decisions. In an integrated system, the process planning function is the nucleus of various production management activities which all draw information input from process planning.

The major objectives of process planning are to:

- Maximize productivity
- Minimize production/operations cost
- Minimize production/operations throughput time (or production lead time)
- Minimize in-process inventory
- Consistently produce quality products or services

The first two objectives are self-evident. The throughput time is the total amount of time required to process the product or its components through the productive system. The shorter the throughput time is, the higher the productivity of the system is. However, if parallel production lines are employed to reduce the throughput time, the productivity of the system may not necessarily be improved. In-process inventory is the inventory on the production floor that waits to be processed by the next process. Industry is paying a great deal of attention to in-process inventory in an effort to reduce it. The last objective in process design concerns the production quality and should not be undermined because of the other objectives.

The basic function of process planning can be summarized as follows (see Figure 4.1):

- Participating in the final stage of product/service design (i.e., designing for production) which predetermines the choices of production processes
- Designing and establishing the process steps of the product and its components (i.e., process design) which may be viewed as macro process planning

- Designing and establishing the detailed arrangement of individual operations (i.e., operation design) which may be viewed as micro process planning

In the previous chapter, we discussed **designing for production** from the product design point-of-view. Once a product/service design is released to production/operations, the process planning function will continuously scrutinize the product/service design in light of the availability of current resources and the updated technological information. For a manufacturing firm, the process planning function would trigger a modification to the product/service design in cases of, for example, a change of a raw material supplier, a persistent quality problem of one specific manufacturing process, or the availability of more productive equipment or new production/operations technology. If the change affects the product/service design, then it is considered to be an extension of designing for production and is often documented and released in the form of an engineering change request (ECR). Once the design and manufacturing databases are integrated, this change should be recorded automatically and should trigger a series of changes in product/service design, facility layout, material planning, maintenance planning, and many other areas. It is important to stress the fact that designing for production is a continuous and dynamic process that has a profound effect on the overall productivity of the organization.

The primary function of **macro process planning** is to design the macro production/operations system that satisfies product/service specifications and quality standards at minimum cost. Its most visible and highly generalized responsibilities are:

- The choice of technology
- The selection of manufacturing equipment and workstations
- The determination and analysis of production/operations flow

Depending on the type of the product/service and the manufacturing/operations process, macro process planning is basically an engineering function of the respective discipline. For discrete parts manufacturers, such as machine tools, automotive parts, hardware, etc., it is a function of mechanical or industrial engineering; for the chemical industries, it is a function of chemical engineering; and for the electronics and computer equipment industries, it is basically a function of electronic engineering or computer software engineering. In the service industries, macro process planning has not been widely engaged as a formal production function due to the relative simplicity of the service operations or its small scale of operations. However, as service industries grow in size and in complexity, more and more of them will adopt some form of formal process planning activities. Those activities are often carried out by their own staff industrial engineers or by outside consultants.

For example, the United States postal service system underwent extensive studies on its mail sorting operation. The process planning function for hospitals and health delivery systems is becoming a specialized profession. Some restaurant chains also have formalized process planning functions where both the food preparation and dining room services are carefully studied and planned. Even when a formal process planning function does not exist due to the small scale of the operation, some sort of informal process planning activity is being carried out in the mind of the operator or the manager. Theoretically speaking, any productive system, manufacturing or service, must have process planning to ensure the success of the operation. In the case of mass production or continuous flow production, a detailed study and analysis of the production process is needed to reach an optimal solution. However, for job-shop or small batch-type operations, the cost of such a study may be way above the potential savings that the study may be able to generate. For those cases, the shop experience of the operators or the shop supervisors often dominate the decision processes of the process planning function.

Basic information required for macro process planning in a manufacturing environment includes the following:

- Production volume (to determine the scale of production)
- Material requirements in product design
- Mechanical requirements in product design (tolerances, surface finish, hardness, etc.)
- Engineering drawings and design databases
- Facility data file
- Planned and actual machine loads
- Existing plant and facility layout
- Methods of material handling
- Vendors, raw material suppliers, and sub-contractors information, etc.

While macro process planning is basically product oriented, **micro process planning** is largely method oriented. Micro process planning is concerned with the localized operation methods and is often referred to as operation planning. The primary function of operation planning is to design micro production systems that provide the most efficient operation methods and operation sequence for the individual work stations. The secondary function of operation planning is to provide means and standards for personnel's and operators' training and control.

Basic information required for micro process planning includes the following:

- Tools and accessories used at the work stations
- Plant or industry work standards for the operations
- Manning condition of the work stations
- Work environment, the workplace organization, and conditions

Operations design is commonly considered as an industrial engineering function. The operation design function or micro process planning is discussed in Chapter 6.

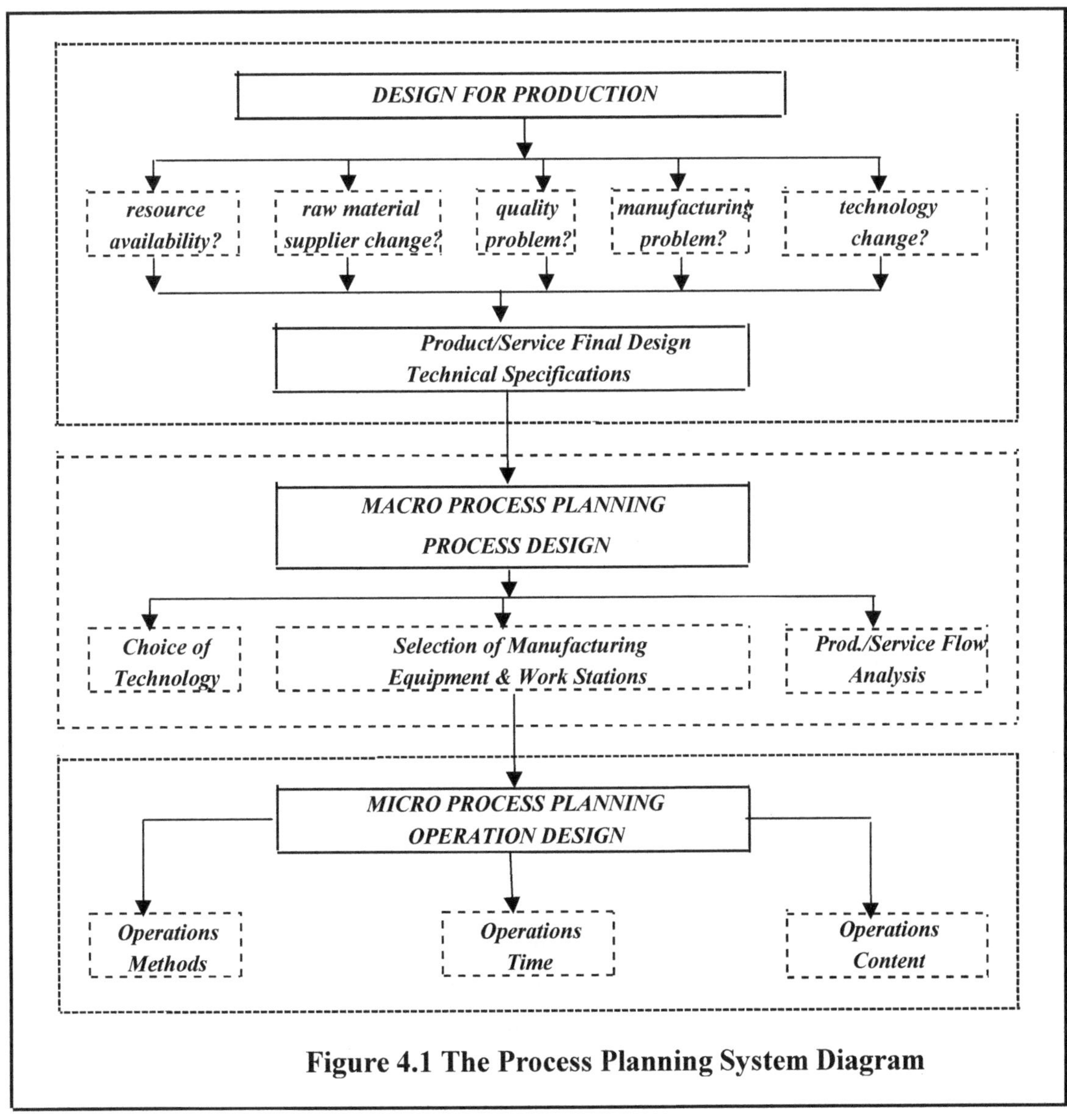

Figure 4.1 The Process Planning System Diagram

2. *FORMS AND DOCUMENTS USED FOR PROCESS PLANNING*

As indicated in the previous section, once the final design is released to production with the engineering bill of materials (BOM), manufacturing BOM, and necessary Gozinto charts (see Figure 4.4), the process planning function can commence in terms of macro process planning and operation design or micro process planning. Figure 4.2 represents the most commonly used documents for such process planning.

3. *ASSEMBLY CHART*

The assembly chart is a schematic model that helps visualize the flow of materials and relationships of parts. It indicates:

- Parts numbers
- Parts descriptions
- Subassemblies
- Assemblies
- Inspections
- Operations

Design stage	Forms and documents
Product Design	Engineering Bill of Materials Manufacturing Bill of Materials Gozinto Chart
Process Design (Macro Process Planning)	Assembly Chart Operations Process Chart Route Sheet Process Maps *Flow Process Chart* *Spaghetti Diagram* *Value Stream Map*
Operation Design (Micro Process Planning)	Man-Machine Chart Right-Left Hand Chart Simulation Motion Cycle Operation Sheets

Figure 4.2 Forms and Documents used for Macro/Micro Process Planning

Two basic symbols are used in the assembly chart. These are the assembly/subassembly symbol and the inspection symbols:

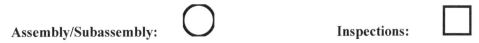

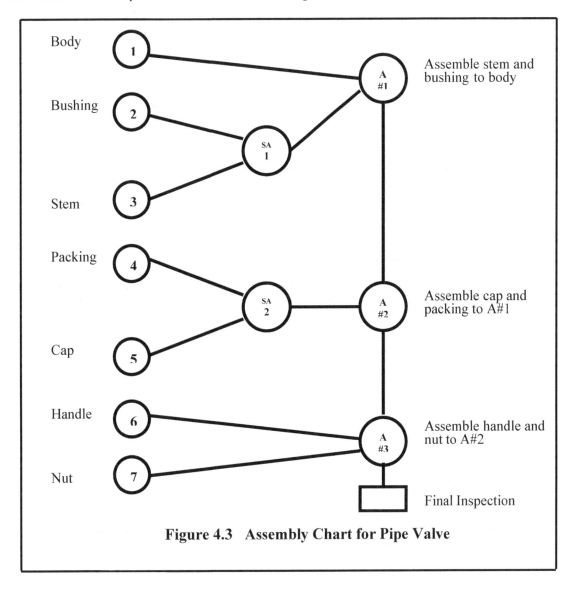

Figure 4.3 represents the assembly chart for the assembly of a pipe valve as shown in Figure 4.4. The pipe valve is made up of seven basic parts: a body, a bushing, a packing, a cap, a stem, a handle, and a nut. The sequence of assembly for this product is fairly straightforward as shown in the assembly chart of Figure 4.3. It consists of the following basic steps:

Step 1: Assemble bushing #002 to stem #003 to form subassembly SA-1
Step 2: Place packing #004 into cap #005 to form subassembly SA-2
Step 3: Assemble to body #001 SA-1 to form assembly #101
Step 4: Assemble to assembly #101 SA-2, forming assembly #102
Step 5: Assemble handle #006 with nut #007 to assembly #102, forming the final assembly #100

Assembly charts are also used in the service industry. For example, an assembly chart is used by McDonalds to show operators how to assemble a Big Mac and other sandwiches.

Body 1
Bushing 2
SA 1
Stem 3
A #1 Assemble stem and bushing to body
Packing 4
SA 2
Cap 5
A #2 Assemble cap and packing to A#1
Handle 6
Nut 7
A #3 Assemble handle and nut to A#2
Final Inspection

Figure 4.3 Assembly Chart for Pipe Valve

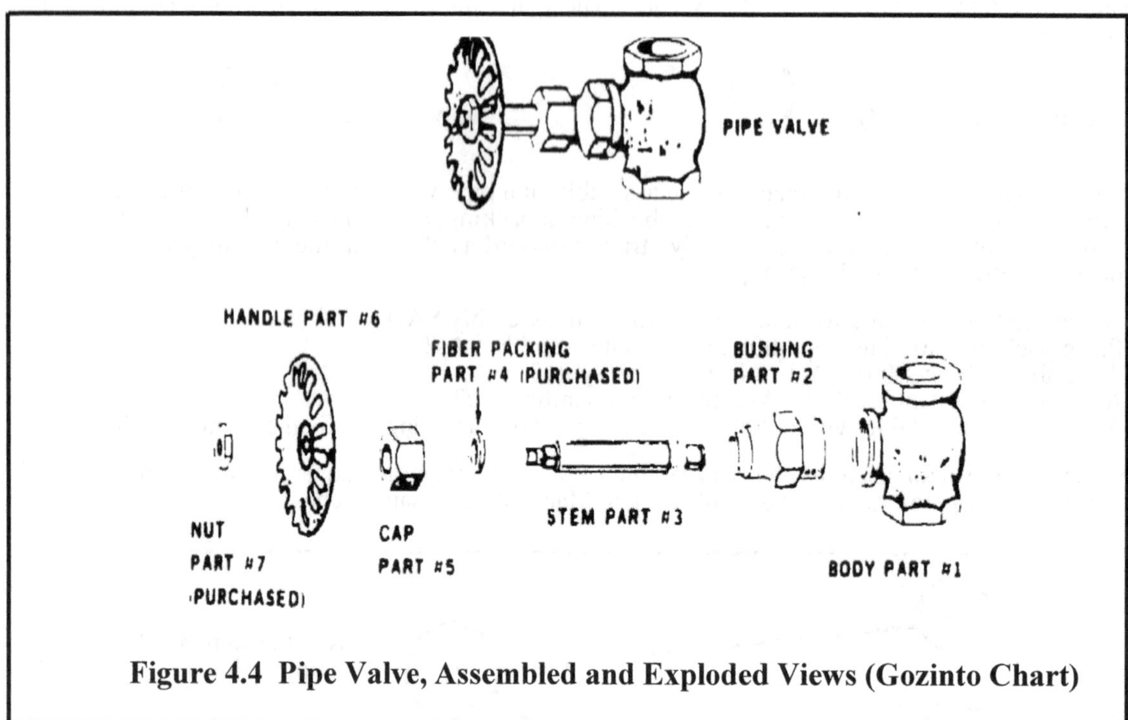

Figure 4.4 Pipe Valve, Assembled and Exploded Views (Gozinto Chart)

4. THE OPERATION PROCESS CHART

The operation process chart can be established after the product is engineered, when drawings and specifications exist as well as the type of equipment to be used to process parts is identified.

The operation process chart is slightly more detailed than the assembly chart and is used to plan the exact manufacturing processes. It includes the run time (the standard time to manufacture one unit), all operations needed to manufacture the parts, and all visual and non-visual inspections. In other words, the operation process chart is like an assembly chart. In addition to what an assembly chart shows, the operation process chart also indicates for each manufactured part the basic flow from machine to machine. The following symbols are used in this chart:

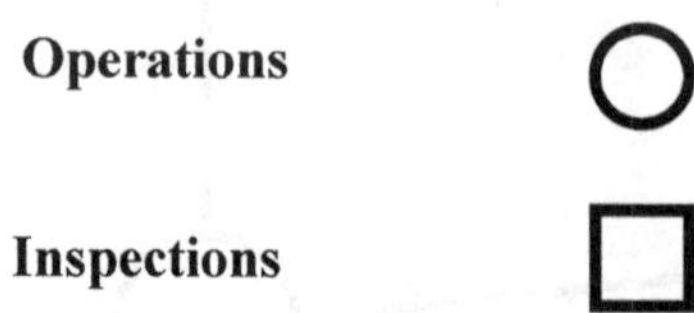

The operation process charts are also used to analyze existing operations.

Figure 4.5 illustrates the operation process chart for the manufacturing of a pipe valve that we discussed earlier. The pipe valve is made up of seven basic parts. Two of the seven parts, the packing and the nut, are purchased; while the company manufactures the body, the bushing, the stem, the cap, and the handle.

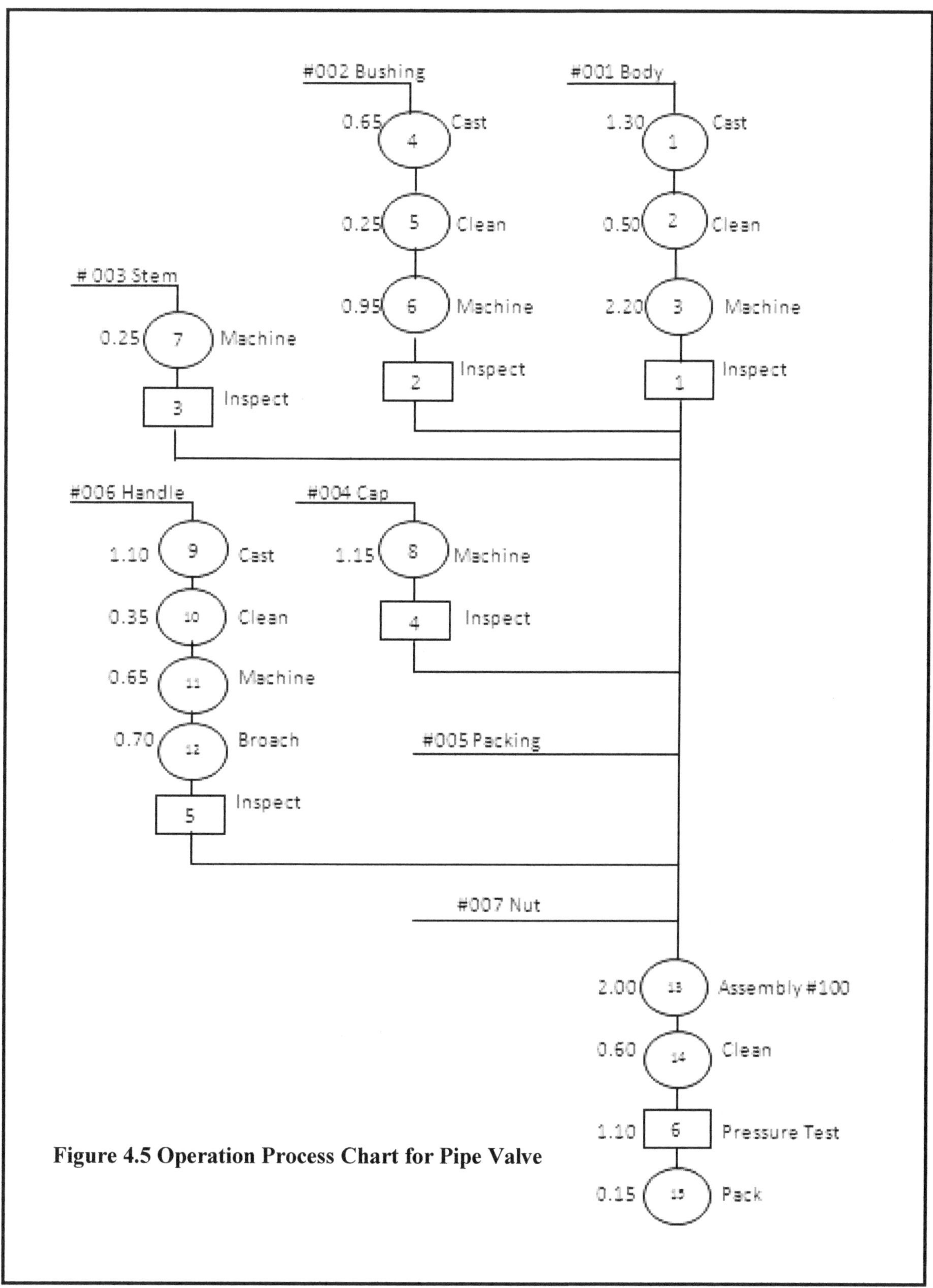

Figure 4.5 Operation Process Chart for Pipe Valve

5. THE ROUTE SHEET

For each individual part of an assembly or product, a route sheet is filled out. For each part, it shows the sequence of operations, the operation numbers, the departments in which the operations are performed, the setup times (if appropriate), production rates, and equipment used. The route sheet for the manufacturing of the handle of the pipe valve is shown in Figure 4.6.

Part Name: Handle
Assembly: A2012
Part number: 006

Date: 5/15/2012
Issued by: Wu

Operation Number	Description	Department	Set Up Time in minutes	Rate /Hour	Equipment
9	Casting	007	15	55	Bench Molding
10	Cleaning	012	08	171	Tumbler Barrel
11	Machining	014	12	92	Turret Lathe
12	Broaching	016	14	86	Broacher
5	inspection	992			Visual

Figure 4.6 Route Sheet for Handle of Valve Assembly

6. THE FLOW PROCESS CHART

The flow process chart is a detailed chart that includes: operations, transportation, temporary and permanent storage, inspections, outside operations, delays, distance traveled, operation times, inspection times, travel times, delay times, and a brief summary of all these. The symbols used for such a chart are shown in Figure 4.7.

The flow process chart is mainly constructed when one wishes to study possible improvements in the flow of materials. It furnishes key data for process layout, to be discussed in Chapter 8. The flow process chart can be used to answer questions, leading towards the elimination of various wastes in the process:

1. Are all operations necessary?
2. Which ones can be eliminated or rearranged?
3. Can the layout be changed to reduce material handling?
4. Are there excessive delays that are avoidable?
5. Can temporary storage be reduced or eliminated?

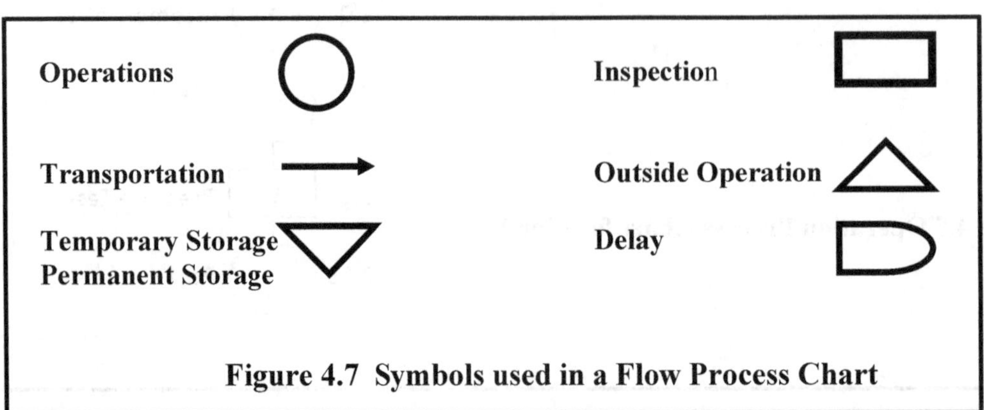

Figure 4.7 Symbols used in a Flow Process Chart

Flow Process Chart	SUMMARY
Process: Water Backyard (flowers and lawn)	
Created by : Nesa Wu	
Number of pages: 1 Page number: 1	
Date: 5/15/2012 **Chart Number: 001**	

Action	No	Time	Feet
▲ Outside Operation	0		
● Operation	10	13.25	100
➡ Transport	11	4.90	490
■ Inspection	1	0.50	
◗ Delays	1	30.00	
▼ Storage	0		

Step	Description	Action	Feet	#	Time	Notes Where, How, Etc.
1	**Walk to garage**	△ ○ ➡ □ D ▽	85		0.85	Right side of house
2	**Open garage**	△ ● ⇨ □ D ▽			0.65	Manual
3	**Walk to locker**	△ ○ ➡ □ D ▽	10		0.10	Left wall
4	**Remove hose**	△ ● ⇨ □ D ▽		1	0.50	50-foot rubber hose
5	**Transport hose to rear**	△ ○ ➡ □ D ▽	15		0.15	Carry
6	**Open rear door**	△ ● ⇨ □ D ▽			0.20	Manual
7	**Walk to faucet**	△ ○ ➡ □ D ▽	10		0.10	Rear of garage
8	**Attach hose to faucet/open faucet**	△ ● ⇨ □ D ▽			1.20	Manual
9	**Inspect for leaks**	△ ○ ⇨ ■ D ▽			0.50	Visual inspection
10	**Water flowers**	△ ● ⇨ □ D ▽	100		7.50	Back of house
11	**Go to tool shed**	△ ○ ➡ □ D ▽	150		1.50	In garage
12	**Get sprinkling system**	△ ● ⇨ □ D ▽		1	0.20	Rotating one
13	**Walk to faucet**	△ ○ ➡ □ D ▽	20		0.20	Rear of garage
14	**Shut off faucet**	△ ● ⇨ □ D ▽			0.50	Manual
15	**Go to end of hose**	△ ○ ➡ □ D ▽	35		0.35	Rear of garage
16	**Attach sprinkling system**	△ ● ⇨ □ D ▽			1.50	Manual
17	**Go to faucet**	△ ○ ➡ □ D ▽	35		0.35	Rear of garage
18	**Turn on faucet**	△ ● ⇨ □ D ▽			0.50	Manual
19	**Go to arm chair**	△ ○ ➡ □ D ▽	50		0.50	On patio
20	**Sit and wait**	△ ○ ⇨ □ ◗ ▽			30.00	On chair
21	**Go to faucet**	△ ○ ➡ □ D ▽	50		0.50	Rear of garage
22	**Close faucet**	△ ● ⇨ □ D ▽			0.50	Manual
23	**Go in house**	△ ○ ➡ □ D ▽	30		0.30	Via side door

Figure 4.8 Flow Process Chart for Watering the Backyard

Changes in layout, methods, jobs, and equipment are a direct result of the analysis of the process flow chart.

Figure 4.8 represents the flow process chart for watering the backyard, based on the following scenario:

- John Smith, who has been sitting on his porch, decides to water his flowers and grass
- He leaves the porch and walks 85 feet to garage door (0.85 minutes), where he takes 0.65 minutes to open the garage door
- He walks 10 feet to locker to get hose
- It takes 0.5 minutes to remove the hose from the locker
- He carries the hose 15 feet to the rear garage door, which he opens in 0.2 minutes
- He walks 10 feet to the faucet at the rear of the garage, attaches the hose to the faucet, and opens the faucet. This operation takes up 1.2 minutes
- He checks the connection for leaks, by observing the connection for 0.5 minutes
- He begins to water the flowers around the house during the next 7.5 minutes, while moving around 100 feet
- He leaves the hose on the grass, walks 150 feet to the tool shed in the garage, retrieves the sprinkling system from the shelves (this takes 0.2 minutes), and walks 20 feet to the faucet to shut it off (this operation takes only 0.5 minutes)
- He walks 35 feet to the hose on the lawn and attaches the sprinkling system to the end of the hose. After 1.5 minutes, he is finished with that job and returns to the faucet to turn it on
- He moves to an armchair, 50 feet away from the faucet, to observe the sprinkling for the next 30 minutes
- He returns to the faucet, closes it completely, and walks into the house through a side door 30 feet away from the faucet

These detailed process steps are shown in Figure 4.8, together with information on distance moved, quantities involved, and times associated with each step. The upper right hand corner summarizes the various actions taken in terms of number of occurrences, accumulated time, and distance traveled.
For this example the summary shows that there are as many operations as there are transports. Though we might assume that watering the grass and flowers requires movement, the number of transports can be reduced. One way of accomplishing this is by locating all tools together, rather than at different places which is the case here. Also, notice the amount of delay of 30 minutes, as compared to the value-added time of 13.5 minutes for operations performed by the operator. Can simultaneous operations, like watering the grass at the same time that the flowers are watered, reduce this delay?

7. SPAGHETTI CHART OR DIAGRAMS

Spaghetti diagrams are used to show the physical flow of processes. A product or activity is shown as it moves through the layout in order to identify possible flow problems such as excessive travel and travel time. In order to create a spaghetti chart and in order to analyze it one must go through the following steps:

1. Identify all necessary steps involved in the task at hand
2. Obtain or make a layout map
3. Picture the sequence of the steps by connecting the dots in the layout map
4. Calculate times and distances and identify the flow problems

An Example

Consider process mapping “getting a cup of coffee at the office”. Some may consider the need of the following few steps:

1. Decide you need coffee
2. Walk to coffee machine
3. Pour coffee
4. Walk to desk
5. Drink coffee

Figure 4.9 The Spaghetti Diagram

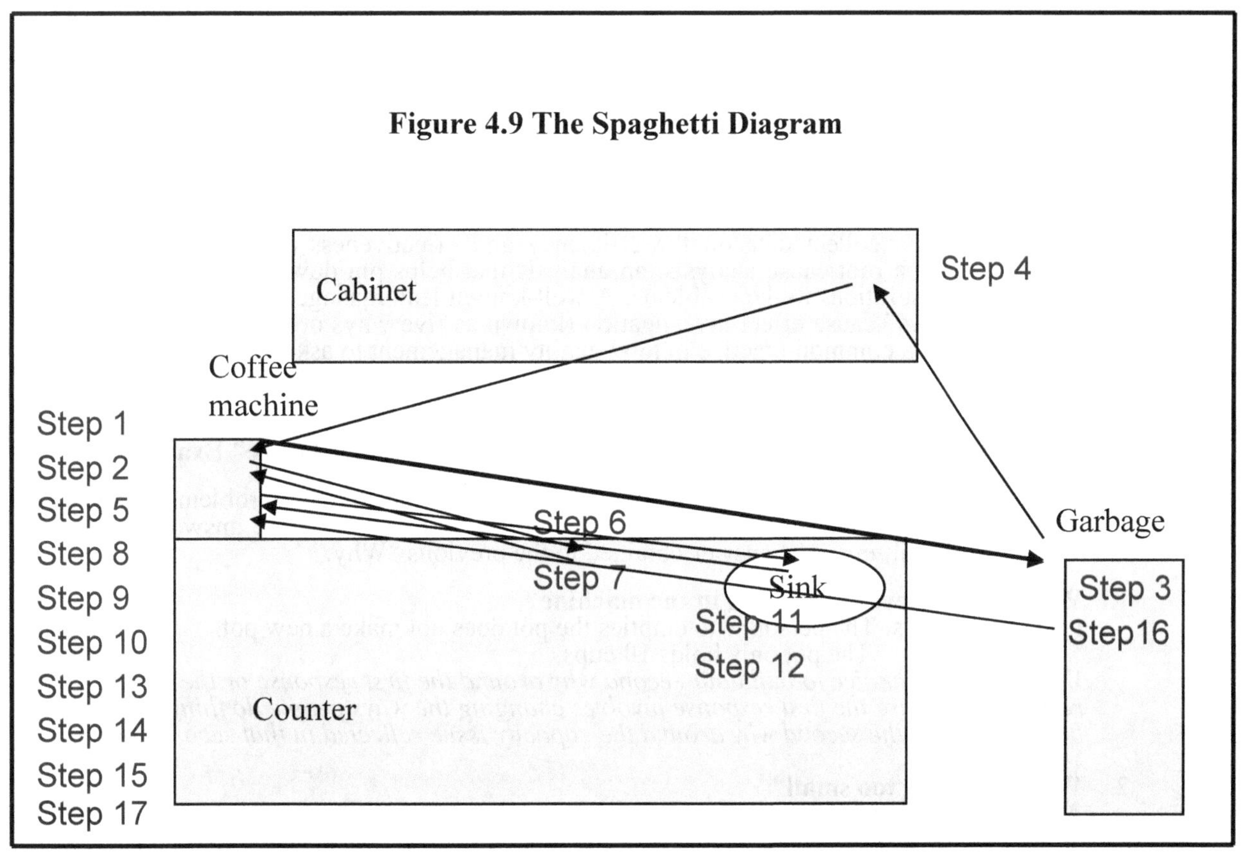

To some this list of steps is not complete. Perhaps more detail needs to be provided in this process. In order to fix any problem, sufficient detail must be provided when listing the steps. So let us make coffee again and represent more detail than is shown in the above list. Now the steps are:

1. Decide you need coffee
2. Stand up
3. Walk to coffee machine
4. Get cup
5. Pour coffee
6. Add cream and sugar
7. Stir coffee
8. Walk to desk
9. Set down coffee on desk
10. Sit down
11. Pick up coffee
12. Drink coffee

Does this represent the complete list? Have we asked ourselves whether all bases are covered here? What if the coffee cup is empty and in order to get coffee you will have to make it? Now additional steps must be added. These are:

1. Open grind drawer
2. Remove old filter and grounds
3. Throw in garbage
4. Get new filter
5. Put filter in machine
6. Get new coffee grounds
7. Open bag (scissors?)
8. Pour into new filter
9. Close grind drawer
10. Get pot
11. Wash pot
12. Fill pot with water
13. Pour water into coffee machine
14. Replace pot in machine
15. Turn on coffee machine
16. Throw empty bag in the garbage
17. Wait for new coffee
18. Return to step 4 of above list

Projecting steps onto a layout map aids in studying the efficiency of the layout of the workroom where this coffee is made! This results in a spaghetti diagram as shown in Figure 4.9. Now observe the map!

Would it not be more efficient to move the coffee machine closer to the sink and to place the filters with the coffee?

Whether we want to improve layouts or rethink the processes, critical thinking is necessary. Critical thinking requires that we ask ourselves whether the processes are necessary or whether they can be improved upon. Improving processes involves group work and often requires training of the workforce; it may require both change management and a cultural change.

One technique used to gather data is a technique called Gemba. Gemba is a process by which team members with their leader go to the site of the activity and collect data on the current state of the process. Thus the team members can collect data on the efficiency and effectiveness of the present process. Problem resolution requires a root cause analysis; an analysis that helps pin down the root cause of the problem and helps suggest solutions to the problems. A well-known lean management technique for root cause analysis is the "5-whys" cause effect investigation (known as five whys or five Ws). According to the *APICS Dictionary*[1], it is a common practice in total quality management to ask "why" five times when confronted with a problem. By the time the answer to the fifth why is found, the ultimate cause of the problem is identified and solutions can be proposed.

Applying the 5-Whys to the Problem in the "Getting a Cup of Coffee at the Office" Example

Finding the coffee pot empty, which necessitate making coffee, seems to be a major problem. Perhaps, the root cause analysis may lead to the following "Whys," with the following possible answers. Note that each successive "Why" is built upon the answer obtained to the previous "Why."

1. **Why is there never any coffee in the machine?**
   Possible answers: The person who empties the pot does not make a new pot.
   The pot only holds 10 cups.
   We now have a choice to build our second why around the first response or the second response. Because the first response involves changing the ways people do things, it might be best to build the second why around the capacity issue reflected in that second response.

2. **Why is 10 cups too small?**
   Answer: There are 50 people using that machine.

3. **Why are 50 people using that machine?**
   Answer: It does not make sense to get a second machine in this office.

4. **Why does it not make sense to get a second machine in this office?**
   Answer: It would need both a sink and a water supply, which is presently not available. (Presently water is being delivered throughout the day in manageable quantities from the restroom around the corner by the secretary)

5. **Why is the water supply not available?**
   Answer: We need a plumber.

Going through these whys, possible solutions may materialize. Some of these could be the following:

1. Get a plumber and a bigger machine (very costly)
2. Get a plumber and a second machine (less costly)
3. < many other solutions>
4. Provide free water bottles in a fridge on the other side of the office (costly)
5. Reduce the number of people (as one joker in the group may suggest!)
   - Maybe by firing the next couple of people who take the last cup and do not make a fresh pot

   <this kind of a response may result in a process put in place to make sure that the person who takes the last cup makes a new pot>
6. Remove the machine and ban coffee (they did it with cigarettes, didn't they?)

---

[1] *APICS Dictionary*, 13th Edition, page 56.

8. VALUE STREAM MAP

Value stream mapping is a process utilized to steer from a current inefficient process to a future lean process environment. The process of value stream mapping begins by documenting the flows of the existing process in a "current state" map. Analyzing the current state map and applying lean manufacturing principles result in the "future state" map. A value stream map is a visual representation of the production/operations path, documenting flow of materials and information. The map is drawn by following a product's production path from beginning to end, and drawing a visual representation of every process in the associated material and information flows. The map is normally drawn by hand, by following a product from the ordering and delivery of raw materials, components and assemblies, through to shipping and delivery to the customer.

While a very detailed flow process chart shows "what" occurs and "where" it occurs, the value stream map is less detailed and shows "why" things are happening. For example: in a flow process chart temporary inventory may be shown at various processes, but does not show what caused this to happen. A value stream map will show the necessary information flow that resulted in the buildup of that inventory.

Value stream maps include both material flows and information flows.

Material flow data constitute:

- Order quantities and order lead time
- Modes of shipment of materials (including transportation frequencies)
- Receiving and storage points (including the warehouse for received materials, work-in-process (WIP), and finished goods inventory)
- Production processes
- Production lead times: the length of time between the release of an order to the shop floor and the shipment to the final customer or receipt into finished stores
- Value-added time: the actual productive time of processes contributing value towards the final product
- Flow of work-in-process (WIP) between production processes
- Mode of shipment of finished product to the customer (including transportation frequencies and time), major customers, distribution centers, or warehouses

Information flows reflect:

- Electronic or manual information control systems
- Material requirement planning (MRP) systems
- Manufacturing resource planning (MRPII) systems
- Enterprise resource planning (ERP) systems
- Supply chain management (SCM) systems

You can create your own icons when you draw a value stream map. Here are some of the often-used icons for manufacturing processes:

Warehouse

Supplier warehouse or customer destination

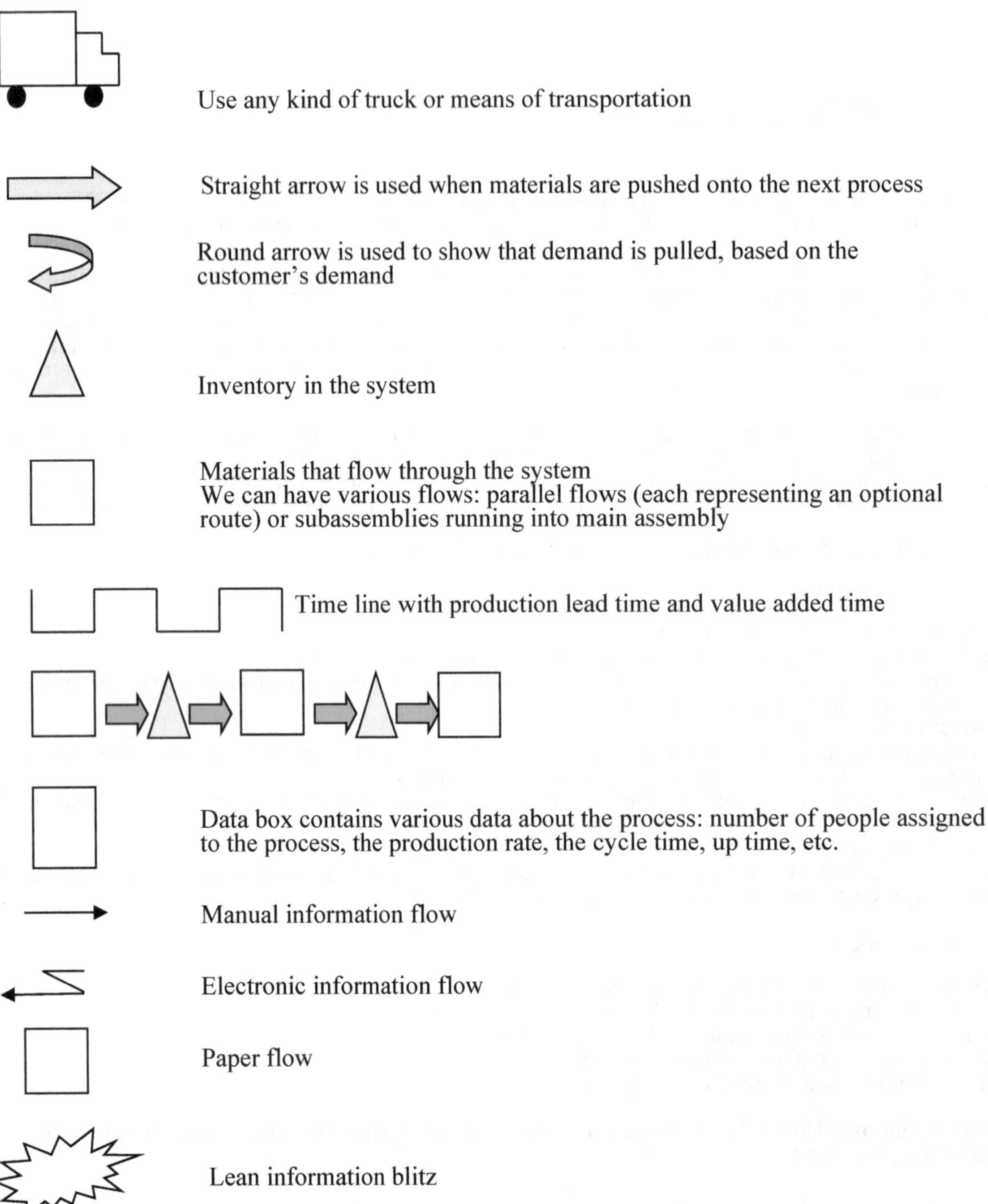
Use any kind of truck or means of transportation
Straight arrow is used when materials are pushed onto the next process
Round arrow is used to show that demand is pulled, based on the customer's demand
Inventory in the system
Materials that flow through the system
We can have various flows: parallel flows (each representing an optional route) or subassemblies running into main assembly
Time line with production lead time and value added time
Data box contains various data about the process: number of people assigned to the process, the production rate, the cycle time, up time, etc.
Manual information flow
Electronic information flow
Paper flow
Lean information blitz

Many more icons exist and as popularity of value stream mapping increases in manufacturing and the service industry, more standard icons will be introduced.

Before drawing a value stream map, a team draws the map by hand on the wall. In doing so, each team member learns the involvement of all members in the process that is being studied. After the map is hand drawn, it is condensed into a format for ease of distribution. Maps can be drawn for any value stream, including manufacturing and service streams.

To illustrate the process of using value stream mapping to improve operations and flows, consider the following examples.

8.1 An Illustrative, Simulated Production Example

Imagine the following abstract scenario. Mr. Andrews wishes to assemble two products, conveniently called black rangers and red rovers. These are relatively simple products consisting of a board, posts, and wires. The difference between the black rangers and red rovers lies in the color of the board.

Mr. Andrews has determined the following seven assembly steps to make any of the two products:

Step 1: Placement and inspection of 1 board (cycle time, C/T = 3.6 seconds)
Step 2: Placement of 3 natural round posts into designated round holes of the board (3.1 seconds)
Step 3: Placement of 1 natural and 2 colored square posts into designated square holes of the board (3.9 seconds)
Step 4: Placement of 3 natural triangular posts into designated triangular holes of the board (3.1 seconds)
Step 5: Looping a metal wire through some posts, as shown on the surface of the board (1.9 seconds)
Step 6: Attaching the front end of the wire to its designated post (4.5 seconds)
Step 7: Attaching the back end of the wire to its designated post (2.9 seconds)

Mr. Andrews has laid out these steps in a very orderly way; one next to each other on a rather long table. All this work is to be executed by one production operator, who can work on any step in whatever way he sees fit. A material handler must provide materials for each step in a timely fashion, in order not to interrupt or stop the assembly.

The value stream map of Figure 4.10 illustrates a possible present state of the production system as designed by Mr. Andrews and executed by his assembler. Note the seven stations and a visual quality control station that make up the production system. In this scenario parts are shipped by truck from a supplier's warehouse. Mr. Andrews is billed for the parts the moment they are shipped to his factory and placed on the production line. Finished goods are shipped by truck, directly after assembly, to the customers. The customer's takt time (the time to finish a complete product in order to meet the customer demand) is 20 seconds. In other words customers wish to pull three units every minute or one unit every 20 seconds.

Taking a snapshot into assembly, a total production lead-time, or production throughput time, of all work in process (WIP) is 518 seconds, while the actual value-added time, the assembly time, is 23 seconds.

How does the total lead time of all work in process add up to 518 seconds? To answer this question one must focus on all work in process and ask how long these parts will remain in the system. In order to figure this time, one must keep in mind that the takt time for each product is 20 seconds. In other words, every twenty seconds a product can be pulled by the customer. The tally for the WIP lead-time at each assembly step for the parts that are waiting to be worked on is as follows:

There are four boards waiting to be processed at station # 1. Since there is only a demand for 1 such board every 20 seconds, these 4 boards will leave the system after 80 seconds (4 x 20 seconds).

There are 5 posts waiting to be processed at station #2. Each board processed at station #2 takes 3 posts. Therefore it will take 34 seconds for all these 5 posts to leave the system (5/3 x 20 seconds).

There are 7 colored and 2 natural posts waiting to be processed at station #3. It takes 1 natural and 2 colored posts for one assembly. The colored posts will take the longest time to leave the system. They will take 70 seconds to clear the production floor [max (7/2, 2/1) x 20 seconds].

There are 5 posts waiting at station #4. Since it takes 3 posts per assembly, they will leave the system within 34 seconds (5/3 x 20 seconds).

There are 7 wires waiting for assembly at station #5. It takes only one wire for each assembly. Therefore these wires will leave the system within 140 seconds (7 x 20 seconds).

There are 5 boards waiting at station #6. Every 20 seconds there is a demand for one such board. Therefore the last one leaves the system within 100 seconds (5 x 20 seconds).

There is 1 board waiting at station #7. This board will be in the system for another 20 seconds.

The two units that are in storage will not leave the system for another 40 seconds (2 x 20 seconds).

These calculations are illustrated in Table 4.1. The total lead time of work-in-process adds up to 518 seconds, whereas the total value added time is 23 seconds.

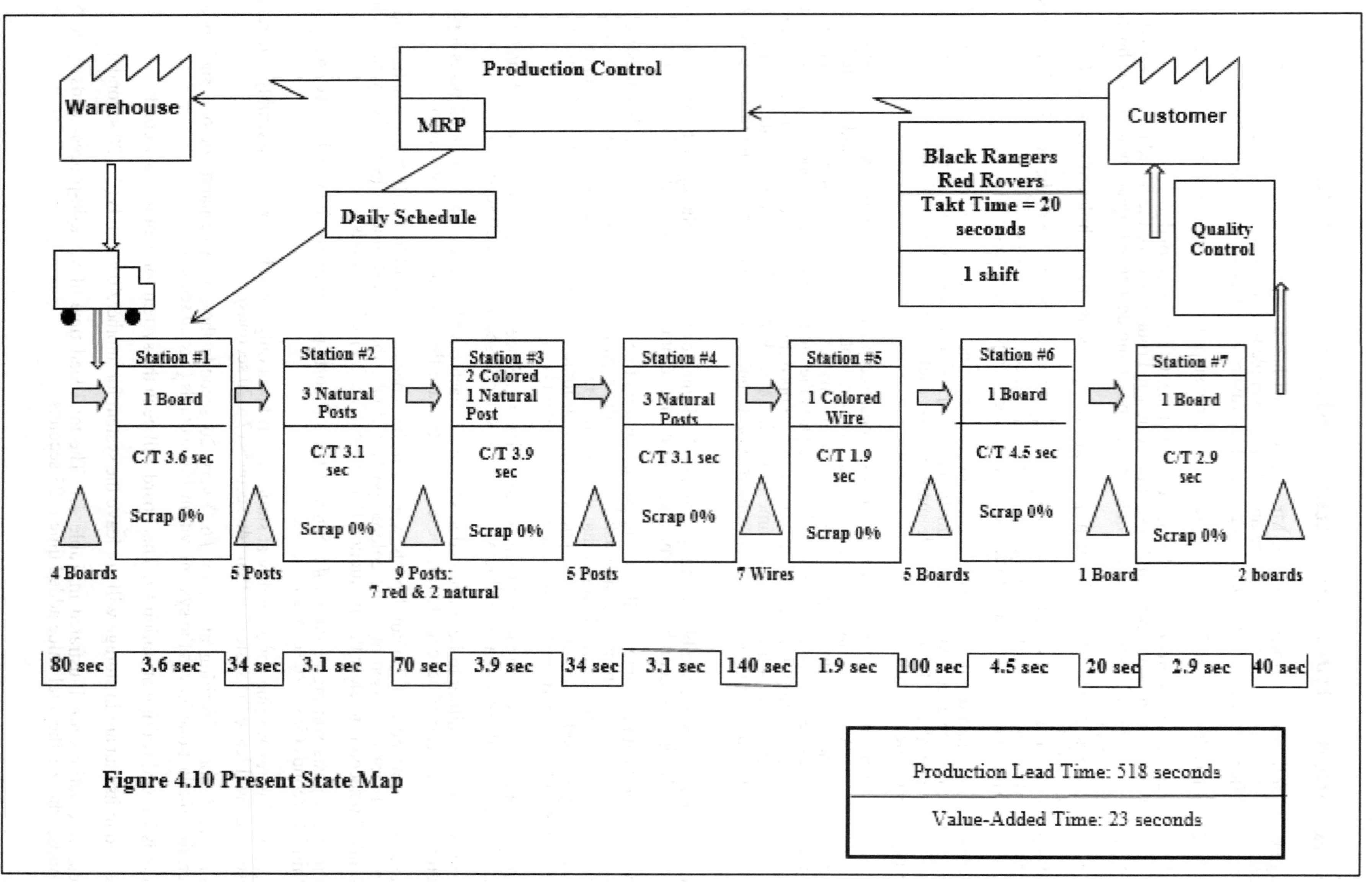

Figure 4.10 Present State Map

Table 4.1: Calculation of Lead Time of Work-in-Process and Value-Added Time

	WIP	Calculations	Total
Process #1:	3.6 seconds of processing		**3.60**
	4 boards are waiting	4 x 20 seconds (takt time)	80.00
Process #2:	3.1 seconds of processing		**3.10**
	5 posts are waiting	it takes 3 posts per one assembly; therefore: (5/3) x 20seconds	34.00
Process #3:	3.9 seconds of processing		**3.90**
	7 colored & 2 natural posts are waiting	it takes 2 colored and 1 natural post for one assembly; therefore: max(7/2, 2/1) x 20 seconds	70.00
Process #4:	3.1 seconds of processing		**3.10**
	5 posts are waiting	it takes 3 posts per one assembly; therefore: (5/3) x 20 seconds	34.00
Process #5:	1.9 seconds of processing		**1.90**
	7 wires are waiting	it takes 1 wire for one assembly; therefore: (7/1) x 20 seconds	140.00
Process #6:	4.5 seconds of processing		**4.50**
	5 boards are waiting	5 x 20 seconds	100.00
Process #7:	2.9 seconds of processing		**2.90**
	1 board is waiting	1 x 20 seconds	20.00
Storage:	2 units in storage	2 x 20 seconds	40.00
		Value-Added Time:	**23.00**
		Lead Time of Work-in-Process:	518.00

When applying lean principles, the "future state map" for this factory could be as shown in Figure 4.11. It shows a re-arrangement of stations, reducing unnecessary work-in-process and activities. The materials are now being delivered on a daily basis directly from the vendors.

A maximum of buffer/safety stock of three boards is stored at the first station. It is a pull system in which work centers signal with a card that they wish to withdraw parts from feeding operations or suppliers. The work-in-process (WIP) lead time is reduced from 518 seconds to 180 seconds. There is also a slim reduction in the value-added time from 23 seconds to 19 seconds. The 19 seconds of value-added time is now sufficient to meet a customer's takt time of 20 seconds. Improvements made to this system are: visual controls, load leveling (9.7 seconds for post-position operation and 9.3 seconds for wire-connection operation), poka-yoke (failsafe techniques or work methods), introduction of signal kanbans (the production and the withdrawal kanban), supermarket (to control inventory limits between processes and allow for pulling inventory from one process to another process), point of use storage of materials that are on consignment, reduction in transportation or movement, and others.

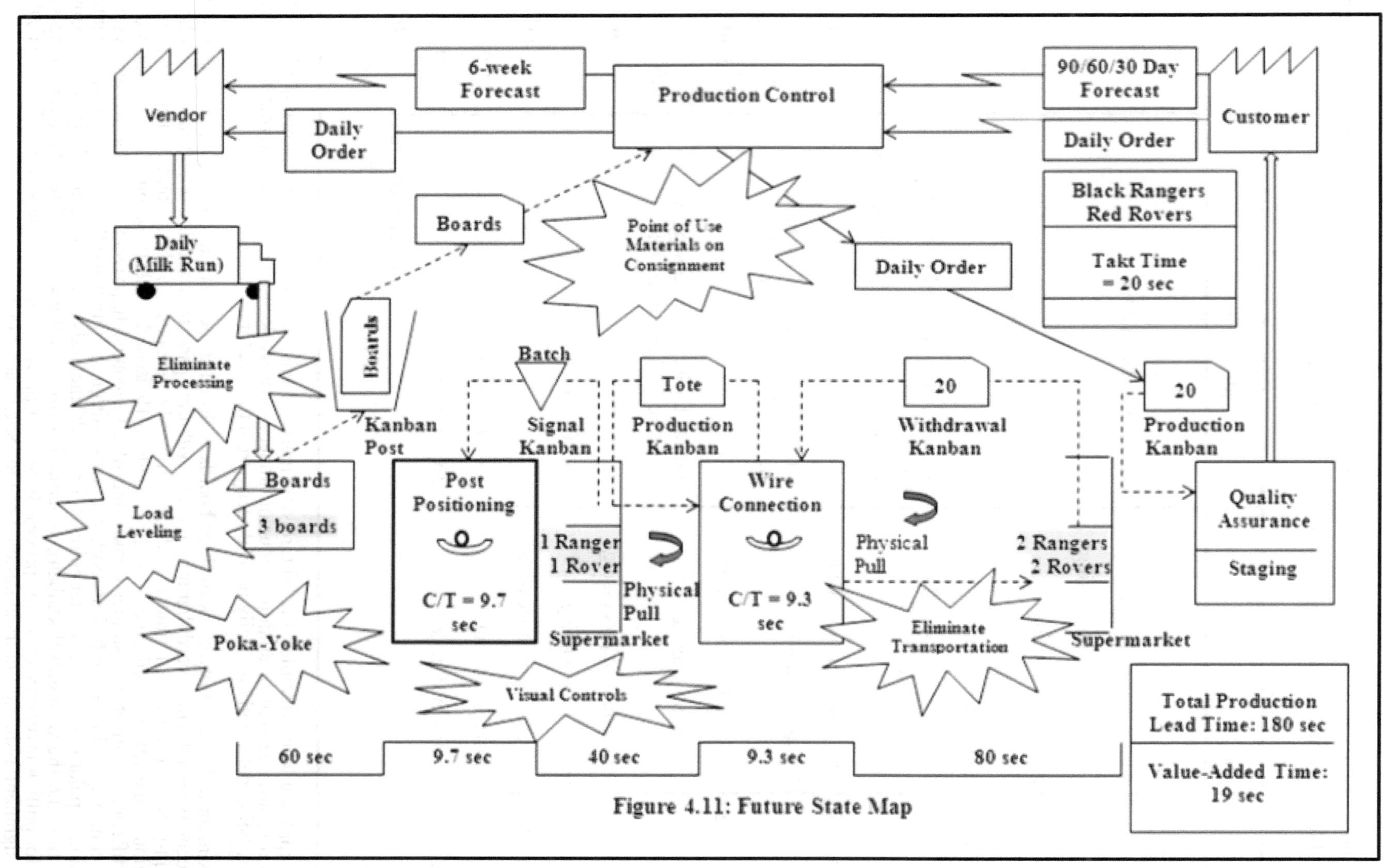

Figure 4.11: Future State Map

Table 4.2: Calculation of Lead-Time of Work-in-Process and Value-Added Time: Future State			
	WIP	**Calculations**	**Total**
Process #1: Post Positioning	9.7 seconds 3 boards are waiting	 3 x 20 seconds (takt time)	**9.70** 60.00
Process #2: Wire Connection	9.3 seconds 2 boards are waiting: one **black** ranger and one **red** rover	 2 x 20 seconds	**9.30** 40.00
Storage:	4 finished products: two **black** rangers and two **red** rovers	4 x 20 seconds	80.00
		Value-Added-Time:	**19.00**
		Lead Time of Work-in-Process:	180.00

Table 4.3: Comparing Results of Present versus Future State Map		
	Present State Map	**Future State Map**
Production Lead Time	518 seconds	180 seconds
Value-Added Time	23 seconds	19 seconds
Meeting Takt Time? (20seconds)	No	Yes
WIP Waste	(518 – 23) = 495 seconds	(180 – 20) = 160 seconds
Reduction in Waste: 495 seconds – 160 seconds = 335 seconds % Reduction in Waste: (335 seconds x 100%) / 495 seconds = 67.68%		

Table 4.3 summarizes the metrics of the present state map and the future state map and shows the calculations of WIP waste. The reduction in waste and % reduction in waste as we change the assembly process from the present state to the future state are also shown. Because of the end "supermarket" that is used in the future state map, and because end products will be shipped to the customer only every 20 seconds, the assembler will experience an unavoidable delay of one second per unit. Therefore, 20 seconds, rather than 19 seconds, are used in the calculation of the WIP waste for the future state map.

8.2 Improving the Process of Preparing Insurance Claims[2]

The M&D Insurance Company spends 29 hours getting claims ready for processing by various claim adjusters.

A company steering committee, made up of representatives from management and union leadership, chartered a cross-functional team. This team included representatives from various functions and was led by a highly experienced facilitator. The members of the team included mailroom and microfilm employees, insurance claim adjudication technicians, information technology professionals, a union steward, and a supervisor from the mailroom.

[2] Data for this case was provided by Ron Crabtree, President of MetaOps

These members walked through the processing of claims and created the hand written current value stream map shown in Figure 4.12. It includes the following steps.

- Picking up mail at the post office
- Unloading mail at the dock
- PO box sort in the mail room on the first floor
- Slitting envelopes in the mail room on the first floor
- Moving the mail from the east mailroom to either the third floor for microfilm prepping, or to the West mail room on the first floor, or to pension on the fifth floor
- Prepping the mail on the third and the first floors (opening envelopes, flattening papers, taping, removing staples, attaching batch sheets, etc.)
- Performing mail sorts on the first and third floors (there are as many as 17 different sorts)
- Microfilming
- Data entry
- Moving claims to the document room for storage

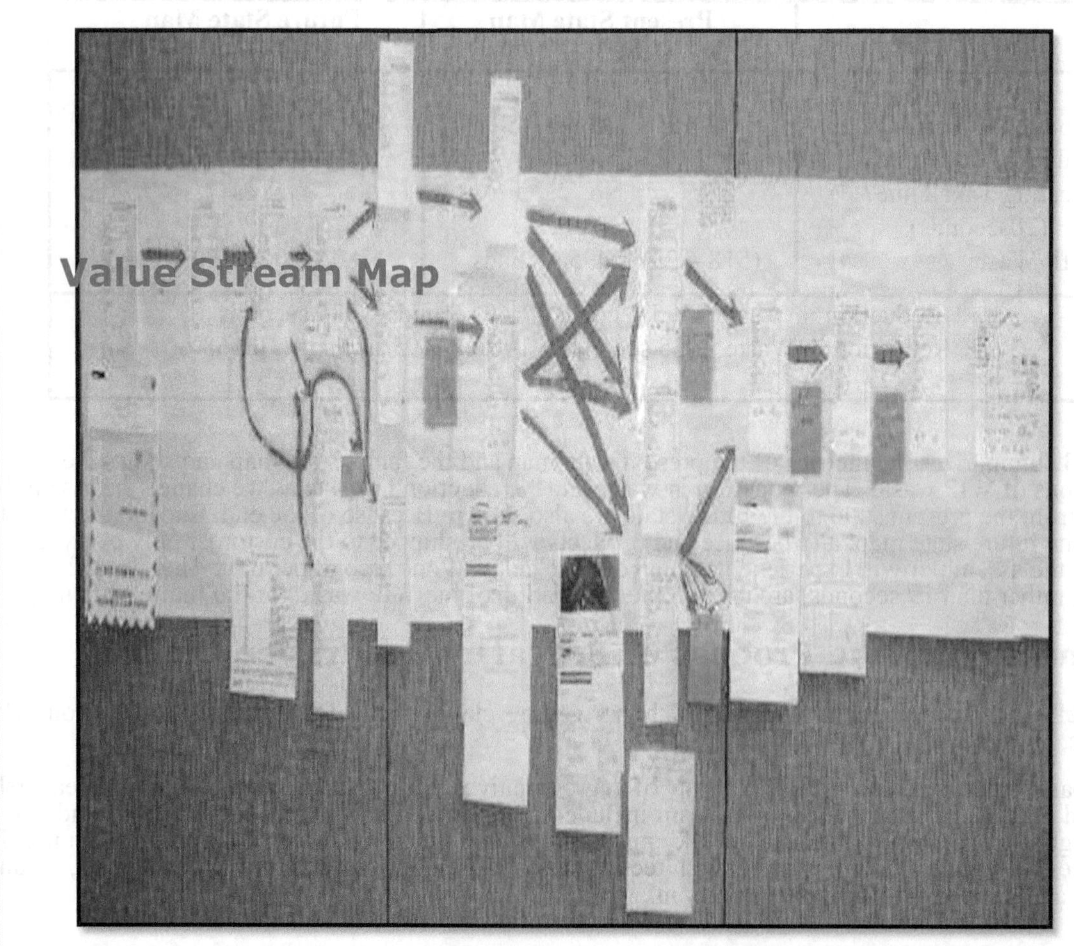

Figure 4.12 Hand drawn Current State Value Stream Map for M&D Insurance Company

This value stream map allows the participants to see the processes from various vantage points in an effort to identify waste in the system and to come up with improvements. It helps create a consensus amongst the participants who have to identify which processes are value-added and which are not. It was done on paper, the length of a wall, where it was pasted. As waste got analyzed, the participants used sticky notes to identify waste, quality problems, inefficiencies, etc.

In addition to the value stream map two spaghetti diagrams of the movement on the first and third floors were created (see Figures 4.13 and 4.14).

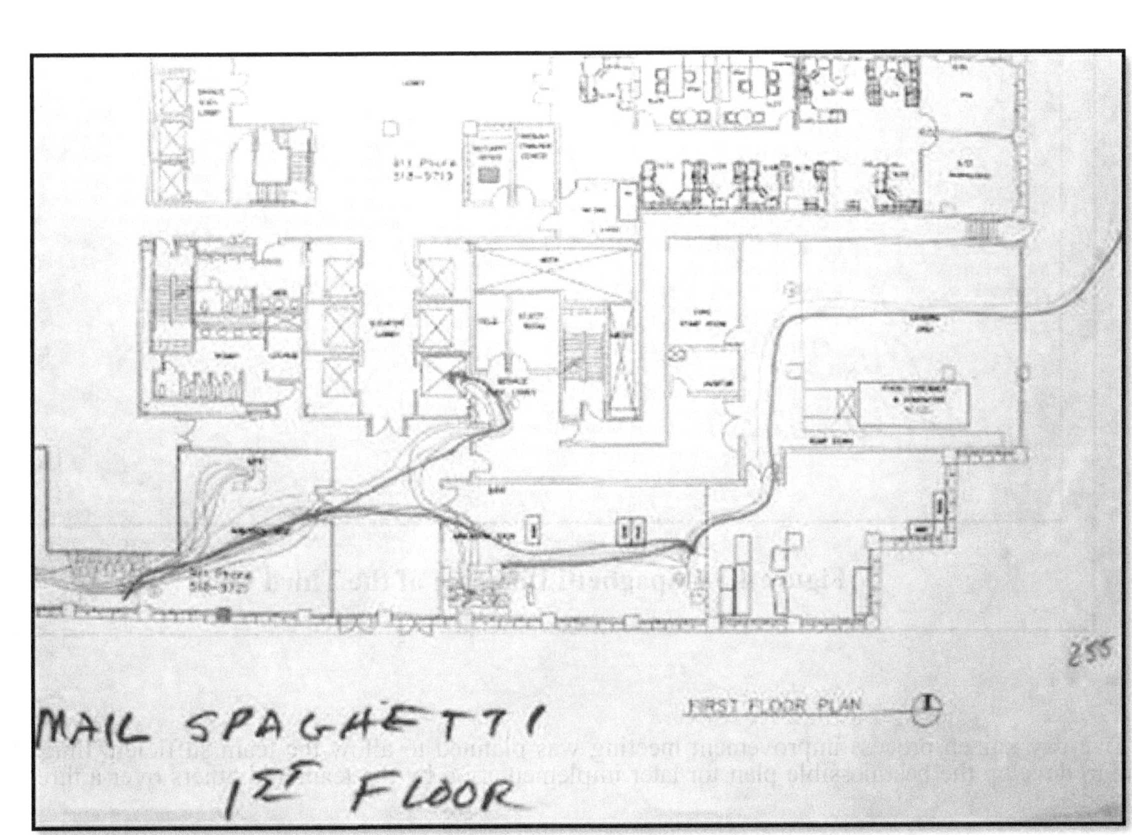

Figure 4.13 Spaghetti Diagram of the First Floor

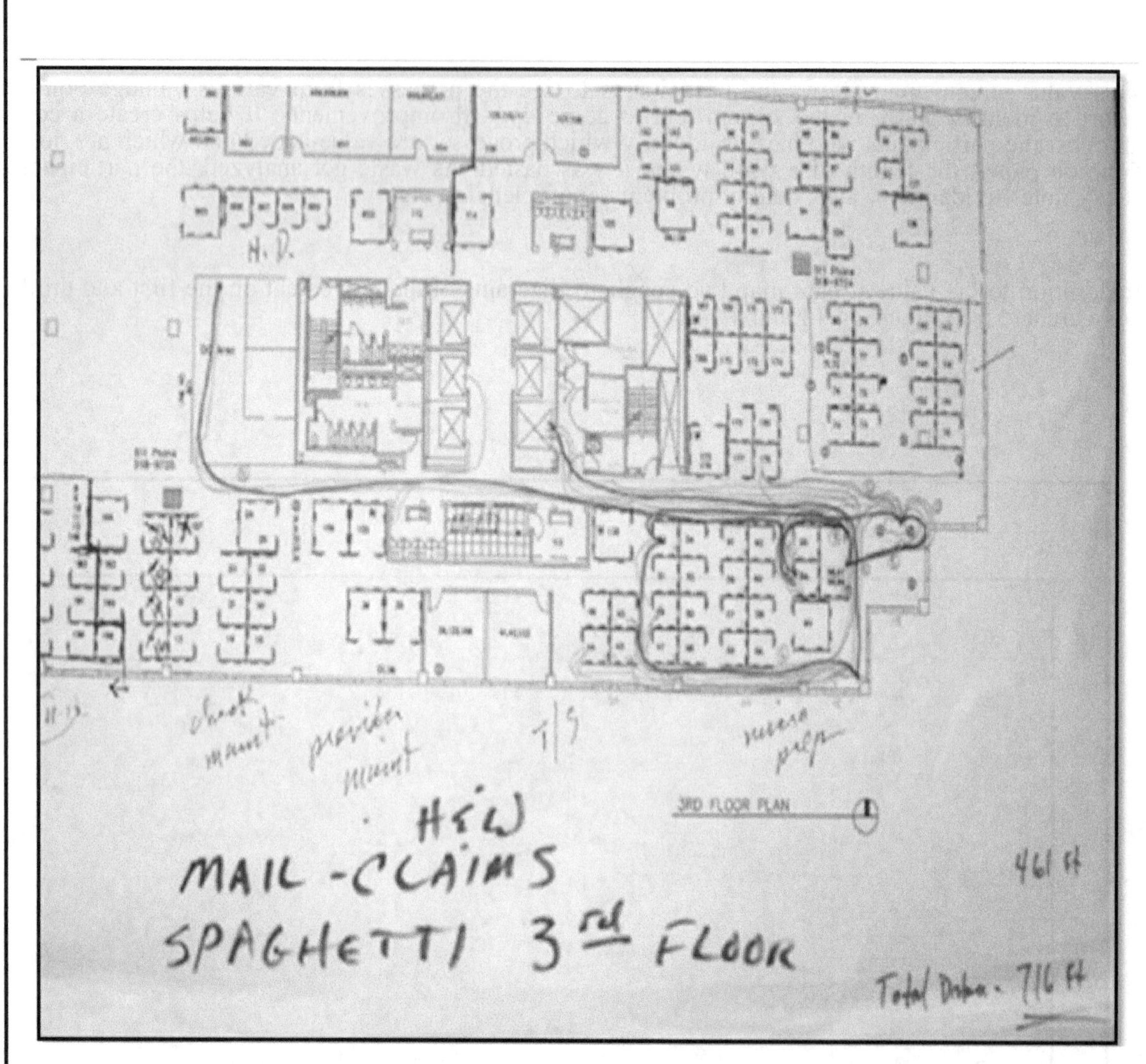

Figure 4.14 Spaghetti Diagram of the Third Floor

A five-day kaizen process improvement meeting was planned to allow the team sufficient time to learn and to develop the best possible plan for later implementation by the team and others over a three month period.

The process improvement had to focus on all of the following:

- Identify and eliminate waste
- Eliminate quality problems and error-proof all activities
- Implement safety improvements

- Create work flow improvements
- Develop standard visual work
- Reduce movement of people and material
- Place all required materials at point of use
- Implement a production communication board
- Improve productivity by at least 20% or reduce the cycle time per piece through workflow improvements and elimination of wasted steps
- Decrease the throughput time for mail to the DC room by at least 50% (this means that the mail will be delivered in less than two working days from the moment it has been delivered to the mail room)
- Reduce the number of sorts by 50% (presently there are as many as 17 sorts)
- Reduce the physical movement of the mail by 50% (presently it is estimated that the movement is approximately 716 feet if all is well)
- The company has given the go-ahead to replace microfilming by computerized scanning. This technology must be considered in implementing the plan

The improvement team members were given the following guidelines and were asked following questions:

- Management has made it very clear that if you are going to move anything or anyone, you had better be able to measure an improvement to the process.
  - First: what is the best strategy to reduce the process time by 50%, so that claims are available for adjusters more quickly?
  - Can we reduce the labor time for this job in a measured way? What is your targeted labor productivity improvement? How do you measure it?
- What will you do to minimize disruption to the business during the transition period?
- What can you do to avoid a big fight with the union before, during, and after making the changes?

The team facilitator generated the cleaned-up version of the current hand drawn present state map, as shown in Figure 4.12. This map can be viewed in Figure 4.15 and shows the present metrics of the system, using the same principles as shown in the previous assembly example. The metrics were obtained by walking one mail item through its various processing steps and its cycle time (in seconds) and throughput time (in hours) were recorded. The value-added time or cycle time for this item was 48.68 seconds. However, the throughput time for that item was 29 production hours. These one-item-specific metrics were recorded and are shown at the bottom of the value stream map. This is a typical batch processing operation, where the various processes are not necessarily synchronized from step to step. The delays are shown in the map and reflect on the enormous throughput time.

Characteristics (including observed issues, quality problems, and concerns) and specific metrics of the present state map of the insurance company are highlighted for each step in Table 4.4.

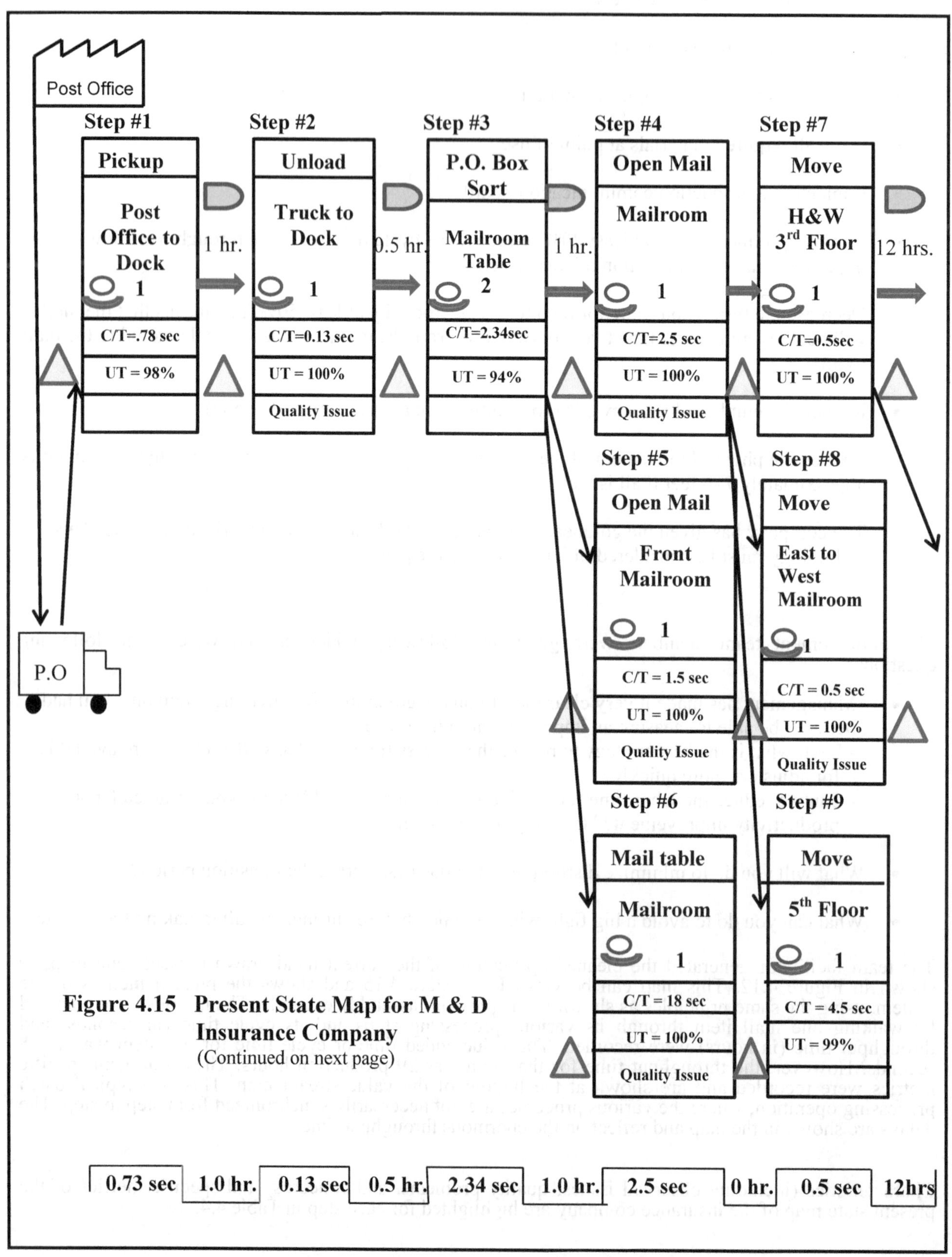

Figure 4.15 Present State Map for M & D Insurance Company
(Continued on next page)

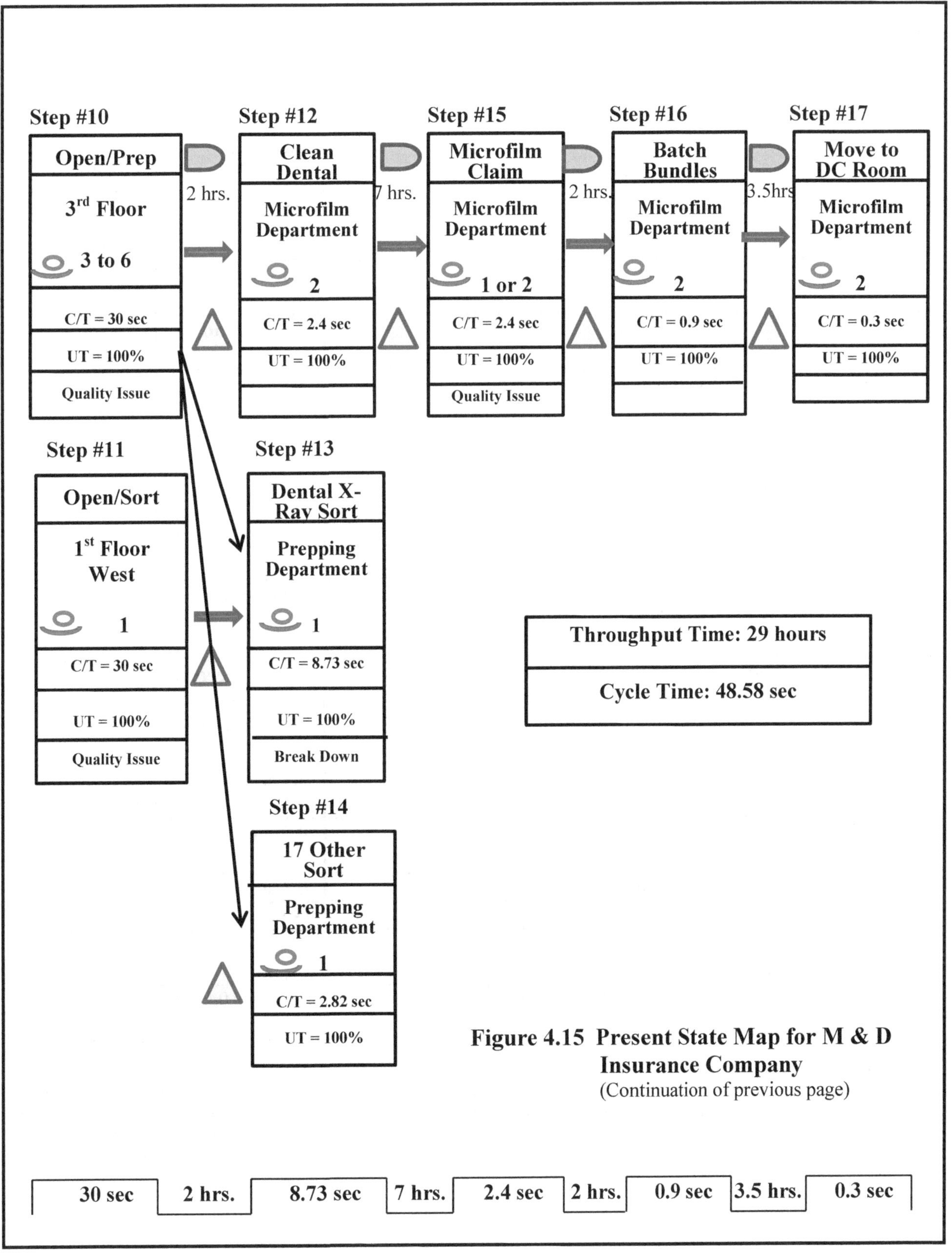

Figure 4.15 Present State Map for M & D Insurance Company
(Continuation of previous page)

Table 4.4: Characteristics and Metrics of the Present State Map			
Steps	**Quality or Rework Issues**	**Value-Added Time (seconds)**	**Throughput Time (delays)**
1. Pickup	Post office errors	**0.78 seconds**	1 hour
2. Unload	Dropping mail	**0.13 seconds**	0.5 hour
3. P.O. Box Sort	Misrouting	**2.34 seconds**	1 hour
4. Slitter	Cut claims	**2.5 seconds**	
5. Small Slitter	Cut letters	1.5 seconds	
6. Hand Open	Misrouting	18 seconds	0 hours
7. Move to 3rd Floor	<no issues noticed>	**0.5 seconds**	
8. Move to 1st Floor	<no issues noticed>	0.5 seconds	
9. Move to 5th Floor	<no issues>	0.5 seconds	12 hours
10. 3rd Floor Open/Prep	Staples missing/not enough tape	**30 seconds**	
11. 1st Floor Open/Sort	Staples missing/not enough tape	30 seconds	2 hours
12. Clean Dental Sort	Comment: could lose a whole day's work	2.4 seconds	
13. Dental X-Ray Sort	Type writer breakdown	**8.73 seconds**	
14. 17 Sorts	Comment: everyone does it different	2.82 seconds	7 hours
15. Microfilming Claims	Machine breakdown and paper jammed	**2.4 seconds**	2 hours
16. Data Entry Batch Bundled	<no issues>	**0.9 seconds**	3.5 hours
17. Move to DC Room	<no issues>	**0.3 seconds**	
Metrics	**For Walk Through Item to 3rd Floor**	**48.58 seconds or 29 hours**	

The value-added time for all processes in the present state map equals 48.58 seconds, while the throughput time or total processing lead time, due to delays, equals 29 hours, or 104,400 seconds.

This yields a **process flow efficiency** of only 0.04653% (**value-added time/total processing lead time**).

Studying the present state map, using the Gemba technique (walking through the processes on the first and the third floor), and measuring waste throughout the system, the team decided that it is possible to perform all operations in the mail room. So they set out designing a proper layout as shown in Figure 4.16. This layout was developed at the same time that the process for readying the mail for the adjusters was re-engineered. The future value stream map, shown in Figure 4.17, reflects this new process.

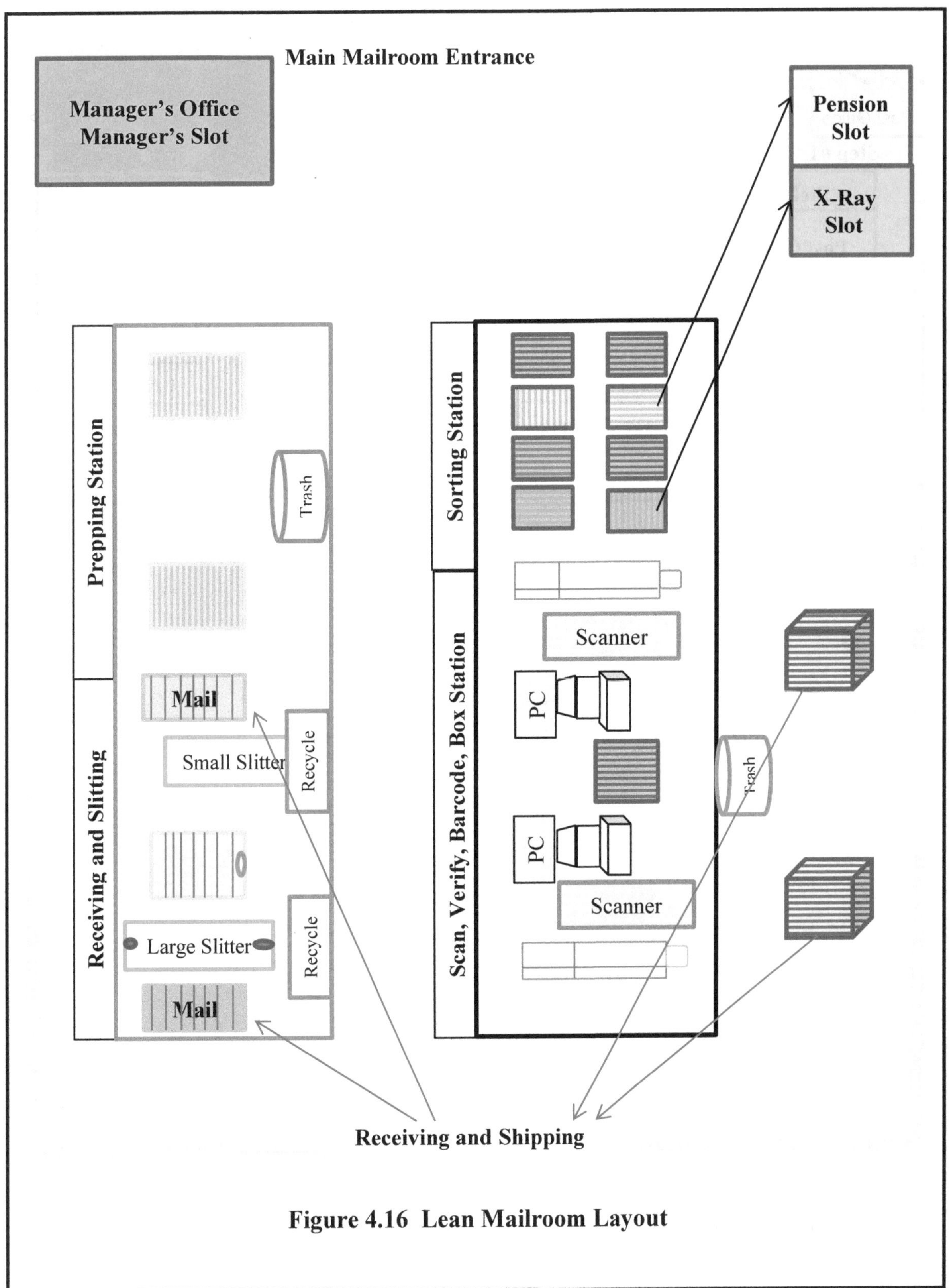

Figure 4.16 Lean Mailroom Layout

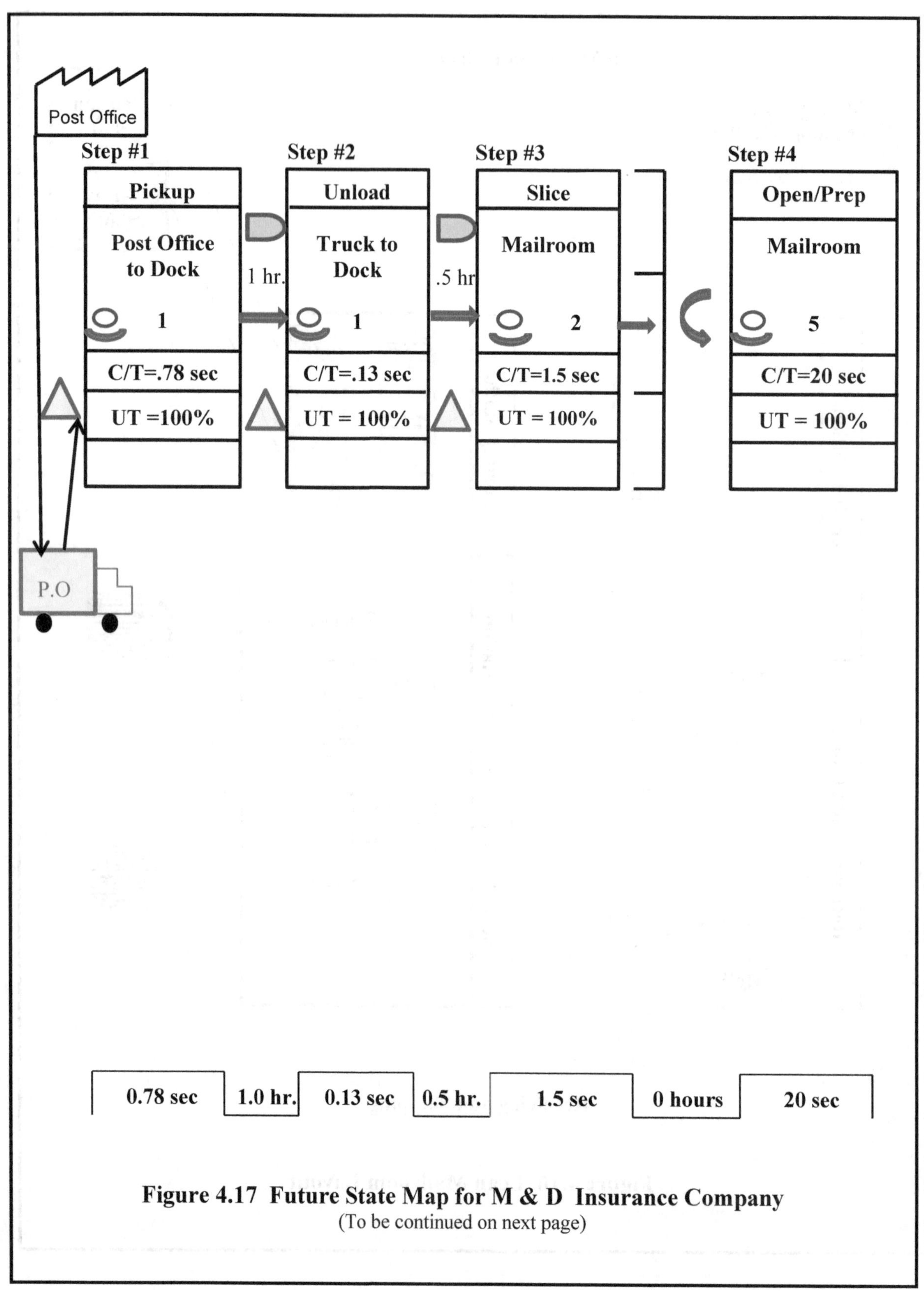

Figure 4.17 Future State Map for M & D Insurance Company

(To be continued on next page)

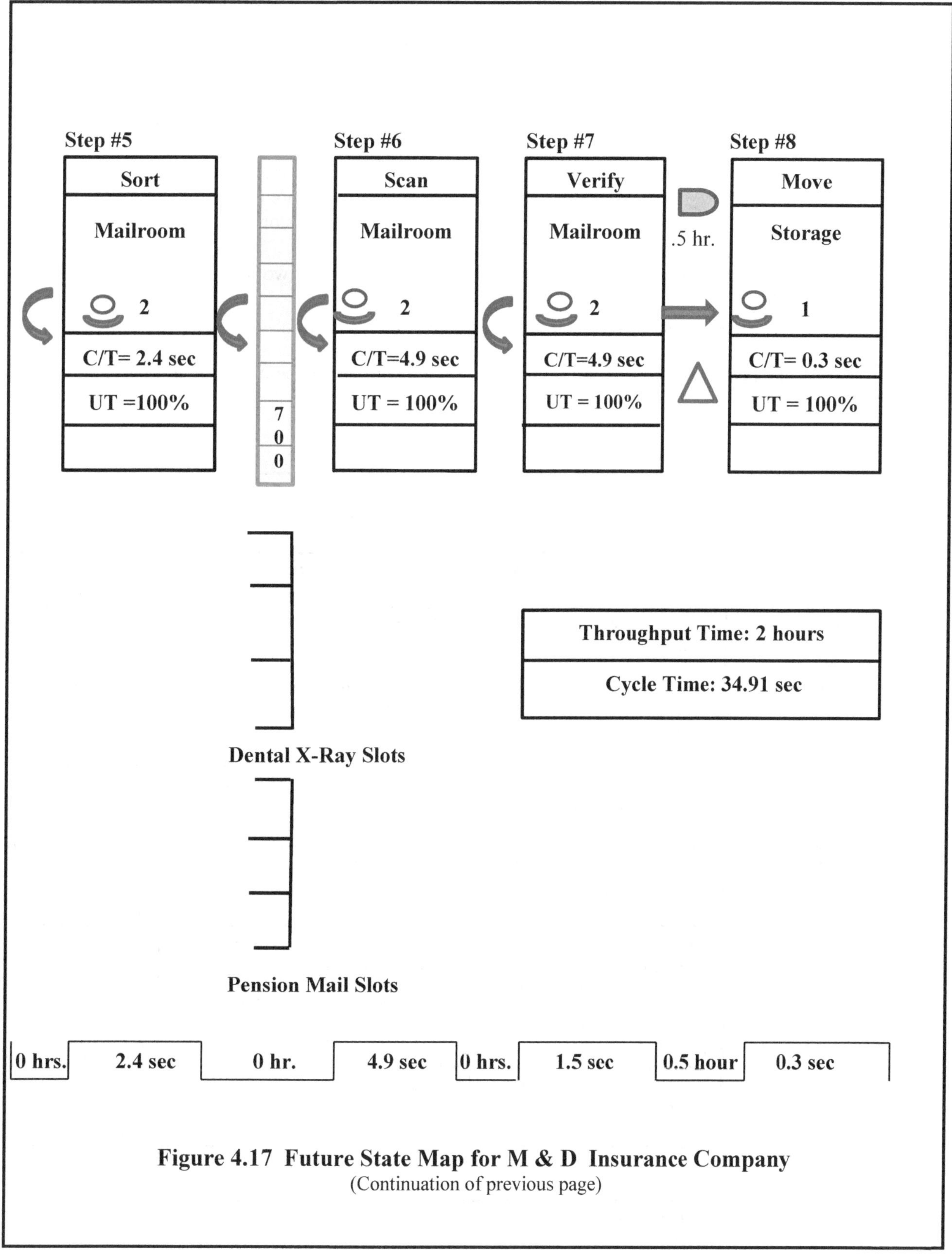

Figure 4.17 Future State Map for M & D Insurance Company
(Continuation of previous page)

Some of the characteristics of that layout are as follows:

- Different colored mail bins are used for each type of mail (X-ray is green, front office mail is blue, pension is yellow, and dental claims are red)
- Front office mail, pension mail, and X-rays (with any referenced dental claims) are moved from the sorting stations directly to the mail slots, for departmental pickup
- Dental claims are scanned, bar coded, and boxed. Scanned claims are electronically sent to the claims department, while boxed hard copies are sent to short-term storage
- Employees are cross-trained and move to a different station every two hours
- Supplies for each station are stored under the counter at each station

Characteristics and specific metrics of the future state map of the insurance company are highlighted for each step in Table 4.5.

Table 4.5: Characteristics and Metrics of the Future State Map

Steps	Quality or Rework Issues	Value-Added Time (seconds)	Throughput Time (delays)
1. Pickup	Company will work with post office to minimize errors	**0.78 seconds**	1 hour
2. Unload	Dropping of mail is minimized through training	**0.13 seconds**	0.5 hour
3. Slice Envelopes	Workers are trained to minimize cutting of content of envelopes	**1.5 seconds**	0 hours
4. Open/Prep	Inventory of staples and tape is controlled on a daily basis	**20 seconds**	0 hours
5. Sort	Workers are trained to sort in the most efficient way, using the colored mail bins	**2.4 seconds**	
6. Scan	A preventive maintenance system is set in place to prevent breakdown of scanners and computers	**4.9 seconds**	0 hours
7. Verify	Necessary step to ensure 100% quality of scanned item	**4.9 seconds**	0.5 hour
8. Move to DC Room	Boxes are moved to DC room every half hour	**0.3 seconds**	
Metrics	**Future State Map**	**34.91 seconds or 2 hours**	

The value-added time for all processes in the present state map equals 34.91 seconds, while the throughput time or total processing lead-time, due to delays, equals 2 hours, or 7,200 seconds.

This yields a **process flow efficiency** of 0.4849% (**value-added time/total processing lead time**).

Comparing the present state map with the future state map shows significant reduction in cycle time, or value-added time, from 48.58 seconds to 34.91 seconds. This reduction of 13.67 seconds [48.58 – 34.91] represents a percentage reduction of 28.14% [100% *(13.67/48.5)].

There is also a significant reduction in the total production throughput time of 27 hours [29 hours – 2 hours], or a 93.10% reduction in throughput time [100% * (27/29)].

The process flow efficiency has also significantly improved from 0.0465% to 0.4849%, for a total improvement of 0.4384% [0.4849 – 0.0465]. This represents a more than nine-fold improvement of 942.8% [100% * (0.4384/0.0465)].

These results are summarized in Table 4.6.

<table>
<tr><th colspan="3">Table 4.6: Comparing Process Maps</th></tr>
<tr><th>Metrics</th><th>Present Value Stream Map</th><th>Future Value Stream Map</th></tr>
<tr><td>Maximum Number of People Involved</td><td>20</td><td>16</td></tr>
<tr><td>Value-Added Time (VAT)</td><td>48.58 seconds</td><td>34.91 seconds</td></tr>
<tr><td colspan="3">Reduction in VAT: (48.58 -34.91) seconds = 13.67 seconds
% Reduction in VAT or Cycle Time: 100% (13.67/48.58) = 28.14%</td></tr>
<tr><td>Throughput Time</td><td>29 hours</td><td>2 hours</td></tr>
<tr><td colspan="3">Reduction in Throughput Time: (29 – 2) hours = 27 hours
% Reduction in Throughput Time: 100% (27/29) = 93.10%</td></tr>
<tr><td>Process Flow Efficiency</td><td>0.0465%</td><td>0.4849%</td></tr>
<tr><td colspan="3">Increase in Process Flow Efficiency: (0.4849 – 0.0465) % = 0 .4384%
% Increase in Process Flow Efficiency: 100% (0.4384 /0.0465) = 942.80%
or More Than a 9-fold Increase in Process Flow Efficiency</td></tr>
</table>

8.3 Improving Health Care Processes via Value Stream Mapping

In health care, a system known as "pay-for-performance" or "P4P" is critical to improve the quality of patient care. This P4P (the "Act") program is an outgrowth of the Deficit Reduction Act of 2005 and was passed by the U.S. Congress. This Act represents attempts by the U.S. government and private enterprise, such as insurance companies and health care purchasing consortiums, to require health care institutions to meet certain objective criteria that will increase the quality of care, while at the same time reducing healthcare cost. Under this Act, hospitals and health care systems are eligible to receive higher Medicare and Medical reimbursements if they can demonstrate certain types of operational efficiencies and productivity improvements. Increased operational efficiency and healthcare productivity gains can be achieved through:

- Focusing on health care enterprise integration (the ability to access data across multiple systems using healthcare information technology)
- Pursuing a more integrated approach to the health care supply chain system for managing activities along the entire chain
- Adapting operations management techniques to the health care industry

A lean technique, like value stream mapping, has become a popular operations management technique for re-engineering many inefficient processes we find in the health care industry.

Anita Craig, DO, summarizes an improvement event as follows:

> "Around 2005, University of Michigan Hospitals began an initiative to bring lean problem solving methods and culture to the health system. As part of that initiative grants and lean coaching support were made available to a number of projects in both the inpatient and outpatient settings. The department of physical medicine and rehabilitation (PMR) received such a grant in 2007 to address the issue of timeliness of patient transfer to the rehabilitation floor. The transfer of a patient from an acute medical service to the rehabilitation service requires coordination between both physicians and nurses on the sending and receiving services, housekeeping to prepare the beds, transport, and multiple steps required to obtain insurance approval for the transfer. Delays in transfer resulted in lack of therapies the first day of the transfer and both patient and staff dissatisfaction. Additionally, with the rise in acute medical census any delay in discharge of patients to the rehabilitation unit potentially could cause delays in admissions of new patients from the emergency department or postoperative holding. The issue of delayed admissions had been a long standing problem, and previous attempts to improve the process were ineffective.
>
> Through the UMHS grant, the department of PMR received a lean coach to assist with the process and educate all participants in lean principles. After an initial scoping phase, a two day workshop was convened to analyze the current process through value stream mapping, to formulate a future state map, and to develop an implementation plan. The group assembled included representatives from all steps in the transfer process, including physicians, nurses from both the rehabilitation floor and from acute medical floors, therapists, discharge coordinators, and the rehabilitation floor admission coordinator. Key deliverables and metrics were identified to bring the desired process change, and specific individuals or groups were tasked with implementation of those changes, with specific time frames and regular process meetings. At the end of the workshop the findings and implementation plan were presented to hospital administration to get leadership buy-in to the project. Another key strategy for process change was close monitoring of key time goals for every admission with analysis of events that fell outside of goal time lines. This allowed daily feedback and early identification of areas for improvement.
>
> Results from the project have been quite dramatic. Prior to initiation of the project in early 2008 only 18% of patients arrived to the floor by 1:00 PM (average admission time 4:30 PM) and no patients received therapies on the day of admission. By early 2010 65% of patients were physically on the rehabilitation unit by 1:00 PM and 92% of patients did receive therapies on that day of admission.

In addition to achieving the goals set out by this project, it served as an example of the power of lean process re-engineering to bring meaningful change and became a springboard for other projects in the department of PMR."

9. E-Blast from Abe Eshkenazi on Visualizing[3]

Consider the following abstract of the e-blast from APICS: **"Yesterday's Visibility to Improve Today's Processes".**

"This week, the *Harvard Business Review* Blog Network featured a piece about a productivity consultant who finds inspiration from his father's clothing factory 40 years ago."

APICS refers to Jordan Cohen, who directs the PA Consulting Group's knowledge worker productivity practice, who mentions that his father's factory was like his personal playground with mountain like stacks of pallets, the dress racks representing jungle gyms.

Cohen, in his blog, goes on to write that while there was little computerization, automation, or reporting software, his father kept on top of the production schedule. By putting his desk on a raised platform in the middle of the factory, Cohen's father could identify bottlenecks and intervene as necessary to ensure orders were completed on time. Employees also could find their boss easily if they needed help. Cohen says that he decided not to become a dressmaker. Instead, he went to graduate school and joined a large corporation. However, he mentions that he sees that the transparency of the factory floor needs to be applied to our modern knowledge work environment.

Referring to Cohen's blog, the e-blast goes on to say: "Of course, therein lays the challenge. Knowledge work happens inside employees' heads. However, Cohen proposes some strategies that help make work more visible. First, he suggests that everyone should know what the inputs are. For example, how many hours were spent on a task or project? How much time was spent in meetings? Employees need to know the outputs, as well. Making the work output **visible** to all workers involved allows them to contribute by **providing insight, identifying short cuts, including innovations, and adding suggestions from their diverse experiences and background**. If knowledge workers, managers, and other company decision makers **can learn to "see"** the work, they can add more value to the product. We know <that>building factories like they were in the 1970s isn't the key to adding value in 2013. What Cohen does is take a core manufacturing **concept of visibility** and apply it throughout the enterprise. Over the years, supply chain and operations management professionals have become more essential to crafting the overall strategy for businesses. During the recession, many professionals applied concepts from the APICS body of knowledge, such as life cycle planning, process mapping, and kaizen, to sustain their businesses."

10. GLOSSARY AND SUMMARY OF METHODS

Assembly Chart – The assembly chart is a schematic model that helps visualize the flow of materials and relationships of parts. It indicates the subassemblies, the assemblies, the position of parts, and the position of purchased parts.

Buffer Stock (or Safety Stock) – Buffer or safety stock is a planned quantity of inventory to safeguard against fluctuations in demand or supply.

Five Whys (or 5-Whys, Five Ws) – Five whys is a lean management technique for root cause analysis. The practice is to ask "why" five times. It is postulated that by the time the answer to the fifth "why" is given the true cause of the problem is found.

Flow Process Chart – The flow process chart is a detailed graphic and sequential representation of work performed on a product or for a service. It includes: operations, transportation, temporary and permanent storage, inspections, outside operations, delays, distance traveled, operation time, inspection time, travel time, delay time, and a brief summary of all the above. The chart uses ASME standard symbols.

[3] Based on an E-blast from Abe Eshkenazi, CEO of APICS, The International Association for Operations Management, February 8, 2013.

Gemba – Gemba is a process by which team members go with their leader to the site of the activity and collect data on the current state of the process

In-Process Inventory (or Work-In-Process WIP) – In-process inventory is the inventory on the production floor that waits to be processed by the next process.

Kanban – Kanban is a method of just-in-time production. It uses standard containers or lot sizes with a card attached to each (kanban = card). The card signals the need for movement from one process to the next (pull kanban), or the need for production at a process (production kanban).

Load Leveling – Load leveling requires that work in successive stations is approximately equal.

Macro Process Planning – Macro process planning is designing and establishing the detailed arrangement of individual operations and processes. It is responsible for the choice of technology, the selection of manufacturing equipment and work stations, and the determination and analysis of production flow.

Micro Process Planning – Micro process planning is often referred to as operation design and is concerned with designing micro production systems that will provide the most efficient operation methods and operation sequence for the individual work stations and that will provide means and standards for personnel's and operators' training and control.

Operations Process Chart (or Process Chart) – In addition to what the assembly chart shows, the operation process chart also indicates for each manufactured part the basic flow from machine to machine. It includes the run time (the standard time to manufacture one unit), all operations needed to manufacture the part, and all visual and non-visual inspections.

Pay-for-Performance (or "P4P") – The P4P (the "Act") program is an outgrowth of the Deficit Reduction Act of 2005 and was passed by the U.S. Congress. This Act represents attempts by the U.S. government and private enterprise, such as insurance companies and health care purchasing consortiums, to require healthcare institutions to meet certain objective criteria that will increase the quality of care, while at the same time reducing health care cost.

Poka-Yoke – Poka-Yoke literally means mistake-proof. Poka-Yoke embraces techniques that prevent workers from making errors that may result in defects.

Process Flow Efficiency – The process flow efficiency is the ratio of the value-added time to the total processing lead time: **value-added time/total processing lead-time**.

Process Planning – The function of process planning is to select and to design the right tools, the right methods, and the right sequence for the production processes consistent with technical specifications from product design.

Route Sheet – A route sheet is filled out for each individual part of a subassembly, an assembly, or a product. It shows the sequence of operations, their operation numbers, and the departments in which the operations are performed, their setup time (if appropriate), production rates, and equipment.

Spaghetti Chart – The spaghetti chart shows the physical flow of processes. A product or activity is shown as it moves through the layout in order to identify possible flow problems such as excessive travel and travel time.

Supermarket – A supermarket is a lean concept to manage inventory between processes, and to aid in easy picking of inventory.

Takt Time (or Tact Time) – Takt time is the heartbeat of a lean production system. It defines the pace of production that meets the customer pull rate. It is the available production time divided by the customer demand rate.

Throughput Time (TT) (or Production/Operations Lead Time) – The throughput time is the total amount of time required to process the product/service through the productive system.

Value Stream Map – The value stream map is a visual representation of the production/operations path, documenting flow of materials and information. The visual representation is a drawing of the production/operations process/flow to produce and deliver a product or a service. The purpose of value stream mapping is to study the flow in the current map, and attempt to improve that flow as one draws the future map.

11. ACRONYMS

BOM Bill of Materials

ECR Engineering Change Request

ERP Enterprise Resource Planning

MRP Material Requirement Planning

MRPII Manufacturing Resource Planning

P4P Pay-for-Performance

PP Process Planning

SCM Supply Chain Management

TT Throughput Time

WIP Work-In-Process

12. REFERENCES

Casey, J.T, T.S. Brinton, and C.M. Gonzalez. "Utilization of Lean Management Principles in the Ambulatory Clinic Setting." *National Clinical Practical Urology*. (2009): pp. 146–154.

Chiodo, A., R. Wilke, R. Bakshi, A. Craig, D. Duwe, and E. Hurvitz. "Using Lean Principles to Manage Throughput on an Inpatient Rehabilitation Unit." *American Journal of Physical Medicine & Rehabilitation*. (November 2012): pp. 977–983.

Paige L. "Getting the Skinny on Lean Management." *Materials Management in Health Care*. (2005): pp. 26–29.

Rother, Mike and John Shook. *Learning to See, Value Stream Mapping to Create Value and Eliminate MUDA*. Brookline, MA: The Lean Enterprise Institute, 1998.

Sunyong, M. "Lean Management and Six-Sigma Yield Big Gains in Hospital's Immediate Response Laboratory. Quality Improvement Techniques Save more than $400,000." *Clinical Leadership Management Review*. (Vol.18, 2004): pp. 255–258.

Wu, N.L., Y. Parfenyuk, A. S. Craig, and M. E. Craig. "Guidelines for Sustaining High Level of Success when Implementing Lean Principles in Business: Some Successful Case Summaries." *International Journal of Accounting Information Science & Leadership*. (Vol. 4, Issue 10, 2011): pp. 67–85.

13. REVIEW QUESTIONS

1. Differentiate between macro process planning and micro process planning.
2. What are some of the objectives of process planning?
3. What are the basic functions of process planning?
4. What forms or documents are used during the product design phase?
5. What forms and documents are used during the process design phase of process planning?
6. What forms and documents are used during the operation design phase of process planning?
7. What is a route sheet? What are its components?
8. What is a flow process chart? What does it contain? Why is it used?

9. What is a gozinto chart? What information is given in a gozinto chart (list)? Should it be used for assembly?
10. What is an operation process chart? What information is given in an operation process chart (list)? Why is it put together?
11. What is value stream mapping?
12. What lean manufacturing principles are used to change a current state value map into a future state value map?
13. What is the purpose of a spaghetti chart? How is it put together?
14. What is meant by Gemba?

14. PROBLEMS

Problem #1

Consider the following process steps:

1. Lift and move via a hand crane a 5x8-ft (1/2-inch thick) steel plate from rack to trimming table: distance = 10 ft.; time = 0.50 minutes.
2. Trim steel plate to correct size with a torch: time = 10 minutes.
3. Inspect for miscalculations: time = 3 minutes.
4. Wait for overhead crane: time = 2 minutes.
5. Transport steel plate via overhead crane to rolling machine: distance = 50 ft.; time = 2.50 minutes.
6. Place plate in rolling machine and adjust machine controls to correct specifications: time = 2 minutes.
7. Roll: 3 minutes
8. Weld edges together to complete cylinder: 3 minutes.
9. Inspect welded seam: 1 minute.
10. Remove from machine by hand crane to floor: 0.5 minute.
11. Roll to storage area: distance is approximately 20 ft. from machine: 0.30 minutes
12. Store for indefinite period.

a) Construct the flow process chart for the above steps (use the blank chart at the end of the chapter).
b) What is the total value-added time?
c) What is the total production throughput time?
d) Calculate the process flow efficiency.
e) Interpret your results.

Problem #2

Read the description of "Water the Backyard" as shown in Figure 4.8.

a) What is the total value-added time?
b) What is the total production throughput time?
c) Calculate the process flow efficiency.
d) Attempt to change the layout and the sequencing of operations in an effort to improve on the flow of this activity. Summarize and analyze the results. What is now the value-added time, the total production throughput time, and the process flow efficiency?

Problem #3

Universal ball point pens consist of the following parts:

Part #1 push button
Part #2 housing
Part #3 refill
Part #4 name cap
Part #5 spring

In order for the pen to work properly, the metal point of the refill must be heated over a flame. You are asked to draw the assembly chart to assemble this pen.

Problem #4

Here is your scenario for "PAINTING THE SPARE ROOM":

After downing your 1st cold drink while sitting on the porch, you decide that it's finally time to paint the spare room. You walk 60 ft. to the garage door. It takes you 0.50 min. to open the door. You then walk 10 ft. to the bench where the paint is stored. You pick up the paint, go out the side door, and over to the house, a total of 45 ft. You then remember that you need paintbrushes and a stirrer, so you walk back to the garage (30 ft.). It takes you 0.25 min. to unlock the side door. You then walk 15 ft. to the bench. It takes you 3.50 min. to locate two brushes and a stirrer. You then walk back through the side door to the house.

You then carry the paint, brushes, and stirrer 30 ft. to the spare room. After inspecting the floor (30 sec.) you decide to get a drop-cloth. This takes you a total of 10 min. You now open the paint and stir it, taking 2 min. Next, you paint the wall to the right of the door, which takes 25 min. You know it will need another coat, so you wander back to the porch (30 ft.) and finish off some more cold drink (time spent sitting is 30 min.). You then return to the spare room. Repainting the wall takes another 20 min. You then decide to let your roommate clean up. It takes him 10 minutes to clean up, so you walk back to the porch and drink some more cold pop.

Assume it takes 0.01 min. to walk 1 foot.

a) Fill out the flow process map.

b) What is the total value-added time?

c) What is the total production throughput time?

d) Calculate the process flow efficiency.

e) Attempt to improve the process by making changes to layout or placement of materials needed for the job. Construct the new flow process chart. Summarize and analyze the results. What are the value-added time, the total production throughput time, and the process flow efficiency now? What are the % gains made for the new procedure shown in the map?

Problem #5

Consider the following parts list and assembly procedure to draw the assembly chart for a stamp holder.

Part #	Description	Material
010	Shaft	Brass
020	Base disk	Steel
030	Base	Marble
040	Lock washer	Steel
050	Flat washer	Steel
060	Hex nut	Steel
070	Felt circle	Felt
080	Lid	Brass
090	Top nut	Brass

The assembly of the stamp holder uses one jig (Jig A). Jig A is used for the assembly of the base section and is retained for the application of the felting. The following activities are performed with the jig:

1. Position the #010 shaft in jig
2. Slide the #020 base disk onto shaft
3. Slide the #030 base onto shaft
4. Slide the #040 lock washer onto shaft
5. Slide the #050 flat washer onto shaft
6. Apply the #060 hex nut to shaft
7. Move the jig to next position
8. Apply the #070 felt to base section
9. Remove the base section from the jig and place the base down, on the line
10. Slide the #080 lid onto the shaft
11. Apply the #090 decorative top nut to the shaft
12. Perform a visual inspection
13. Box each unit
14. Crate units, 12 boxes per crate

Problem #6

Look at Figure 4.10. Can you verify that the total production lead time or throughput time for work-in-process (WIP) is 518 seconds?
Look at Figure 4.11. Can you verify that the total production lead time or throughput time for work-in-process (WIP) is 180 seconds?

Problem #7

You are to draw a value stream map for the following scenario:

A patient has been admitted to the hospital and meets with his physician who orders some very needed tests. The process for having these tests done is as follows:

1. Doctor hand writes the request for the test on a requisition: 2 minutes
2. It takes 2 hours to enter this order into the system
3. Entering the order into the system automatically triggers the request for transport
4. The transport arrives 20 minutes after it is requested
5. The transport orderly moves the patient to the testing area: 20 minutes
6. Here the patient waits for 10 minutes, before being called for the test
7. Time to perform the test: 5 minutes
8. Patient waits for transfer back to room: 30 minutes
9. The transport orderly moves the patient back to his room: 20 minutes
10. Immediately after tests are finished, the technician waits for the expert to read the results: 2 hours
11. The expert reads the results of the test(10 minutes) and sends the results to the doctor instantly
12. The patient waits for the doctor to explain the results: 3 hours
13. The doctor explains the results to the patient: 5 minutes

In drawing the value stream map, understand that there are some simultaneous activities taking place (steps 8, 9, & 12 and steps 10& 11).

a) From a patient's standpoint, what is the value-added time?

b) From the patient's standpoint, what is the non-value-added time?

c) What is the process lead time or the total process throughput time?

d) What is the flow efficiency?

You may duplicate this form to do the flow processing charting problems

Flow Process Chart	
Process:	
Created by :	
Number of pages:	**Page number:**
Date:	**Chart Number:**

SUMMARY

Action	No	Time	Feet
△ Outside Operation			
○ Operation			
⇨ Transport			
□ Inspection			
D Delays			
▽ Storage			

Step	**Description**	**Action**	Feet	#	Time	Notes Where, How, Etc.
1		△○⇨□D▽				
2		△○⇨□D▽				
3		△○⇨□D▽				
4		△○⇨□D▽				
5		△○⇨□D▽				
6		△○⇨□D▽				
7		△○⇨□D▽				
8		△○⇨□D▽				
9		△○⇨□D▽				
10		△○⇨□D▽				
11		△○⇨□D▽				
12		△○⇨□D▽				
13		△○⇨□D▽				
14		△○⇨□D▽				
15		△○⇨□D▽				
16		△○⇨□D▽				
17		△○⇨□D▽				
18		△○⇨□D▽				
19		△○⇨□D▽				
20		△○⇨□D▽				
21		△○⇨□D▽				
22		△○⇨□D▽				
23		△○⇨□D▽				

Chapter 5

WORKPLACE ORGANIZATION AND STANDARDIZED WORK PROCEDURES

Many companies have spent huge amounts of dollars in an effort to "lean out" their businesses and their processes. They have not all been very successful, falling back into their old habits and ways of operation. Successful implementation of lean principles starts with good, sustainable workplace organization and standardized work procedures.

Whether it is an office or a manufacturing floor, a workplace needs to be organized. A work area should be laid out properly and standardized work procedures followed so that all employees can perform their jobs in the most efficient manner. If not, some type of non-value-added activity could be identified, such as waiting for tools, searching for tools and inventory causing delays, creation of excessive inventories, creation of obsolete inventories, extra motions to find what is needed, defective items due to inappropriate storage procedures and retrieval methods, and many others. Hence, all employees ought to perform their jobs using the principles of a lean workplace: a workplace that is organized, properly laid out, has lean standardized work procedures or process steps, and exhibits respect towards the workforce.

1. WORKPLACE ORGANIZATION

5 Japanese words

- Seiri **Sort (Housekeeping)**
- Seiton **Set in Order (Organization)**
- Seisou **Shine (Cleanup)**
- Seiketsu **Standardize (Keep Cleanliness)**
- Shitsuke **Sustain (Discipline)**

Figure 5.1 Where Does the 5S System Come from?

Elements of a 5S Program

- Sort - what is not needed, sort through, then sort out: "When in doubt, throw it out!"
- Straighten - what must be kept; make it visible and self explanatory so everyone knows where everything goes.
- Shine - everything that remains. Clean equipment, tools, and workplace.
- Standardize - develop a standard to keep the workplace clean and organized.
- Self-discipline - is making a habit of properly maintaining correct procedures.

Figure 5.2 The Five S System

Workplace organization is defined as a ***safe, clean, and neat*** arrangement of the work place. One must provide for **a specific location for everything** that is needed and we must eliminate anything that is not required to do the job. The principles used for the organization of the workplace are defined by the 5S program or system. The 5S program was initially introduced in Japan and represents five Japanese words: *seiri* for sort; *seiton* for straighten, simplify, or set in order; *seiso* for shine or scrub; *seiketsu* for standardize; and *shitsuke* for sustain or self-discipline. They relate to housekeeping, organizing, cleaning, maintaining, and sustaining a clean workplace. This deceptively simple, yet very powerful, program is supposed to work as follows:

Sort what is needed and what is not needed. What is not needed must be eliminated from the work place. When you are in doubt, throw it out. When implementing this principle you will get rid of excess waste, thus gaining significant space. In order to separate the needed items from the unneeded items you can use red, green, and yellow tags. Use the red tags for unneeded items (these are the items that need to be eliminated, tossed out); use the green tags for items that are needed and must be kept in the immediate area; and use the yellow tags for items you do not need all the time and must not be kept in the immediate area. You must designate a person to organize this activity and to manage the consolidation.

Set in order what must be kept. Make what is kept visible and self-explanatory, so everyone knows where everything goes. There must be a designated place for everything and everything must be set in its place. Use an appropriate and logical filing system for your paperwork and organize your parts inventory so it can easily be retrieved, used, and put away. Organize your inventory so that the first-in-first-out (FIFO) rule can be used. Place all items close to point of use. Vertical storage is preferred over horizontal storage. Store similar items together and different items on different levels. Consider color coding and labels.

Scrub and shine everything that remains. Like you clean equipment and tools, clean the work place and keep it shining.

For the Workers	For the Company
Pleasant Environment	**Improved Quality**
Satisfying Job	**Cost Reduction**
Pride in Workplace	**Increased Profitability**
Positive Mental Attitude	**Improved Maintenance**
Easier Job Performance	**Increased Customer Satisfaction**
Job Procedure makes Sense	

Figure 5.3 Benefits of the Five S System

This leads to standardization. Standardization requires discipline, sticking to the rules of organization, and making these rules a habit. Set up some standardized procedures to sort and straighten in a timely fashion, so that the above 3Ss can be maintained. It will be necessary to schedule this into regularly assigned work duties. A proper standardized procedure will prevent unneeded items from accumulating and thus falling back into unacceptable habits.

Sustain, through self-discipline, an organized workplace to avoid future problems. Do not allow yourself to fall back into old habits. You may want to use visuals to sustain the 5S program: label filing cabinets, restrict the space of labeled inventory areas, etc. Unless time is integrated into the work schedule, the 5S program will fall apart. Management must support this effort, perform regular audits, and recognize great efforts through a reward system.

This **5S system** is a powerful system that companies around the world are using to eliminate waste, dirt, clutter, inefficiency, and other stumbling blocks to excellence.

Both the company and the workers benefit from a good 5S program. Workers find they are working in a more pleasant work environment and find their jobs more satisfying. This gives them more pride in the workplace and generates a positive mental attitude. Their jobs become easier to execute because the procedures make sense. The bottom line is that the workers are spending less time on tasks and are able to perform these tasks to perfection.

The company will experience improved maintenance and increased work quality. These generate cost reductions and increased profitability. It ultimately leads to increased customer satisfaction.

2. *STANDARDIZED WORK PROCEDURES*

The workplace principle of standardized work requires that operations be safely carried out with all tasks organized in the best-known sequence and by using the most efficient and effective combination of resources. Resources include, but are not limited to, people, materials, methods, and machines. In other words, the way all operators are performing their tasks must be standardized. This implies that the best way to perform a task or execute a process must be determined. In determining the best way one must focus on eliminating non-value-added tasks, while improving customer satisfaction. Once this best method is determined, all operators involved in performing the tasks must be trained using standardized work tools that lead to standardized work performance.

Some of these standardized work tools are:

- Time observation sheets
- Flow diagrams
- Standard work sheets
- Standard work layout or work instructions
- Standard inspection sheets
- Standard visual controls

Standardized work procedures require the performance of work studies. Work study is, first of all, the systematic investigation and analysis of contemplated and present work systems and methods in order to formulate the most effective systems and methods for achieving necessary functions. It is also the establishment of measurement standards by which this work may be planned, scheduled, and controlled (Reuter, 1980, p.1). It includes work measurement, motion time study, methods engineering, work simplification, work design, and value stream mapping. Its objectives are to search for the best methods, to determine operation time standards, and above all to improve customer satisfaction.

Work study and measurement are necessary to aid in determining manpower requirements, to evaluate plant or department efficiency, to calculate productivity indexes, to determine machine/operator utility, to establish time standards and time allowances, to allocate cost, to schedule work, to evaluate alternate methods of operation, to define an acceptable day's work, to balance operations and work, and to lean out the productive system while focusing on customer satisfaction. Chapter 6 discusses some of the popular work study and measurement techniques for both direct and indirect work.

Successful implementation of a 5S improvement program, standardized work, and re-engineering processes (as discussed in Chapter 4 with value stream mapping) require the implementation of change management. It is commonly known that organizations that have introduced lean principles of workplace organization, standardized work procedures, and change management have re-engineered many of their processes, thus significantly improving the level of their product/service quality. Many of these companies were also able to introduce and implement lean six sigma (LSS) (discussed in Chapter 13).

3. *CHANGE MANAGEMENT*

APICS defines change management as a "business process that coordinates and monitors all changes to the business process and applications operated by the business as well as to their internal equipment, resources, operating systems, and procedures." Its purpose is to "minimize the risk of problems that will affect the operating environment and service delivery to the users" (APICS, 2010, p. 22).

Change management is a structured approach to transition organizations from a current state to a desired future state. It is an organizational process that aims at ensuring the changes are smoothly and successfully implemented, and that the lasting benefits of change are achieved. As a result of the dissatisfaction many leaders felt in the late 1980s and throughout the 1990s with the implementation of changes using a top-down approach, many companies created the position of "Change Leader." McKinsey consultant Julien Phillips first published a change management model in 1982 in the journal Human Resource Management; though it took a decade for his change management peers to catch up with him (Julien Phillips). Change management presents most senior executives, who used to focus their attention on devising the best strategic and tactical plans, with an unfamiliar challenge. Change management requires that management must have a profound understanding of the human side of change — the alignment of the company's culture, values, people, and behaviors—to generate the desired results and have these results sustained. Any value that change creates is now sustained because of the collective actions of numerous employees who are responsible for designing, executing, and living with the changed environment.

3.1 Obstacles to Overcome

To successfully implement change, the organization must overcome obstacles because of the legal environment of the operations, financial situations and economic conditions, company policies and procedures, the organizational structure and culture, the IT environment, and people's natural resistance and tolerance level to change.

Legal Environment

Organizations operate in an environment where legal or institutionalized constraints may slow down the change. If the environment is unionized, the labor contract may stipulate that any change to the nature and scope of work must be negotiated with the union. Although, respecting any contractual requirements to "meet and confer" are mandatory, a union's interest is usually to protect and preserve jobs, and they recognize that staying competitive in a globalizing environment is necessary if they are going to succeed in their mission.

Financial Situation and Economic Conditions

Recent changes in regulation of financial activities impact change management. As a response to accounting scandals such as Enron and WorldCom, Congress enacted the Sarbanes-Oxley Act of 2002, which is the most important and influential security legislation since the Security Exchange Act of 1934 (Nazareth, 2006, p.134). Since the inception of this legislation, sections 302 and 404 of the Act have influenced organizations' operations and triggered the need for change in public companies. Section 302 requires the CEO and the CFO of public companies to certify the appropriateness and fairness of financial statements and disclosures, while section 404 requires management of public companies to perform assessments of their internal controls and control environment. For many organizations conformance with those requirements, in the short term, means an increase of paperwork and implementation of additional activities, which interfere with the principles of lean manufacturing and the concept of non-value-added activities elimination. However, in the long run, developing a strong control environment may contribute towards achieving standardization and simplification of the processes and thus indirectly contributes to sustaining a lean business.

A strong, as well as a weak, economy may influence change management: on the one hand it may slow down change, and on the other hand it may increase the need for change. When the economy is strong, management focuses on developing strategic goals, increasing market share, implementing new technologies, and introducing new products, which translate into an increase of complexity of operations as well as a need for change. It is relatively easy to promote ideas and justify budgets for change implementation when the economy is strong. However, the complexity of the operating environment may slow down change and increases the need for financial resources required for implementation. Since all organizations have limited resources, financial implications of changes need to be considered, and a cost-benefit analysis for all changes should be performed at the onset of the implementation stage.

During tight times, businesses must focus on simplification to stay competitive. We recently experienced one of the longest recessions since the Great Depression, when in February 2009 the consumer confidence level in the United States decreased to 25.0 from an average of 58.0 in 2008, and 100 in 1985. For many companies it meant a decrease in sales, operations, and income, and an increase in inventory. In these situations many organizations shifted their focus to survival and "freeze" implementation of change until "better times." However, slow times are the best times for change implementation. During recessions, operations are at the lowest point, which means that some resources can be allocated to the change implementation effort without the need to compromise current production activities. For example, average capacity utilization in the U.S. manufacturing industry in February 2009 was 66.7 percent as compared to 78.9 percent in 2008 (Kutyla, 2009, p. 4). Low utilization provides room for flexibility, reduction in lead time, and opportunity for change and process improvement.

Also, difficult financial situations may trigger the need for change in some organizations. For example, realignment and structural changes in companies may increase the need for process change due to lack of personnel. This is often labeled "spontaneous" change management. If it is handled in an organized manner, it can improve processes and contribute to enlargement or empowerment of the jobs.

Policies and Procedures

Policies and procedures are the rule of organizations' operations. They should be communicated to and understood by the personnel of the company to ensure that people understand their roles and that processes are carried out consistently throughout the organization. Policies and procedures may impact change management in the following ways: they may slow down change or restrict the company's ability to make change.

Firstly, existing rules may slow down the change. For example, governmental and quasi-public non-profit organizations (special districts, hospitals, public universities) often have policies and procedures in place that slow down the pace of change, because citizens do not want a rapidly changing government. These types of constraints may take forms such as public bidding procedures; systems of purchases or contract approvals over a certain amount by the governing board; laws that allow any action by a board to be contested within 30 days; or laws that any new ordinance (law) passed by a board may not go into effect for 60 days. In fact, in addition to their role as public policy makers, the significant other role of public institution boards is to provide fiduciary oversight to the organization, which is usually focused on constraining anyone in the organization from doing anything too crazy and too quickly.

Secondly, absence of documented policies and procedures may restrict a company's ability to implement change successfully. Formulating and documenting of policies and procedures may be a time-consuming process, but it is a prerequisite for standardization. Unfortunately, some companies undervalue the importance of developing documented policies and rely on oral agreements about operations, which may lead to confusion amongst the participants in the process. Change management starts with realizing that there is a need for change. Documented policies and procedures are essential during this stage. They reflect the current processes and can be used as a starting point for change. It is very hard to change the processes if it is unclear what the processes are.

Finally, often when it comes to the desire to change policies and procedures, management forgets that they are documented as rules in the various IT applications that are networked together to form the flow of data in the company. To implement a change to any policy or procedure requires documenting how it must change and analyzing which applications must have their code altered to reflect these changes, then granting approval, funds, and resources to the IT organizations to implement the changes. When these changes are ready to be released to the personnel, training must be provided so that everyone understands what policy or procedure has changed, why, and how to use the applications with these new changes, including what audit criteria will be enforced to ensure the changes are done correctly and consistently.

Organizational Structure

Organizational structure may significantly impact change management. For successful implementation of change appropriate authority must be granted. A hierarchical corporate structure can delay the implementation of change and negatively impact the effectiveness of change management. For example, to purchase new tooling equipment that is required for a change implementation, a U.S. subsidiary company may have to send a request to the foreign parent corporation. It usually takes 6 to 8 months to get the approval for the purchase; thus the project may get delayed. To compete in a fast-paced environment, companies should reduce the lead time and eliminate delays in change implementation by providing necessary authority to the change management team and flatting the organization structure.

Cultural differences also play an important role in change management. For example, in collective cultures such as Japan's, workers are more submissive to the ideas of those in authority than are workers in individualist cultures such as American's, which slows the process of change implementation in the United States. The drawback of a high level of submissiveness is that the change may not be challenged at early stages and some opportunities for improvement may be missed.

IT Environment

The IT environment (both the organization and the infrastructure) should be considered during the change implementation as well. The IT infrastructure includes hardware and software. The software aspect can be products purchased as "off-the-shelf," such as Microsoft Office, and in-house applications that are developed using tools like SQL, Oracle Database, and JAVA to create rules for processing the input data (orders, contracts, receivables, supplier invoices for payment, delivery dates, methods of delivery, etc.) as outputs (order delivery, customer credit verification, supplier delivery reconciliation, etc.). For example, one of the common mistakes made by manufacturing departments is planning change and deploying lean without getting IT involved. Not involving IT can contribute to "lean dip" or stagnation of the continuous improvement process. The role of the IT function is to support the operations and generate statistical information and analysis. Companies practicing the kaizen philosophy sometimes undervalue the importance of the IT department in change management due to the supporting nature of its function.

Human Factor

The human factor is the key to change management. In general, people do not like the uncertainty surrounding any change. Workers may resist change because they do not understand the objectives of change or how it will impact their jobs. However, people operate on a continuum of change tolerance. It is important to note that while some employees will embrace and even drive change, others will resist change, even to the point of leaving if the changes are too dramatic and/or happening too fast. Minimizing the loss of such employees is very important, because recruitment is one of the most disproportionally costly things an organization can do, and that is not lean. So, the goal of change management is to go lean and achieve sustainable change while retaining employees.

Many people have tried to change others, but have failed miserably doing so. The only reliable way to "change people" is by helping them to learn so that they can change themselves. This is where training comes in. Good training in all aspects of the job in the context of a lean, organized workplace with standard tools, methods, and procedures is vital to accomplish any change. Sufficient time and resources must be allocated to such training.

Every change involves two groups of people: the team that implements the change and the users impacted by the change. There is a misconception that top-down changes are perceived to be easy, are common, and have the patina of being efficient. To succeed in the implementation process, however, changes must be organic and grow from the ground up. Sustainable change that grows from the ground up is best accomplished through the formation a well-trained group of diverse membership.

Bringing the right team to the table is one of the key aspects of change management. A cross functional team serves this purpose best. The team should consist of managers of all departments that will be affected by the change. The change implementation effort should be supported by people who have the authority to implement change and people who have the knowledge of the operations to ensure that the change improves the process. Therefore, all personnel should be involved in the change implementation process for the following three reasons. Firstly, floor workers are the people who understand the process best. They perform tasks on a routine basis and can be helpful in identifying the weaknesses and non-value-added activities of current processes. Secondly, "you can lead a horse to water, but you cannot make it drink." The team should ensure that changes are carried out consistently throughout the organization. However, it will be the workers who will carry the implementation and incorporate it in their everyday activities. Thirdly, people are more likely to accept change if they are part of the change. Employees' job satisfaction is directly correlated with how much of a sense of control they have about their work and their work environment. Involving the workers into the change implementation process will contribute to empowerment of their jobs and will make change implementation organic.

3.2 Change Management Implementation

An organization undertaking the implementation of improvement programs based on lean principles should recognize that, while it may seem easy enough to contemplate changes to a factory layout or changes in a process or procedures, those changes will affect all the employees who work in or interface with that place or process. As such, the opportunity for successfully implementing an improvement will be increased if thought and planning regarding change management take place at the very beginning.

There are many ways to implement change. One of the most effective approaches today is the ADKAR model developed by Prosci. This model consists of five elements: Awareness, Desire, Knowledge, Ability, and Reinforcement. Each element is critical for the success of change implementation. It is important that sufficient attention is given to each aspect of the model. People in the organization need to be aware of change. They need to understand the desire for change and the benefits to being willing to accept the change. The team and people affected by the change must possess appropriate information, skills, knowledge, and practical ability. Finally the team must perform reinforcement of change.

The roadmap that clarifies the direction in which an organization needs to move is its vision. It is the role of the leaders to articulate that vision that includes change implementation steps that are in alignment with overall organization goals. The role of the teams is then to figure out how to get there. The leaders should inspire the teams and make sure that that the teams and employees are confident about the change. Once the teams understand what the vision state looks like and embrace it, they will probably be more creative, more effective, and more committed to creating that vision than anything management could accomplish with a top-down change mandate. This is when employees really feel empowered in their jobs!

The implementation of change does not happen overnight. The team needs to ensure that key people in the change implementation process are freed up from existing responsibilities so they can concentrate on the new effort. In order to continuously monitor the success of the implementation process the team needs to ensure that a feedback system that provides information from the shop floor is in place. Thus analysis of the collected data can be performed and corrective actions can be prescribed in a timely fashion.

Recovery should be an integral part of any change management implementation process and should not be skipped. Just like your muscles need a day of rest to recover and rebuild their strength after an intense workout, so does the organization undergoing change need a recovery period. Sustained continuous change without respite will do more damage than a period of intense change followed by a period of status quo.

Successful implementation of change management requires a budget, cultural criteria, leadership and organizational criteria, communication and people criteria, policies and procedures, and technological criteria.

Budget

To ensure success a budget must be created at the onset of the change and one must stick to that budget to ensure success. Change management often fails because of initial lack of financial support by management or reduction in the budget as change management is implemented.

Cultural Criteria

Develop a baseline culture, define an explicit end-state or desired culture, and define a comprehensive plan to achieve that culture goal. A "collective" culture such as the Japanese culture, where workers are more submissive to the idea of change is perhaps not the ideal culture to pursue, because this culture does not challenge the change at early stages of the change, thus missing some opportunities for improvement. However, "individualistic" cultures such as American cultures slow the process of change implementation.

As change programs cascade down through the organization assess the culture landscape at each level of the organization in a timely fashion. Doing so will enable the organization to assess its readiness for change, identify resistance to change and existing conflicts, and ultimately find ways to identify elements that need be changed to allow for a successful implementation of the change.

Leadership and Organizational Criteria

Leaders must embrace the new approach of change, so they can motivate, have the ability to communicate, and inspire others towards a vision for an improved future state. So start at the top and involve every layer in the organization that will be affected by the change. Identified leaders from each layer of the organization must be trained, aligned to the company's vision, equipped to execute their specific mission, and motivated to make change happen.

Leaders must make a formal case for change through confronting reality and articulating in a convincing manner the need for change; through demonstrating that the company has a great future; and through providing a specific road map to accomplish the proposed change. Leaders must prepare for the unexpected because problems will present themselves as the external environment in which people work will shift. Understand that workers will resist change, a problem that needs to be addressed at a very early stage of change management implementation. They must address this human side systematically, not on a reactive case-by-case basis, thus integrating it in the program design and decision making process.

Communication and People Criteria

The message for change must be communicated properly. The company cannot assume that all involved understand the problems, feel a need for change, or see the new direction as clearly as the leaders do. Such messages must be both inspirational and practical. They are the direct response to communications coming from the bottom, responded to by the top leadership. Individuals need to know how their work will change, what can be expected of them, how their performance will be measured, and how their success or failure affects those around them.

Change requires the creation of a cross functional team. This team consists of managers and workers of all departments that will be affected by the change. The change implementation effort should be supported by people who have the authority to implement change and people who have knowledge of the operations to ensure that change improves the process. Leaders and all involved in the change must create ownership of the change. It can be reinforced by both tangible and intangible incentives and rewards at the end of the change.

Policies and Procedures

Policies and procedures that are necessary for implementing change must be formulated and documented, while policies that hinder change must be eliminated.

Technological Criteria

The IT environment must be involved to avoid a "lean dip" or stagnation of the continuous improvement process.

4. 5S PROGRAM IMPLEMENTATION

The following 5S implementation approach for change management has proven to be very successful for both manufacturing and service companies. It has been used by practitioners as a first step towards leaning out or improving various companies such as: processing plants, parts and tool manufacturers, mining companies, assembly plants, hospitals, medical offices, resorts, hotels, etc.

Before implementing a 5S system a company must set objectives, build teams, and train these teams. The ultimate goal that companies must set is that personnel are maintaining all 5S standards with no direction from their supervisors and they are active in devising ways to improve workplace organization. Implementation attempts showing any other reasonable lower level goal, like where Sort, Straighten and Shine requirements are met and where personnel are maintaining all 5S standards with direction from their supervisors, have led towards failure of the 5S implementation system.

In order to attain a high level of success, the following requirements must be met:

- Management leadership and support
- Change management
- Worker/management compromises
- Team building and training
- Auditing
- Financial resources

Leadership is the ability to communicate and inspire others towards a vision for an improved future state. Leadership involves working on the process or status quo in an effort to improve it. It requires personal passion, courage, patience, and commitment. Leaders who embed 5S into the culture have demonstrated their ability to create employee mindsets that are aligned with ideals and principles that serve the organization and the customer. This is leadership in its purest form. This is a 5S system that people want to be part of. Management is the skill to ensure that maximum results are obtained from the existing process or situation. It entails effectively setting expectations, establishing timely and accurate feedback systems, and having the discipline, tactfulness, and courage to respond quickly and appropriately to out-of-control situations. Management is all about working within the process or current situation. It requires discipline, courage, personal skill, and commitment.

A reasonable amount of training is necessary. Workers must be introduced at least to the concepts of lean, waste reduction, total quality management (TQM), and the 5S system. Appropriate teams, consisting of people from maintenance and operations, must be formed.

A good auditing system, with the aim to continuously improve the system, is essential for a successful implementation. This can be aided by developing good lean metrics. APICS defines lean metrics as "a metric that permits a balanced evaluation and response-quality without sacrificing quantity objectives" (APICS, 2010, p.79). These metrics include financial, behavioral, as well as core-process performance metrics.

Initially workers may not be very anxious to participate in this 5S process. It may be difficult for the company to break workers' paradigms. However, after good training and involvement of managers and supervisors, the workers will understand the importance of the process and become committed to the task. After the formation of teams and at the conclusion of their training, schedules and implementation guidelines must be developed for each of the five phases of the program.

Phase 1: Sort what is needed and what is not needed.

The main objectives of this phase are to identify all items within the work area that are not required to do the job and to remove these items from the work area, so that work can now be performed without obstacles or unnecessary searching.

This housekeeping activity places items in the "necessary" and the "unnecessary" categories. For the "necessary" group a "goal number" must be set (allowing for a maximum number of items to be present in the area). The practical approach here is to take out of the area any item that would not be used within a certain number of days.

This can be accomplished using a "Team Blitz System" and a "Red/Green/Yellow Tag Event." The "Team Blitz System" requires that all personnel work as a team as they try to identify excess supplies, obsolete forms and materials, broken or excess tools, broken or unused gauges, outdated work instructions, defective parts, excess furniture, excess or obsolete equipment, unused cleaning materials, trash, etc. A predetermined amount of time must be given to the teams to place green/red/yellow tags on the items in various areas. At the end of the period all red tagged items must be removed and disposed of with the supervisor's approval. Yellow tagged items normally require more investigation before removal is approved.

Phase 2: Set in order what must be kept.

The objective here is to place every item in its place. This implies that the team, after removing unnecessary items from the workplace, has to place and demarcate all necessary items in the workplace; has to label all shelves and storage units; and has to arrange all items so that they can easily be found, used, and replaced. All users of these items must be informed and trained on the storage system in use, the labeling system introduced, and the procedures for storing and selecting items for use.

Phase 3: Scrub and Shine everything that remains.

The objective here is to get a clean, safe, and comfortable workplace, so that the production of goods and services is facilitated. At the same time, machines, equipment, and tools must be evaluated for quality performance and, if deemed necessary, maintenance must be performed.

Phase 4: Standardize.

The objectives here are to establish and standardize the procedures and routines of daily maintenance of the workplace, its equipment, machinery, and others; to have the opportunity to participate and collaborate with individual and collective creativity to improve the quality and safety of the work environment; and to establish a quick and effective visual control of the conditions of the workplace, equipment, and machines.

In order to implement standardized routines for areas common to more than one group (specialty tool areas, file storage rooms, hazardous materials rooms, computer software, files and break areas, etc.) the various teams must have meetings to assign responsibilities for these areas. A chart must be developed listing these common areas and responsibilities must be assigned on a rotating basis. In order to facilitate rotation and minimize effort, names that can easily be removed for rotation purposes must be applied to the chart (this can be done by using Velcro).

Phase 5: Sustain through self-discipline.

The objectives of this phase are to get everybody to practice the previous steps on an ongoing basis; to motivate all workers to sustain the accomplishments through creation of a high culture of cooperation and teamwork aimed at doing things right and better all the time; and to have management and supervisors show leadership through their good examples.

Because of the importance of this phase, auditing and a policy of housekeeping must be introduced. Initially this may consist of the following: a five-minute, twice a week team meeting to recall the concepts of the 5S system; monthly rotation of responsible people and adjustments of the charts; and weekly three-hour housekeeping of selected areas with participation of plant manager, supervisors, area workers, and invited workers from other areas.

An auditing team must be formed for each area and each area must initially be audited on a weekly basis. Over time the auditing frequency can be reduced. The auditing system is based on the previously listed four areas of workplace organization. The auditing team preferably consists of at least the division manager, area supervisor, and one area worker.

It helps if the auditing process implements a recognition program. Most companies that successfully implement a 5S system recognize all their participants during a special public event. At that time the general manager of the company may award a special prize to all outstanding participants.

Best practices when it comes to starting a 5S program suggest to start small, to keep the focus tight and confined to one manageable area, go an inch wide and a mile deep, and raise the level of 5S so high that people cannott help but notice. You must develop and practice sustainment skills before you begin work in the next area. It does you no good to run rampant through the factory or office if you can't sustain. You must build on your success and use that success to get 5S expectations for all areas of the business and move through the entire company one step at a time. In the process of moving through the entire company, remember that the most challenging and important part of 5S is to change behaviors!

5. *EXAMPLES of 5S IMPLEMENTATIONS*

Here are some highlights of diverse and successful implementations of the 5S program where the implementation guidelines, as described above, were followed.

5.1 A Mining Company: to better manage and control inventory

A mining company producing copper concentrate in their processing plant implemented the 5S system. Its purpose was to better manage and reduce its inventory on the shop floor. Here are some of the highlights of their implementation.

The 5S system implementation went through various phases: setting an objective; team building and training; classifying so they could sort out and keep what is needed; creating order resulting in straightening what must be kept; cleaning and shining the worksite; standardizing; sustaining through self-discipline; auditing through visual inspection; rewarding at project closure; and implementing a continuous improvement program.

In order to achieve the highest level of success, management was willing to show leadership and support, compromise, introduce change management, create an auditing system, and contribute financial resources. Additionally workers were introduced to the concept of total quality management (TQM) and the 5S system. Four teams, consisting of people from maintenance and operations, received two days of introductory training, followed by two months of detailed training. Once people were committed to start the implementation process, schedules were developed. Initially workers were not very keen on participating in this process. It was difficult for the company to break workers' paradigms. Only after good training and involvement of managers and supervisors did the workers understand the importance of the process and became committed to the task. They used the team blitz system to successfully perform all phases of the program.

An auditing team was formed to sustain the 5S system. Initially each area was audited once a week and after the auditing process got improved it was done once a month. Their auditing team consisted of the plant manager, area supervisor, metallurgist, a safety advisor, and one area worker.

At the conclusion, during a public event, the general manager of the company recognized all workers at the plant and a special prize was given to each of them.

5.2 Kreisler Manufacturing[1]: to improve quality and productivity

Kreisler Manufacturing is a family-owned company with a long history of success and problems. In 1914 the company began doing business as a fine jewelry manufacturer selling to upscale jewelry and department stores throughout the country. The company was founded by Marcus Stern and Jacques Kreisler. When the depression hit in 1932 the company closed its doors. The company started up again the following year manufacturing watchbands, with Bulova Watch Company as a primary customer. During the Second War, in 1941, Kreisler started manufacturing parts for cathode ray tubes and various war-related products such as aircraft tubes and manifold assemblies. After the war they went back to producing watches and briefly got involved in a new product line of writing instruments. After closing its jewelry division in 1979, Kreisler Industrial Corp. became the sole operating subsidiary of Kreisler Manufacturing Corp. A complete history of the company can be found on the internet.

According to William Green (Green, 1997), Kreisler Corp. was in trouble in 1996. It had lost $923,000 in fiscal year 1996 and had losses for the past five years. With poor sales and dwindling cash reserves, the company did not have enough business to keep going. Miraculously, demand for aircraft engines surged in 1997, just in time to save the company. The company now prides itself on quality performance in all aspects of design, process planning, and manufacturing. They have manufactured precision components for the aerospace industry for over half a century by delivering a consistently high quality product and helping their customers solve complex engineering and manufacturing challenges. The company's technical capability is complemented by continuous improvement efforts and certified quality systems that help improve quality and reliability. Two of Stern's sons have significantly improved productivity of the company and they pride themselves in properly implementing the 5S system with weekly 5S cleanliness audits.

5.3 Hospital: to reduce time spent on documentation[2]

The literature tells us that as much as 40% of a staff nurse's work time is spent in documentation. Whether electronic or manual, documentation is an essential component of a nurse's responsibilities. It provides for a more consistent approach to patient care as practitioners share information about their patients with other clinicians. Also, documentation regarding care giver observations,

[1] Based on http://www.Kreisler-ind.com/ retrieved 4/20/2009 and "Fasten Your Seat Belts," by William Green, *Forbes Magazine*, December 15, 1997.

[2] Contributed by Mrs. Mayble E. Craig, MS, RN.

treatments/medications administered, and the patients' responses are important in order to maintain continuity of care and to track patients' progress and daily status. Furthermore, documentation on a patient's records is essential to meet requirements of regulatory agencies and provide lawyers in litigation investigations a record of the patient's care that was rendered. Notwithstanding the importance of documentation, added efficiency and cost savings would result if the percentage of time spent by professional nurses in documentation could be reduced by even a fraction. Reducing documentation time without sacrificing any of the important quality objectives of said documentation is a challenge that when addressed satisfactorily would allow professional nurses additional time in actual value-added direct care activities. These enhanced direct care activities could include patient and family education, comprehensive discharge planning, and participation in patient care team conferences.

One way an organization can embark on this goal is through the use of the 5S system for workplace organization. The following is a sample of how an organization can utilize the 5S system in order to reduce nursing documentation time. To achieve success in this endeavor, an organization would do well to designate one person, the team leader, to coordinate the process from the beginning to the final stage. At the project's conclusion, a permanent overseer should be appointed to avoid reverting back to previous behaviors of adding additional forms in the workplace without due process.

Step #1 Sort (Housekeeping). This is the step in which the project manager, in consultation with his/her work teams, decides which forms contain information that is needed and which forms can be safely discarded. Eliminating forms at this juncture eliminates the needs for storing excessive inventory of paper and/or allows for the reduction of screens nurses check when doing electronic documentation. This step can take significant time as the project manager needs to make sure he has collected and assessed all forms/screens currently in use by all nursing departments of the organization. This includes the Emergency Department, the Preoperative Services, the Outpatient and Inpatient Services, and any additional specialty area that may exist in the healthcare organization. While this is a big undertaking, it is nevertheless an essential step in the overall process.

Step #2 Set in Order (Organization). After non-essential forms have been purged, further reductions are achieved by the organization of the remaining forms through condensing, consolidating, and eliminating duplication. This is where the teams are most active as they determine how to succinctly combine forms and make them user friendly, simple to use, and inclusive. During this stage, teams may take two or more forms and reduce them to one form that contains the essential data from the initial variety of forms. During this stage "experts" from the Nursing Departments as well as the Quality Department, Medical Records, Compliance, Risk Management, IT, etc. are asked to review the newly condensed forms. These experts will check to make sure critical elements have not been inadvertently omitted and new regulatory requirements are included. At this time, these experts may recommend even more forms to be merged, combined, or condensed.

Step #3 Shine (Cleanup). This is where the forms and screens are prepared for review by each institution's designated approving body and/or where those doing electronic documentation can work with their vendor or in house experts to incorporate any desired changes to the screens. At this point, the forms are prepared for final printing.

Step #4 Standardize (Keep cleanliness). Training on the proper use of the forms/screens is done at this stage in order to maximize the proper use of newly revised, simplified, condensed forms. It is important that all parts of the organization receive consistent training on all shifts. Additionally, it is also essential that the workplace is "cleaned" of any of the old forms that may be in any decentralized location so that there is no error in their continued use. Only the new forms should now be available in the organization's inventory.

Step #5 Sustain (Discipline). During this final stage, monitoring of the proper use of the forms/screens is done. This could be done in any number of ways, including concurrent or retrospective audits of a pre-established percentage of the weekly or monthly charts. Ongoing monitoring can be reduced in frequency based on the degree of compliance observed. The best of all systems need periodic reviews and enhancements, so this process becomes a cyclical undertaking with the goal of continuous process improvement.

5.4 A Vacation Time Share Company: to improve and consolidate maintenance planning

In early 2006, a methodology for assessing lean operations in small to midsize service companies was developed by Wu/Walker (Wu, Walker, pp. 211–222). This methodology requires the calculation of a "lean office score" based on four surveys. It not only measures the level in which each operation is lean, but also points out the areas of deficit, so improvements can be suggested and made.

This methodology has been applied to a multiple location time share company (TSC). The application involved an initial analysis of its main office operations in the U.S.A., followed by an evaluation of three of its multiple time share locations in Mexico.

The workplace organization in the main office of TSC exhibited all of the 5S system lean principles. As you walked in this office you immediately noticed that everything that is needed has been sorted, organized, and given a place. What is needed and kept is visible and self-explanatory so everyone knows where it goes. The office is clean and exhibits no clutter. This organizational discipline is spread to all areas of the office because of its open cellular layout. This has led to standardization that requires discipline, sticking to the rules, and making the rules a habit. The principle of standardized work at TSC manifests itself when one looks at the procedures that have been established over the years with input from all employees, and at the technology all workers have been trained on to perform all activities in the most optimal way. Many processes are computer driven, which makes cross training easy. Furthermore, many of the activities/processes are well documented and easy accessible and known by all members of the office staff, including the president.

Upon the request of its Board of Directors, the maintenance management function at three of their nine resorts in Mexico was evaluated. We will refer to these locations as A, B, and C. A 5S system score card, capturing maintenance specific entities, was developed for each location. Location B received the best average score (3.9 out of 5), whereas locations A and C received poor average scores (2.8 and 2.4 respectively).[3] It was suggested that location C needed to implement the 5S system of work place organization first, before implementing and executing various aspects of Total Productive Maintenance (such as visual scheduling and control of preventive and routine maintenance) that were being developed for all locations. With proper training, help from the supervisor of location B, support of all maintenance workers, and good leadership of management, "the dirty dungeon" of a maintenance office got transformed into a "spic and span" well organized area, where all 5S system principles became and still are visible. What was helpful in this implementation of the 5S system was that any change that was made to the office and its organization was made with active involvement of its supervisor. People like to feel they have a say in what they do and how they do it. This ownership helped sustain the organization that was put in place at this location.

In developing the 5S system score card, it was clear that each location had designed its own order forms and inspection forms. In order to reduce the number of different forms that the main office had to print and deal with it was suggested that the maintenance supervisors consolidate these forms and generate a set of forms that could be used at all locations. Again, with proper training and leadership of management, it was agreed that the work order generation forms and inspection forms of location B could serve as an initial blue print for this endeavor, and that all maintenance supervisors would get involved in the creation of common maintenance forms.

Additionally, each location had developed its own tedious, inefficient way of tracking and planning routine and preventive maintenance activities. This was mostly due to lack of use of computers. Maintenance supervisors were spending an enormous amount of time going through files, data forms, lists of past work done, and other documents to ensure the timely execution of all future inspections, preventive maintenance (PM), and routine maintenance (RM) activities. This process got re-engineered using value stream mapping. This led to the development of a sound, quick to act visual control system for routine and preventive maintenance. Because of the Excel-based system, computers were introduced in the maintenance department at each location. The now computerized system eliminated bundles of paperwork, thus freeing up space and clutter in the maintenance office.

5.5 Thought Organization/Proposal Formulation

In Chapter 2, section 5, "The Idea Development Lifecycle Process" suggests the use of the 5S principles as a process for thought organization/proposal formulation. The 5S principles of lean thinking, originally implemented to leaning out the workplace, applied to the "Idea Development Lifecycle Process" certainly is very novel, thought provoking, and demonstrates that the sky is the limit when it comes to applying principles of lean thinking.

Reviewing the process of idea development, as outlined in Chapter 2, the following 5Ss emerge:

[3] For more detailed results see Wu/Walker, 2006.

1. **Sorting Out and Communicating Your Idea.** One way to do this is to distinguish between needs and nice-to-haves.

2. **Setting Up and Organizing Your Idea's Concept.** Unless you communicate the concept of your idea in sufficient detail, it will remain a figment of your imagination. The purpose of this stage is to set out a list of requirements necessary to see your idea all the way through to actual production. Through your conversations, presentations, and discussions you communicate in sufficient detail what the product or service is, so everyone will share the "vision."

3. **Scrubbing and Documenting Your Idea.** This stage begins with formalizing your idea by writing it down and creating the requirements of a **specification document.** This set of written requirements provides a permanent means to describe, explain, and communicate your idea to others. This process allows you to scrub your idea, clean it up, and refine it with the help of experts, novices, owners, and anyone else who is part of your team or interested in your idea.

4. **Standardizing or Establishing a Baseline for Your Idea.** Once all the requirements are documented and scrubbed for accuracy, it is then called a **baseline document** or a **specifications document.** This document is labeled "Version 1.0." This key milestone is noted by all stakeholders or their representatives through signed approval, signaling their agreement to proceed with materializing your idea through the production phase.

5. **Sustaining Your Idea's Baseline with Changes.** Throughout the idea lifecycle, it is important to recognize that changes do occur. Therefore, it is necessary to establish a **change management process** very early in your idea development lifecycle. Each change must be defined and written down: what it is, its purpose, and its benefits to the baseline. Once established, the change can be measured and analyzed with respect to how it would be integrated into your idea without causing the idea to lose its essence. Thus your idea is sustained.

6. *READY TO IMPLEMENT THE 5S SYSTEM?*

You begin by removing everything from the closet. As you sort and grasp each article of clothing, each box, each forgotten treasure, you set them in an order as you place them into specific piles: keep returning to the closet, donate to charity, and lastly, toss into the trash.

Once the closet is empty, you dust and sweep, or scrub and shine it clean. As you return all your Keep items, you standardize where each one goes, all your shirts, each on a hanger, grouped together by color, then all your pants, in a similar fashion, then all your paired shoes lined up on the floor, and so on—everything has a place and everything in its place. Now you must sustain this sense of tidiness and order through self-discipline. So the next time you are putting away your laundered clothes or returning your shoes to the closet at the end of the day, you must return them to "their" designated place.

This discipline will keep your closet looking tidy and allow you the ability to find your things the next time you want to wear them, thus sustaining your tidiness standard. Perhaps you might add labels to help you remember where to place everything!

7. *GLOSSARY AND SUMMARY OF METHODS*

5S System – The 5S system was initially introduced in Japan and represents five Japanese words that relate to housekeeping (Seiri for Sort), organizing (Seiton for Set in Order), cleaning (Seisou for Shine), keeping cleanliness (Seiketsu or Standardize), and sustaining a clean workplace (Shitsuke for Discipline).

Change Management – Change management, according to the *APICS Dictionary*, is a business process that coordinates and monitors all changes to the business process and applications operated by the business as well as their internal equipment, resources, operating systems, and procedures. Its purpose is to minimize the risk of problems that will affect the operating environment and service delivery to the users. It is an organizational process that aims at ensuring that changes are smoothly and successfully implemented, and that the lasting benefits of change are achieved.

Change Management Obstacles – Change management obstacles are the lean environment, financial situations, economic conditions, policies and procedures, organizational structure, IT environment, and the human factors.

Change Management Successful Implementation – Change management successful implementation requires addressing the following:

1. Budget requirements
2. Cultural requirements
3. Leadership and organizational requirements
4. People criteria
5. Policies and procedures
6. Technological criteria

Lean Workplace – A lean workplace is a workplace that is organized, that is properly laid out, that has lean standardized work procedures or process steps, and that exhibits respect towards the workforce.

Standardized Tools – Standardized tools are time observation sheets, flow diagrams, standard work sheets, standard work layout or work instructions, standard inspection sheets, and standard visual controls.

Standardized Work – Standardized work implies standardized tools.

Successful Implementation of the 5S System – Successful implementation of the 5S system requires management leadership, change management, worker/management compromises, team building and training, auditing, and financial resources.

Workplace Organization – Workplace organization is defined as a safe, neat arrangement of the work place. It entails providing a specific location for everything that is needed and eliminating anything that is not required to do the job.

8. ACRONYMS

5S Sort, Straighten, Shine, Standardize, Self-Discipline

IT Information Technology

APICS American Production and Inventory Control Society, the operations management organization

CEO Chief Executive Officer

CFO Chief Financial Officer

TQM Total Quality Management

RM Routine Maintenance

PM Preventive Maintenance or Productive Maintenance

9. REFERENCES

Anderson, D. and L.A. Anderson. *Beyond Change Management: Advanced Strategies for Today's Transformational Leaders.* San Francisco: Jossey-Bass/Pfeiffer, 2001.

APICS Dictionary, Thirteenth Edition, 2010.

Brimeyer, Rick. "How to Avoid Common 5S Mistakes – Six lessons learned from a proven Lean leader." www.pdgconsultants.com, PDG, Inc., 2008.

DeCamara, D. "To Survive or Thrive?" *Chief Executive*, www.deloitte.com, March 6, 2008.

Green, William. "Fasten Your Seat Belts." *Forbes Magazine.* (December 15, 1997)

Gotsill, G. and M. Natchez. "From Resistance to Acceptance: How to Implement Change Management." *T+D.* (Vol. 61, Iss. 11, November 2007)

Grasley, M. "Changing a process? Ask MON for help." *Control Engineering.* (Vol. 54, Iss. 5, May 2007).

Katz, J. "Bridging the Great Divide." *Industry Week.* (Vol. 256, Iss. 8, August 2007).

Kotter, J. P. "Leading Change: Why Transforming Efforts Fail." *Harvard Business Review.* (March/April 1995).

Kutyla, D. M. "Economic Update. It's Spring. Things Have Sprung!" *Deloitte,* www.deloitte.com, March, 2009.

Long, S. and D.G. Sputlock. "Motivation and Stakeholder Acceptance in Technology-driven Change Management: Implications for the Engineering Manager." *Engineering Management Journal.* (Vol. 20, No. 2, June 2008).

Marden, R.E., R.K Edwards, and W.D. Stout. "The CEO CFO Certification Requirement." *The CPA Journal.* (Vol 73, Iss. 7, July 2003).

Maylett, T. and K. Vitasek. "For Closer Collaboration, Try Education." *Supply Chain Management Review.* (Vol. 11, Iss. 1, January 2007).

Nazareth, A.L. "Keeping SarbOx is Crusial." *Business Week.* (Iss. 4009, November 13, 2006).

Parrinder, Joann O. "Lean Thinking Applied in Your Idea Development Lifecycle." *Driving Operational Excellence: Successful Lean Six Sigma Secrets to Improve the Bottom Line.* Ron Crabtree, editor. Livonia, MI: MetaOps Publishing LLC, pp. 237-250.

Reuter, Vincent G. "A Productivity Implementation Plan." *Industrial Management.* (September-October, 1980).

Sande, T. "Taking Charge of Change with Confidence." Strategic Communication Management. (Vol. 13, Iss. 1, December/January 2009).

Stanleigh, M. "Effective Successful Change Management Initiatives." *Industrial and Commercial Training.* (Vol. 40, Iss. 1, 2008).

Woodward, N.H. "To Make Change, Manage Them." *HR Magazine.* (Vol. 52, No.5, May 2007).

Wu, N. L. and Curtis Walker. "Assessing Lean Operations: Methodology for the Service Industry." *Productivity.* (October-December 2006).

www.Kreisler-ind.com/ retrieved 4/20/2009.

10. REVIEW QUESTIONS

1. What are the three principles of a lean workplace?
2. What are the principles used for workplace organization?
3. What is required or meant by the principle of standardized work?
4. Explain the 5S system of organization.
5. How would you implement the 5S system at your work or at home?
6. What are the requirements for success when implementing the 5S system? Explain.
7. How does one differentiate between good leadership and good management?
8. What are the 5 major criteria that need to be addressed for successful implementation of change management? Explain each of them.
9. What are some of the obstacles when implementing change management?

11. PROBLEMS

Problem #1

How would you implement the 5S system at your work or at home?

Explain in detail how you would go about implementing it; implement it; and explain what you have accomplished.

Problem #2

Consider the following case scenario and explain how workplace organization can help this ABC Company. Explain this in as much detail as possible.

The ABC American Company:

The ABC Company is a privately held, 38-year-old, corporation. It has 50 employees, $6 million in sales, and a facility of 40,000 square feet with height of 24 feet at the eaves. The company is located on 8 acres adjacent to rail and 2 miles from an interstate. The company produces fabricated tube assemblies for the diesel engine market. The company has 60 customers and 60% of their sales volume comes from one customer (CAT) and 80% of that customer's volume comes from 60 part numbers. The company has 10,000 active part numbers in its item master. This is a job shop that builds to customer specifications. Manufacturing lead times are relatively high because the firm likes to produce in large lot sizes with a 1 to 2 months production rotation on regular orders (which make up about 80% of the business). It currently takes 6 to 8 weeks for an order to move from shop floor release to shipping. All inventories are high (raw, work-in-process, safety stock, and finished goods) as they purchase to accommodate those large production runs.

ABC's aggregate inventory accuracy is about 80%, but individual part inventories are very questionable. In fact, accounting requires physical inventories quarterly and they involve all personnel and take 1 to 3 days (so no production occurs during physical inventory taking). The biggest issue is not whether or not they have the materials, but where they are inside the building. Their vendors like them because they always pay and they order a lot.

The processes required to produce the parts are: cutting, cleaning, brazing, bending, end forming, drilling, testing, packaging, and various combinations of all or some of the above activities. 95% of the products only need cutting, cleaning, end forming, bending, and testing before they are ready to ship. Equipment in the plant consists of: 2 mechanical pipe cutters (one is dedicated to cut 3/8" pipe as 70% of the parts use that material), 2 large cleaning tanks, 6 brazing stations, 2 CNC benders, 12 manual bending tables (98% of the bent parts use the CNC machines), 1 mechanical tester, a tool room where drilling and other custom applications are performed, 2 fork lifts, and 1 overhead hoist. All released shop orders go to the CHECKER for 1 week before hitting the shop floor/cutting list. ABC does not use any vertical storage (except bending patterns are kept above the office).

ABC's largest customer has embraced just-in-time (JIT) and is now requiring smaller, more frequent shipments. This has been problematic as ABC is running out of space to store finished goods inventory, especially due to the large dedicated containers used in the JIT packaging which are un-stackable. The company is being strained financially because of the inventory investment and they have been very close to missing some JIT deliveries to that big customer. Morale is low and they are always fighting fires. Also, there is friction between departments as work spills over from one area to the other and people are viewed as specialists, not generalists. Business is booming and ABC is turning down business, mostly the smaller lot, high margin jobs. They have also neglected some of the high margin, small lot size, quick turn, custom orders and risk losing some customers because of focus on Mr. Big (their largest customer).

Problem #3

Just concentrating on process planning, workplace organization, and the 5S system, explain how L Corp should be leaned out.

The L Corp Case:

This L Corp plant is a tier 1 automotive supplier that has grown to 175,000 square feet over 65 years. The firm competes with 299 other L Corp plants located around the world (150 in USA and 150 outside USA) for business. L Corp handles sales for all plants based on their individual capabilities. Going into 1999, sales for the plant were down to $80 million (previously they had been: $100 million in 1998, $140 million in 1997, $130 million in 1996, and $120 million in 1995). Coincidentally, employment is down to 470 from 525 over the same period and morale is low. The factory is showing its age and the perception within the corporation reflects that physical appearance. Also, lighting is bad, process flow is complex, inventory levels are high, and lead times are longer than anyone would like. The plant recently lost a sizable piece of business from a major automotive company and the trend is not improving. On the positive side, this plant has always produced outstanding quality which has continually remained the saving grace of this plant. The company has been forcing improvement via strict numeric criteria: 1) Exceed 15% profit margin you are golden, 2) Achieve 10% to 15% margin you will be left alone, 3) Drop below 10% margins and you will be watched and possibly shut down. The plant has grown the margin to 10% in 1999. Also, 10 years ago the Corporation enacted a mandate: "No plant can add new brick and mortar to increase capacity (i.e., new square footage for an existing facility)." However, each plant manager can spend up to $100,000 for facility improvements within the current shell.

During this time period, L Corp was aggressively expanding sales by merger and acquisition. Talks had begun with another tier 1 supplier called D Corp, and a specific product line was being purchased from a plant not far from the this plant. This 50,000-square foot-facility is responsible for $58 million in sales that utilizes similar capabilities as this L Corp. Final decisions on which plants will stay and which will be closed should be made within 9 months.

John Smith was recently (1 ½ years ago) promoted to plant manager at this L Corp plant, after spending 2 years as the materials manager there. John knew he had to do something substantial in order to save the plant. He began by creating a 20 member cross functional planning team (consisting of hourly workers, union reps, and salaried people) to bring in fresh ideas and develop some plant goals. The team produced a 5-year plan to grow the business, and their goals suggested going for new and different automotive markets/products, they identified the other L Corp plants as their competition, and they had to find a way to modernize the plant and its processes to make it all happen.

The team did a floor space utilization study for the manufacturing "shop floor" area and found the available space (175,000 square ft.) being used for: 20% isles, 10% shop offices, 40% inventory storage (materials, work-in-process, and finished goods), and 30% for production. The shop was divided into functional departments (i.e., shipping & receiving, production, assembly, warehouse, mold storage, tool room, R&D, maintenance, etc.) and as the plant grew, many expansions added new exterior/structural walls. The material handling department, with 22 workers (13 on shift 1, 6 on shift 2, and 3 on shift 3) and 23 fork lifts, moves all materials. Fork lifts are used with modified booms to set up equipment. Each equipment set-up uses 2 lifts and takes 6 hours or more. All tooling is stored in the tool crib, where accuracy is low, which sometimes causes delays for set ups and /or repairs. This plant has 260 operating days and plant-wide inventory turns are 40. L Corp has trained all plants in a hybrid kaizen approach called "compass" which utilizes a 15-person group (75% of participants are hourly) to tackle an issue in 4 days.

The products tend to go through complex routings and employees refer to product flow diagrams as "spaghetti charts" because of the overlapping and looping material movements. The small building along the main plant contains 6,000 square feet and is currently used for storage of materials, equipment, and old molds. Per customer requirements, some inventory storage is dedicated to spare parts and the equipment to make them. One of its clients, an automotive company, requires replacement parts (spares/service parts) to be available for 15 years after model change. Margins on service parts are at least two times that of current parts, and their lead times are longer than two times the lead times of the current parts.

CHAPTER 6

WORK DESIGN AND MEASUREMENT

Work study is the systematic investigation and analysis of contemplated and present work systems and methods. Its purpose is to formulate the most effective systems and methods for achieving necessary company objectives. It is also the establishment of measurement standards by which any work may be planned, scheduled, and controlled.

Work study, therefore, includes work measurement, motion time study, work sampling, methods engineering, work simplification, and work design. Its objectives are to search for the best operation methods and to determine operation time standards.

Work study and measurement are necessary to aid in determining manpower requirements, evaluating plant or department efficiency, calculating productivity indexes, determining machine/operator utility, establishing time standards and time allowances, allocating cost, scheduling work, evaluating alternate methods of operation, defining an acceptable day's work, and balancing operations and work.

1. DIRECT TIME STUDY METHODS

Frederick W. Taylor, who is believed to be the founder of time study, worked through the ranks from laborer to management.

Midvale Steel Company hired Frederick Taylor in 1878 as an ordinary laborer. Soon he was promoted to time clerk, journeyman, lathe operator, gang boss, foreman of the machine shop, and finally, at the age of 31, he became chief engineer. He strongly believed that it was the responsibility of management to develop spirit and hearty cooperation between workers and management. In his book, *The Principles of Scientific Management*, published by Harper and Bros., New York, in 1929, Taylor refers to enormous obstacles to harmonious cooperation between workers and management. One such obstacle lies in the ignorance of management as to what really constitutes a proper day's work for a workman.

In an attempt to improve the spirit and hearty cooperation between workers and management, Taylor received permission and financial support in the 1880's to conduct a scientific study of the time required to do various kinds of work in the Midvale Steel Company. Taylor's main objective in this study was to learn what really constituted a full day's work for a first class man; the best day's work that a man could properly do year in and year out and still thrive.

In doing his experiment, Taylor noticed that the amount of work a person is able to do in one work day depends on the amount of time he is actually working, the amount of time he is resting, and the length and frequency of the rest periods. The use of the stop watch time study method was considered as the greatest contribution Taylor made to the field of scientific management.

As is evident from Taylor's investigation of shoveling at the Bethlehem Steel Works in 1898, he used time study as a tool in order to increase overall labor productivity. For this work and time study, Taylor selected two good people to shovel, each measured by a well-trained time study man. Various shoveling loads were evaluated and it was found that the optimal load for maximum daily production output is 21.5 pounds. Taylor ordered the redesign of all shovels to accommodate that load. He instigated a planning department to issue orders to foremen as to daily production requirements, tools to be used, and the exact nature of the job to be done. Savings from this change were tremendous. There was a 50% reduction in material handling cost that translated into a $78,000 savings per year according to F.B. Copley in his works, *Frederick W. Taylor*, Harper & Bros., New York, 1923, Volume II, (p. 56).

Several time measuring methods are used in direct time study: the calendar method, the TV or movie method, the electronic circuit breaking method, and the stop watch method.

The Calendar Method assumes that identical or a few different jobs are performed over a long period of time and that each day approximately the same amount of time is spent working. A relatively long period of time (a week or more) is then divided by the total output quantity produced over that period to establish the standard for one unit produced.

The TV or Movie Method suggests that a TV tape or movie is made while an operator is at work performing a repetitive job, such as sewing clothes, pressing shirts, forming records, drilling holes, etc. By dividing the time period during which the tape was made by the overall production, one can come up with a time per unit estimate. When a clock is introduced into the TV or movie picture, this method has the advantage that we can evaluate the operation time of each operation or item produced, and that we can identify and eliminate from the analysis any unusual circumstances.

The Electronic Circuit Breaking Method allows us to measure time extremely accurately, to about 0.001 seconds. Here, a flashlight battery and target, together with a strip chart recorder, can be used to record time when the operator touches the target. Different targets can be set up for different operations. It also can be programmed to perform a complete data analysis.

The Stop Watch Method is the oldest and most frequently used method in industry. A fairly extensive discussion of this method follows.

2. STOP WATCH METHOD

Measuring work for repetitive direct labor jobs, like the assembly of a product or the production of parts on a machine, can best be done using the stop watch method. This method, as introduced by Taylor, is the most frequently used method in work study and measurement. Setting time standards via the stop watch method must be carefully planned. The following reflects the sequence of operations necessary to properly establish such standards.

1. Make ready the job for the time study. The method for doing the job must be standardized. This includes defining the optimal way of doing the job, planning the appropriate layout for the job, and designing or obtaining the correct tools for the job.
2. Find an experienced operator who is trained to do the job in its standardized fashion. Obtain not only the acceptance and cooperation from the operator, but from his foreman and union as well.
3. Break down the operation into work elements. Seek cooperation of supervisor and worker to correctly identify appropriate work elements. Identify which operations are repeated in cycles and which are performed periodically. On the time study observation sheet it will be necessary to first list in order all work elements that occur regularly, followed by the elements that are part of the job but are repeated in cycles. When operations are broken down in work elements it will be possible to show when excessive time is being taken to perform certain elements.
4. Record the actual time to perform the work elements. Work can be measured via continuous timing, repetitive timing, or accumulative timing. With continuous timing the observer starts the watch at the beginning of the execution of the first work element and permits the watch to run continuously during the study. The stop watch is read at the conclusion of the performance of each work element and the accumulated time is recorded on the observation sheet. When the recording is finished, the time of each work element is determined by subtracting two consecutive recorded times. When repetitive timing is used, the stop watch is snapped back to zero at the end of the performance of each work element. Accumulative timing uses two stopwatches that are connected by a lever mechanism. When the lever mechanism is snapped, the first watch is started, while the second watch is stopped. Now the time for the just performed work element can be read from the second watch, while the first watch is measuring the time for the following work element. This method allows us to read the times with the greatest degree of accuracy and ease because the hands of the watch that are being used are stationary. Times must be carefully recorded! Any foreign element, irregular element, or outlier must be identified on the observation sheet. A dash on the recording sheet may, for example, indicate that the worker omitted that element. The watch need not be stopped when avoidable or unavoidable delays occur. These delays should, however, be identified on the observation sheet.
5. Observe carefully the work pace while measuring and recording element times so that performance rating for the operator and for each element can be established. Performance rating requires that the time study technician is able to "normalize" the times he is recording for each work element. The performance rating should be 100% if the performance appears to be normal. A rating larger than 100% should be assigned if the time study technician notices an abnormally fast performance. For a slow performance a performance rating smaller than 100% should be assigned. The performance

rating must be as objective as possible. It must reflect the rating of the operator's speed and effort and difficulty of the job. This activity is often the most difficult task of a time study. Experience has shown that it is easiest to establish performance ratings for the average experienced operator. This is perhaps why it is preferred to select amongst all experienced workers the average worker for a time study.

6. Based on the sample data obtained in step 4, determine how many observations are necessary to obtain a reasonable accuracy of the performance times at an acceptable confidence level. If not enough data was collected, gather more data as required. The number of observations needed, the sample size, largely depends on the desired accuracy, the desired confidence, and the variability of the data. Realize that the true average time is being estimated via a sample of times. One may expect our estimate to deviate from the true standard by a certain percentage. A maximum allowable deviation from the sample mean is often set at 5% of the sample mean (called accuracy). This accuracy is expected to be obtained with a certain confidence that can be expressed in standard units. For example, a 95.5% confidence means that there is a 95.5% chance that the sample means or average standard time will not be in error by more than the desired accuracy. A 95.5% confidence level is commonly used in time study. The formula for calculating the sample size, using an allowable deviation of 5% (0.05) of the sample mean and a 95.5% confidence level (z = 2), is as follows:

$$Sample\ size = \frac{z^2 * sample\ variance}{(allowable\ deviation)^2} = \frac{2^2 * sample\ variance}{(0.05 * sample\ mean)^2}$$

Table 6.1 shows commonly used z values:

Table 6.1: Commonly Used Z Values	
Required Confidence Level (%)	**Z value**
90	1.65
95	1.96
95.5	2.00
96	2.05
97	2.17
98	2.33
99	2.58

← COMMON

7. When sufficient data is gathered, calculate the normal time (t_n) for each work element as follows:

$$t_n = Average\ Observed\ Time * Performance\ Rating$$

8. Calculate the overall normal time (T_n) for the job which is the sum of all individual normal times of the work elements of the job.

$$T_n = \sum t_n$$

So, the normal time for a job is the time that a qualified operator needs to perform that job while working at a normal tempo.

9. Determine the allowance percentage. Allowance must be given for personal time, fatigue and other unavoidable delays. For light work, two to five percent personal time must be given. When work is heavy, more personal time is needed. Modern management has attempted to eliminate fatigue as much as possible, so rarely does one have to assign allowance for this factor. Organizing rest periods is one way of taking care of the fatigue factor. When delays are unavoidable, such as delays caused by machines, material handling equipment, or other outside forces, a delay percentage must be assigned. The sum of personal time allowance, fatigue allowance, and delay allowance constitute the total allowance percentage that will be used to calculate the standard time for the job (T_S).

$$T_s = T_n / (1 - Allowances)$$

An Example: The Assembly of a Fountain Pen

1. A bench assembly is chosen for this job. The method for doing the job has been standardized which includes: defining the optimal way of doing the job, planning the appropriate layout for the job, and designing or obtaining the correct tools for the job.
2. The cooperation of an experienced operator who is trained to do the job in its standardized fashion is sought. The cooperation of his foreman and union are obtained to use this operator.
3. The supervisor and worker have aided in identifying 4 distinct work elements for this job. These work elements are all repeated in cycles, none of them are performed periodically. On the time study observation sheet we will refer to these work elements as work element #1, #2, #3, and #4.
4. This work is measured via the continuous timing method. With the continuous timing method the observer starts the watch at the beginning of the execution of the first work element and permits the watch to run continuously during the study. The stop watch is read at the conclusion of the performance of each work element and the accumulated time is recorded on the observation sheet:

Table 6.2: Time Observation Sheet for the Fountain Pen Assembly

Date: April 3, 2013	Operator: Johnsons			Approval: Jonsons			Observer: Nesa W'U			
Work Elements	Cycles									
	1	2	3	4	5	6	7	8	9	10
Work Element #1	4.5	1)	74.5	113	149.8	187	224	261	299	336.7
Work Element #2	16.5	50.5	86.5	125	161.8	198	236	273	311	348.4
Work Element #3	24	58.5	95	133	170.3	206	244	281	320	356.6
Work Element #4	37.5	70.5	109	146	182.8	219	256	294	333	369.8

1) work element was not performed during this cycle

The time measurement unit used for the assembly of the fountain pen is seconds. When the recording is finished, the time of each work element is determined by subtracting two consecutive recorded times. This is shown in the finalized Table 6.2 as follows:

	A	B	C	D	E	F	G	H	I	J	K
1	Table 6.2: Time Observation Sheet for the Fountain Pen Assembly										
2	Date: April 3, 2013		Operator: Johnsons		Approval: Jonsons			Observer: Nesa Wu			
3	Work Elements	Cycles									
4		1	2	3	4	5	6	7	8	9	10
5	Work Element	4.5	1)	74.5	113	149.8	187	224	261	299	336.7
6	#1	4.5	1)	4	4	3.8	4	4.5	4.5	4.7	4
7	Work Element	16.5	50.5	86.5	125	161.8	198	236	273	311	348.4
8	#2	12	13	12	12	12	11.5	12	12	12.5	11.7
9	Work Element	24	58.5	95	133	170.3	206	244	281	320	356.6
10	#3	7.5	8	8.5	8	8.5	8	8	8.5	8.5	8.2
11	Work Element	37.5	70.5	109	146	182.8	219	256	294	333	369.8
12	#4	13.5	12	13.5	13.5	12.5	13	12.5	12.7	13	13.2
13	1) work element was not performed during this cycle										

=B5

=B11-B9

=C7-B11

=D7-D5

=D5-C11

Sample Excel equations

5. While measuring and recording element times, following work pace or performance ratings were recorded by the observer:

    For work element #1: performance rating = 1.20 (20% above normal)

    For work element #2: performance rating = 1.10 (10% above normal)

    For work element #3: performance rating = 1.20 (20% above normal)

    For work element #4: performance rating = 0.85 (15% below normal)

6. Given the sample of 9 or 10 observations, now calculate the sample size for each work element to determine whether more data need be collected or whether we can proceed with the calculation of the normal and standard times. The formula for calculating the sample size, using an allowable deviation of 5% (0.05) of the sample mean and a 95.5% confidence level ($z = 2$), is as follows:

$$\textit{sample size} = 2^2 * (\textit{sample standard deviation})^2 / (0.05 * \textit{sample mean})^2$$

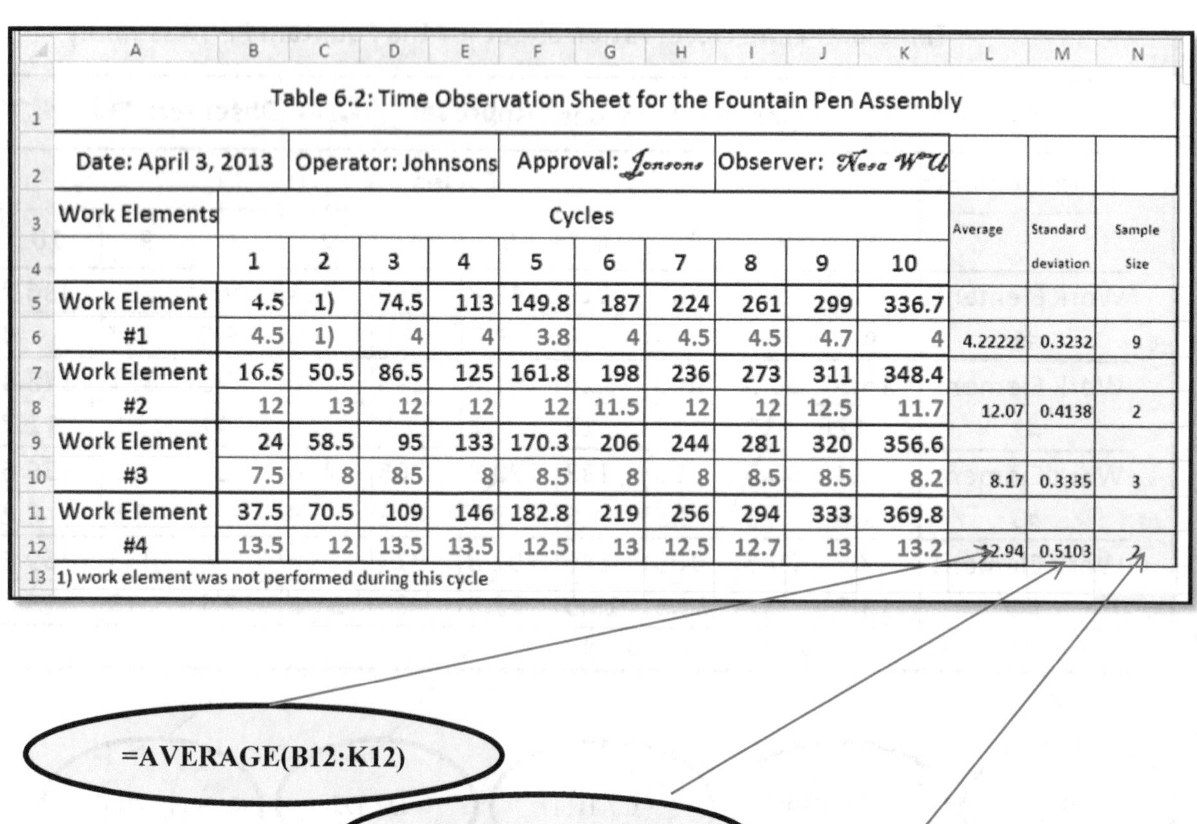

Table 6.2: Time Observation Sheet for the Fountain Pen Assembly

Date: April 3, 2013 | Operator: Johnsons | Approval: Johnsons | Observer: Nesa Wu

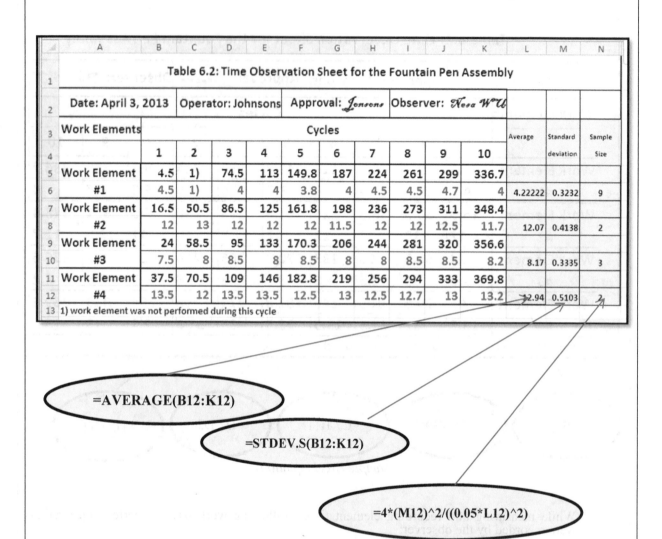

Work Elements	Cycles 1	2	3	4	5	6	7	8	9	10	Average	Standard deviation	Sample Size
Work Element	4.5	1)	74.5	113	149.8	187	224	261	299	336.7			
#1	4.5	1)	4	4	3.8	4	4.5	4.5	4.7	4	4.22222	0.3232	9
Work Element	16.5	50.5	86.5	125	161.8	198	236	273	311	348.4			
#2	12	13	12	12	12	11.5	12	12	12.5	11.7	12.07	0.4138	2
Work Element	24	58.5	95	133	170.3	206	244	281	320	356.6			
#3	7.5	8	8.5	8	8.5	8	8	8.5	8.5	8.2	8.17	0.3335	3
Work Element	37.5	70.5	109	146	182.8	219	256	294	333	369.8			
#4	13.5	12	13.5	13.5	12.5	13	12.5	12.7	13	13.2	12.94	0.5103	2

1) work element was not performed during this cycle

=AVERAGE(B12:K12)
=STDEV.S(B12:K12)
=4*(M12)^2/((0.05*L12)^2)

The sample sizes calculated are less than or equal to the present sample sizes. Therefore, sufficient data is collected to proceed to the next step of calculating the normal times for each work element, the normal time for the job, and the standard time for the assembly of a fountain pen.

7. Now that sufficient data is gathered, we can calculate the normal time (t_n) for each work element as follows: (these calculations and results are shown in the table that follows)

$$t_n = \text{Average Observed Time} * \text{Performance Rating}$$

8. The overall normal time (T_n) for the job is then the sum of all individual normal times of the work elements of the job as follows: (this calculation is shown in the table that follows):

$$T_n = \sum t_n$$

Table 6.2: Time Observation Sheet for the Fountain Pen Assembly													
Date: April 3, 2013	Operator: Johnsons		Approval: *Jonsons*		Observer: [illegible]								
Work Elements	Cycles										Average	Perf. Rating	Normal Time
	1	2	3	4	5	6	7	8	9	10			
Work Element	4.5	1)	74.5	112.5	149.8	186.8	223.8	260.8	298.7	336.7			
#1	4.5	1)	4	4	3.8	4	4.5	4.5	4.7	4	4.222	1.2	5.067
Work Element	16.5	50.5	86.5	124.5	161.8	198.3	235.8	272.8	311.2	348.4			
#2	12	13	12	12	12	11.5	12	12	12.5	11.7	12.07	1.1	13.277
Work Element	24	58.5	95	132.5	170.3	206.3	243.8	281.3	319.7	356.6			
#3	7.5	8	8.5	8	8.5	8	8	8.5	8.5	8.2	8.17	1.2	9.804
Work Element	37.5	70.5	108.5	146	182.8	219.3	256.3	294	332.7	369.8			
#4	13.5	12	13.5	13.5	12.5	13	12.5	12.7	13	13.2	12.94	0.85	10.999
1) work element was not performed during this cycle													
											Total Normal Time:		39.147

= L6 * M6

= SUM(N6:N12)

9. For this job a total allowance of 10% is appropriate. It consists of 5% for personal allowance and 5% because the job is quite tedious. The standard time for this job is then:

$$T_s = 39.147/(1 - 0.10) = 43.50 \text{ seconds}$$

A standard time of 43.50 seconds for the assembly of one fountain pen means that the production rate per hour is 82.76 units:

$$\text{Production Rate} = \text{Seconds in one hour}/T_s = 3600/43.50 = 82.76 \text{ units/hour}$$

1) A Final Note: Note that no time was recorded for work element #1 of the second observation! Perhaps the operator did not perform that work element. It is ignored in the analysis.

3. *ELEMENTAL TIME DATABASE*

Validated time study standards are stored in the company's elemental time database. This database becomes helpful when setting standards for newly designed jobs that may have work elements that are similar to existing jobs. Examples of such similar work elements include reaching for a container of parts from a rack, positioning a part on a jig, placing a finished part in a bin, and many others.

Using elemental time databases can significantly reduce a company's time when setting standards and therefore reduce workplace disruptions that often occur when collecting data for setting standards. So the procedure for setting standards when the company relies on elemental time databases is as follows:

1. Determine the work elements of the job
2. Identify which work elements have been done in the past by consulting the database
3. Do a time study for these work elements that are not in the database
4. Add all work element times to get the normal time and adjust for allowances to determine the standard time
5. Update the elemental time database by adding the data obtained for the new work elements

4. *INDIRECT TIME STANDARDS*

Contemporaries of Taylor are Frank and Lillian Gilbreth, who are known for motion study. Frank Gilbreth became interested in motion study when he learned the bricklayer's trade. He soon noticed the various motions used by many bricklayers, which he analyzed carefully. It made him realize that, with the correct tools, the proper set-up of the work place, and the efficient sequencing of various operations, bricklaying time could be reduced significantly. Gilbreth spent endless time taking and analyzing photographs of the bricklaying activities. He learned to substitute longer and fatiguing motions with shorter and less tiring ones. He invented the scaffold, equipped with a bench for holding bricks and mortar, that could be raised and lowered a short distance at a time in order to keep the bricklayer at the most convenient level to perform his work. Later Gilbreth developed the technique of micro motion study, whereby fundamental elements of an operation can be analyzed and timed by the use of a motion picture camera and an accurate timing device indicating time intervals on the motion picture film.

As a result of his detailed motion analysis, Frank and Lillian Gilbreth broke work down into 17 micro elements, called "therbligs." After an efficient work method has been established, motion study and its timing require that all its therbligs are defined and time values assigned to their micro elements. The total task time of the job is then the sum of these element times. Thus Frank introduced universal units of work with predetermined amounts of time. This resulted in various **predetermined time standards** (PTS), of which **methods time measurement** (MTM), as developed by Maynard, Stegemerten, and Schwab (1948) ,and **work factor,** as developed by Philco Radio Corporation in Philadelphia (1930–34), are the most popular ones. More information on some of these methods is in the following section.

Occurrence sampling or **work sampling** was introduced by Tippett in 1934 as an alternate method for setting time standards. Work sampling has been used to measure work as well as delays, idle time, and performance. It is especially useful when measuring long cycle operations of work where people are employed in groups. Work sampling requires that a large number of observations are made and that a tally of idle and working conditions is created. The principle behind such work sampling is then that the number of observations working or idling is proportional to the amount of time spent in a working or idle state.

5. *PREDETERMINED TIME STANDARDS*

Predetermined time standard (PTS) systems have been developed since the establishment of fundamental hand motions by Frank B. Gilbreth. Frank B. Gilbreth, who was mainly interested in improving work methods, broke work down into 17 micro elements, called therbligs (the name "therblig" comes from spelling his name "Gilbreth" backwards). These 17 therbligs are: assemble (A), disassemble (DA), avoidable delay (AD), unavoidable delay (UD), grasp (G), hold (H), inspect (I), plan (PL or PN), position (P), pre-position (PP), release load (RL), rest to overcome fatigue (R), search (SH), select (SE or ST), transport empty (TE), transport loaded (TL), and use (U). A description of these therbligs can be found in Table 6.3.

Table 6.3: Description of the Original Therbligs, as defined by Frank Gilbreth and Redefined by Barnes.

Therblig	**Letter**	**Description**
1. Assemble	A	Place one object on or into another object. This motion starts when the hand starts to move one part into place and ends when the assembly is completed.
2. Disassemble	DA	Remove one part from another part of which it is an integral part. This motion starts when the hand starts to remove one part from the assembly and ends when the hand has completed the removal of the part from the assembly.
3. Avoidable Delay	AD	A delay over which the operator has control. It is a delay that the operator can avoid. It starts when the standard work method is interrupted and ends when these standard methods are resumed.
4. Unavoidable Delay	UD	A delay over which an operator has no control. It can be caused due to failure of equipment. It starts when the hand stops its activity and ends when the activity is resumed.
5. Grasp	G	The hand takes a hold of an object and closes the fingers around it so that the hand gets in position to pick it up, to hold it or to manipulate it. It starts at the first contact of the fingers with the part and ends when the hand obtains control of the part.
6. Hold	H	No movement takes place and the part is retained after having been grasped. It starts when movement of the part stops and ends when the next therblig begins.
7. Inspect	I	Examine a part for compliance with standards, such as size, odor, shape, color, taste, etc. It is often a mental reaction that is often performed together with other therbligs.
8. Plan	PL PN	A mental reaction that precedes a physical movement. It starts when the operator begins to determine the next step of the operation and ends when that step starts to be executed.
9. Position	P	Turn or orient a part so that it becomes properly placed as to fit in the location for which it is intended. It starts when the hand starts orienting the object and ends when the hand has placed the object in the desired location.
10. Pre-position	PP	Locate an object in a predetermined place or correct position for the next motion. The object is located in the appropriate position, rather than the exact position, as is the case in 'Position' motion.
11. Release Load	RL	Let go of a part or object. It starts from the moment the object leaves the hand until it is completely separated from the hand and fingers.
12. Rest to Overcome Fatigue	R	A fatigue or delay factor given to the worker so that he can recover from fatigue incurred by his work. It starts when the worker stops working and ends when he resumes his work.
13. Search	SH	Activity whereby eyes or hands are looking or seeking for an object. It starts when the eyes or hands begin the hunt and ends when the object has been located.
14. Select	SE ST	Find one object from among others. It is often combined with the search activity and is difficult to discriminate between both the search and the select activity. Therefore it is appropriate to refer to both as the select activity.
15. Transport Empty	TE	Move an empty hand without any resistance towards or away from the object. It starts when the empty hand starts moving without resistance and ends when it stops moving.
16. Transport Loaded	TL	Move an object from one place to another in the hands, or on the fingers, or through pushing, sliding, pulling, or dragging. It is also used when the empty hand is moved against some type of resistance.
17. Use	U	The hand manipulates a tool, instrument, apparatus, or device. It starts when the hand starts to manipulate and ends when the hand terminates that manipulation.

Table 6.4: Right-Left Hand Chart With Therbligs for Assembling a Nut to a Bolt			
Left Hand		Right Hand	
TE	Transport empty to reach for the bolt	TE	Transport empty to reach for the nut
G	Take hold of the bolt	G	Take hold of the nut
TL	Transport loaded, carry the bolt in assembly position	TL	Transport loaded, carry the nut in assembly position
H	Hold the bolt on position	PP	Pre-Position the nut to the bolt for proper assembly
TL	Transport the bolt/nut assembly to the collection bin	U	Assemble nut to bolt
		RL	Release assembly
RL	Release bolt/nut assembly in to the collection bin	UD	Unavoidable delay

Breaking down work in elementary work elements is fundamental to work improvement. Therefore, one must practice to learn the names of such therbligs. Table 6.4 is an example where fundamental motions for the right hand and the left hand are defined when assembling a nut to a bolt.

Frank B. Gilbreth, who established the original list of therbligs, was never interested in establishing any manual of universal standard data. However, a number of people and groups of people have used the pioneering work of Gilbreth to establish such standards. Companies such as Western Electric, Westinghouse, DuPont, General Motors, and others became interested in establishing predetermined motion time data systems. Some of these systems are: **motion time analysis** (MTA) developed by Segur in 1924; **work factor** system developed by Quick and others in 1938; **elemental time standard** for basic manual work developed at Western Electric in 1920; and **methods time measurement** (MTM) systems developed in 1948 at Westinghouse. The most popular systems are work factor and MTM and it is believed that the MTM systems are perhaps the most widely used systems throughout the world.

Companies that have similar work elements can use the predetermined time databases, just like elemental time databases are used by individual companies. Using predetermined time standards have many advantages over other methods. There is no need to seek the cooperation of a worker. Additionally, the subjective element of performance rating is automatically included in the predetermined time standard. However, a major disadvantage of using the predetermined time standards is that each motion is considered independently of all other motions.

5.1 Methods Time Measurement (MTM) Systems

The basic MTM system, called MTM-1, breaks down motions into 10 categories: reach (R), move (M), turn (T), apply pressure (AP), grasp (G), position (P), release (RL), disengage (D), body motions (B), and eye motions (E). Times have been established for these motions based on: distance moved, difficulty level, weight of object, etc. The time unit used by the MTM system is called the "**time-measuring unit**" (TMU). A TMU is a unit of time defined so that 100,000 TMU = 1 hour, or if you wish, 1 TMU equals 0.00001 hr, or 0.0006 min, or 0.036 sec.

Therbligs can easily be converted to MTM motions by the use of Table 6.5. Note that MTM provides for assigning allowances for rest to overcome fatigue and for avoidable delays.

The therbligs versus MTM motions for left hand and right hand motions for the assembly of a nut to a bolt is shown in Table 6.6.

Table 6.5: Converting Therbligs to MTM System Motions	
Therbligs	**MTM System Motions**
1. Assemble 2. Disassemble	Combination of Reach (R), Move (M), Grasp (G), Release (RL), and Position (P)
3. Avoidable Delay	This is handled by assigning allowances for specific jobs
4. Unavoidable Delay	Is non-existing, since the other hand is usually in control
5. Grasp	Grasp
6. Hold	Is non-existing, since the other hand is usually in control; sometimes Apply Pressure (AP)
7. Inspect	Combination of Reach (R), Move (M), Grasp (G), Release (RL), Position (P), eye travel (E), and focus (E)
8. Plan	Is non-existing for repetitive operations
9. Position 10. Pre-Position	Position
11. Release Load	Release (RL)
12.Rest to Overcome Fatigue	This is handled by allowances
13. Search 14. Select	Part of Reach
15. Transport Empty	Reach (R)
16. Transport Loaded	Move (M); sometimes Turn (T)
17. Use	Combination of Reach (R), Move (M), Grasp (G), Release (R), and Position (P)

Table 6.6: Therbligs versus MTM Motions for Assembly of a Nut to a Bolt							
Left Hand				**Right Hand**			
Therbligs		**MTM Motions**		**Therbligs**		**MTM Motions**	
Transport empty	TE	Reach for bolt	R	Transport empty	TE	Reach for nut	R
Grasp bolt	G	Grasp bolt	G	Grasp nut	G	Grasp nut	G
Transport loaded	TL	Move bolt	M	Transport loaded	TL	Move nut	M
Hold	H			Pre-position Use Release	PP U R	Position Release	P R
Transport loaded	TL	Move	M	Unavoidable delay	UD		
Release	R	Release	R				

The following general procedure can be used to establish the MTM time.

Step 1: Visually analyze all work elements and record the therbligs

Step 2: Evaluate therbligs so that the necessary therblig elements can be identified and retained and the unnecessary elements disregarded

Step 3: Convert all necessary therbligs to MTM elements

Step 4: Use MTM tables to assign time values to all MTM elements and add up all such time elements

Step 5: Apply work allowances to the total job time when appropriate

Table 6.7 is the "Move (M)" MTM element table. The times in the table are in TMUs and depend on:

- The distance moved in inches (first column)
- Whether the object is moved to the other hand or a stop (column A), or whether the object is moved to approximate or indefinite location (column B), or whether the object is moved to an exact location (column C), or whether the hand was already in motion when the move started (next column)
- The weight in pounds that gives a multiplier factor and a constant to the established times

Table 6.7: TMUs for the Move MTM Element (based on: MTM Association for Standards and Research)

Distance Moved (inches)	A	B	C	Hand in Motion B	Weight (lbs.) Up to:	Multiplier Factor	Constant factor TMU	Case and Description
¾ or less	2.0	2.0	2.0	1.7				
1	2.5	2.9	3.4	2.3	**2.5:**	1.00	0	
2	3.6	4.6	5.2	2.9				**A.** Move object to other hand or against stop.
3	4.9	5.7	6.7	3.6	**7.5:**	1.06	2.2	
4	6.1	6.9	8.0	4.3				
5	7.3	8.0	9.2	5.0	**12.5:**	1.11	3.9	
6	8.1	8.9	10.3	5.7				
7	8.9	9.7	11.1	6.5	**17.5:**	1.17	5.6	
8	9.7	10.6	11.8	7.2				
9	10.5	11.5	12.7	7.9	**22.5:**	1.22	7.4	**B.** Move object to approximate or indefinite location.
10	11.3	12.2	13.5	8.6				
12	12.9	13.4	15.2	10.0	**27.5:**	1.28	9.1	
14	14.4	14.6	16.9	11.4				
16	16.0	15.8	18.7	12.8	**32.5:**	1.33	10.8	
18	17.6	17.0	20.4	14.2				
20	19.2	18.2	22.1	15.6	**37.5:**	1.39	12.5	
22	20.8	19.4	23.8	17.0				
24	22.4	20.6	25.5	18.4	**42.5:**	1.44	14.3	**C.** Move object to exact location.
26	24.0	21.8	27.3	19.8				
28	25.5	23.1	29.0	21.2	**47.5:**	1.50	16.0	
30	27.1	24.3	30.7	22.7				
Additional per inch over 30 in.	0.8	0.6	0.85					

Table 6.7 can, for example, be used to figure the TMUs for moving a 20-pound object over 14 inches to an exact location as follows:

$$TMUs: 16.9x1.22 + 7.4 = 28.018\ TMUs$$

This translates into 1.01 seconds to move a 20-pound object over 14 inches to an exact location:

$$28.018\ TMUs\ x\ 0.036\ seconds/TMU = 1.008648$$

The TMUs for the "Reach (R)" MTM element depends on the following difficulty characteristics:

- Distance moved to reach object
- Whether the reach is to an object in a fixed location or to an object in the other hand or on which the other hand rests (column A), or whether the reach is to a single object in a location that may vary slightly from cycle to cycle (column B), or whether the reach is to an object jumbled with other objects in a group so that search and select occur (column C), or whether the reach is to a very small object or where an accurate grasp is required (column D), or whether the reach is to an indefinite location to get the hand in position for body balance or the next motion or out of the way (column E)
- Therbligs for columns A and B are different if the hand was already in motion

Table 6.8 is the Reach MTM Table, reflecting the above difficulty levels.

Table 6.8: TMUs for the Reach MTM Element (based on: MTM Association for Standards and Research**)**

Distance Moved (inches)	**A**	**B**	**C or D**	**E**	Hand in Motion **A**	Hands in Motion **B**	**Cases and Descriptions**
¾ or less	2.0	2.0	2.0	2.0	1.6	1.6	**A.** Reach to object in fixed location or to object in other hand or on which other hand rests.
1	2.5	2.5	3.6	2.4	2.3	2.3	
2	4.0	4.0	5.9	3.8	3.5	2.7	
3	5.3	5.3	7.3	5.3	4.5	3.6	
4	6.1	6.4	8.4	6.8	4.9	4.3	**B.** Reach to single object in location, which may vary slightly from cycle to cycle.
5	6.5	7.8	9.4	7.4	5.3	5.0	
6	7.0	8.6	10.1	8.0	5.7	5.7	
7	7.4	9.3	10.8	8.7	6.1	6.5	
8	7.9	10.1	11.5	9.3	6.5	7.2	
9	8.3	10.8	12.2	9.9	6.9	7.9	**C.** Reach to object jumbled with other objects in a group so that search and select occur.
10	8.7	11.5	12.9	10.5	7.3	8.6	
12	9.6	12.9	14.2	11.8	8.1	10.1	
14	10.5	14.4	15.6	13.0	8.9	11.5	
16	11.4	15.8	17.0	14.2	9.7	12.9	
18	12.3	17.2	18.4	15.5	10.5	14.4	**D.** Reach to a very small object or where accurate grasp is required.
20	13.1	18.6	19.8	16.7	11.3	15.8	
22	14.0	20.1	21.2	18.0	12.1	17.3	
24	14.9	21.5	22.5	19.2	12.9	18.8	
26	15.8	22.9	23.9	20.4	13.7	20.2	**E.** Reach to indefinite location to get hand in position for body balance or next motion or out of the way.
28	16.7	24.4	25.3	21.7	14.5	21.7	
30	17.5	25.8	26.7	22.9	15.3	23.2	

The MTM handbook has ten such tables, one for each of the ten MTM elements.

5.2 Work Factor System

The work factor system was initiated by Philco Radio Corporation of Philadelphia. Times developed through work factor are based on the output level of the average experienced skillful operator. MTM times are 20% larger than work factor times. In other words, if the MTM time for a special task equals 400 TMU's, then the corresponding work factor time is:

$$\frac{400\,TMUs\ \times 0.036\,sec/TMU}{1.20} = 12.00\,seconds$$

Work factor times do not include work allowances and assume that a skillful worker can achieve these standard times within 200 to 400 cycles.

6. WORK SAMPLING OR OCCURRENCE SAMPLING

Tippet introduced work- or occurrence sampling for the first time in the British textile industry in the early 1930s. It was introduced in the US. a decade later under the name of "ratio delay," because its main purpose at that time was to study operator delays.

Since the principle behind work sampling is that the number of observations is proportional to the amount of time spent in the working or idle state, work sampling is a technique that can be used to estimate time utilization of workers, machines, and their operators by making a sufficient number of instantaneous, random observations.

Work sampling is the most popular probability-oriented tool that ever emerged from the postwar era. It has been used to:

- Determine time allowances
- Determine machine utilization or operator utilization
- Determine cycles of work load
- Expose causes of delays
- Aid in identifying problems
- Aid in establishing goals for supervision
- Aid in determining manpower requirements
- Define plant/departmental efficiencies or productivity
- Evaluate conformance to management policy
- Establish time standards

There are many advantages of work sampling that make it more attractive than the stop watch approach or the predetermined time standards approach. These are:

- It is relatively inexpensive to use
- If used correctly, the results are very accurate
- The union prefers this technique over others
- It is adaptable to ever-changing objectives of the firm
- It is relatively easy to train supervisors to use it as a management tool
- It provides management with an economical and convenient yardstick for measuring any change

6.1 Managing Work Sampling

Work sampling is best managed when the following 12 steps are followed:

Step1: Decide upon the work sampling objectives

There are many different reasons why a work sampling may be undertaken. The objective could be: 1) to perform a general survey; 2) to aid in defining certain problems; 3) to aid in establishing goals for supervision; 4) to study various delay ratios; 5) to determine the extent of cyclical fluctuations in various activities; 6) to study production efficiency or inefficiency;7) to determine work content; 8) to determine time standards and allowances; 9) to aid in manpower planning, etc.

Step 2: Inform the supervisor, foreman, and workers

The objective of the work sampling study must be explained to the supervisor and/or the foreman of the area. It is then also the responsibility of the foreman to inform all workers to obtain their co-operation and understanding for this study.

Step 3: Conduct a preliminary survey

This preliminary survey is necessary to determine the work time contents, the people covered by this study, and the general area in which the activities are performed.

Step 4: Establish a quantitative measure for various production outputs

Based on the principle of work sampling, sampling results will be correlated with their appropriate quantitative measures. Therefore, one needs to accurately define such measures. Some of these measures could be the number of parts produced or assembled, the number of technical pages typed, the number of professional calls made, the number of personal calls made, etc...

Step 5: Classify work activities

Work activities must be classified into different categories. The three major categories are: 1) productive work, 2) unavoidable delay, and 3) avoidable delay.

Step 6: Determine the observation schedule

After one determines the correct sample size (as discussed in next section) it is necessary to determine the frequency of observations. The appropriate frequency of observations largely depends on how soon one needs the results and how long it takes to make observations. Based on the frequency of observations an observation schedule can be set up. It is best that the observation times are selected at random by the use of a random number table.

Step 7: Prepare the observation sheets

Step 8: Perform the observations

It is necessary, in order to eliminate bias, that all observations are made from the same location and that observations are made instantaneously. There should be no hesitation on the part of the observer in recording a delay, even though the operator might be getting ready to start working seconds after the observer arrives at the location.

Step 9: Analyze daily sampling results

Results of sampling observations must be analyzed on a daily basis and results must be accumulated as days go on. As will be discussed in the next section, this will also enable the work sampling analyst to evaluate the correctness of the initial defined sample size. If necessary, sample size must be adjusted.

Step 10: Set up a control chart

The control chart is set up after all sampling results are in. This chart (that is based on the final sampling results) will exhibit the variation of the work performance on a daily basis. Any unusual daily sampling results must be identified and eliminated from the final analysis. Control limits are based on $\pm$ 3 standard deviations from the overall sampling mean.

For example, assume that the percent of occurrence of a drilling activity during a 10-day study is 80% and that a daily sample of 40 observations has been taken, then the control limits are 61% and 99%, based on the following calculations:

$$0.80 \pm 3\sqrt{\frac{p(1-p)}{n}} = 0.80 \pm 3\sqrt{\frac{0.8(1-0.8)}{40}} = 0.80 \pm 3(0.06325) = 0.80 \pm 0.19$$

Any daily percent of occurrence of a drilling activity that falls outside these limits should be eliminated in order to achieve statistical reliability. If data must be eliminated, then perhaps additional sampling may be necessary.

Step 11: Summarize study results

Study results are summarized when sampling is complete and summaries must be presented to management.

Step 12: Store sampling results and plan for future study and follow-up

6.2 Sample Size

The same reasoning that was used for the stop watch time study can be used to define the number of observations that are needed in a work sampling study. Based on the sample data obtained in step 10, determine how many observations are necessary to obtain a reasonable accuracy of the percentage of occurrence at an acceptable confidence level. If not enough data was collected, gather more data as required. The number of observations needed, the sample size, largely depends on the desired accuracy, the desired confidence, and the variability of the data. Realize that the true percentage of occurrence is being estimated via a sample. One may expect our estimate to deviate from the true standard by no more than a certain percentage. This accuracy is expected to be obtained with a certain confidence that can be expressed in standard units. For example, a 95.5% confidence means that there is a 95.5% chance that the occurrence percentage will not be in error by more than the desired accuracy. A 95.5% confidence level is commonly used in time study. The formula for calculating the sample size, using an allowable error e (expressed as a percentage, like 2%, 3%, or any other %) and a 95.5% confidence level (z = 2), is as follows:

$$Sample\ size = \frac{z^2 * sample\ variance}{(e)^2} = \frac{2^2 * p(1-p)}{(e)^2}$$

For example, if the occurrence percentage as obtained through sampling is 85% (p = 0.85) and the allowable error is 4% (p = 0.04), then for a 95.5% confidence level the sample size is:

$$Sample\ size = \frac{z^2 * sample\ variance}{(e)^2} = \frac{2^2 * 0.85(1-0.85)}{(0.04)^2} = 319$$

The sample size, though initially defined at the onset of the study, must be monitored and re-evaluated during the collection of sampling results. As the true sampling proportions become known it may be necessary to increase the initially defined sample size. This monitoring and adjustment of the number of observations is described and illustrated in the following steps:

Step 1: Calculate the initial sample size

At the onset of work sampling an educated guess is made with respect to the estimate of the percentage occurrence of the measured element. For demonstration purposes, let us assume that this estimate equals 0.85 (p = 0.85). If management allows a maximum deviation error of 4% (e = 0.04), then the initial sample size (N_1) is 319 observations:

$$N_1 = \frac{2^2 * 0.85(1-0.85)}{(0.04)^2} = 319$$

Now, 319 observations must be made and the sample proportion p_1 is calculated based on these sampling results. If p_1 is within four percentage points of p ($0.81 \leq p_1 \leq 0.89$) then N_1 is the correct sample size and the sample proportion, p_1, is an acceptable estimate for the percentage occurrence of the measured element. If p_1 is not within 4 percentage points of p, consider the next step.

Step 2: Re-estimate the sample size

Use now the sample proportion p_1 to re-estimate the sample size. For demonstration purposes let us assume that the obtained sample proportion, p_1, equals 0.80. This is indeed less than the acceptable lower limit of 0.81. Therefore, the sample size must be re-evaluated as follows:

$$N_2 = \frac{2^2 * 0.80(1-0.80)}{(0.04)^2} = 400$$

Step 3: Continue Sampling

If $N_2 \geq N_1$, then additional sampling of $(N_2 - N_1)$ observations is necessary. In our case it will be necessary to make at least 81 additional observations (400 – 319). After all 400 observations are made a new overall sample proportion, p_2, is calculated and checked to be within 4 percentage points of the previously calculated proportion, p_1. If it is, then N_2 is the correct sample size and the sample proportion, p_2, becomes an acceptable estimate for the percentage occurrence of the measured work element. If p_2 is not within four percentage points of the previously calculated proportion, then proceed to step 4.

Step 4: Continue

Continue to repeat steps 2 and 3 until p_i is within the allowable maximum deviation of p_{i-1}. Then p_i becomes the reliable estimate for the percentage occurrence of the measured work element.

An Example: Percentage of Time Nurses Spend on Documentation

In Chapter 5, section 5.3, a 5S implementation to reduce time spent on documentation by nurses is presented. Mrs. Mayble E. Craig suggests that the literature tells us that as much as 40% of a staff nurse's work time is spent on documentation. This can easily be verified for a specific hospital through work or occurrence sampling.

A reasonable, initial sample size can be established using as p value the suggested 40%. If one wants to estimate p for a hospital, using a reasonable 3% error at a 95% confidence level, the sample size can be calculated as follows:

$$N_1 = \frac{z^2 * \textit{sample variance}}{(e)^2} = \frac{1.96^2 * 0.40(1-0.40)}{(0.03)^2} = 1025$$

If one plans to sample over a period of 10 days, then 103 observations need to be made each day. These observations must be made at random, by the use of a random number generator that assigns 103 random times over the duration of a nurse's shift, for each of the 10 days a nurse is observed.

Step 9 of work sampling suggests that results of sampling observations must be analyzed on a daily basis and results must be accumulated as days go on. This will also enable the work sampling analyst to evaluate the correctness of the initial defined sample size. If necessary, sample size must be adjusted.

Therefore, if at any time the work occurrence proportion p falls outside the range of 0.40 ± 0.3 (0.37-0.43), a new sample size needs to be calculated and the remaining data that needs to be collected adjusted.

For example, half way through sampling, at the end of the fifth day, when 515 (5x103) observations have been made the sampling results suggest that the nurses are spending 45% (p_1) of their time on documentation. Because 45% (p_1 = 0.45) falls outside the range of 40% ± 3% (p range of 0.40 ± 0.3), a new sample size needs to be calculated, using the sample result of p_1 = 0.45, as follows:

$$N_2 = \frac{1.96^2 * 0.45(1-0.55)}{(0.03)^2} = 1057$$

N_2 suggests that 542 (1057 – 515) additional observations need to be taken. If during these additional observations the overall occurrence percentage remains within ± 3% of 45%, then the final overall occurrence percentage becomes a reasonable estimate for the percentage of time that the nurses are documenting.

6.3 Setting Work Standards with Work Sampling

Since the principle behind work sampling is that the number of observations is proportional to the amount of time spent in working or idle state, the following general formula can be used to calculate the Normal Time to perform a certain job.

$$\text{Normal Time} = \frac{\begin{array}{ccc}\text{total time} & \text{percentage of} & \text{average perf.} \\ \text{of study} \times & \text{time working} \times & \text{rating} \\ \text{in minutes} & \text{from sampling} & \text{in decimals}\end{array}}{\text{total number of pieces produced}}$$

The use of this formula is illustrated in the following example.

An Example: Establishing Time Standards for Secretarial Work

Let us assume that one wishes to determine time standards for four major activities performed by a departmental secretary. These activities are phone calls, typing of letters, typing of professional papers, and filling out forms. Full co-operation of the secretary and her boss is obtained before commencing with the study. After surveying the layout of her work area it is agreed to make all observations from the main entrance to her office, since this would minimize the interference with her work.

In accordance with step 4 of the work sampling procedure, the following quantitative measures are defined for the various activities being measured: 1) number of phone calls made, 2) number of letters typed, 3) number of professional pages typed, and 4) number of forms filled out.

Table 6.9 shows the work sampling results.

Table 6.9: Sampling Results for Secretarial Activities

	A	B	C	D	E
2	Activities	Initial Estimate p	Sample Size N (e = 0.05)	Sampling Results Occurrences	Sampling Results p
3	Non-personal Calls	0.13	181	58	0.1510
4	Typing Letters	0.29	329	123	0.3203
5	Typing Professional Papers	0.10	144	27	0.0703
6	Filling out Forms	0.08	118	38	0.0990
7	Others	0.40	384	138	0.3594
8			Total:	384	1.0000

= (2^2)*B3*(1-B3)/(.05^2)   = D3/$D$8

Initial estimates were established during a 20 minute discussion with the secretary. These estimates were consequently used to define the initial sample size N, using a 95.5% confidence level (z = 2) and an error of 5%. (e = 0.05). Based on the sample size results, we will select the largest sample size of 384 observations. If we do not wish to take more than 20 observations a day, the collection of all 384 observations will take 4 weeks or 20 working days:

20 observations per day for 19 days, and
4 observations on the 20th working day

A random number table is used to randomly select the observation times. Note that the sampling results are all well within 5 percentage points of the initial estimates, so that further sampling is not necessary.

The estimated total time spent on each activity over a period of four weeks can now be calculated by multiplying each activity's sampling proportion, *p*, with the total amount of time spent sampling, 9600 minutes (4weeks x 40hrs./week x 60 min/hr. = 9600 minutes). Finally, the ratios of these estimated total times in minutes to their respective output volumes yield the estimated time per activity. These results are shown in Table 6.10.

Table 6.10: Estimated Time per Unit Activity through Work Sampling

	A	B	C	D	E
2	Activities	Occurrence %	Estimated Total Time in Minutes	Output over 4 Week	Estimated minutes per Unit Activity
3	Non-personal Calls	15.10%	1449.6	483	3.00
4	Typing Letters	32.03%	3074.88	170	18.09
5	Typing Professional Papers	7.03%	674.88	31	21.77
6	Filling out Forms	9.90%	950.4	380	2.50
7	Others	35.94%	3450.24		
8		100.00%	9600.00		

=B3 * 9600 **=C3/D3**

During the work sampling period it was possible to estimate performance ratings for three of the four activities (typing letters, typing professional papers, and filling out forms). Estimated times, performance ratings, and job allowances allow us to set up standards as shown in Table 6.11.

Table 6.11: Establishing Time Standards through Work Sampling (in minutes)

	A	B	C	D	E
2	Activities	Estimated Time in Minutes	Performance Rating	Normal Time	Standard Time (10% allowance)
3	Non-personal Calls	3.00		3.00	3.33
4	Typing Letters	18.09	1.05	18.99	21.11
5	Typing Professional Papers	21.77	0.90	19.59	21.77
6	Filling out Forms	2.50	1.15	2.88	3.19

= B3 **= B4 * C4** **= D/(1 – 0.10)**

7. HUMAN FACTORS IN WORK DESIGN

Human factor systems deal with relationships between workers, machines, and the work environment, and their effects on work performance and productivity. The body of knowledge pertaining to human factors can be utilized in designing and improving the functional effectiveness of man-made systems and objects, including tools, fixtures, work stations, facilities, man-machine systems, and the work environment.

The science of studying the human capability and limitations in performing the various tasks under various conditions is called **ergonomics**. Human activities in manufacturing and service industries can be classified in three basic groups of tasks:

- Strenuous manual tasks
- Motor tasks
- Mental tasks

Each of these groups prescribes a different set of constraints and requirements to the human body, both mentally and physically. Strenuous manual tasks demand large muscular strength and always result in increased energy transformation that can be measured by monitoring changes in vital functions, such as heartbeat, blood pressure, oxygen consumption, etc. The prolonged changes in those vital functions will result in physical stress and fatigue. This aspect of the ergonomic study is also called **work physiology**. Experiments have been conducted where volunteers from the plant were asked to run on treadmills in order to measure oxygen consumption, blood pressure, and heart rate. Work performed in factories has been simulated in laboratories in order to set proper guidelines for the performance of tasks. When physical demands of a task exceed the acceptable range of changes in vital functions as determined through work physiology experiments, the job needs to be redesigned. We may use a two-man team instead of one person to do the job; we may employ some sort of device to help the worker to do the job; or we may design a robot for this job which is not subjected to the same restrictions as a human worker is. Some of the strenuous manual tasks that are still commonly utilized in our industries are: longshoremen's cargo handling, lumbering, small scale earthwork, highway maintenance, mining, etc. The trend is to eliminate the strenuous manual tasks and to substitute them with machines.

Motor tasks require a predetermined precision and speed of body reflexes which may also cause physical and mental strain. Machines perform repetitive activities in a highly reliable fashion and maintain such performance over an extended period of time. This is not necessarily true for humans. Localized muscular fatigue is often associated with motor tasks. The physical demand of a motor task is in proportion to the speed and the precision requirement of the task. To study the capability and limitations in performing motor tasks, workers are required to perform a set of tasks at various speeds for various durations. The accuracy of the performance is used to measure the degree of fatigue. Many mental and environmental conditions also have a profound effect on the performance of motor tasks, such as temperature, humidity, light, noise, mood, etc. The major problem associated with motor tasks is boredom, which, in turn, is the major cause of fatigue. Machines are superior to human beings in performing motor tasks in terms of consistency and endurance. Therefore, many of the motor tasks in our industries have gradually been taken over by machines. Typical motor tasks that can still be found in our industries are paced assembly, packaging, mail sorting, keyboard operations, etc.

Mental tasks studied under ergonomics relate to the processing of information. People have the ability to process information rapidly; sense low levels of various types of stimuli such as visual, tactual, olfactory, and palpable; feel unusual and unexpected events in the environment; and are well equipped for all types of mental tasks such as inspection, process control, and monitoring, etc. Like for motor tasks, the human capability in performing mental tasks can be measured in terms of speed and accuracy of information processed by the subject. Since modern computers have enormous capabilities in processing information in terms of speed and accuracy, the trend is that computers are gradually taking over the performance of mental tasks in work design. The branch of ergonomics that is concerned with mental as well as motor tasks is called **human engineering**. It should be noted that decision making and creative mental activities are not normally considered as part of ergonomics. Table 6.12 is a summary of the scope and the key elements of ergonomics.

In addition to the human capability and limitations, human factor groups are also concerned about the human worker as he interacts with machinery, equipment, processes, facilities, and his environment in general. Therefore, these groups play an important role in the design of products, processes, facilities, and safety devices. They are concerned about the functional effectiveness of tools and equipment and have an interest in maintaining and enhancing human values in the manufacturing processes. In this sense, they care about safety, health, work comfort, and job satisfaction, which are the four important attributes of quality of life and which have a profound impact on productivity.

Table 6.12: Elements of Ergonomics			
Sub-Disciplines:	**Work Physiology**	**Human Engineering**	
Type of Tasks Covered	**Strenuous Manual Tasks**	**Motor Tasks**	**Mental Tasks**
Typical Examples:	Lumbering Loading and Unloading Earthwork	Key Punching Paced Assembly	Inspection Process Monitoring
Physical Limitations:	Rate of Energy Transformation	Reflexes	Information Processing Capacity
Measurement of Work Intensity:	Change in Vital Functions	Speed and Precision in Movement	Time to Respond to Number of Errors

Studies have shown that human values are enhanced on the job and productivity is improved through job enrichment, job enlargement, the creation of flexible work schedules, flextime, the four-day work week, and the formation of work teams.

Job enrichment and **job enlargement** reduce boredom and monotony. Instead of assigning to each worker a limited and specialized set of tasks, he is given a variety of activities. Through **job enrichment** (vertical work integration), workers have the opportunity to increase their knowledge and skills, to take more responsibilities on the job, and to take pride in their work. Besides executing their jobs, they get involved in planning, organizing and controlling their work. For example, a press operator, in addition to operating his press, gets involved in setting up the press and performing daily routine maintenance activities.

Through **job enlargement** (horizontal work integration) workers have the opportunity to perform a variety of similar activities. Job enlargement was introduced with assembly work teams in the early 1970s. Here subassembly lines are replaced by teams of assemblers who are assigned to assemble part of a product collectively. Each individual worker is not only concerned with his/her own set of operations but also takes an interest in the team effort of the entire operation. Unlike controlling each individual assembly operation on a paced continuous assembly line, the assembly work team is responsible for part of a product which is technologically identifiable. Therefore, the team has a clear-cut responsibility with respect to the quality and productivity of the subassembly. The team experience shows that product quality and workers' productivity are improved and that the boredom and monotony, which characterize the paced assembly line, are reduced.

A very important side benefit of job enrichment and job enlargement is a reduction in effort and time required in future job retraining. When our industries gradually and unmistakably move from traditional manufacturing methods to computer assisted and automated manufacturing, the firms with teams of highly diverse and highly motivated workers will most likely excel and be most compatible.

Flexible work schedules and **flextime** are relatively new concepts in our industry. While flexible work schedules allow employees freedom to work whatever hours they prefer, flextime allows employees to work a fixed number of hours whenever they choose. The flexible work schedules enable the employees to work more or less hours than the traditional eight-hour workday schedule. With flextime, employees are allowed to arrive on the job as early as 6:30 a.m. and as late as 8:30 a.m. They may take up to two or more hours for lunch and are allowed to go home between, say, 3:30 and 5:30 p.m., with the understanding that the traditional eight-hour workday and five-day workweek are observed. Flextime has been successful in Europe and Japan and is highly desirable for working mothers. It works well for the service industry and some offices, but it creates some problems for factory work and where a team effort of a job is required.

The application of ergonomics and the consideration of human factors in design and in improving man-made systems are called **human factors engineering**. While the ergonomic scientists seek scientific knowledge about human characteristics, capabilities, and limitations, the human factors engineers integrate and apply this knowledge in the development of products and systems of all kinds. In work design, human factors engineering integrates physiological and anthropometric data in designing a work station. This includes selecting and designing tools, fixtures, and facilities; the arrangement of the work place; and the specifications of the work environment. There exist more human factors than the ones we have discussed in this section that need to be considered in job design.

8. REST ALLOWANCES FOR VARIOUS WORK CLASSES

Rest allowances are classified under constant allowances and variable allowances. Constant allowances are for personal and basic fatigue. Variable allowances are necessary to accommodate standing, abnormal position, use of muscular force for lifting, pulling or pushing based on weight, bad lighting, poor atmospheric conditions, close attention, noise level, mental strain, monotony, and tediousness. Approximate ranges for such allowances are summarized in Table 6.13.

Table 6.13: Rest Allowances

Type	Reason	Level	%
Constant	Personal		5
	Basic		4
Variable	Standing		2
	Position:	Awkward (bending)	2
		Very awkward (lying, stretching)	7
	Use of Force	0 – 5 pounds	0
		10 – 30 pounds (1% per 5 lbs.)	1 – 5
		31 – 50 pounds (2% per 5 lbs.)	7 – 13
		51 – 60 pounds	17
		61 – 70 pounds	22
	Light	Well below recommended level	2
		Quite inadequate	5
	Atmosphere		0 – 10
	Attention	Fine or exact work	2
		Very fine or very exacting	5
	Noise	Intermittent loud	2
		Intermittent very loud	5
		High pitched loud	5
	Mental Strain	Fairly complex process	1
		Complex or wide span of attention	4
		Very complex	5
	Monotony	Medium	1
		High	4
	Tediousness	Tedious	2
		Very tedious	5

9. LEAN MOTIONS AND LEAN USE OF STANDARDS

Frank Gilbreth developed a list of 17 elemental motions with the purpose of studying work and improving it. Gilbreth felt that, by eliminating unnecessary motions and training workers to perform only necessary motions, a job can be standardized. From a lean manufacturing standpoint only very few of these 17 motions add value. The value-added motions are: assemble (A), disassemble (DA), and use (U).

Initially, when work standards were set and used, workers were encouraged to beat the standards and were rewarded for producing more work than what the standard asked for. Special pay scales were developed to encourage workers to produce more. This individual operator efficiency, which focuses on maximizing the output of each individual operator without regard for the effect on the total system, is not advocated by lean principles. It results in overproduction, excess inventory, obsolescence, poor quality, and ultimately in customer dissatisfaction.

Setting work standards and developing lean standard work methods are necessary to balance the workload for each operation to the actual demand rate (or takt time). This will eliminate overproduction, excess inventory, and optimize the total system's performance.

Non-Lean: Individual Operator

Focus: maximize output of operation without regard for the effect on the total system

Lean: Standard Work Methods & Line Balance

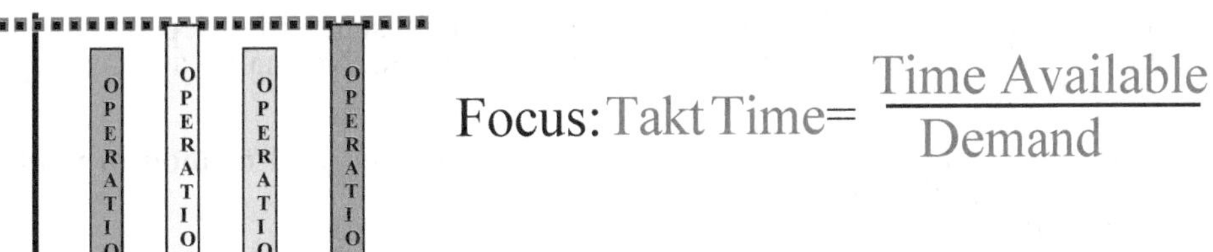

Figure 6.1 Lean versus Non-Lean Purpose for Setting Work Standards

10. GLOSSARY AND SUMMARY OF METHODS

Calendar Method – The calendar method can be used when identical or a few different jobs are performed over a long period of time and when approximately each day the same amount of time is spent working. This method generates a standard by dividing the total amount of time spent on the same job by the total number of units produced.

Direct Time Study – Direct time study consists of various methods that enable the company to set standards in a direct way. These methods are the calendar method, the TV or movie method, the electronic circuit breaking method, and the stop watch method.

Electronic Circuit Braking Method – The electronic circuit breaking method uses a flashlight battery and target, together with a strip chart recorder, to record the time when an operator touches a target.

Ergonomics – Ergonomics is the science of studying the human capability and limitations in performing strenuous manual, motor, and mental tasks under various conditions.

Flexible Work Schedules – Flexible work schedules allow employees the freedom to work whatever hours they prefer.

Flextime – Flextime allows employees to work a fixed number of hours whenever they choose.

Human Engineering – Human engineering is the branch of ergonomics that is concerned with mental as well as motor tasks.

Human Factor Systems – Human factor systems deal with relationships between workers, machines, and the work environment and their effects on work performance and productivity.

Job Enlargement – Job enlargement is similar to job enrichment; here the workers do not get involved in planning, organizing, and controlling their work. Workers, however, get the opportunity of performing more similar tasks. This is often referred to as horizontal job improvement.

Job Enrichment – Through job enrichment, workers have the opportunity to increase their knowledge and skills, to take more responsibilities on the job, and to take pride in their work. Besides executing their jobs, they get involved in planning, organizing, and controlling their work. In the literature this is often referred to as vertical job improvement.

Predetermined Time Standards – Predetermined time standards divide manual work into fundamental motions that have established times. The overall time for the job is obtained by adding up the predetermined times of its motions. Popular predetermined systems are: motion time analysis (MTA), work factor system, elemental time standard, and methods time measurement (MTM).

Sample Size – The sample size, for the purpose of setting time standards, depends on the desired accuracy, the desired confidence, and the variability of the data. Normally, an accuracy of 5% and a confidence of 95% are used.

Stop Watch Method – The stop watch method is the most frequently used method in work study and measurement. The method consists of the following steps:

1. Prepare the job for time study
2. Find an experienced operator
3. Break down the job into work elements
4. Record the actual time over various cycles of the work elements
5. Observe and record performance ratings for each work element
6. When sufficient data is gathered, calculate the normal time for each work element:

   $$t_n = \text{Average Observed Time} \times \text{Performance Rating}$$

   Calculate the overall normal time: $T_n = \sum t_n$
7. Determine the allowance percentage for unavoidable delays.
8. Calculate the standard time: $T_s = \dfrac{T_n}{1 - \text{allowance}}$

TV or Movie Method – The TV or movie method suggests that a TV tape or movie is made while an operator is at work performing a repetitive job. By dividing the time period during which the tape was made by the overall production, one can come up with a time per unit estimate.

Work Sampling – The principle behind work sampling or occurrence sampling is that the number of observations is proportional to the amount of time spent in the working or idle state:

$$\text{Normal Time} = \frac{\begin{matrix}\text{total time} & \text{percentage of} & \text{average perf.} \\ \text{of study} \times & \text{time working} \times & \text{rating} \\ \text{in minutes} & \text{from sampling} & \text{in decimals}\end{matrix}}{\text{total number of pieces produced}}$$

Work Study – Work study is the systematic investigation and analysis of contemplated and present work systems and methods in order to formulate the most effective systems and methods for achieving necessary functions. It is also the establishment of measurement standards by which the work may be planned, scheduled, and controlled.

11. ACRONYMS

MTA Motion Time Analysis

MTM Methods Time Measurement

PTS Predetermined Time Standards

TMU Time Measurement Unit

12. REFERENCES

Bridger, R. S. *Introduction to Ergonomics*. New York: McGraw-Hill, Inc., 1995.

Cudney, E. and J.S.W. Fargher Jr. *Standard Work.* APICS Educational & Research Foundation, Inc. Chicago, IL. 2003.

Fein, M. *Wage Incentive Plans*. WM and ME Division Publication 2. Atlanta, GA: American Institute of Industrial Engineering, 1970.

Konz, S. *Work Design*. Columbus, OH: Grid Publishing, Inc., 1979.

Niebel, B. W. *Motion and Time Study*. Homewood, IL.: Irwin, 1993.

Reuter, V. G. "A Productivity Implementation Plan." *Industrial Management.* (September-October, 1980): p.1.

Savage, J. A. "Incentive Programs at Nucor Corporation - Employee Relations Geared to Productivity Improvement in a U. S. Company." *Three Day Seminar on KANBAN, Quality Control and Quality Management*, The Cambridge Corporation, April, 1983.

Wu, J. A. and Nesa L. Wu. "Productivity Management of Indirect Labour through Variable Measurement and Control." *International Journal of Operations and Production Management.* (Vol. 11, No.8, 1991).

13. REVIEW QUESTIONS

1. Since 1900, three different ways for measuring work have been developed. What are they called? Who developed them? Briefly describe them.
2. List and explain the various direct time study methods.

3. Briefly explain the sequence of operations necessary to properly establish a standard via the stop watch method.
4. When setting standards, what is meant by performance rating, work allowance, sample size, confidence, and accuracy?
5. Briefly explain how confidence, accuracy, and variability in data affect the sample size.
6. When are allowances used when setting standards?
7. What is the normal level of confidence and accuracy when used for setting work standards?
8. What are predetermined time standards?
9. What is a therblig? Who developed the concept of therbligs?
10. What is contained in the right-left hand chart? List some of the predetermined time standards that have been developed out of the pioneering workof Frank Gilbreth.
11. Of the predetermined time standards, which ones are the most popular ones? Briefly describe them.
12. What is the principle behind work sampling?
13. What do human factor systems deal with?
14. What is meant by ergonomics? What are its elements?
15. What is meant by work physiology and human engineering?
16. Describe the following terms: job enlargement, job enrichment, flexible work schedules, flextime, and group assembly. How do they improve productivity?
17. What motions are value-added motions?

14. PROBLEMS

Problem #1

A task was observed and timed for five repetitions. The times recorded (in minutes) were: 2.50, 2.60, 2.70, 2.40, and 2.30. The worker was rated performing at 90% of normal. The company used a 15% allowance for personal time, fatigue, etc. What is the average time, the normal time, and the standard time?

Problem #2 (Excel)

A portion of a time study observation sheet is shown below. The continuous method of stop watch timing was used. For each operation it is estimated that an operator has 420 minutes out of a 480-minute work day to apply to production.

The continuous stop watch time study yielded the following accumulated times (in seconds):

Element	1	2	3	4	5	Performance Rating
1	11	45	81	113	148	0.95
2	28	63	97	130	165	1.10
3	35	70	104	137	173	1.05

a) What is the normal time for this task?
b) What is the standard time for this task?
c) How many pieces will be produced in a standard hour?

Problem #3

Forty hours of observations were made during the work sampling of a machine operator who had to drill the holes in the main frame of an air breaker. During that forty-hour period, the work sampling results indicated that the operator was actually working 80% of the time, drilling a total of 280 main frames. His performance rating was judged to be 35% above normal. The work allowance for this job is 10%.

a) If an accuracy of 5% was desired at a confidence level of 95%, how many observations had to be made during this 40-hour period?
b) What is the normal time?
c) What is the idle time?
d) What is the standard time?

Problem #4 (Excel)

A work measurement study of a bank teller's operation was concerned with the time required to count out $100. The $100 consisted of the following: six $10 bills, seven $5 bills, and five $1 bills. Before the work measurement study began the following work elements were identified:

- Element #1: count the $10 bills
- Element #2: count the $5 bills
- Element #3: count the $1 bills
- Element #4: count total
- Element #5: give the money to the customer

The continuous stop watch time study yielded the following accumulated times (in minutes):

Element	1	2	3	4	5	6	7	8	9	10
#1	0.12	0.75	1.41	2.05	2.70	3.46	4.07	4.71	5.37	6.18
#2	0.27	0.90	1.55	2.19	2.85	3.60	4.23	4.86	5.52	6.33
#3	0.37	1.02	1.64	2.31	2.96	3.68	4.33	4.98	5.65	6.42
#4	0.57	1.21	1.85	2.51	3.15	3.88	4.54	5.18	6.00	6.62
#5	0.64	1.29	1.93	2.58	3.23	3.95	4.60	5.25	6.06	6.69

The following performance ratings were assigned to the above work elements:

- Element #1: 110%
- Element #2: 105%
- Element #3: 100%
- Element #4: 120%
- Element #5: 90%

a) What is the normal time for the above data?
b) Assuming an allowance of 15%, what is the standard time for the above data?

Problem #5 (Excel)

Consider a Fuse Holder Assembly. Each of the following work elements (I, II, and III) is a grouping of sub-elements/tasks performed on each of the three jigs/fixtures (a, b, c) used to assemble the Fuse Holder Assembly. The specific elements are composed of the following:

Elements	Tasks	Jig	Products
I	1-12	a	#090 Base Assembly
II	13-29	b	#091 Contact Assembly
III	30-64	c	#100 Fuse Holder Assembly

The stop watch methodwas used to collect data for this assembly. The initial results for the first five observations are as follows (times are in minutes):

Element	1	2	3	4	5
I	0.3841	0.3841	0.4008	0.3841	0.3006
II	0.6179	0.6179	0.6012	0.6346	0.6680
III	0.8851	1.0020	1.0855	1.0020	1.0354

In order to ensure appropriate accuracy and confidence, an additional time study resulted in 14 additional observations for work element #I and 4 additional observations for work element #III. The times in minutes are as follows:

Work Element #I

0.3006; 0.3507; 0.4342; 0.3674; 0.3674; 0.3674; 0.3841; 0.4175; 0.4342; 0.3674; 0.3841; 0.4008; 0.4008; and 0.3707.

Work Element #III

1.0688; 1.0354; 1.0521; and 1.0187

a) Use initial data to calculate the normal time and the standard time. The performance ratings are as follows:
   - Work Element I: 85%
   - Work Element II: 105%
   - Work Element III: 95%

   Work allowances for this type of work add up to 10%.

b) Verify the need for having more observations for work element I and III, assuming a z value of 2 and an error of 5% of the average.

c) Use all data to calculate the normal and standard time.

Problem #6 (Excel)

The following data represent the time study data for the manufacturing of a stainless steel top collar for hydraulic filtering systems. Initially, ten observations were made. The job was broken down into the following four standardized work elements:

#1: get a stainless steel top collar and load it into the NC machine
#2: push the buttons to start the machine and to machine the first side
#3: take the part out and to use an air chuck to blow away loose chips
#4: turn the part over to its other side and to machine the second side

Consider the following 10 observations with times in minutes:

Element	1	2	3	4	5	6	7	8	9	10
#1	0.21	0.22	0.22	0.21	0.24	0.24	0.25	0.23	0.22	0.25
#2	7.17	7.18	7.17	7.16	7.17	7.17	7.17	7.18	7.18	7.17
#3	0.07	0.08	0.09	0.07	0.08	0.09	0.08	0.09	0.07	0.09
#4	1.96	1.93	1.92	1.91	1.92	1.92	1.93	1.92	1.92	1.93

a) Calculate the normal time using the following performance ratings:

   Work element #1: 90%
   Work element #2: 100%
   Work element #3: 90%
   Work element #4: 100%

b) Consider the following allowances in establishing the standard time for this job:

Basic fatigue allowance	4%	Standard allowance	2%
Weight lifted (10 lbs.)	1%	Fairly fine work	1%
Intermittent loud	2%	Fairly complex process	1%
Tediousness	2%		

Problem #7 (Excel)

A work study was performed to set standards for the assembly of a remote control unit. The work was broken down into the following 7 work elements:

Work element #1:	reach for the base and putting it on jig A
Work element #2:	reach for the electrical panel and placing it on the base
Work element #3:	take the screws and securing the electrical panel to the base
Work element #4:	place both the negative and positive cables on their respective slots
Work element #5:	reach for the cover and putting it in place
Work element #6:	use the two remaining screws to tie the cover to the base
Work element #7:	cover the battery compartment with its cap

The following 10 observations were made for this job (times in seconds):

Element	1	2	3	4	5	6	7	8	9	10
#1	1.23	0.91	0.94	1.04	0.77	1.03	0.82	1.60	1.41	1.52
#2	2.59	2.03	1.86	2.28	2.31	1.98	3.22	2.22	2.40	2.53
#3	39.35	39.78	36.10	42.54[2]	37.78	36.89	38.72	36.88	45.03[2]	42.56
#4	6.31	4.16	6.04	6.09	6.96	7.26	5.24	7.47	4.28	4.81
#5	5.65[3]	3.78	5.32[3]	3.22	4.32	5.63[3]	2.26	3.74	2.48	3.19
#6	22.28	17.06	17.24	20.50	21.27	19.87	23.47[1]	20.94	18.83	23.03[1]
#7	2.22	3.38	3.72	2.50	2.00	2.54	2.78	1.82	2.13	1.88

[1] dropped screw, [2] mishandled screw driver, [3] mishandled work piece

Use the following performance ratings:

Work element #1:	0.95
Work element #2:	1.05
Work element #3:	0.90
Work element #4:	0.95
Work element #5:	0.85
Work element #6:	0.95
Work element #7:	1.05

a) Calculate the normal time.
b) Calculate the standard time (what would be a reasonable allowance for this type of a job?).

Problem #8 (Excel)

Develop a table in Excel that generates the sample sizes for various combinations of proportions (p = 0.01, 0.02, 0.03, …, 0.47, 0.48, 049, 05) versus various error levels (e = 0.01, 0.015, 0.02, 0.025,….., 0.045, 0.05). Use a confidence level of 95% (z = 1.96).

Without making additional calculations can you look up in your table the sample size for p = 0.80 and an allowable error of 0.03?

Chapter 7

LOGISTICS OF LOCATION ANALYSIS

1. INTRODUCTION

The design of a supply chain requires proper location of plants and warehouses. In locating these facilities, one must analyze the logistics of the company: "the art and science of obtaining, producing, and distributing material and product in the proper place and in proper quantities,"[1] from suppliers to the end-users, the customers. This chapter does not discuss how to transport or move goods from suppliers to facilities, or from facilities to customers, but rather how to best locate facilities so as to minimize both tangible and intangible costs. Decisions on where to locate facilities and warehouses must be based on cost factors, speed of delivery, flexibility of ever-changing demand, quality of work, reliability of the supply chain to track inventory, the carbon footprint of manufacturing and transporting, and many other characteristics.

Facilities location decisions are made very infrequently. However, since factors affecting facilities location are constantly changing, top management regularly wonders whether its facility should be altered at the present location or moved to another location. Expansion, decentralization or relocation, and diversification are situations which lead to decisions concerned with facilities location analysis. Expansion is considered when one has outgrown the present plant and facilities. Rather than enlarging the present facilities, management may prefer to establish a new facility somewhere else. When there is a need to meet competition in an emerging market, or when management wishes to get away from industrialized areas because of labor or union problems, decentralization or relocation might be the solution. Companies that wish to diversify may decide to buy other companies, or they may decide to produce new products requiring different facilities.

2. FACTORS AFFECTING FACILITIES LOCATION

2.1 Transportation Availability and Cost

This factor applies to both incoming materials and outgoing finished products. The transportation cost normally consists of the terminal cost at the point of origin (T_O), the terminal cost at the point of destination (T_d), and the line-haul cost (H).

$$C_{transportation} = T_O + T_d + H$$

Since both terminal costs (the one at the point of origin and the one at the destination) are affected by the weight, the size, and the type of commodity, the overall transportation cost may not be linearly related to the distance of transportation.

Transportation availability and the time required to reach the market, the raw materials, and supplies are equally important. For example, transportation availability was the primary reason why the steel industry

[1] *APICS Dictionary*, 13th edition, The Educational Society for Resource Management, page 81.

originally located in the Great Lakes region, Pennsylvania, and Ohio. This factor is of great importance to mining, quarrying, heavy manufacturing, and warehousing.

2.2 Labor Cost and Labor Supply

Here we are concerned with the availability of the potential labor force, local wage rates, and labor and union relations. The quality of the labor force—skilled or unskilled—is also important.

The high cost of doing business, particularly because of an uneven single business tax, high unemployment insurance, workman's compensation, health care cost, high wage and salary structures, and a regulatory climate that places uncompetitive costs on business, were some of the reasons cited for the negative business climate in Michigan in the early- and mid- 1980s. Together with a poor economy, these same problems have resulted in the present high unemployment rate in Michigan. Michigan's average wage rate is the highest in the nation and the state is dominated by high-wage-paying industries. Should a Michigan automotive company wish to relocate to Texas, for example, it could have a competitive advantage, since Texas workers receive less in wages than the national average, though the state is dominated by high-wage-paying industries.

Figure 7.1 shows the relationship of a state's industrial mix (manufacturing industry only) and the prevailing wage rates (labor cost for blue color workers) for that state.

The availability of labor and its cost are factors that are of extreme importance to light manufacturing and customer services for-profit organizations. They are also important, but to a lesser degree, in mining, quarrying, heavy manufacturing, warehousing, retailing, local government services, health, and emergency services. Labor and union relations need to be reckoned with in mining, quarrying, and heavy industry, and light manufacturing. The degree of unionization is also becoming more important in warehousing, retailing, and other service industries, such as health and emergency services.

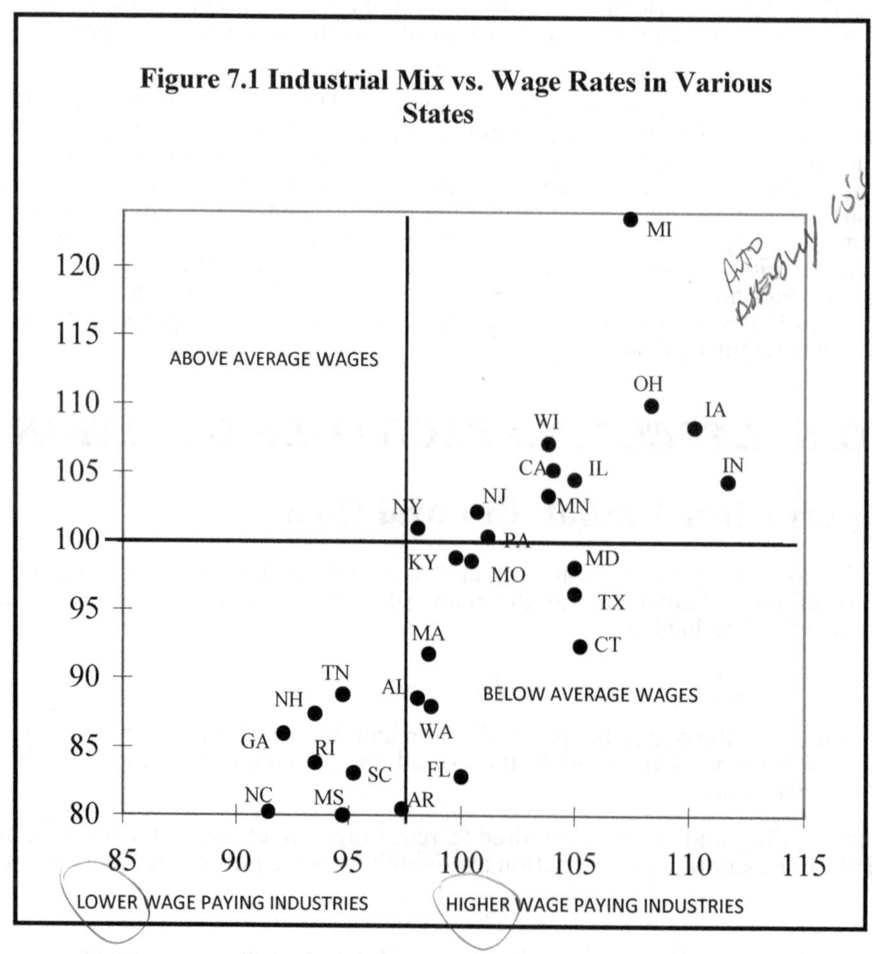

2.3 Capital Costs

Capital cost items are land cost, construction cost, and equipment cost. Within the U.S.A., capital cost factors have become less important in recent years when selecting a region, a specific community, or a site. What is more important than the land cost is the size of the piece of property. "Is the site large enough for possible future expansion?" is often asked when selecting the specific site for the firm.

2.4 Operating and Materials/Supplies Costs

Utilities cost for power, fuel, water, and waste disposal is a very important factor in mining, quarrying, and heavy manufacturing. Present and future availability of such utilities, their quality and service, are equally important. The availability of utilities and their costs are factors that are less important in warehousing, retailing, customer services for profit, health and emergency services, and, most of all, service companies.

An Example: GM's Saturn Location

The importance of utilities, their quality, service, and availability, to the GM-proposed Saturn plant was described in a metropolitan Detroit newspaper on March 31, 1985, under the heading "Saturn Needs Healthy Utility." It mentioned that one of GM's criteria for the plant site was the need for service by a financially healthy utility system. GM did not wish to build the plant in an area where a utility company has large amounts of capital invested in facilities that have been abandoned, or are about to be abandoned. GM expressed in a document it had given to the states who were competing for Saturn that it was looking for a location that could provide the company with sufficient power several years from now.

2.5 Tax Rates and Insurance Rates

Tax rates, assessment practices, and insurance rates for workman's compensation, property, inventory, and liability are all very important operating expenses.

Two Examples: Mercedes and Quantum Learning get state tax credit to expand

In *The Ann Arbor News,* Stephanie Murray reported on March 17, 2009, that two companies have been attracted to the Ann Arbor area because of state tax credits: the luxury automaker Mercedes-Benz and Quantum Learning Technologies.

The $10 million hybrid technology research and development center that Mercedes-Benz planned to build in Washtenaw County would create 223 jobs over a period of ten years. It was announced by the Michigan Economic Growth Authority that Mercedes-Benz will receive for this project a tax credit of $7.5 million over a period of ten years. Because of the tax break and available experienced engineers, Mercedes-Benz chose to build its 65,000-square feet facility in Washtenaw County, rather than a competing site in South Carolina. Other factors that affected the location decision were Ann Arbor's talent pool, the University of Michigan, and the proximity to the U.S. Environmental Protection Agency emission lab.

Quantum Learning planned to invest $930,000 to launch its first computer game for the consumer market from its local office in Ann Arbor, rather than from a location in Illinois or Texas, thanks to the tax break. At that time the company employed 11 people, but planned to add another 47 jobs over a period of five years. These jobs would pay an average of $63,000 and would most likely include marketing, sales, software, and Web site development work.

2.6 Miscellaneous Intangible Factors

Other intangible factors are:

- Climate (such as process-required, personal preference, or environmental impact)
- National defense (dispersion of industry related to the national defense)
- Living facilities (residential housing, schools, churches, recreation facilities, etc.)
- Community talent pool and proximity to higher learning institutions
- Customers and constituents

Since the 1970s, the following factors have become very important for manufacturing companies: water/ air/ noise pollution, energy availability and cost, all sorts of government regulations, and the carbon footprint for manufacturing and transport.

Because of the ever-changing economic climate and variables, firms have found it difficult to perform proper location analysis. Often decisions have been made with incomplete information, resulting in costly relocations down the road. This is what many U.S. firms are experiencing as they are slowly bringing their operations home from China.

3. CLASSICAL FACILITIES LOCATION DECISION PROCESS

Coming up with a proper location for one's facility normally involves a sequence of decisions. First, a general region is selected by management. A general region could be a county, a state, several states, or a country. Factors affecting the regional location decision are:

- cost and availability of transportation
- cost and supply of labor
- capital cost
- cost and availability of utilities
- cost and availability of materials and supplies
- customers and constituents

Soon after a general region is selected, management will pick an appropriate community in which to locate. In addition to all regional factors, the following factors are likewise considered:

- taxes and zoning
- insurance rates for workman's compensation
- property inventory and liability
- banking services
- community attitude
- pollution and government regulations

Because climate is uniform within most regions, it is not a factor when selecting a specific community.

Within the chosen community a specific plant site must be considered. At this time, the following factors are most important:

- transportation facilities
- proximity to highway, waterway or railway, and (major) airport
- availability of water, gas, electricity, and sewers
- efficient waste water treatment facilities
- industrial waste disposal
- zoning restrictions in industrial districts
- soil characteristics and bearing loads
- drainage
- space for expansion
- land cost
- existing buildings and services

Table 7.1 summarizes sample factors for a facility location decision. The process of selecting a location can be quite time consuming and complex. The regional/community/site evaluation sequence can be looping and backtracking. Often a site in one community could be compared with a site in another community, before a final decision can be made.

Table 7.1: Sample Factors Affecting Facility Location Decision

Factors	Regional	Community	Site
Transportation Cost & Availability	*	*	*
Labor Cost and Supply			
- labor force availability	*	*	
- local wage rates	*	*	
- labor & union relations	*		
Capital Cost			
- land cost	*	*	*
- land size			*
- construction cost	*	*	
- equipment cost	*	*	
Operating & Materials Cost			
- utilities	*	*	*
- taxes		*	
- zoning			*
- insurance		*	
- materials & supplies	*	*	
Climate	*		
Banking Services		*	
Community Attitude		*	*
Customers & Constituents	*	*	*
Pollution Relations		*	*
Government Regulations		*	

4. *FACILITIES LOCATION METHODS - AN OVERVIEW*

There are many different types of location problems. When one wishes to locate one facility that will not interact with the company's other facilities, then we are dealing with a **single facilities location problem**. Many methods have been developed and utilized to determine the preferred single plant location for a factory or warehouse, for a government facility or a hospital, or even for an electric power plant. Such type of location problems are concerned with multiple criteria such as labor cost, labor supply, unionization problems, wage structure, taxes, community attitude, building cost, and many others.

Decision tree models can be an important tool in facilities location decision making when the investment is large and, in many cases, distinctions among the final communities under consideration are not great. In other words, decision trees are used when no town is either clearly attractive or clearly unattractive due to uncertainty of possible important events. While the decision tree method only takes tangible data into consideration, there are other methods that allow us to incorporate both tangible and intangible data such as the point rating systems, the relative merits method, and the analytical hierarchy process. This method is illustrated in section 5 of this chapter.

The point rating systems are widely used for locating both manufacturing and service companies. These methods come in a variety of formats, but are all additive methods. One version of the point rating method is explained by the use of an example in section 6 of this chapter.

When it is important that all factors have relatively high ratings for the alternative selection, then the **relative merits method** is preferred over the point rating system. In other words, a multiplicative model of the relative merits method is more appropriate than the additive scoring method of the point rating system. This method is illustrated with an example in section 7 of this chapter.

The **analytical hierarchy process** (AHP) can deal with both tangible and intangible criteria simultaneously. As is the case with the other methods, the first step in the AHP is to determine what criteria will be used in making the decision as to which location would provide the best potential benefit to the organization. Several people, called judges, may be involved in the selection of these appropriate criteria. The second step in the AHP is to find appropriate locations that may be beneficial to the organization. In case of a possible relocation, it is essential to include in the list of appropriate locations the present location as well.

The AHP is based on a "trade off" concept that is accomplished by structuring the problem and assigning weights in the form of a series of pair-wise comparison matrices. The modeling process is carried out in three phases, namely 1) structuring the problem, 2) assessing of weights (in the form of pair wise comparison matrices), and 3) analyzing.

The AHP is perhaps the most powerful and accurate procedure for single plant location analysis. It can handle many alternatives at one time (which is not the case with the relative merits method). It can handle complex situations where different weights are assigned to the same factors by various people involved in the decision making process, because judges' opinions may vary when determining how important a factor is. Also, a weight could be assigned to the judges' authority in the decision making process. For instance, the president of the firm may have more say than the vice-president. Therefore, the president's opinion can be weighted at 0.65 and the vice-president's opinion at 0.35.

When a new facility may affect existing shipping patterns and production levels of present facilities, then we are dealing with a **multiple facilities location problem**. In this case one usually formulates a production distribution network of facilities and distribution centers with the objective of minimizing variable cost. The **transportation method** is often used for such an analysis. It requires all of the following:

1) Defining all possible alternate locations (the alternatives or proposed new locations of the model)
2) Defining all unit variable costs for all facilities/distribution combinations for all present and alternate locations
3) Using a transportation method to solve for the optimal allocation (the optimal allocation shows for all facilities the best allocation of produced goods to markets at an overall minimum yearly variable cost) for each individual alternative (proposed new location), together with all existing locations
4) Performing the final payoff analysis of the alternatives incorporating all fixed costs

The transportation method only uses tangible data such as: labor cost, material cost, shipping cost, variable burden, projected demand in various demand centers, and capacity at various existing and proposed facilities.

Section 8 of this chapter illustrates how Microsoft Excel's Solver function can be used to find the best allocation for goods to markets.

5. DECISION TREE MODEL

A schematic model, called a decision tree, can be employed to represent a decision problem visually. When applied to location analysis the tree shows all **alternatives or decisions** (the possible locations to choose from), all **events or chance nodes** (factors affecting the facilities location choices), **probabilities** associated with possible state of nature of uncertain events, and the overall **payoff values** (operating costs).

Rectangles, such as the one marked **A** in Figure 7.2, represent the decision points or the decision nodes. Here management will have to make a decision. If this decision point is imbedded in the tree, then management will elect to take one, and only one, of the paths that lead through the tree. Circular nodes, or chance nodes, represent points at which uncertain events occur. The **expected payoffs** at the chance nodes depend on the probabilities assigned to the various states of nature and the payoff values.

The **rollback updating method** is used to evaluate a decision tree: it will determine which decision or decisions are preferred. Simply defined, the rollback updating procedure means moving backward through the decision tree, from the rightmost point in the tree to the leftmost point by calculating the expected payoffs at chance or event nodes and by choosing the most favorable course of action at each decision node.

Building a decision tree and finding the best solution are illustrated in the following example.

An Example: Locating a Manufacturing Company

An entrepreneur, who is ready to make a large investment in a plant, has identified two possible locations to manufacture his ladders: location A and location B. He recognizes that the distinction between these two communities is not great. In other words, no town is either clearly attractive or clearly unattractive.

Established wage patterns, local raw materials, and tax concessions are the uncertain factors that the entrepreneur needs to consider in making his decision.

The uncertainties for town A include:

- Whether or not the company will be faced with a national or local wage pattern: research has shown that the company has a 65% chance of having to deal with a national wage pattern and a 35% chance of having to deal with a local wage pattern
- Whether or not local materials will be usable: there is a 70% chance that the local materials will be unusable and a 30% chance that they are usable
- Whether or not the company will receive a tax concession from the community: the entrepreneur speculates that he has a 60% chance that he will receive a tax concession, or a 40% chance that he may not get a tax concession

A combination of the above three events, each having two possible outcomes, leads to 8 (2x2x2) possible operating costs as estimated by the entrepreneur.

Since town B does not offer any concession there are only two uncertainties to consider:

- Whether or not the company will be faced with a national or local wage pattern: research has shown that the company has a 60% chance of having to deal with a national wage pattern and a 40% chance of having to deal with a local wage pattern
- Whether or not local materials will be usable: there is a 90% chance that the local materials will be unusable and a 10% chance that they are usable

These two events, each having two possible outcomes, yield 4 (2x2) possible operating costs.

Figure 7.2 shows the decision tree that represents this location problem. It starts with one decision node, node **A**, and has several event or chance nodes (1 through 10). To the right of the tree you find twelve estimated operating costs.

Finding the location that minimizes the expected operating cost is the goal of this location problem.

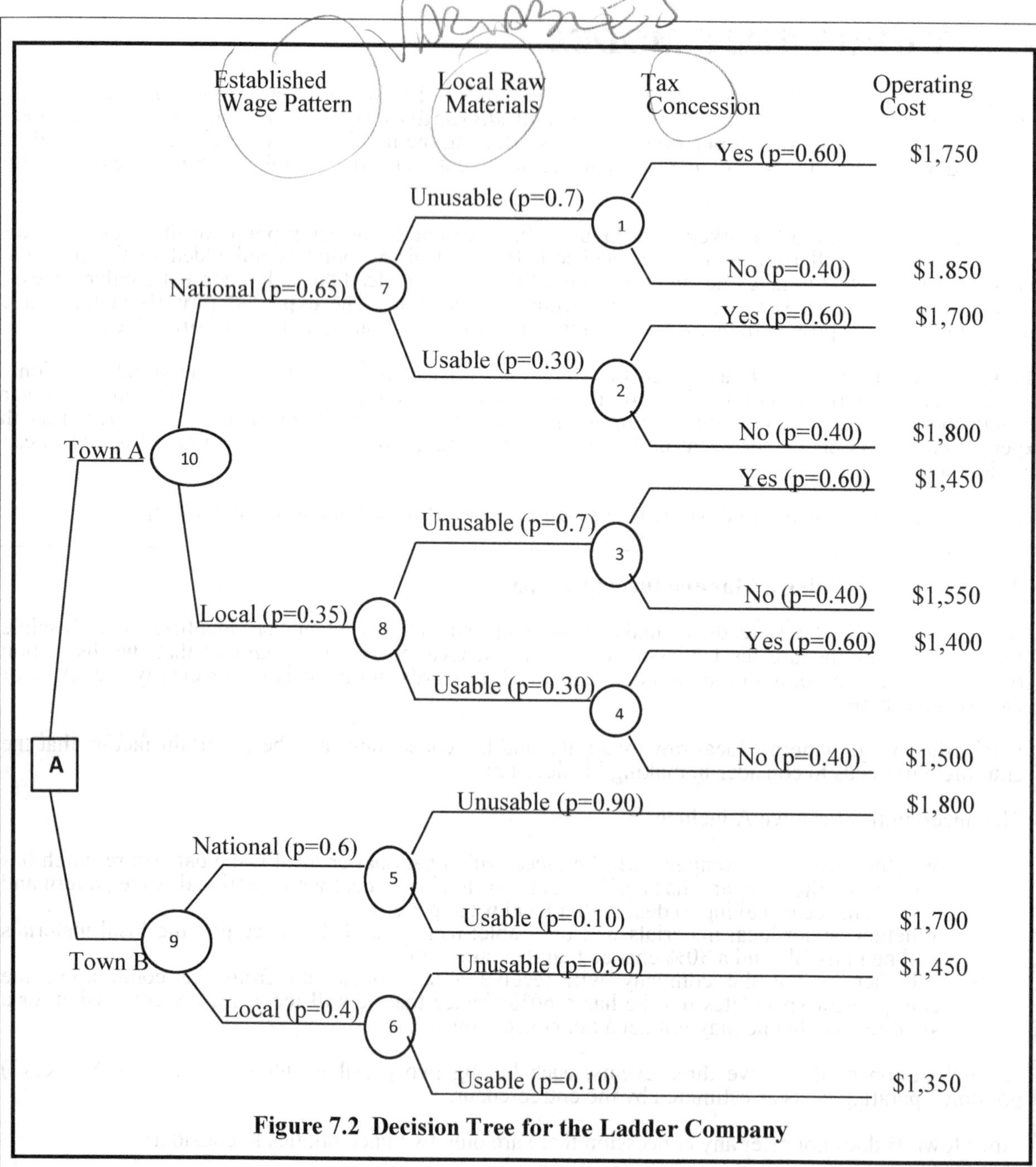

Figure 7.2 Decision Tree for the Ladder Company

Moving backward through the tree the analysis consists of the following steps:

Step 1: Chance nodes 1, 2, 3, 4, 5, and 6 can be evaluated in any order, calculating expected operating costs:

At node #1: ($1,750)(0.60) + ($1,850)(0.40) = $1,790
At node #2: ($1,700)(0.60) + ($1,800)(0.40) = $1,740
At node #3: ($1,450)(0.60) + ($1,550)(0.40) = $1,490
At node #4: ($1,400)(0.60) + ($1,500)(0.40) = $1,440
At node #5: ($1,800)(0.90) + ($1,700)(0.10) = $1,790
At node #6: ($1,450)(0.90) + ($1,350)(0.10) = $1,440

Step 2: Now chance nodes 7, 8, and 9 can be evaluated, using the above calculated expected operating costs:

At node #7: (\$1,790)(0.70) + (\$1,740)(0.30) = \$1,775

At node #8: (\$1,490)(0.70) + (\$1,440)(0.30) = \$1,475
At node #9: (\$1,790)(0.60) + (\$1,440)(0.40) = \$1,650

Step 3: Now node 10 can be evaluated using the expected values calculated for nodes #7 and #8:

At node #10: (\$1,775)(0.65) + (\$1,475)(0.35) = \$1,670

Step 4: Making the decision. Select the path with the smallest expected payoff, as calculated in nodes #9 and #10: therefore Town B must be selected.

As the rollback updating method is used one normally shows the calculations in the tree, as shown in Figure 7.3.

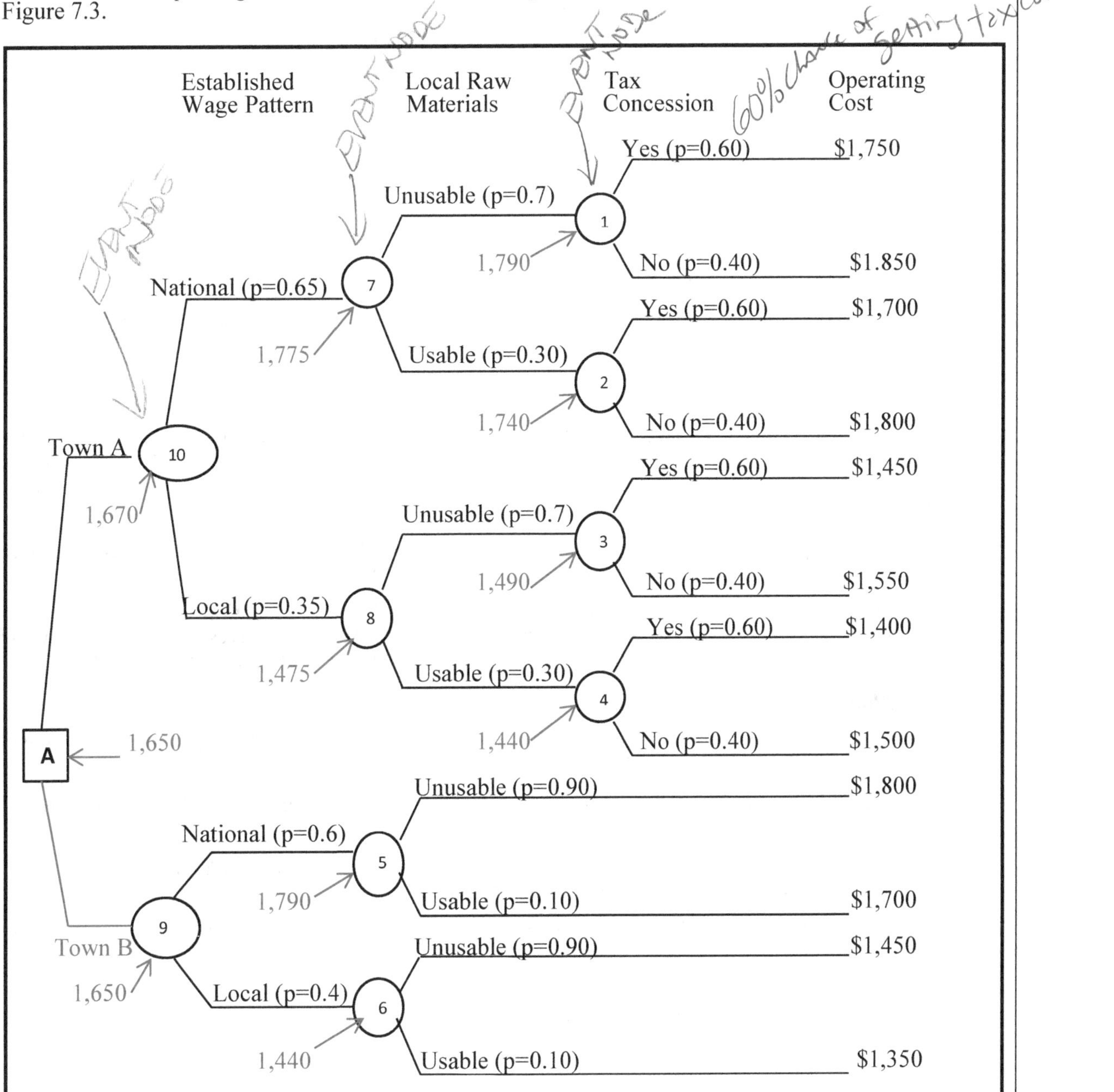

Established Wage Pattern
Local Raw Materials
Tax Concession
Operating Cost
A
1,650
Town A
1,670
10
National (p=0.65)
1,775
7
Unusable (p=0.7)
1,790
1
Yes (p=0.60) \$1,750
No (p=0.40) \$1.850
Usable (p=0.30)
1,740
2
Yes (p=0.60) \$1,700
No (p=0.40) \$1,800
Local (p=0.35)
1,475
8
Unusable (p=0.7)
1,490
3
Yes (p=0.60) \$1,450
No (p=0.40) \$1,550
Usable (p=0.30)
1,440
4
Yes (p=0.60) \$1,400
No (p=0.40) \$1,500
Town B
1,650
9
National (p=0.6)
1,790
5
Unusable (p=0.90) \$1,800
Usable (p=0.10) \$1,700
Local (p=0.4)
1,440
6
Unusable (p=0.90) \$1,450
Usable (p=0.10) \$1,350

Figure 7.3 Decision Tree for the Ladder Company

6. POINT RATING SYSTEM

Point rating systems are widely used for single facility location problems. One of the various types of point rating systems is presented here. In this method, variable integer weights are assigned to each location factor i (W_i) and relative weights are calculated (R_i). Each location (j) is then rated by a common point scale for each factor ($P_{i,j}$). The location factor value ($V_{i,j}$) is then obtained by multiplying the location rating for each factor ($P_{i,j}$) by its relative weight (R_i):

$$V_{i,j} = R_i \times P_{i,j}$$

Where:
- i = the ith factor
- j = the jth location
- $V_{i,j}$ = value of the ith factor for location j
- R_i = relative weight assigned to the ith factor
- $P_{i,j}$ = point rate of the ith factor for location j (10 being the most preferred, highest value that can be assigned to any site)

The sum of these resulting location values are then calculated (S_j) for each location.

$$S_j = \sum_{i=1}^{w} V_{i,j}$$

The location with the largest S value is the preferred one.

If correctly assigned, the actual weights (W_i) rather than the relative weights (R_i) can be used to calculate the factor value ($V_{i,j}$)

Managing Intangible Data:

When assigning point values for intangible factors, a point value of 10 should only be assigned if we cannot imagine a better outcome. In the example that follows, a point value of ten (10) is assigned to location Y for community attitude towards the industry because the folks in that location expressed an overwhelming interest in having the company locate there (the reception just could not be better).

Furthermore, if for a particular factor, point values of ten (10) and five (5) have been assigned to different locations, then these point values reflect a two (2) to one (1) relative value of importance.

Weights also reflect relative importance. In our example that follows, the location factor "availability of labor" receives a weight of one (1) and the location factor "schools" receives a weight of five (5). Therefore the factor "schools" is five (5) times more important than the factor "availability of labor."

Managing Tangible Data:

For each tangible factor, cost data must be transformed into point values and appropriate weights must be given to each factor. This is done using the following steps:

Step 1: For each factor assign 10 points to the lowest cost site. For the example that follows we have thus assigned 10 as follows:

For "yearly manufacturing cost": 10 points are assigned to locations Y and Z.
For "yearly freight cost": 10 points are assigned to location X.

Step 2: For each ith factor, calculate equivalent point values for all j locations by using the following formula:

$$P_{i,j} = \frac{10 \times \min(C_{i,1}, \ldots\ldots, C_{i,n})}{C_{i,j}} \quad \text{for all } j \text{ locations: 1 through } n$$

For the example that follows this is calculated as follows:

Factor 1: Manufacturing cost $P_{1,j} = \dfrac{10 \times \min(C_{1,x}, C_{1,y}, C_{1,z})}{C_{1,j}}$ for j = locations x, y and z

Factor 2: Freight cost $P_{2,j} = \dfrac{10 \times \min(C_{2,x}, C_{2,y}, C_{2,z})}{C_{2,j}}$ for j = locations x, y and z

For the yearly manufacturing cost: $\min(C_{1,x}, C_{1,y}, C_{1,z}) = \min(20,15,15) = 15$

$$P_{1,x} = \frac{10 \times \min(20,15,15)}{20} = \frac{10 \times 15}{20} = 7.5 \qquad P_{1,y} = \frac{10 \times \min(20,15,15)}{15} = \frac{10 \times 15}{15} = 10$$

$$P_{1,z} = \frac{10 \times \min(20,15,15)}{15} = \frac{10 \times 15}{15} = 10$$

For the yearly freight cost: $\min(C_{2,x}, C_{2,y}, C_{2,z}) = \min(4,6,5) = 4$

$$P_{2,x} = \frac{10 \times \min(4,6,5)}{4} = \frac{10 \times 4}{4} = 10 \qquad P_{2,y} = \frac{10 \times \min(4,6,5)}{6} = \frac{10 \times 4}{6} = 6.7$$

$$P_{2,z} = \frac{10 \times \min(4,6,5)}{5} = \frac{10 \times 4}{5} = 8$$

Step 3: When assigning weights to each of the cost factors, they must reflect the relative importance of the cost factors. One way of establishing these weights is by adding the cost values for each factor. In the example that follows, the following weights are calculated for each cost factor:

Yearly Manufacturing cost: 20 + 15 + 15 = 50
Yearly Freight cost: 4 + 6 + 5 = 15

Procedure for Identifying the Best Location Using the Point Rating System

Step 1: Define the weights for both tangible and intangible factors. These weights are normally given as data for the intangible factors. They need to be calculated for the tangible factors, by adding up the cost values at each location.

Step 2: Determine the relative weights for each set of tangible and intangible factors.

Step 3: For each tangible factor calculate the point values of the cost elements at each location. This is done by the use of the "min" function as explained above.

Step 4: For each factor and each location multiply the relative factor weight with the point value to calculate the weighted point values.

Step 5: For the tangible set and intangible set of weighted point values, calculate for each location the total of the weighted point values.

Step 6: For each location, add the tangible and intangible totals obtained in step 5, while assigning proper weights that are reflecting the relative importance of the tangible versus intangible factors.

This procedure is illustrated with the following example and all calculations are done, using Excel.

An Example: Locating a Specialty Furniture Manufacturing Company

A very successful Irish specialty furniture manufacturing company wishes to expand its business, while capturing a new market in England. The owners have identified three possible locations (X, Y, and Z) and have collected the data as shown in Tables 7.2 and 7.3.

Table 7.2: Intangible Data for the Specialty Furniture Manufacturing Company

Location Factors	Weight	Point Value Location X	Point Value Location Y	Point Value Location Z
1. Community Attitude (COM-A)	2	3	10	6
2. Water Availability (W-A)	2	5	2	5
3. Availability of Labor (A-L)	1	1	5	9
4. Availability of Transportation (A-CTR)	2	1	10	2
5. Cultural Attributes (CUL-A)	3	4	2	5
6. Schools (SCH)	5	6	1	4
7. Labor Climate (L-CL)	4	10	2	5

Table 7.3: Tangible Cost Data (x100K) for the Specialty Furniture Manufacturing Company

Location Factors	Cost at Location X	Cost at Location Y	Cost at Location Z
1. Yearly Manufacturing Cost	20	15	15
2. Yearly Freight Cost	4	6	5

Excel is used to find the best location. Figure 7.4 shows the tangible and intangible data, while Figure 7.5 shows the calculations and results.

Chapter 7, Point Rating Method

Location Analysis for the Tangible Factors

Factors		Relative Weights	Location X Cost 100k	Location X Point Value	Location X Weighted Value	Location Y Cost 100k	Location Y Point Value	Location Y Weighted Value	Location Z Cost 100k	Location Z Point Value	Location Z Weighted Value
Manufacturing			20			15			15		
Freight			4			6			5		
				TOTAL:			TOTAL:			TOTAL:	

Location Analysis for the Intangible Factors

Factors	Weights	Relative Weights		Location X Point Value	Location X Weighted Value		Location Y Point Value	Location Y Weighted Value		Location Z Point Value	Location Z Weighted Value
COM-A	2			3			10			6	
W-A	2			5			2			5	
A-L	1			1			5			9	
A-CTr	2			1			10			2	
CUL-A	3			4			2			5	
SCH	5			6			1			4	
L-CL	4			10			2			5	
				TOTAL:			TOTAL:			TOTAL	

Figure 7.4 Data for the Specialty Furniture Manufacturing Company

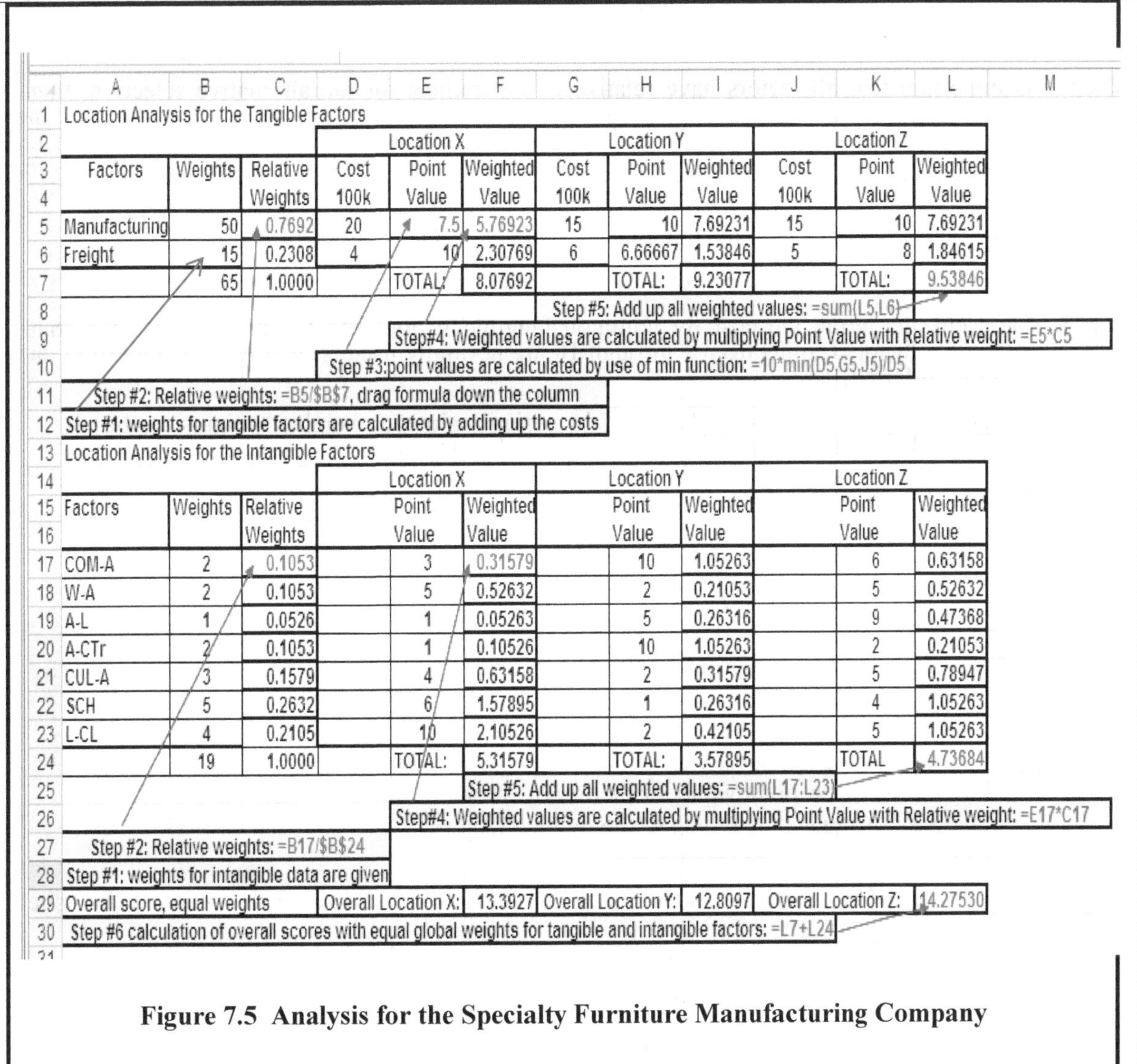

	A	B	C	D	E	F	G	H	I	J	K	L	M
1	Location Analysis for the Tangible Factors												
2				Location X			Location Y			Location Z			
3	Factors	Weights	Relative	Cost	Point	Weighted	Cost	Point	Weighted	Cost	Point	Weighted	
4			Weights	100k	Value	Value	100k	Value	Value	100k	Value	Value	
5	Manufacturing	50	0.7692	20	7.5	5.76923	15	10	7.69231	15	10	7.69231	
6	Freight	15	0.2308	4	10	2.30769	6	6.66667	1.53846	5	8	1.84615	
7		65	1.0000		TOTAL:	8.07692		TOTAL:	9.23077		TOTAL:	9.53846	
8							Step #5: Add up all weighted values: =sum(L5,L6)						
9					Step#4: Weighted values are calculated by multiplying Point Value with Relative weight: =E5*C5								
10				Step #3:point values are calculated by use of min function: =10*min(D5,G5,J5)/D5									
11	Step #2: Relative weights: =B5/$B$7, drag formula down the column												
12	Step #1: weights for tangible factors are calculated by adding up the costs												
13	Location Analysis for the Intangible Factors												
14				Location X			Location Y			Location Z			
15	Factors	Weights	Relative		Point	Weighted		Point	Weighted		Point	Weighted	
16			Weights		Value	Value		Value	Value		Value	Value	
17	COM-A	2	0.1053		3	0.31579		10	1.05263		6	0.63158	
18	W-A	2	0.1053		5	0.52632		2	0.21053		5	0.52632	
19	A-L	1	0.0526		1	0.05263		5	0.26316		9	0.47368	
20	A-CTr	2	0.1053		1	0.10526		10	1.05263		2	0.21053	
21	CUL-A	3	0.1579		4	0.63158		2	0.31579		5	0.78947	
22	SCH	5	0.2632		6	1.57895		1	0.26316		4	1.05263	
23	L-CL	4	0.2105		10	2.10526		2	0.42105		5	1.05263	
24		19	1.0000		TOTAL:	5.31579		TOTAL:	3.57895		TOTAL	4.73684	
25						Step #5: Add up all weighted values: =sum(L17:L23)							
26					Step#4: Weighted values are calculated by multiplying Point Value with Relative weight: =E17*C17								
27	Step #2: Relative weights: =B17/$B$24												
28	Step #1: weights for intangible data are given												
29	Overall score, equal weights			Overall Location X:		13.3927	Overall Location Y:		12.8097	Overall Location Z:		14.27530	
30	Step #6 calculation of overall scores with equal global weights for tangible and intangible factors: =L7+L24												

Figure 7.5 Analysis for the Specialty Furniture Manufacturing Company

With equal weights given to the tangible and intangible factors the overall scores are as follows:

- Location X: 13.39271
- Location Y: 12.80972
- Location Z: 14.27530

It seems like location Z is the preferred one! However, there does not seem to be a significant difference at the **5% error level** between the weighted point values of locations X and Z:

The average of their weighted point values is 13.8340 [(13.39271 +14.27530)/2] . The weighted point values for locations X and Z lie within the range of this **average ± 5%** [Range: **13.1423, 14.5257**].

Therefore, it is difficult to choose one location over the other location, and we must conclude that locations X and Z are equally preferred.

7. RELATIVE MERITS METHOD

When it is important that all factors have relatively high ratings for the alternative selection, then the **relative merits method** is preferred over the point rating system. In other words, a multiplicative model of the relative merits method is more appropriate than the additive scoring method of the point rating system. The procedure of the relative merits method can be summarized in the following five steps for all locations under consideration:

Step 1: Enumerate all tangible and intangible factors affecting the site selection

Step 2: Select the most appropriate common tangible and intangible factors

Step 3: For each site define the cost for common tangible factors and the point values for common intangible factors (points from 1 through 10 are normally used, with 1 as most preferred and 10 as least preferred)

Step 4: Weigh all tangible and intangible factors by assigning integer weights: weights can be determined either by the individual in charge of the project or by group consensus

Step 5: For all possible combinations of two sites define the selection factor $S_{x,y}$.

$$S_{x,y} = \prod_{i=1}^{n} \left(\frac{F_{i,x}}{F_{i,y}} \right)^{W_i}$$

Where: i = tangible and/or intangible factors
x = site x
y = site y
W_i = weight associated with factor i
F_{ix} = cost or point value for factor i of site x
$\prod$ = denotes the product of the relative factors

If $S_{x,y}$ is larger than one (1), then site y is preferred, however if $S_{x,y}$ is smaller than one (1), then site x is preferred.

An Example: Locating a Medical Research Lab

Amongst the numerous tangible and intangible factors affecting the site selection, the company has decided that the following factors are most appropriate:

Tangible factors are: land cost, building cost, and taxes.
Intangible factors are: labor supply, research climate, and community attitude.

Data for this company are summarized in Table 7.4

Table 7.4: Data for Locating a Medical Research Lab

Factors	Alternative x	Alternative y	Weight
1. Land Cost	600,000	300,000	3
2. Building Cost	1,600,000	2,000,000	3
3. Taxes	50,000	40,000	3
4. Labor Supply	(adequate) 2	(plentiful) 1	2
5. Research Climate	(excellent) 1	(good) 2	1
6. Community Attitude	cooperating 1	(ambivalent) 3	2

Using Excel, the relative merits analysis is shown in Figure 7.6.

	A	B	C	D	E
1	Factors	Alternative x	Alternative y	Weight	(Factor x/Factor y)^Weight
2	1. Land Cost	600,000	300,000	3	8
3	2. Building Cost	1,600,000	2,000,000	3	0.512
4	3. Taxes	50,000	40,000	3	1.953125
5	4. Labor Supply	2	1	2	4
6	5. Research Climate	1	2	1	0.5
7	6. Community Attitude	1	3	2	0.111111111
8	Calculating the product of values in column E:				1.777777778
9					
10			Formula: =(B2/C2)^D2		
11					Formula: = Product(E2:E7)

Figure 7.6 Analysis to Locate the Research Lab Using the Relative Merits Method

In Figure 7.6 the formula "= (B2/C2)^D2" represents the ratio of alternative x's land factor to alternative y's land factor, raised to the weight of the factor.

Cell E8 calculates the final result or:

$$S_{x,y} = \prod_{i=1}^{6} \left(\frac{F_{i,x}}{F_{i,y}} \right)^{W_i} = 1.7777779$$

Because the $S_{x,y}$ value is larger than 1, the best site for our research lab is location y.

8. *TRANSPORTATION METHOD*

The transportation method, a special linear programming method, is a procedure that solves transportation problems. The transportation problem, as it relates to location analysis and distribution of goods to centers, is formulated in a transportation tableau that generally consists of the following information:

- Sources: manufacturers, factories, warehouses, and others
- Destinations: products, distribution centers, retailers, and others
- Cost values: cost for shipping/producing one unit at a source, destined for a certain destination

There is no set rule that columns must be sources and that rows must be destinations. A transportation tableau simply tells the story of a "commodity" that is available at a given set of "sources" (manufacturers, factories, warehouses, and so on) and that needs to be "shipped" to a given set of "destinations" (products, distribution centers, retailers, and so on) in some best way (usually minimum cost or maximum profit). The availability of the "commodity" at each source is limited and so is the desire at each destination. Shipments are not allowed between sources or between destinations.

A Supply Chain Example: The Optimal Toyland Enterprise Supply Chain

Three regional toymakers (Worth, Selkirk, and Henry) can be engaged to manufacture three types of bears (pandas, grizzly bears, and polar bears). They will ship these bears to a central warehouse. Each toymaker has a limited capacity of toys they can make and the demand for these toys is limited too. Table 7.5 exhibits the demand for these toys, the capacity or maximum amount that each regional toymaker can make, and the combined per unit shipping and manufacturing cost.

Table 7.5: Toyland Enterprises Transportation Problem

Destinations: / Sources:	Worth	Selkirk	Henry	Demand
Pandas	2.2	2.4	2.1	250
Grizzly Bears	3.4	3.2	3.6	300
Polar Bears	1.9	1.8	2.1	200
Available Capacity:	180	250	320	750/750

It is the goal of Toyland Enterprises to assign manufacturing of these toys to the three regional toymakers in such a way as to minimize its total shipping and manufacturing cost. In doing so it must meet the demand for each of these toys and cannot exceed the available capacity of each regional toymaker. In this example, the total demand equals the available capacity. Therefore all available capacity will be utilized.

This type of a problem can best be solved using the Microsoft Excel's Solver function that can be found under "Tools"/"Add-Ins."

Data as shown in Figure 7.7 provides the input to Microsoft Excel's Solver function to solve the Toyland Enterprises problem.

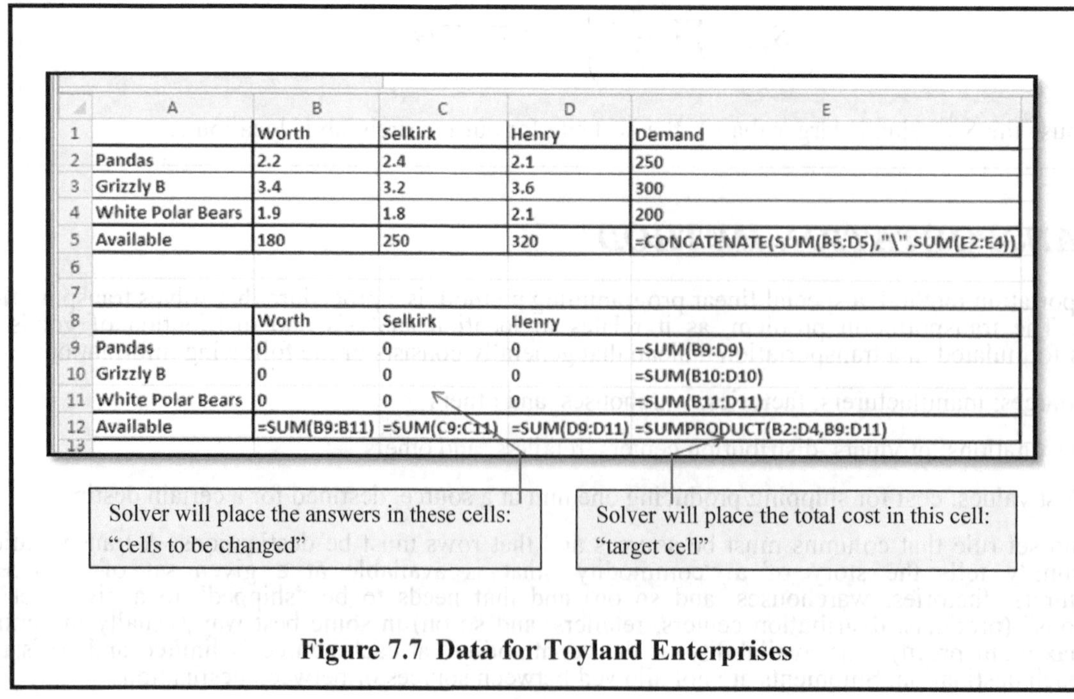

	A	B	C	D	E
1		Worth	Selkirk	Henry	Demand
2	Pandas	2.2	2.4	2.1	250
3	Grizzly B	3.4	3.2	3.6	300
4	White Polar Bears	1.9	1.8	2.1	200
5	Available	180	250	320	=CONCATENATE(SUM(B5:D5),"\",SUM(E2:E4))
6					
7					
8		Worth	Selkirk	Henry	
9	Pandas	0	0	0	=SUM(B9:D9)
10	Grizzly B	0	0	0	=SUM(B10:D10)
11	White Polar Bears	0	0	0	=SUM(B11:D11)
12	Available	=SUM(B9:B11)	=SUM(C9:C11)	=SUM(D9:D11)	=SUMPRODUCT(B2:D4,B9:D11)
13					

Figure 7.7 Data for Toyland Enterprises

Cell E12: will have the total cost value (objective function) and is the "target cell" in Solver that will be either maximized or minimized. In our example we wish to minimize total cost.

Cells B9:D11 are the cells where the answers will be placed and are the "cells to be changed" in Solver. These cells are currently empty because no assignments have been made yet..

Cell E5 has the "CONCATENATE" function. This function allows us to calculate two results and place these in one cell. Here we wish to sum the total available capacity and the total demand. In our example these sums are the same. It is important to know whether these are equal or not, because it will direct us as to how to formulate the constraints of the model.

Now, use "Solver" function under "Tools"/"Add-Ins" to solve this transportation problem. "Solver" for this transportation tableau needs to be filled in as shown in Figure 7.8.

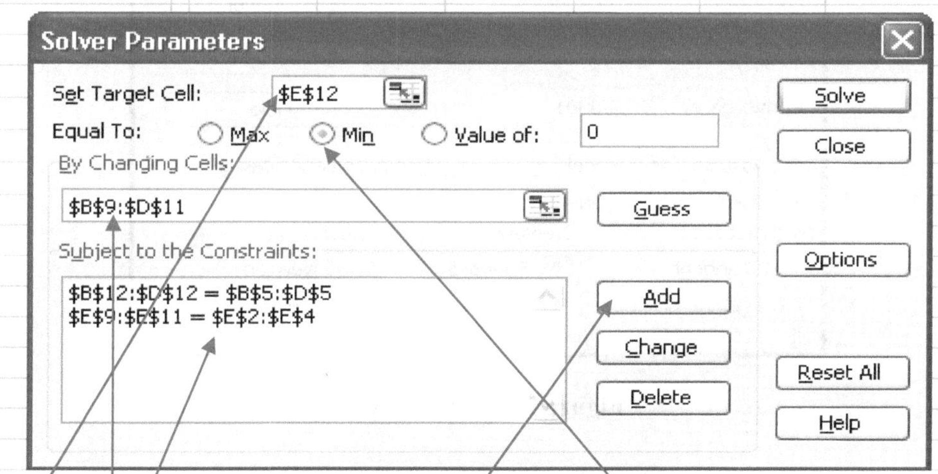

Figure 7.8 Excel Solver Function

The "target cell" is E12. It contains the objective function or the cost function that needs to be minimized. It is the objective to minimize this objective function: "Min" is checked on the solver parameter.

The "cells that need to be changed" are located in the squares B9 through D11: therefore cells B9:D11 will contain the final assignments for this problem.

There are two sets of constraints: the demand and supply "constraints." These constraints can be introduced by clicking on the "Add" box. An "Add Constraint Box" will appear through which constraints can be repeatedly added. In our example this box is used twice to enter two global constraints.

Because the total demand equals the total supply, these sets of constraints will all be equal to (=) constraints. In other words: the sum of assignments in rows and columns must be equal to the stated row and column totals:

"$B$12:$D$12 = $B$5:$D$5" relates that B12 = B5, C12 = C5, D12 = D5

"$E$9:$E$11 = $E$2:$E$4" relates that E2 = E9, E3 = E10, E4 = E11

If the supply would have been larger than the demand, then the sum of the assignments in columns (supply) must be less than or equal to the stated column totals, whereas the sum of the assignments in the rows (demand) must be equal to the stated row totals. Similarly, if the demand would have been larger than the supply, then the sum of the assignments in the rows (demand) must be less than or equal to the stated row totals, whereas the sum of the assignments in the columns (supply) must be equal to the stated column totals.

The "CONCATENATE" function will steer you in defining the correct signs for the constraints, because it will show the relationship between total supplies versus (\) total demand.

Now that all data has been entered, proceed to Solver "Options" to indicate that it is a linear model and that we can only assume non-negative values for the variables of the model. This can be achieved by clicking on the "Options" screen in the "Solver" window. The "Solver Options" window is shown in Figure 7.9 (this may look slightly different on your Word version).

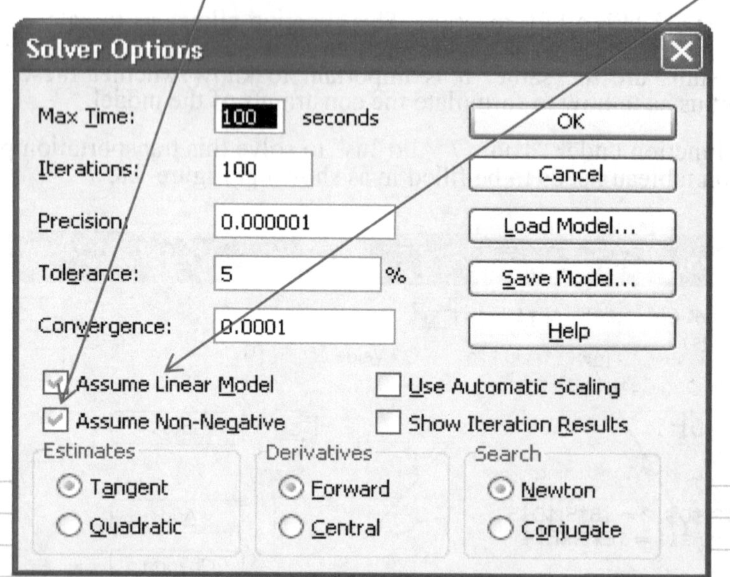

Figure 7.9 Solver Options

Hit "OK" in the "Solver Options" window and you will return to the "Solver" window. Now click on "Solve" to have Solver solve the problem. You may wish to keep the solution and generate various reports.

The solution is shown in Figure 7.10.

	A	B	C	D	E
1		Worth	Selkirk	Henry	Demand
2	Pandas	2.2	2.4	2.1	250
3	Grizzly B	3.4	3.2	3.6	300
4	White Po	1.9	1.8	2.1	200
5	Available	180	250	320	750\750
6					
7					
8		Worth	Selkirk	Henry	
9	Pandas	0	0	250	250
10	Grizzly B	50	250	0	300
11	White Po	130	0	70	200
12	Available	180	250	320	1889

Figure 7.10 The Solution

The supply chain solution that minimizes the production and the shipping cost is as follows:

- Mr. Worth will make and ship 50 grizzly bears and 130 polar bears
- Mr. Selkirk will produce and ship 250 grizzly bears
- Mr. Henry will make and ship 250 pandas and 70 polar bears

This satisfies the demand at a minimum cost of $1,889.

A Location Expansion Example:

Consider a manufacturing firm with present locations in Saint Louis and Boston that must expand its production in order to meet the demand of four distribution centers. A preliminary analysis points at two possible locations, Denver and Dallas. Though the fixed cost for establishing these plants in any of these locations is the same, the operating and shipping costs are different, as shown in Table 7.6. Table 7.6 also shows available capacity and demand.

Table 7.6: Cost, Capacity, and Demand Data for the Location Expansion Problem

Plants: Warehouses:	Saint Louis (capacity: 35,000)	Boston (capacity: 30,000)	Denver or (capacity: 25,000)	Dallas (capacity: 25,000)
Warehouse #1 (demand: 20,000)	20	26	22	21
Warehouse #2 (demand: 20,000)	21	28	19	26
Warehouse #3 (demand: 26,000)	23	25	26	23
Warehouse #4 (demand: 24,000	24	24	27	27

In order to find the best choice, two transportation tableaus must be solved: the first one considers the existing plants at Saint Louis and Boston with the proposed plant in Denver, and the second one includes the existing plants at Saint Louis and Boston with the proposed plant in Dallas.

	A	B	C	D	E
1		Saint Louis	Boston	Denver	Demand
2	Warehouse #1	20	26	22	20000
3	Warehouse #2	21	28	19	20000
4	Warehouse #3	23	25	26	26000
5	Warehouse #4	24	24	27	24000
6	Capacity	35000	30000	25000	=CONCATENATE(SUM(B6:D6),"\",SUM(E2:E5))
7					
8					
9		Saint Louis	Boston	Denver	Demand
10	Warehouse #1	0	0	0	=SUM(B10:D10)
11	Warehouse #2	0	0	0	=SUM(B11:D11)
12	Warehouse #3	0	0	0	=SUM(B12:D12)
13	Warehouse #4	0	0	0	=SUM(B13:D13)
14	Capacity	=SUM(B10:B13)	=SUM(C10:C13)	=SUM(D10:D13)	=SUMPRODUCT(B2:D5,B10:D13)

Figure 7.11 Data for Denver Alternative

Microsoft Excel's Solver function is used to generate the optimal allocations for each of the alternatives and the results are exhibited in Figures 7.12 through 7.14.

	A	B	C	D	E
1		Saint Louis	Boston	Denver	Demand
2	Warehouse #1	20	26	22	20,000
3	Warehouse #2	21	28	19	20,000
4	Warehouse #3	23	25	26	26,000
5	Warehouse #4	24	24	27	24,000
6	Capacity	35,000	30,000	25,000	90000\90000
7					
8					
9		Saint Louis	Boston	Denver	Demand
10	Warehouse #1	15,000	-	5,000	20,000
11	Warehouse #2	-	-	20,000	20,000
12	Warehouse #3	20,000	6,000	-	26,000
13	Warehouse #4	-	24,000	-	24,000
14	Capacity	35,000	30,000	25,000	1,976,000

Figure 7.12 Optimal Allocation for Denver Alternative

	A	B	C	D	E
1		Saint Louis	Boston	Dallas	Demand
2	Warehouse #1	20	26	21	20000
3	Warehouse #2	21	28	26	20000
4	Warehouse #3	23	25	23	26000
5	Warehouse #4	24	24	27	24000
6	Capacity	35000	30000	25000	=CONCATENATE(SUM(B6:D6),"\",SUM(E2:E5))
7					
8					
9		Saint Louis	Boston	Dallas	Demand
10	Warehouse #1	0	0	0	=SUM(B10:D10)
11	Warehouse #2	0	0	0	=SUM(B11:D11)
12	Warehouse #3	0	0	0	=SUM(B12:D12)
13	Warehouse #4	0	0	0	=SUM(B13:D13)
14	Capacity	=SUM(B10:B13)	=SUM(C10:C13)	=SUM(D10:D13)	=SUMPRODUCT(B2:D5,B10:D13)

Figure 7.13 Data for Dallas Alternative

A	B	C	D	E
	Saint Louis	Boston	Dallas	Demand
Warehouse #1	20	26	21	20,000
Warehouse #2	21	28	26	20,000
Warehouse #3	23	25	23	26,000
Warehouse #4	24	24	27	24,000
Capacity	35,000	30,000	25,000	90000\90000

	Saint Louis	Boston	Dallas	Demand
Warehouse #1	15,000	-	5,000	20,000
Warehouse #2	20,000	-	-	20,000
Warehouse #3	-	6,000	20,000	26,000
Warehouse #4	-	24,000	-	24,000
Capacity	35,000	30,000	25,000	2,011,000

Figure 7.14 Optimal Allocation for Dallas Alternative

The overall variable cost for operating a plant in Denver ($1,976,000) is less than for operating a plant in Dallas ($2,011,000). Therefore the choice location is Denver.

Accordingly, Figure 7.12 illustrates the proper allocation of goods to warehouses when the Denver plant becomes operational. Only that allocation will yield the lowest yearly variable cost of $1,976,000.

It can be summarized as follows:

- Produce in Saint Louis 15,000 units for warehouse #1
- Produce in Saint Louis 20,000 units for warehouse #3
- Produce in Boston 6,000 units for warehouse #3
- Produce in Boston 24,000 units for warehouse #4
- Produce in Denver 5,000 units for warehouse #1
- Produce in Denver 20,000 units for warehouse #2

These allocations satisfy, at minimum yearly cost, the required demand at all warehouses and do not exceed plant capacities. Any different allocation may increase the yearly variable cost.

9. GLOSSARY AND SUMMARY OF METHODS

Analytical Hierarchy Method – The analytical hierarchy method is based on a "trade off" concept that is accomplished by structuring the problem and assigning weights in the form of a series of pair-wise comparison matrices. These weights are then mathematically combined to come up with normalized weights for all locations under consideration. The location with the highest normalized value is the preferred one.

Decision Tree Method – The decision tree method calculates the expected cost differential amongst alternate locations.

Multiple Facilities Location Problem – We are dealing with multiple facilities location problems when a new facility may affect existing shipping patterns and production levels of presently existing facilities.

Classification of Facilities Location Methods – **Single Plant Location Methods**: decision trees method, point rating methods, relative merits method, and analytical hierarchy process. **Multiple Plant Location Method:** transportation method.

Facilities Location Decision Process – There are three steps followed in the process of selecting a site. These are:

Step 1: Management first selects a general region
Step 2: Management then picks a community within that region
Step 3: Finally, management selects a specific plant site in the community

Facilities Location Factors – The following are the most important factors that affect facilities location decisions: availability and cost of transportation; labor cost and labor supply; capital cost; operating and materials/supplies cost; miscellaneous intangible factors such as climate, natural defense, living facilities, community administration, attitude, and customers and constituents; new factors such as water-, air- , and noise pollution, availability of energy and cost; and all sorts of government regulations.

Point Rating Methods – Point rating methods calculate a weighted point value for alternate locations, after assigning weights and points to appropriate tangible and intangible factors. The method selects that location that has the significantly highest weighted point value.

Relative Merits Method – The relative merits method evaluates two locations at a time by calculating a ratio of two geometric averages of factors. If that ratio is smaller than one, then the location which has its geometric average in the numerator of the ratio is the preferred one. If that ratio is larger than one, then the location which has its geometric average in the denominator of the ratio is the preferred one.

Rollback Updating Method – The rollback updating method is used to evaluate a decision tree. It will determine which decision or decisions are preferred. The rollback updating procedure means moving backward through the decision tree, from the rightmost point in the tree to the leftmost point by calculating the expected payoffs at chance or event nodes and by choosing the most favorable course of action at each decision node.

Single Facilities Location Problem – We are dealing with single facilities location problems when we desire to locate one facility that will not interact with the company's other existing facilities.

Transportation Method – The transportation method was originally developed to find the optimal, minimum cost allocation of goods shipped from factories to destinations. It is used to evaluate alternate locations in addition to existing locations by considering both production and shipping cost data.

10. REFERENCES

Anderson, D. R., Dennis J. Sweeney, and Thomas A. Williams. *An Introduction to Management Science - Quantitative Approaches to Decision Making.* West Publishing Company, Sixth Edition, 1991.

Cerveny, Robert P. "An Application of Warehouse Location Technique to Bloodmobile Operations." *Interfaces.* (Vol. 10, December 1980): 89–93.

Conway. "The Checklist of Site Selection Factors." *Site Selection Handbook.* Atlanta, GA: Conway, 1978.

Craig, C. S. "Models of Retail Location Process." *Journal of Retailing.* (Vol. 60, April 1984): 5–36.

Drayer, W. and Steve Seabury. "Facilities Expansion Model." *Interfaces - TIMS/ORSA.* (Vol. 5, February 1975): 104–109.

Dutton, R., G. Himman, and C. B. Millham. "The Optimal Location of Nuclear Power Facilities in the Pacific Northwest." *Operations Research.* (Vol. 22, May-June 1974): 478–487.

Fitzsimmons, James A. "A Warehouse Location Model Helps Texas Comptroller Select Out-of-State Audit Officers," *Interfaces*. (Vol. 13, October 1983): 40–45.

Ford, L. R. "Solving the Transportation Problem." *Management Science*. (Vol. 3, 1956): 24–32.

Hitchcock, Frank L. "The Distribution of a Product from Several Sources to Numerous Locations." *Journal of Mathematical Physics*. (Vol. 20, 1941): 224–230.

Molinero, C. Mar. "Schools in Southampton: A Quantitative Approach to School Location, Closure, and Staffing." *Journal of Operational Research Society*. (Vol. 39, No. 4, 1988): 339–350)

Saaty, T. *The Analytical Hierarchy Process*. New York: McGraw-Hill, 1980.

Szwarc, W. "The Initial Solution of the Transportation Problem." *Operations Research*. (Vol. 8, 1960): 727–729.

Wu, Jack A. and Nesa L. Wu. "Analyzing Multi-Dimensional Attributes for the Single Plant Location Problem, via the Analytic Hierarchy Process." *International Journal of Operations and Production Management*. (Vol. 4, Fall 1984): 13–21.

11. REVIEW QUESTIONS

1. When is the relative merits method used?
2. What kinds of data are needed to perform an analysis of alternate sites within a general location?
3. Name two mathematical models that can be used in evaluating single facilities location problems and that simultaneously consider and evaluate tangible and intangible factors.
4. Briefly describe the relative merits method. When is that method preferred over the point rating method?
5. How is data collected for the analytical hierarchy method?
6. Of the ones mentioned in the text, which is the best single plant location method?
7. What data are required for the transportation method?

12. PROBLEMS

Problem #1

Consider the annual operating costs of:

Location A: $10,000,000

Location B: $8,000,000

Location C: $6,000,000

Convert these costs to values on a positive oriented point scale (scale from 1 to 10, with 10 equal to the best outcome).

Problem #2

The following factors and weights have been used in a location planning rating system (1 to 10, where 10 is the highest rating value).

Factors	Weights	Rating
Taxes	15	8
Utilities	27	6
Transportation Cost	9	8
Land Cost	10	7

What is the score that this site will receive in the rating analysis?

Problem #3 (Excel)

An NC manufacturing company is evaluating two locations for its facility.

Tangible data and intangible data are as follows;

Factors	Weights	Locations	
		Location A	**Location B**
Annual Operating Cost	10	$5,000,000	$4,000,000
Degree of Unionization	1	Excellent	Good
Zoning	2	Good	Average
Community Attitude	2	Poor	Average

There is a 1 (one) to 2 (two) relative relationship between good and excellent.

There is a 1 (one) to 3 (three) relative relationship between average and excellent.

There is a 1 (one) to 5 (five) relative relationship between poor and excellent..

Use the point rating method (scale 1 through 10, with 10 being best and 1 being worst) to identify the location that is the most attractive one for this company.

Problem #4 (Excel)

A toy manufacturing company is considering relocating. Two locations were suggested, City A and City B. The data that were collected are shown in the following table.

Use the point rating method to evaluate the two locations. Which location is preferred?

Composite Ratings for Intangible Factors			
Factors	City A	City B	Weight
Labor Attitude	4	6	10
Community Attitude	10	3	5
Research Climate	5	5	10
Schools	3	8	10
Yearly Cost Values for Tangible Factors			
Factors	City A	City B	Weight
Taxes	$15,000	$35,000	1
Transp. Cost	$80,000	$120,000	4
Building & Equip.	$600,000	$400,000	20
Manufacturing Cost	$300,000	$200,000	10

Problem #5 (Excel)

A potential robotics manufacturing company is evaluating three locations for its new facility. The important tangible and intangible data are as follows:

	Locations		
Factors	San Diego	Cincinnati	Orlando
Tangible Factors			
Annual Operating Cost	$5,000,000	$4,000,000	$3,000,000
Transportation Cost	$300,000	$200,000	$500,000
Intangible Factors			
Research Climate	average	excellent	below average
Degree of Unionization	excellent	excellent	average
Zoning Restrictions	average	excellent	below average
Proximity to Customers	poor	excellent	average
Recreation Facilities	excellent	below average	average
Cost of Living	excellent	poor	average
Community Attitude	poor	average	excellent
Urban Transport System	excellent	excellent	below average
Housing Availability	below average	excellent	good

Use the following relative rating scale: excellent (1), good (2), average (3), below average (4), poor (5). In other words, there is a one (1) to two (2) relative relationship between "good" and "excellent," etc.

Use the point rating method (as presented in the text) to identify the location that is the most attractive one for the robotics manufacturing firm. Tangible factors, as a group, are twice as important as the intangible factors, as a group. Assume that "excellent" is the best outcome and will be assigned a value of 10 on the point rating scale.

Problem #6 (Excel)

A small appliance manufacturing company is considering relocating. Two locations were suggested, City A and City B. The following comparative data were collected.

There is a one (1) to two (2) relative relationship between "good" and "excellent" and between "poor" and "good", and there is a one (1) to three (3) relative relationship between "fair" and "excellent."

a) Verify that the weights for tangible data are correct (when rounded to integer weights)

b) Use the point rating method to find which location, A or B, is the preferred one. Assume that "excellent" is the best outcome and will be assigned a value of 10 on the point rating scales.

Factor	City A	City B	Weight
Annual Bldg/Equipment Cost	$400,000	$300,000	32
Taxes	$10,000	$12,000	1
Transportation Cost	$9,000	$13,000	1
Manufacturing Cost	$300,000	$450,000	34
Labor Attitude	good	good	10
Community Attitude	poor	excellent	5
Research Climate	good	good	15
Schools	fair	good	10

Problem #7 (Use Excel's Solver)

Reconsider the location expansion problem (Example is on page 169).

a) Verify using Solver that the assignments shown in the text for each option are optimal.

b) Assume that the upcoming product lifecycle is approximately 10 years and that the Denver plant will cost half a million more than the Dallas plant. Which location is the preferred one if you wish to minimize overall cost, both variable and fix costs?

Problem #8 (EXCEL's Solver)

Midnight Auto Supplies has 5 factories that supply 6 warehouses. The total cost of manufacturing and shipping (per ton) from each factory to each warehouse is shown in the table below. The production capacities at the 5 factories and the demand at the 6 warehouses are shown in the margins of the table.

Note that the sum of the demand (40 + 20 + 55 + 30 + 40 +50 = 235) is less than the available total capacity (75 + 45 +30 + 50 + 60 = 260). Therefore, there is plenty of capacity to meet the demand.

a) Use solver to allocate factory production to the warehouses in such a way that overall cost, both manufacturing and shipping costs, is minimized. The allocation must be such that the demand at each warehouse is satisfied. In Microsoft Excel Solver this means that the warehouse demand equations will be of the equal type (=). Because the accumulated capacities at the factories are larger than the accumulated demand at each warehouse the capacity constraints in Microsoft Excel Solver will be of the less than or equal type (<=).

b) Suppose we can reduce manufacturing costs at factory #3 by $3/ton. Will this change the optimal solution? Why or why not? If there is a change in allocation, find the new solution.

c) Suppose that manufacturing costs at factory #2 are actually $4/ton higher than originally thought. Does this change the solution? Why or why not? If there is a change in allocation, find the new solution.

Factories Destinations	F1	F2	F3	F4	F5	Demand
W1	9	6	8	15	10	40
W2	17	13	11	9	12	20
W3	18	15	12	13	11	55
W4	14	15	8	6	12	30
W5	8	6	9	7	12	40
W6	10	16	10	12	13	50
Capacities	75	45	30	50	60	260/235

Problem #9 (Use Excel's Solver)

Small Toy Robotics Inc. has three factories and three warehouses. The accumulated demand at the warehouses, however, currently exceeds the accumulated production capacities at the three existing factories. The capacities at each of the three factories are as follows:

Chicago, IL: 250 units
Detroit, MI: 130 units
Louisville, KY: 180 units

The present projected demand at each of the three warehouses is as follows:

Fort Wayne, IN: 290 units
Dayton, OH: 210 units
Evansville, IN: 160 units

Because the projected demand of 660 units exceeds the total plant capacity of 560 units by 100 units Small Toy Robotics Inc. considers expansion of its production operation. Presently the company is considering one of two locations, namely a plant in Saint Louis, MO or a plant in Indianapolis, IN.

The shipping department came up with the shipping cost, while the operations manager estimated the per unit variable production cost and the yearly building and equipment cost. These costs are summarized in the following tables.

Per Unit Shipping Cost			
To warehouses:	Fort Wayne	Dayton	Evansville
From Plants:			
Chicago	9	11	8
Detroit	6	7	13
Louisville	11	6	5
Saint Louis	10	8	7
Indianapolis	9	8	4

Variable Production and Other Yearly Fixed Cost Data		
Plants	Per Unit Variable Production Cost	Yearly Building & Equipment Cost
Chicago	$105	$ 8,550
Detroit	$120	$13,550
Louisville	$100	$11,550
Saint Louis	$125	$22,550
Indianapolis	$155	$19,050

a) When considering shipping cost only, which new location is the preferred one? What is the company's yearly shipping cost when selecting that location?

b) When considering all variable cost elements, which new location is the preferred one? What is the company's total variable cost when selecting that location?

c) When considering all costs, which location is the preferred one? What is the company's overall yearly cost when considering that location? Describe the supply assignment of goods from factories to demand centers for Small Toy Robotics Inc.'s new optimal manufacturing system.

Problem #10 (Use Excel's Solver)

Your manager is faced with a plant location problem. He comes to you for help and supplies you with all the data he received from his boss. Considering it a challenge, you agree to help him out. You will use Microsoft Excel's Solver to figure the best allocation of goods from factories to demand centers. The manager expects to receive from you a carefully written report that contains all the information, data, results, together with your analysis and recommendations. Remember, though, that your manager is of the "old school" and never had a chance to study the "transportation method." However, he is a careful person and will only implement what he understands is correct. Whatever you suggest or write must be sufficient for him to choose the best alternative and to implement production and distribution assignments. The marketing department of your company developed a large market in Western Europe, in the Far East, and in Central America. The projected yearly average demand over the next ten years for all regions is as shown in the following table.

Projected Average Demand by Regions	
Regions	Units
Western Region	110,000
Midwestern Region	180,000
Eastern Region	125,000
Far East	40,000
Western Europe	55.000
Central America	30,000

The present plant capacities in the three existing plants are as shown in the following table.

Plant Capacity	
Plants	Capacity
San Diego, CA	100,000
Detroit, MI	200,000
Richmond, VA	120,000

Because the stable projected demand of 540,000 units exceeds the total plant capacity of 420,000 units by 120,000 units the company is considering expansion of its production operation. In this expansion the possibility of overtime in the present locations is an alternative.

In consideration of the emerging markets and a preliminary analysis of various regions, the following options are considered for expansion of this business:

Option #1: Introduce overtime in the present facilities. The maximum amount of overtime capacity is 60% of the regular capacity; however, it costs the company 150% of direct labor cost.

Option #2: In addition to overtime in the present locations consider the construction of a new plant in Japan with a capacity of 60,000 units per year at a fixed cost for construction of $1,500,000.

Option #3: In addition to overtime in the present locations consider the construction of a new plant in France with a capacity of 60,000 units per year at a fixed cost for construction of $4,500,000.

Option #4: In addition to overtime in the present locations consider the construction of a new plant in Mexico with a capacity of 60,000 units per year at a fixed cost for construction of $3,000,000.

In order to evaluate each of these four alternatives, the operations and shipping departments are requested to come up with information on the variable production costs and shipping costs. The operations department has submitted the following information on variable production costs for the six facilities (data for regular shift only).

Estimated Average per Unit Variable Production Cost			
Plants	Raw Materials Cost	Direct Labor Cost	Variable Burden
San Diego	$13.30	$6.00	$23.00
Detroit	14.50	4.50	23.00
Richmond	13.00	7.50	21.50
Japan	12.70	5.60	20.80
France	12.90	6.00	21.70
Mexico	12.60	3.30	21.70

Estimated Average per Unit Shipping Cost						
To: From:	Western R	Midwest R	Eastern R	Far East	W. Europe	Central America
San Diego	$3.00	$9.00	$12.00	$18.00	$24.00	$15.00
Detroit	9.00	6.00	7.50	22.50	22.50	13.50
Richmond	12.00	7.50	4.50	24.00	24.00	12.00
Japan	21.00	24.00	25.50	3.00	31.50	27.00
France	25.50	24.00	25.50	30.00	4.50	28.50
Mexico	16.50	15.00	13.50	33.00	30.00	1.50

A ten-year horizon for paying off the fixed construction cost must be considered. You may assume that the demand will not change over that planning horizon.

Problem #11

A rural community clinic regularly sends patients via ambulance to a major hospital in Newport. The distance on the state highway is 80 miles. The distance on a shortcut via a country road is only 50 miles. The ambulance can drive 65 miles per hour on the highway and 55 miles per hour on the country road, provided that there is no rain. If there is rain, the driver can average 60 miles per hour on the highway and 50 miles per hour on the country road. Twenty miles down the country road there is a bridge. Due to river water levels, this bridge has a 50 percent (p =0.50) chance of being closed to traffic when it rains. There is no broadcasting whatsoever if the bridge is closed! If the driver encounters a closed bridge, he may still try another bridge that is 5 miles out of the way. This second bridge, however, has a 20 percent (p = 0.20) chance of being closed without warning. These data are summarized in the Figure below.

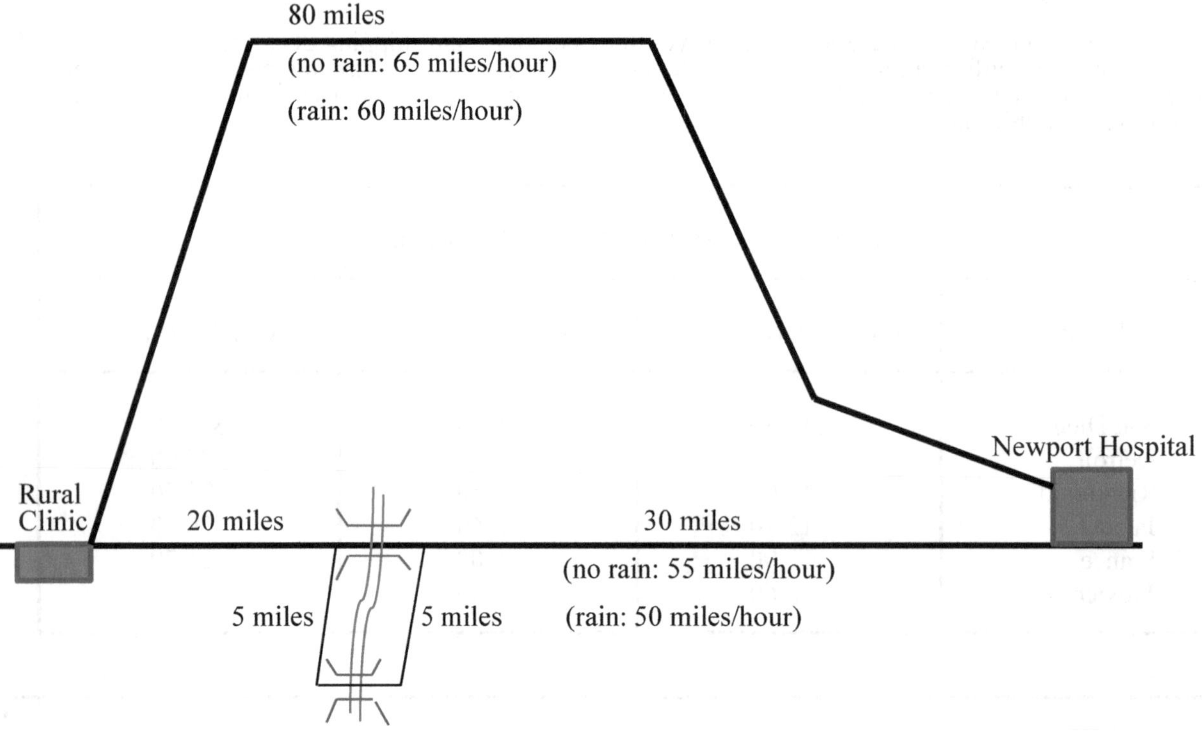

Weather bureau statistics show that it rains 50% of the time in this area.

a) Which road should the ambulance driver take if he wishes to minimize the expected time to reach Newport Hospital? You will have to construct the decision tree, calculate the payoff times for all possible alternatives, calculate expected times in event nodes, and make decisions in decision nodes. Narrate your answer.
b) Because of the high cost of fuel, the rural clinic wishes to choose the route that would minimize the expected distance of traveling. Find that route and narrate your answer.

(Hint: if you do this problem correctly you will have seven (7) payoff branches for the first part of the problem (a.) and six (6) payoff branches for the second part of the problem (b.). These include returning from the first bridge and/or second bridge to travel via the highway if these bridges are closed!)

Chapter 8

FACILITIES PLANNING

LAYOUT AND CAPACITY PLANNING

Facility planning (i.e., the layout of physical facilities and figuring its proper capacity), is a continuous, ongoing activity in an organization because of product proliferation, innovation, competition, expansion, etc. Facility layout includes the layout of new facilities in a newly constructed building, a to-be constructed building, or an existing building, the re-layout within an existing organization due to changes in processes, products, or services, or the relocation or adding of new equipment within the present layout (various computer aided packages have been developed to assist the facility planner in such layout projects.)

In this chapter you will learn what constitutes a good layout and how to plan for expansion. Additionally, you will study various types of layout, such as: the product layout, the process or functional layout, the lean layout, the fixed material layout, the project layout, and the layout of a lean warehouse. A brief overview of various computer aided tools available to properly layout a product and a functional layout are briefly discussed. Because the layout of a facility, together with its equipment and labor, defines the facility's design capacity, a brief section on capacity planning concludes this chapter.

1. LAYOUT CONSIDERATIONS AND OBJECTIVES

A good layout of machines, work places, offices, warehouses, equipment, tools, and material handling systems must provide for an integrated system's layout in the capacities required, so that feasible work schedules can be determined at minimum cost. All layout decisions are, therefore, concerned with the relative allocation and actual positioning of all physical components to the floor space, so that the manufacturing of goods or the creation of services can be accomplished in a most productive way. An efficient layout is the result of a careful blending of many tangible and intangible factors. It must:

- Provide for an efficient flow of workers and materials
- Consider the human and social impact of the layout
- Provide a comfortable and efficient working environment for all concerned
- Attempt to minimize in-process inventory and reduce travel time of people and goods
- Provide a smooth flow of material and effective communication amongst departments
- Encourage a reasonable production throughput time
- Maximize space utilization and minimize construction costs
- Be flexible to changes in process design that may require re-layout of facilities
- Be modular for ease of expansion

— ALSO MUST CREATE A SAFE ENVIRONMENT

2. PANNING FOR EXPANSION

There are four basic designs available for modern modular facility planning: the mirror image expansion design, the centralized expansion design, the decentralized expansion design, and the spine expansion design.

2.1 The Mirror Image Expansion Design

The expanded layout of a mirror image expansion design becomes the mirror image of the original design, thus duplicating similar departments at different locations in the plant. This is shown in Figure 8.1. This design, as opposed to the following two designs, may result in a reduced production throughput time, a better flow of materials, a reduced travel time for workers, a reduced materials movement, and less in-process inventory. However, such design always requires stoppage of production during the expansion process. The mirror image design requires that products receive a designation as to where they will be processed or worked on, because there are now two distinct processing areas. This design may lead towards cellular layout, as discussed later in this chapter.

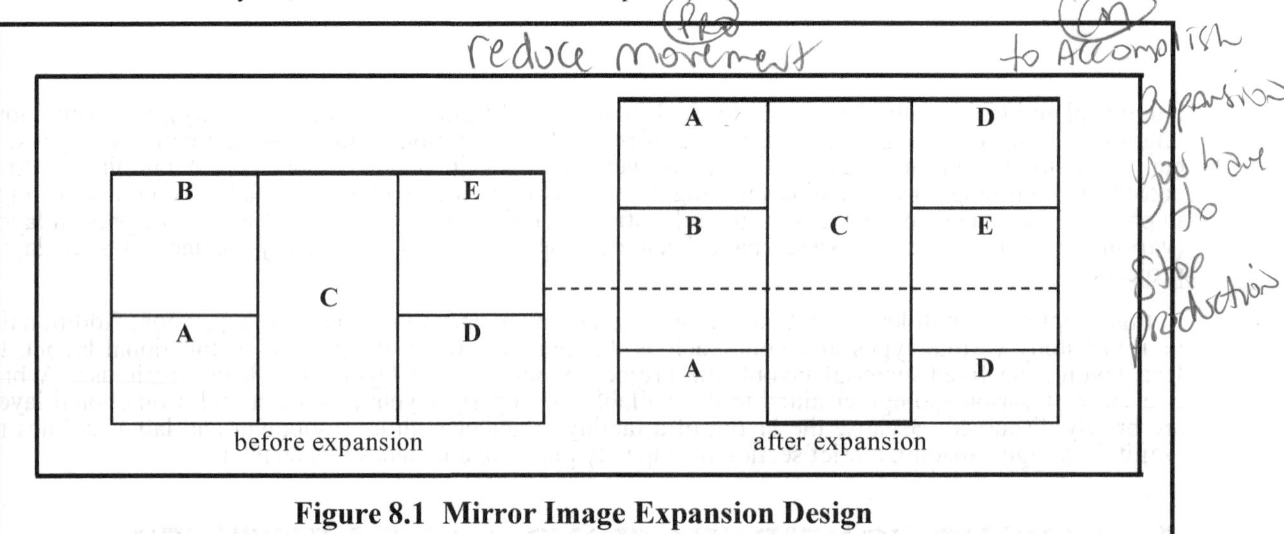

Figure 8.1 Mirror Image Expansion Design

2.2 The Centralized Expansion Design

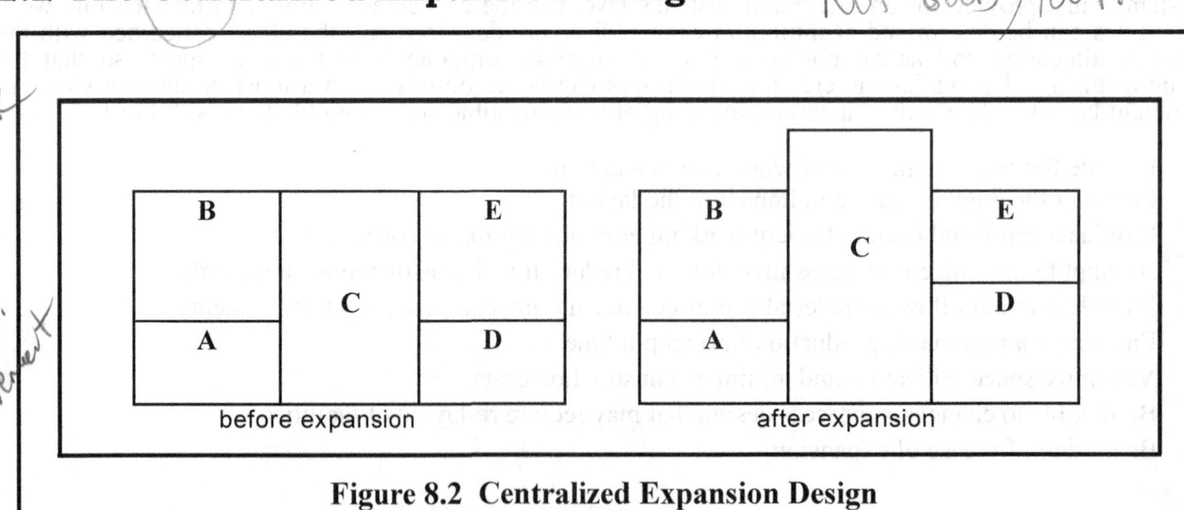

Figure 8.2 Centralized Expansion Design

The centralized expansion design is shown in Figure 8.2. This design does not have duplicate departments at different locations. Expansion occurs by adding space to the original departments. In the centralized expansion design no space is left idle in the original design and expansion is accomplished by adding to the outskirts of the original departments. The expansion activity requires production to stop until the conclusion of the expansion. After expansion we normally see an increase in travel and move time of people and materials, an increase in production throughput time, and more work-in-process. This non-lean design is not recommended.

2.3 The Decentralized Expansion Design

Like in the centralized expansion design, the decentralized expansion design, as shown in Figure 8.3, does not have duplicate departments at different locations. In this expansion design, empty space between departments is added within the original layout. This space can then later be utilized when certain departments need to be expanded. Unfortunately, before expansion can take place, such empty space is often used to hold unnecessary inventory. By the time expansion takes place it will be necessary to liberate the place of such inventory, which is not always an easy task. Because this design invites excess inventory on the shop floor, it is not a recommended design.

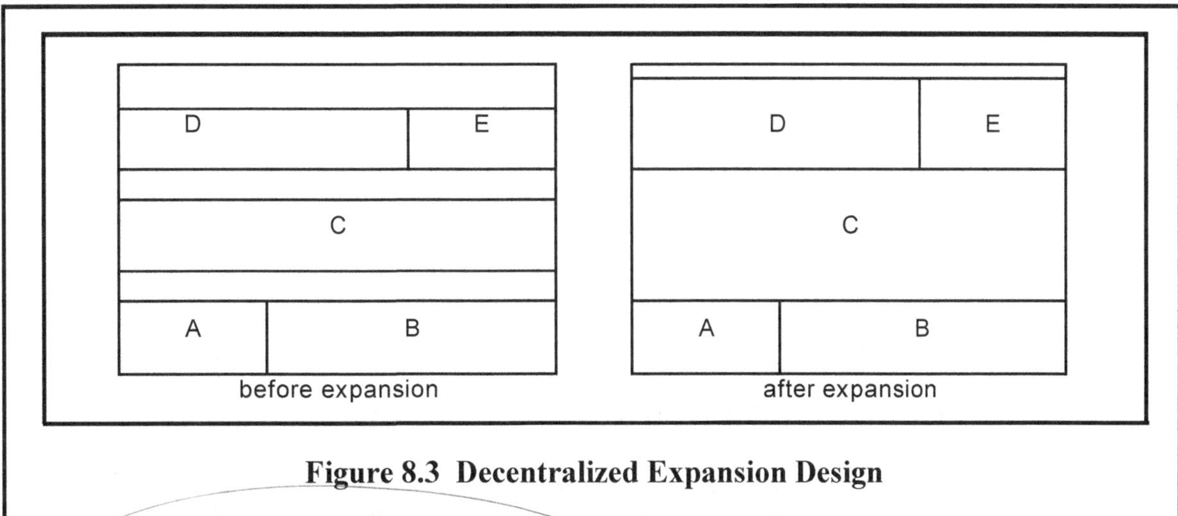

Figure 8.3 Decentralized Expansion Design

2.4 The Spine Expansion Design

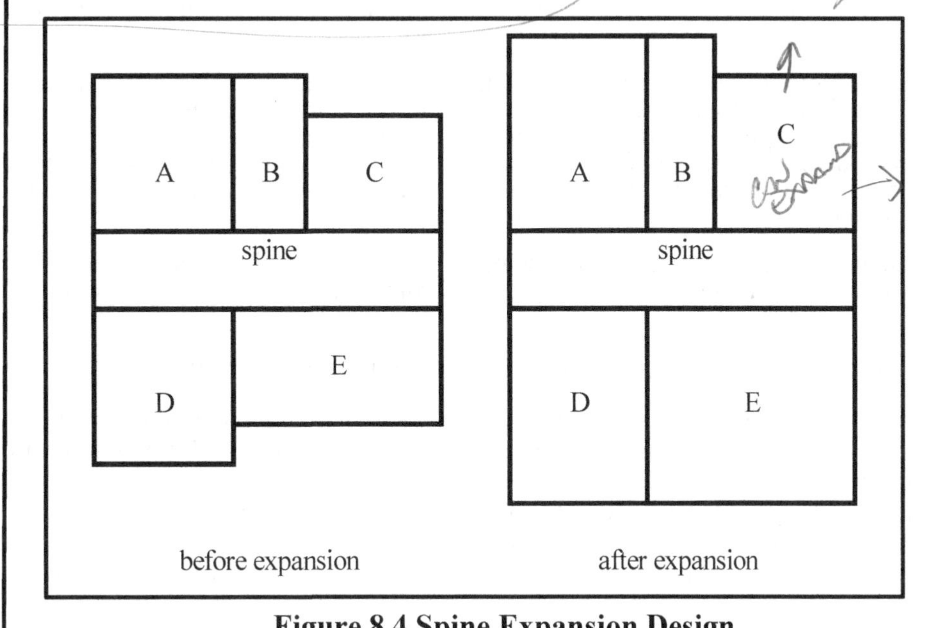

Figure 8.4 Spine Expansion Design

A relatively new design, the spine expansion design, lends itself to great ease of expansion (see Figure 8.4). It is far superior to the three previously discussed designs, since the expansion of a spine facility requires no changes in the primary facility services, in personnel travel patterns, or in material handling and storage systems.

Primary facility services, such as electricity, gas, compressed air, telephone lines, plumbing, etc., are routed through the spine and fed into the departments via so-called feeder connections. Similarly, material handling of goods is carried from departments via feeder systems into the spine. In order to avoid congestion of movement in the spine, the movement of personnel, facility services, and material handling may occur on various levels, creating multi-level spines. Thus personnel may move on the first level, the material handling system on the second level, and the facility services on the third level.

Industrial engineers, who traditionally have been engaged in layout activities of manufacturing organizations, are increasingly using their expertise in the layout of hospitals, banks, offices, restaurants, warehouses, and manufacturing organizations.

In general, dozens of areas need to be studied and evaluated before the actual construction or change of a layout can occur. These are: receiving and storage of raw materials and parts, the production processes and assembling of goods, the material handling system, the packaging/warehousing and shipping of finished goods, personnel and maintenance services, plant safety and energy use, offices, buildings, external facilities, parking lots and grounds, community attitude and regulations regarding noise, pollution control, etc.

Based on the purpose or function for which layouts are designed, typical layouts are: product layouts, functional or process layouts, group layouts, fixed material layouts, project layouts, and storage layouts. A company's layout most likely will reflect a combination of these typical layouts. These layouts are discussed in what follows.

3. PRODUCT LAYOUT

3.1 Basic Characteristics of a Product Layout

The basic organization of a product layout (see Figure 8.5) is determined by the production sequence of a part or product in a continuous production system. In this fashion, product departments are established by grouping all of the processes together that are necessary to manufacture the part or product. Product departments are highly efficient, since material movement and storage are kept to a bare minimum. However, they exhibit low flexibility in response to changes in product and/or processes. The objective of a product layout is to sequence properly, in a continuous fashion, all work and to assign work elements to workstations so that workload is balanced amongst workers.

A product layout is recommended if the production volume is adequate and thus yields reasonable equipment utilization. In order to ensure production continuity, the product demand must be reasonably stable, and the material supply must be continuous. Therefore, product layouts can be found in the assembly of washers, dryers, ranges, refrigerators, automobiles, etc. On such assembly lines that move the product from one station to another, appropriate equipment, tools, and machinery are positioned for efficient task performance.

Examples of product layouts are traditional assembly lines, transfer lines and automated assembly systems, kitchens in some fast food restaurants, the maternity ward in most hospitals, and a car wash operation.

The following summarizes the characteristics of continuous production in a product layout environment:

- There are only a few standard products/services, each with a high volume of demand
- The systems utilize special purpose machines, designed to perform highly specialized operations on single product designs
- Equipment is arranged so that products flow through facilities in direct paths
- Departments are often established on the basis of products
- Equipment for moving products and materials through facilities is usually of the fixed path type such as conveyers

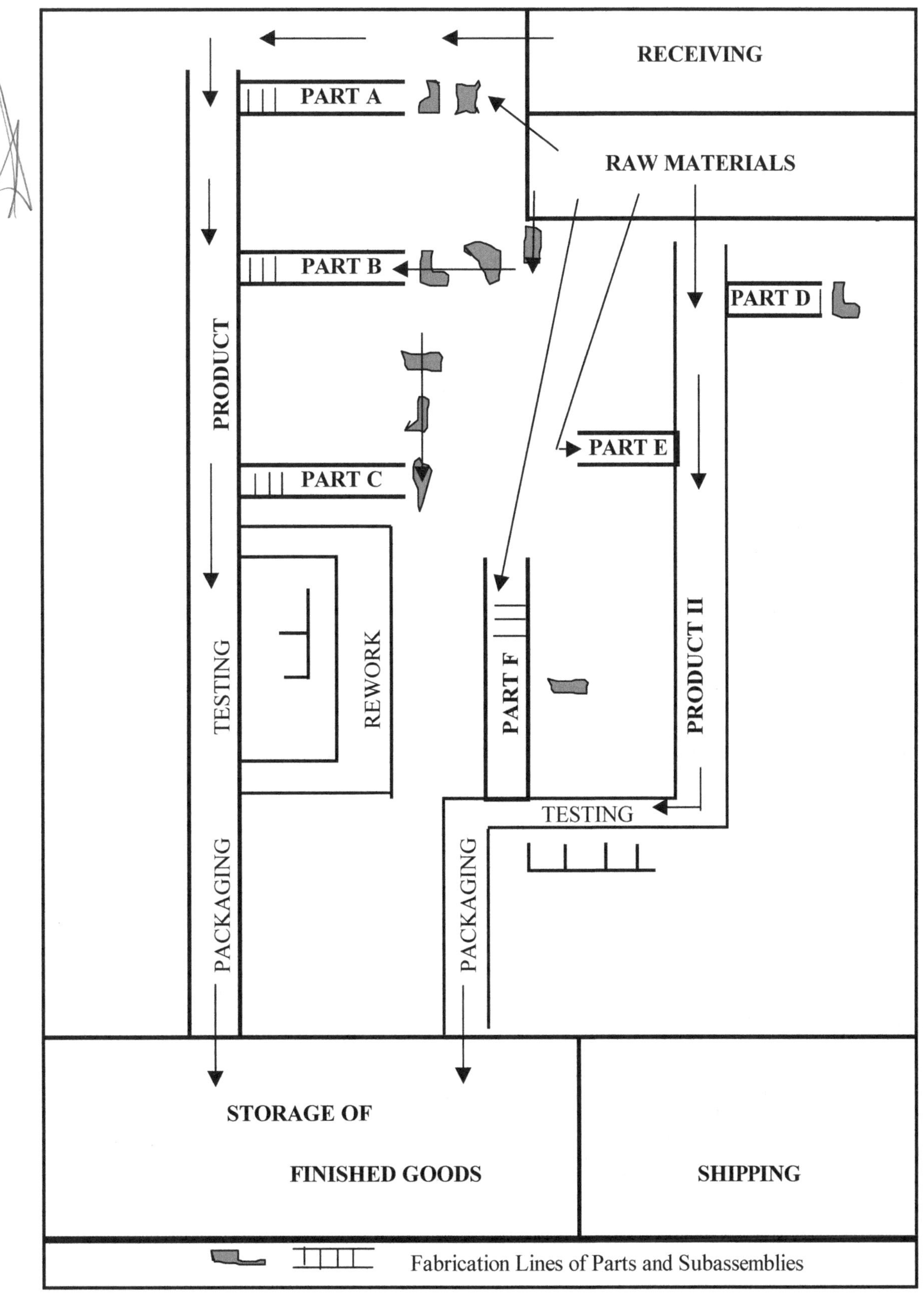

Figure 8.5 Product Layout for the Assembly of two Products

- Little or no inventory builds up between steps of the productive system
- Worker skill level tends to be low, requiring little job training
- Supervision tends to be easy and good, with low supervisor-to-worker ratios
- Process planning is complex but occurs only occasionally when major changeovers to new products are made
- The system is inflexible: it cannot easily be changed to different product designs
- The system offers the lowest per unit cost for most standard high volume products/services
- The system is vulnerable to breakdowns (preventive maintenance is necessary)

3.2 Transfer Lines and Automated Assembly Systems

The transfer line is one of the most highly automated and versatile examples of our modern industrial equipment. On a transfer line, workstations are arranged in a straight line flow pattern and parts are transferred automatically from one station to the other station on the line.

Even though transfer lines originally were designed for machining a single product in high quantities over long production runs, more recently these machines have been designed for ease of changeover, thus allowing different but similar work parts to be produced on the same line. Transfer lines can be synchronous or non-synchronous, can have buffer storage, and may have a variety of monitoring and control features to manage the line.

Automated assembly systems contain all of the following elements: 1) transfer systems; 2) automatic workstations for performing automatic assembly steps; 3) manual assembly stations, where assemblers perform non-mechanized assembly steps; and 4) automatic inspection devices.

The transfer lines used to move parts from one station to the other are dealing with a variety of parts. For each different part or component, careful and timely positioning of the part at each workstation is a problem that needs to be solved. Several devices have been developed to orient and feed assembly components on such lines.

The automatic assembly stations can perform a variety of non-assembly and assembly type of operations. Automatic non-assembly operations are sheet metal forming, drilling and tapping operations, plastic molding, painting, and inspection operations. The following assembly operations are performed on automatic assembly lines: screw driving, press fitting, welding, soldering, riveting, staking, swaging, and adhesive bonding.

U.S. auto makers are introducing more and more automated assembly systems in an effort to produce more efficiently and productively a quality product to compete effectively in the domestic and world marketplaces.

Chrysler Corporation in Kokomo, IN, has one such automated assembly system designed by Ingersoll-Rand's Automated Production Systems Division (APS), Farmington Hills, MI, for the production of trans-axle assemblies. The system up-time, its achieved capacity, is maximized and quality rejects are cut to a near-irreducible minimum, because the system constantly monitors its own performance. The built-in system computer continually charts trends at all stations and signal operations that are heading out of control. In this way, the system can be corrected before a bad assembly is produced. The transfer line is non-synchronous, offering flexibility to accommodate for variable time requirements for the manual operations that are still featured in this system. Production rates exceed 200 per hour at 100% efficiency and assembly reject rates are close to nil.

Control and monitoring capabilities of this system are extraordinary. The supplier can monitor and even re-program stations from its Michigan headquarters through a modern tie-in with the Kokomo plant. In other words, whatever problem may arise in the assembly line operation, engineers at APS can query the system using a computer monitor or data printout on their headquarters' computer and can input corrective measures directly as required when requested by Chrysler.

4. PROCESS OR FUNCTIONAL LAYOUT

4.1 Basic Characteristics of a Process or Functional Layout

A functional layout, also called a process layout (see Figure 8.6), contains process departments, each of which is formed by grouping equipment of the same functional type. Typically, job shops, hospitals, department stores, universities, etc.; consist of process or functional departments. In a manufacturing environment, when the same facilities are used to fabricate and assemble a wide variety of low volume parts for products whose design is not stable, then a functional layout is preferred over a product layout. Though process departments exhibit low efficiency, they represent a high degree of flexibility. When developing a functional layout, the planner is concerned about the relative location of the various functions or process departments, so as to minimize material flow. Functional/process departments have the advantage that they can handle a variety of products/services. Each function or department has its own specialized general purpose equipment and technicians or operators are trained to use any of its equipment for a variety of jobs that can be scheduled for the department.

Functional layouts are not as vulnerable to work stoppages as product layouts are. In a product layout whole lines are doomed to shut down when one or two machines fail. Failure of equipment in a process layout, however, often results in a rescheduling of work on similar equipment within the department. However, there are disadvantages to functional layouts, as well. Because of the slow and dense movement of parts and products from one department to others, excessive in-process inventory is unavoidable.

The following summarizes the characteristics of intermittent production in a process or functional layout environment:

- There are many highly variable nonstandard product/services, each with a low volume of demand
- The systems utilize general purpose machines designed to perform a great variety of general operations on a variety of products
- Equipment is arranged by the type of process performed
- Products follow a variety of paths through facilities depending upon which processes are required
- Departments are based on processes such as painting, forming, and machining. Equipment for moving products and materials through facilities is usually mobile, variable path type of equipment such as fork-lift trucks
- Inventory build-ups frequently occur between steps of the production process sequence
- Worker skill level tends to vary, but is generally high
- Supervision tends to be difficult and is often poorly done, with a high supervisor-to-worker ratio
- Process planning is complex and performed often
- The productive system adapts easily to different product/service designs
- The systems offer the lowest per-unit cost for most non-standard low-volume products/services
- The intermittent productive systems are not as vulnerable to breakdowns as the continuous productive systems

Examples of process or functional layouts can be found in:

- Manufacturing environments that exhibit cut and sheer departments, press departments, plastic extrusion departments, paint departments, and others
- Hospitals with emergency departments, pharmacies, operating rooms, general hospital bed areas, X-ray departments, labs, and others

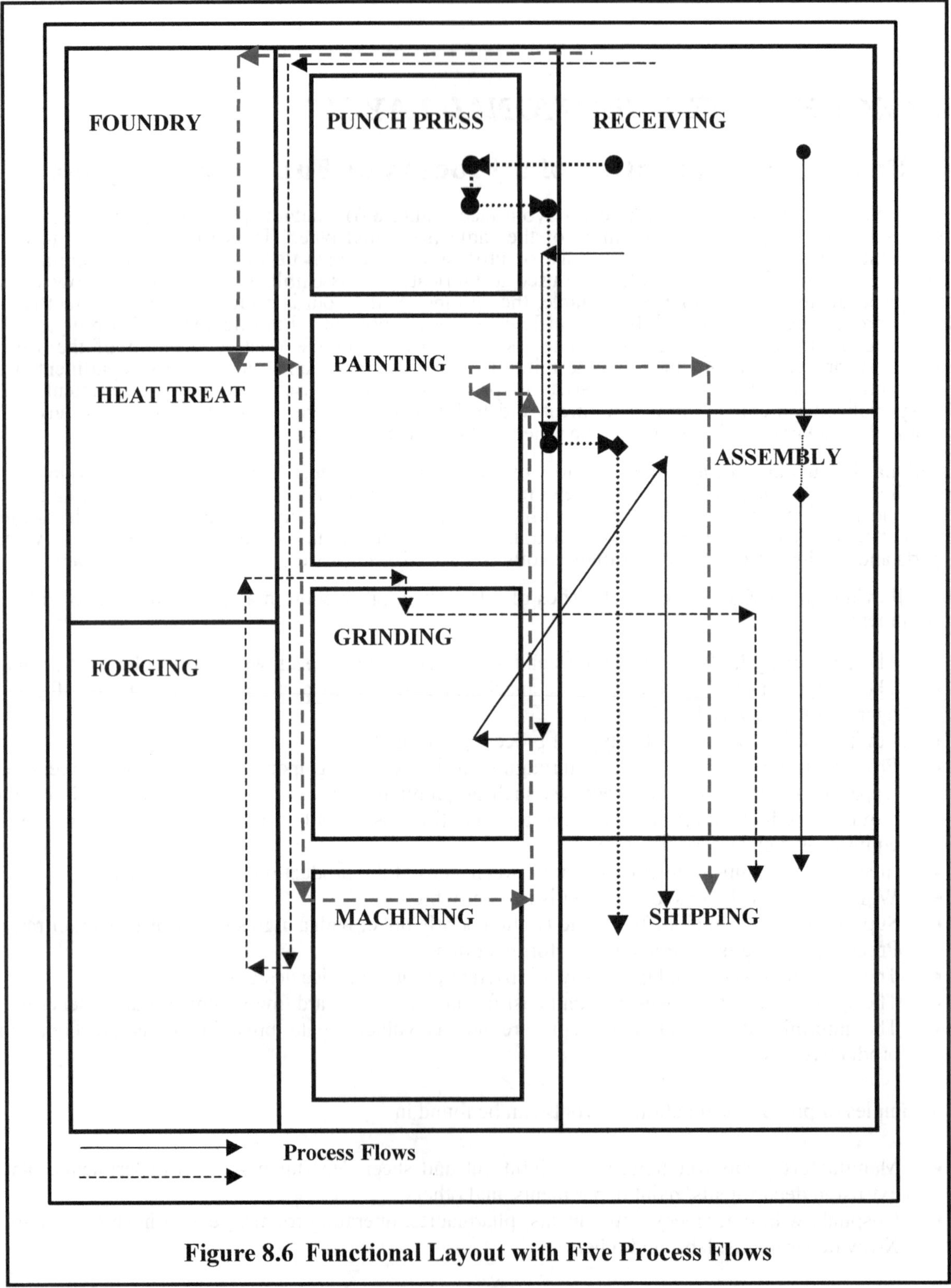

Figure 8.6 Functional Layout with Five Process Flows

4.2 Batch Manufacturing with Conventional and Numerically Controlled Equipment

Twenty-five percent of the parts in the United States are produced by mass production systems. Seventy-five percent of U.S. manufactured parts are produced in lot sizes that may range from 1 to 500, or 1000 or more.

Conventional machinery in job shops produce batches of small quantity (1–10 pieces) with virtually no repeats. Job shops and machine shops are traditionally organized to respond to endless streams of random part orders. A typical job shop or machine shop has more equipment than it usually needs. A survey in Germany (based on a year of 365 days and 24 hours) found that a tool manufacturer using conventional machine tools was actually chipping metal only five percent of the time or less than 500 hours per year and spent 95% of its time in idleness. Conventional machinery in job shops is general purpose equipment. This type of equipment is designed to do one kind of work, rather than one job. Highly skilled operators man this type of equipment. The equipment is very flexible to perform a very wide variety of jobs.

To reduce set-up time, reduce operator time, and increase production speed and accuracy, **numerically controlled (NC) equipment** has been designed for metal cutting. These machines are well suited for parts made in small to medium size lots (1 to 1,000 pieces per batch). Numerically controlled machines are general purpose machines that are controlled using a computer to select the proper tool, to insert the tool into the machine, to set the proper machine operating speed, to control the machine motions, and to sequence different tools, motions, and operations of the job. Thus the machine operator of an NC machine does not need to be as skilled as the operator who works with a conventional machine.

NC machines are expensive and require constant complex maintenance. NC equipment comes under the form of DNC or CNC machines. DNC machines are direct numerically controlled machines that are directly linked with a remote computer from which they obtain their instructions on a time sharing basis. If the equipment has its own microprocessor or minicomputer then the equipment is referred to as computerized numerically controlled (CNC) equipment.

5. GROUP, GT, CELLULAR, LEAN LAYOUTS

5.1 Basic Characteristics of Group, GT, Cellular, Lean Layouts

The trade-off that needs to be made between the efficiency of a product layout and the flexibility of a functional layout does not need be made with a group layout (see Figures 8.7 and 8.8). Group departments of a group layout handle specific groups or families of products. The concept of group layout evolved from the field of group technology. Group technology is a manufacturing philosophy whose basic concept is to arrange the required machines, tools, and other equipment for a part family into groups or cells to produce the parts. In this fashion, parts of the same family are completed within the same cell, without leaving it. Within that cell we, therefore, have straight line production of all different parts belonging to the family of parts. This concept significantly reduces the movement of parts within the plant. It also results in a significant reduction of work-in-process inventory, throughput time, and machine set-up time. In this way, overall manufacturing productivity is improved.

Families of items are established by classifying them into categories by shape, material, and/or manufacturing processing characteristics. Before engaging in group technology analysis and subsequent group layout, all of the following must exist:

- Many parts exhibit design redundancy
- There are many similar parts requiring similar processing
- The present equipment is laid out functionally (according to a process layout)
- The present set-up cost is relatively high
- Work-in-process inventory is high and costly
- Shop lead times are long
- Material handling time is significantly larger than the actual manufacturing time of parts
- Similar parts are processed in diverse ways

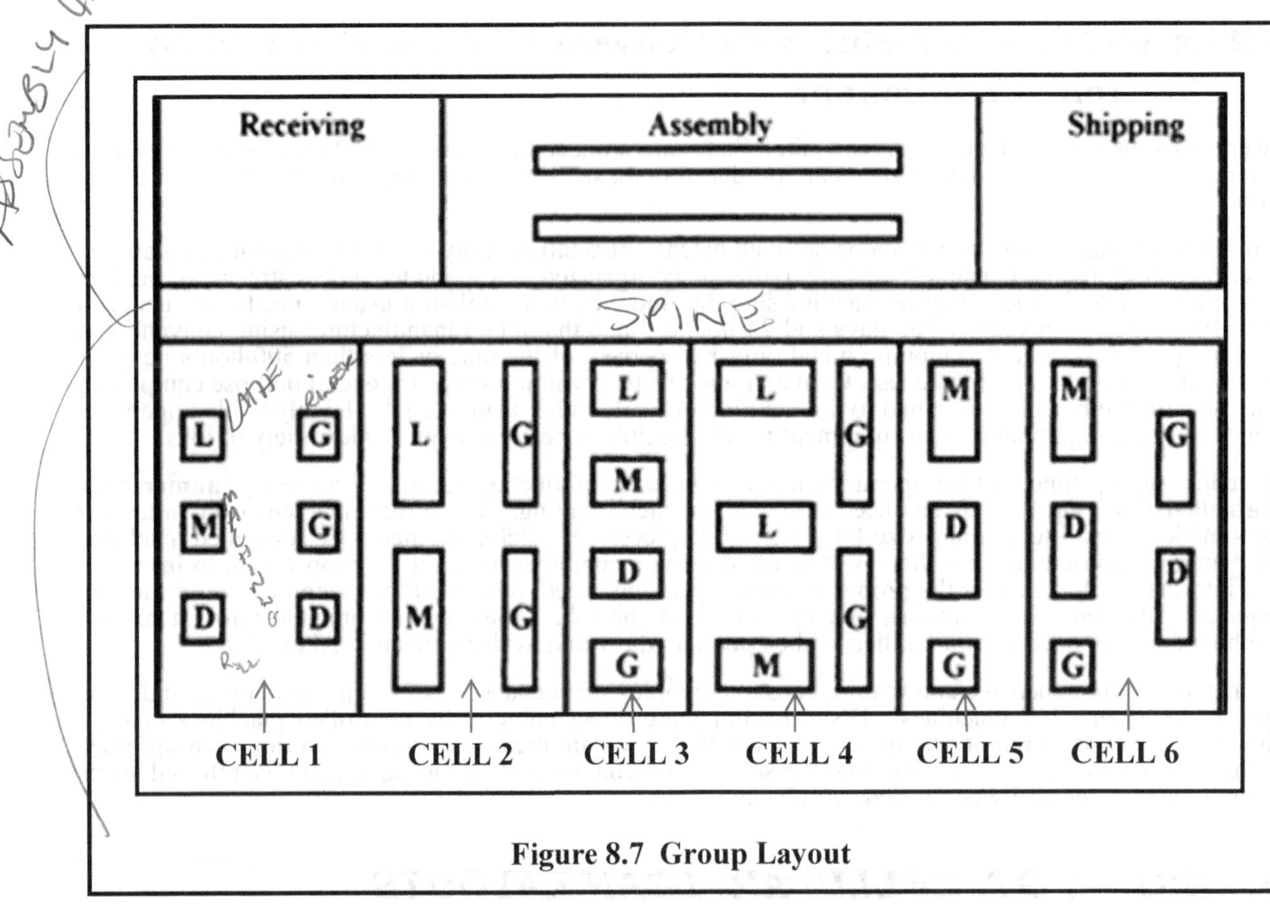

Figure 8.7 Group Layout

The goal of a lean layout is to allow for the production of quality parts or services at takt time (the amount of time available to produce one unit based on the customer demand rate), while minimizing non-value-added activities. A lean layout accomplishes all of the following:

- Facilitates the flow of material and work
- Minimizes walking
- Minimizes travel
- Reduces work-in-process inventory
- Decreases production or shop lead times
- Allows for the immediate flow of information and feedback
- Promotes a good balance among workers.
- Allows for changes in demand
- Encourages sharing of work
- Promotes communication within the cell
- Creates flexibility in managing the cell according to set rules
- Leads to a pull production system, rather than a push production system

If a company's layout (whether functional, line, cellular, or a combination of these) does not exhibit all of these characteristics, then a change is needed. For a process or activities to flow correctly, all these criteria must be met. Operations ought to be located as closely together as possible. This is where the concept of cellular production/operations, based on group technology, comes into play. Placing progressive operations in a U-shaped cell that flows counter clockwise is one of the best options.

Manufacturing in a group layout or a cell is called cellular manufacturing.

Research on the use of group technology in U.S. companies has revealed that group layout of diverse equipment in manufacturing cells has reduced set-up times and cost by 20 to 30%, has reduced work-in-process inventory by 25 to 40%, and has reduced lead time by as much as 80%.

If it is not possible to cellularize the entire process, then various cells can be linked with supermarkets. A supermarket is similar to a warehouse, where the stored product is policed by a kanban system. Only when the operation downstream pulls the product, depleting the inventory to the re-order point, does the operation upstream begin producing the required amount. This is communicated between the two operations via kanban triggers, or signal cards.

Look at the value stream map of Figure 4.10. There are many problems with that layout. It does not promote a good balance between operations. There are other problems with the layout as well. Besides poor communications between operations, excessive inventory has been placed on the shop floor. Figure 4.11 exhibits an improved layout with two work cells that are well balanced. This layout has a supermarket to link the two cells properly and a kanban system is introduced to pull production through the system. This improved layout now meets the customer's demand.

The cellular layout of Figure 8.8 suggests that workers can be added to a cell or taken out of a cell, depending on an increase or decrease of takt time. More workers can be added to a cell if product demand increases. Likewise, people can be removed from a cell if demand rate decreases. This is easily done in a lean environment, where workers are generalists and trained to operate a variety of equipment. Workers are not necessarily assigned to one specific machine. Rather, they may be assigned to operate more than one machine on a rotating basis, as shown in Figure 8.8. Flexible manufacturing systems (FMS) as discussed below are examples of automated cellular layouts.

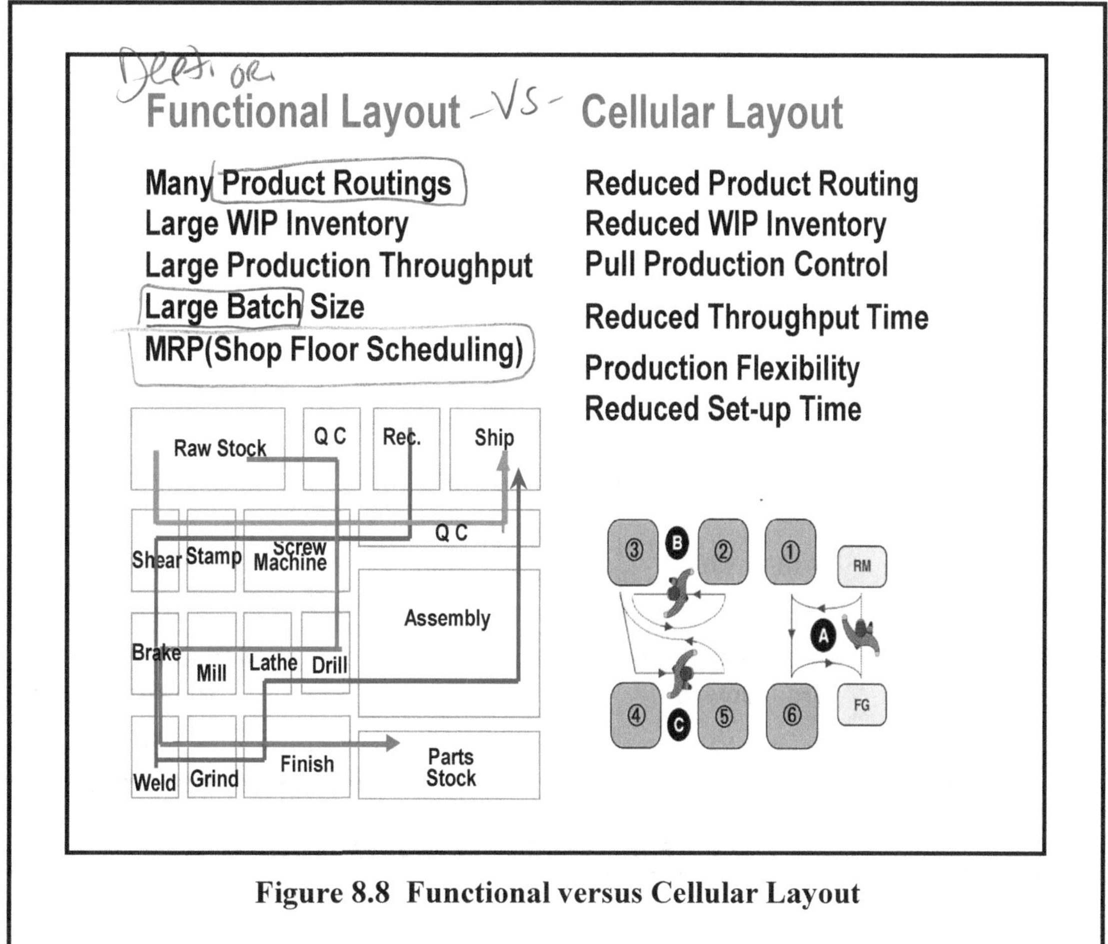

Figure 8.8 Functional versus Cellular Layout

Figure 8.9 presents a comparison between the product layout, the functional layout, and the GT layout for the following ten basic layout characteristics that have been addressed in this chapter: product type, equipment type, product flow, material handling, inventory, worker skill, supervision, process planning, system flexibility, and maintenance. The table also lists some of the available layout methods that are briefly discussed in this chapter.

Most lean layouts, like the GT or cellular layouts, allow for multiple products at relatively low volume. This production most likely is performed with variable purpose equipment that is laid out in flexible manufacturing cells. The materials often follow a fixed or variable flow on fixed or variable material handling equipment. Movement in these cells occurs over relatively short distances. Because of the relatively high level of production synchronization in these cells, in-process inventory tends to be low. These characteristics are listed in the third column of Figure 8.9. As compared to the product layout and the functional layout, the GT layout is clearly the preferred layout.

	PRODUCT	*PROCESS*	*GT*
PRODUCT TYPE	Few Products and High Volume	Multiple products and Low Volume	Multiple Products Medium Volume
EQUIPMENT TYPE	Special Purpose	Variable Purpose	Variable Purpose
PRODUCT FLOW	Fixed Flow	Variable Flow	Variable Flow
MATERIAL HANDLING	Fixed Path	Variable Path	Fixed/Variable Path
INVENTORY	Low	High	Reasonably Low
WORKER SKILL	Low	Higher	Higher
SUPERVISION	Good	Poor	Reasonably Good
PROCESS PLANNING	Rarely	Often	Often, Aided by GT
SYSTEM FLEXIBILITY	Non flexible	Flexible	Flexible
MAINTENANCE	PM, Vulnerable to Breakdowns	Not Vulnerable to Breakdowns	Medium Vulnerable to Breakdowns
METHOD	Line Balancing	Travel Chart	GT

Figure 8.9 Layout Characteristics

5.2 Flexible Manufacturing Systems

The automated random or flexible manufacturing system (FMS) is designed for medium quantity production (1,000 to 10,000 pieces) with some repetition of parts. These systems can handle "families" of similar parts, as defined by group technology, in different process sequences.

If several numerically controlled machine tools are linked through an integrated material handling system and if the mainframe computer is programmed to operate the tools in a specified sequence, then we have a flexible manufacturing system. In such a system, families of parts are selected through group technology for machining. As soon as a pallet of work pieces is set in place, these work pieces move automatically from tool to tool and are thus machined in a proper sequence. Many FMS systems require being loaded and unloaded only once a day. One person can oversee the whole operation. The percent of time a machine spends cutting work pieces during a shift can be as high as 50 to 90 percent in an FMS. This compares to 10 to 30 percent for standalone computer numerically controlled machine tools.

A flexible manufacturing system is a dedicated machining facility and/or assembly line that utilizes following four automation concepts and technologies in a single system:

- Numerically controlled and CNC (computerized numerically controlled) machine tools
- Automated material handling system between machine tools
- A supervisory direct numeric control over the material handling system and the machine tools
- Group technology principles

According to the processing requirements, a FMS can be classified as a dedicated (or fixed sequence) FMS or a random FMS system. A dedicated FMS is more flexible than a transfer line, but only produces a limited variety of parts. The number of parts in a family is from 3 to 10 and the average batch size is 1,000 to 10,000 units.

A random FMS handles a greater variety of parts in a random sequence. It can accommodate from 4 to 50 different parts in a family with an average batch size of 50 to 2,000 units. Several different parts can be machined simultaneously on standard general purpose NC machines, and the layout configuration makes it possible to route parts to any choice of machines. Machine tools can perform the following operations: assembling (fasting, placement, welding), machining (boring, drilling, facing, grinding, milling, tapping), inspecting, loading/unloading of work piece, heat treating, painting, and finishing. General purpose machine tools are used in this kind of a system.

Material handling systems are used to transport in-process parts from one machine to another one. Some successful examples of material handling systems are towlines, robots, automated storage/retrieval systems, roller conveyer systems, car-on-track systems, automated guided vehicle systems (AGV), shuttles ,and monorails. Typical characteristics of a FMS material handling system are the absence of floor obstructions and low cost per unit and per foot transport. FMS material handling systems are very reliable, quiet, flexible, and expandable.

Automation in a FMS is accomplished through a variety of computer control systems that supervise the machine tools and material transportation systems. The computer control systems perform the following general functions: computer control of the production operations on the individual machines (CNC), direct numerical control of all the machine tools (DNC), computer control of the material handling system, collection of production- and maintenance- related data (monitoring system), and the overall supervisory control functions related to production control, traffic control, and tool control.

A Flexible manufacturing system can furnish major improvements in productivity at every phase of the metal working process. Here are some success stories:

- The FMS installed at General Electric's locomotive plant (Erie, Pennsylvania) reduced the previous time of 16 days to finish a motor housing to a mere 8 hours.
- The $8 million system installed by the Harris Corporation (Melbourne, Florida) reduced the previously required 120,000 machine hours to produce printing press rollers to 40,000 machine hours, while greatly improving the quality of the parts.
- Other companies, including the Hughes Tool Co., Renault, General Motors, and Acme Cleveland Corporation have experienced the increase in production and quality that FMS affords.

- The flexible manufacturing system utilized by John Deere Component Works in Iowa helped the company to increase productivity, reduce work-in-process inventory, cut lead times, eliminate extra handling, and save floor space. The Deere operation was successful because of a special make-ready operation. Parts are mounted on pallets that carry identification codes. Computer controlled towline carts arrive at palletizing stations carrying fixtures by workers who report part numbers and pallet codes at a computer terminal and release the carts to the towline. The identification codes are "read" at transfer points, routing the parts to the right machine tools.
- One of the most successful FMS is that at Messerschmidt in Germany. The small firm was at a disadvantage in the costly move to automation.
- After applying FMS concepts, Toshiba Tungoloy Co. in Japan reported great reductions in the number of machine tools used (from 50 to 18), in production personnel (from 70 to 16), in average production time (from 15.6 days to 4.2 days), and in floor space (from 16,000 ft^2 to 3,767 ft^2). Shortly after the installation of the FMS systems, its machine utilization increased from 20% to 64%.

6. FIXED MATERIAL LAYOUT

In a fixed material layout the final product does not move, instead, the processes and materials are brought to the final production area. This layout is productive for extremely large or heavy products, such as airplanes and ships or for goods with an extremely low volume of output. (In a fixed material layout the product is removed from the construction area when the job is completed.). Some airplane assemblies have moved from a fixed material layout to an assembly type of product layout, creating huge assembly lines. These layouts have increased, sometimes doubled, the speed of assembly, thus resulting in a leaner way of assembly.

7. PROJECT LAYOUT

This layout is quite similar to the fixed material layout. It is used in the construction industry for buildings, roads, bridges, dams, sea walls, etc. Here, too, the end product is fairly large, and material, equipment, and manpower are moved to the construction site. The main difference between the project layout and the fixed material layout is that at the completion of the job the product is not removed from the site of the project. Rather, material, scrap, equipment, and manpower move on to another construction site.

8. STORAGE AND WAREHOUSE LAYOUTS

Storage and warehouse layouts fulfill an inventory function. Quick storage and retrieval is the main objective of such layouts. Because incoming material and finished goods can occupy a relatively large area of a facility, efficient space utilization is another objective of storage layouts. Efficient storage layouts require efficient material handling equipment. The first patented material handling and storage system, LOAD BANK, is a flow-through storage system that combines the forces of air and gravity to give loads a safe and gentle ride with a first-in-first-out control on inventory retrieval.

An efficient storage layout addresses following fundamental lean storage principles:

1. Slotting
2. Zoning
3. Space sizing for minimum and maximum inventory requirements
4. Vertical product orientation
5. Ergonomics of picking
6. 5S system implementation

Slotting requires segmenting the warehouse into at least three areas: a fast moving section, a midrange moving section, and a slow moving section. In a warehouse used for redistribution the fast moving items must be closely located to receiving and shipping docks, whereas the slow moving items are located the farthest away from the shipping and receiving docks. This approach significantly reduces the travel time when storing and picking items. It implies that we study the picking path history of various orders over at least a one-month period to determine which items belong to each group. There exist warehouse management systems that perform such analysis and help slot your inventory items. This principle is often referred to as storing by velocity. This slotting principle is exhibited in Figure 8.10.

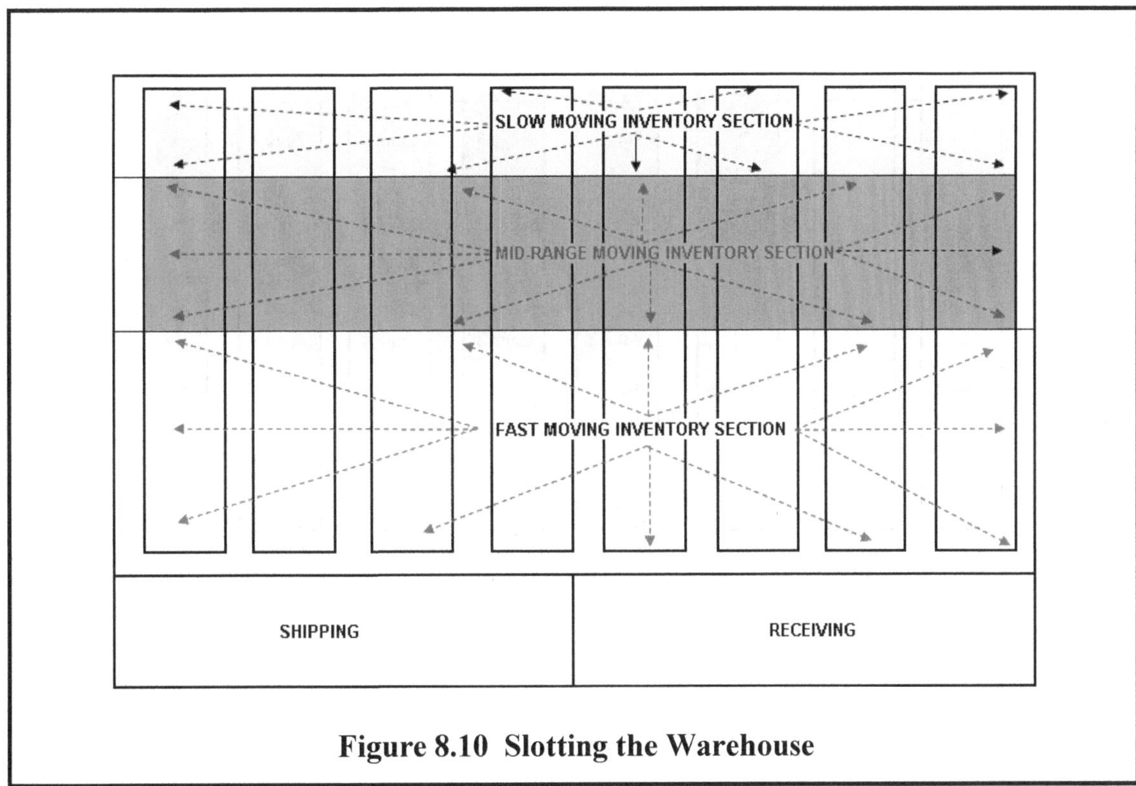

Figure 8.10 Slotting the Warehouse

Zoning implies that items being stored are grouped based on various characteristics such as weight, size, packaging, small or large boxed items, pallet size, wrapped or unwrapped items, etc. In the example shown in Figure 8.11, the warehouse is divided into five zones for each of the three slotted areas. It is conceivable that not all three slotted areas have the same number or type of zones. Different zones may require different storing/picking equipment that must be located in the vicinity of their zones.

Space sizing refers to allocating the correct amount of space for inventory items. This requires defining the minimum and maximum inventory quantity levels and analyzing required volume and square footage for products being warehoused, so that sufficient space can be allocated and demarcated on the shelves. Assigning too much shelf space for inventory items is not desirable, because it will increase picking time and underutilize warehouse space. Not allocating sufficient space for inventory items tend to spill inventory into the wrong shelf space or aisles, which is equally undesirable. Lean warehouses stock inventory tightly, ideally reflecting an average of 80% space utilization.

Vertical storage orientation is especially necessary if the shelf depth does not accommodate the longest measurement of the product. Vertical storage orientation tends to minimize shelf requirements and improves the visibility of all inventory items.

Ergonomics of picking relates to storing products within easy reach of the pickers, and placing heavy items close to the floor, preferably at waist height. Using stools to reach products on high shelves is not only dangerous but also requires more time for the storing and picking activity. This may require reducing shelf height to make the top shelf accessible. Placing heavy items on top shelves makes the warehouse unsafe and makes storing and picking physically stressful.

SLOW MOVING INVENTORY SECTION

Zone 1	Zone 2	Zone 3	Zone 3	Zone 3	Zone 4	Zone 4	Zone 5

MID-RANGE MOVING INVENTORY SECTION

Zone 1	Zone 2	Zone 3	Zone 3	Zone 3	Zone 4	Zone 4	Zone 5
			Zone 3	Zone 3	Zone 4	Zone 4	

FAST MOVING INVENTORY SECTION

Zone 1	Zone 2	Zone 3	Zone 3	Zone 3	Zone 4	Zone 4	Zone 5
			Zone 3	Zone 3	Zone 4	Zone 4	

SHIPPING	RECEIVING

Figure 8.11 Zoning the Slotted Warehouse

5S system implementation relates to sorting, straightening, shining, standardizing, and sustaining an organized functional warehouse. **Sorting** requires that only those items that move must be placed on shelves. All obsolete items must be removed from the warehouse. **Straightening** the warehouse requires storing items in appropriate zones of designated slots. Inventory items with different SKUs must have a separate demarcated location on the shelves. It is necessary that inventory records match up with the warehouse locations for each SKU. Visual controls can be introduced to keep the shelves organized: product labels, demarcation lines, etc. Finally, aisles, shelves, or racks and bins must be clearly marked. **Shining** requires that the warehouse has no clutter or unwanted items in aisles and on racks. The area must be clean and safe for all workers. **Standardized** procedures must be developed to work in the warehouse. Value stream mapping or flow process mapping can be used to develop the best way for performing warehousing tasks. Only warehouse workers must be allowed in the warehouse. All others must be accompanied by an authorized warehouse worker. When storing and picking procedures are standardized and when the warehouse is properly organized, it should take a minimum amount of time to train new workers. Literature on leaning the warehouse suggests that it should not take longer than two days to train a worker to pick. **Sustaining** warehouse organization is not an easy task. Under supervision of the supervisor, it is the responsibility of the warehouse workers to sustain order. This requires proper training. Regular auditing of the warehouse may help sustain an orderly warehouse.

9. OVERVIEW OF METHODS

9.1 The Travel Chart Method for Functional Layouts

In many applications, there are a large variety of products and/or activities flowing between departments in many different sequences. The arrangement of these departments in such a way as to reduce the material handling cost to a reasonably low value becomes a challenging task. Factors affecting material handling costs include the following: volume of material moved, weight, and distance.

It is intuitive that it is desirable to put those work centers that have the greatest amount of interaction adjacent to each other. Good layout involves considering and reconciling all competing and offsetting costs. By working through several alternative plans and costing each, the layout engineer will finally arrive at a layout which is superior even though there is no guarantee that it is the best.

The heuristic travel chart method is a method that can aid the layout engineer in properly planning the location of the departments. The travel chart that shows in matrix format the amount of material moved from each function/department to each of the other functions/departments is used to facilitate the engineer in preparing the initial layout plan. Once the travel chart is established it is scanned to find the largest entry. These two departments, between which the largest amount of material is moved, are then diagrammatically placed adjacent to each other. The travel chart is now repeatedly re-scanned for the next largest entry and appropriate departments are located, until all departments have been considered. This method yields a good initial layout diagram. Minor improvements (e.g., reduction in material handling) might still be possible by changing the relative location of one or two departments at a time. When all departments are satisfactorily diagrammatically placed, the diagram must now be adjusted to give each department its required area within the company's floor plan.

The input to the heuristic travel chart method consists of the following basic items:

- Name and number by which each department is to be referenced
- Dimension of the floor space on which the layout must fit
- Flow patterns of most jobs worked on during a representative period of time
- Number of different items, the average annual volume, and the average difficulty rating for each of the flow patterns

Experiments have shown that computer assistance in layout does not necessarily yield better layouts in terms of material handling cost, since experienced engineering planners have been able to come up with equally good low-cost final layouts as computer programs have. It seems that the only major advantage of computer aided layout is that they can be generated more quickly than what human planners can do.

In conclusion, interactive heuristic programming is the key to efficient plant layout. It utilizes the best talents of both man and machine. On the one hand, humans can grasp, understand, and manipulate large amounts of information when presented in graphical format; whereas, on the other hand, heuristic computer programming is effective in reducing the amount of computer search required to find acceptable solutions and program decision rules are able to internally modify the direction of the search to reduce time in finding improved layouts.

9.2 Assembly Line Balancing for Product Layouts

Since the introduction of the progressive assembly technique via a conveyor into the manufacturing industry in 1913, line balancing has been recognized as one of the most important factors of production efficiency. The work pace of each individual worker no longer can be set by him- or herself, but completely depends upon the line cycle time. Therefore, any bottleneck station(s) (where the workers are highly loaded) along the line would slow down the normal working pace of all other stations. Industry is estimated to waste from five to twenty percent of the time of its assembly workers due to the loss caused by the balance delay. This loss results in lower production efficiency, or higher direct labor cost, which can never be recovered.

An unequal allocation of workload among the assembly workers also results in grievances by and dissatisfaction of workers who have heavier workloads than others. Those workers who are under-loaded may become accustomed to a lower than normal work pace and tend to retain this slower work pace even though this under-load condition in these stations may be changed at some later time. Then, it would take time for those workers to re-establish their normal work pace. As a result, the line change time may be prolonged and an unnecessary bottleneck condition on the assembly line may develop.

For years, industrial engineers have devoted a majority of their time to balancing and re-balancing assembly lines. Due to the extreme complexity of line balancing under practical production conditions there has been no guarantee, or absolute measure, of achieving an optimal balanced line. In an attempt to resolve this problem, numerous methods or techniques have been developed and adopted by different manufacturers. A definite trend in industry today is to use a computer aided line balancing system for reducing the engineer's time and for achieving consistency in line balancing results. However, the quality of line balancing will still largely depend on the line balancing technique itself.

The traditional method for assembly line balancing is often **the simple trial-and-error procedure.** This method can still be found in many assembly manufacturing companies today. The results of line balancing by trial-and-error method are largely dependent on the experience of the individual industrial engineers. Chance also plays an important role in the final result. With this method, there is no definite way or assurance that it leads towards optimal line assignments. Furthermore, this is a time consuming procedure.

An improvement to this trial-and-error procedure is sorting of assembly element description cards into pigeon holes representing assembly workstations. The **pigeonhole** approach can reduce the engineer's time but it has very little effect on the final result.

The first analytical approach towards the line balancing problem is the use of a precedence diagram to show the ordered relationship of the assembly operations. Many companies that use the precedence diagram approach, balance their assembly lines by pencil and paper, or manual methods. However, the precedence diagram is also the basis for computerized line balancing techniques. It is accepted by most companies and industrial engineers that computerization is the definite trend and direction of assembly line balancing today and tomorrow. Several computer assisted line balancing techniques have been formulated and tested with varying degrees of success. Some of these are:

- **Ranked Positional Weight Method**, by Helgeson and Birnie in early 1961, gives a good initial station assignment, but it makes no attempt to smooth station time or to minimize station idle time.
- **Dual-Matrices Method**, by Dr. C. Moodie & J. Mize of Purdue University, 1964, considers only the time value of each individual work element, by assigning the job that has the largest time value and meets the precedence relationship.
- **Target-Job Line Balancing (TJLB) Method**, by the Ford-Motor Company, 1965-66, is based on a target job list. The jobs that are associated with either fixed tools or stock supplies are assigned as target jobs. The allocation of work stations is started from one of the target jobs and then traced back to all its predecessors in order to free this target job from precedence restrictions. If there is any choice among its predecessors, the job with the largest element time will be assigned first. This system is written to balance assembly lines that are unique to the automobile industry.
- **Computer Aided Line Balancing (CALB) Program**, by the Advanced Manufacturing Methods Program at Illinois Institute of Technology Research, 1967, is one of the most popular computerized assembly line balancing programs in the industry. Users are: General Motors Corporation, Bell Helicopter Textron, IBM Corporation, etc. Important aspects of CALB are that no programming knowledge is needed for the use of the program and it is capable of handling many complex assembly situations such as mixed models, multi-man stations, cooperative work, and physical restrictions.
- **Multiple Decision Rules (MDR) Assembly Line Balancing Technique**, by Jack and Nesa Wu, 1970, is a line balancing procedure that consists of two phases. The first phase is a systematic procedure whereby work elements are assigned on an individual basis to each workstation. The last two job assignments in a workstation may be considered jointly in order to generate minimum slack times. For most cases, the MDR line balancing technique gives a good initial assignment. However, further improvement of the initial assignment is often possible. For the MDR technique, further improvement of the initial assignment is done by a smoothing procedure, the second phase of the method. This smoothing procedure can only be used to increase the line speed or the line productivity. The number of workstations will not be reduced by this procedure.

9.3 Terminology of Line Balancing

Cycle Time (*C*) is the time that the product spends at each station and is thus the time that is normally available to an operator to perform his assigned tasks. It is therefore also the elapsed time between units coming off the production line.

Station Time (*S*) is the actual amount of work assigned to a specific station on the assembly line.

Minimum Rational Work Element (E_i) is a rational division of the total work content in natural minimum work units.

Total Work Content or Total Direct Time (*T*) is the aggregate amount of work of the total assembly:

$$T = \sum_{i=1}^{n} E_i$$

Station Slack Time or Idle Time is the difference between the cycle time and the sum of work element times assigned to the station.

Total Slack or Idle Time is the total amount of time that the workers on a line are not performing any value-added task:

$$\text{the number of stations} \times \text{cycle time} - \sum \text{work element times}$$

Balance Delay (*BD*) is the degree or the percent of unbalance. It is the ratio between the total idle time and the total time spent by the product in moving from the beginning to the end of the line.

Precedence Diagram is a graphical description of any ordering in which elements must be performed in achieving the total assembly of the product.

Minimum Number of Stations (K_{min}) is the number of work stations required on the assembly line when the balance delay between any two stations could be zero.

$$K_{min} = \left[\frac{T}{C}\right]^{+}$$

9.4 Objectives of Line Balancing

The objectives of line balancing are

- Given the cycle time (C), minimize the number of work stations, or
- Given the number of stations (K), minimize the line cycle time, or
- Minimize the balance delay time for given conditions (optimize the C and K combination).

An Example: Analysis of a Balanced Line

Consider the precedence Diagram in Figure 8.12.

This precedence diagram consists of 11 work elements and their precedence relationships. The times for each of the work elements are placed next to the element nodes and are in decimal minutes. If the desired rate of production for this example is 60units/hour (60 units per hour = 1 min. cycle time), the assignment to stations is as shown in Table 8.1, resulting in the following line characteristics:

Proposed cycle time: $C = 1$ min.

Optimal cycle time: 0.95 min (is defined by the slowest station)

Total work content: $T = \sum_{i=1}^{11} E_i = 5.25$ min.

Total line content: $6 \text{ (stations)} \times 0.95 \text{min/ station} = 5.70 \text{ min}$

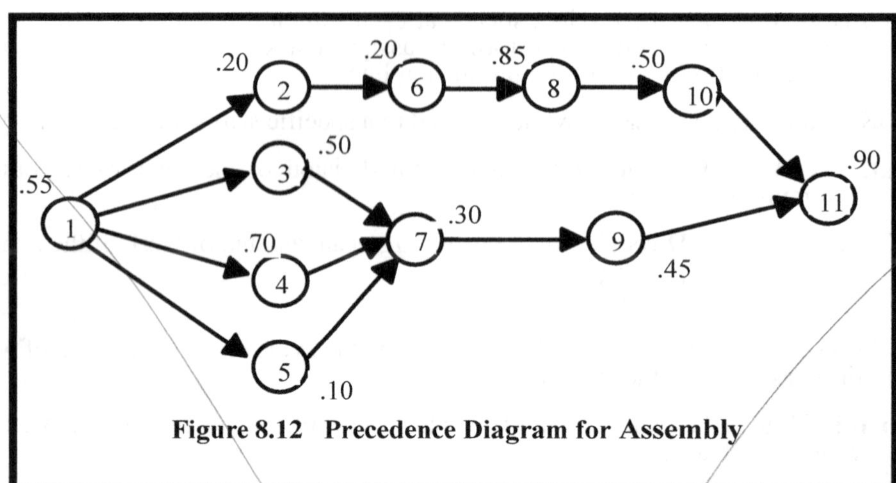

Figure 8.12 Precedence Diagram for Assembly

Total idle time: 5.70 min.–5.25 min. = 0.45 min.

Balance delay: $\dfrac{0.45}{5.70} \times 100\% = 7.89\%$

Minimum number of stations: $K_{min} = \left[\dfrac{5.25}{1}\right]^{+} = 6$

Line efficiency: 100%–7.89% = 92.11%

Table 8.11: Assignment of Work Elements to Stations

Station #	Work Element #	Work Element Time (E_i)	Sum of Work Element Times	Unassigned Cycle Time	Slack Time
1	1 2 6	0.55 0.20 0.20	0.55 0.75 0.95	0.45 0.25 0.05	0.00
2	4 5	0.70 0.10	0.70 0.80	0.30 0.20	0.15
3	8	0.85	0.85	0.15	0.10
4	3 7	0.50 0.30	0.50 0.80	0.50 0.20	0.15
5	9 10	0.45 0.50	0.45 0.95	0.55 0.05	0.00
6	11	0.90	0.90	0.10	0.05

Because the total work content is 5.25 minutes and the proposed cycle time is 1 minute, the minimum number of stations that are needed to perform this assembly is 6 stations. A maximum efficiency of 92.11% reflects a fairly well balanced line.

10. CAPACITY PLANNING

Capacity planning starts before any other decisions on location or layout are made. Capacity issues, such as meeting short- and medium-term demands, are complex. Companies use various strategies to manage capacity and adjust capacity to meet changes in demand. Short- to medium-term capacity issues are concerned with providing adequate capacity in a timely fashion to meet the demand over a certain planning period. Defining such capacity is known as capacity planning and control.

A company's capacity can be measured in terms of output or input; however, in the service industry measuring capacity can be fairly complex.

In this section we will discuss the complexity of measuring capacity, look at three major strategies in order to balance demand and capacity; define three types of capacity measures (design capacity, effective capacity, and achieved capacity); and discuss machine utilization, efficiency, and overall equipment effectiveness including considering the capacity of a company's IT infrastructure to support the company business.

10.1 The Complexity of Measuring Capacity

Capacity can be measured in terms of input or output. It can be defined in a very straightforward way in certain industries and become more complex in others. To understand the complexity in measuring capacity, let us look at certain production systems as defined in Chapter 1.

In continuous flow production systems, such as paper mills, the food processing industries, TV, radio, home appliance manufacturing companies, many automobile assembly plants, refineries, and institutional feeding systems (at prisons, army, etc.) defining capacity is fairly straight forward:

- In typical assembly line operations, the flow rate of materials and the production output rate are defined by the speed of the line. Here we can talk about the output capacity of the line that can be measured as the maximum possible output of that line over a specific time period.
- A refinery operates on a continuous basis and its various columns, such as the topping, the reformer, the thermic reformer, the vacuum unit, the catalytic cracking unit, and the catalytic polymerization unit, together with its pipes, valves, and pumps, determine the output capacity of the refinery in terms of its product mix. This product mix consists of gas, propane, butane, P.F.D, benzene, naphthalene, kerosene, gasoline, residue, and others. However, capacity can also be determined in terms of the number of barrels of crude oil that is processed during a given time unit.
- Institutional feeding systems can determine their capacity by the number of meals served during a fixed amount of time: breakfast period, lunch period, or dinner period.

In intermittent production systems, often synonymous to batch production systems in a manufacturing environment, defining capacity is more complex. Examples of job shops are auto parts production centers, machine parts production centers, parts production centers for any kind of assembly, bakeries, general education centers, general hospitals, etc. Here materials and inputs are used in a variety of ways and the batches in which they are produced may vary. This can cause unavoidable down time because of equipment changeover or because of scheduling problems. Therefore the actual theoretical capacity of an operation in the system is often quite different from what it is able to do:

- In a typical parts manufacturing company, with parts being produced in batches, moving from one process to the other, downtime caused by maintenance, quality adjustment problems, machine set-up, scheduling problems, and others may significantly reduce capacity utilization. Companies with standalone, variable purpose, and non-automated equipment could have a capacity utilization of 30 to 50%. When production becomes more synchronized, such capacity utilization may increase to 85% (like in FMS systems). Capacity in such companies is best defined by its input measure: available equipment.
- The capacity of a general hospital is often defined by the number of beds it has. This is a typical input measure by which the capacity of a hospital could be defined. However, a hospital offers a variety of services with variable service times, making it very difficult to predict the flow of patients through the system. Perhaps an output measure, like the number of patients treated, might be used as a capacity measure. However, this measure very much depends on the mix of services the hospital performs.
- The capacity of a restaurant, serving customers a variety of meals, can best be determined by an input measure: the available number of seats.

- The capacity of a company's IT infrastructure (servers, storage, network architecture) is often defined in how many users are accessing the company's business applications (e.g. ERP system for order processing, inventory management, shipping and receiving, accounts receivable, accounts payable, financial systems, and procurement) during peak hours. If the utilization has reached 80 percent utilized and the line of business has forecasted that it will continue to grow, then plans have to be made to upgrade capacity. Perhaps this upgrade would be in the form of procuring larger servers which may include upgrading operating systems and the middleware software to the next releases requiring in turn license upgrades or renewal, more storage, and/or possibly additional network equipment to improve response time. The company has to monitor and control the capacity of their IT infrastructure constantly and keep the licenses and software maintenance current.

10.2 Strategies for Balancing Capacity and Demand

Companies use many strategies to balance capacity and demand. Here we will examine three such strategies: level capacity, chase demand, and demand management.

Level Capacity

This strategy aims at keeping the level of capacity constant during a given planning horizon, regardless of the fluctuations in demand. Because output is set at a fixed rate, inventory will be created when demand goes down and backlogs will be created when demand cannot be met with production capacity or available inventory. The cost for inventory and the cost for creating backlogs must be considered when choosing such a policy. This strategy should not be used for perishable goods or when the company is not sure that it can sell the goods that are placed in inventory. If backlog cost is high or if the company may lose valuable customers if it cannot meet their demand, then the level of capacity a firm must carry can be rather high.

Because inventory cannot be stored in the service industry, such a strategy requires a higher level of inventory.

Chase Demand

With this strategy the company seeks to adjust capacity, based on changes in demand. The adjustment policies could be creating overtime, hiring more people, or subcontracting work when demand increases. Creating under-time, rather than laying people off could be policies to adjust capacity when demand goes down. These strategies for adjusting to changes in demand can be very costly in a manufacturing environment:

- Laying off skilled labor that is scarce, may require expensive training cost when they need to be hired when demand increases
- Overtime cost requires higher pay per hour
- Subcontracting reduces profits and the firm may run the risk that the subcontractor may take over a portion of its market
- Under-time requires paying workers for no work done

This strategy is not often advantageous in the manufacturing industry. However, it could serve well in the service industry, where inventory cannot be stored. There are some interesting strategies that the service industry can use to adjust to changes in demand:

- Staggered work shift schedules, where the number of workers available meets the demand
- Multi-skilled floating staff is a lean way to adjust capacity
- Multi-skilled nurses in a hospital can be assigned and reassigned to various floors, based on the demand of such floors
- Self-service, where customers' demand changes according to their arrival patterns, like at supermarkets where the customers represent the capacity, and as they pull their merchandise from the racks, they are meeting their demand

Demand Management and Yield Management

This strategy attempts to adjust demand to meet capacity. It requires working with marketing and sales people to change product pricing, to increase or decrease advertising, to provide rebates or coupons to increase demand, delaying deliveries, etc.

In the service industry, when capacity cannot be stored and where demand fluctuates, one may wish to maximize customer revenue as one segments the customer base into different types of customers. This demand strategy is called yield management. It is practiced in the airline industry when customers are initially charged relatively high fares. These fares later on, closer to flight time, are reduced, so all seats get sold.

Demand management is also generally used for monitoring, controlling, and planning IT infrastructure capacity needs. We mentioned earlier that the focus is to ensure satisfactory response time during peak hours for the employees, suppliers, and clients to access the appropriate company business applications. Sometimes this demand is managed by adding additional servers when needed and removing them when the demand has decreased in a flexible manner that is opaque to the user. This is generally true today as many applications are web applications that are accessible from users' mobile devices or laptops. If the user cannot access his or her account quickly, securely, and accurately, then the user will take his or her business elsewhere.

10.3 Defining Capacity Measures

Design Capacity

The design capacity is the maximum capacity a process, an operation, or a service system can offer. This assumes that the process, operations, or systems run at full capacity. Examples are:

- If all the beds in a hospital are occupied, the hospital is running at full or design capacity
- If a refinery is running at full capacity, it is running at its design capacity
- If an operation in a process department did not experience downtime for maintenance, set up, or other causes, then it is running at full or its design capacity
- If a resort has all rooms sold out, then it is operating at its design capacity
- If all teller windows in a bank have a teller serving the customers, then it is operating at its design capacity
- If assembly lines are continuously assembling products, then they are operating at design capacity

It is possible that at times the capacity exceeds the design capacity:

- After a major disaster, hospitals, in addition to having all beds occupied, may have patients waiting for treatment on makeshift beds in hallways
- During rush hour trains and busses are carrying more passengers than the number of seats they have

In most companies, however, design capacity is rarely met because of changes in demand; the need for breakdown-, routine-, or preventive maintenance; the need for setting up equipment for product change over; etc.

Effective Capacity

Because of unavoidable delays, such as scheduled routine- and preventive maintenance and the need to set up equipment for product changeover in a batch environment, companies are not running at their design capacity, but rather at their effective capacity.

Effective Capacity = Design Capacity – Unavoidable Delays

Achieved Capacity

The output of an operation could be less than its effective capacity. This happens because of avoidable down time caused by breakdowns, staff shortages, poor scheduling, etc.

Achieved Capacity = Effective Capacity – Avoidable Delays

Utilization, Efficiency, and Overall Effectiveness

Utilization compares the achieved capacity to the design capacity. It is the ratio of the achieved capacity to the design capacity:

Utilization = Achieved Capacity/ Design Capacity

Efficiency, however, compares the achieved capacity to the effective capacity. It is the ratio of the achieved capacity to the effective capacity:

$$Efficiency = Achieved\ Capacity/Effective\ Capacity$$

The overall effectiveness of a process or an operation includes an assessment of the output quality and the performance of the operation or process:

$$Overall\ Effectiveness = Utilization * Performance\ ratio * Quality\ ratio$$

Where: Performance ratio is the ratio of actual run rate to its design rate.
Quality ratio is the ratio of good process outputs to total process outputs.

Utilization, efficiency, and overall effectiveness are normally high in continuous flow production systems, such as in processing companies, on assembly lines, and transfer lines. They are generally lower in intermittent production systems, such as batch production systems.

Example #1: Measuring Utilization, Efficiency, and Effectiveness at the Jiffy Mix Filling Station

The Jiffy Mix filling station is designed to operate during two shifts, five days a week. However, during one week the machine encountered six hours of down time due to product change over and planned preventive maintenance. Additionally, five hours were lost because of breakdown maintenance. During that week the machine was running below its normal speed (rather than filling 1800 boxes of Jiffy Mix per hour, it was only filling 1500 boxes per hour). It was also noted that 5% of the filled boxes weighed in below their required weight and could not be packed for shipping.

Design Capacity: (5 days/week) * (16 hours/day) = 80 hours/week

Effective Capacity: (80 hours/week) – (6 hours/week) = 74 hours/week

Achieved Capacity: (74 hours/week) – (5 hours/week) = 69 hours/week

Machine Utilization: (69/80) * 100% = 86.25%

Machine Efficiency: (69/74) * 100% = 93.24%

Overall Machine Effectiveness: [(0.8625)(1500/1800)(0.95)] * 100% = 68.28%

Example #2: Monitoring Overall Effectiveness and Adjusting Capacity of an IT Infrastructure

When considering the company's IT infrastructure, it is the user's response time that must be satisfactory (effective) and quick enough that the user does not realize that there is a delay, which can be measured in a matter of a few seconds. Any longer and it is considered a very slow system that will prompt the user to call support to inform and complain of the delay if it does not resolve quickly by itself. Frequent delays may and sometimes will cause the user to seek business elsewhere. Response time, computer processing unit utilization, and database access response time are just some of the measurements that are captured by the servers' various monitoring systems. Given the volume of data that is available today, monitoring and controlling has gotten more complicated, requiring the company to look for new tools. One type is the predictive analytics tools that collect, display, monitor, and create statistics for an established period (e.g., two weeks of data) of time to create and display patterns of the data viewed as "normal" (overall effectiveness) based on the company's set thresholds or upper and lower control limits. Should any of the variables exceed their threshold, an alert is sent to the designated personnel who had established them for possible immediate investigation and resolution. In order for its employees, suppliers, and clients to access the appropriate applications when doing or supporting business operations, the server utilization could be managed by percent utilized and when it has reached 80 percent utilization, the company may plan to upgrade capacity, possibly by procuring a larger server, which may include upgrading operating systems and the middleware software to the next releases, requiring license upgrades or renewals.

11. GLOSSARY AND SUMMARY OF METHODS

Achieved Capacity – Achieved capacity is less than its effective capacity. This happens because of avoidable down time caused by breakdowns, staff shortages, poor scheduling, etc.

Achieved Capacity = Effective Capacity – Avoidable Delays

Assembly Line Balancing – Assembly line balancing is a procedure that attempts to assign a balanced workload amongst stations in a product type of layout. Heuristic methods used for balancing assembly lines are: ranked positional weight method, dual-matrices method, target job line balancing method, largest job first method, multiple decision rule assembly line method, etc.

Balance Delay – The balance delay is the degree or the percent of unbalance. It is the ratio between the total idle time and the total time spent by the product in moving from the beginning to the end of the line.

Centralized Expansion Design – In the centralized expansion design no space is left idle in the original design, and expansion is accomplished by adding to the outskirts of the original departments.

Computerized Numerically Controlled Equipment (CNC) – If equipment has its own microprocessor or minicomputer then the equipment is referred to as computerized numerically controlled equipment.

Cycle Time – The cycle time is that time that a product spends at each station, or it is the amount of time between units coming off the production line.

Decentralized Expansion Design – In the decentralized expansion design empty space between departments is added within the original layout and this space is then utilized when certain departments need to be expanded.

Design Capacity – The design capacity is the maximum capacity a process, an operation, or a service system can offer. This assumes that the process, operation, or system runs at full capacity.

Direct Numerically Controlled Equipment (DNC) – Direct numerically controlled equipment is directly linked with a digital computer, operating on a time-shared, sampled-data basis, to monitor a host of processing variables.

Effective Capacity – Because of unavoidable delays, such as scheduled routine- and preventive maintenance, and the need to set up equipment for product changeover in a batch environment, companies are not able to run at their design capacity, but rather at their effective capacity:

Effective Capacity = Design Capacity – Unavoidable Delays

Fixed Material Layout – The fixed material layout is a layout for the manufacturing or the assembly of large products that do not move during production. Instead, the processes and materials are brought to the final production area. Only when the job is completed is the product removed from the construction area.

Flexible Manufacturing Systems (FMS) – Flexible manufacturing systems are designed for medium quantity production (1,000 to 10,000 pieces) with some repetition of parts. They utilize the following four automation concepts and technologies in one system: 1) numerically controlled and CNC machine tools, 2) automatic material handling system, 3) supervisory direct numeric control over the material handling system and the machine tools, and 4) handles families of parts, using group technology principles.

Functional or Process Layout – A functional or process layout contains process departments, each of which is formed by grouping equipment of the same functional type.

Group Layout – Group departments of a group layout handle specific groups of families of products. The concept of group technology is used to arrange the required machines, tools, and other equipment for a part family into groups or cells to produce the parts.

Heuristic Travel Chart Method – The heuristic travel chart method is a procedure used to layout a functional layout. It reduces material handling to a minimum level by attempting to place the departments or work centers that have the greatest amount of interaction adjacent to each other.

Lean Layout – A lean layout allows for the production of quality parts or services at takt time (the amount of time available to produce one unit based on the customer demand rate), while minimizing non-value-added activities. A lean layout must accomplish the following:

- Facilitate the flow of material and work
- Minimize walking
- Minimize travel
- Allow for the immediate flow of information and feedback
- Promote a good balance among workers
- Allow for changes in the demand

Mirror Image Expansion Design – The expanded layout of a mirror image expansion design becomes the mirror image of the original design, thus duplicating similar departments at different locations.

Precedence Diagram – The precedence diagram is a graphical description of any ordering in which elements must be performed in achieving the total assembly of the product.

Process Efficiency – Process Efficiency compares the achieved capacity to the Effective capacity. It is the ratio of the achieved capacity to the effective capacity:

Efficiency = Achieved Capacity/Effective Capacity

Process Overall Effectiveness – The overall effectiveness of a process or an operation includes an assessment of the output quality and the performance of the operation or process:

*Overall Effectiveness = Utilization * Performance ratio * Quality ratio*

Process Utilization – Process utilization compares the achieved capacity to the design capacity. It is the ratio of the achieved capacity to the design capacity:

Utilization = Achieved Capacity/ Design Capacity

Product Layout – Product departments are established by grouping all of the processes together that are necessary to manufacture or assemble a product in a continuous fashion. It is recommended if the production volume is adequate and thus yields reasonable equipment utilization.

Project Layout – The project layout is similar to the fixed material layout, except that the final product is not removed from the construction site. Instead, materials, scrap, equipment, and manpower move on to another construction site.

Slotting the Warehouse – Slotting the warehouse requires segmenting the warehouse into at least three areas: a fast moving section, a midrange moving section, and a slow moving section.

Spine Expansion Design – In the spine expansion design departments are located alongside the main aisle in such a way that the expansion in such a facility requires no changes in the primary facility services, personnel travel patterns, material handling, and storage system.

Station Slack Time – The station slack time is the difference between the station time and the sum of work element times assigned to the station.

Station Time – Station time is the actual amount of work (measured by time) assigned to a specific station on the assembly line.

Total Work Content or Total Direct Time – The total work content is the aggregate amount of work (measured by time) of the total assembly.

Transfer Lines – Transfer lines are used in automated dedicated batch manufacturing systems to move parts from one process to the other or from one machine to the other, while orienting and locating the part in the correct position for processing at the next station or machine.

Zoning the Warehouse – Zoning the warehouse implies that items being stored are grouped based on various characteristics such as weight, size, packaging, small or large boxed items, pallet size, wrapped or unwrapped items, etc.

12. ACRONYMS

CNC Computerized Numerically Controlled Equipment

DNC Direct Numerically Controlled Equipment

FMS Flexible Manufacturing Systems

13. REFERENCES

Arcus, A. L. "COMSOAL: A Computer Method for Sequencing Operations for Assembly Line." *International Journal of Production Research.* (Vol. 4, No.4, 1966).

Armour, G. C. and E. S. Buffa. "A Heuristic Algorithm and Simulation Approach to Relative Location of Facilities." *Management Science.* (Vol. 9, No. 1, 1963): 294–309.

Buffa, E. S., G. S. Armor, and T. E. Vollman. "Allocating Facilities with CRAFT." *Harvard Business Review.* (Vol. 42, No. 2, March-April 1984): 136–159.

Choobineh, F. "A Framework for the Design of Cellular Manufacturing Systems." *International Journal of Production Research.* (Vol. 26, No. 7, 1988): 1161 –72

Chase, R. B. "Strategic Considerations in Assembly Line Selection." *California Management Review, Fall.* (1975): 17–23.

Dreckshage, Brian. "Leaning the Warehouse." *Proceedings APICS International Conference & Expo,* 2007.

Francis, R. L., and J. A. White. *Facilities Layout and Location: An Analytical Approach.* Englewood Cliffs, NJ: Prentice Hall, 1987.

Ghosh, Soumen, and R. Gagnon. "A Comprehensive Literature Review and Analysis of the Design, Balancing and Scheduling of Assembly Systems." *International Journal of Production Research.* (Vol. 27, No. 4, 1989): 637 –70.

Helgeson, W. B., and D. P. Birnie. "Assembly Line Balancing Using the Ranked Positional Weight Technique." *Journal of Industrial Engineering.* (Vol. 12, No. 6, Nov-Dec. 1961): 394–398.

Kaiman, L. "Computer Programs for Architects and Layout Planners." Proceedings of the 22nd Annual Meeting of the American Institute of Industrial Engineers, Boston, 1971.

Muther, Richard. *Practical Plant Layout.* New York: McGraw-Hill Book Company, Inc., 1955.

Thompkins, J., A., and James M. Moore. *Computer Aided Layout: A User's Guide*, Publication #1, Facilities Planning and Design Division, American Institute of Industrial Engineers, Inc., AIIE, Inc., 1978.

Wu, J., A. and Nesa L. Wu. "Assembly Productivity." *Productivity Quarterly.* (Vol. 25, No. 2, July-Sept. 1984): 143 –149.

Wu, J., A. and Nesa L. Wu. "Wu/Wu Heuristic Assembly Line Balancing Model." *Taiwan Journal of Industrial Engineering.* (Vol. 1, No. 1, Jan. 1981): 85–96.

14. REVIEW QUESTIONS

1. When would you prefer a process layout to a product layout?
2. Explain how general purpose equipment is more likely to be used in process layouts, rather than product type of layouts.

3. Rank the following layouts in terms of material handling cost (1 = lowest MH cost, 3 = highest MH cost): product layout, process layout, group layout.
4. Rank the following layouts in terms of density of special purpose equipment (1 = most special purpose equipment, 3 = least number of special purpose equipment): product layout, process layout, group layout.
5. Briefly explain the concept behind the travel chart method. When is it used?
6. Briefly discuss product layout and group layout in terms of
   a) Production volume
   b) General purpose vs. special purpose equipment
   c) NC/DNC/CNC control
   d) Material handling problem/consideration
   e) Flexible manufacturing
   f) Production scheduling
   g) Machine utilization
7. Discuss the various types of expansion designs. Which one is the preferred one? Why is it the preferred one?
8. What is a transfer line?
9. What are the objectives of assembly line balancing?
10. What constitutes a lean layout?
11. Differentiate between a project layout and a fixed material layout.
12. What are the six lean storage principles? Explain these principles.
13. Give some examples of capacity measures in different types of industries.
14. Differentiate between design capacity, effective capacity, and achieved capacity.
15. What is meant by process utilization, process efficiency, and process overall effectiveness?

15. PROBLEMS

Problem #1

An assembly line is to be balanced. There are 35 individual tasks, totaling 928 seconds of required time. The task of the longest duration requires 38 seconds, the quickest task takes 10 seconds. The manager wants a 50 seconds/item cycle time. What is the minimum number of workstations to achieve this cycle time?

Problem #2

An item has a work content of 54 minutes and is produced at the rate of 10 units per hour. What is the minimum number of stations required to do this assembly?

Problem #3

General Products Company is planning an assembly line for one of its small products. The plan is for a line which will turn out 75 units an hour. The assignment to stations is as follows:

WORKSTATION	WORK ELEMENTS	TIME REQUIRED (SECONDS)
1	1, 2, 16, 17	45
2	5, 6, 15	45
3	4, 8, 12, 19	45
4	3, 14	45
5	9, 10, 11	46
6	7, 13, 23, 24	45
7	18, 21	45
8	25, 27	47
9	20, 22, 26	47
10	31, 34, 35	45
11	23, 33	37
12	28, 29, 30	42

a) What is the maximum cycle time that can be considered before assigning work elements to stations?

b) What is the optimal cycle time?

c) What is the maximum rate of production per hour?

d) What is the total slack time?

e) What is the balance delay or line balance loss?

Problem #4

It takes seven work elements to assemble a cassette tape. The work elements, the work element standard time in minutes, and precedence relationships for the assembly is given in the table below. The assembly of the seven elements will occur alongside a conveyer and the demand is such that 600 cassettes must be produced within a seven-hour workday.

WORK ELEMENT	TIME (min)	PRECEDING ELEMENT
1	0.66	none
2	0.35	none
3	0.30	1, 2
4	0.32	3
5	0.31	3
6	0.35	5
7	0.33	4, 6

a) What is the proposed cycle time (in minutes) if 600 cassettes must be produced in 7 hours?

b) Draw the precedence diagram.

c) Try to manually assign work to stations. Do not exceed the proposed cycle time and respect the precedence relationships amongst work elements in assigning work to stations.

d) What is your optimal cycle time? (Explain)

e) What is the actual optimal hourly production rate?

f) How well is the line balanced?

Problem #5 (use your imagination on this problem!)

A table lamp is constructed from the following components:

lamp shade (frame and covering)

housing assembly (shade support and light bulb housing)

power assembly (conduit, cord, and plug)

base

The following activities and standard times (minutes) describe the assembly process:

ACTIVITY	DESCRIPTION	TIME (min)
1	Cut cover from the sheet	3
2	Form lamp shade frame	10
3	Cover shade frame with shade covering	10
4	Form lamp shade support	7
5	Assemble housing	4
6	Measure and cut electric cord	2
7	Attach plug to cord	2
8	Assemble power assembly	3
9	Assemble base assembly	6
10	Assemble table lamp	8
11	Insert bulb, test, and remove	4
12	Package lamp	3

The expected demand for the lamp ranges between 1,500 and 9,000 units per year. You may assume that there are 50 working weeks in a year, that one week has 5 working days, and that there are 6 hours in one workday.

a) Draw the fabrication/assembly precedence diagram for the table lamp.

b) Determine the minimum number of workstations required for a production rate of 1,500; 3,000; 4,500; 6,000; 7,500; or 9,000 units per year

Problem # 6

Reconsider the ABC American Company introduced in Problem 2 of Chapter 5 and consider its present layout as shown in Figure 8.13.

a. Criticize that layout in terms of inventory, type of layout, and space utilization.

b. Is this a lean layout? Why or why not?

c. Is this layout conducive towards creating a JIT production system for ABC's largest customer, Mr. CAT.? Why or why not?

d. Propose an approach to improve this layout (include a brief discussion of what tools are available to study this layout in an attempt to improve it).

e. Though you may not be able to redraw an accurate new layout, describe how your layout might look different from the one shown in Figure 8.13. Make an effort to draw such a layout.

f. Describe all the advantages of your new layout (be as complete as possible).

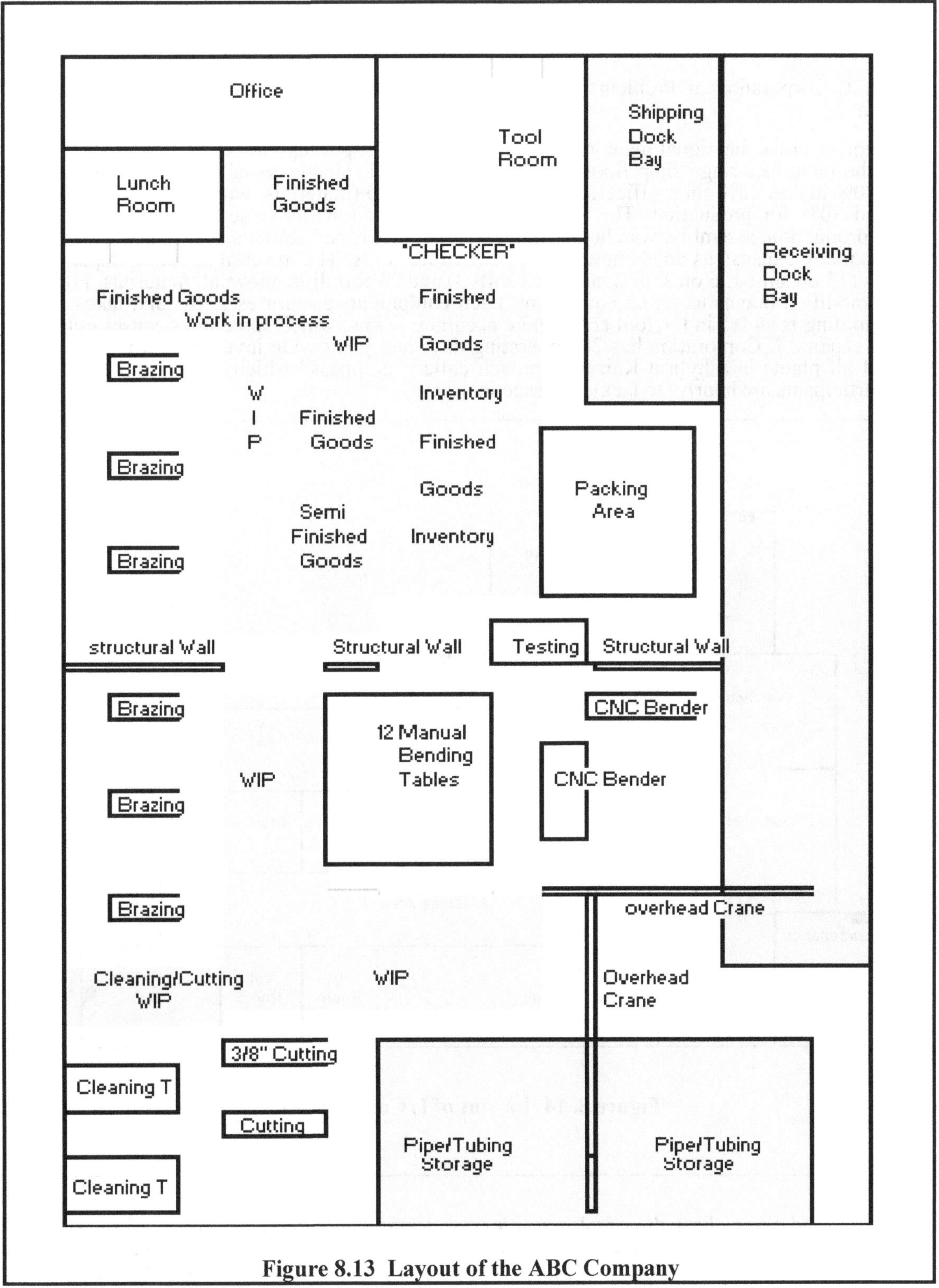

Figure 8.13 Layout of the ABC Company

Problem #7

Reconsider L Corporation of Problem 3 in Chapter 5 and pay attention to the following plant layout information:

The 20-member cross functional planning team that John Smith put together did a floor space utilization study for the manufacturing "shop floor" area and found the available space (175,000 square ft.) being used for: 20% aisles, 10% shop offices, 40% inventory storage (materials, work in process, and finished goods), and 30% for production. The shop was divided into functional departments (i.e. shipping & receiving, production, assembly, warehouse, mold storage, tool room, R&D, maintenance, etc.) and as the plant grew, many expansions added new exterior/structural walls. The material handling department with 22 workers (13 on shift 1, 6 on shift 2, and 3 on shift 3) and 23 fork lifts, move all materials. Fork lifts are used with modified booms to set up equipment. Each equipment set-up uses 2 lifts and takes 6 hours or more. All tooling is stored in the tool crib, where accuracy is low, which sometimes causes delays for set ups and/or repairs. L Corporation has 260 operating days and plant wide inventory turns are 40. L Corp has trained all plants in a hybrid Kaizen approach called "compass" which utilizes a 15-person group (75% of participants are hourly) to tackle an issue in 4 days.

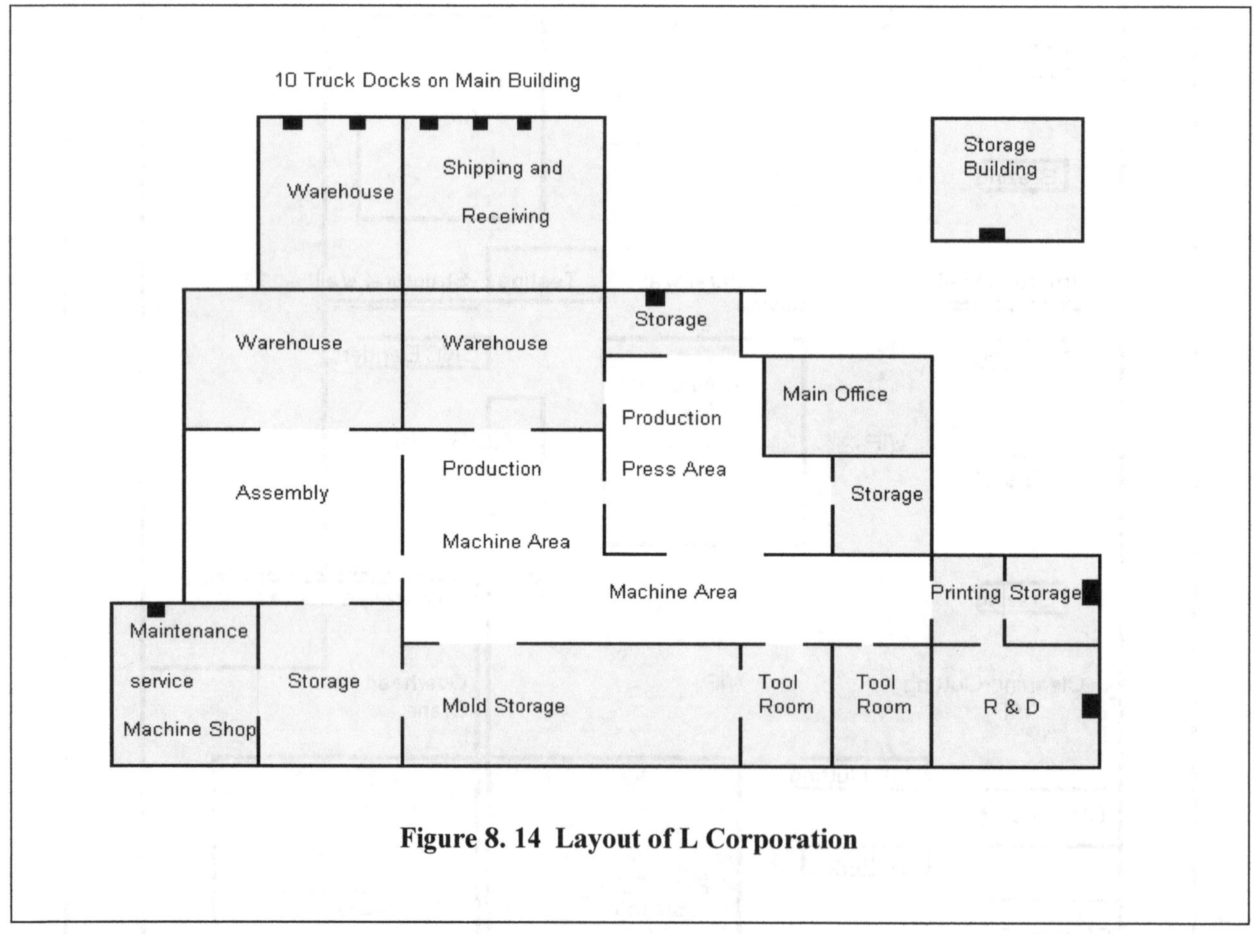

Figure 8. 14 Layout of L Corporation

The products tend to go through complex routings and employees refer to product flow diagrams as "spaghetti charts" because of the overlapping and looping material movements. The small building along the main plant contains 6,000 square feet and is currently used for storage of materials, Equipment, and old molds. Per customer requirements, some inventory storage is dedicated to spare parts and the equipment to make them. Ford requires replacement parts (spares/service parts) to be available for 15 years after the model was changed. Margins on service parts are at least two times that of current parts, and their lead times are longer than two times the lead times of the current parts.

a) Criticize that layout in terms of inventory, type of layout, and space utilization.

b) Is this a lean layout? Why or why not?

c) Propose an approach to improve this layout (include a brief discussion of what tools are available to study this layout in an attempt to improve it).

d) Though you may not be able to redraw an accurate new layout, describe how your layout might look different from the one shown in Figure 8.14. Make an effort to draw such a layout.

e) Describe all the advantages of your new layout (be as complete as possible).

Problem #8

The Jiffy Mix box-making station

Jiffy Mix boxes are made through the following process:

- Cutting of the boxes out of cardboard that are fed into the cutting machine from a hopper
- Applying the glue to the box
- Folding the box into shape
- Optically checking the box to see whether it is correct. If it is not correct, the box gets rejected and goes into the reject bin. All other boxes go to the filling stations.

During one shift of eight hours the glue machine malfunctioned and it took the maintenance crew 20 minutes to restore production. At one o'clock the machine was shut down for scheduled preventive maintenance that took 30 minutes.

This machine can produce in one hour 3200 boxes. However, to keep quality at a reasonable level the engineers suggested running the machine that day at a rate of 3000 boxes per hour. At the end of the day the reject bin contained 500 defective boxes.

Calculate all of the following:

a) Design capacity in minutes per shift, in production output per shift and per hour.

b) Effective capacity in minutes per shift, in production output per shift and per hour.

c) Achieved capacity in minutes per shift, in production output per shift and per hour.

d) Machine utilization

e) Machine efficiency

f) Overall machine effectiveness

Chapter 9

FORECASTING

1. THE SALES FORECASTING SYSTEM

Forecasting, in general, is a technique whereby past experience is transformed into general predictions of "things to come." In this format, forecasting techniques can be employed for a variety of reasons: 1) to predict sales volume of individual end products; 2) to predict gross sales; 3) to determine facility capacity requirements; 4) to define the labor force capacity over time; 5) to predict the gross national product; 6) to forecast changes in the national labor productivity; and 7) to estimate future energy reserves; and many more.

The information framework for sales forecasting is represented in Figure 9.1. For the purpose of initial sales projections, the information that is analyzed consists of data on the economy and industry, company past sales records, field reports, and market research or surveys. Based on the type of information, different types of analysis can be performed to come up with either initial mechanical projections or a sales force composite.

The marketing group is normally interested in company sales records, field reports, market research, and surveys to come up with a sales force composite. To compose the sales force composite the marketing manager will heavily rely on subjective information provided by the sales staff. Because of the immediate contact of the sales people with the customer they may provide the marketing group with valuable information. However, their input can and must not be the sole data inputted into the overall forecasting mechanism. After all, since sales people may not always be able to distinguish between what the customer "wants" and what he is "willing to buy," their suggestions and information that are channeled to the marketing group are highly subjective.

The reliability of such data very much depends on the success of the sales people. Experience indicates that a sales person tends to be overly pessimistic in estimating the need for a product when past sales have dwindled and very optimistic when such sales were great. In addition to the input obtained from the sales force, marketing managers should also rely on subjective input obtained from consumer surveys, from managers and executives, and from panels of experts.

Mechanical projections are normally obtained through statistical and mathematical analysis of data on the economy and industry, and company's past sales records. Various techniques can be employed to make mechanical projections, such as: moving averages, exponential smoothing, Box-Jenkins, trend projections, regression, econometrics, leading indicators, life-cycle analysis, etc.

It is the task of the operations manager to review both mechanical projections and sales force composites in order to finalize demand forecasts.

Forecasting is an essential input to proper production planning. However, for forecasting to be useful for such planning, it must not only define the expected demand in terms of physical units, but also exhibit the variation in that forecasted demand. In order to timely schedule all production tasks that are required to achieve necessary outputs, all sales and demand forecasts must be available on time. Moreover, demand forecasts must be made regularly, so that all necessary production and inventory adjustments can take place on time.

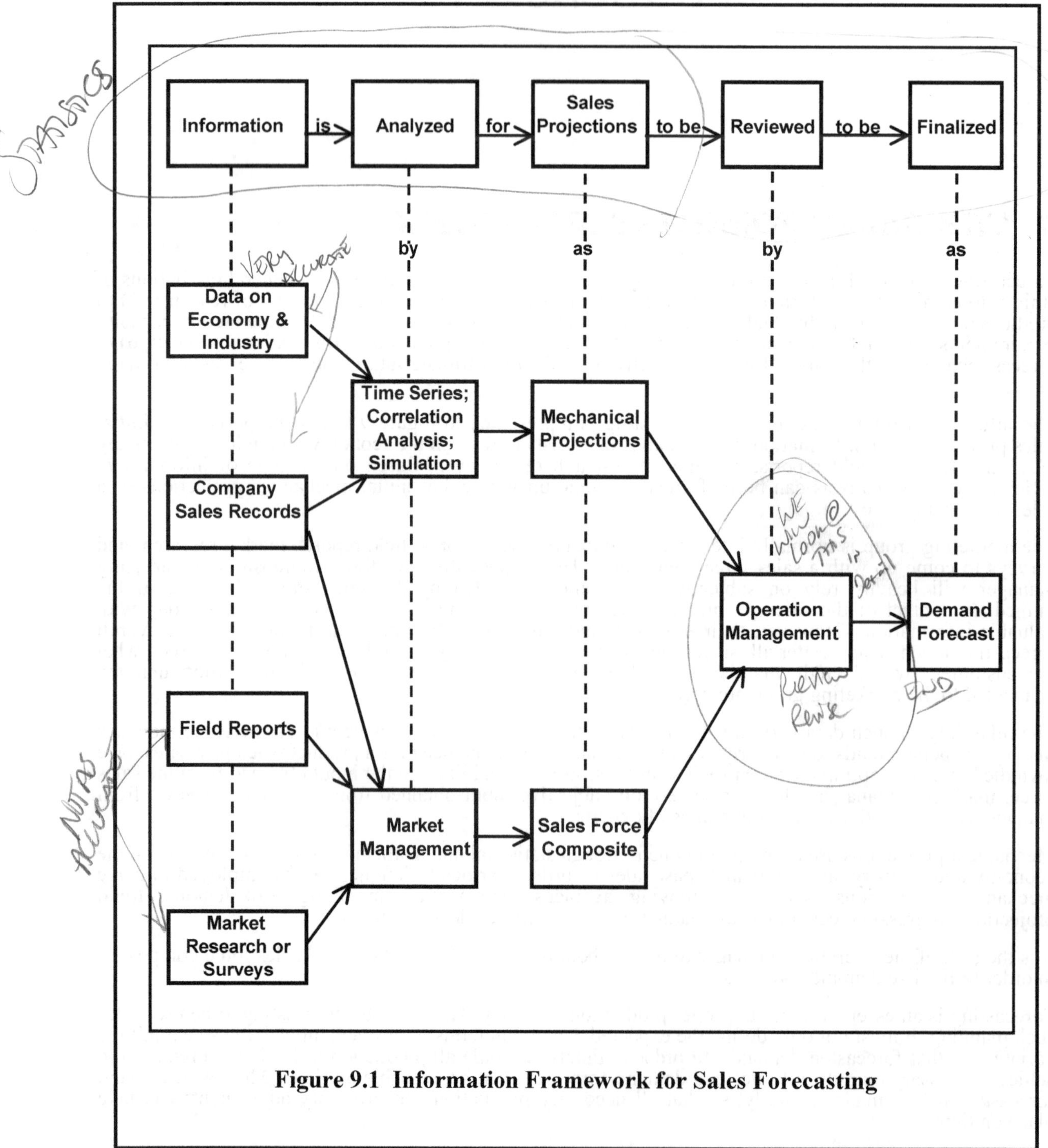

Figure 9.1 Information Framework for Sales Forecasting

2. CHOOSING AN APPROPRIATE FORECASTING TECHNIQUE

There are three types of forecasting methods: qualitative or predictive methods, time series analysis or projection methods, and causal forecasting methods (see Figure 9.2).

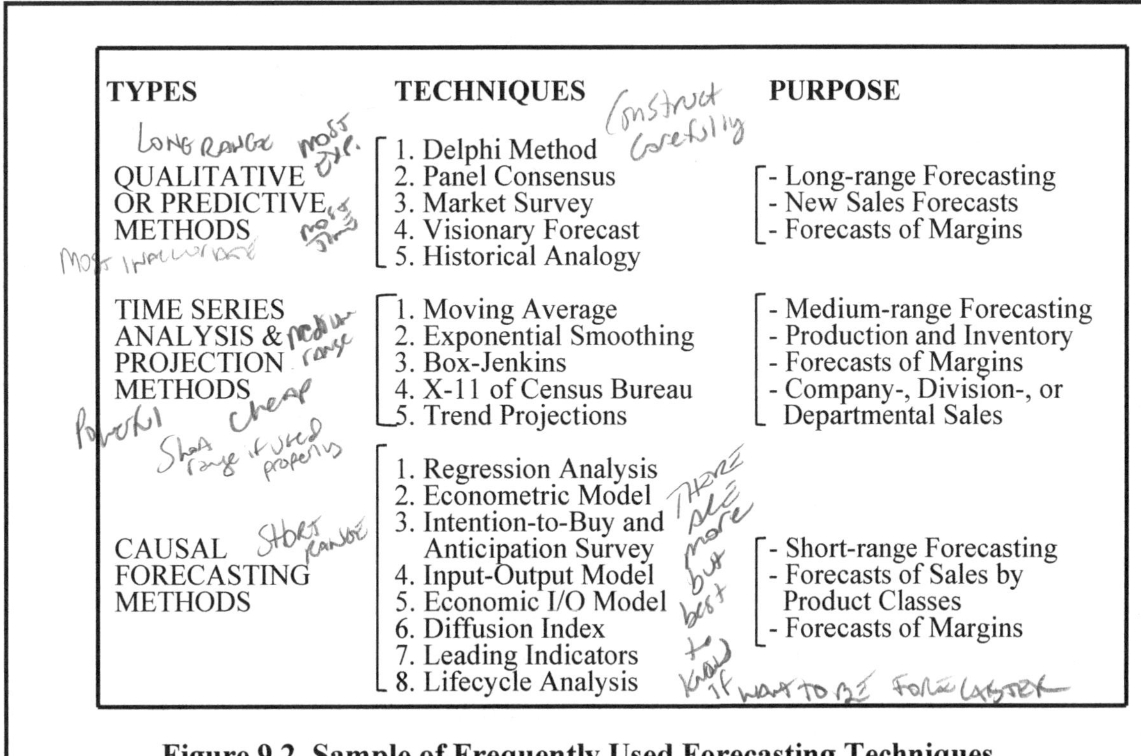

TYPES	TECHNIQUES	PURPOSE
QUALITATIVE OR PREDICTIVE METHODS	1. Delphi Method 2. Panel Consensus 3. Market Survey 4. Visionary Forecast 5. Historical Analogy	- Long-range Forecasting - New Sales Forecasts - Forecasts of Margins
TIME SERIES ANALYSIS & PROJECTION METHODS	1. Moving Average 2. Exponential Smoothing 3. Box-Jenkins 4. X-11 of Census Bureau 5. Trend Projections	- Medium-range Forecasting - Production and Inventory - Forecasts of Margins - Company-, Division-, or Departmental Sales
CAUSAL FORECASTING METHODS	1. Regression Analysis 2. Econometric Model 3. Intention-to-Buy and Anticipation Survey 4. Input-Output Model 5. Economic I/O Model 6. Diffusion Index 7. Leading Indicators 8. Lifecycle Analysis	- Short-range Forecasting - Forecasts of Sales by Product Classes - Forecasts of Margins

Figure 9.2 Sample of Frequently Used Forecasting Techniques

Qualitative or Predictive Methods employ human judgments and rating schemes to convert intangible data into quantitative estimates. Forecasts are made based on information and judgments which are obtained in a systematic, logical, and unbiased fashion. Delphi method, market research, panel consensus, visionary forecasting, and historical analogy are frequently used qualitative forecasting techniques for long-range planning, new product sales estimation, and forecasting of margins. Cost for computer analysis can range from approximately $500 for visionary forecasting to well over $25,000 for market survey analysis.

Time Series Analysis and Projection Methods are statistical techniques that can be employed for forecasting if sufficient historical data exist for the product or product line. With these methods we use past performance in an attempt to predict the future. The principle that lies at the base of time series analysis, namely that "history repeats itself," only applies to short-term and average-range forecasting. Therefore, time series analysis and projection methods are valuable and reasonably accurate for medium-range and short-range forecasts. Time series analysis helps to identify seasonal patterns (systematic variation in series of data), cyclical patterns (patterns that repeat themselves every two or three years), trends, and growth rates. Time series analysis and projection methods, such as moving average, exponential smoothing, Box-Jenkins, X-11 of Census Bureau, and trend projections, are used for medium- range forecasting, for production and inventory, for forecasting margins, and for estimating company-, division-, or departmental sales. They are all relatively cheap methods for computing forecasts, ranging from a few pennies for the computer calculation of a moving average or an exponential smoothing value to well over $50 for a Box-Jenkins or an X-11 of Census Bureau estimate.

Causal Forecasting Methods are forecasting techniques that employ mathematical relationships amongst two or more variables. Causal models take into account economic and business variables that may contribute to the forecast of specific business phenomena. They are one of the most sophisticated forecasting techniques that are used for short-range predictions, for forecasts of sales by product classes, or forecasts of margins. Some causal forecasting methods use, in addition to outcomes of related events (variables), market survey information as well as results of time series analysis. The computational cost of causal forecasts varies. They can be as low as $100 for regression analysis, $50,000 for input-output models, and well over $100,000 for economic input-output models.

In order for a manager to successfully cope with sudden changes, such as changes in demand levels, seasonal changes, competitive price cutting, changes in the economy, strikes, and inflation, he must inform his forecaster as to the purpose of the forecast and how its results are going to be used.

Many factors need to be considered when choosing an appropriate forecasting technique. Some of these factors are: the age of the product within its lifecycle, the relevance of available information, the availability of historical data, the desired degree of accuracy, the cost/benefit of the forecast to the organization, the time available within which a forecast needs to be made, the amount of control the company has over the distribution of the product, etc.

As a product develops and grows through its lifecycle, from conception to maturity, different forecasting techniques must be employed by the forecaster to aid the manager in making typical company decisions.

During the product development stage a company must decide on the amount of effort it is willing to allocate to the development and design of the product. It must make decisions with respect to appropriate business strategies for the new product. At this stage many questions need to be answered, such as:

- How have similar products fared in the market?
- Should we really enter this business?
- How much R&D funds need to be allocated to this product?
- What will be the demand for this product five years hence?

Systematic market research will help answer many of these questions. However, the accuracy of such research very much depends on the time span over which predictions need to be made, with two years being the limit for decent accuracy and reliability of forecasting results. When the market is defined, one may be able to compare the proposed product with our competitor's present or planned products, or one may wish to compare a planned product with a former product that had similar characteristics. This forecasting technique has been referred to as historical analysis of comparable products or historical analogy. However, the market is not always defined. If it is not, then industry prefers to apply the Delphi method to solicit and consolidate experts' opinions or it may use panel consensus. When projecting future technology, input/output techniques are most appropriate.

During the market testing and early introduction of the product in the marketplace, management is interested in defining the optimum facility size and must come up with appropriate marketing strategies for distribution and pricing of the product. At this point, good short-, medium-, and long-range forecasts need to be made. Now, no funds need to be spared in determining when rapid sales will set in; in defining the rate of market penetration during this rapid sales period; and in figuring the optimal level of market penetration. Consumer surveys, statistical tracking methods and routine market studies may aid in determining the onset of the rapid growth stage and the extent of that rapid growth.

During the rapid growth stage of the product, management is concerned with facilities expansion, marketing strategies, and product planning. During this stage forecasters often use techniques such as statistical techniques for identifying turning points (time series methods and regression), and surveys (market surveys and intention-to-buy surveys).

Finally, during the steady state period of the product, forecasters use short-term forecasting methods to control production and inventories and to define the need for promotions, specials, and various pricing techniques. Specifically, the following methods are used during this stage of the product: time series analysis, projection methods (such as moving averages, exponential smoothing, Box-Jenkins), and causal forecasting methods. At this stage the manager also needs a good tracking and warning system in order to detect declining demand for the product.

In the following section some of the above-mentioned methods will be closely examined.

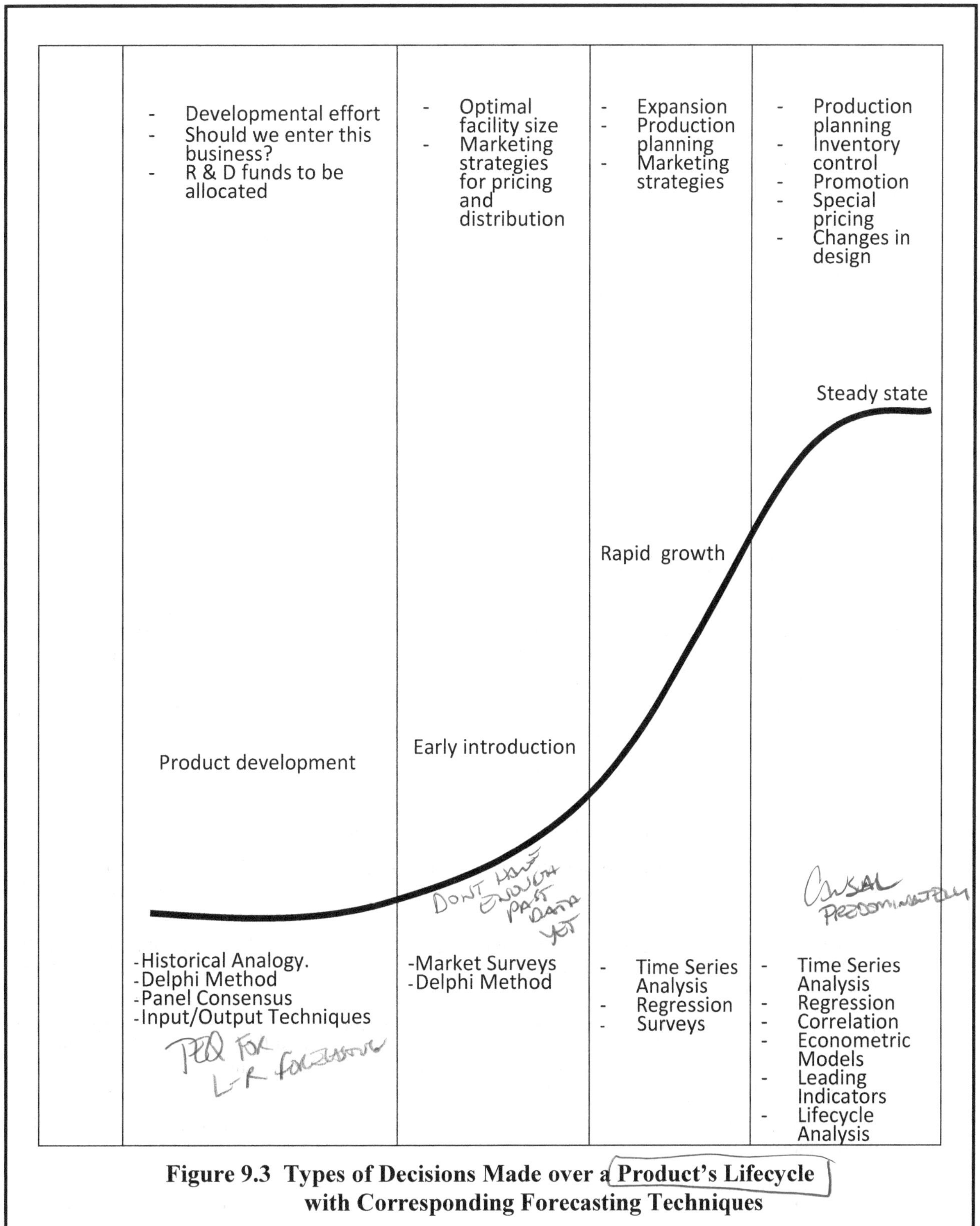

Figure 9.3 Types of Decisions Made over a Product's Lifecycle with Corresponding Forecasting Techniques

3. DELPHI METHOD

The Delphi method generates subjective information provided by experts. Here a panel of experts is asked to answer a series of well-designed questions of the Delphi questionnaire. Certain criteria are set up for these experts under which they have to respond to the various questions. Answers and information provided by the experts are kept confidential. However, after the answers of one questionnaire are all summarized, they are made available to all experts before they are asked to answer a second questionnaire. This communication ensures that information that is available to a few experts is now given to all other experts on the panel. The process of collecting information and channeling it back to all experts is normally repeated a number of times in order to improve the quality of experts' judgments. Finally all experts will have access to all available facts that are needed for quality forecasting purposes. In this fashion the Delphi method constructively expands shared knowledge and eliminates the "bandwagon effect" of majority opinion. The objective of this method will be met if it increases the body of reliable information and if no confusion is being created as to what the true facts are.

The Delphi method has often been quite satisfactory in generating forecasts, because convergence of experts' opinions has been observed in most cases. It produces fair to very good forecasting accuracy at a relatively medium to high cost. More than two months' time is often needed to produce reliable forecasting results via this technique. The Delphi method is especially useful in forecasting long-range and new product sales as well as the forecasts of margins. Until the early seventies the Delphi method, together with trend extrapolation, was the most frequently used technique in technological forecasting. By 1976, however, computer and mathematical modeling was preferred over the Delphi method for such forecasting.

4. MARKET SURVEYS

Market surveys can result in valuable information for forecasting purposes, if the prepared questionnaire is properly worded and satisfactorily presented and administered by trained and well instructed interviewers. Market surveys are systematic, formal or informal, and conscious methods whereby certain hypotheses about the actual market can be defined and tested.

Before engaging in the planning stage of a market survey one must decide what information is needed and sought, one must decide on the best technique to collect such information and above all one must establish which of the three types of questionnaire survey techniques is most appropriate. There are three types of market survey techniques: the mail or e-mail survey, the personal interview and the telephone survey.

The mail survey approach is effective if all of the following conditions exist:

- The questionnaire is constructed in such a way that it is easy to respond to all questions. This is the case when multiple choices are provided for various questions or when a simple "yes" or "no" answer is sufficient.
- The majority of people receiving the questionnaire have had at least a high school education. In other words, the questionnaire should be addressed to people who are willing and able to respond through the mail.
- The universe being sampled for the survey is relatively homogeneous; this is people with similar interests, education, social standing, etc. No identical surveys should be distributed to groups of people with diverse backgrounds, since the language employed in the survey questionnaire must be familiar to the people being surveyed.
- The company can wait at least one to four weeks for the respondents to reply to the questionnaires.
- Sufficient funds have been allocated to such surveys. The budget must provide for pre-testing the questionnaire, for acquiring mailing lists, for follow up letters and personal interviews or phone calls, etc.
- Complete, reasonably priced mailing lists can be obtained. These mailing lists may have to contain up-to-date phone numbers if follow up by phone may become necessary.

Personal interviews, though expensive, are the most satisfactory survey technique. They should be used when the following conditions are met:

- A personal interview is necessary to ensure a quality response that is needed for the forecast.
- Interviewers can be properly trained to conduct the survey in a satisfactory fashion.
- There is no personal or financial information sought that may become embarrassing to ask in a face-to-face interview.
- There is sufficient time to collect the information through personal interviews.
- Adequate funds have been allocated to recruit, train, supervise, and compensate the interviewers.

The telephone survey technique is not a preferred way of obtaining market information for the sake of product or sales forecasting. It should be used onlywhen all of the following circumstances are met:

- The population that is being tested or surveyed is well represented in and can be easily defined by the telephone directories.
- Only a few, non-ambiguous questions need to be answered over the phone and the caller or interviewer does not need to observe the respondent or his social environment.
- Very little time is available to conduct the survey.
- The survey material is sufficiently interesting and well-presented so that the interviewee is willing to remain on the phone in order to respond completely to all questions asked.

If surveys are carefully planned and conducted, they will generate good to excellent results at a relatively high cost. In general, except for the telephone survey, market surveys could require at least three months in order to obtain adequate results which are useful for forecasting. This technique is employed for product and sales forecasting during the entire life span of the product. It is used for long-range as well as short-range planning and is also an effective tool for the forecasting of margins. When product development people know what product classes they want to scan, survey data can monitor market behavior and help locate market driven innovation opportunities to be considered for future product designs or redesigns.

5. MOVING AVERAGES

Patterns in time series vary widely and can usually be classified under the following groups: averages, trends in averages, cyclic effects, seasonal effects, and random variations. In most forecasting models averages are meaningless, because trends, cycles, and seasonal patterns may prevail. A variation of simple averages is moving averages, which emphasize recent values and therefore estimate trend effects and patterns. The basic assumption underlying the moving average technique, as well as any other time series analysis, is that trends and patterns of the past will continue in the future. None of the time series analysis methods, however, can predict turning points in the economy.

Though the method of moving averages is useful in isolating cyclical components and has the advantage of not needing any trend computation, this method tends to lag a trend and raise the valleys and depress the peaks of cyclic patterns. When calculating moving averages, only data from more recent time periods are used. The number of data points used in calculating a moving average needs to be determined very carefully, because the magnitude of the lag and the smoothing of cyclic patterns depend on the number of data points used. The fewer data points a forecaster uses, the quicker the model will react to dramatic changes. When a dramatic change that is depicted by an outlier data point is a true indication of a new demand level, then early detection of that point and weighting it heavily in the model is advantageous. However, when such an outlier data point is just random noise, then the forecaster should not react to it too quickly, by placing a lesser weight on that element or by using more data points in the calculation of moving averages. In general, the number of points that are chosen must be such that seasonal effects or irregularities in the data are eliminated.

Even though theoretically as little as one data point is required to make a forecast based on the moving average, at least one year's historical data is necessary. Though its forecasting accuracy is poor to good, the method has been used to forecast inventories for low volume items, for scheduling, and for the timing of special promotions.

5.1 Simple Moving Averages (MA)

Each point of a simple moving average of a time series is the arithmetic average of several consecutive points of the time series. The general formula for computing the simple moving average, when n consecutive data points are used, is:

$$F_{t+1} = \frac{D_t + D_{t-1} + \cdots + D_{t-n+1}}{n} = \text{Average of most recent n sales values}$$

$$F_{t+1} = \sum_{i=t-n+1}^{t} \frac{D_i}{n}$$

Where: F_{t+1} is the demand forecast for period $t+1$, made after period t has ended
D_i is the actual sales in period i
n is the number of consecutive data points used in the forecast

In order to reduce the required calculations, the simple moving average can be rearranged algebraically to its updating form:

$$MA = F_{t+1} = F_t + \frac{D_t - D_{t-n}}{n}$$

Forecasting with moving averages for n=3 and n=5 is illustrated, using Excel's "Analysis ToolPack". This "Analysis ToolPack" must be added and placed on the "Data" tool bar of Excel.

With "Analysis ToolPack" you have available for use a limited statistical analysis package that provides you with some forecasting tools such as the moving average, basic exponential smoothing, and linear regression, as shown in Figure 9.4

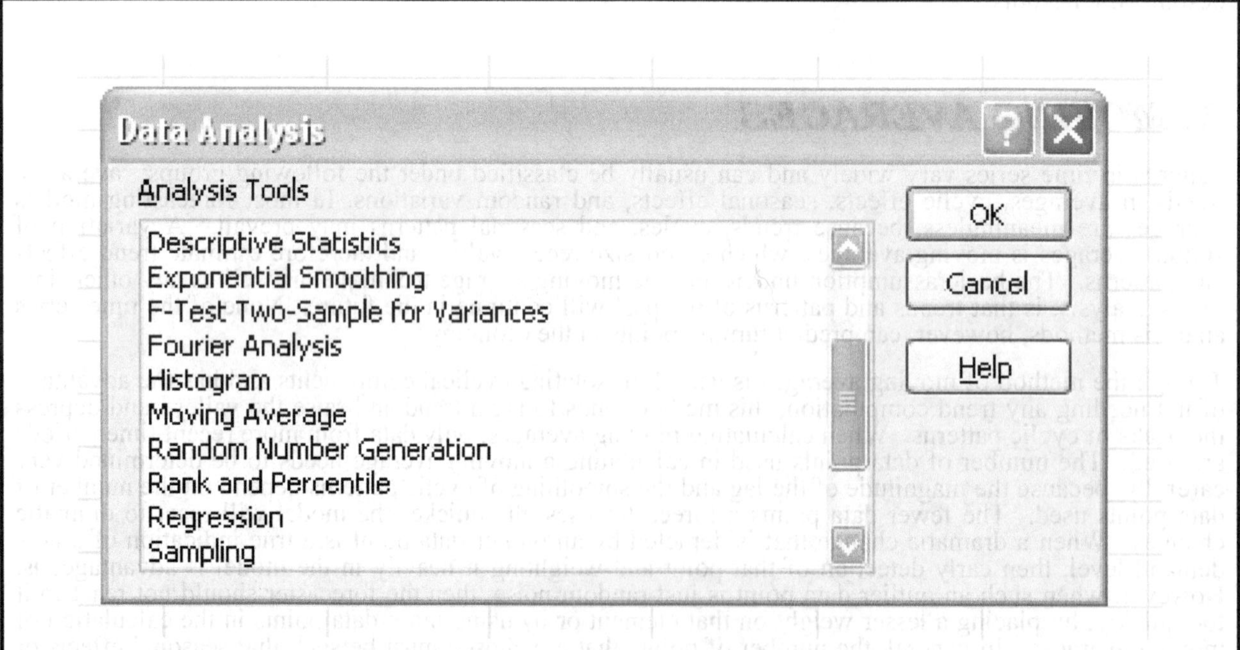

Figure 9.4 Sample Data Analysis Tools Available in Excel's "Analysis ToolPak"

Data Preparation

Before using a forecasting technique, data must be prepared: demand data are placed in data columns. It is a good habit to label your demand and all other input data. Likewise, label all output or results that you generate. This is shown in Figure 9.5 for demand over 23 periods. Columns indicate that moving averages over three and five periods will be calculated, together with their absolute errors, sum of absolute errors, and average absolute errors.

	A	B	C	D	E	F
1	Period	Demand	Moving Average	Absolute	Moving Average	Absolute
2			n = 3	Error	n = 5	Error
3	1	113				
4	2	100				
5	3	97				
6	4	103				
7	5	122				
8	6	113				
9	7	88				
10	8	71				
11	9	69				
12	10	85				
13	11	92				
14	12	96				
15	13	121				
16	14	117				
17	15	124				
18	16	133				
19	17	152				
20	18	149				
21	19	167				
22	20	161				
23	21	148				
24	22	158				
25	23	165				
26			Total:		Total:	
27			Average:		Average:	
28						

Figure 9.5 Data Preparation in Excel

Using Excel

To calculate the simple moving averages for three and five periods, go now to "Data Analysis" on your "Data" toolbar. Click on "Data Analysis." You will obtain the screen as shown in Figure 9.6.

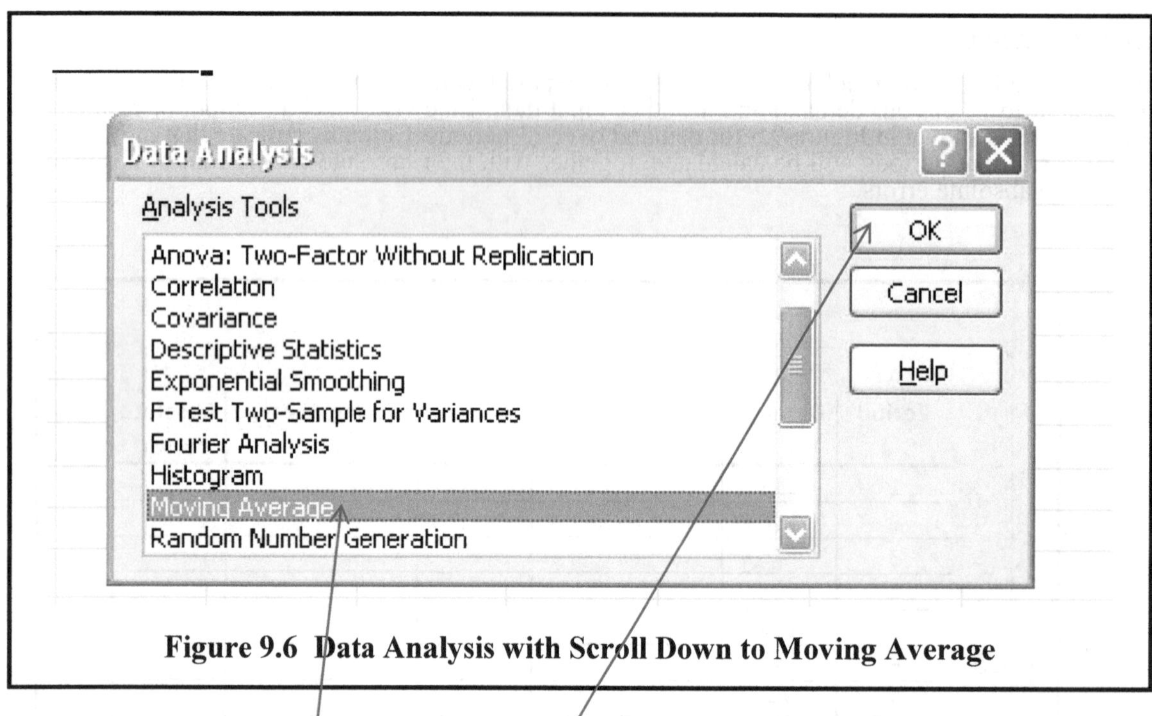

Figure 9.6 Data Analysis with Scroll Down to Moving Average

After scrolling down to "Moving Average," click "OK." This will generate the moving average input box as shown in Figure 9.7.

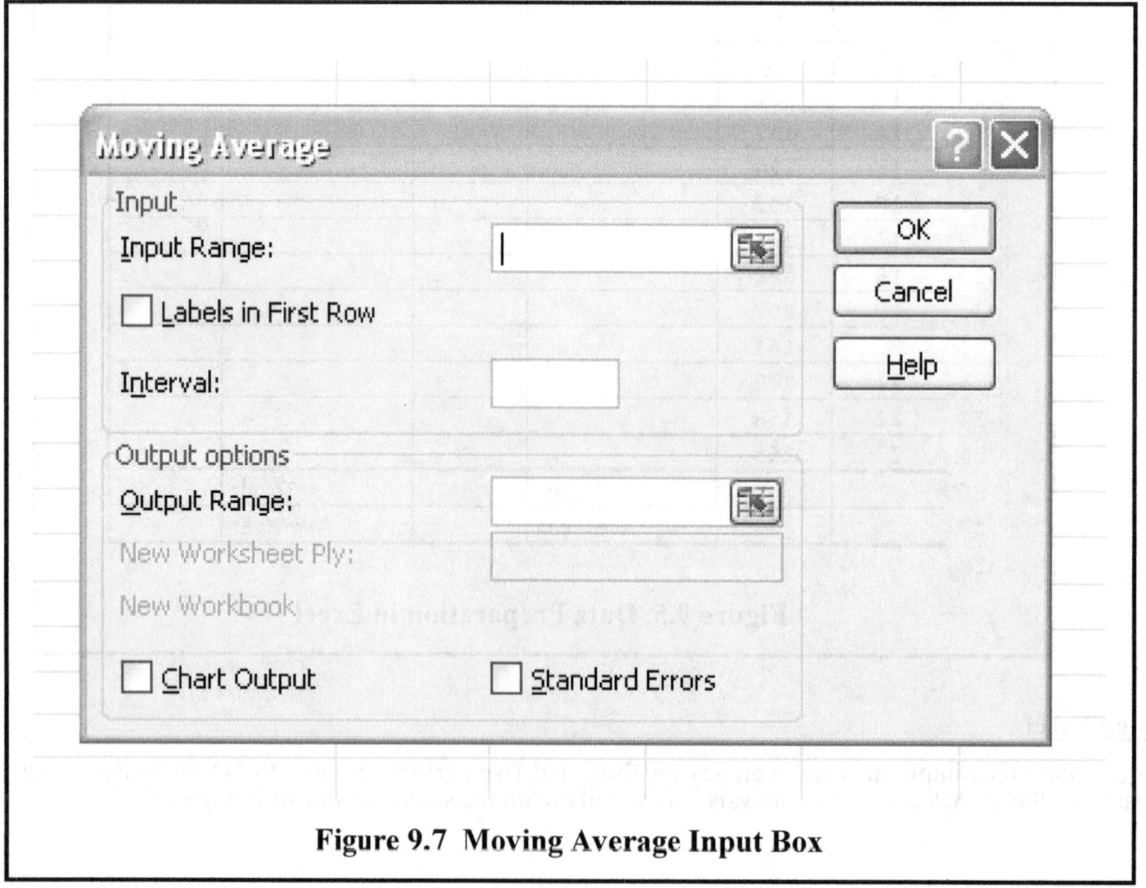

Figure 9.7 Moving Average Input Box

The following minimum input is required to generate moving averages, as shown in Figure 9.8.

"Input Range": you can show the input range by dragging the mouse over the input data.

"Interval": is the number of periods or the number of data items you wish to use in the calculation of the moving average. Here is illustrated an interval of three periods.

"Output Range": you can show the output range by dragging the mouse over the area where the forecasted values need to be printed (always omit the first data line; it is never part of the output range). Therefore, our output range starts in cell C4.

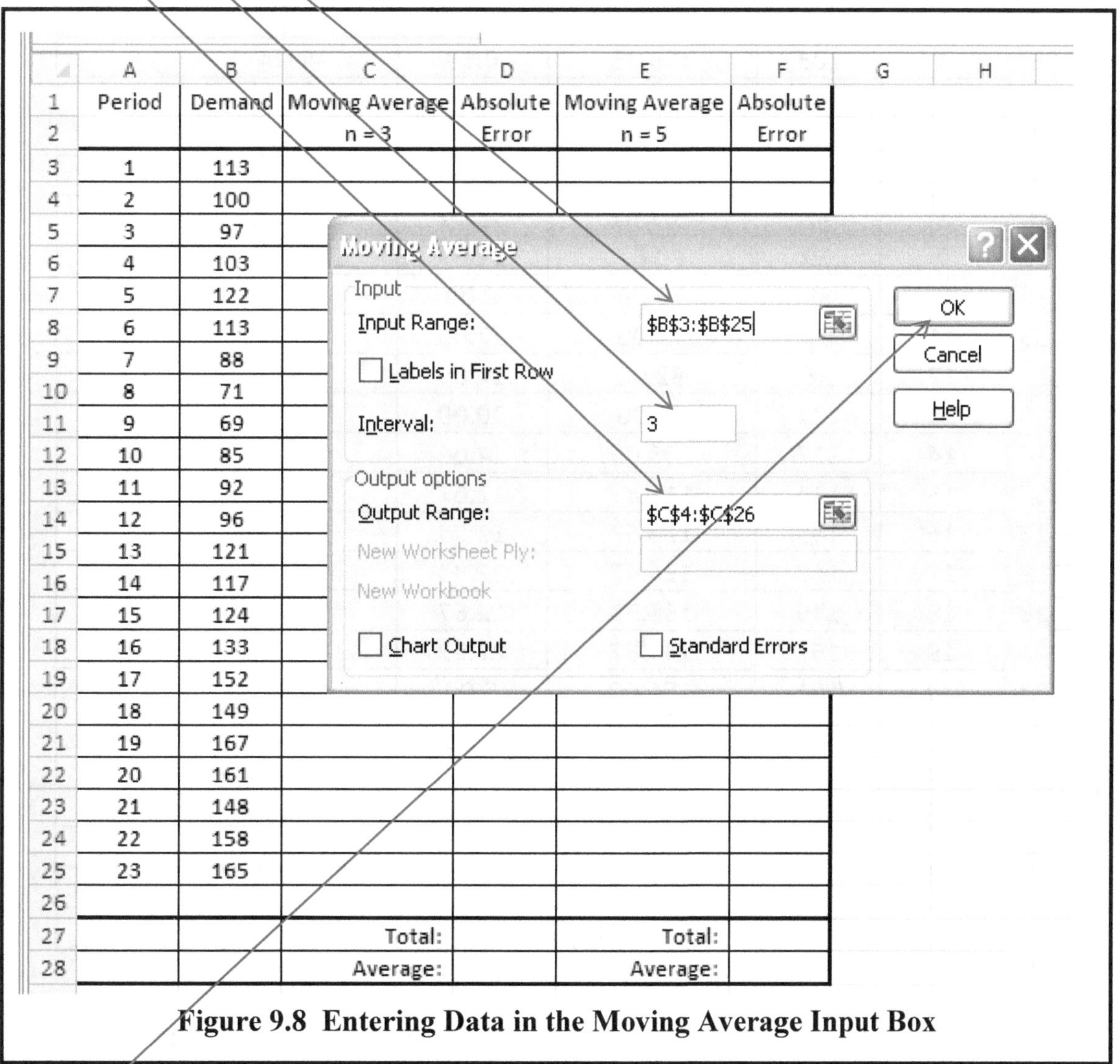

	A	B	C	D	E	F
1	Period	Demand	Moving Average	Absolute	Moving Average	Absolute
2			n = 3	Error	n = 5	Error
3	1	113				
4	2	100				
5	3	97				
6	4	103				
7	5	122				
8	6	113				
9	7	88				
10	8	71				
11	9	69				
12	10	85				
13	11	92				
14	12	96				
15	13	121				
16	14	117				
17	15	124				
18	16	133				
19	17	152				
20	18	149				
21	19	167				
22	20	161				
23	21	148				
24	22	158				
25	23	165				
26						
27			Total:		Total:	
28			Average:		Average:	

Figure 9.8 Entering Data in the Moving Average Input Box

Click "OK" after all data are entered in the moving average input box. This generates the results as seen in Figure 9.9. Note that the forecast is generated and placed in column C, under the "Moving Average *n*=3" column heading.

We could have checked the "Standard Errors" box in the moving average input box! Instead of calculating the "Standard Errors," we will calculate the absolute errors, or the absolute difference between the demand and the forecasted demand, using the **ABS** function. This is shown in column D, with its total and its average absolute error.

This process is repeated with the same demand data for 5 periods. The results are shown in column E and F of Figure 9.9.

	A	B	C	D	E	F
1	Period	Demand	Moving Average	Absolute	Moving Average	Absolute
2			n = 3	Error	n = 5	Error
3	1	113				
4	2	100	#N/A		#N/A	
5	3	97	#N/A		#N/A	
6	4	103	103.33	0.33	#N/A	
7	5	122	100.00	22.00	#N/A	
8	6	113	107.33	5.67	107.00	6.00
9	7	88	112.67	24.67	107.00	19.00
10	8	71	107.67	36.67	104.60	33.60
11	9	69	90.67	21.67	99.40	30.40
12	10	85	76.00	9.00	92.60	7.60
13	11	92	75.00	17.00	85.20	6.80
14	12	96	82.00	14.00	81.00	15.00
15	13	121	91.00	30.00	82.60	38.40
16	14	117	103.00	14.00	92.60	24.40
17	15	124	111.33	12.67	102.20	21.80
18	16	133	120.67	12.33	110.00	23.00
19	17	152	124.67	27.33	118.20	33.80
20	18	149	136.33	12.67	129.40	19.60
21	19	167	144.67	22.33	135.00	32.00
22	20	161	156.00	5.00	145.00	16.00
23	21	148	159.00	11.00	152.40	4.40
24	22	158	158.67	0.67	155.40	2.60
25	23	165	155.67	9.33	156.60	8.40
26			157.00		159.80	
27			Total:	308.33	Total:	342.80
28			Average:	15.42	Average:	19.04

= (B3+B4+B5)/3 =ABS(B6–C6) =sum(F8,F25) =F27/18

Figure 9.9 Moving Average Forecasting Results for *n* = 3 and n = 5

In Figure 9.10, observe how the five period moving averages lag the trend, raise the valleys, and depress the peaks. Increasing *n*, from three (3) periods to five (5) periods, results in moving averages that become less sensitive to noise and require more time to respond to trend changes. There will also be a poorer response to valleys and peaks.

When demand is unstable or when a trend is present, it is recommended that fewer, rather than many, periods are considered when calculating moving averages.

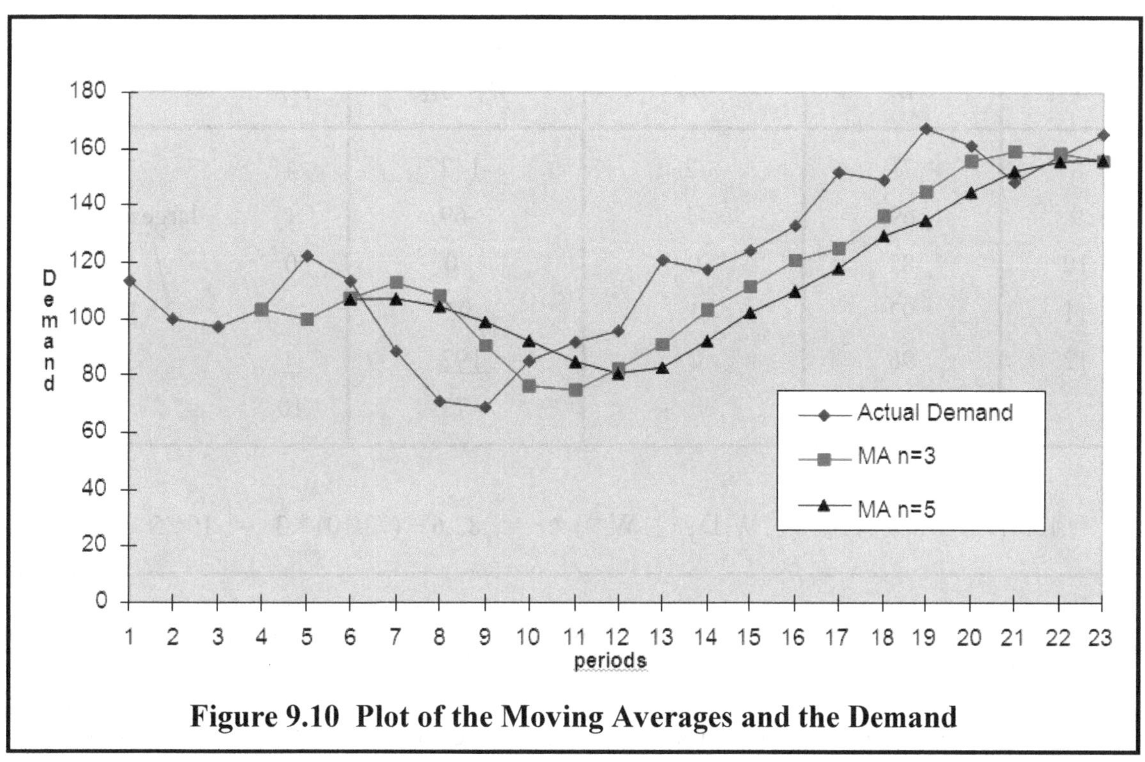

Figure 9.10 Plot of the Moving Averages and the Demand

5.2 Adjusted Weighted Moving Averages (AMA)

Adjusted weighted moving averages are preferred when the data exhibit a definite trend. The general formula is:

$$F_{t+1} = AMA = MA + \frac{\sum_{i=t-n+1}^{t} W_i D_i}{\sum_{i=t-n+1}^{t} W_i^2} \times r$$

Where: *MA* is the simple moving average

W_i is the weighted factor in the *ith* period

D_i is the demand in the *ith* period

r is the number of periods since the base period (including the base period) or it equals the largest weight + 1

In the *AMA* equation the slope or the trend is calculated as $\sum W_i D_i / \sum W_i^2$ and the simple moving average, *MA*, is corrected by augmenting it with the slope times the number of periods since the base period (including the base period). An odd number of periods are required for adequate performance of the AMA formula.

Consider the data as shown in Figure 9.5 and note that a definite trend has set in around the 13th period. So, let us examine how to calculate the AMA at the end of the 12th period to determine the forecast for the 13th period. We will take the data of the last five periods to calculate the simple moving average and the trend.

These calculations are shown in Table 9.1.

Table 9.1: AMA Calculation for $t = 13$ and $n = 5$

i	D_i	W_i	$W_i * D_i$	W_i^2	
8	71	-2	-142	4	
9	69	-1	-69	1	largest weight
10	85	0	0	0	
11	92	1	92	1	$r = 2 + 1 = 3$
12	96	2	192	4	
			73	10	

$$AMA(13) = MA(13) + \left(\sum W_i D_i \Big/ \sum W_i^2\right) * r = 82.6 + (73/10) * 3 = 104.5$$

The calculations in Table 9.1 show that for $n = 5$ (when 5 periods are used) the weights are –2, –1, 0, 1, and 2. Because the largest weight is 2, the r value in the calculations is 3 ($r + 1$).

Adjusted weighted moving averages only make sense when a definite trend exists. To illustrate how poorly it performs if no trend is present and how good it performs if a definite trend exists, consider Figures 9.11 and 9.12.

In the illustrated example, the adjusted weighted moving average does wonders for predicting the next period's demand, starting with period 12 end ending with period 19. During these periods a definite trend exists that started materializing itself in periods 10 and 11. However, it should not have been used before period 12, because there was no evidence of a trend in the periods before the 12th period.

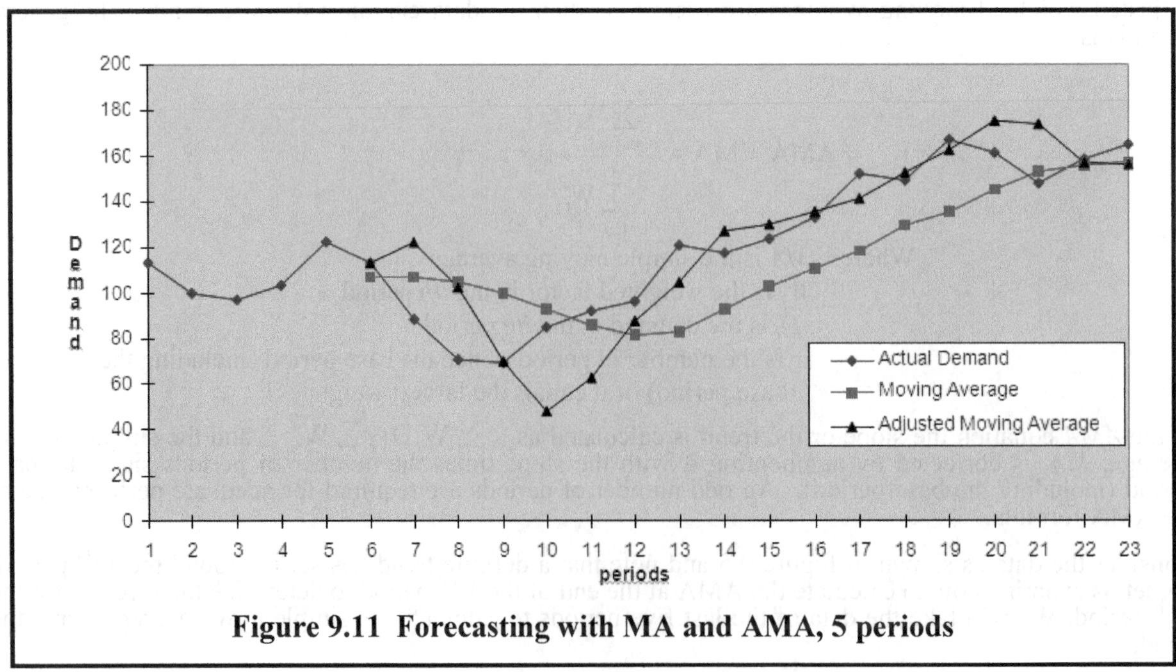

Figure 9.11 Forecasting with MA and AMA, 5 periods

Though Excel aids in quickly calculating simple moving averages, it does not directly aid in calculating the trend part of the formula. So, this formula must be entered as shown in Figure 9.12.

	A	B	C	D	E	F	G
1	Period	Demand	Moving Average	Absolute	Adjusted MA	Absolute	Preferred
2			n = 5	Error	n = 5	Error	Method
3	1	113					
4	2	100	#N/A				
5	3	97	#N/A				
6	4	103	#N/A				
7	5	122	#N/A				
8	6	113	107.00	6.00	113.30	0.30	MA
9	7	88	107.00	19.00	122.30	34.30	MA
10	8	71	104.60	33.60	102.20	31.20	MA
11	9	69	99.40	30.40	70.00	1.00	MA
12	10	85	92.60	7.60	48.20	36.80	MA
13	11	92	85.20	6.80	62.70	29.30	MA
14	12	96	81.00	15.00	87.60	8.40	AMA
15	13	121	82.60	38.40	104.50	16.50	AMA
16	14	117	92.60	24.40	127.10	10.10	AMA
17	15	124	102.20	21.80	130.10	6.10	AMA
18	16	133	110.00	23.00	135.50	2.50	AMA
19	17	152	118.20	33.80	141.30	10.70	AMA
20	18	149	129.40	19.60	152.80	3.80	AMA
21	19	167	135.00	32.00	162.60	4.40	AMA
22	20	161	145.00	16.00	175.60	14.60	AMA
23	21	148	152.40	4.40	173.70	25.70	AMA
24	22	158	155.40	2.60	156.60	1.40	MA
25	23	165	156.60	8.40	156.30	8.70	MA
26			159.80				
27			Total:	342.80	Total:	245.80	
28			Average:	19.04	Average:	13.66	

=C9+(((−2)*(B4)+(−1)*(B5)+(0)*(B6)+(1)*(B7)+(2)*(B8))/10)*3
(after entering this formula, drag your mouse down the column!)

Figure 9.12 Moving Average versus Adjusted Moving Average (*n*=5)

This simple demonstration clearly indicates that the forecaster must be prudent in selecting a forecasting method and may have to change the forecasting technique, based on long-term general changes in the demand.

There are other less complicated ways that weighted moving averages can be calculated. For example, the simple weighted moving average is:

$$F_{t+1} = \sum_{i=t-n+1}^{t} W_i D_i$$

Where D_i is the actual demand in period i
W_i is the weight attached to D_i
with $0 < W_i < 1$ and $\Sigma W_i = 1$

6. EXPONENTIAL SMOOTHING

The exponential smoothing forecasting method is quite similar to the moving average forecasting method. Some of the problems associated with using the moving average techniques are non-existing with the exponential smoothing techniques. For example, there is no need to maintain long records of demand or sales data, because exponential smoothing in its simplest format only uses the previous forecast plus some proportion of the previously made forecasting error. In this way, more recent data are given a higher weight.

Forecasting models using exponential smoothing have gained widespread application in business and industrial forecasting. Many simple, inexpensive exponential smoothing models have been developed, making it often difficult to select the most appropriate smoothing model for a particular set of circumstances.

Despite the general acceptance of the exponential smoothing models, the predicting accuracy ranges from poor to good. Applications are in the areas of production and inventory control, forecasting of margins, and other financial data. As indicated earlier, a forecast can be made in one day with any of the exponential smoothing techniques at a very inexpensive cost.

When using exponential smoothing techniques, decision makers and forecasters can choose between fixed smoothing and adaptive smoothing models. Each type of such model can be further enriched with adaptive trends, seasonal adjustments, or both. In order to appreciate the easy use of exponential smoothing techniques as a forecasting method, let us examine some of the methods in their simplest format.

6.1 Basic Model

In its simplest format, the new forecast equals the old or previously made forecast plus some proportion of the previously made forecasting error:

$$F_{t+1} = F_t + \alpha(D_t - F_t)$$

Or

$$F_{t+1} = \alpha D_t + (1 - \alpha)F_t$$

Where: F_{t+1} is the next period's ($t+1$) forecast, made in the present period (t)
D_t is the actual demand in the present period (t)
α is the smoothing constant, $0 < \alpha < 1$ (typically, $0.01 < \alpha < 0.30$)

Note that, if the actual demand for the last period exceeded the forecast that was made for that period, then the next forecasted demand will reflect this and will be higher than the old one. The smoothing factor (α) will define how much higher it will be. This factor is a weight that must be chosen carefully by management. The selection of a higher alpha factor, such as α = 0.30 or higher, naturally results in weighting very heavily the difference between the actual demand and the forecasted one. Therefore, it will lead to a quicker response to changes in the actual demand over time. This is the same as saying that older data has less influence on the calculation of the new forecasted demand. Consequently, a lower alpha factor has just the opposite effect. A low alpha factor, such as α = 0.10, only moderately weights the difference between actual demand and its forecasted value. In this way greater forecasting stability is obtained over time. One could compare exponential smoothing with a high alpha factor with a moving average over a few time periods, whereas exponential smoothing with a small alpha factor is similar to a moving average over many time periods.

The basic model is now illustrated with the same data we used for the moving average techniques, using α values of 0.2 and 0.7.

Data Preparation

Use the same data preparation guidelines as outlined for the moving average technique.

Using Excel

Go to "Data Analysis" on your "Data" toolbar to calculate the exponential smoothing forecast for α = 0.2. Click on "Data Analysis." You will obtain the screen as shown in Figure 9.13. Now scroll down to "Exponential Smoothing" and hit "OK." This will bring you to the Exponential Smoothing input box as seen in Figure 9.14.

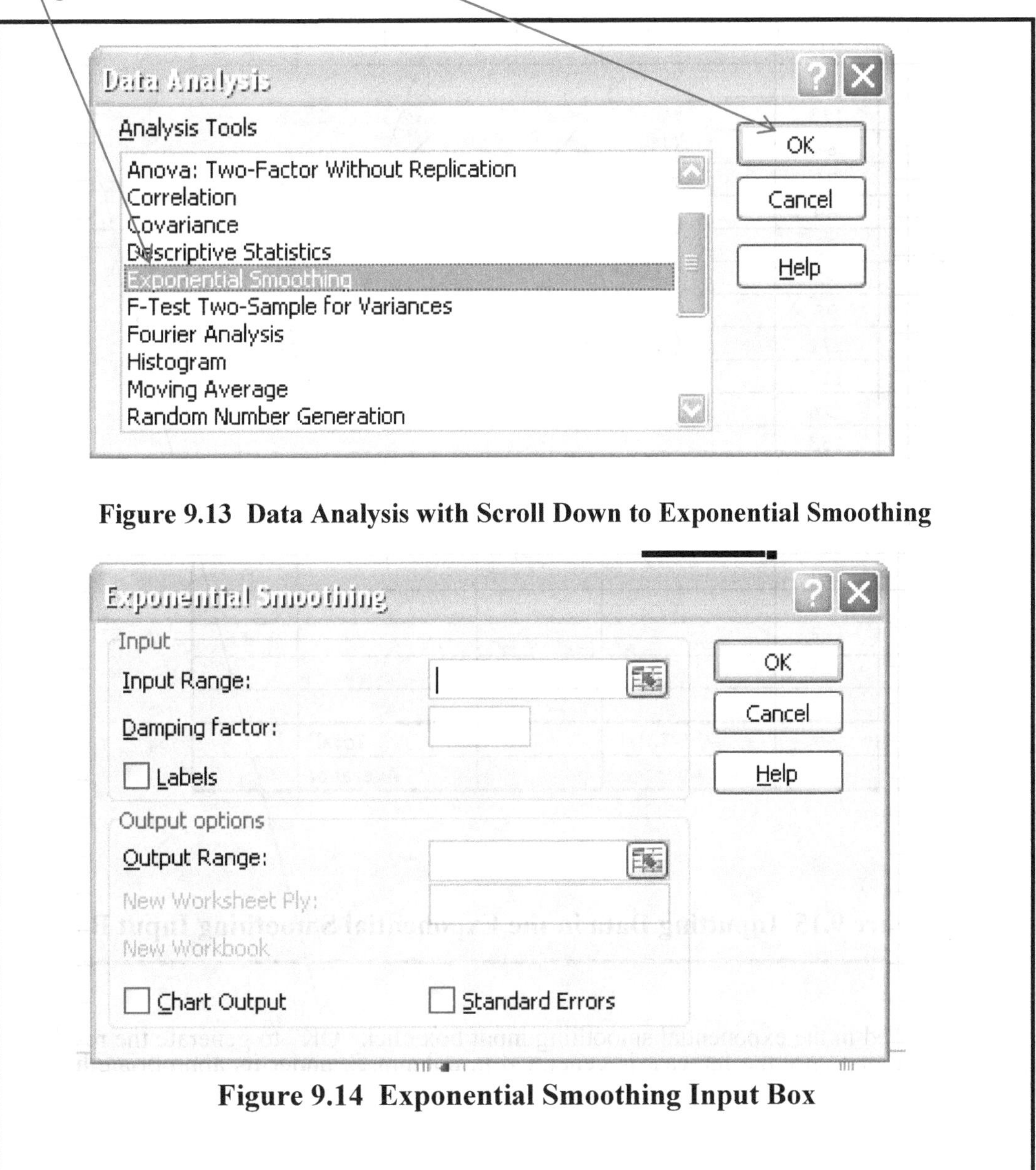

Figure 9.13 Data Analysis with Scroll Down to Exponential Smoothing

Figure 9.14 Exponential Smoothing Input Box

The following minimum input is required to generate exponential smoothing forecasts:

"Input Range": you can show the input range by dragging the mouse over your input data.

"Damping Factor": the damping factor is one minus the smoothing factor as defined in the text $(1-\alpha)$. If α is 0.2, then the damping factor is 0.8. This is used in our example.

"Output Range": you can show the output range by dragging the mouse over the area where the forecasted values need to be printed (note, however, that the first data line needs to be included!!!!). Therefore the first data output starts in cell C3.

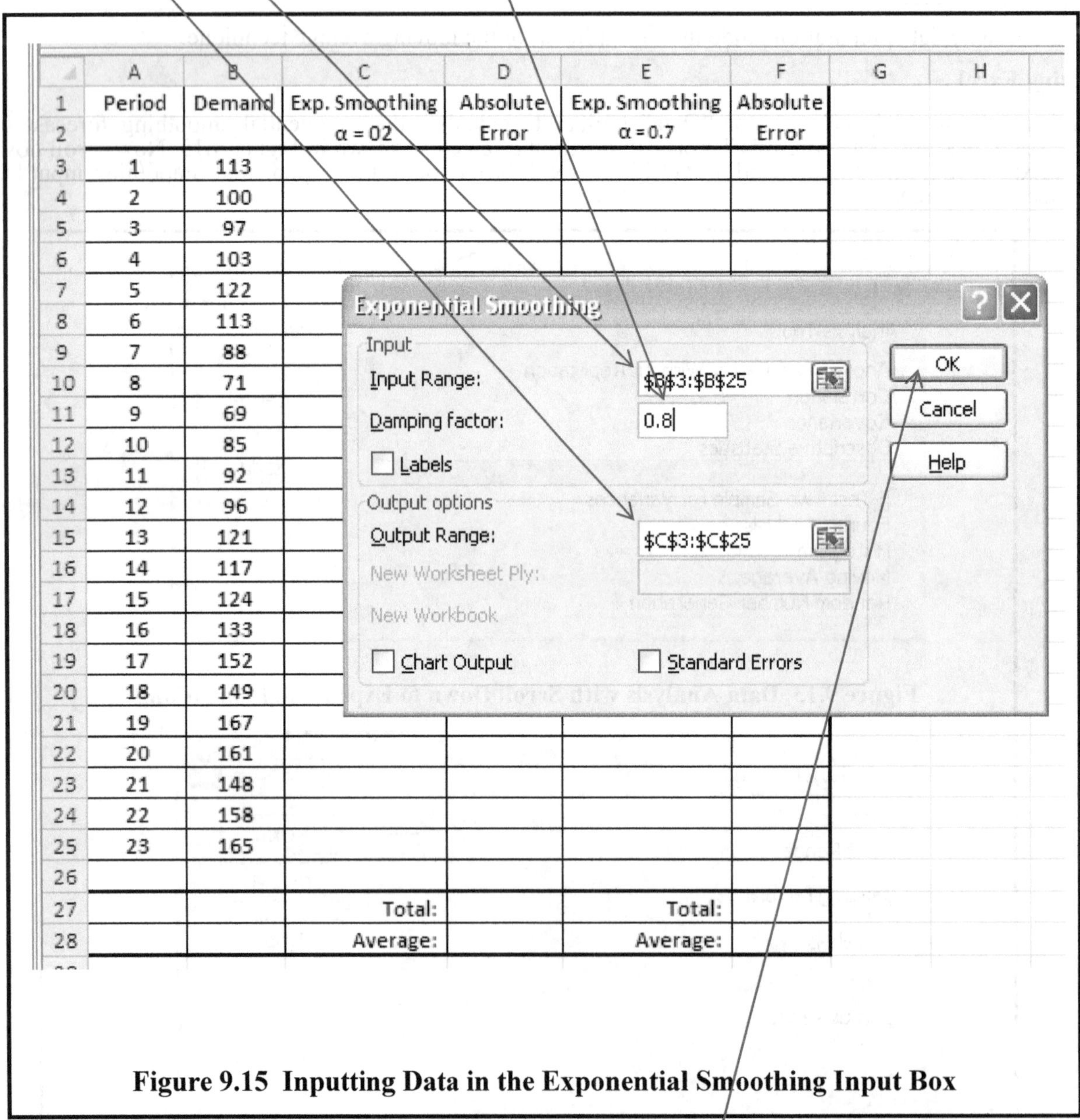

Period	Demand	Exp. Smoothing α = 02	Absolute Error	Exp. Smoothing α =0.7	Absolute Error
1	113				
2	100				
3	97				
4	103				
5	122				
6	113				
7	88				
8	71				
9	69				
10	85				
11	92				
12	96				
13	121				
14	117				
15	124				
16	133				
17	152				
18	149				
19	167				
20	161				
21	148				
22	158				
23	165				
		Total:		Total:	
		Average:		Average:	

Figure 9.15 Inputting Data in the Exponential Smoothing Input Box

After data is entered in the exponential smoothing input box click "OK" to generate the results as seen in Figure 9.16. Note that only the forecast is generated in column C, under its appropriate heading. Again you will have to formulate the absolute error calculation, using the ABS function.

	A	B	C	D	E	F
1	Period	Demand	Exp. Smoothing	Absolute	Exp. Smoothing	Absolute
2			α = 0.2	Error	α = 0.7	Error
3	1	113	#N/A		#N/A	
4	2	100	113.00	13.00	113.00	13.00
5	3	97	110.40	13.40	103.90	6.90
6	4	103	107.72	4.72	99.07	3.93
7	5	122	106.78	15.22	101.82	20.18
8	6	113	109.82	3.18	115.95	2.95
9	7	88	110.46	22.46	113.88	25.88
10	8	71	105.97	34.97	95.77	24.77
11	9	69	98.97	29.97	78.43	9.43
12	10	85	92.98	7.98	71.83	13.17
13	11	92	91.38	0.62	81.05	10.95
14	12	96	91.51	4.49	88.71	7.29
15	13	121	92.40	28.60	93.81	27.19
16	14	117	98.12	18.88	112.84	4.16
17	15	124	101.90	22.10	115.75	8.25
18	16	133	106.32	26.68	121.53	11.47
19	17	152	111.66	40.34	129.56	22.44
20	18	149	119.72	29.28	145.27	3.73
21	19	167	125.58	41.42	147.88	19.12
22	20	161	133.86	27.14	161.26	0.26
23	21	148	139.29	8.71	161.08	13.08
24	22	158	141.03	16.97	151.92	6.08
25	23	165	144.43	20.57	156.18	8.82
26						
27			Total:	430.69	Total:	263.04
28			Average:	19.58	Average:	11.96

= 0.2*B17 + 0.8*C17 =ABS(B18–C18)

Figure 9.16 Basic Exponential Smoothing with α = 0.2 and 0.7

The actual and the forecasted demand are plotted in Figure 9.17. The plot clearly shows that better results are obtained with α (the smoothing factor) equal to 0.7.

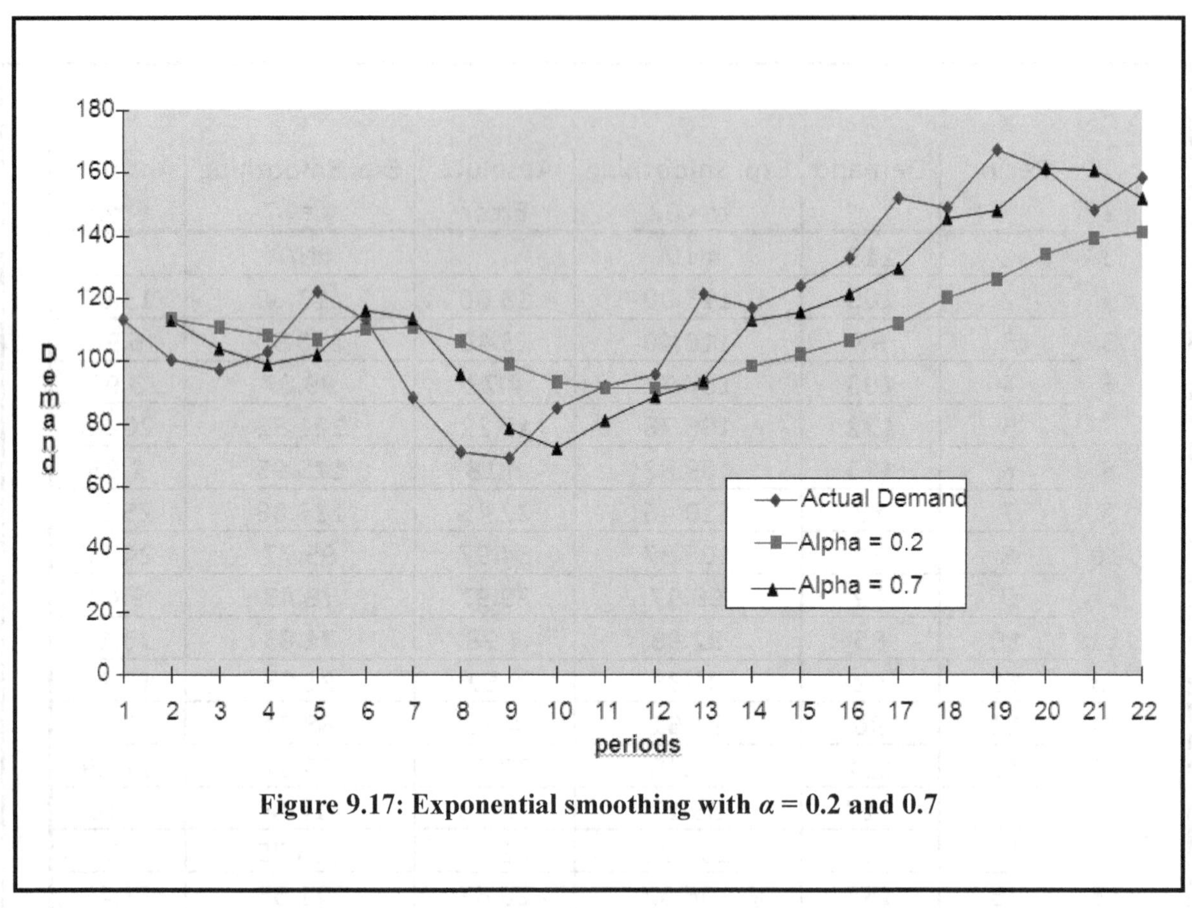

Figure 9.17: Exponential smoothing with α = 0.2 and 0.7

6.2 Basic Model with Trend Effect and Seasonal Effect

The simple exponential smoothing model can be adjusted for trend and seasonal effects. Let us first consider the trend effect.

Many forecasting models with trend effect have been suggested and used. One relatively simple exponential smoothing model with linear trend correction is presented here. The lead time for predicting purposes is assumed to be one period. The general formula is:

$$F_{t+1,1} = F_{t+1} + \frac{1-\alpha}{\alpha} T_{t+1}$$

With: $F_{t+1} = \alpha.D_t + (1-\alpha)F_t$

$$T_{t+1} = \alpha(F_{t+1} - F_t) + (1-\alpha)T_t$$

Where: $F_{t+1,1}$ is the Trend Effect forecast for the next period ($t+1$)

F_{t+1} is the basic exponentially smoothed estimate

D_t is the actual demand in the present period (t)

T_t is the smoothed estimate of the slope in period t

α is the smoothing constant, $0 < \alpha < 1$

Let us use these formulas to forecast the demand for our typical data and with □ = 0.2. In order to do this in an organized fashion, we will proceed through the following steps for each period *t*, where *t* starts with 1 and ends with 23:

Step 1: Calculate $F_{t+1} = 0.2D_t + 0.8F_t$ using the Exponential Smoothing forecast

Step 2: Evaluate the trend: $t_{t+1} = F_{t+1} - F_t$

Step 3: Calculate the smoothed trend: $T_{t+1} = 0.2t_{t+1} + 0.8T_t$

Step 4: Compute the forecast for the next period: $F_{t+1,1} = F_{t+1} + \frac{0.8}{0.2}T_{t+1}$

Calculations for period 2:

Since there is no value for the exponentially smoothed average for the period preceding period 1, we will assume that the trend is zero. As a starting value it is appropriate to set the forecasted value for the second period equal to the demand of the first period.

For t = 2: $F_2 = D_1 = 113$

$t_2 = 0$

$T_2 = 0$

Therefore: $F_{2,1} = F_2 + 4T_2 = 113$

Calculations for period 3:

Now we can calculate the simple exponential smoothing forecast, F_3. To get the trend factor, t_3, started we will calculate the difference between F_3 and F_2.

For t = 3: $F_3 = 0.2D_2 + 0.8F_2 = 0.2(100) + 0.8(113) = 110.4$

$t_3 = F_3 - F_2 = 110.4 - 113 = -2.6$

$T_3 = 0.2t_3 + 0.8T_2 = 0.2(-2.6) + 0.8(0) = -0.52$

Therefore: $F_{3,1} = F_3 + 4T_3 = 110.4 + 4(-0.52) = 108.32$

Calculations for period 4: (continues as above)

For t = 4: $F_4 = 0.2D_3 + 0.8F_3 = 0.2(97) + 0.8(110.4) = 107.72$

$t_4 = F_4 - F_3 = 107.72 - 110.4 = -2.68$

$T_4 = 0.2t_4 + 0.8T_3 = 0.2(-2.68) + 0.8(-0.52) = -0.952$

Therefore: $F_{4,1} = F_4 + 4T_4 = 107.72 + 4(-0.952) = 103.91$

Calculations for period 5: (continues as above)

For t = 5: $F_5 = 0.2D_4 + 0.8F_4 = 0.2(102) + 0.8(107.72) = 106.776$

$t_5 = F_5 - F_4 = 106.776 - 107.72 = -0.944$

$T_5 = 0.2t_5 + 0.8T_4 = 0.2(-0.944) + 0.8(-0.952) = -0.9504$

Therefore: $F_{5,1} = F_5 + 4T_5 = 1\ 06.776 + 4(-0.9504) = 102.9744$

This calculation procedure continues for all other time periods. All results are summarized in Figure 9.18, where calculations are done in Excel, and plotted in Figure 9.19.

	A	B	C	D	E	F	G
1	Period	Demand	Exp. Smoothing	Trend	Smoothed Slope	Predicted	Absolute
2			α = 0.2	Estimate	Estimate	Demand	Error
3	1	113	#N/A				
4	2	100	113.00	0.00	0.00	113.00	13.00
5	3	97	110.40	-2.60	-0.52	108.32	11.32
6	4	103	107.72	-2.68	-0.95	103.91	0.91
7	5	122	106.78	-0.94	-0.95	102.97	19.03
8	6	113	109.82	3.04	-0.15	109.22	3.78
9	7	88	110.46	0.64	0.01	110.48	22.48
10	8	71	105.97	-4.49	-0.89	102.39	31.39
11	9	69	98.97	-6.99	-2.11	90.52	21.52
12	10	85	92.98	-5.99	-2.89	81.42	3.58
13	11	92	91.38	-1.60	-2.63	80.86	11.14
14	12	96	91.51	0.12	-2.08	83.19	12.81
15	13	121	92.40	0.90	-1.48	86.47	34.53
16	14	117	98.12	5.72	-0.04	97.95	19.05
17	15	124	101.90	3.78	0.72	104.78	19.22
18	16	133	106.32	4.42	1.46	112.16	20.84
19	17	152	111.66	5.34	2.24	120.60	31.40
20	18	149	119.72	8.07	3.40	133.33	15.67
21	19	167	125.58	5.86	3.89	141.15	25.85
22	20	161	133.86	8.28	4.77	152.95	8.05
23	21	148	139.29	5.43	4.90	158.90	10.90
24	22	158	141.03	1.74	4.27	158.11	0.11
25	23	165	144.43	3.39	4.09	160.81	4.19
26							
27						Total:	340.79
28						Average:	15.49

=0.2*B4+0.8*C4 =C5–C4 =0.2*D5 + 0.8*E4 =C5 + 4*E5 =ABS(B5–F5)

Figure 9.18 Exponential Smoothing with Trend and α = 0.2

In order to appreciate the effect of the trend factor when making forecasts with the exponential smoothing models, one must compare their forecasting results. Note that the sum of the absolute errors when forecasting with the model that considers the trend factor is significantly smaller than the one that does not use the trend factor. According to Figure 9.16 the sum of the errors for the basic model is 430.69 while Figure 9.18 exhibits a reduced value of 340.79 for the sum of the absolute errors in the exponential smoothing model with trend factor. Looking at their plots in Figure 9.19 one can observe how much better the forecast is with the model that contains the trend factor. Therefore, it can be concluded that when past demand exhibits a trend, the forecaster must choose a model that considers a trend factor.

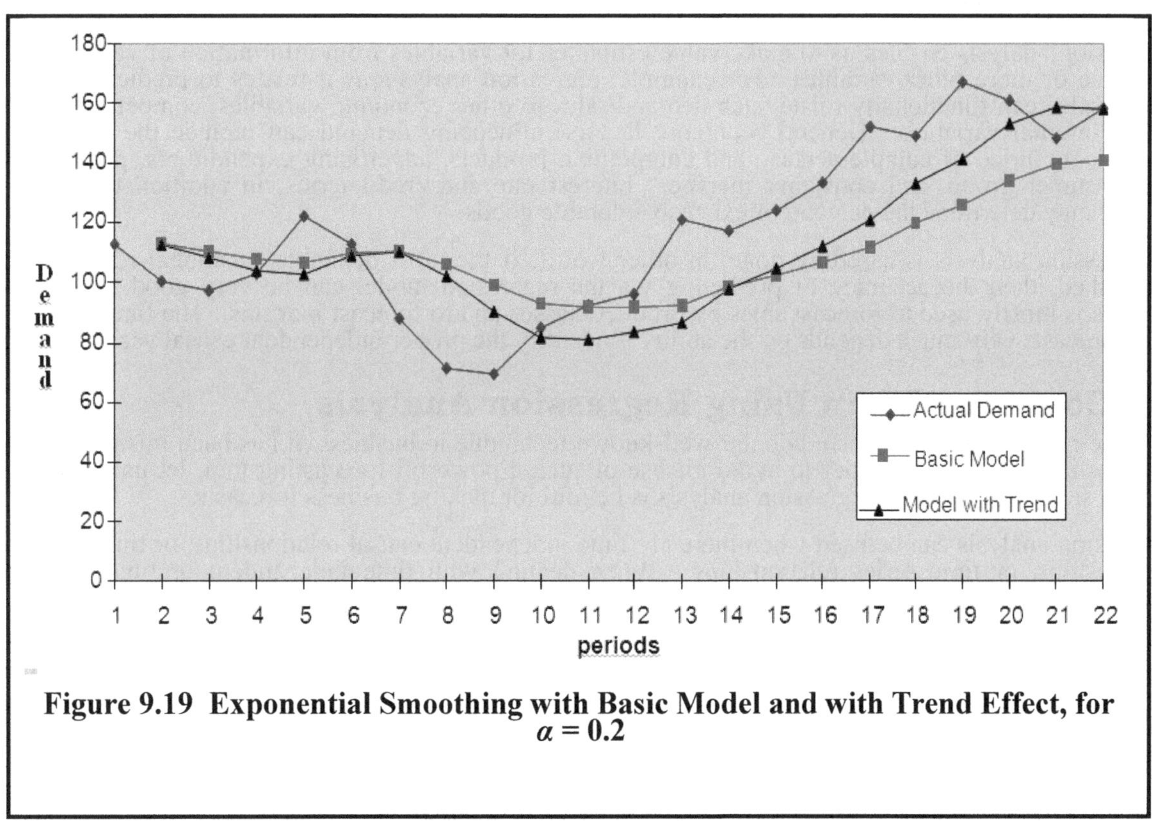

Figure 9.19 Exponential Smoothing with Basic Model and with Trend Effect, for $\alpha = 0.2$

In addition to adjusting the basic exponential smoothing models for trend, they can also be adjusted for seasonal changes. The following formulas are used for such forecasting.

$$F_{t+1,1} = F_{t+1} + \left(\frac{1-\alpha}{\alpha}\right) T_{t+1}$$

$$\text{With } F_{t+1} = \frac{\alpha D_t}{S_{t+1-L}} + (1-\alpha) F_t$$

$$T_{t+1} = \alpha\left(F_{t+1} - F_t\right) + (1-\alpha) T_t$$

$$S_{t+1-L} = \beta \frac{D_{t-L}}{F_{t+1-L}} + (1-\beta) S_{t-L}$$

Where L is the seasonality period (i.e., for period t+1-L to t) and $0 < \beta < 1$

Because of $F_{t+1} = \frac{\alpha D_t}{S_{t+1-L}} + (1-\alpha) F_t$ and $S_{t+1-L} = \beta \frac{D_{t-L}}{F_{t+1-L}} + (1-\beta) S_{t-L}$, forecasting with seasonality requires keeping track of many previous demands and forecasts.

7. CORRELATION AND REGRESSION ANALYSIS

Regression analysis enables us to make value estimates for variables from information of values coming from one or more other variables. For example, regression analysis as it relates to predicting demand and/or sales can functionally relate such demand/sales to other economic variables, competitive factors, and/or internal variables. General economic factors influencing demand can include the price of the product, the price of complementary and competitive products, advertising expenditures, population of the consumer group, and consumer income. Interest rate and credit terms, in addition to the above factors, may determine the demand of expensive durable goods.

If regression analysis is carefully done, in other words, if the most desirable functional relationship is established, then the accuracy of predicting via the regression model can be very good. Regression analysis is mostly used to forecast sales by product classes and to forecast margins. The time to perform such forecasts very much depends on the ability to identify the proper independent causal variables.

7.1 Concerns When Using Regression Analysis

Because regression analysis is a popular well-known technique in business, it has been misused in many business applications. In order to avoid misuse of such a powerful forecasting tool, let us examine the various situations in which regression analysis is helpful for making business forecasts.

Regression analysis can be used when there are time independent causal relationships, or time lag causal relationships, or time series relationships. When dealing with time independent or time lag causal relationships, the forecaster must be concerned with selecting the appropriate independent causal variables.

The following examples exhibit appropriate causal relationships amongst independent and dependent variables:

- Profit changes can be estimated when there is an increase in wage rates
- Absenteeism depends on job complexity
- Replacement parts depend on general business indicators such as consumer price index, disposable income, labor price, unemployment rate, prime interest rate, etc.
- The number of people employed in spring constructing depends on the value of all building permits applied for during the winter months for spring construction
- Yield of the corn crop depends on the amount of rain during the growing season, etc.

The forecaster must be very prudent in deciding when there does exist a causal relationship or association between independent and dependent variables. Just because there exists a significant mathematical association, called correlation, amongst independent and dependent variables does not necessarily mean that these variables are truly associated. Such type of association could be sheer chance. Also, when both dependent and independent variables simultaneously increase or decrease, then there is a possibility that they both depend on a third variable and they should not be considered in a regression formula. It is the task of the researcher/forecaster to use his knowledge and experience in defining appropriate predictive independent variables for purposes of forecasting economic elements. However, any chosen independent causal variable in a regression model must highly correlate with the dependent variable it is chosen to predict.

In regression models we often employ independent variables that lead their dependent variables. When such variables are used in predicting business phenomena, the lead time must be sufficient so that business and industry can react and adjust to any unexpected forecasted result. Leading indicators are mostly used to predict turning points in business cycles and to assess the magnitude of rising or declining economic activities. The National Bureau of Economic Research routinely assesses and publishes the most useful indicators for forecasting and for measuring changes in business activities. Useful leading indicators are fiscal policies, monetary policies, GNP deflators, productivity, consumer spending, residential construction, the stock market, population trends, and others.

In general, causal relationships are useful in making short-term predictions when the forecaster successfully uses his ingenuity and knowledge to pinpoint the most appropriate and effective variables to employ in the prediction.

Regression can also be used to forecast time series. In this context the forecast is referred to as trend analysis. It is only appropriate to use regression to project trends if past data are randomly distributed around the trend line. If there is a pattern in the data around the trend or regression line, then serial correlation exists and predicting future outcomes via such a regression line is not appropriate. Figure 9.20 suggests no serial correlation, because the time series data are randomly distributed around the trend line. However, serial correlation is certainly present in the data points shown in Figure 9.21.

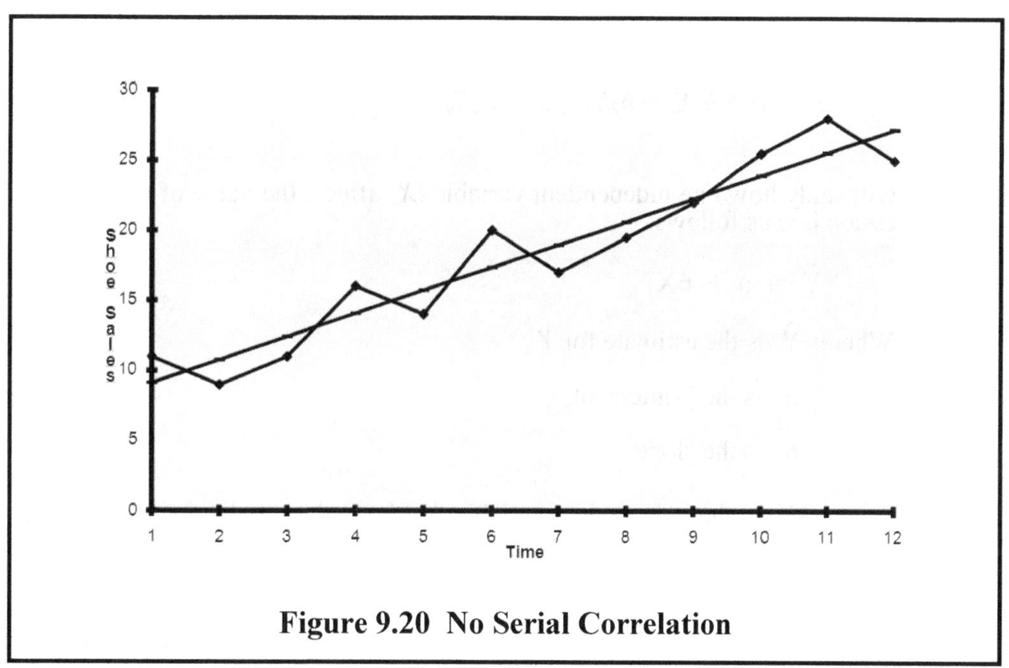

Figure 9.20 No Serial Correlation

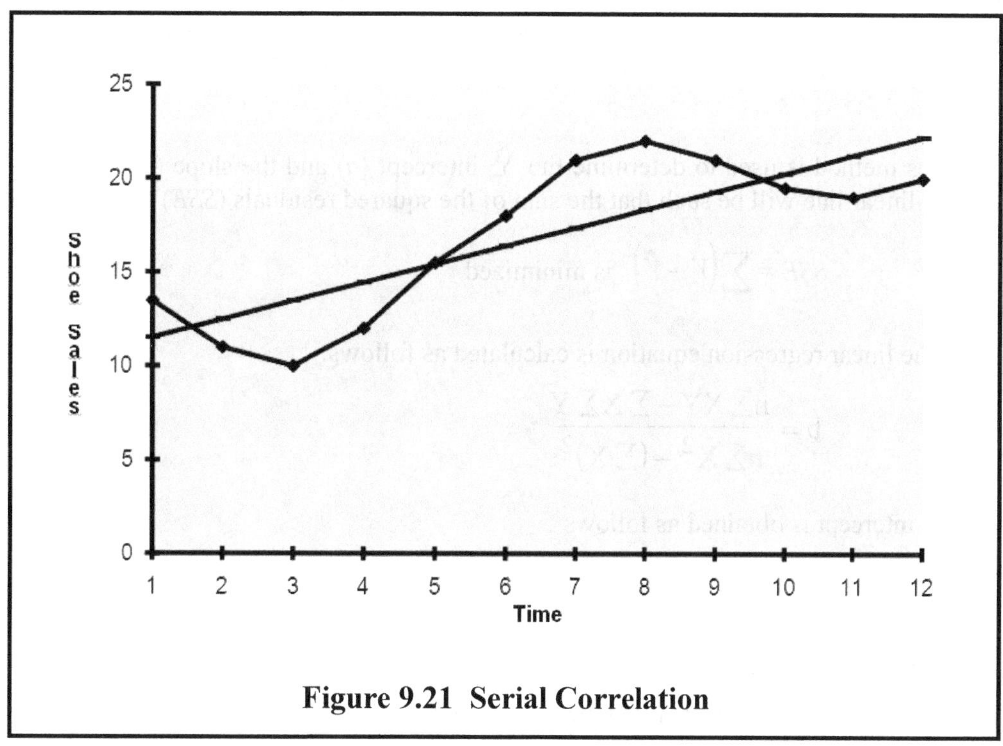

Figure 9.21 Serial Correlation

7.2 Linear Regression Analysis

Linear regression refers to the use of a linear equation to estimate one variable from others. The linear regression is then as follows:

$$Y = a + b_1X_1 + b_2X_2 + \ldots + b_nX_n$$

In this section we will study how one independent variable (X) affects the value of the dependent variable (Y) in a linear regression line as follows:

$$\hat{Y} = a + bX$$

Where: $\hat{Y}$ is the estimate for Y

a is the y-intercept

b is the slope

X is the independent variable that is used to predict $Y(\hat{Y})$

$\hat{Y} = a + bX$ is a single variable linear regression line where the b coefficient represents the amount by which $\hat{Y}$ changes for each unit change in the independent variable X. Simple linear regression analysis makes sense if past records indicate a fairly good linear relationship between the variable X and the variable Y that depends on the outcome of X. In other words, our linear equation makes sense if historical data demonstrates that $X - Y$ points fall about a straight line and seem to be randomly distributed about this line. For example, this seems to be the case with the distribution of the points about the trend line in Figure 9.20.

The least squares method is used to determine the $\hat{Y}$ intercept (a) and the slope (b) of $\hat{Y} = a + bX$. In this sense the linear line will be such that the sum of the squared residuals (SSE) are minimized:

$$SSE = \sum \left(Y - \hat{Y}\right)^2 \text{ is minimized}$$

The slope b in the linear regression equation is calculated as follows:

$$b = \frac{n\Sigma XY - \Sigma X \Sigma Y}{n\Sigma X^2 - (\Sigma X)^2}$$

Whereas the $\hat{Y}$ intercept is obtained as follows

$$a = \frac{\Sigma Y}{n} - b\frac{\Sigma X}{n}$$

Where: n is the sample size used to calculate the linear regression line

X is the original independent variable

Y is the original dependent variable

The sum of squared residuals (*SSE*) is the basis of two important measures: the standard error of the regression equation (*S*) and the correlation coefficient (*R*). These two statistical measures reflect the discrepancy between the observed values of *Y* and their respective estimated values from the regression line or $\hat{Y}$.

The **standard error (*S*)** of the line (regression equation) is the square root of the sum of squared residuals (*SSE*) divided by the number of degrees of freedom (number of total observations (*n*) minus the number of regression coefficients in the linear equation or two (2)). Thus the standard error is:

$$S = \sqrt{\left(\frac{\sum\left(Y_i - \hat{Y}_i\right)^2}{n-2}\right)}$$

The **correlation coefficient (*R*)** is obtained by comparing the sum of squared residuals (*SSE)* to sum of the squared deviation of *Y* about the mean $\bar{Y}$ (*SST*) and is defined by the following equation:

$$R = \sqrt{\frac{SST - SSE}{SST}}$$

Where: $SST = \sum\left(Y_i - \bar{Y}_i\right)^2$

$SSE = \sum\left(Y_i - \hat{Y}_i\right)^2$

The correlation coefficient is given the sign of the regression coefficient of the explanatory variable (*b*). It explains the relative importance of the association between *Y* and *X*. Its range is from –1 to +1, where –1 reflects a perfect negative relationship between X and *Y* and +1 means a perfect positive relationship between *X* and *Y*.

An Example

The following example illustrates the single linear regression line for ten data points.

All calculations are made in Excel and their results are shown in Figure 9.22.

The linear line represents the estimated values of *Y* ($\hat{Y}$) for various values of *X*:

$$\hat{Y} = 24.6 + 4.4X$$

These estimated values deviate from the actual *Y* values and their differences are recorded in column G. This column contains the residuals for this particular regression line, whose sum of their squared values (*SSE*) are extremely important entities in regression analysis.

A correlation coefficient of 0.935, as calculated here, reflects an excellent relationship between *X* and *Y*.

	A	B	C	D	E	F	G	H	I	J
1	Points	X	Y	X*Y	X*X	Ŷ=a+b*X	e = Y -Ŷ	(Y-Ŷ)*(Y-Ŷ)	Y-Ȳ	(Y-Ȳ)*(Y-Ȳ)
2	1	2	30	60	4	33.4	-3.4	11.56	-19	353.44
3	2	3	30	90	9	37.8	-7.8	60.84	-19	353.44
4	3	4	50	200	16	42.2	7.8	60.84	1.2	1.44
5	4	8	60	480	64	59.8	0.2	0.04	11.2	125.44
6	5	5	40	200	25	46.6	-6.6	43.56	-8.8	77.44
7	6	1	35	35	1	29	6	36	-14	190.44
8	7	6	53	318	36	51	2	4	4.2	17.64
9	8	10	70	700	100	68.6	1.4	1.96	21.2	449.44
10	9	9	62	558	81	64.2	-2.2	4.84	13.2	174.24
11	10	7	58	406	49	55.4	2.6	6.76	9.2	84.64
12	Sum:	55	488	3047	385		SSE:	230.4	SST:	1827.6

15 Slope = b =(10*∑(X*Y) - ∑X*∑Y)/(10 *∑(X*X) - (∑X*∑X)): 4.4

17 Intercept = a = (∑Y/10) - (b *∑X/10): 24.6

19 Estimate = Ŷ = 24.6 + 4.4X

21 Average of Ys = Ȳ = ∑Y/10: 48.8

23 Standard Error = S = √(SSE/(10-2)): 5.366563

25 Correlation Coefficient = R= √((SST-SSE)/SST): 0.934844

=SQRT((J12–H12)/J12)

=SQRT(H12/8)

=C12/10

=(C12/10) – J15*(B12/10)

=(10*D12 –B12*C12)/((10*E12) – (B12*B12))

Figure 9.22 Regression Analysis (Long Hand)

Using Excel

The regression analysis that is shown in Figure 9.22 can quickly be done using "Data Analysis" on your "Data" toolbar. This is illustrated in what follows using the same data as shown in Figure 9.22.

Use the same data preparation guidelines as outlined for the moving average technique!

Go now to "Data Analysis" on your "Data" toolbar to perform a complete regression analysis. You will obtain the screen as shown in Figure 9.23. Now scroll down to "Regression" and hit "OK." This will bring you to the Regression input box as seen in Figure 9.24.

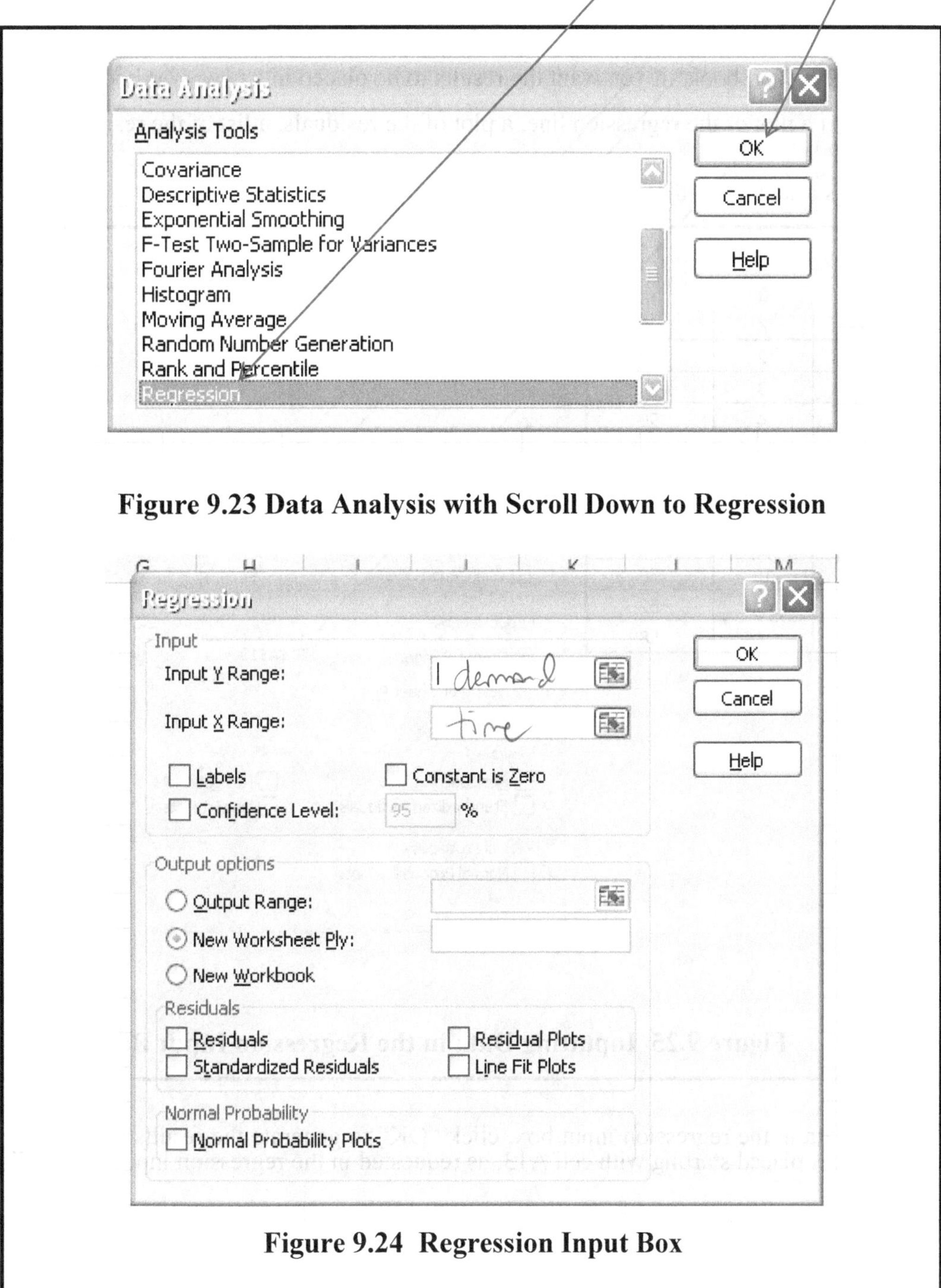

Figure 9.23 Data Analysis with Scroll Down to Regression

Figure 9.24 Regression Input Box

The following minimum input is required to perform regression analysis:

"Input Y Range": drag the mouse over the dependent data values (Y column)

"Input X Range": drag the mouse over the independent data values (X column)

You have various options for the Output:

Click on "Output Range" if you want to show where to place the output; or

Click on "New Worksheet" if you want the results to be placed on a new worksheet; or

Click on "New Workbook" if you want the results to be placed in a new workbook.

If you wish to get a plot of the regression line, a plot of the residuals, a list of the residuals, etc., then click the appropriate boxes.

Limited output is asked for in the input box shown in Figure 9.25.

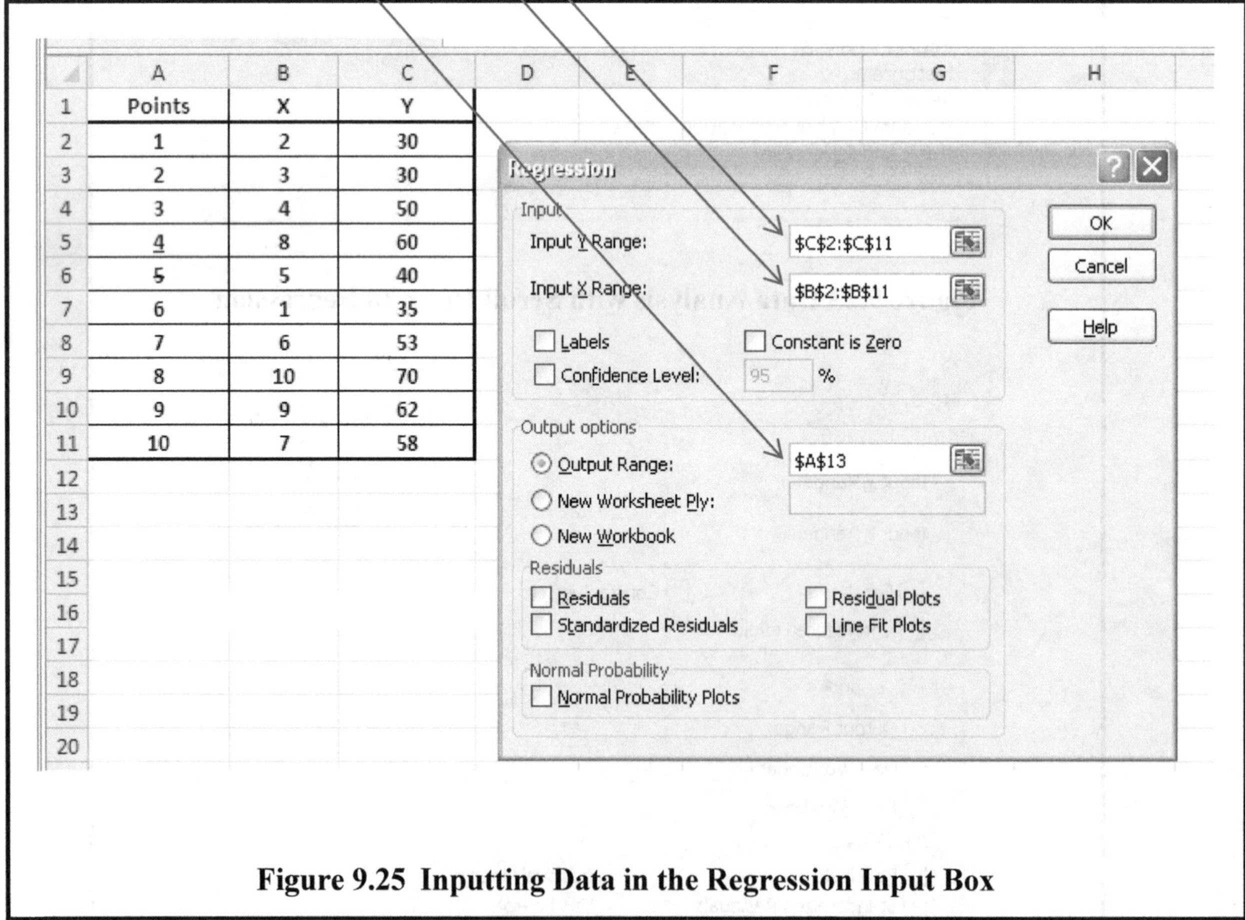

Figure 9.25 Inputting Data in the Regression Input Box

After entering data in the regression input box, click "OK" to generate the results as seen in Figure 9.26. Note that output is placed starting with cell A13, as requested in the regression input box of Figure 9.25.

	A	B	C
1	Points	X	Y
2	1	2	30
3	2	3	30
4	3	4	50
5	4	8	60
6	5	5	40
7	6	1	35
8	7	6	53
9	8	10	70
10	9	9	62
11	10	7	58

SUMMARY OUTPUT

Regression Statistics		
Multiple R	0.93484385	← this is the correlation
R Square	0.87393303	
Adjusted R Square	0.85817466	
Standard Error	5.36656315	
Observations	10	

ANOVA

	df	*SS*	*MS*	*F*	*Significance F*
Regression	1	1597.2	1597.2	55.458	7.28504E-05
Residual	8	230.4	28.8		
Total	9	1827.6			

	Coefficients	*Standard Error*	*t Stat*	*P-value*	*Lower 95%*	*Upper 95%*	*Lower 95.0%*	*Upper 95.0%*
Intercept	24.6	3.666060556	6.7102	0.0002	16.1460492	33.053951	16.1460492	33.0539508
X Variable 1	4.4	0.590839157	7.447	7E-05	3.037522461	5.7624775	3.03752246	5.76247754

this is the b value of the line

this is the a value of the line

Figure 9.26 Regression Output

The highlighted part in Figure 9.26 shows the information needed to define the linear regression line and to understand its fit ("Multiple R," the correlation, or "R Square").

$$Y = 24.6 + 4.4X$$

This function can now be used to forecast values for ***Y***, for various given values of ***X***.
For a complete interpretation of the "ANOVA," "t Stat," and upper and lower limits for the "intercept" and the "X variable 1" consult your statistics text.

Figure 9.27 shows the plot for this regression line and the original data points.

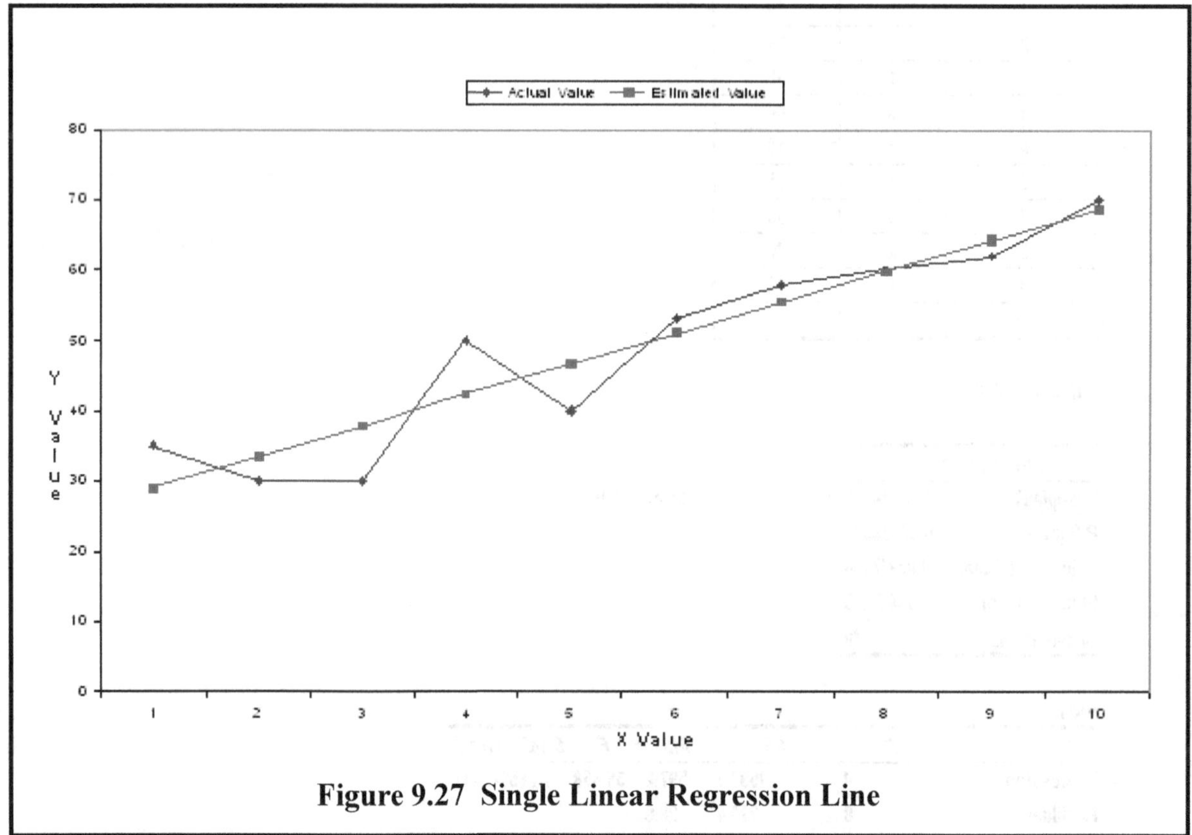

Figure 9.27 Single Linear Regression Line

8. *TECHNOLOGICAL FORECASTING*

8.1 Defining Technological Forecasting

Technological forecasting can be used when the need for a new product can be forecasted based on current and future trends in applied research and projections of possible breakthroughs in technology. In other words, technological forecasting aims at predicting future technological capabilities, attributes, and parameters in an attempt to bring about tomorrow's evolving technologies.

Technological forecasting can be helpful in estimating the realization of new needed advancements in processes, tools, machinery, equipment, etc. to reduce manufacturing cost or improve production productivity. In the last decade research has focused on forecasting health information technology that can significantly impact health services by improving patient care, and that improve organizational efficiencies within the U.S. health care services delivery system.

When dealing with industrial process technology, it is important to forecast the rate at which some new technology will replace the old one. In this case the promoter of technology wishes to know how fast his research and development investment in new technology will be recovered. Technological forecasting can also lead to the identification of a new future need for an existing product.

An Example : DuPont's Teflon Invention

A good example that technological forecasting can lead to the identification of a new future need for an existing product is DuPont's Teflon invention. Teflon was originally developed by DuPont to solve the need for high heat resistance in space vehicles. This invention eventually led to the creation and the identification of a commercial need for Teflon in the fabrication of cookware.

Often technological forecasting is also employed when the research manager has neither a product/service nor a foreknowledge of need. Here one may start with new discoveries in science. The current event of such discoveries can lead to certain innovations. Technological forecasting can then be used to predict when certain actions may take place leading to specific events in the product design area and eventually the product use area.

An Example: The Laser Invention

The event of the birth of the laser set off a myriad of chain reactions in various fields, resulting in various services and events. Researchers in the field of medicine, metal works, graphic arts, astronomy, surveying, etc. were motivated to find applications for the laser in their respective areas. This eventually lead to the events of eye surgery with the laser beam, the diamond punch in metal works, the hologram in graphic arts, the measurement of moon distance in astronomy, etc.

Technological forecasting does not only consist of planning "what" will evolve out of an invention, but also with "when," "where," "why," "how," and "the probability of success."

Examples of Successful Inventions for the Health Care Industry

Health information technologies are changing the future of health care delivery in a very successful way. Here are some examples.

Telemedicine with its infrastructure that includes physical facilities and equipment used to capture, transmit, store, process, and display voice, data, and images is still in its infancy, but here to stay.

Technological advances in fiber optics, satellite communications, and compressed video are gaining the interest of the public and the private health care sectors as their implementation cost is decreasing.

Emerging technologies are dictating that people take a more active role in maintaining their own health. This will result in a more proactive prevention-oriented consumer driven health care system, using the technology of "smart devices" that can 'think," customized wearable devices, electronic patient records, and internet-linked systems.

Research supports that at least five emerging technologies have a future in the healthcare industry: Radio Frequency Identification (RFID), Semantic Web, Wearable Devices, e-Health, and Artificial Intelligence (AI). RFID is a technology that uses radio waves to automatically identify people and objects. The semantic Web makes it easier for data on the Web to be shared and reused by people and applications. Wearable devices are vital to the world's ever growing aging population. They are patient monitoring devices that measure, display, and document physiological information at regular time intervals. E-health relates to convenience in exchanging medical information from one source to another, via electronic communications, in order to improve and monitor patient health. Artificial intelligence (AI) is the study of how computer systems simulate learning, reasoning, and understanding symbolic information in context. AI overcomes the limitation of humans' short term memories.

8.2 An Overview of Technological Forecasting Methods

During the early 1970s only two important methods of technological forecasting existed, namely the Delphi method and Trend Extrapolation. However, since then many new techniques of technological forecasting have evolved and are gaining respect in the field of forecasting. These newer techniques are: Dynamic Modeling, Computer Modeling (System Dynamics), Mathematical Modeling, Cross Impact Modeling, Trend Impact Analysis, Growth Curves, Scoring Models, Probabilistic System Dynamics, Patent Analysis, Bibliometrics, and Scenario Analysis.

Mathematical Modeling and **Computer Modeling**, such as **Systems Dynamics** and **Probabilistic Systems Dynamics** are the most commonly used technological forecasting techniques. In **Systems Dynamics** models, events happen with certainty. Thus, the effects of some variables on others are fully known with only one possible outcome for any set of initial conditions of the model.

Probabilistic Systems Dynamics evolved out of the fact that technological forecasters realized that they were faced with events which are not certain, and whose impacts are not certain either if the events were to occur. It allows for stochastic events in system dynamics simulation.

Cross Impact Models take into account the interactions among events in large-scale technological forecasting. These models require nominal forecasts for each event, so that the initial forecast for each event specifies a time of occurrence and a probability of occurrence. These forecasts of occurrence and probability of occurrence may be altered through cross impacts (resulting from interactions amongst events). The cross impact algorithms are generic models and are supplied as input data models. Therefore, the cross impact model is highly flexible since major changes in the model are brought about through changes in input data.

Trend Impact Analysis is another technique where the forecaster begins with projecting a trend and extrapolates it under the assumption that there are no changes that may affect the trend. Changes are introduced through a computer program and result in the alteration to the initial trend. In this way the forecaster generates a spread of trends around the initial baseline. Now the forecaster has, in addition to the baseline trend, an estimate of how much deviation from that baseline trend might occur.

Growth Curves are used to forecast the substitution of one technology for another one. When plotted these growth curves look like product life cycle curves. Initially, the substitution is slow since barriers must be overcome. This changes when the rate of substitution accelerates. Finally, it tapers off when the last "old-timers" adopt the new technology.

Scoring Models expect that the forecaster develops a figure of merit or a performance rating for a technology. In this way he may be able to predict the application and the performance of that technology in the future. The figure of merit or performance rating includes various factors such as power, speed, weight, and others. These factors must be properly combined into a functional relationship by the use of mathematical techniques.

Patent Analysis and **Bibliometrics** have been used to trend emerging technologies that, while under exploration, reach a plateau of granted patents at a certain time period. They are very useful forecasting technique for health care information technology and are solely based on numeric data.

Example #1: The Blue Laser Diode

Based on United States Patent and Trademark Office data, the blue laser diode reached its high level plateau at the turn of the century, when its number of U.S. patents reached 60. However, it took six years before we saw its first commercial application in 2006. So, it took six years to commercialize this technology.

Example #2: The five Emerging Technologies in Health Care

Searching the U.S. patents database and a comprehensive review of the current literature identified the five emerging technologies in health care: Radio Frequency Identification (RFID), Semantic Web, Wearable Devices, e-Health, and Artificial Intelligence (AI).

Scenario Analysis, as opposed to patent analysis, is a judgmental method and is appropriate for studying technologies that are more suggestive of an evolving concept.

9. POLITICAL AND SOCIOLOGICAL FORECASTING

Political decisions and social concerns largely determine the economic and technical background against which business organizations operate. Therefore, business enterprises get involved in evaluating and predicting political decisions and sociological changes that affect various aspects of their businesses, such as their:

- Corporate planning
- Strategic planning
- Marketing strategies
- Advertising strategies
- Process and product development
- Employment policies such as labor relations and communications
- Search for new technologies

There does not exist a generally accepted comprehensive model of how society works and how it affects business planning. After all, with social matters there is no accepted unit of accounting, nor a comprehensive database. Various centers have done a considerable effort to create a comprehensive database. The Hensley Center that grew out of James Morrell and Associates, which made economic forecasts way back in the early sixties, has attempted to create a comprehensive database. Key input elements of that database were the MONITOR survey of public attitudes. This survey consisted of a detailed set of about 7,000 questions. This database consists of attitudinal data, information on population factors, health care, crime, educational statistics, divorce rates, etc.

Using tools of survey research, the researcher can measure, monitor, and consequently predict national, political, and social issues that may have significant impacts on business. Such survey research must draw information from two distinctly different sets of interviews:

- A large scale statistically valid general public survey
- A series of probing in-depth interviews of key opinions, leaders in government, industry, trade unions, televising, press, financial community, and pressure groups

All information generated through these interviews must be carefully analyzed in order to predict the importance and the type of impact certain political and social issues will have on business.

Here follows an example on how sociological research affected one industry:

An Example: Shell Oil Creates a Unique Customer Service Program

In the early 1980s, sociological research on energy and the oil industry revealed that public and leader attitudes towards the oil industry were very negative, making traditional product marketing and public issue advertising very ineffective. The public seemed to view public issue advertising as non-credible and it viewed traditional product advertising as wasteful, unnecessary, and as a sign of excess profits. Shell Oil, consequently, created a unique customer service program with its advertisement of "Come to Shell for Answers" and with the publication of a series of pamphlets to aid motorists in maintaining their vehicles and improving their driving skills. This campaign gave Shell Oil a most positive public rating amongst major oil companies.

10. GLOSSARY AND SUMMARY OF METHODS

Causal Forecasting Methods – Causal forecasting techniques employ mathematical relationships amongst two or more variables. They take into account economic and business variables that may contribute to the forecast of specific business phenomena (regression analysis, econometric model, intention-to-buy and anticipation surveys, input-output model, economic I/O model, diffusion index, leading indicators, lifecycle analysis).

Delphi Method – The Delphi method generates subjective information provided by experts who answer a series of questions on several questionnaires over an extended period of time. Results of one questionnaire are reflected on consecutive questionnaires, so that all information that is available is made available to all experts answering the next questionnaire.

Exponential Smoothing – In the basic model of exponential smoothing the forecast is made by using the previous forecast plus some portion of the previously made forecasting error. The basic exponential smoothing model, however, can be adjusted for trend and seasonal effect.

Forecasting – In general terms, forecasting is a technique whereby past experience is transformed into general predictions of "things to come" in order to: 1) predict sales volume of individual end products, 2) predict gross sales, 3) determine facility capacity requirements, 4) define the labor force capacity over time, 5) predict gross national product, 6) forecast changes in the national labor productivity, etc.

Market Survey – Market surveys are systematic, formal or informal, and conscious methods whereby certain hypotheses about the actual market can be defined and tested. Surveys can be mail surveys, personal interviews, or telephone surveys.

Mechanical Projection Techniques – Some mechanical projection techniques are: moving averages, exponential smoothing, Box-Jenkins, trend projections, regression analysis, econometrics, leading indicators, lifecycle analysis, etc.

Moving Average – When calculating moving averages, only data from more recent time periods are used. The moving average methods tend to lag a trend, raise the valleys, and depress the peaks of cyclic patterns.

Political and Sociological Forecasting – Political and sociological forecasting measure, monitor, and consequently predict national, political, and social issues that may have a significant impact on business.

Qualitative or Predictive Methods – Qualitative forecasting methods employ human judgments and rating schemes to convert intangible data into quantitative estimates (Delphi method, market research, panel consensus, visionary forecasting, and historical analogy).

Regression Analysis – Regression analysis enables us to make value estimates for variables from information of values coming from one or more other variables. Leading independent variables are used to predict their dependent variable, using a variety of mathematical relationships (linear and non-linear models).

Technological Forecasting – Technological forecasting aims at predicting future technological capabilities, attributes, and parameters in an attempt to bring about tomorrow's evolving technologies (mathematical modeling, computer modeling, probabilistic systems dynamics, cross impact models, trend impact analysis, growth curves, scoring models, patent analysis, bibliometrics, and scenario analysis).

Time Series Analysis and Projection Methods – Time series methods are statistical techniques that use historical data to predict the future (moving average, exponential smoothing, Box-Jenkins, X-11 of Census Bureau, and trend projections).

11. REFERENCES

Ashley, R. and J. Guerard "Applications of Time Series Analysis to Texas Financial Forecasting." *Interfaces*. (Vol. 13, No. 4, August 1983): 46–55.

Becker, B. C., and A. Sapienza. "Forecasting Hospital Reimbursement." *Hospital and Health Services Administration*. (Vol. 32, November 1987): 521–530.

Bowerman, B. L. and R. T. O'Connell. *Time Series Forecasting*. Boston: PWS-Kent Publishing Company, 1987.

Box, G. E. P., and G. Jenkins, *Time Series Analysis, Forecasting and Control*. San Francisco: Holden Day, 1970.

Cauffiel, D., and A. Porter. "Electronics Manufacturing in 2020: A National Technological University Management of Technology Mini-Delphi." *Technological Forecasting and Social Change*. (Vol. 51, 1996): 185–194.

Chambers, J. C., C. Satinder, S. K. Mullick, and D.D. Smith. "How to Choose the Right Forecasting Technique." *HarvardBusiness Review* (Vol. 49, Vol. 4, July-August 1971): 45–74.

Cohen, A. and R. Hanft. Technology in Healthcare. 2004.

Daim, T., G. Grueda, and H. Martin. "Forecasting Emerging Technologies: Use of Bibliometrics and Patent Analysis." *Technological Forecasting and Social Change*. (Vol. 73, 2006): 981–1012.

Dielman, T. E. Applied Regression Analysis for Business and Economics. Boston: PWS-Kent Publishing Company, 1991.

Farnum, N. R. and L. W. Stanton. *Quantitative Forecasting Methods*. Boston: PWS-Kent Publishing Company, 1989.

Gardner, E. S. "Exponential Smoothing: The State of the Art." *Journal of Forecasting*. (Vol. 4, No.1, March 1985).

Geisler, E., K. Krabbendam, and R. Schuring. *Technology: Healthcare, and Management in the Hospitals of the Future*. Westport, CT: Greenwood Publishing Group, 2003.

Kayal, A. "Measuring the Pace of Technological Process: Implication for Technological Forecasting." *Technological Forecasting and Social Change*. (Vol. 60, 1990): 237–245.

Kleinbaum, D. G., Kupper, L. L., and K. E. Muller. *Applied Regression Analysis and other Multivariable Methods*. Boston: PWS- Kent Publishing Company, 1988.

Myers, R. H. *Classical and Modern Regression with Applications*. 2nd Ed. Boston: PWS-Kent Publishing Company, 1990.

Neter, J., Wasserman, W. and M. H. Kutner. *Applied Linear Statistical Models*. 2nd Ed. Homewood, IL: Richard D. Irwin, Inc., 1985.

Parker, G. C., and E. L. Segura. "How to Get a Better Forecast." *Harvard Business Review*. (Vol. 49, No. 2, March-April 1971): 99 –109.

Schnaars, S. P., and R. J. Bavuso. "Exponential Models on Very Short Term Forecasts." *Journal of Business Research*. (Vol. 14, 1986): 27–36.

12. REVIEW QUESTIONS

1. Briefly discuss the sales forecasting system. Include in your discussion the types of information used; how that information is analyzed; and what types of sales projections are obtained.
2. Distinguish between qualitative or predictive methods, time series analysis or projection methods, and causal forecasting methods. Give some examples for each of the three groups.
3. Consider the product lifecycle. What types of decisions are made over the course of the product life cycle and what types of forecasting methods are used to enable making these decisions?
4. Briefly describe the process used when forecasting with the Delphi method.
5. What conditions must be met for a mail survey approach to be effective?
6. What conditions must be met for personal interviews to be effective?
7. What conditions must be met for a telephone interview to be effective?
8. How can a simple moving average be adjusted to incorporate a definite trend?
9. What is the main difference between a moving average and exponential smoothing?
10. How are trend and seasonal effects incorporated in exponential smoothing?
11. Discuss the selection of the smoothing factor in exponential smoothing. How does it affect the forecast?
12. List some general economic factors that may influence the demand. How can these be used in forecasting the demand for goods?
13. Discuss the concerns when using regression analysis.
14. What measures can be used to evaluate the accuracy of linear regression models? Briefly discuss these measures.
15. What is meant by technological forecasting?
16. Explain some of the technological forecasting techniques.
17. How have some of these techniques impacted health care technologies?
18. Differentiate between patent analysis and scenario analysis as a technological forecasting technique.
19. What is meant by political and sociological forecasting?
20. Why must businesses get involved with sociological and political forecasting?
21. What aspects of businesses are affected by sociological and political events?
22. Survey research must draw information from two distinctly different sets of interviews. Explain these interviews.

13. PROBLEMS

Problem #1 (Excel)

The Amdex Corporation produces industrial air filters. Past demand for the units is as follows:

Month	2006	2007
January	18	41
February	24	58
March	34	79
April	41	92
May	45	93
June	38	71
July	40	76
August	39	72
September	41	68
October	37	60
November	34	58
December	32	48

a) Plot the above 24 demand data and describe what you see.

b) Is a trend present? Does the data show any seasonality?

Problem #2 (Excel)

If you observed a trend in the above demand pattern, compute the constant and the slope of the demand line (linear trend) as indicated by the following equation:

$$Y = a + bT$$

Where: Y is the estimated demand trend

a is the constant or the y-intercept

b is the slope

T is the time period (1, 2, 3, 4, ... ,24)

Problem #3 (Excel)

Use the regression output for Problem #2 to answer all of the following questions:

a) What is the correlation coefficient?

b) Is the trend model a good model for forecasting purposes?

c) Use the above trend equation to estimate the demand for June 2008 and December 2008.

Problem #4 (Excel)

Reconsider the data of Problem #1.

a) Use a simple moving average over 5 periods to predict the demand.

b) Calculate the accumulated absolute error over last year's period (2007).

c) Use the adjusted weighted moving average (adjusted for trend) over 5 periods to predict the demand.

d) Calculate the accumulated absolute error for the AMA forecast over last year's period (2007).

e) Compare the results of b) and d). Which of the two methods is the preferred one? Why?

Problem #5 (Excel)

Reconsider the demand data of Problem #1.

a) Use the basic exponential smoothing model for predicting the demand for smoothing constants equal to 0.1, 0.3, 0.5, 0.7, and 0.9. Calculate the accumulated absolute errors.

b) Which smoothing constant gives you the best results?

c) Can you explain why the above best smoothing factor gives you the best results (hint: look at the graph you plotted for Problem #1)?

Problem #6 (Excel)

Reconsider the demand data of Problem #1.

a) Use the basic exponential smoothing model with trend effect for smoothing constants 0.1, 0.3, 0.5, 0.7 and 0.9 to predict the demand. Calculate the errors.

b) Which smoothing constant gives you the best results?

Problem #7 (Excel)

Compare the results of Problems #5 and #6. Which model is better, the basic exponential smoothing model or the basic exponential smoothing model with trend effect?

Problem #8 (Excel)

Compu Inc. believes that there is a relationship between the sales of computers and computer games sold to individual households. The owner feels that there is a two-week lag between the hardware and the software sale. Therefore, the owner wishes to use sales of hardware to predict the sales of the computer games. He has collected the following data:

Observation	$X(t)$	$Y(t+2)$
1	29	370
2	45	415
3	91	490
4	54	403
5	86	480
6	77	475
7	51	415
8	38	235
9	28	360
10	29	390
11	42	
12	40	

a) Use the first 10 observations to obtain a linear regression line to predict $Y(t+2)$, using $X(t)$.

b) Calculate the correlation coefficient.

c) Use your linear regression line to predict the demand for games for periods 13 and 14.

Problem #9 (Excel)

Quick Auto Lube System has been in business for the past year. Its operations have been expanding fast and the owner believes that the past trend of expansion will continue for at least another year. He has collected the following data over the past 16 months of operation.

Month	Year	Number of Auto Lubes
January	2007	660
February		1120
March		1550
April		1500
May		1400
June		1660
July		1860
August		2240
September		2600
October		2730
November		2900
December		2890
January	2008	2900
February		3160
March		3350
April		3570

a) Calculate the trend in the data using regression analysis.

b) Use the calculated trend to estimate the number of lubes for May, June, and July of 2008.

Problem #10 (Excel)

Reconsider the data of Problem #9.

a) Generate a forecast using the adjusted weighted moving average method (use 5 periods)

b) Calculate the errors by comparing the actual with the forecasted demands.

Problem #11 (Excel)

Reconsider the data of Problem #9.

a) Generate a forecast using the basic exponential smoothing method with trend effect and a smoothing factor equal to 0.6.

b) Calculate the errors by comparing the actual with the forecasted demands.

Problem #12

Compare the results of Problem #10 and Problem #11 to determine the best method.

Chapter 10

PRODUCTION PLANNING AND CONTROL SYSTEMS

1. INTRODUCTION

The production planning and control system relates to the total supply/production/distribution network of a productive system—the backbone of the industrial society. The fluctuations of the system are monitored and the activities of the network are adjusted by the production/inventory planning and control functions. In modern society, the productive systems are complex and mutually related in many different ways. Each firm can be viewed as a sub-system within a much larger socioeconomic system. The planning and control of the total socioeconomic system is studied in macro economics and political science. Our primary concern about the production/operations management function is the planning and control of the productive activities within the producer's domain, that is from raw materials and supplies entering the factory (in a broader sense) to the finished products leaving the factory.

1.1 Basic Objective of Production Planning & Control

The basic objective of production planning and control is to plan and to control the flow of materials into, through, and out of the productive system in such a manner that an optimal amount of value is added through the transformation process of the system. For manufacturing and service operations, the added value is measured by its profit position achieved within the framework of the established goals of the organization. For non-profit operations, the added value is measured by the level of output against its established goals.

To achieve its objective, the production planning and control function must establish a way to monitor and to evaluate the current customer orders and future market demand, the production capacity, the manpower resources, and the production lead time. The production lead time is often treated as a constant in production planning and control models. In reality, it can be as volatile and unpredictable as the market demand if the control function fails. The frequency and the time span of continued evaluation of the above-mentioned factors depend on many factors which will be discussed in this chapter.

1.2 Timing the Supply Chain Response

The supply chain consists of the network that delivers products and services from raw materials to end customers. It includes flows of information, physical distribution and movement of goods, and cash. The management of the supply chain includes its design, planning, execution, control, and monitoring of its activities. Its main objective is to create added value in its productive system, while synchronizing supply with demand. This primary objective must be accomplished at the right time, in the right quantity, and with the right cost. To achieve this objective, it is important to control and to shorten the market response time. Within our highly competitive marketplace, the market response time of a firm often plays a very critical role in the success or failure of a business.

Lean operations management focusses on shortening the market response time by eliminating waste in the system that adds time and no value to the end product.

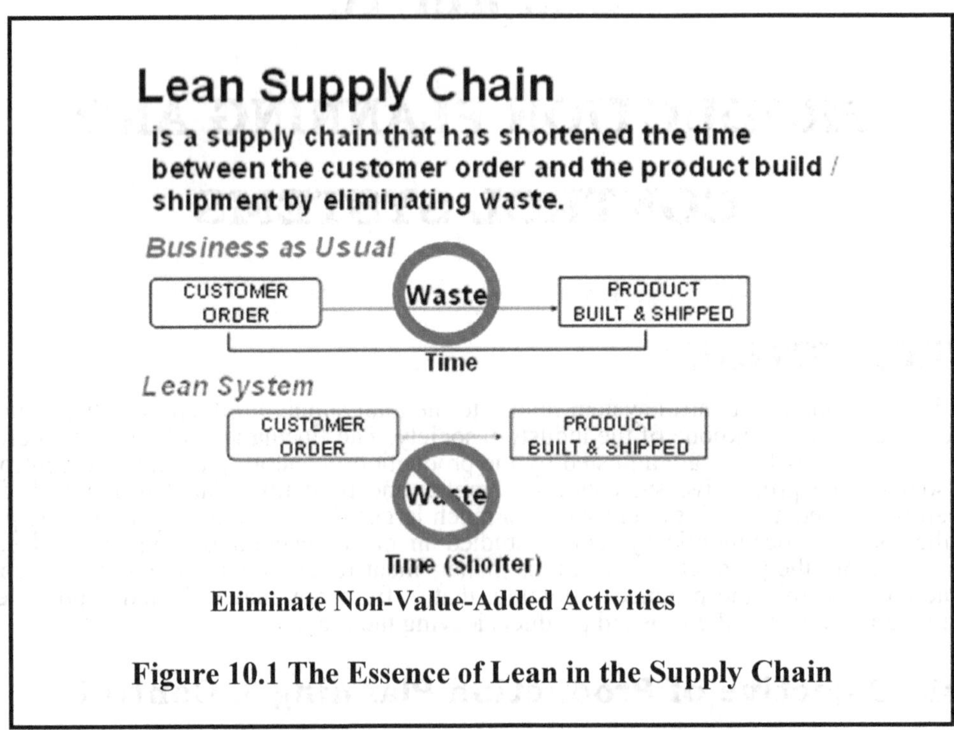

Figure 10.1 The Essence of Lean in the Supply Chain

Per definition, the **market response time** is determined by the elapsed time of all information flows plus the elapsed time of the materials flows. This definition is correct for a **produce-to-order system**, but needs to be modified for a **production-to-stock** system.

In a **produce-to-order** system there is no inventory in place and no production activity is scheduled before the customer's actual order is received. Here the market response time is determined by the information flow time, the production lead time, and the market lead time. The **production lead time (PLT)**, often called the **manufacturing lead time** for a manufacturing firm, is the elapsed time between the release of the production order to the shop floor and the delivery of the final product to the finished goods warehouse. The **market lead time (MLT)** is the elapsed time of the transfer of the customer's order from the sales department to the factory plus the needed time for delivering the finished goods to the customer.

In a **production-to-stock** system the MLT (market response time) is equal to market lead time and, theoretically speaking, is independent from the PLT (production lead time). However, unless a perfect forecasting system or an unlimited finished goods inventory is in place, the actual market response time is very much affected by the PLT (production lead time).

The PLT (production lead time) can further be divided into two time elements: the **operation time** (OT) and the **inter operation time** (IT). The OT (operation time) includes the time during which the transformation process is actually taking place and the time required to set up the production machines or equipment. The inter operation time (IT) is nonproductive time during which the production orders are in queue (before entering the next operation), in storage between two consecutive operations, or in transit from one operation to the next operation. The waiting time, for both in storage and in queue, is controllable and, at times, avoidable. Yet, this waiting time is often the largest time element in the PLT. Therefore, lean operations management pays special attention to reducing the inter operation time.

An Example: Calculating the Market Response Time

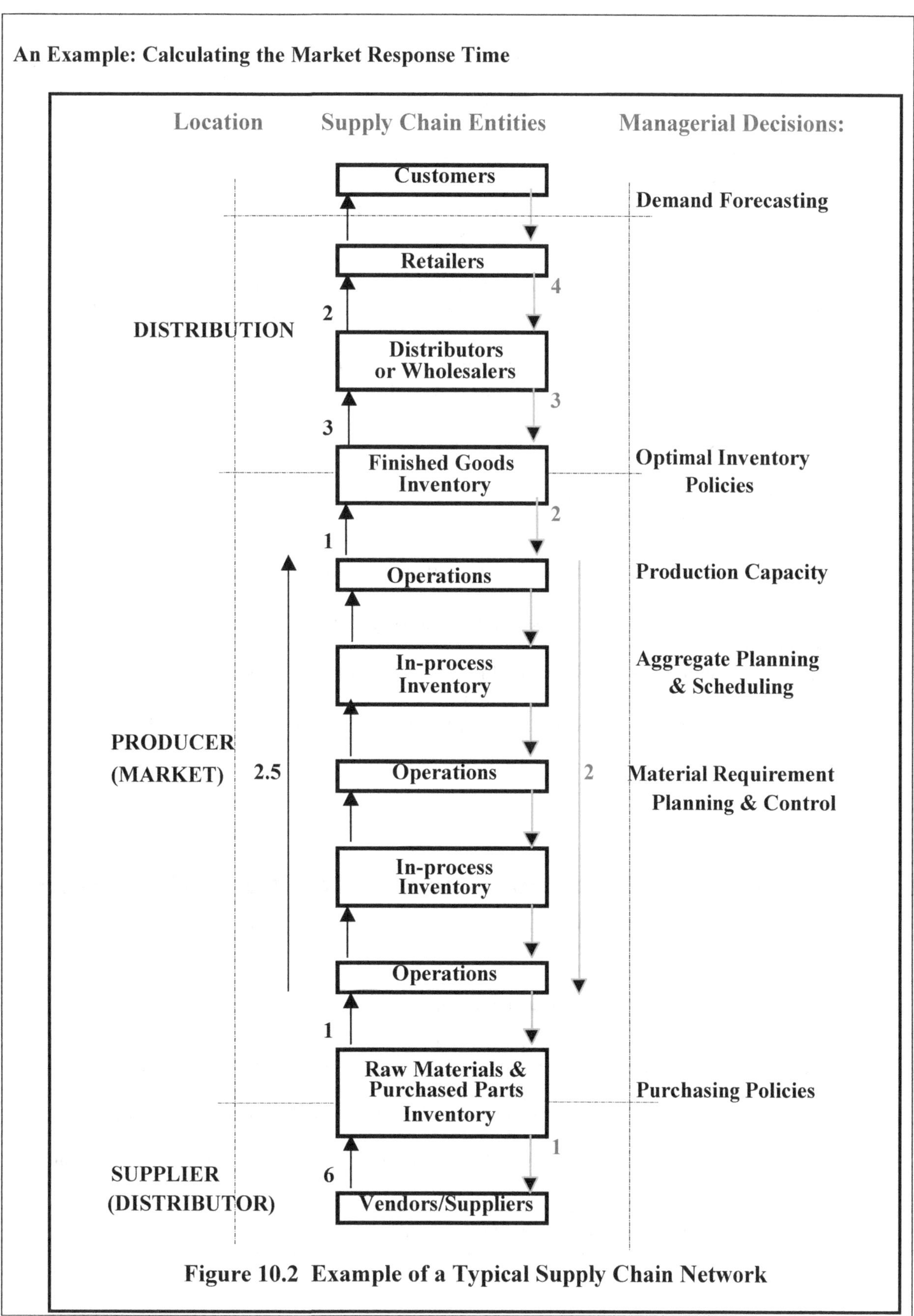

Figure 10.2 Example of a Typical Supply Chain Network

Consider the supply chain network as shown in Figure 10.2.
Figure 10.2 shows that the market response time is determined by the elapsed time of all information flows (as shown by the blue arrow lines) plus the elapsed times of the materials flow (as shown by the solid black arrow lines).

The information flow consists of a total 12 days as follows:

Within the Distribution System:

- Wholesalers reacting to retailer's demand for the product: **4 days**
- Pricing, order processing, and mailing: **3 days**

Within the Factory:

- Checking inventory, releasing engineering drawings, and scheduling production: **2 days**
- Checking on availability/requirements of tools and releasing purchasing requisitions: **2 days**

Within the Supplier Network:

- Contracting vendors and releasing purchasing orders: **1 day**

The materials flow consists of a total of 15.5 days as follows:

From Supplier to Factory:

- Delivering all required raw materials and supplies: **6 days**

Within the Factory:

- Releasing purchased items to the shop floor: **1 day**
- Setting up equipment and in-process waiting: **2 days**
- Processing the order: **½ a day**
- Labeling, recording, and stacking in the finished goods warehouse: **1 day**

Within the Distribution System:

- Shipping, receiving, inspecting, unpacking, re-packing: **3 days**
- Reaching the retailers: **2 days**

Thus, the **market response time** as shown in this example **takes 27.5 days**.
However, if the orders can be totally filled by the finished goods inventory, the market response time consists of 7 days of information flow plus 5 days of materials flow, for a total of 12 days.

1.3 Functions and Managerial Decisions of Production Planning and Inventory Control

The functions of production planning and inventory control include:

1. Forecasting the market demand for products and/or services as a function of time
2. Monitoring actual demand against forecasted demand, and revising forecasts, if necessary
3. Establishing economical lot sizes for purchased and for manufactured products
4. Setting a production plan based on the actual and the forecasted demand, the production capacity, and the desired lot size
5. Establishing production requirements and inventory levels for all input materials, parts, and sub-assemblies based on the production plan of the final products
6. Making detailed production schedules, job assignments, and machine loads
7. Monitoring inventory levels and production schedules
8. Revising production plans or expediting some work orders, when and if necessary
9. Making basic managerial decisions in production planning and control

Basic managerial decisions with respect to production planning and inventory control are:

1. Demand forecasting decisions
2. Inventory policy decisions
3. Purchasing policy decisions
4. Production capacity decisions
5. Aggregate planning and scheduling decisions
6. Material and resource requirement planning decisions

Figure 10.2 depicts a typical supply-production-distribution network of a firm (a factory, an office, a restaurant, etc.) and the typical managerial decisions at each of the decision points in the network. In viewing the industrial society as a total productive system, each network, in fact, is a subsystem of the total supply system. All of the subsystems are in some way interdependent and interrelated. The decision points and their related operational functions in the supply network are connected through information and materials flows. The above basic managerial decisions direct the desired actions that will serve the overall objectives of the productive system.

2. CAPACITY ADJUSTMENT AND PRODUCTION SMOOTHING

2.1 Capacity Adjustment

Based on the production requirements and operations' standard times, we can determine the total production hours and the production capacity required at each workstation. The difference between the actual production capacity and the required production capacity can be resolved through several capacity adjustment policies. Cost effectiveness is a major consideration when determining the appropriate type of policy decision.

Capacity adjustment can be achieved through:

1. Increasing or reducing the number of production shifts to adjust production capacity without actually changing the physical capacity
2. Using subcontracting to reduce in-house production load
3. Hiring to adjust for an increase in demand or laying off employees when demand decreases
4. Using overtime in case of insufficient capacity or under-time in case of excess capacity
5. Creating inventory when demand decreases or backlogs when production is not sufficient to cover the demand
6. Combining above pure policies

Each of these capacity adjustment measures results in a different cost penalty. The decision makers must weigh the cost of meeting production demand against the cost of not meeting the production demand. Linear programming, mathematical models, and simulation can be used to resolve this type of problem.

2.2 Production Smoothing

The function of production smoothing is to level the production man-hours required through the entire planning period. Demand fluctuations that may be caused by seasonal effects, model change, contract terms, and social/political events are often very costly to production operation runs. Through production smoothing, some production demand is removed from the peak-demand period and is filled during the slow-demand period. The variables that are under management control and are often used to smooth out demand fluctuations are similar to those used in capacity adjustment. Those variables are: overtime/under-time, hiring/layoff, inventory/backorders, subcontracting/in-house manufacturing, etc. If the cost associated with each of the variables is known, the production smoothing problem can be resolved by using mathematical programming techniques or simulation.

3. AGGREGATE PLANNING

3.1 Function of Aggregate Planning

Aggregate planning is concerned with the overall operation of an organization over a specified time horizon. The overall operation is usually measured by the number of man-hours required to accomplish the planned production level and the time horizon that is normally covered by the aggregate production plan (from 6 to 24 months).

The primary function of aggregate planning is to utilize—at minimum cost—the potential production capacity in such a manner that the market can be best served. Or, it can be simply stated as, "to match the supply and demand at a minimum cost." The minimum production cost normally requires a consistent and smooth production rate. However, market demand is based on demand forecasts and changes from time to time. Therefore, the major activity in aggregate planning is to balance the conflict between supply and demand. Long-term production capacity is determined by facilities planning and constraints of aggregate planning decisions. Even though the capacity of production facilities can be increased through technology and engineering innovations, in aggregate planning it is considered to be fixed.

3.2 Strategic Variables of Aggregate Planning

There are three basic operational strategies that are used in the effort to balance supply and demand on a continuous basis. These three strategies are:

1. Increase or decrease the size of the work force through hiring and layoff, thus directly responding to the fluctuations in the market demand
2. Maintain a constant workforce and respond to the fluctuations in the market demand through using temporary help, going into overtime or under-time, subcontracting, creating inventory or backlogs, etc.
3. Maintain a constant rate of supply and influence demand patterns through pricing policies, promotions, coupons, rebates, and product mixing, which are also the strategies of the marketing function

Each of the above strategies is an extreme case and normally does not provide the optimal solution to the supply/demand equilibrium equation. Therefore, in aggregate planning a combination of the above strategies is employed and the pro and cons of each of the strategies are normally evaluated. While intangible factors are often assessed through judgmental methods, tangible factors are often evaluated on the basis of cost/benefit analysis in analytical decision making models.

3.3 Cost Factors of Aggregate Planning

The most economical production plan is the one in which the constant market demand equals the constant production rate. Some sort of cost will occur if there is any deviation from this ideal plan. Unfortunately, it is very difficult to obtain most of the cost data associated with strategic variables and to express this data in a simple mathematical formula. Therefore, for planning purposes, some degree of approximation of the cost information is acceptable. The cost factors that are often considered are as follows:

1. **Unit Production Cost**. In general, as the production rate increases, the unit production cost decreases. However, the range of production rates which is feasible for a limited time horizon, as covered by the aggregate production plan, normally is very narrow. Therefore, a constant unit production cost is normally assumed in aggregate planning models. With mixed products situations, the aggregated unit of measure needs to be carefully defined. If different products are similar in terms of production resource requirements, then the unit measure can be the equivalent number of "standard" products. If the types of products are very different, the aggregated unit measure can be weight, volume, dollar value, or man or machine hour requirements.

2. **Normal Labor Cost**. Usually, labor cost is based on the average hourly wage plus fringe benefits as a percentage of the base wage. Only these types of labor hours that are directly affected by workload fluctuations should be considered in computing the average hourly wage rate.

3. **Overtime and Under-Time Cost**. The overtime cost is based on the difference between the regular hourly wage rate and the overtime wage rate. The overtime wage rate is normally 50% more than the regular hourly wage rate. However, the fringe benefit portion of the total wage may not be affected by overtime and should be analyzed carefully when computing the overtime cost. The under-time cost is the labor cost of un-utilized man-hours that is paid by the company either at the regular wage rate or at a reduced wage rate, depending upon company policy and/or union-management agreement.

4. **Hiring and Layoff Cost**. The hiring cost includes recruiting cost, training cost, and reduced production rate cost as a result of the learning curve effect. The layoff cost includes solvency cost and increase in unemployment tax.

5. **Part-Time and Temporary Help Cost**. In reality, the hourly wage rate of part-timers may be lower than the normal wage rate. However, the hourly wage rate of temporary help as supplied by temporary employment agencies is normally much higher. In either case, the productivity of part-timers and temporary help is usually lower than that of the regular workers. Therefore, in computing the cost for hiring part-timers and temporary help, both the difference in basic wages and in productivity need to be considered.

6. **Subcontracting Cost**. When internal resources cannot meet the production demand, management may decide to purchase some components or to subcontract a portion of the customer orders to outside producers. Once the make/buy decision at the process planning stage is made in favor of making the product, the cost "to buy" is normally higher than the cost "to produce." The difference between these two cost elements is the subcontracting cost. It must also include the procurement cost and receiving cost.

7. **Inventory and Backlog Cost**. The inventory cost of finished, but unsold, goods includes the holding cost and the opportunity cost. The backlog cost includes the penalty cost and/or the lost sales cost which is normally expressed as a percentage of the value of the backlog orders.

8. **Promotion and Lost Sales Cost**. For retail items, the overproduced products can be sold through store coupons, discounts, factory rebates, and other promotional measures. In these cases, the promotion cost may be estimated through past experience or from marketing research data. The cost of lost sales for retail items is very difficult to determine in dollars and cents. Since products to satisfy that potential demand were never produced and thus no actual cost was incurred, the lost sales cost should be viewed as a shift in royalty in the marketplace which translates into a reduction in the demand from the original forecasted demand for future months.

3.4 Planning Procedures

Aggregate planning is an on-going process which reviews and extends the planning periods regularly and continuously. Though the regularity of aggregate planning may not be established or may be occasionally interrupted due to market-, product-, policy-, or other re-adjustments, the continuity of aggregate planning is absolutely essential for continuous functioning of modern business organizations. Once the method and the system for aggregate planning are established, maintaining the system and applying the methods become a clerical routine. However, no system or method can adequately reflect the dynamic business environment and thus completely substitute for human experience. Therefore, the result of aggregate planning still requires management review and adjustment.

When initially setting up aggregate planning procedures, the following management decisions must be made:

1. Determining the time period and the planning time horizon to be used for the planning system that must be in agreement with the forecasting system
2. Determining the aggregate units of production to be used as standard measurement of production volume
3. Determining strategic variables to be included in the planning process based on the organizational policy
4. Determining relevant cost structures as the basis for planning tradeoffs in applying different strategic variables
5. Selecting the appropriate planning method based on the availability of input information, the cost of applying the method, and the relative benefit of using this method

Once a planning system is selected and a relevant data base is established, aggregate plans should be generated at regular time intervals (weekly, biweekly or monthly, which normally correspond to the time periods used in aggregate planning). Since activities of an entire organization are scheduled based on an aggregate production plan, once production requirements are established, they should remain relatively stable.

3.5 Defining the Production Requirements

An Example: In what follows an example is developed that is based on an aggregate plan that will cover a six-month period starting in January and ending in June. Based on the forecasted demand and production data for that time horizon, the production requirements are generated as shown in Table 10.1.

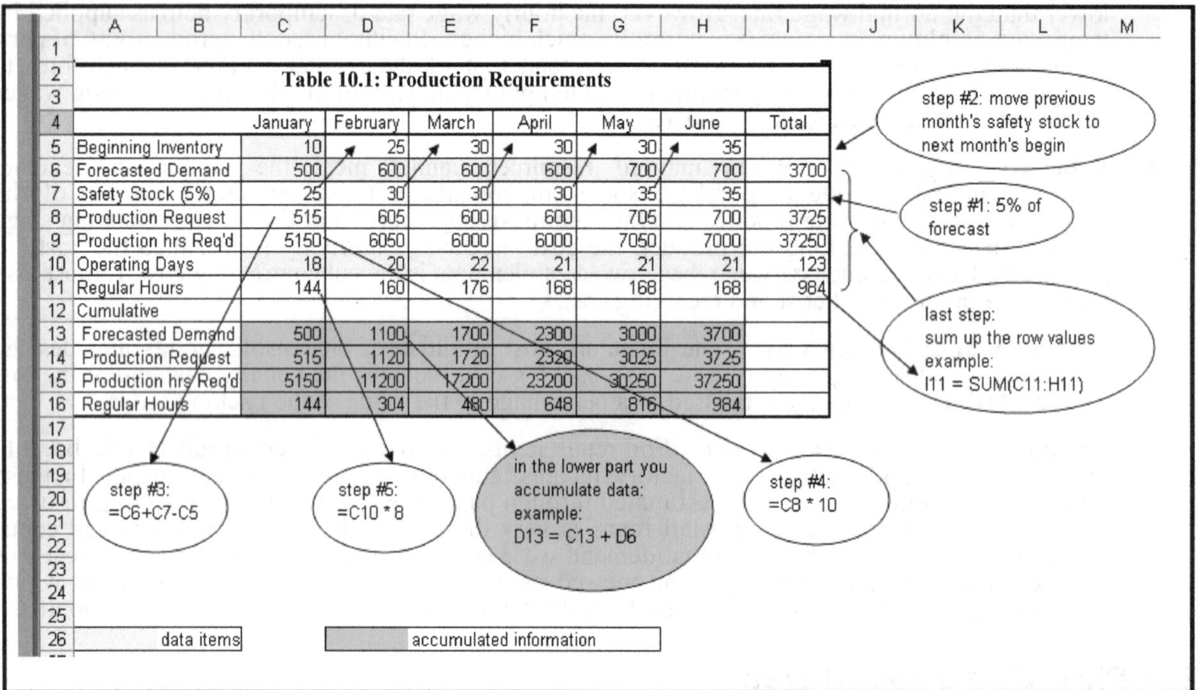

Table 10.1: Production Requirements

	January	February	March	April	May	June	Total
Beginning Inventory	10	25	30	30	30	35	
Forecasted Demand	500	600	600	600	700	700	3700
Safety Stock (5%)	25	30	30	30	35	35	
Production Request	515	605	600	600	705	700	3725
Production hrs Req'd	5150	6050	6000	6000	7050	7000	37250
Operating Days	18	20	22	21	21	21	123
Regular Hours	144	160	176	168	168	168	984
Cumulative							
Forecasted Demand	500	1100	1700	2300	3000	3700	
Production Request	515	1120	1720	2320	3025	3725	
Production hrs Req'd	5150	11200	17200	23200	30250	37250	
Regular Hours	144	304	480	648	816	984	

The required data consist of:

- The beginning inventory in the month of January (10 units)
- The forecasted demand for the months of January through June (500, 600, 600, 600, 700, 700)
- The number of operating days for the months of January through June (18, 20, 22, 21, 21, 21)

The step-by-step procedure for calculating all entries in Table 10.1 is:

Step 1: The safety stock is calculated by figuring 5% of the forecasted amount (example: C7 = 0.05*C6)

Step 2: The beginning inventory of a month is the safety stock of the previous month (example: D5 = C7)

Step 3: The production request equals the forecasted demand, plus the safety stock, minus the beginning inventory (example: C8 = C6 + C7 – C5)

Step 4: The number of production hours required is equal to the production request times the aggregate production time per unit or 10 hours per unit (example: C9 = C8 * 10)

Step 5: The regular hours one person works in each month equals the number of working days per month (data is given) times 8 hours per working day (example: C11 = C10 * 8)

After calculating all entries in the Excel file, as explained in steps 1 through 5, you may wish to accumulate the calculated results (as shown in Table 10.1)

3.6 The Charting Method for Aggregate Planning

The fluctuations in the monthly production demand and in the available line-hours per worker, as shown in Table 10.1, cause the monthly fluctuations in workload. The production department can now manipulate strategic variables and come up with different production plans. Each plan will reflect different economical and non-economic consequences. The economic consequences can be evaluated via spread sheet calculations and tabulations as follows.

The classical method and also the most commonly used aggregate planning method is the **charting method**. With this method, a set of selected, strategic variables is tabulated in table format. Using trial and error, only one or a few variables are evaluated at a time. If this is done manually, without the help of a computer, this method is crude and often time consuming. The optimality of this procedure largely depends upon the skill of the planner and the number of trials he makes. However, due to recent advancements in computer applications and simulation techniques, the charting method, combined with simulation, can produce high quality and dynamic aggregate plans.

The production requirements of Table 10.1, together with the following accounting data, are used to evaluate four capacity adjustment plans: three pure plans and one combination of pure plans. The assumption is made that, at the end of December/beginning of January, the beginning manpower is 35.

Accounting cost data:

1. Overtime Wage Rate: $15/hour (so, an extra $5/hr. is paid when workers do overtime production)
2. Under-Time Cost is the labor cost: $10/hour
3. Hiring (& Training) Cost: $1,200/person
4. Layoff Cost: $1,600/person
5. Inventory Holding Cost: $25/unit/month
6. Backlog Cost: $50/unit-month

Plan I: Provide for the Exact Amount of Manpower through Hiring and Laying Off Workers

The hiring and layoff plan, Plan I-1 is shown in Table 10.2.

Some of the input for this plan comes from output generated in Table 10.1 and can be moved from that Excel sheet into this new Excel sheet as shown. The data consist of:

- Define the number of workers employed at the beginning of the first month (35)
- Based on Table 10.1, enter the production hours required for each month (5150, 6050, 6000, 6000, 7050, and 7000) and the regular hours that each worker will work in each month (144, 160, 176, 168, 168, and 168)

There are two important functions that must be used to make the calculations for Plan I. These functions are:

- The ROUNDUP function: ROUNDUP(*number, num_digits*)
  where*: number*: is a real number you wish to round up
  num_digits: is the number of digits behind the decimal point
- The IF function: IF(*logical test, value if true, value if false)*
  where: *logical test*: is a logical expression that results in either being true or false

The ROUNDUP function is used to generate an integer value for the required manpower, because no part-time employment is acceptable.

The IF function is used to define the number of people who need to be either hired or laid off in a particular month.

The steps needed to generate Plan I are shown in Table 10.2 and consist of the following:

Step 1: The manpower required to do the job is calculated by rounding up the ratio between production hours required and the regular hours one worker has available in each month

Step 2: The number of people who will be hired equals the difference between the manpower required and the beginning manpower of the month, if and only if the manpower level required is larger than the available manpower in the beginning of the month

Step 3: The number of people being laid off equals the difference between the available manpower in the beginning of the month and the required manpower level, if and only if the available manpower is larger than the required manpower

Step 4: The hiring cost is the product of the number of people the company hires and the unit hiring cost ($1,200)

Step 5: The layoff cost is the product of the number of people being laid off and the unit layoff cost ($1,600)

Finally, all costs are accumulated to figure the adjustment cost of Plan I over the six-month period.

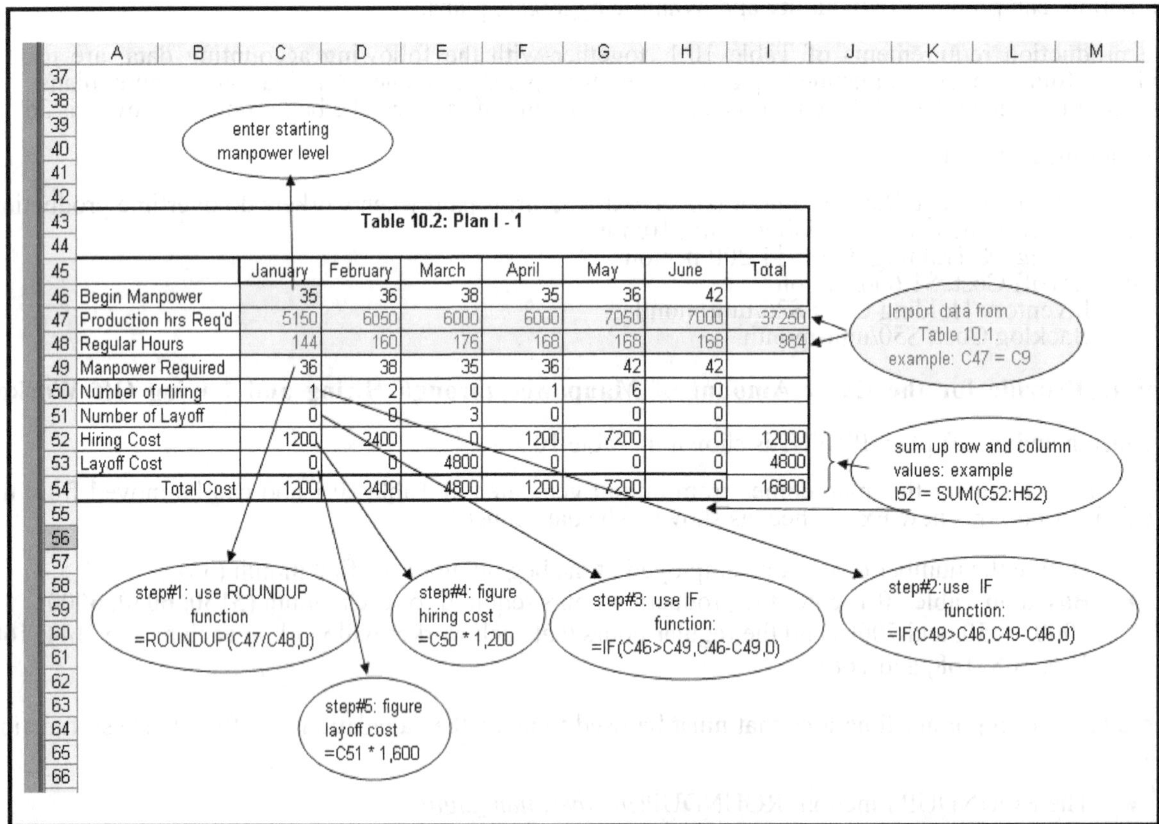

Table 10.2: Plan I - 1

	January	February	March	April	May	June	Total
Begin Manpower	35	36	38	35	36	42	
Production hrs Req'd	5150	6050	6000	6000	7050	7000	37250
Regular Hours	144	160	176	168	168	168	984
Manpower Required	36	38	35	36	42	42	
Number of Hiring	1	2	0	1	6	0	
Number of Layoff	0	0	3	0	0	0	
Hiring Cost	1200	2400	0	1200	7200	0	12000
Layoff Cost	0	0	4800	0	0	0	4800
Total Cost	1200	2400	4800	1200	7200	0	16800

Table 10.2 assumes that the beginning manpower level is 35 workers. Since the production requirement for January calls for 36 workers, one new worker must be hired for this month. In February, the production plan calls for hiring two additional workers. However, in March the manpower requirement drops to 35, resulting in the layoff of three workers. The total hiring/layoff cost of this plan is $16,800. However, if the starting manpower level for January is exactly 36 as required for that month, then the total hiring/layoff cost will drop to $15,600, as can be seen in Table 10.3.

Table 10.3: Plan I-2

	January	February	March	April	May	June	Total
Beginning Manpower	36	36	38	35	36	42	
Production Hrs. Req'd	5150	6050	6000	6000	7050	7000	37250
Regular Hours	144	160	176	168	168	168	984
Manpower Required	36	38	35	36	42	42	
Number of Hiring	0	2	0	1	6	0	
Number of Layoff	0	0	3	0	0	0	
Hiring Cost	$0	$2,400	$0	$1,200	$7,200	$0	$10,800
Layoff Cost	$0	$0	$4,800	$0	0	$0	$4,800
Total Cost	$0	$2,400	$4,800	$1,200	$7,200	$0	**$15,600**

Plan II: Hold Manpower Levels Constant and Schedule Overtime or Under-Time as Needed

The overtime and under-time plan is shown in Table 10.4 for the present manpower level of 35 people.

Like for the previous plan, some of the input for this plan comes from output generated in Table 10.1 and can be moved from that Excel sheet into this new Excel sheet as shown. The data consist of:

- Define level of manpower (this is set at 35 people for each of the six months)
- Based on Table 10.1, enter the production hours required for each month (5150, 6050, 6000, 6000, 7050, and 7000) and the regular hours that each worker will work in each month (144, 160, 176, 168, 168, and 168)

Like for Plan I, an IF function is used. Here the IF function is used to determine the hours of overtime or under-time required in each of the six months.

The steps needed to generate Plan II are shown in Table 10.4 and consist of the following:

Step 1: The regular hours available equal the product of the regular manpower available (35 over each of the six months) and the regular hours each worker has available in each of the six months

Step 2: The amount of overtime required is the difference between the production hours required and the available production hours, if and only if the production hours required are larger than the available production hours

Step 3: The amount of under-time required is the difference between the available production hours and the required production hours, if and only if the available production hours are larger than the required production hours

Step 4: The overtime cost is the product of the number of hours of overtime performed and the additional labor cost for performing overtime, or 50% of labor cost per hour ($5)

Step 5: The under-time cost is the product of the number of hours not worked, but paid for, by the employees (called under-time) and the labor cost per hour ($10)

Finally, all costs are accumulated to figure the adjustment cost of Plan II over the six-month period.

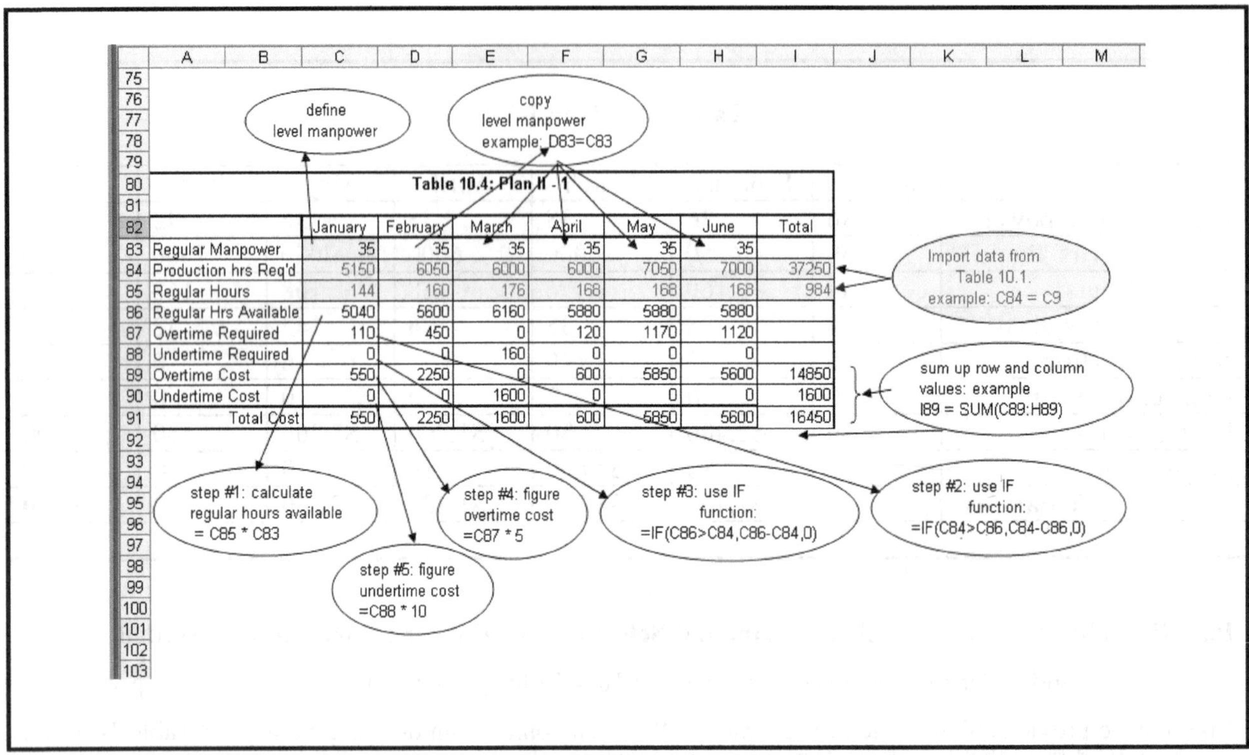

In an effort to find the best manpower level for this plan, the following manpower levels are tried: 36 and 37.

Their results are shown in Tables 10.5 and 10.6 respectively.

Table 10.5: Plan II-2

	January	February	March	April	May	June	Total
Regular Manpower	36	36	36	36	36	36	
Production Hrs. Req'd	5150	6050	6000	6000	7050	7000	37250
Regular Hours	144	160	176	168	168	168	984
Regular Hrs. Available	5184	5760	6336	6048	6048	6048	
Overtime Required	0	290	0	0	1002	952	
Under-time Required	34	0	336	48	0	0	
Overtime Cost	0	1,450	0	0	5,010	4,760	11,220
Under-time Cost	340	0	3,360	480	0	0	4,180
Total Cost	340	1,450	3,360	480	5,010	4,760	**15,400**
Adjusting for the cost of hiring one worker ($1,200), the final cost for this plan is							**$16,600**

Table 10.6: Plan II-3

	January	February	March	April	May	June	Total
Regular Manpower	37	37	37	37	37	37	
Production Hrs. Req'd	5150	6050	6000	6000	7050	7000	37250
Regular Hours	144	160	176	168	168	168	984
Regular Hrs. Available	5328	5920	6512	6216	6216	6216	
Overtime Required	0	130	0	0	834	784	
Under-Time Required	178	0	512	216	0	0	
Overtime Cost	0	650	0	0	4,170	3,920	8,740
Under-Time Cost	1,780	0	5,120	2,160	0	0	9,060
Total Cost	1,780	650	5,120	2,160	4,170	3,920	**17,800**
Adjusting for the cost of hiring two workers ($2,400), the final cost for this plan is							**$20,200**

Viewing the total costs of all Plan IIs, the lowest combined under-time/overtime cost is $16,450 for keeping the manpower level at 35.

Plan III: Hold Manpower Level Constant and Use Inventory and Backlog to Absorb Monthly Demand Fluctuations

Since inventory can be in the form of finished-goods inventory or in-process inventory, a fraction of a unit of inventory or backlog is allowed. The resulting inventory or backlog levels when the manpower level is held at 35 are shown in Table 10.7.

For Table 10.7, the input consists of the following (some of the data can be transferred from Table 10.1)

- The beginning inventory for January (10)
- The safety stock for each of the six months (25, 30, 30, 30, 35, 35)
- The manpower is set at the present available manpower of 35 workers for each of the 6 months of the aggregate planning horizon
- Regular working hours a worker has available for each of the six months (144, 160, 176, 168, 168, and 168)
- Production request for each of the six months (515, 605, 600, 600, 705, and 700)
- Finally, note that the adjusted production requirement for the first month equals the production request of the first month

The following eight steps must be performed in the following order for each of the six months of this aggregate planning horizon:

Step 1: The regular hours available equal the product of the regular manpower available (35 over each of the six months) and the regular hours each worker has available in each of the six months

Step 2: The aggregate capacity equals the ratio of the regular hours available (of all workers) and the aggregate time for producing one unit (10 hours/unit)

Step 3: The amount of scheduled inventory equals the difference between the aggregate capacity and the adjusted production requirement, if and only if the aggregate capacity is larger than the adjusted production requirement

Step 4: The amount of backlog is the difference between the adjusted production requirement and the aggregate capacity, if and only if the adjusted production requirement is larger than the aggregate capacity

Step 5: The inventory cost is the product of the scheduled inventory and the cost of holding one unit of inventory ($25)

Step 6: The backlog cost is the product of the amount of units backlogged and the cost of backlogging one unit ($50)

Step 7: Beginning inventory for next month equals the safety stock of the previous month, plus the scheduled inventory of the previous month, minus the backlog of the previous month

Step 8: The adjusted production request (starting with the second month) equals the production request of the month, plus the backlog of the previous month, minus the scheduled inventory of the previous month

Finally, all costs are accumulated to figure the adjustment cost of Plan III over the six-month period. This cost is $30,450, the least attractive cost so far.

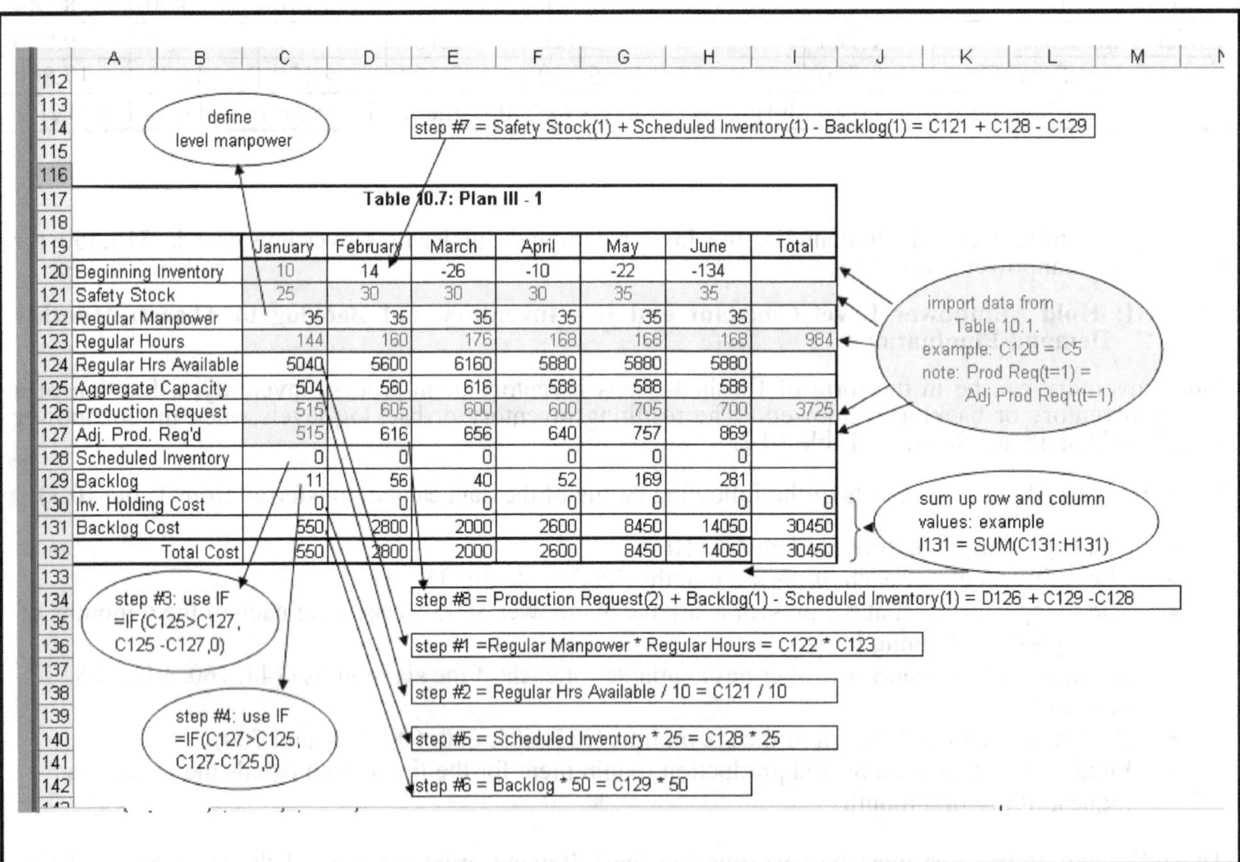

Table 10.7: Plan III - 1

	January	February	March	April	May	June	Total
Beginning Inventory	10	14	-26	-10	-22	-134	
Safety Stock	25	30	30	30	35	35	
Regular Manpower	35	35	35	35	35	35	
Regular Hours	144	160	176	168	168	168	984
Regular Hrs Available	5040	5600	6160	5880	5880	5880	
Aggregate Capacity	504	560	616	588	588	588	
Production Request	515	605	600	600	705	700	3725
Adj. Prod. Req'd	515	616	656	640	757	869	
Scheduled Inventory	0	0	0	0	0	0	
Backlog	11	56	40	52	169	281	
Inv. Holding Cost	0	0	0	0	0	0	0
Backlog Cost	550	2800	2000	2600	8450	14050	30450
Total Cost	550	2800	2000	2600	8450	14050	30450

In an effort to find the optimal manpower level for this capacity adjustment scenario, three other manpower levels are evaluated: 36, 37, and 38 workers. Their results are shown in Tables 10.8 through 10.10.

Table 10.8: Plan III-2

	January	February	March	April	May	June	Total
Beginning Inventory	10	28.4	4.4	38	42.8	-52.4	
Safety Stock	25	30	30	30	35	35	
Regular Manpower	36	36	36	36	36	36	
Regular Hours (one worker)	144	160	176	168	168	168	984
Regular Hours Available	5184	5760	6336	6048	6048	6048	
Aggregate Capacity	518.4	576	633.6	604.8	604.8	604.8	
Production Request	515	605	600	600	705	700	3725
Adj. Prod. Req'd	515	601.6	625.6	592	692.2	787.4	
Scheduled Inventory (Excluding Safety Stock)	3.4	0	8	12.8	0	0	
Backlog	0	25.6	0	0	87.4	182.6	
Inventory Holding Cost	85	0	200	320	0	0	605
Backlog Cost	0	1,280	0	0	4,370	9,130	14,780
Total Cost	85	1,280	200	320	4,370	9,130	**15,385**
Adjusting for the cost of hiring one worker ($1,200), the final cost for this plan is							**$16,585**

Table 10.9: Plan III-3

	January	February	March	April	May	June	Total
Beginning Inventory	10	42.8	34.8	86	107.6	29.2	
Safety Stock	25	30	30	30	35	35	
Regular Manpower	37	37	37	37	37	37	
Regular Hours (one worker)	144	160	176	168	168	168	984
Regular Hours Available	5328	5920	6512	6216	6216	6216	
Aggregate Capacity	532.8	592	651.2	621.6	621.6	621.6	
Production Request	515	605	600	600	705	700	3725
Adj. Prod. Req'd	515	587.2	595.2	544	627.4	705.8	
Scheduled Inventory (Excluding Safety Stock)	17.8	4.8	56	77.6	0	0	
Backlog	0	0	0	0	5.8	84.2	
Inventory Holding Cost	445	120	1,400	1,940	0	0	3,905
Backlog Cost	0	0	0	0	290	4,210	4,500
Total Cost	445	120	1,400	1,940	290	4,210	**8,405**
Adjusting for the cost of hiring two workers ($2,400), the final cost for this plan is							**$10,805**

Table 10.10: Plan III-4

	January	February	March	April	May	June	Total
Beginning Inventory	10	57.2	65.2	134	172.4	110.8	
Safety Stock	25	30	30	30	35	35	
Regular Manpower	38	38	38	38	38	38	
Regular Hours (one worker)	144	160	176	168	168	168	984
Regular Hours Available	5472	6080	6688	6384	6384	6384	
Aggregate Capacity	547.2	608	668.8	638.4	638.4	638.4	
Production Request	515	605	600	600	705	700	3725
Adj. Prod. Req'd	515	572.8	564.8	496	562.6	624.2	
Scheduled Inventory (Excluding Safety Stock)	32.2	35.2	104	142.4	75.8	14.2	
Backlog	0	0	0	0	0	0	
Inventory Holding Cost	805	880	2,600	3,560	1,895	355	10,095
Backlog Cost	0	0	0	0	0	0	0
Total Cost	805	880	2,600	3,560	1,895	355	**10,095**
Adjusting for the cost of hiring three workers ($3,600), the final cost for this plan is							**$13,695**

Viewing Tables 10.7 through 10.10, the lowest combined inventory/backorder capacity adjustment plan is for a work force level of 37 workers. Its adjustment cost is **$10,805**.

Notice the relatively high monetary penalty of backlog that is due to loss of sales, erosion of customer base, and/or deterioration of public relations, which may prove to be very costly in the long run. This brings us to the next plan.

Plan IV: Hold Manpower Level Constant, Use Inventory and Overtime to Absorb Monthly Demand Fluctuations

In an effort to drive the cost of **$10,805**, as shown for Plan III with 37 workers, further down we can combine Plan II with Plan III, creating Plan IV. This plan should be run at a worker level of 37 workers.

The most reasonable strategic variable for Plan II is "overtime" and the most reasonable strategic variable of Plan III is "creation of inventory." These then become the strategic variables at which to run Plan IV.

Just like for Plan III, the following are the input data for this plan:

- The beginning inventory for January (10)
- The safety stock for each of the six months (25, 30, 30, 30, 35, 35)
- The manpower is set at 37 workers for each of the 6 months of the aggregate planning horizon
- Regular working hours a worker has available for each of the six months (144, 160, 176, 168, 168, and 168)
- Production request for each of the six months (515, 605, 600, 600, 705, and 700)
- Again, note that the adjusted production requirement for the first month equals the production request of the first month

The following nine steps must be performed in the following order for each of the six months of this aggregate planning horizon:

Step 1: The regular hours available equal the product of the regular manpower available (37 over each of the six months) and the regular hours each worker has available in each of the six months

Step 2: The aggregate capacity equals the ratio of the regular hours available (of all workers) and the aggregate time for producing one unit (10 hours/unit)

Step 3: The production hours required is the product of the adjusted production requirement and the aggregate time for producing one unit (10 hours/unit)

Step 4: The amount of scheduled inventory equals the difference between the aggregate capacity and the adjusted production requirement, if and only if the aggregate capacity is larger than the adjusted production requirement

Step 5: The amount of overtime is the difference the production hours required and the regular hours available, if and only if the production hours required is larger than the regular hours available

Step 6: The inventory cost is the product of the scheduled inventory and the cost of holding one unit of inventory ($25)

Step 7: The overtime cost is the product of the amount of overtime and the additional cost of doing one hour of overtime ($5)

Step 8: Beginning inventory for next month equals the safety stock of the previous month plus the scheduled inventory of the previous month

Step 9: The adjusted production request (starting with the second month) equals the production request of the month minus the scheduled inventory of the previous month

Finally, all costs are accumulated to figure the adjustment cost of Plan IV over the six months period. This cost is **$10,515**, the lowest cost so far.

Table 10.11: Plan IV

	January	February	March	April	May	June	Total
Beginning Inventory	10	42.8	34.8	86	107.6	35	
Safety Stock	25	30	30	30	35	35	
Regular Manpower	37	37	37	37	37	37	
Regular Hours (one worker)	144	160	176	168	168	168	984
Regular Hours Available	5328	5920	6512	6216	6216	6216	
Aggregate Capacity	532.8	592	651.2	621.6	621.6	621.6	
Production Request	515	605	600	600	705	700	3725
Adj. Prod. Req'd	515	587.2	595.2	544	627.4	700	
Production Hrs. Required	5150	5872	5952	5440	6274	7000	
Scheduled Inventory (Excluding Safety Stock)	17.8	4.8	56	77.6	0	0	
Overtime Required	0	0	0	0	58	784	
Inventory Holding Cost	445	120	1,400	1,940	0	0	3,905
Overtime Cost	0	0	0	0	290	3,920	4,210
Total Cost	445	120	1,400	1,940	290	4,210	**8,115**
Adjusting for the cost of hiring two workers ($2,400), the final cost for this plan is							**$10,515**

In summary the charting method has generated the following adjusted costs for each of the four plan groups, with a starting workforce of 35 people:

Plan I: Exact Number of Workers - Hiring and Laying Off Workers -

Start with 35 workers	$16,800

Plan II: Constant Manpower Level - Overtime and Under-Time -

Level: 35 People	$16,450
Level: 36 People	$16,600 ($15,400 + $1,200 for hiring one worker)
Level: 37 People	$20,200 ($17,800 + $2,400 for hiring two workers)

Plan III: Constant Manpower Level - Inventory and Backlog -

Level: 35 People	$30,450
Level: 36 People	$16,585 ($15,385 + $1,200 for hiring one worker)
Level: 37 People	$10,805 ($8,405 + $2,400 for hiring two workers)
Level: 38 People	$13,695 ($10,095 + $3,600 for hiring three workers)

Plan IV: Constant Manpower - Inventory and Overtime- (Combine Plans II and III) -

Level: 37 People	$10,515 ($8,115 + $2,400 for hiring two workers)

Plans I, II, and III are pure plans, whereas Plan IV is the combination of two pure plans, Plan II and Plan III. It is this combination that yields the lowest capacity adjustment cost.

In what follows, this plan that allows for inventory will be used to create the disaggregated plan and the master production schedule.

4. MASTER PRODUCTION SCHEDULE (MPS)

4.1 Function of Master Schedule

Master scheduling is the production planning function that determines the kinds and quantities of products to be manufactured in each time period and within the framework of the aggregate plan. In other words, master scheduling dis-aggregates the production requirements for product groups as defined in the aggregate plan. Unlike the aggregate plan, the master schedule provides a detailed production schedule for each individual product over smaller time segments (which will be referred to as planning periods) within a shorter time horizon. Normally, the time horizon covered by the master production schedule is equal to or shorter than the aggregate plan (which runs between six months to two years), but greater than or equal to the longest production lead time. While the aggregate plan presents the production volume by month, the master production schedule normally presents the production volumes of individual products by week. As new demand and production information become available, the master production schedule is updated, revised, and/or extended as often as weekly.

4.2 Planning Period and Time Horizon of Master Scheduling

During the initial set-up of the master scheduling system, the longest product lead time must be determined in order to define the minimum planning time horizon. The length of the planning horizon, normally expressed in weeks, is expressed as a number of planning periods. For example, if the longest lead time amongst all products is nine (9) working weeks, then the minimum planning time horizon must include at least nine (9) periods. However, when taking production interruptions and production adjustments into consideration, the actual production lead time will be longer than this nominal lead time. Also, since the planning periods are measured by calendar weeks and since the length of each working week may be shortened by holidays and vacations (if the vacation period is longer than a week, then, the non-working week is not included in the schedule), it is desirable to select a number of planning periods within the planning time horizon to be greater than nine.

Furthermore, since business activities are often timed on a monthly basis, it is desirable (but not necessary) to round off the planning horizon in months. In our example, we may elect to use 3 months, or 12 time periods, as the planning horizon for the master schedule. However, if the longest lead time is exceptional and its product represents only a small percentage of the total workload, it may be desirable to use a shorter time horizon, say, eight (8) time periods. In general, the shorter the planning horizon is, the more accurate the master schedule will be.

Additionally, there will be fewer changes in the schedule and it will be less expensive to generate and maintain the schedule. Special attention should be given to the products that have an accumulated lead time that exceeds the planning horizon. Make sure that for these products there is adequate inventory to meet the demand.

4.3 Priority Planning

In aggregate planning, fluctuations in production requirements are met through manipulating the actual production capacity. Production capacity can be adjusted by changing the manpower level, the inventory/backlog level, the overtime/under-time, etc. The master schedule must operate within the stated capacity constraint as determined by the aggregate plan. However, the capacity as defined by the aggregate plan is the rough-cut capacity which does not distinguish production capacity requirements on a product basis. Through the master schedule, the rough-cut production capacity as specified by the aggregate plan is allocated to different products over their planning periods. The capacity allocation specifies the orders of various products to be produced during the planning period and is referred to as priority planning. The determination of the production priority is based on production capacity, demand information, and production lead times. Demand information dictates which products need to be delivered first and production lead times indicate how soon a product needs to be scheduled for production in order to meet its delivery requirement.

In the case of single product operations, the question of production priority is non-existing and thus there are very little differences between the aggregate plan and the master schedule. With multiple-product operations, the characteristics of the product-mix in each planning period define the production priorities for that planning period. The production priority determines what product to make, when to make it, and how many to make. If the master scheduling system is aware of any scarcity in raw materials and/or production supplies for which various products are competing, then the master schedule must take materials constraints into consideration in order to redefine the product mix. However, materials requirement information is generally not explicitly expressed in master scheduling systems. Unless the shortages are severe and obvious, they are difficult to detect directly from the master schedule. Consequently, these undetected materials shortages may cause production interruptions and delays when the master schedule is executed. This deficiency in the master schedule can be improved upon by the use of a Material Requirement Planning system (MRP) that breaks down the material requirements of individual parts and components as discussed later in this chapter.

4.4 Scheduling Procedure

Like aggregate planning, master scheduling is an on-going process. It is not only directly affected by changes in the aggregate plan, but also by the materials requirement plan when the status of any material supply is altered or its deficiency is detected. The inputs into a master production scheduling consist of the aggregate plan, dis-aggregated work orders, and/or the demand forecast. Master scheduling allocates these production requirements for each product into different time periods within a planning horizon. When thus assigning production schedules for each product economic production lot size requirements are observed. The total workload within each time period must be in agreement with the rough-cut capacity as determined by the aggregate plan. However, unless a production lead time is less than the length of one time period of the master schedule (i.e., one week) the master schedule will not provide accurate information on work load requirements during each time period. Therefore, both capacity requirements (in terms of man-hours available) and priority requirements (in terms of available materials) must be checked at the materials requirement planning stage, when job orders are actually generated.

The master production schedule is updated periodically when scheduled production is carried out and when a new time period is added, when any finished production work is deleted from the schedule, and when unfinished and delayed work is rescheduled.

An Example: (Continuation of the Aggregate Planning example)

Assume that our manufacturing firm makes three different products, A, B and C. Their normal required production hours, their production lead times, and their economic lot sizes are shown in Table 10.12.

Table 10.12: Product Characteristics

	Standard Time Hours/Unit	Lead Time Weeks	Economic Lot Size Units
Product A	15	7	10
Product B	10	5	20
Product C	7	5	10

Since the longest production lead time is seven weeks, the planning horizon for this master schedule is selected to be eight weeks. Based on Table 10.11, or Plan IV-I, the dis-aggregated market demand for each week during the eight-week planning horizon is shown in Table 10.13. Note the accumulated scheduled inventory of 18 and 5 units, as figured in Table 10.11. Also, note that the beginning inventory for week 2 is 43 units. It is the sum of the safety stock in week 1 (25 units) and the scheduled inventory of week 1 (18 units).

Based on market demand information and lot size requirements, a trial master schedule is developed as shown in Table 10.14. Its associated capacity requirement (based on required production hours/unit) is shown in Table 10.15. Finally, the cumulative capacity requirement resulting from the trial master schedule is shown in Table 10.16. As compared to the cumulative production hours required for the first two months planning horizon or 8 weeks (see Table 10.11: Plan IV-I, best aggregate plan), the planned capacity of 5,150 hours for the first 4 weeks and 11,022 hours for the entire 8 weeks is reasonable to meet the demand. It will require less than 50 hours per week in overtime (398 hours/8weeks).

Through trial and error an alternate, adjusted master schedule is generated as shown in Table 10.17. This schedule is preferred over the previous one because of the smaller fluctuations in weekly capacity requirements (see Table 10.18) and its larger production runs.

Table 10.13: Disaggregated Production Requirements (based on Plan IV-1)

	WK1	WK2	WK3	WK4	WK5	WK6	WK7	WK8	SUM
Demand - A	90	0	0	0	120	0	0	0	210
Demand - B	260	0	0	0	280	0	0	0	540
Demand - C	150	0	0	0	200	0	0	0	350
TOTAL Demand:	500	0	0	0	600	0	0	0	1,100
Beginning Inventory - A	2	8	8	8	8	6	6	6	
Beginning Inventory - B	5	21	21	21	21	20	20	20	
Beginning Inventory - C	3	14	14	14	14	9	9	9	
TOTAL Beginning Inventory:	10	43	43	43	43	35	35	35	
Safety Stock - A	5	5	5	5	5	5	5	5	40
Safety Stock - B	12	12	12	12	17	17	17	17	116
Safety Stock - C	8	8	8	8	8	8	8	8	64
TOTAL Safety Stock:	25	25	25	25	30	30	30	30	220
Scheduled Inventory - A	3	3	3	3	1	1	1	1	16
Scheduled Inventory - B	9	9	9	9	3	3	3	3	48
Scheduled Inventory - C	6	6	6	6	1	1	1	1	28
TOTAL Scheduled Inventory:	18	18	18	18	5	5	5	5	92
Production Requirement - A	96	0	0	0	118	0	0	0	214
Production Requirement - B	276	0	0	0	279	0	0	0	555
Production Requirement - C	161	0	0	0	195	0	0	0	356
TOTAL Production Requirement:	533	0	0	0	592	0	0	0	1,125

The calculations for the last section of the table are as follows:

Production requirement for product A at the beginning of the first month: 90 – 2 + 5 + 3 = 96
Production requirement for product B at the beginning of the first month: 260 – 5 + 12 + 9 = 276
Production requirement for product C at the beginning of the first month: 150 – 3 + 8 + 6 = 161
Production requirement for product A at the beginning of the second month: 120 – 8 + 5 + 1 = 118
Production requirement for product B at the beginning of the second month: 280 – 21 + 17 +3 = 279
Production requirement for product C at the beginning of the second month: 200 – 14 + 8 + 1 = 195

When considering economic lot sizes of ten (10), twenty (20), and ten (10) for products A, B, and C respectively, the master production schedule calls for the production of 100 units of A, 280 units of B, and 170 units of C during the first month. Likewise, during the second month 120 units of A, 280 units of B, and 200 units of C must be scheduled.

Table 10.14: Master Schedule

Product	WK1	WK2	WK3	WK4	WK5	WK6	WK7	WK8	SUM
A	20	20	30	30	30	30	30	30	220
B	80	60	80	60	80	60	80	60	560
C	40	30	50	50	40	50	50	50	360
TOTAL	140	110	160	140	150	140	160	140	1,140

Table 10.15: Capacity Requirements

Product	WK1	WK2	WK3	WK4	WK5	WK6	WK7	WK8	SUM
A	300	300	450	450	450	450	450	450	3,300
B	800	600	800	600	800	600	800	600	5,600
C	280	210	350	350	280	350	350	350	2,520
TOTAL	1,380	1,110	1,600	1,400	1,530	1,400	1,600	1,400	11,420
Deviation from Mean	-48	-318	172	-28	102	-28	172	-28	148*

*Standard Deviation

Table 10.16: Cumulative Capacity Requirements

	Product	WK1	WK2	WK3	WK4	WK5	WK6	WK7	WK8
Production Requirement	A	96	96	96	96	214	214	214	214
	B	276	276	276	276	555	555	555	555
	C	161	161	161	161	356	356	356	356
All Products		533	533	533	533	1,125	1,125	1,125	1,125
Scheduled	A	20	40	70	100	130	160	190	220
	B	80	140	220	280	360	420	500	560
	C	40	70	120	170	210	260	310	360
All Products		140	250	410	550	700	840	1,000	1,140
Capacity Requirements	A	300	600	1,050	1,500	1,950	2,400	2,850	3,300
	B	800	1,400	2,200	2,800	3,600	4,200	5,000	5,600
	C	280	490	840	1,190	1,470	1,820	2,170	2,520
All Products		1,380	2,490	4,090	5,490	7,020	8,420	10,020	11,420
Planned Capacity					5,150				11,022
Deviation from PC					340				398

Table 10.17: Adjusted Master Schedule

Product	WK1	WK2	WK3	WK4	WK5	WK6	WK7	WK8	SUM
A	50	0	50	0	100	0	20	0	220
B	0	140	0	140	0	140	0	140	560
C	80	0	90	0	0	10	170	10	360
TOTAL	130	140	140	140	100	150	190	150	1,140

Table 10.18: Adjusted Capacity Requirements

Product	WK1	WK2	WK3	WK4	WK5	WK6	WK7	WK8	SUM
A	750	0	750	0	1,500	0	300	0	3,300
B	0	1,400	0	1,400	0	1,400	0	1,400	5,600
C	560	0	630	0	0	70	1,190	70	2,520
TOTAL	1,310	1,400	1,380	1,400	1,500	1,470	1,490	1,470	11,420
Deviation from Mean:	-118	-28	-48	-28	72	42	62	42	62*

*Standard Deviation

Table 10.19: Adjusted Cumulative Capacity Requirements

	Product	WK1	WK2	WK3	WK4	WK5	WK6	WK7	WK8
Production	A	96	96	96	96	214	214	214	214
Requirement	B	276	276	276	276	555	555	555	555
	C	161	161	161	161	356	356	356	356
All Products		533	533	533	533	1,125	1,125	1,125	1,125
Scheduled	A	50	50	100	100	200	200	220	220
	B	0	140	140	280	280	420	420	560
	C	80	80	170	170	170	180	350	360
All Products		130	270	410	550	650	800	990	1,140
Capacity	A	750	750	1,500	1,500	3,000	3,000	3,300	3,300
Requirement	B	0	1,400	1,400	2,800	2,800	4,200	4,200	5,600
	C	560	560	1,190	1,190	1,190	1,260	2,450	2,520
All Products		1,310	2,710	4,090	5,490	6,990	8,460	9,950	11,420
Planned Capacity					5,150				11,022
Deviation from PC					340				398

5 MATERIAL REQUIREMENT PLANNING (MRP)

5.1 Function of Material Requirement Planning

All of the production planning activities that have been discussed thus far, including demand forecasting, aggregate production planning, and master production scheduling, deal with independent demand for the end products, which may or may not be the final assemblies. All independent demand items are sold as end products and are subject to market fluctuations and production management decisions. For a discrete part type of manufacturing organization, the end products are normally made up of a number of parts and subassemblies, called dependent demand items. These dependent demand items are not necessarily unique to any specific single end product or final assembly, but can be shared by several end products or final assemblies. Thus the required demand for these dependent demand items directly depends on the collective demand for the independent demand items.

Scheduling for dependent demand items is the most time-consuming and the most difficult part of the production planning and control function. As the number of dependent demand items increases, the complexity of scheduling increases at an even faster rate. The major difficulty in scheduling production is the large amount of data and information that is dynamically involved during the scheduling process. Before we had high speed, large capacity computers, and capable software to handle and to process large amounts of information, production management simply ignored the distinction between dependent and independent demand items and handled production scheduling by using a great deal of guess work and some type of reactive inventory control system.

Material Requirement Planning (MRP) is a computer based production planning and inventory control system designed to generate production and purchasing orders for dependent demand items. MRP creates schedules that identify, for all demand items, their amounts available in inventory, their exact required production quantities, and their production starting dates. MRP simply extends and interprets the information specified by the master production schedule and performs, therefore, strictly a data processing function. However, with detailed and precise information, it can also verify the feasibility of the original master schedule, and is therefore a very valuable tool for assisting the production manager in executing and following up on the master production schedule.

5.2 Objectives of MRP

The three major objectives of MRP include:

1. Minimizing inventory requirements
2. Maximizing production efficiency
3. Improving customer service

Prior to the MRP era, it was common practice in production scheduling to provide for sufficient inventory for all dependent demand items in order to safeguard against uncertainties in the market demand for end products or the independent demand items. The amount of such inventories was governed by various inventory control systems, such as the ABC system, the two-bin system, and others as discussed in Chapter 11. The need for such inventories was a direct result of insufficient information. MRP determines precisely when and how many dependent demand items are needed in order to meet the scheduled independent demand items. It takes all of the guess work out of scheduling. Therefore, if MRP is properly implemented, there is no longer a need for providing any inventory for dependent demand items. The only inventories required are safety stocks for independent demand items.

MRP provides time-phased material requirement information for purchasing orders and production orders. With the timely release of purchasing orders to suppliers and of work orders to work centers and/or production departments, all production activities for component parts, subassemblies, and final assemblies can be closely coordinated. Consequently, loss of productivity due to order expediting, order de-expediting, stock chasing, and other production interruptions are drastically reduced with MRP systems.

MRP provides the sales department with accurate and realistic product due date information and aids the production department by supplying production scheduling information, so that production activities can be carried out in an orderly and streamlined fashion. When material shortages or production interruptions occur, MRP provides a means for quickly detecting these irregularities such that proper actions can be taken to correct these problems on time.

5.3 Input Requirements of the MRP System

The input information required by the MRP system includes:

1) The bill of materials (BOM)
2) The master production schedule (MPS)
3) The inventory records and characteristics

A **bill of materials** (BOM) is a listing of all items, including materials, component parts, subassemblies, and assemblies that are required to make up a final product. The information on all items in a BOM includes their identification codes, their quantities required to make one unit of a product, their sources of supplies, their order lead times, their production lead times, their production lot sizes, etc. The structure of the bill of materials used by an MRP system is hierarchical and its graphical presentation is called the product structure tree. Recall that the product structure tree identifies the level of each item in the tree and shows the quantity of each item needed to complete one unit of the next higher level item. The level of the end product is designated as level 0, the next lower level to the end product is level 1, and so on.

An Example (Continuation of previous example)

The product structure trees for products A, B, and C are as shown in Figure 10.3.

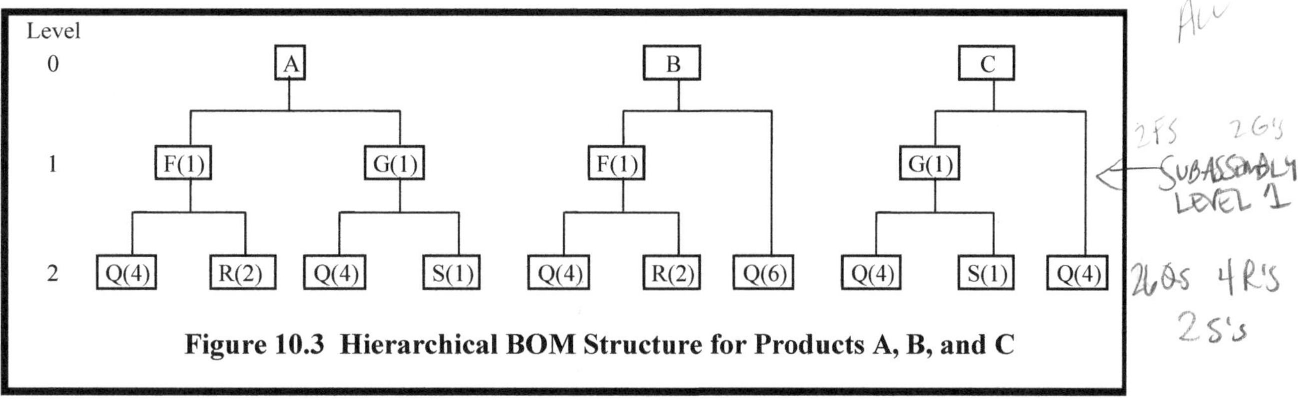

Figure 10.3 Hierarchical BOM Structure for Products A, B, and C

The product structure tree for product A has three levels: 0, 1, and 2. Level 0 is the end product A that needs one unit of component F and one unit of component G from level 1. In turn, one unit of level 1 component F requires four units of component Q and two units of component R from level 2. One unit of level 1 component G requires also four units of component Q and one unit of component S from level 2.

The product structure tree for product B has also three levels. At level 0, final product level, B needs one unit of component F from level 1 and six units of component Q from level 2. Note that, an item is normally designated one level higher than the item into which it feeds. However, in the case of component Q, six of that item feed directly into level 0, the end product B, and four of its items feed into B through level 1 component F. Therefore, item Q is designated as a level 2 item since the highest level item it feeds into is level 1 (items F and G). Similarly, end product C (level 0) needs one unit of component G from level 1 and four units of component Q from level 2.

The Master Production Schedule (MPS) is the key driving force of MRP planning. An MPS, as shown in Table 10.17, gives the timing and the quantities required for the independent demand items. Note that independent demand items do not necessarily have to be level 0 items in a BOM. For example, a lamp shade on a post lamp is not a level 0 item in the product structure tree of a post lamp factory; however, it is an independent demand item since it is also sold as a replacement item.

Due to fluctuations in production capacities at different production stations, an initial master schedule may or may not be feasible under current capacity constraints. MPS checks only rough-cut capacity and is not equipped to check the actual capacity requirements for each individual work center and each type of resource. Because the MRP system explodes the master schedule into production requirements of all components from all levels of the product structure tree, it can also check the feasibility of the initial master schedule. If it turns out that the master schedule is not feasible because of insufficient capacity, then a decision must be made to either increase production capacity or to revise the master schedule.

The **inventory records and characteristics file** keeps track of information on each component, subassembly, and assembly for netting purposes. This information includes the number of units on hand at the beginning of the MRP schedule, the number of units already allocated, the quantity of safety stock required (for independent demand only), the production lot size, and the production lead time. The "units on hand" are based on a physical inventory count, the accuracy of which is vitally important to maintain an effective MRP system. The "units allocated" are the independent demand items which have been previously committed to the end user(s) but are temporarily held in the warehouse for pick-ups or delivery. Therefore, those items cannot be counted against future demand. The difference between the number of "units on hand" and the number of "units assigned for safety stock" and "allocated to past orders" is the number of units "projected on hand" which are used to offset the "gross requirement" from the MPS. A sample inventory records and characteristics file that is used to describe our sample production example is shown in Table 10.20.

Table 10.20: Inventory Records and Characteristics File

Item	Lot Size	Lead Time	On Hand	Safety Stock	Items Allocated	Low Level Code
A	10	4	7	5	2	0
B	20	2	17	12	5	0
C	10	2	11	8	3	0
F	20	2	0	0	0	1
G	20	2	0	0	0	1
Q	500	1	680	0	280	2
R	100	1	50	0	10	2
S	100	1	40	0	0	2

5.4 Output Information of the MRP System

The basic output information generated by MRP systems is the planned and time-phased order releases. MRP releases purchasing orders for purchased items and work orders for manufactured items at predetermined time intervals. The gross requirements of the dependent demand items are generated directly from the end items' product structure tree and are adjusted with the inventory record. The times at which orders are released to the shop floor are based on the master production schedule and are obtained by working backwards through the product structure tree, level by level, incorporating lead times.

Continuing with our sample production example as previously described, Table 10.21 shows an MRP schedule for products A, B, and C.

Table 10.21: MRP Format for our Master Schedule Requirement

MASTER SCHEDULE								
Product	1	2	3	4	5	6	7	8
A	50	0	50	0	100	0	20	0
B	0	140	0	140	0	140	0	140
C	80	0	90	0	0	10	170	0

Lot Size	Lead Time	On Hand	S. S.	Al'd	Low L. C.	Item	- Period -	PD	1	2	3	4	5	6	7	8
10	4	7	5	2	0	A	Gross Requirements		**50**	**0**	**50**	**0**	**100**	**0**	**20**	**0**
							Scheduled Receipts		50	0	50	0	0	0	0	0
							Projected Available	0	5	5	5	5	5	5	5	5
							Net Requirements		0	0	0	0	100	0	20	0
							Planned Order Receipts		0	0	0	0	100	0	20	0
							Planned Order Releases	**OK**	100	0	20	0	0	0	0	0
20	2	17	12	5	0	B	Gross Requirements		**0**	**140**	**0**	**140**	**0**	**140**	**0**	**140**
							Scheduled Receipts		0	140	0	0	0	0	0	0
							Projected Available	0	12	12	12	12	12	12	12	12
							Net Requirements		0	0	0	140	0	140	0	140
							Planned Order Receipts		0	0	0	140	0	140	0	140
							Planned Order Releases	**OK**	0	140	0	140	0	140	0	0
10	2	11	8	3	0	C	Gross Requirements		**80**	**0**	**90**	**0**	**0**	**10**	**170**	**0**
							Scheduled Receipts		80	0	0	0	0	0	0	0
							Projected Available	0	8	8	8	8	8	8	8	8
							Net Requirements		0	0	90	0	0	10	170	0
							Planned Order Receipts		0	0	90	0	0	10	170	0
							Planned Order Releases	**OK**	90	0	0	10	170	0	0	0
20	2	0	0	0	1	F	Gross Requirements		**100**	**140**	**20**	**140**	**0**	**140**	**0**	**0**
							Scheduled Receipts		100	140	0	0	0	0	0	0
							Projected Available	0	0	0	0	0	0	0	0	0
							Net Requirements		0	0	20	140	0	140	0	0
							Planned Order Receipts		0	0	20	140	0	140	0	0
							Planned Order Releases	**OK**	20	140	0	140	0	0	0	0
20	2	0	0	0	1	G	Gross Requirements		**190**	**0**	**20**	**10**	**170**	**0**	**0**	**0**
							Scheduled Receipts		200	20	0	0	0	0	0	0
							Projected Available	0	10	30	10	0	10	10	10	10
							Net Requirements		0	0	0	0	170	0	0	0
							Planned Order Receipts		0	0	0	0	180	0	0	0
							Planned Order Releases	**OK**	0	0	180	0	0	0	0	0
500	1	680	0	280	2	Q	Gross Requirements		**440**	**1,400**	**720**	**1,440**	**680**	**840**	**0**	**0**
							Scheduled Receipts		1,500	0	0	0	0	0	0	0
							Projected Available	400	1,460	60	340	400	220	380	380	380
							Net Requirements		0	0	660	1,100	280	620	0	0
							Planned Order Receipts		0	0	1,000	1,500	500	1,000	0	0
							Planned Order Releases	**OK**	0	1,000	1,500	500	1,000	0	0	0
100	1	50	0	10	2	R	Gross Requirements		**40**	**280**	**0**	**280**	**0**	**0**	**0**	**0**
							Scheduled Receipts		200	0	0	0	0	0	0	0
							Projected Available	40	200	20	20	40	40	40	40	40
							Net Requirements		0	80	0	260	0	0	0	0
							Planned Order Receipts		0	100	0	300	0	0	0	0
							Planned Order Releases	**OK**	100	0	300	0	0	0	0	0
100	1	40	0	0	0	S	Gross Requirements		**0**	**0**	**180**	**0**	**0**	**0**	**0**	**0**
							Scheduled Receipts		200	0	0	0	0	0	0	0
							Projected Available	40	240	240	60	60	60	60	60	60
							Net Requirements		0	0	0	0	0	0	0	0
							Planned Order Receipts		0	0	0	0	0	0	0	0
							Planned Order Releases	**OK**	0	0	0	0	0	0	0	0

Table 10.22: Typical MRP Showing Backward Scheduling for Product B

MASTER SCHEDULE

Product	1	2	3	4	5	6	7	8
A	50	0	50	0	100	0	20	0
B	0	140	0	140	0	140	0	140
C	80	0	90	0	0	10	170	0

Lot Size	Lead Time	On Hand	S. S.	Al'd	Low L. C.	Item	- Period -	PD	1	2	3	4	5	6	7	8
							Gross Requirements		**50**	**0**	**50**	**0**	**100**	**0**	**20**	**0**
							Scheduled Receipts		50	0	50	0	0	0	0	0
10	4	7	5	2	0	A	Projected Available	0	5	5	5	5	5	5	5	5
							Net Requirements		0	0	0	0	100	0	20	0
							Planned Order Receipts		0	0	0	0	100	0	20	0
							Planned Order Releases	**OK**	100	0	20	0	0	0	0	0
							Gross Requirements		**0**	**140**	**0**	**140**	**0**	**140**	**0**	**140**
							Scheduled Receipts		0	140	0	0	0	0	0	0
20	2	17	12	5	0	B	Projected Available	0	12	12	12	12	12	12	12	12
							Net Requirements		0	0	0	140	0	140	0	140
							Planned Order Receipts		0	0	0	140	0	140	0	140
							Planned Order Releases	**OK**	0	140	0	140	0	140	0	0
							Gross Requirements		**80**	**0**	**90**	**0**	**0**	**10**	**170**	**0**
							Scheduled Receipts		80	0	0	0	0	0	0	0
10	2	11	8	3	0	C	Projected Available	0	8	8	8	8	8	8	8	8
							Net Requirements		0	0	90	0	0	10	170	0
							Planned Order Receipts		0	0	90	0	0	10	170	0
							Planned Order Releases	**OK**	90	0	0	10	170	0	0	0
							Gross Requirements		**100**	**140**	**20**	**140**	**0**	**140**	**0**	**0**
							Scheduled Receipts		100	140	0	0	0	0	0	0
20	2	0	0	0	1	F	Projected Available	0	0	0	0	0	0	0	0	0
							Net Requirements		0	0	20	140	0	140	0	0
							Planned Order Receipts		0	0	20	140	0	140	0	0
							Planned Order Releases	**OK**	20	140	0	140	0	0	0	0
							Gross Requirements		**190**	**0**	**20**	**10**	**170**	**0**	**0**	**0**
							Scheduled Receipts		200	20	0	0	0	0	0	0
20	2	0	0	0	1	G	Projected Available	0	10	30	10	0	10	10	10	10
							Net Requirements		0	0	0	0	170	0	0	0
							Planned Order Receipts		0	0	0	0	180	0	0	0
							Planned Order Releases	**OK**	0	0	180	0	0	0	0	0
							Gross Requirements		**440**	**1,400**	**720**	**1,440**	**680**	**840**	**0**	**0**
							Scheduled Receipts		1,500	0	0	0	0	0	0	0
500	1	680	0	280	2	Q	Projected Available	400	1,460	60	340	400	220	380	380	380
							Net Requirements		0	0	660	1,100	280	620	0	0
							Planned Order Receipts		0	0	1,000	1,500	500	1,000	0	0
							Planned Order Releases	**OK**	0	1,000	1,500	500	1,000	0	0	0
							Gross Requirements		**40**	**280**	**0**	**280**	**0**	**0**	**0**	**0**
							Scheduled Receipts		200	0	0	0	0	0	0	0
100	1	50	0	10	2	R	Projected Available	40	200	20	20	40	40	40	40	40
							Net Requirements		0	80	0	260	0	0	0	0
							Planned Order Receipts		0	100	0	300	0	0	0	0
							Planned Order Releases	**OK**	100	0	300	0	0	0	0	0
							Gross Requirements		**0**	**0**	**180**	**0**	**0**	**0**	**0**	**0**
							Scheduled Receipts		200	0	0	0	0	0	0	0
100	1	40	0	0	0	S	Projected Available	40	240	240	60	60	60	60	60	60
							Net Requirements		0	0	0	0	0	0	0	0
							Planned Order Receipts		0	0	0	0	0	0	0	0
							Planned Order Releases	**OK**	0	0	0	0	0	0	0	0

- In order to understand how MRP works, move backwards from period 8, for product B, as highlighted in Table 10.22. Note that there is a net requirement of 140 units for product B.
- Because the production lead time for product B is 2 weeks, 140 units are planned to be released to the shop floor in the 6th week. The 12 units in inventory cannot be used because it is equal to the required safety stock.
- In order to make one unit of F (for product B) we need 2 units of R and 4 units of Q. Therefore, gross requirements of 280 units of R (2x140) are scheduled for period 4 and gross requirements of 560 units of Q (4x140) are scheduled for period 4 (note that gross requirements of 1440 units of Q for period 4 reflect accumulated gross requirements of Q for all level 1 and level 0 products!). Because there are 340 units in inventory ("projected available" in period 3) for Q, the "net requirement" for production is 1,100 units (1440 – 340) and because its production lot size is 500, 3 batches or 1500 units will be released to the shop floor ("planned order releases"). Similar reasoning explains why the 280 units of "gross requirements" of R result in 300 units of "planned order releases" in period 3.
- Finally, in order to make one unit of B, we also need an additional 6 units of Q. These units must be available by period 6. These 840 units of Q (6 x 140) are reflected in the accumulated gross requirements (840) for product Q in period 6. Because of a 1-period lead time for producing these items, 220 "projected available." a net requirement of 620 units (840 – 220), and a required lot size of 500 units, 1,000 units of Q will be released to the shop floor in period 5.

5.4 MRP Follow-Up

Production action will not start until a production or purchasing order is released by the dispatching function of the MRP system to the production floor or to the purchasing department in case of purchased items. Dispatching is the actual release of orders to responsible areas.

After production orders are dispatched to the production floor, the production function must continuously follow-up on the orders until they are completed. If there is any deviation between inventory/production levels and scheduled inventory/production levels, an expediter or a stock chaser must take proper action and see to it that the deviation is properly resolved. Since the follow-up cost is a function of the stock-out cost and/or the back-order cost, it is important to design an effective and efficient order control and follow-up system.

5.5 Managing Changes with MRP

In the real world, any plan or schedule is subject to change. Any change in input information to the MRP system will result in changes in the MRP output schedule. Some common changes in input information are:

- Increase/decrease in customer orders
- Revision of the demand forecast
- Modification in product design
- Substitution of scarce materials by more available ones
- Adjustments in inventory counts
- Changes in production methods
- Replacement of suppliers

Changes in production methods and suppliers may alter lead time requirements.

There exist two different approaches in managing changes with MRP. They are the regenerative approach and the net change approach. With the **regenerative** approach, the MRP system periodically recalculates the entire schedule, based on the latest master schedule requirements and inventory records. The system re-explodes the entire bill of materials to regenerate valid priorities and scheduling information for all items on all levels of the product structure tree. The regenerating process is carried out in a batch processing mode and, in most of the cases, requires extensive data processing time. Normally, the frequency of the regenerating process is once per time period or, typically, a week.

When there is a change in the master production schedule, in the inventory status, or in the bill of materials, the **net change approach** will carry out a partial explosion for only those items affected by the change. All other MRP information and output for the items that are not affected by the change are left untouched. Net changes may be applied instantaneously or at the end of the day when the change has taken place. The net change approach reduces the need for repetitive explosions of the complete master schedule and, consequently, significantly reduces the data processing time required to run the system. Therefore, the net change approach is designed primarily for a highly volatile environment where changes occur frequently and for a productive system with an extensive master schedule.

5.6 Manufacturing Resource Planning (MRP II)

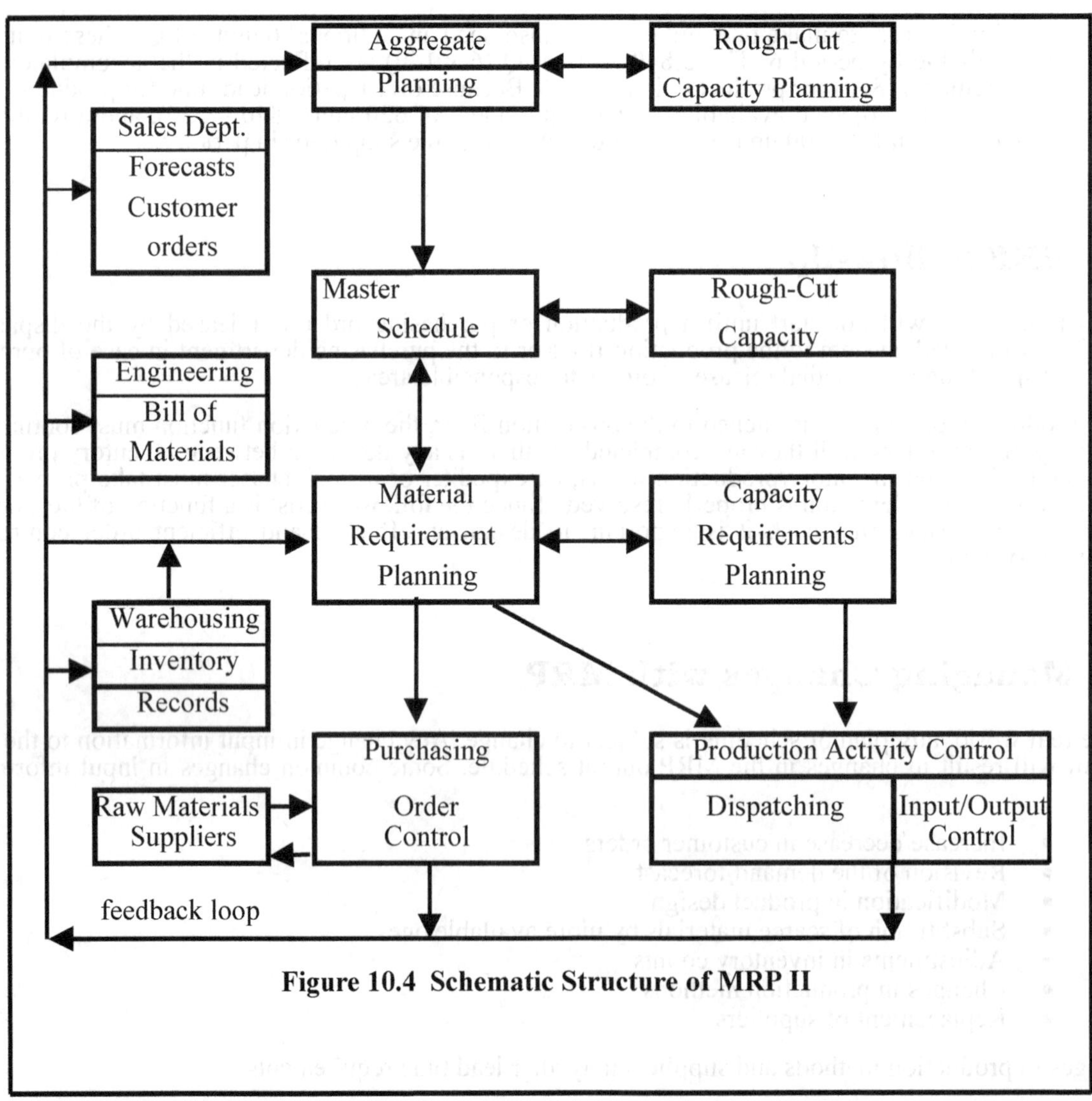

Figure 10.4 Schematic Structure of MRP II

Manufacturing Resource Planning came about as a gradual extension to the MRP system and is referred to as MRP II. The gradual extension started with adding computer software features to the MRP system. It obtained full recognition with the application of a common database, shared with other company functions, including purchasing, marketing, finance, engineering, manufacturing, and maintenance functions. This shared operational database became the foundation for an integrated information system. With this integrated information system, the MRP II system is able to generate output information for various departments, such as:

- Shipping schedules and shipping budget for the shipping department
- Inventory projections for the inventory control department
- Cost estimation and due-date commitments for the sales department
- Purchasing commitment reports for the purchasing department, etc.

The schematic structure of a typical MRP II system is shown in Figure 10.4.

The MRP II system, as pictured in Figure 10.4, is a closed loop system that links output to input upon the execution of the system and that checks capacity requirements against available capacity when generating detailed production schedules. In this sense, the master schedule and sometimes also the aggregate plan is adjusted to satisfy capacity constraints. Upon execution of the schedule, production activities and the purchasing order status are monitored and measured. Any discrepancy in scheduled activities is fed back immediately to all levels of the MRP II system and any required adjustments are incorporated into the next run of the MRP program.

The production planning function of the MRP II system includes aggregate production planning, master production scheduling, material requirement planning, and capacity planning. It not only carries these planning functions out sequentially, but also interactively via the feedback feature of MRP II. In this sense, production schedules will become more realistic as more information becomes available at each stage of the planning hierarchy. The MRP II system is thus better equipped to keep production schedules up-dated and to react quickly, or self-adjust, upon the detection of changes in market demand or in production conditions.

5.7 Capacity Requirement Planning

In comparison with material requirement planning (MRP), the most important added feature in manufacturing resource planning (MRP II) is detailed capacity requirement planning (CRP). Thus far we have discussed capacity planning at the aggregate planning level (rough-cut capacity planning) and its explosion at the master production level. Though the rough-cut capacity is somewhat realistic, there is no guarantee that it will be adequate when scheduling production as defined by the master schedule. In the MRP system, the "planned order release" is offset from the "net requirement" to accommodate the production or purchasing lead time; however, there is no provision to identify and check for the actual workload required during different production time periods. In an MRP system, we often infinitely load the shop floor.

Capacity requirement planning in MRP II generates a more detailed capacity requirement profile by exploding the production orders from the MRP output through the routing specified by the production activity control system. This profile details what capacity is required for each job type, in each work center, and even on each key machine during each time period of the planning horizon. The available capacity for each job type, in each work center, and on each key machine during each time period is measured against the required capacity. Any under-load or overload condition can be quickly identified and necessary adjustments to the production schedule can be made. Thus, MRP II leads towards a finite loading of the shop floor.

6. GLOSSARY AND SUMMARY OF METHODS

Aggregate Planning – Aggregate planning is concerned with the overall, aggregate operation of an organization (usually measured by the number of man-hours required) over a specified time horizon (6 months to 2 years).

Bills of Materials – A bill of materials is usually established by the engineering department and is a list of all component items that constitute the subassemblies and the main assembly. It shows how each end product is manufactured by defining all its sub-component items, their sequence of assembly, and their required quantity in each finished unit.

Capacity Requirement Planning (CRP) – Capacity requirement planning is a feature of MRPII that generates a more detailed capacity requirement profile by exploding the production orders from MRP output through the routing as specified by the production activity control system. It details what capacity is required for each job type, in each work center, and on each key machine during each time period of the planning horizon.

Dispatching – Dispatching is the actual release of orders to the responsible areas.

Inter Operation Time – The inter operation time is the nonproductive time during which the production orders are in queue (before entering the next operation), in storage between two consecutive operations, or in transit from one operation to the next operation.

Manufacturing Resource Planning (MRP II) – Manufacturing resource planning extends the material requirement planning system with an integrated information system that can generate information for various departments of the company (purchasing, marketing, finance, engineering, manufacturing, maintenance, shipping, etc.).

Market Lead Time – The market lead time is the elapsed time of the transfer of the customer's order from the sales department to the factory plus the needed time for delivering the finished goods to the customer.

Master (Production) Scheduling (MPS) – Master scheduling is the production planning function which determines the kinds and quantities of products to be manufactured in each time period and within the framework of the aggregate plan. Master scheduling dis-aggregates the production requirements for product groups over smaller time segments than the aggregate plan does.

Material Requirement Planning (MRP) – Material requirement planning is a computer based production planning and inventory control system designed to generate production and purchasing orders for dependent demand items. It creates schedules that identify, for all demand items, their amounts available in inventory, their exact required production quantities, and their production starting dates.

Operation Time – The operation time includes the time during which the transformation process is actually taking place and the time required to set up the production machines or equipment.

Priority Planning – Priority planning is the capacity allocation as specified by the order in which various products are to be produced. It is based on available production capacity, demand information, due dates, and production lead times.

Procurement Time or Lead Time (t_l) – Procurement time, or lead time, is the time that elapses between placing and receiving an order.

Production Lead Time – The production lead time is often referred to as the manufacturing lead time and is the elapsed time between the release of the production order to the shop floor and the delivery of the final product to the finished goods warehouse. It is the sum of the operation time and the inter operation time.

Production Planning and Control Function – The production planning and control function stores, analyzes, and distributes data and information from and to other production functions in an effort to guide the productive activities of the physical system.

Production Smoothing – The function of production smoothing is to level the production man-hours required through the entire planning period.

7. ACRONYMS

BOM Bill of Materials

CRP Capacity Requirement Planning

IT Inter Operation Time

MLT Market Lead Time

MPS Master Production Scheduling

MRP Material Requirement Planning

MRP II Manufacturing Resource Planning

OT Operation Time

PLT Production Lead Time

8. REFERENCES

APICS. *Material Requirement Planning Reprints*. Falls Church, VA: APICS, 1986.

Arnold, Tony J. R. *Introduction to Materials Management*. Englewood Cliffs, NJ: Prentice Hall, 1991.

Blackstone, J. H. *Capacity Management*. Cincinnati, OH: South-Western Publishing Co., 1989.

Fogarty, D. W., J. H. Blackstone, and T. R. Hoffman. *Production and Inventory Management*. Cincinnati, OH: South-Western Publishing Co., 1991.

Fogarty, D. W., F. R. Hoffmann, and P. W. Stonebraker. *Production Operations Management*. Cincinnati, OH: South-Western Publishing Co., 1989.

Green, J. H. *Production and Inventory Control Handbook*. New York: McGraw Hill Book Company, 1987.

Harris, F. W. *Operations and Cost*. Chicago: A. W. Shaw Company, 1915, pp. 48–52.

Hax, A. C., and D. Candea. *Production and Inventory Management*. Englewood Cliffs, NJ: Prentice-Hall, 1984.

Mather, Hal. *Bills of Materials*. Homewood, IL: Dow Jones-Irwin, 1987.

McLeavey, D. W., and S. L. Narasimhan. *Production Planning and Inventory Control*. Boston: Allyn and Bacon, 1985.

Orlicky, Joseph. *Material Requirement Planning, The Newest Way of Life in Production and Inventory Management*. New York: McGraw-Hill Book Company, 1975.

Reinfeld, N. V. *Handbook of Production and Inventory Control*. Englewood Cliffs, NJ: Prentice-Hall, 1987.

Vollman, T. E., W. L. Berry, and D. C. Whybark. *Manufacturing Planning and Control Systems*. Homewood, IL: Business One Irwin, 1988.

Wallace, Thomas F. *MRP II: Making it Happen, The Implementers' Guide to Success with Manufacturing Resource Planning*. Essex Junction, VT: Oliver Wight Ltd Publications, Inc., 1990.

Wight, Oliver W. *Manufacturing Resource Planning: MRP II, Unlocking America's Production Potential*. Essex Junction, VT: Oliver Wight Publications, Inc., 1984.

Wight, Oliver W. *The Executive's Guide to Successful MRP II*. Essex Junction, VT: Oliver Wight Ltd. Publications, Inc., 1982.

Wight, O. W. *Production and Inventory Management in the Computer Age*. New York: Van Nostrand Reinhold Company, 1984.

9. REVIEW QUESTIONS

1. What is the basic objective of production planning and control?
2. How can the objective of production planning and control be achieved through the control of the market response time and the production lead time?
3. What does lean operations management focus on with respect to the market response time?
4. What are the major functions of production planning and control?
5. What are the basic managerial decisions with respect to production planning and control?
6. How can capacity be adjusted to resolve the difference between the available and the required production capacity?
7. What is the function of aggregate planning and what operational strategies can be employed to accomplish that function?
8. What is the time horizon for aggregate planning?
9. What does the charting method accomplish?
10. What is the charting method?
11. What is usually the best aggregate plan?
12. What is meant by rough-cut capacity and what defines it?
13. When are priorities determined?
14. What is the input to master production scheduling?
15. How is the time horizon of master production scheduling defined?
16. How is a master production schedule generated?
17. What are the inputs for the MRP system?
18. What is the bill of materials?
19. Differentiate between independent demand (inventory) and dependent demand (inventory).
20. What is meant by a finite loading system and an infinite loading system?
21. Which of the systems we discussed in this chapter is a finite loading system and which one is an infinite loading system?
22. Is MRP and MRP II a backward or a forward scheduling system? Explain.
23. Differentiate between the regenerative and the net change approach in managing changes with MRP.
24. What is meant by capacity requirement planning?

10. PROBLEMS

Problem #1

PDC Corporation is currently manufacturing four (4) different products: A, B, C, and D. Product A is made up of two (2) different sub-assemblies: one (1) unit of subassembly E and two (2) units of sub-assembly F. Product B is made up of one (1) unit of subassembly E, four (4) units of component G and four (4) units of component H. Product C is similar to product B, except no separate H components are used. Subassembly E is also sold separately as product D in the market. Subassembly E is made up of two (2) units of component H and two (2) units of component J, while sub-assembly F consists of four (4) units of component K and two (2) units of component G.

a) Draw the bill of materials charts.

Problem #2

Work yourself through the bill of materials, from Level 0 (end product) to Level 2 (component parts), to determine the production requirements for each of the four products, the subassemblies, and all components, given the following forecast for next month.

A.	300 units
B.	50 units
C.	90 units
D.	10 units

Problem #3

Work yourself through the bill of materials to determine the net production requirements for all products, subassemblies, and components of PDC Corporation for next month, based on the forecasted demand as determined in problem #2 and on the following end of month inventory records:

A:	20 units
C:	10 units
E:	60 units
F:	100 units
G:	200 units
H:	20 units
K:	500 units

Problem #4 (Excel)

Use the 9 steps for Plan IV to generate the results that are shown in Table 10.11 in Excel.

Problem #5 (Excel)

Determine the monthly and the cumulative, aggregate production demand, in terms of man-hours, for each of the six months of next year under the following assumptions:

- Forecasted aggregate demand for the first six months of next year is as follows: 450, 250, 250, 300, 400, and 450
- There are 22, 20, 22, 21, 22, and 22 working days in January through June, respectively
- The expected inventory at the beginning of next year is 20 aggregate units
- The company's inventory policy requires maintaining a 10% safety stock level
- The normal production standard for each aggregate unit is 35 hours

Problem #6 (Excel)

Based on the production schedule as described in Problem #5, what would be the hiring and layoff costs during each of the six months and what would be the total cost during the entire six-month period? Use the following assumptions:

Management has freedom in hiring/laying off employees as dictated by production demand.

- The company starts the planning period with 80 workers
- The cost of hiring a new employee is $1,000
- The cost of laying off an employee is $3,000

Problem #7 (Excel)

Reconsider the data of Problem #5 and assume that it is company policy to freeze the manpower level for the planning period. Therefore, the fluctuations in workload can only be absorbed through working overtime or under-time. Given that the regular labor rate is $16 per hour and the overtime rate is $24 per hour, determine the optimal manpower level over the planning period of six months, so that the accumulated overtime and under-time cost during this six-month period is minimized. In determining the optimal manpower level you must use the simulation technique of the charting method. Print all appropriate tables that show your work sequence that leads to the best solution. In determining the cost, consider that the company starts the planning period with 80 workers.

Problem # 8 (Excel)

At the optimal manpower level as determined in Problem #7, what will it cost if a full load work schedule is maintained at all times and only inventories and backlogs are used to absorb the fluctuations in the production demand? Assume that the inventory holding cost is $20 per unit and per month and that the backlog cost is $25 per unit and per month. In determining the cost, consider that the company starts the planning period with 80 workers.

What is the optimal manpower level under this holding and backlog cost?

Problem #9 (Excel)

If management policy allows only for overtime and inventory to be used in absorbing fluctuations in production demand during the next six months planning period, determine the optimal manpower level. In determining the cost, consider that the company starts the planning period with 80 workers.

What is the cost consequence of this policy?

Problem #10 (Excel)

The master production schedule of our PDC Corporation is based on a two months' time span. The standard production times in number of hours per unit for products A, B, C, and D are 40, 34, 32, and 10 respectively. The economical lot size for the four different products is 10, 5, 5, and 1 respectively. Over the next two months of the master scheduling period, the forecasted demand for each of the four products by month are 150, 140, 150, and 10 units for the first month and 100, 140, 60, and 10 for the second month. There is no scheduled inventory for the first month. Based on the aggregate production schedule, as determined by the aggregate plan, there are 81 units of scheduled inventory for the second month. The materials manager suggests allocating these 81 units of scheduled inventory over the four products as follows: 40, 15, 20, and 6 units respectively.

The inventory report shows that the number of units on hand at the beginning of the next scheduling period is 10, 0, 5, and 5. The safety stock levels are set at 10% across the product line. Determine the production requirements for each of the two months. In other words, develop the disaggregated plan.

Problem #11 (Excel)

By using computer simulation, determine the Master Schedule for the next eight weeks. Use charts to show the weekly and cumulative capacity requirements for each of the eight weeks. Compare the planned capacity (rough-cut capacity) against scheduled capacity.

Chapter 11

INVENTORY MANAGEMENT

Simply defined, **inventory** is a stock of physical goods that are stored for later use or sale. Inventories exist ***continuously*** in all industries: manufacturing industries, such as textile, automotive, appliance, and others have raw materials, work-in-process, finished goods, and supply inventories, which are necessary to ensure continuity in the production process. Businesses dealing in repairs have inventories of spare parts and other supplies. Banks keep inventories of deposit and withdrawal slips, savings books, loan payment coupons, and so on. Hospitals keep inventories of disposable surgical goods, medication, linens, blood, and other critical supplies.

Inventories are maintained for various reasons. Inventories kept to meet demand during transit time are called **pipeline inventories**. In order to synchronize various production activities **in-process inventories** or **decoupling inventories** are necessary. **Buffer or safety inventories** are created to protect against unpredictable variation in demand and supply. **Seasonal inventories** are generated when one decides not to change production rates over time for goods affected by a seasonal demand. In this case, seasonal inventories accumulate during periods of low demand rate and deplete during periods of high demand rate. To take advantage of economic order sizes, **lot size or cycle inventories** are generated.

Various systems exist to monitor and control inventory. Some of these systems discussed here are the two-bin reorder-point system, the fixed reorder-point system, the fixed time-interval system, and the ABC system.

If management carries cycle inventory, then it is necessary to determine the optimal or best order quantity. In this chapter we will discuss various inventory models that management can use to define the optimal, best, order, or production quantity.

1. INVENTORY AND CYCLE COUNTING

Inventory quantities that are on record for various inventory items do not necessarily reflect an accurate count of what is in storage or in the facility. For this reason, on a regular basis, ***physical inventory*** ought to be taken. The technique whereby physical inventory is taken is called **cycle counting**. The review period can vary from less than 30 days to over 180 days and largely depends on the annual dollar usage. Items with high annual dollar usage get counted more often than items with low annual dollar usage. Many companies will tolerate a difference between the physical inventory and its record. But on an annual basis, it behooves them to have an accurate count with obsolete items removed if possible.

APICS, the leading professional association of supply chain and operations management, recommends 0.2% accuracy for high annual dollar use items (class A goods), 1.0% accuracy for medium annual dollar use items (class B goods), and 5.0% accuracy for low annual dollar use items (class C goods).

2. INVENTORY CONTROL SYSTEMS

2.1 Two-Bin Reorder-Point System

The **two-bin reorder-point system** is a ***continuous control system*** and is pictured in Figure 11.1. The items are distributed into two bins whereby Bin #2 receives the **reorder-point (ROP) quantity** and Bin #1 the remains of the original order. Material handlers remove needed items from Bin #1 as long as they can. The first item retrieved from Bin #2 triggers the next order (the reorder-point). Because it contains the number of items needed to meet demand during the replenishment lead time for this item plus safety stock (the reorder-point quantity), it should meet the demand until the order arrives. When the next order arrives, Bin #2 is filled to the reorder-point quantity, the remains are put into Bin #1, and the cycle begins again.

An Example: The 2-Bin Reorder-Point System

Figure 11.1 shows that Bin #1 only has 150 units of stock left in it. This is the bin that was used to satisfy the demand in the previous period. The second bin has not been used, and therefore still contains its reorder quantity of 250 units. As soon as Bin #1 is depleted, the need for goods will be satisfied by using the units in Bin #2. At that time, the quantity in Bin #2 falls below 250, so then an order for 250 units will be placed to replenish the inventory.

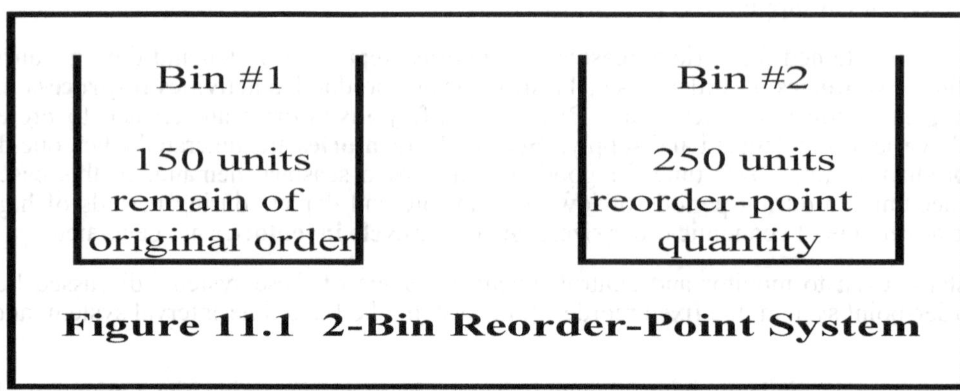

Figure 11.1 2-Bin Reorder-Point System

In this continuous review ordering system the **order or lot size, Q**, is normally determined by the use of various quantitative inventory models, such as the **EOQ (Economic Order Quantity**) or the **EPQ (Economic Production Quantity) model**, or by management. In either case the order quantity much depends on three main variables: the size of the demand, the lead time, and the price of an item.

One of the most important criteria is the size of the demand. The higher the demand is, the higher the order quantity is. Lead-time is important since the quantity that is in Bin #2 of our example must be sufficient to meet the demand during the replenishment period. Finally, if the price for an item is low, then more can be held in storage for a small cost. Some or all of these variables can be used to determine the lot size as will be discussed later.

2.2 Fixed Reorder-Point System

In the fixed reorder-point system, a **predetermined fixed quantity of units (Q)** is ordered when the inventory reaches a predetermined limit. If the replenishment is instantaneous, then the order can be placed when the inventory reaches zero (theoretically). Figure 11.2 pictures the inventory movement when the demand rate remains constant and when replenishment is instantaneous.

The optimal order quantity in this system is normally defined by management who considers minimizing yearly inventory cost. As discussed earlier, the following components or variables determine such yearly inventory cost: yearly demand, ordering cost, holding cost, unit cost, and possible quantity discounts. The EOQ model or a variation of it (when considering quantity discounts) can be used to establish the optimum order quantity in this system.

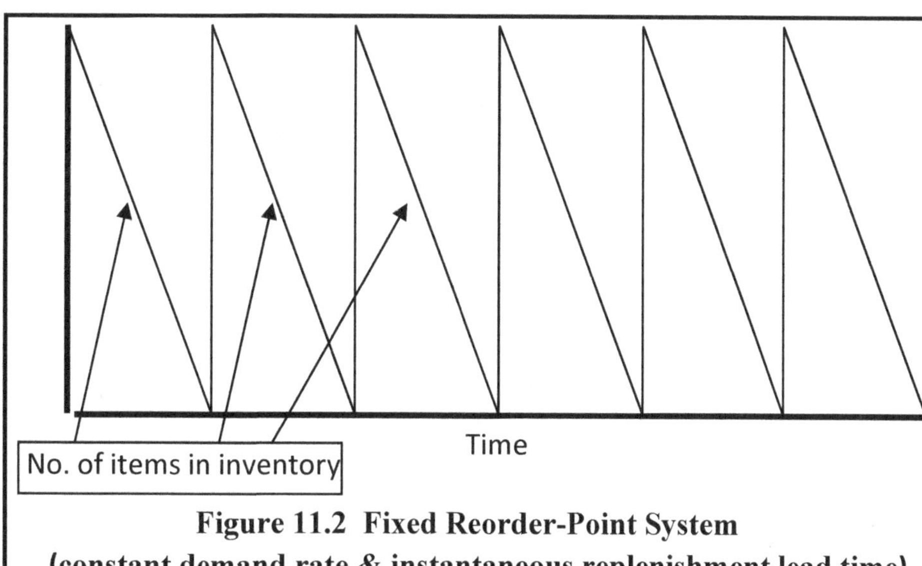

Figure 11.2 Fixed Reorder-Point System (constant demand rate & instantaneous replenishment lead time)

The condition of instantaneous (zero lead time) replenishment described above is not realistic. Normally, it takes some time to order and receive a new batch of inventory. This time is referred to as the **lead time**. If this lead time is constant and if the demand rate for the product is also constant, then the reorder-point can easily be defined. The inventory on hand at the time of placing an order must be such that it is sufficient to cover the demand during the lead time. Figure 11.3 shows the inventory movement when the demand rate is constant and when the lead time for replenishing the inventory is a constant of *t* days.

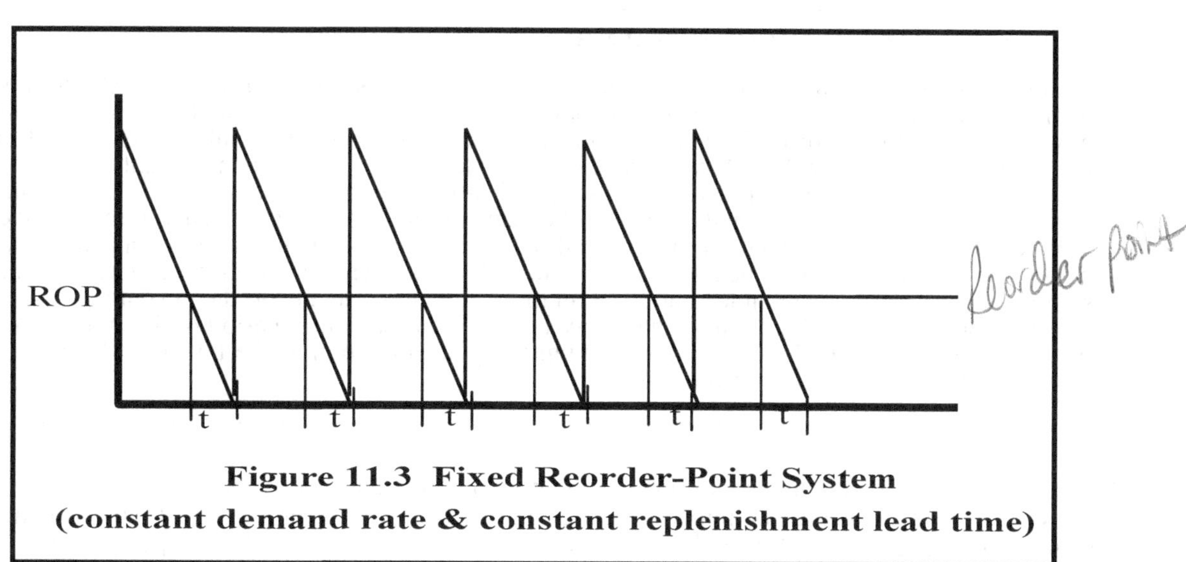

Figure 11.3 Fixed Reorder-Point System (constant demand rate & constant replenishment lead time)

In this case the inventory movement is the same as in Figure 11.2. However, given the constant replenishment period of *t* days, an order of Q units must be placed as soon as the inventory reaches R units, the reorder point level. After *t* days of lead time, the inventory level reaches the zero level. It is at that time that the new order comes in and the inventory reaches its maximum level of Q units.

The most realistic scenario for the fixed-reorder-point system is the one that is shown in Figure 11.4. Here both the demand rate and the lead-time may vary. In order to safeguard against **stock-out** as a result of an increase in the lead time or an increase in the demand rate, a **safety stock or buffer stock of S units** is required. The size of the safety stock very much depends on the variability of the lead time and the demand, the standard of service one wishes to maintain, and the cost of running out of stock. The larger the lead time and its variability, the larger the safety stock must be. Likewise, the larger the demand variability, the larger the safety stock must be.

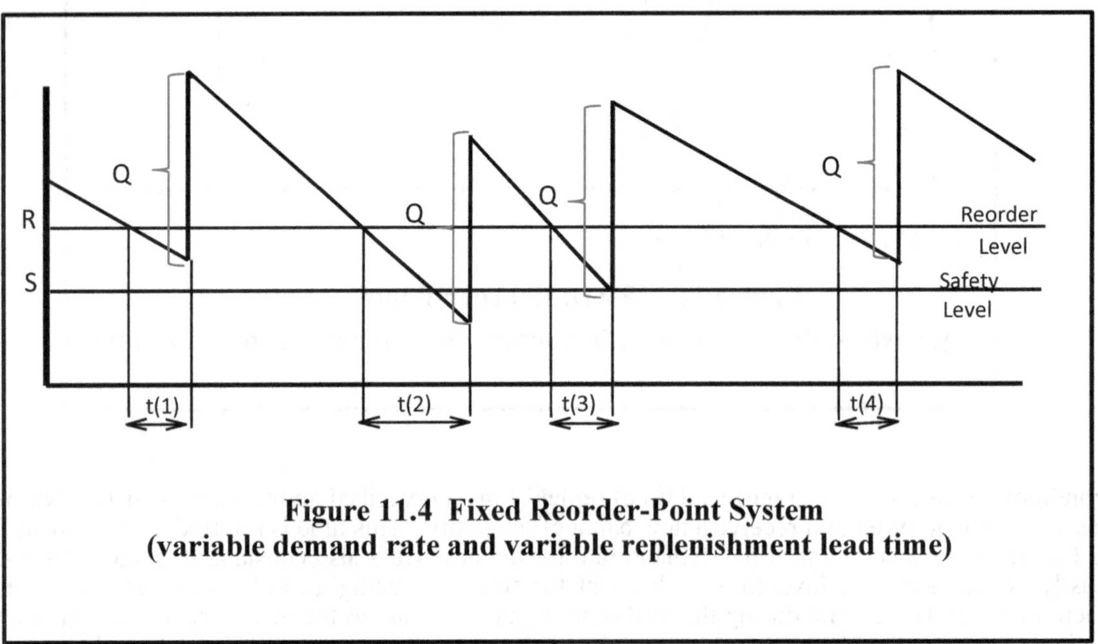

Figure 11.4 Fixed Reorder-Point System (variable demand rate and variable replenishment lead time)

An Example: The Fixed Reorder-Point System:

Examine the inventory movements of Figure 11.4. Let us here assume that period 1 exhibits a normal demand rate and a normal lead time of *t*(1) days. During period 2 the demand rate has not changed, however the lead-time for replenishing the inventory has approximately doubled. As a result of this, the inventory dips below the safety stock level of S. Because of a sufficient amount of safety stock, the company will not experience any stock-out before its inventory is replenished. During the third period the lead time *t*(3) is normal; however, the demand rate has increased. Therefore, the inventory will deplete faster than normal during the lead time period. This again causes the inventory to drop below the safety level S. When the demand rate decreases and the lead time does not increase significantly, then it is possible that the minimum inventory level, or the inventory level when replenishment occurs, is higher than the safety level. This is shown in period 4 of Figure 11.4. In all periods shown in Figure 11.4, an order of Q units is placed as soon as the inventory level reaches a level of R units, or the reorder point level.

Note that the two-bin system, as described in the previous section, is a special case of the fixed-reorder-point system. As soon as the first bin is depleted, an order is placed to replenish that bin, while the second bin is being engaged to fulfill, at least, the demand during the replenishment period. Therefore, the minimum amount of inventory in any bin must be sufficient to cover the average demand during the replenishment cycle plus a certain safety margin to absorb demand and lead-time variability.

2.3 Fixed Time-Interval System

The fixed time-interval system, also known as the **optional replenishment system**, is a ***periodic review inventory system***. In this inventory control system management sets upper and lower limits for all inventory items. The lower inventory level is usually denoted by s, whereas the upper limit is denoted by S. In this sense, this system is also known as the **(s, S) inventory system**. In setting both limits for inventory items, management is normally guided by the following factors: the yearly demand for the product, the relationship of the product to the production of other products (parts, subassemblies, raw material, etc.), availability of warehouse space and holding cost, the ordering cost, and the cost of the item itself.

When the fixed time-interval system is used, the level of an inventory item is reviewed periodically to make sure that the level has not dropped beyond its lower limit, s. If during a review period it occurs that the inventory level of an item is less than its minimum level, then an order will be placed to restore the inventory to its upper level. However, if during a review period the inventory level is above the minimum level, then no action will be taken during that review period. The following example illustrates this system.

An Example: The Fixed Time-Interval System

Consider the data in Table 11.1. Note that the X item is below its lower level of 100 units! Therefore, 340 (400–60) units of the X item must be ordered to return the level to its upper limit of 400 units. The Y item is still above its lower limit of 50 units, so no units of the Y item must be ordered. However, as the Z item is below its lower limit of 150 units, it is necessary to order 250 (350–100) units to restore it to its upper level of 350 units.

Table 11.1: Inventory Status Information for the Periodic Review Inventory System

Item	s, Lower Limit	S, Upper Limit	Inventory Status	Reorder Quantity
X	100	400	60	340
Y	50	250	75	n/a
Z	150	350	100	250

The fixed time-interval system requires larger safety stocks than the fixed reorder-point system, because the inventory is not constantly monitored, but only reviewed periodically. The longer the review periods the larger that safety stock ought to be. In the fixed reorder-point system we are constantly monitoring the inventory level, while this monitoring only occurs at certain intervals of time in the fixed time interval system.

3. *THE ABC INVENTORY SYSTEM*

Inventory control becomes tedious when the system consists of many items. Keeping track of hundreds of different order quantities and reorder points is impractical. The ABC inventory system is used to control inventory systems that consist of numerous items. This system classifies the inventory into three basic groups: the A group, the B group, and the C group. Approximately 5 to 20 percent of the goods belong to the A group and represent the high-dollar-volume group. The moderate volume group is the B group that represents approximately 25 to 30 percent of the inventory goods. The largest group (approximately 60 percent of the inventory) is the low-dollar-volume group, or C group. The dollar volume is the product of the dollar value of the item and the number of units required per year.

The high dollar volume of items in group A requires that these goods be more closely controlled than the goods in either the B or the C groups. This implies that goods belonging to the A group are ordered more frequently than the ones in either the B or C group.

A typical illustration of the ABC inventory system is the gasoline station. Here, gasoline and oil inventories need to be controlled daily and therefore belong to the A group. The B group may consist of transmission fluid, windshield solvent, tires, and batteries. The C group consists of hoses, gasoline tank caps, radiator caps, windshield wiper blades, fan belts, car wax, valve stems, grease, and so on. If a medium- or low-volume item becomes a critical item, then it may be placed in the A group. (This is the case for certain hospital inventories such as oxygen or blood. Since a hospital cannot afford to run out of these supplies, daily controls and relatively high safety stocks are necessary.)

Example #1: ABC Book Distributors

Last year, ABC Book Distributors decided to improve the management of its inventory of over 35,000 titles. Their goal was to reduce the total cost of handling and carrying inventory and at the same time improve inventory turnover. Since the company stocked a large number of titles and since less than 35% of its titles represents 90% of dollar sales, it realized that monitoring all titles very closely was not realistic. Therefore, it decided to stratify its titles in three main categories in order to focus buyer attention on the items which gave the highest return for their investment of time and resources. The stratification would also be used to define different safety stock levels. The inventory data for three inventory strata at ABC Book Distributors as of January of last year is shown in Table 11.2.

Table 11.2: ABC Book Distributors Inventory Strata

Class	Annual Sales per Title	# of Titles	Percent of Titles	Total Annual Sales/Class	Percent of Sales
A	$3,500 – Up	2,400	7%	$24.6MM	60%
B	$501-$3,500	9,800	26%	12.6MM	30%
C	$0 - $500	25,000	67%	$3.9 MM	10%

Note that a relatively small percentage of titles (7%) represented 60% of the sales at ABC Book Distributors and 33% (7% + 26%) of the titles (strata A and B) accounted for 90% of its sales. The last stratum included 67% of the titles, but only contributed 10% to annual sales dollars. Therefore, it was quite natural that ABC Book Distributors wished to set up a system, where buyers' attention and stock control became proportional to the percentage of sales, rather than the percentage of titles in each class. In other words, about 60% of effort and resources must be spent on the 7% of items in stratu A, 30% on the 26% of items in stratum B, and only 10% on all 67% of titles that constitute strata C. This was feasible because the company had the capability to automate the re-ordering of class B and C stocks and also class A stock with considerable buyer intervention.

The company established the following inventory policy: define economic order quantities for all A and B strata items and, in defining the reorder point, only formally define safety stock for A stratum items.

Example #2: Controlling Hospital Inventories

In the early sixties, Reed and Stanley designed a procedure to improve the economic control of hospital general inventories for the J. Hillis Miller Health Center of the University of Florida. The emphasis of their work was placed on defining the order points and order quantities for stored inventory items.

They classified the inventories in three categories: high-value-class items (class A), middle-value-class items (class B), and low-value-class items (class C).

For the high-value-class items, the average demand for an item during the replenishment period is the product of the average demand and the average lead time. However, since there is variation expected in the demand and the lead time, the thus defined order point would result in a stock out of 50% of the orders during the replenishment period. To reduce this stock-out probability, safety stock is figured. The size of the safety stock depends on the variability of the demand during the replenishment period, the variability of the replenishment period, and the desired service level. This method provides overprotection, which is desirable because many of the items in this category, such as medical gases and surgical and medical supplies, are life-and-death items.

For the middle-value-class items, cost for data collection was significantly reduced by calculating the lead-time estimate for the class, rather than the individual inventory items. This value was then applied to each inventory item in that class.

For the low-value-class that represents very little of the total inventory investment, larger safety stocks are considered more economic than detailed, accurate data collection. Here the assumption was made that there is no variance in the expected demand during the lead time and a fixed time factor is added to the lead time. In this case, the fixed time factor is determined by qualitative means. It will be greater if the lead time for the item is relatively long and variable, or if the stock-out of the low-value-class item in question is particularly undesirable.

4. ECONOMIC ORDER QUANTITY MODEL (EOQ)

The economic order quantity model, the first inventory model, was suggested and derived by F. W. Harris (1915). R. H. Wilson (1926) made the EOQ model popular when, as a consultant, he applied it to many companies. The basic objective of the EOQ model is to find the optimal (constant) order quantity using the following basic assumptions:

- Demand is deterministic
- Demand rate is constant
- Inventory is replenished instantaneously and lead time (t) is fixed
- No shortages are allowed
- Order or replenishment size is constant (Q)
- There is a constant per-unit holding cost and a constant ordering cost

With these assumptions in mind, the inventory model can be graphed as shown in Figure 11.5.

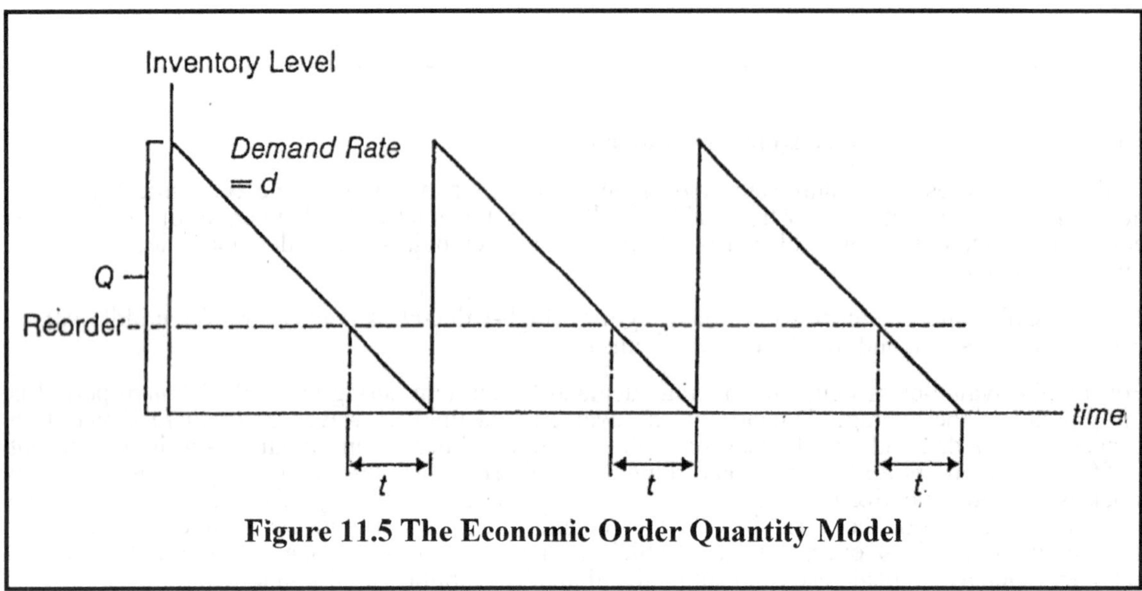

Figure 11.5 The Economic Order Quantity Model

4.1 Demand

The demand in the economic order quantity model is deterministic, and the demand rate (*d*) is predetermined. As the demand rate is constant, the inventory decreases linearly at a rate equal to the demand rate. Yearly demand is denoted by the capital letter *D*.

4.2 Inventory Level

When the inventory level reaches zero, it is replenished instantaneously by an amount equal to *Q*. Therefore the inventory level fluctuates between the maximum quantity *Q* units and the lowest possible level, zero units. Because of the daily constant demand rate of *d* units, the inventory decreases linearly, as shown by the series of triangles in Figure 11.5. Due to the triangular pattern in inventory movement, on the average *Q/2* units of goods are carried in inventory.

4.3 Lead Time and Reorder Time

The reorder point *R* is that level of inventory at which an order has to be placed so that inventory will reach zero when the new order arrives. The lead-time *t* – the period that must be allowed for ordered goods to arrive - is a constant for the EOQ model. Since both the demand rate *d* and the lead-time *t* are constant, the reorder point *R* must also be constant:

$$R = (d)*(t)$$

4.4 Yearly Inventory Cost

To develop the economic order quantity, the yearly inventory cost is established, since it is the objective to find the order quantity that minimizes yearly inventory cost. Two cost elements that must be considered here are the yearly ordering cost and the yearly holding or carrying cost:

$$C = C_o + C_h$$

Where: C = yearly inventory cost
C_o = yearly ordering cost
C_h = yearly holding cost

4.5 Yearly Ordering Cost (C_o)

Ordering cost occurs when inventory is ordered and results from salaries and wages in the accounting and purchasing departments, from postage, and from telephone calls to vendors. Ordering cost is not exactly a constant amount each time an order is placed, but it is certainly incorrect to assume that the order cost is directly related to the order size. To determine the yearly ordering cost, we multiply the average ordering cost by the number of orders per year:

$$C_o = c_o\left(\frac{D}{Q}\right)$$

Where: C_o = yearly cost for placing orders
c_o = average cost for placing an order
D = yearly demand
Q = order quantity
D/Q = number of orders placed per year

As the order quantity (Q) increases, fewer orders (D/Q) are placed during one year, thus decreasing the yearly ordering cost.

An Example: Understanding the Order Cost Curve of Big George's Appliance Store

George's Appliance Store sells approximately 60 Litton microwave ovens per year. Each time the store manager places an order, ordering costs amount to $20 per order. Table 11.3 and Figure 11.6 represent the yearly ordering cost for various order quantities.

Table 11.3: Ordering Costs for George's Appliance Store

Order Quantity Q	**Yearly Ordering Cost** $C_o = c_o(D/Q) = \$20(60/Q)$
60 units	$20(60/60) = $20
50 units	$20(60/50) = $24
40 units	$20(60/40) = $30
30 units	$20(60/30) = $40
20 units	$20(60/20) = $60
10 units	$20(60/10) = $120
5 units	$20(60/5) = $240

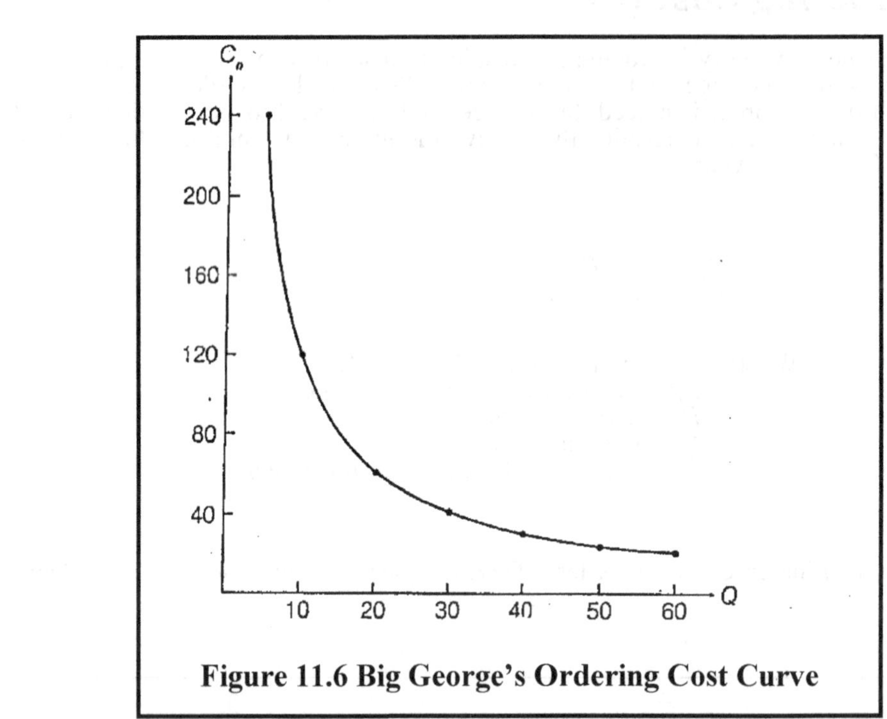

Figure 11.6 Big George's Ordering Cost Curve

Viewing Figure 11.6, the yearly ordering cost as a function of the order quantity is non-linear.

4.6 Yearly Holding or Carrying Cost (C_h)

Holding, or carrying, costs result from placing and keeping goods in inventory. When goods are placed in inventory or removed from inventory, there is handling cost. Other costs in keeping goods are insurance, taxes, rent, utilities, and capital investment. The yearly holding cost depends upon either the average inventory or the maximum inventory. If the holding cost reflects capital investment in goods, then the yearly holding cost is a function of the interest rate, price of the unit, and the average number of units carried in inventory. If, however, the holding cost reflects rent, utilities, and insurance, then the yearly holding cost is most likely to be a function of the per-unit yearly holding cost (the sum of the per-unit insurance, rent, and annual utility costs) and the maximum number of units carried in inventory.

Clearly, if other costs are held constant, high per-unit yearly holding costs will result in low inventory levels and therefore frequent replenishments, or orders. Low per-unit holding costs will favor high inventory levels and infrequent replenishments.

If the yearly holding cost is a function of the average inventory, then for the EOQ model the yearly holding cost is as follows:

$$C_h = c_h\left(\frac{Q}{2}\right)$$

Where: C_h = yearly holding cost
c_h = per-unit yearly holding cost
$Q/2$ = average inventory

4.7 Optimal Order Quantity

Now that the two major cost factors of the yearly inventory cost function are defined we can provide a complete expression for the yearly inventory cost:

$$C = c_o\left(\frac{D}{Q}\right) + c_h\left(\frac{Q}{2}\right)$$

Where: C = yearly inventory cost
c_o = average ordering cost
D = yearly demand
Q = order quantity
c_h = per-unit yearly holding cost
$Q/2$ = average inventory

We know the yearly holding cost ($c_h(Q/2)$) will increase as the order quantity (Q) increases, whereas the yearly ordering cost ($c_o(D/Q)$), will decrease as the order quantity increases. Figure 11.7 gives a graphic view of the total inventory cost.

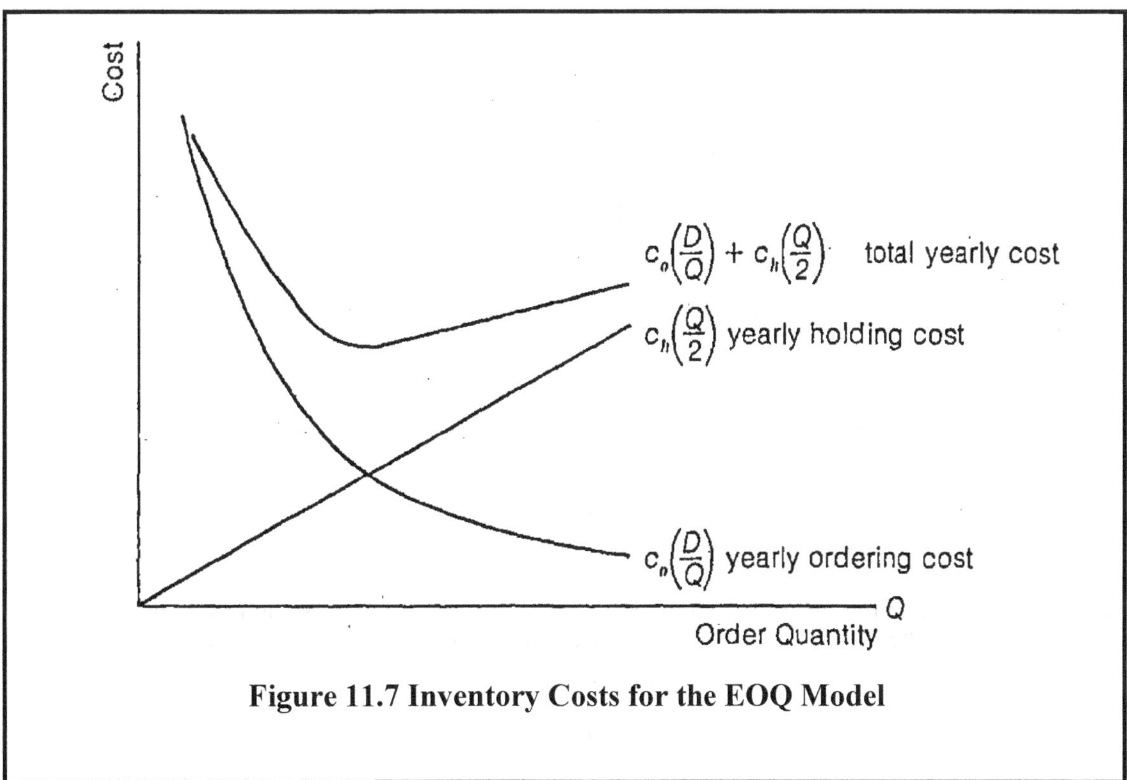

Figure 11.7 Inventory Costs for the EOQ Model

Note from the figure that the total yearly inventory cost is minimized when the cost of ordering equals the cost of carrying inventory, or when:

$$c_o\left(\frac{D}{Q}\right) = c_h\left(\frac{Q}{2}\right)$$

This relationship can now be solved to find the economic order quantity (EOQ):

$$EOQ = Q = \sqrt{\frac{2 \times D \times c_o}{c_h}}$$

As expected, the economic order quantity confirms that the optimal order quantity decreases as the holding cost (c_h) increases, and the optimal order quantity increases as the ordering cost (c_o) increases.

Example #1: Big George's Economic Order Quantity for Litton Microwave Ovens

Reconsider the case of George's Appliance Store. Sixty Litton microwave ovens are sold each year. Ordering cost is $20 per order. Big George's has plenty of storage room but is concerned about the 10% interest paid for borrowing to keep goods in inventory. Each Litton microwave oven costs $180.

To define George's optimal order quantity we must consider the ordering cost of $20 per order and the capital holding cost of $18 (0.10 x 180) per microwave oven. The economic order quantity can now be defined with the following data:

Annual demand: $D = 60$ units

Ordering cost: $c_o = \$20$ per order

Holding cost: $c_h = \$18$ per unit per year.

The economic order quantity is therefore:

$$Q = \sqrt{\frac{2 \times D \times c_o}{c_h}}$$

$$= \sqrt{\frac{2(60)20}{18}}$$

$$Q = 11.55 units$$

If it takes Big George's 10 days to receive the order, then the reorder point is:

$$R = d(10\text{days})$$

$$= (60\text{units}/356\text{days})(10\text{days})$$

$$= 1.64 \text{ units}$$

Rounding off all calculations, Big George's will order 12 microwave ovens each time an order is placed, and orders are made when the inventory drops to two units. Thus, the total yearly inventory cost will be:

$$C = c_o\left(\frac{D}{Q}\right) + c_h\left(\frac{Q}{2}\right)$$

$$= \$20\left(\frac{60}{12}\right) + \$18\left(\frac{12}{2}\right)$$

$$C = \$208$$

Note, however, that the yearly ordering cost [$100 = $20(60/12)] does not quite equal the yearly holding cost [$108 = $18(12/2)] in the above example. This is due simply to the rounding of the order quantity from 11.55 units to a workable 12 units.

Example #2: ABC Book Distributors Determines its Ordering Cost, Holding Cost, ROP, and Economic Order Quantity

The cost of placing an order for one item depends on the annual cost of ordering and receiving merchandise and the number of product orders generated. The annual cost of ordering and receiving consists of buying cost, receiving cost, data processing cost, and supplies. Work sampling indicated that approximately 76% of the buyers' time was spent on ordering titles, 44% of the work time in the warehouse was dedicated to receiving and shelving titles, and approximately 4.7% of data processing time was dedicated to ordering titles and generating reports for buyers. Supplies, consisting of product orders and other reports cost the company $9,600 annually. This data was used in Table 11.4 to determine the yearly order cost.

Table 11.4: Determining the Yearly Ordering Cost

Category	Yearly Cost	Work Sampling %	Attributed to Orders
Buying Center	$300,000	76%	$228,000
Receiving Center	$591,000	44%	$260,000
Data Processing Center	$954,000	4.70%	$44,838
Supplies	$9,600	100%	$9,600
		Total Yearly Ordering Cost:	$542,478

Since in the past approximately 336,000 product orders had been generated yearly, the approximate order cost per product line was:

$$C_o = \frac{\$542,478}{336,000} = \$1.61$$

The cost for holding inventory, c_h, was set at 18%, of which 13% was the capital cost and 5% was for shelf space, taxes on inventory, insurance, etc.

Various forecasting techniques were evaluated in an effort to determine the annual sales. It was decided that a reasonable way of calculating such sales each time an order had to be placed was by taking the past two months sales and multiplying them by 6. The cost of each item was figured by taking the average cost maintained in the inventory file.

The reorder point was defined using the following formula:

$$ROP = B + S_d\,(L + R)$$

Where: ROP = the reorder point (units)
B = the safety or buffer stock (units)
S_d = the average daily sales (units)
L = the vendor lead time (days)
R = the review period (time between the buyers reports in days)

In the proposed model, buyers' reports would be run weekly for all items. A decision to reorder would be made whenever the on-hand plus on-order inventory was less than the ROP. The quantity to reorder would be the EOQ. For practical reasons, each EOQ got appropriately adjusted, so that at least a two week supply was ordered and so that each order represented a full case or a multiple thereof.

The average daily sales, S_d, was defined by taking the average daily sales over the past two months, whereas the review period between buyers reports was assumed to be seven days. The vendor file provided data for determining vendor lead-time.

Buffer or safety stock levels were only calculated for A-stratum items, or those items that had an annual dollar volume of over $3,500. Given the approximate sales distribution and company policy that stock-out cannot exceed 2% of total sales, the appropriate buffer or safety stock was defined as:

$$B = 2 \times S_d \times L$$

Where: S_d = the average daily sales (units)
L = the vendor lead-time (days)

The immediate effect of calculating EOQs was that high-volume and high-ticket items were ordered more frequently and in smaller quantities than was typically done previously. Low-volume and low-ticket items were ordered in larger quantities and less frequently.

There was a significant increase in inventory turnover for high- volume and high-ticket items. The overall inventory turnover was more than six times a year for class A items, and over five times for class B items. This was well above the average for this industry.

5. EOQ MODEL AND QUANTITY DISCOUNTS

In the economic order quantity model, as discussed in the previous section, it is assumed that the price of one inventory item is fixed, regardless of the quantity ordered or produced. We all know that in reality discounts are given based on order size. If this is the case, then we must know whether it is in our best interest to take advantage of quantity discounts.

Let us analyze, in general, what effect quantity discounts have on the EOQ model. Remember that the yearly handling cost will increase as the order quantity increases. Therefore, quantity discounts are advantageous only if the added yearly inventory cost is less than the savings obtained from the discount. For a more careful analysis, reconsider the economic order quantity formula:

$$Q = \sqrt{\frac{2(D)c_o}{c_h}}$$

In many applications the per-unit yearly holding cost (c_h) is expressed as a percentage (i) of the unit cost (c). The economic order quantity then becomes:

$$Q = \sqrt{\frac{2(D)c_o}{(i)(c)}}$$

Note that the order quantity (Q) will increase as the per-unit cost (c) decreases as a result of quantity discounts. Unfortunately, however, the new increase order quantity of

$$Q = \sqrt{\frac{2(D)c_o}{(i)(c_d)}}$$

Where c_d = price with discount
$c_d < c$

is often less than the minimum order quantity required to enjoy the discount. If this is the case, then we must consider the total yearly product cost in addition to the total yearly inventory cost in order to determine the optimal order quantity. The following procedure will yield that optimal order quantity when considering quantity discounts:

Step 1: Compute the total yearly cost; this is the total of inventory and product costs for the lowest quantity at each price break.

Step 2: Calculate the EOQ for the lowest unit price.

Step 3: If the EOQ is feasible, that is, if it is in the range for that price, then calculate its total yearly cost (inventory and product cost). The optimal quantity is the amount that yields the smallest total yearly cost among the ones calculated in Step 1 and 3. Go to Step 4 if the EOQ is not feasible.

Step 4: Calculate the EOQ for the next higher unit price.

Step 5: Repeat Steps 3 and 4 until the optimal quantity is defined in Step 3.

This five-step procedure is illustrated with an example using a small hardware store.

An Example: Quantity Discounts for the Small Hardware Store

Cases of hardware are ordered by a local hardware store and sold at a constant rate of 25 cases per month. The hardware cases that contain nuts and bolts are bought by the store at an approximate price of $21, depending on the order size. To be exact, the following prices are quoted by the manufacturer: the price is $20 if more than 75 cases are ordered; $20.50 for 51 to 75 cases; $21 for 26 to 50 cases, and the base price is $21.50 if fewer than 26 cases are ordered. It costs the hardware store $16 to place an order, and the inventory carrying cost is 20 percent of the dollars invested in inventory.

The economic order quantity for the hardware store will be derived with the following data:

Annual Demand: $D = 300$ cases (25 cases per month)
Ordering Cost: $c_o = \$16$ per order
Capital Cost: $i = 20$ percent $= 0.20$
Base Price: $c = \$21.50$ per case (for $0 \leq Q \leq 25$)
First Price Break: $c = \$21$ per case (for $26 \leq Q \leq 50$)
Second Price Break: $c = \$20.50$ per case (for $51 \leq Q \leq 75$)
Final Price Break: $c = \$20$ per case (for $76 \leq Q$)

Now the optimal order quantity is defined through the five-step procedure. We first compute the total cost (inventory and product cost) for the lowest quantity at each price break.

$$TC = c(D) + c_o\left(\frac{D}{Q}\right) + i(c)\left(\frac{Q}{2}\right)$$

Where: $c(D)$ = yearly product cost
$c_o(D/Q)$ = yearly ordering cost
$i(c)(Q/2)$ = yearly holding cost

Use above equation for all three price breaks at their lowest acceptable quantity. For the first price break with $c = \$21$ and minimum $Q = 26$:

$$TC_1 = 21(300) + 16\left(\frac{300}{26}\right) + 0.20(21)\left(\frac{26}{2}\right)$$

$$TC_1 = \$6{,}539.22$$

For the second price break with $c = \$20.50$ and the minimum $Q = 51$:

$$TC_2 = 20.50(300) + 16\left(\frac{300}{51}\right) + 0.20(20.50)\left(\frac{51}{2}\right)$$

$$TC_2 = \$6{,}348.67$$

For the third price break with c = \$20 and minimum Q = 76:

$$TC_3 = 20(300) + 16\left(\frac{300}{76}\right) + 0.20(20)\left(\frac{76}{2}\right)$$

$$TC_3 = \$6{,}215.16$$

Note that the total cost is the lowest for the third price break.

According to the second step we now calculate the EOQ for the lowest unit price, or the third price break, of \$20 as follows:

$$EOQ = \sqrt{\frac{2(16)(300)}{0.20(20)}}$$

$$Q = 48.99 \ or \ 49 cases$$

This EOQ is not feasible since it is not in the range for that price (Q must be larger than or equal to 76). Therefore we now proceed with the next higher unit price to calculate the EOQ (c=\$20.50):

$$EOQ = \sqrt{\frac{2(16)(300)}{0.20(20.50)}}$$

$$Q = 48.39 \ or \ 48 cases$$

Again, this optimal quantity is not within the range for that price ($51 \leq Q \leq 75$). So we must continue our EOQ calculation for the next price break (c = \$21):

$$EOQ = \sqrt{\frac{2(16)(300)}{0.20(21)}}$$

$$Q = 47.81 \ or \ 48 cases$$

Since the EOQ of 48 cases is feasible for the price of \$21 ($26 \leq Q \leq 50$), its total yearly cost must be calculated (step 3):

$$TC = 21(300) + 16\left(\frac{300}{48}\right) + 0.20(21)\left(\frac{48}{2}\right)$$

$$TC = \$6{,}500.80$$

The total yearly cost of \$6,500.80 is larger than the lowest total cost of \$6,215.16 previously calculated for the third price break. The optimal order quantity is therefore the quantity that yields a \$6,215.16 total yearly cost, or 76 cases. Thus, the manager of the hardware store must order 76 cases each time an order is placed at a cost of $20 per case. The yearly inventory cost will be:

$$C = 16\left(\frac{300}{76}\right) + 0.20(20)\left(\frac{76}{2}\right)$$
$$C = \$215.16$$

6. ECONOMIC PRODUCTION QUANTITY (EPQ)

In manufacturing situations, inventory grows as a result of production. When inventory reaches zero, management decides to replenish inventory by producing a new batch. As goods are produced, they are placed in inventory and customers then draw units from that inventory. This situation is, of course, only possible when the production rate is at least as large as the demand rate. When the production rate (p) is larger than the demand rate (d), then inventories will increase during the production cycle. The objective of the economic production quantity model is to establish the optimal production lot size under the following basic assumptions:

- Demand is deterministic
- Demand rate is a constant at a daily rate equal to d
- Goods are produced at a constant production rate equal to p
- The production rate is larger than the demand rate ($p>d$)
- Inventory is replenished over a fixed production period (t) at a rate equal to the production rate minus the demand rate ($p - d$)
- Production lot size or batch size is constant (Q)
- There is a constant per-unit holding cost and a constant set-up cost
- No shortages are allowed

By using these assumptions, the production quantity inventory model can be drawn and appears as shown in Figure 11.8.

We now proceed in a fashion similar to the EOQ model procedure. First we will discuss the changes in the inventory level. Then the yearly inventory cost is derived using production change or set-up cost and holding cost. Finally, the economic production quantity is defined.

6.1 Inventory Level

There are two distinct phases in the economic production inventory model (EPQ). During the first phase, the inventory level increases linearly during the production period (t). It increases at a rate of ($p - d$), the production rate minus the demand rate, until it reaches a maximum level of I_m. We can define the maximum inventory level (I_m) as a function of the production rate (p), the demand rate (d), and the production period (t). According to geometry, the slope ($p - d$) equals the rise (change in inventory or height, I_m) divided by the run (change in time, t):

$$(p-d)=\frac{I_m}{t}$$

Where: p = production rate
d = demand rate
I_m = maximum inventory level
t = production period

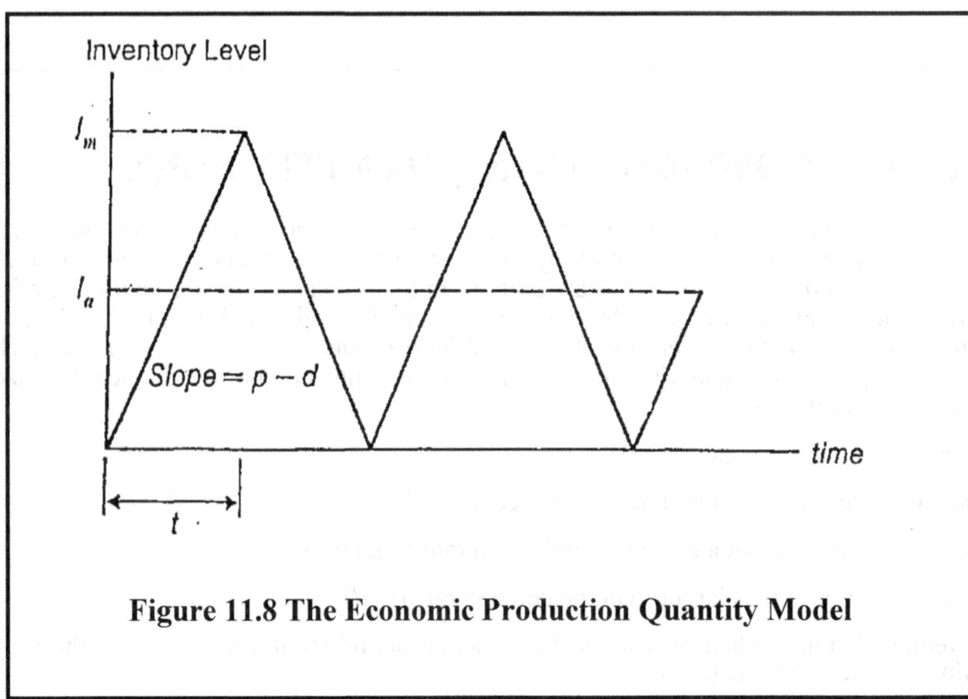

Figure 11.8 The Economic Production Quantity Model

Since the length of the time (t) to produce a lot of size Q equals the production quantity (Q) divided by the production rate (p), the maximum inventory is now:

$$I_m=\frac{Q}{p}(p-d)$$

Once the inventory level has reached its maximum, it decreases at a rate equal to the demand rate (d) until the inventory equals zero. During the second phase no goods are produced while inventory reduces. Because the inventory level changes linearly from zero to I_m (maximum inventory), from I_m to zero, and so on, the average inventory equals half of the maximum inventory.

$$I_a=\frac{I_m}{2}$$

Substituting I_m for the equation as defined above, we can redefine the average inventory:

$$I_a=\frac{Q}{2}\left(\frac{p-d}{p}\right)=\frac{Q}{2}(1-\frac{d}{p})$$

This average inventory will be used later to define the yearly holding cost.

6.2 Yearly Inventory Cost

The yearly inventory cost for the economic production quantity model consists of the **yearly production change**, or *set-up*, **cost (C_p)** and the **yearly holding**, or ***carrying*** **cost (C_h).** The yearly production change cost occurs when the equipment changes for the production of a different product. This may entail costs such as changing dies on machinery, obtaining necessary materials, clearing the area of all previous stock, filling out papers, and performing other administrative duties, such as laying off workers, and allowing for temporary work stoppage. Production change, or set-up, cost affects inventory models when inventories are generated by in-plant manufacturing. In some industries, extensive or expensive production changes will result in high set-up costs. The greater this cost, the fewer the changes are made and the larger the size of the production run is. This, of course, results in larger inventories. Consequently, if the production change cost is low, many small lots of goods can be produced, thus reducing the inventory. The yearly production change, or set-up, cost (C_p) is defined in a fashion similar to the yearly ordering cost (C_o), as follows:

$$C_p = c_p\left(\frac{D}{Q}\right)$$

Where: c_p = average setup cost
D = yearly demand
Q = production lot size
D/Q = number of setups per year

If one plots the yearly production change cost as a function of the production lot size, then a plot similar to the one drawn in Figure 11.6 will be obtained. If the yearly holding cost is a function of the average inventory, then, using the average inventory formula, the yearly holding cost is:

$$C_h = c_h\left(\frac{Q}{2}\right)\left(1-\frac{d}{p}\right)$$

Where: p = production rate
c_h = per-unit yearly holding cost
d = demand rate

Putting these two equations together, the yearly inventory cost (C) is as follows:

$$C = c_p\left(\frac{D}{Q}\right) + c_h\left(\frac{Q}{2}\right)\left((1-\frac{d}{p}\right)$$

6.3 Optimal Production Quantity

Similar cost functions of the yearly setup cost and the holding cost can be drawn as for the EOQ model in Figure 11.7. As in the EOQ model, the yearly inventory model for the EPQ model is minimized when the yearly setup cost equals the yearly holding cost:

$$c_p\left(\frac{D}{Q}\right) = c_h\left(\frac{Q}{2}\right)\left((1-\frac{d}{p}\right)$$

This equation can now be solved for Q, yielding:

$$EPQ = Q = \sqrt{\frac{2(D)c_p}{c_h\left(1-\frac{d}{p}\right)}}$$

Calculus can also be used to derive the EPQ formula. The EPQ formula can also be used when ordered goods arrive in small shipments at a daily rate of p units per day. Note the similarity between the EOQ and the EPQ formulas!

An Example: Alpha Corporation Making Refrigerator Parts

The Alpha Corporation manufactures refrigerator parts at a rate of 500 pieces per month. These parts are delivered to Philco Ford Corporation at a constant rate of 100 units per month. The direct and indirect costs, including labor and material, total $62.50 per piece. The carrying costs are estimated to be equal to 20% per year. Each time Alpha Corporation sets up the equipment to manufacture a batch of these parts, it encounters a set-up, or preparation, cost of $60. What is the optimal production quantity for Alpha Corporation, so that its inventory cost is kept to a minimum?

There are two basic costs that will affect the optimal order quantity: the setup cost and the per-unit yearly holding cost. The setup cost is defined as $60 and is a fixed cost, independent of the production quantity. The per-unit yearly holding cost equals 20% of the capital investment in one unit of the product and is, therefore, $12.50 ($62.50 x 0.20). the economic production quantity can now be derived with the following data:

Annual Demand:	D = 1,200 pieces (100 per month)
Setup Cost:	c_p = $60 per setup
Holding Cost:	c_h = $12.50 per unit and per year
Demand Rate:	d = 100 pieces per month
Production Rate:	p = 500 pieces per month

The economic production quantity is now calculated as follows:

$$EPQ = Q = \sqrt{\frac{2(D)c_p}{c_h\left(1-\frac{d}{p}\right)}}$$

$$= \sqrt{\frac{2(1{,}200)60}{12.50\left(1-\frac{100}{500}\right)}}$$

$$= 120 \text{ pieces}$$

The economic production quantity of 120 pieces can be manufactured in approximately one week:

$$t = \frac{Q}{p} = \frac{120}{500} = 0.24 \text{ months (one-quarter month)}$$

At the end of the production period of approximately one week (120/500 = t) the inventory has reached its maximum of 96 units:

$$I_m = (p-d)t$$

$$= (500-100)\frac{120}{500}$$

$$= 96 \text{ units}$$

The total inventory cost for Alpha Corporation is:

$$C = c_p\left(\frac{D}{Q}\right) + c_h\left(\frac{I_m}{2}\right)$$

$$= \$60\left(\frac{1{,}200}{120}\right) + \$12.50\left(\frac{96}{2}\right)$$

$$= \$1{,}200$$

Note that the yearly set-up cost $\left[\$60\left(\frac{1{,}200}{120}\right)\right]$ equals the yearly holding cost $\left[\$12.5\left(\frac{96}{2}\right)\right]$.

7. LEANING IN-PROCESS INVENTORY

The Japanese were the first to define **waste**, or ***muda***, in context of inventory. Some examples of muda as it relates to inventory and materials include: mistakes requiring rework, production of items without immediate orders that create excessive in-process inventory; unnecessary processing steps or movement of employees, material, or inventory; keeping inventory longer in the production system; waiting for materials; and any good or service that does not meet the needs of the customer.

Some of our currently accepted production methods, like batch production and mass production, produce a great amount of waste. Mass production calls for the production of a large volume of goods without immediate orders, using large machines with large queues and wait times, pushing large amounts of finished goods towards their end customers. In a mass production system one normally produces in large production quantities because it takes a large effort or cost to set up equipment. Batch production on large machines with expensive set-up cost slows the production throughput, creating enormous in-process inventory.

Change in companies that utilize mass production is slow because master production schedules are created months before the product is produced, and any down time is unacceptable because standard cost accounting states that a machine must be operating for as long as possible to get the best cost out of it, leading to massive amounts of over-production—yet more inventory muda. Lean is the answer to mass and batch production.

Lean principles, such as ***inventory waste reduction***, require a pull system, with significant reduction in batch or lot sizes. When optimized production technology, OPT, was introduced as a preferred pull system it was argued that more frequent set-ups that need to occur when decreasing batch size will have no significant effect on the total yearly set-up cost. The initial argument used was that most companies are overstaffed with production set-up workers and an increase in the number of set-ups will absorb the overstaffing and force the workers to become more efficient. This argument is of course not satisfactory for those companies that utilize proper staffing models so as not to overstaff any of their functions. The correct argument, however, is found in the equilibrium between the yearly set-up cost and the yearly inventory holding cost. Let us revisit the simplified EPQ model, where inventory is being pulled at a rate of d, while being produced at a rate of p, with $p>d$. Its yearly inventory cost and its associated economic production quantity equations are:

Yearly inventory cost: $C = c_p\left(\frac{D}{Q}\right) + c_h\left(\frac{Q}{2}\right)\left(1 - \frac{d}{p}\right)$

$$\text{Economic production quantity: } EPQ = Q = \sqrt{\frac{2(D)c_p}{c_h\left(1 - \frac{d}{p}\right)}}$$

Where: C = yearly inventory cost
c_p = production change, or setup, cost
D = yearly demand
p = production rate
c_h = per-unit yearly holding cost
Q = production quantity
d = demand rate

A considerable reduction in both EPQ (the economic production lot size) and C (the total yearly inventory cost) demands for a reduction in the per-unit set-up cost, c_p. Theoretically speaking, an increase in the per- unit holding cost, c_h, would also reduce the EPQ, but does not reduce the yearly inventory cost. This, however, would not be considered a lean move, since it would translate into increased cost of product and/or increased cost for holding goods in inventory and an increase in the yearly inventory cost. Cost reduction is lean, cost increase is not lean! So, how can the firm reduce the set-up cost significantly, so that, while batch sizes decrease, they also enjoy a significant reduction in the total yearly inventory cost?

The Japanese were first in attempting to reduce set-up cost. Traditional thinking defines set-up cost as consisting of material cost, equipment cost, tool cost, and labor cost. The labor cost is based on the time it takes to perform a set-up, multiplied by the people involved, and multiplied by their wages. It often far outweighs the other set-up cost elements.

By using set-up reduction techniques, companies have experienced the following lean benefits:

- Lower set-up times
- Ability to do more frequent set ups, thus gaining production flexibility
- Ability to run smaller batches
- Shorter production lead times
- Less in-process inventory
- Implementation of just in time manufacturing and one piece flow
- Cellular manufacturing
- Extra floor space
- Reduced yearly inventory cost
- Added productive time on bottleneck processes, increasing company profits

A significant reduction in machine set-up time is one of the most important pre-requisites for decreasing production batch quantities if the firm wishes to simultaneously minimize its total inventory cost and operate in a lean just-in-time way. Many companies have done a great job in reducing set-up time. One of the authors still remembers when it took more than one day (10 hours to be exact) to set up a Ferguson or a Niagara press in 1968 at Philco Corporation in Connersville, Indiana. Over time the set-up time of a similar type of equipment has been reduced to one hour or less. The Japanese were the first to find ways to reduce set-up time to less than one minute. Where there is a will, there is a way!

So, a significant reduction in set-up time - reducing set-up time to a mere fraction of the old set-up time (for example, less than 5% when reducing set-up time from 10 hours to less than 10 minutes for presses and heavy manufacturing equipment, as initially achieved by the Japanese) - lowers the traditionally defined "set-up cost, c_p". Additionally, a significant reduction in set-up time also gives the company numerous lean benefits that must be used to redefine the "real" reduced "set-up cost, c_p". What needs to be valued to redefine the set-up cost are:

- The value of a decrease in production through-put time, by measuring increased customer satisfaction
- The value of decreased obsolete inventory as a result of a decrease in in-process inventory
- The value of an increase in productive time on bottleneck processes that results in an increase in company profits
- The value of a quicker response of the productive system and its inventory to changes in demand, driving down safety stock

It stands to reason that these savings can be so significant that they could drive the "redefined set-up cost" down to a very insignificant value. Placed in the EPQ model, this cost would yield small production batch sizes. How small will these economic batch sizes be? Nobody really knows until we do the data collection and the math to figure it.

Though the above exposé on lean inventory management and the EPQ model and its associated yearly inventory cost explain the justification for the joint efforts of batch size reduction and reduction in equipment set-up time, it is becoming increasingly difficult to calculate the exact yearly inventory cost and EPQ value. The problem lies in accurately defining the real, nontraditional, set-up cost, c_p, and in the dynamic nature of in-process inventory itself because of variations in demand. Any analytic model, like the EPQ model, is non-dynamic, using constant cost values for its parameters and a reasonable fixed demand. When a company is in the process of driving down set-up time, these inventory characteristics will change.

Perhaps, a reliable method for defining the value associated with the lean inventory benefits of batch size reduction is through the work of the before-mentioned dedicated product teams consisting of members of all functional areas of the organization. While a company is driving down a product's batch size, each member of the team must observe and measure the savings/cost from their perspective. As data is being accumulated, computer inventory simulation—the programmed simulation of real inventory movement and its effect on the lean benefits—can be used to study and define the optimal smaller batch size. This asks for a significant effort, but is nevertheless a reasonable recommendation for defining the appropriate cost effective small batch size.

8. GLOSSARY AND SUMMARY OF METHODS

ABC Inventory System – The ABC inventory system is a system that classifies the inventory into three basic groups (A, B, and C group). The A group represents 10 to 20% of goods and is the high-dollar-volume goods that require closer control than either the B or the C group.

Buffer Inventory – A buffer inventory is created to protect against unpredictable variations in demand and supply. It is also called safety inventory.

Cycle Counting – Cycle counting is the act of physically taking inventory on a regular basis.

Cycle Time (T) –The cycle time is the time that elapses between the receiving of two orders.

Dispatching – Dispatching is the actual release of orders to the responsible areas.

Decoupling Inventory - A decoupling inventory is an inventory that is necessary to properly synchronize various production activities. It is also called in-process inventory.

Economic Order Quantity Model (EOQ Model) – The EOQ model defines the optimal (constant) order quantity using the following basic assumptions: demand is deterministic, demand rate is constant, inventory is replenished instantaneously, lead time (t) is fixed, shortages are not allowed, order or replenishment size is constant (Q), and per-unit holding cost and ordering cost are constant. The equation for the EOQ model is:

$$EOQ = Q = \sqrt{\frac{2 \times D \times c_o}{c_h}}$$

Economic Production Quantity Model (EPQ Model) – The objective of the economic production quantity model is to establish the optimal production lot size under the following basic assumptions: demand is deterministic, demand rate is a constant at a daily rate equal to d, goods are produced at a constant production rate equal to p, production rate is larger than demand rate ($p>d$), inventory is replenished over a fixed production period (t) at a rate equal to the production rate minus the demand rate ($p - d$), production lot size or batch size is constant (Q), per-unit holding cost and setup cost are constant, and shortages are not allowed. The equation for the EPQ model is:

$$EPQ = Q = \sqrt{\frac{2(D)c_p}{c_h\left(1 - \frac{d}{p}\right)}}$$

Fixed Reorder-Point System – The fixed reorder-point system is an inventory system that is controlled by ordering a fixed quantity of units, when the inventory reaches a certain level.

Fixed Time-Interval System – The fixed time-interval system is also known as the optional replenishment system and is a periodic review system. If during the review period the inventory level of an item is less than its minimum level (s), then an order is placed to restore the inventory to its upper level (S). If during the review period, the inventory has not fallen below the minimum level (s), then no action is taken.

Holding, or Carrying, Cost (C_h, c_h) – The holding cost results from placing and keeping goods in inventory. It covers costs such as handling, insurance, taxes, rent, utilities, and capital investment in stocks. The yearly holding cost depends on the average and/or maximum inventory level.

In-Process Inventory – In-process inventory is inventory that is necessary to properly synchronize various production activities. It is also called decoupling inventory.

Lot size, or Cycle, Inventory – Lot size inventory is created to take advantage of the economic order size.

Ordering Cost (C_o, c_o) – Ordering cost occurs when goods are ordered. It covers salaries, wages, postage, and telephone calls and is not a function of the order quantity. Yearly ordering cost is related directly to the number of orders placed per year.

Pipeline Inventory – Pipeline inventory is inventory that is kept to meet demand during transit time.

Procurement Time or Lead Time (t_l) – The procurement time, or lead time, is the time that elapses between placing and receiving an order.

Production Change, or Set-Up Cost (C_p,c_p) – The production change or set-up cost occurs when one changes the equipment for production from one product to another. It covers the cost for changing dies on machines, obtaining necessary materials, cleaning the area of all previous stock, filling out papers, and performing other administrative duties. Yearly set-up cost is directly related to the number of set-ups per year.

Production Lead-Time – The production lead time is often referred to as the manufacturing lead time and is the elapsed time between the release of the production order to the shop floor and the delivery of the final product to the finished goods warehouse. It is the sum of the operation time and the inter operation time.

Quantity Discounts – Customers pay lower per-unit cost when they order larger quantities. This affects the economic order quantity in the sense that it tends to increase the economic order quantity.

Reorder Point (R) – The reorder point is that level of inventory at which it is necessary to place an order.

Safety Inventory – Safety inventory is created to protect against unpredictable variations in demand and supply. It is also called buffer inventory.

Seasonal Inventory – Seasonal inventory is generated when one decides not to change production rates over time for goods affected by seasonal demand.

Two-Bin-Reorder-Point System – The two-bin reorder-point system is also known as the lot-size-reorder-point system. It is a system that controls inventory via two bins. When the first bin is emptied, the second bin, containing the reorder quantity *ROP*, is used to satisfy demand while an order is placed of size *Q*.

9. ACRONYMS

ABC Inventory system with classification of inventory in three basic groups (A, B, and C)

EOQ Economic Order Quantity

EPQ Economic Production Quantity

ROP Re-Order Point

10. REFERENCES

APICS. *Inventory Management Reprints*. Falls Church, VA: APICS, 1986.

Buffa, Frank P. "A Model for Allocating Limited Resources When Making Safety-Stock Decisions." *The Journal of the American Institute of Decision Sciences.* (8, April 1977): 415–26.

Fourre, J. P. "Applying Inventory Control Techniques." *American Management Association Bulletin.* (129, 1969): 1–20.

Goldratt, Eliyahu, and Jeff Cox. *The Goal, Excellence in Manufacturing.* North River Press, Inc.

Hadley, G. and T. M. Whitin. *Analysis of Inventory Systems*. Englewood Cliffs, NJ: Prentice-Hall, 1963.

Hebbar, B. A. and A. R. Brani. "Inventory Control System." *Journal of Industrial Engineering.* (8, February 1976): 41–45.

McLeavey, D. W., and S. L. Narasimhan. *Production Planning and Inventory Control.* Boston: Allyn and Bacon, 1985.

Parsons, James A. "Multi-product Lot Size Determination when Certain Restrictions are Active." *Journal of Industrial Engineering.* (XVII, July 1966): 360–65.

Reed, R., Jr., and W. E. Stanley. "Optimizing Control of Hospital Inventories." *Journal of Industrial Engineering.* (XVI, January-February 1965): 48–51.

Reinfeld, N. V. *Handbook of Production and Inventory Control.* Englewood Cliffs, NJ: Prentice-Hall, 1987.

Rother, Mike, and John Shook. *Learning to See. Version 1.3.* Brookline, MA: Lean Enterprise Institute, Inc., 2003.

Wight, O. W. *Production and Inventory Management in the Computer Age.* New York: Van Nostrand Reinhold Company, 1984.

Wu, Nesa. "Set-up Time Reduction and Lean Shop Floor Control: Accounting for Redefining Setup Cost in the Economic Production Quantity Model." *International Journal of Accounting Information Science & Leadership.* (2, 2008).

11. REVIEW QUESTIONS

1. What is pipeline inventory, in-process inventory, safety inventory, and seasonal inventory?
2. What is the relationship between safety stock and non-deterministic demand rate?
3. What determines the amount of safety stock needed by a company?
4. How does the lot-size or the two-bin-reorder-point system work?
5. Compare the fixed reorder-point system with the fixed time-interval system.
6. Which one of these systems requires a larger safety stock? Explain!
7. How does the ABC inventory system work?
8. Explain how the principles of the ABC inventory system are implemented in the case of the "ABC Book Distributors Inventory Control System."
9. How is the economic order quantity defined?
10. How is the economic production quantity defined?

12. PROBLEMS

Problem #1

A company has a steady demand for 200,000 units per year. To determine the optimal order quantity, the company must consider the following data:

- The order cost is $150, regardless of the order size
- The unit cost to the wholesaler is $1.20 per unit
- There is a $0.08 per unit and per year holding cost
- The interest charge is 16 percent
- Both the interest charge and the holding cost are based on the average inventory level

a) What is the economic order quantity?
b) What is the total annual stocking cost?
c) Given 250 working days per year, what is the time between orders?

Problem #2

Reconsider problem #1 and assume that everything remains the same except that the $0.08 per-unit and per-year is based on the maximum inventory level, rather than on the average inventory level.

a) Derive the economic order quantity formula.
b) What is the economic order quantity?
c) What are the annual procurement cost, the annual holding cost, and the total yearly stocking cost?
d) If the procurement time is exactly 4 days, what is the reorder point (assume that there are 250 working days per year)?

Problem #3

Examine the EOQ and the EPQ formula. If $c_p = c_o$ and if c_h and D are the same in both cases, which formula leads to a larger Q? Why?

Problem #4

Great Lakes Tool Manufacturers have agreed to manufacture certain tools for the Carbide Corporation in lots of 150 pieces. Carbide Corporation, which is next door to Great Lakes Tool Manufacturers, will be supplied with these tools at a constant rate of 7 pieces per day (175 pieces per month under the assumption that there are 25 work days per month). Find out whether the production batch size of 150 pieces is a good choice based on the following data:

- Production speed: 3,000 pieces per month
- Demand: 7 pieces per day (175 pieces per month)
- Production cost: $24 per piece
- Holding cost: 20 percent per year plus $1.25 per piece per year
- Set-up cost: $30 per setup

Problem #5

You are in charge of the inventory control system at Good Samaritan Hospital. Up to now you have been buying packages of surgical gloves at $1.20 per package. However, the supplier proposes to sell gloves for $1.15 per package if you order in quantities of 2,000 or more. Since you use 12,000 packages per year, this means a savings of $600 per year (12,000 x $0.05). However, this may mean larger inventories. Your records indicate that the cost for processing each order is $30 and that the holding cost is 20 percent per year plus $0.06 per package per year.

a) Given this information, do you think it is wise to order in quantities of at least 2,000 packages at a cost of $1.15 per package?

b) Assume that the quantity discount is $1.18 for orders of at least 5,000 packages. What will you do now? Why?

Problem #6

Approximately 36,000 water pipes are sold per year by a major plumbing firm. Its carrying cost is $0.40 per pipe per year, the ordering cost is $111 per order, and the procurement time is one month.

a. What is the optimal order quantity?
b. How many orders will be placed per year?
c. What is the reorder point?
d. What is the annual inventory cost?

Problem #7

Walton Appliance Corporation needs 804 rolls of sheet metal for its yearly operation. There are 240 working days per year. To safeguard against strikes, the company wishes to keep a safety stock that covers 15 days of its needs. The fixed reorder time consists of three days for the preparation and approval of the requisition, one day for transmitting the requisition, two days for processing the order, and five days for delivery. The procurement cost is rather steep and amounts to $80. Each roll costs the company $120. The yearly holding cost equals 20 percent of the average inventory value. For lot sizes of 10, 20, 50, 100, and 200:

a) Calculate the average inventory quantity and average inventory value
b) Calculate the total yearly cost (price and inventory cost) given the following quantity discounts:
    - $120 per unit for orders of 10 units
    - $117.50 per unit for orders of 20 units
    - $115 per unit for orders of 50 units
    - $112.50 per unit for orders of 100 units
    - $110 per unit for orders of 200 units
c) What is the reorder point?

Problem #8

Allison Tool and Die Corporation uses 40,000 widgets per year. These items are purchased from a local supplier, who sells them at $2 apiece. The ordering cost is $45 per order and the yearly carrying cost amounts to 20% of the purchase price. The company is considering buying a machine that can produce these parts at a rate of 400,000 units per year. In this way it will cost the company only $1 a piece, half of what they are paying now. Since the capacity of the machine is ten times larger than the actual need, the widgets will be produced in batches. Each time a batch is produced there is a $36 set-up cost. Allison Tool and Die Corporation will buy the new machine if the total savings (product cost plus inventory cost) for producing this part versus buying it will cover at least one-third of the cost of the machine. The economic life of the machine is eight years. At that time the salvage value will be zero. What is the maximum amount that Allison Tool and Die Corporation should pay for the machine?

Chapter 12

DAILY JOB SCHEDULING AND CONTROL

Traditionally, in many American manufacturing firms, parts have been transported to the next production stage as soon as they were ready, regardless of whether the next process was ready for these parts or not. Similarly, raw materials were released to the shop floor as soon as the first process could process them. In other words, the process occurred "***just-in-case***" the product was needed later on. This total just-in-case system is a typical **push system**: materials and parts are pushed from one process to the next process, regardless of whether they are needed or will be worked on by that next process. This leads to extra inventory being carried because everyone wants to guard against bringing the production line or system to a halt.

Pushing raw materials into a production system based on economic production quantities or based on anticipated demand leads to an enormous buildup of inventory on the production floor. This problem came to a head at the end of 1984, as many companies had very high inventory levels in relation to profits. American businesses have been attempting to reduce such inventory pile-ups, but large fluctuations and serious drops in sales have made this very difficult. The serious downturn of the economy that we experienced during the recession of 2007–2009 has somewhat helped in reducing these inventories.

Over many years American companies have been experimenting with other production/inventory control systems in an effort to reduce inventories. The **just-in-time (JIT)** inventory and manufacturing system developed in Japan has become increasingly popular among American manufacturers. At the vanguard of the US's JIT movement were companies such as John Deere, IBM, Motorola, Eastman Kodak, Hewlett Packard, Apple, and GM, to name a few.

Another revolutionary manufacturing system that has gained great popularity in the U.S. and Western European countries is **optimized production technology (OPT)** developed by Eliyahu Goldratt, an Israeli physicist, and being marketed by Creative Output, Inc.

In this chapter, we will examine the conventional approach to the day-to-day production control for the intermittent, low-to-medium-volume job shop type of operations. This control consists of the following:

1. Assignment of jobs to work centers or machines
2. Sequencing of jobs in each workplace or on each machine
3. Determination of the start and finish times of each job on each machine or work center
4. Conditions for when expediting and de-expediting may occur on the shop floor
5. Management of queues that form as customers or jobs wait for processing

Besides this conventional approach, the alternate, more sophisticated, scheduling technique, called optimized production technology, for controlling low-medium production volume systems is discussed. Finally, the flow control for high volume, repetitive manufacturing systems is presented with emphasis on the Japanese just-in-time production system.

1. TRADITIONAL LOW-MEDIUM VOLUME JOB SHOP SCHEDULING AND CONTROL

Low-medium intermittent production systems produce at ***low-to-medium volume rate*** of products that are based on specific customer orders. Many manufacturing systems, except for a typical job shop type of operation, are neither low-medium nor high volume production systems but a combination of both.

As soon as production planning has identified that certain products need to be manufactured by a certain due date, these plans need to be translated into active operational plans to be executed on the production floor. These active plans include developing master route sheets, loading the jobs in the various work centers, scheduling and sequencing jobs in each work center, and expediting/de-expediting of jobs.

1.1 Master Route Sheet

Master route sheets are developed by a product manufacturing engineer for each part that is planned to be manufactured. A sample master route sheet was introduced in Chapter 4, Figure 4.6. It is derived from information coming from either the operation process chart or the flow process chart as discussed in Chapter 4. For each individual part of an assembly or a product, a route sheet must exist. It shows the sequence of operations, their operation numbers, the departments in which the operations are to be performed, their set up times (if appropriate), and the production time per unit or the production rate. In addition, the master route sheet may also exhibit the acceptable or normal in-between-operation dead or idle time, the kind of raw materials needed, the quantity of these materials needed to produce one unit, worker classification, and acceptable piece rate (if appropriate).

Besides the master routing sheets, workers also need to receive product drawings and specific instructions on quality and process control.

1.2 Work Loading

As soon as the production inventory planning and control department gives the factory the authority to produce and to process parts and products, specific jobs can be allocated to work centers. This allocation of jobs to work centers and commitment of people or machine time to jobs is called **loading (or job shop-, or machine-, or work loading)**. Just like work center or department loads are normally expressed in terms of time, the capacity of each work center is also expressed in terms of time. For example, for a fixed upcoming period of time, say a week, a work center may have 3 days of capacity remaining. In this case already 2 days of capacity have been committed as a result of releasing an order to the shop floor and therefore one can say that a backlog of two days has been created.

Many organizations assign work to workstations regardless of the available capacity. In this sense the company exercises the **infinite loading principle** when releasing work orders to the shop floor. The released work orders merely exhibit what needs to be done, rather than what can be done under normal production circumstances. When the infinite loading principle is used, the load planning reports for various work stations may exhibit a required capacity or a backlog that is larger than 100%. This then in turn may call for temporary capacity adjustments or a change in the master production schedule. Most computerized machine loading systems are infinite loading type of systems. Too often we notice that jobs and materials are released to the shop floor to keep workers working, regardless of whether there are resources or capacity available for downstream processing of these jobs. This then results in bottleneck operations and an enormous buildup of in-process inventory. This often happens when a simple MRP system is used to release orders to the shop floor.

Finite loading systems are concerned with checking prior allocations of capacity to orders, before committing capacity to new orders. The detailed **capacity requirement planning function (CRP)** in MRP II accomplishes this. In this chapter we will also discuss another computerized finite loading system, the Optimized Production Technology system (OPT).

A **Gantt load chart** can be drawn for exhibiting valuable information with respect to relative workloads in the productive system. It may, for example, show that one work center is ***under-loaded*** and that another center is ***overloaded.*** If it is the objective of the organization to level loads in various work centers, then resources, such as labor or capital, can be shifted from the under-loaded center to the over loaded center. A typical Gantt load chart is shown for five jobs and two machines in Figure 12.1.

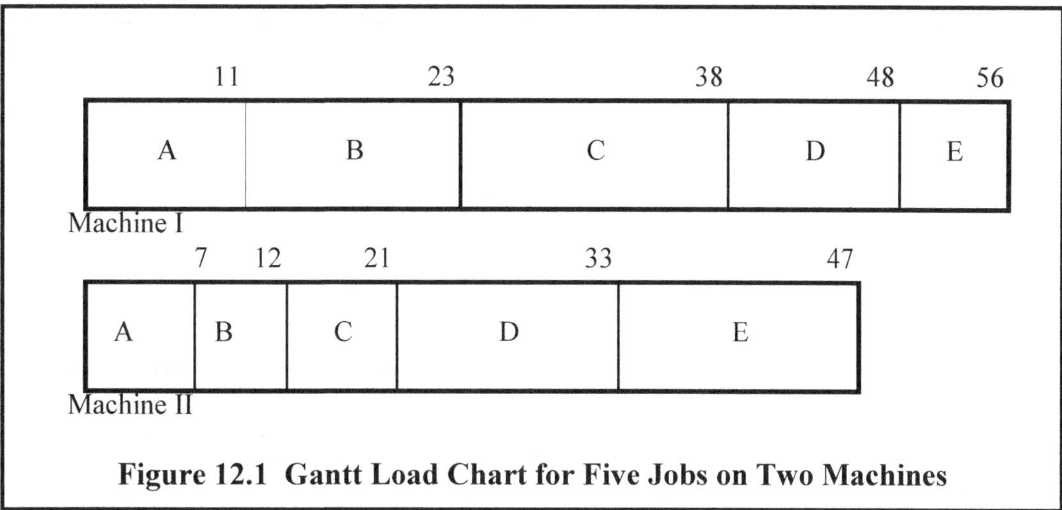

Figure 12.1 Gantt Load Chart for Five Jobs on Two Machines

2. SEQUENCING AND SCHEDULING

Sequencing jobs is defining the order in which jobs will be performed in a work center.

Various sequencing rules can be used to order jobs in the queues of work centers. In selecting a sequencing rule, management is guided by a set of criteria. Some of these criteria are: minimize in-process inventory, minimize average job lateness, minimize average number of the jobs in the system, minimize average job completion or flow time, minimize number of late jobs, *etc.*

Industry has simulated and tested many priority rules in an effort to find the best rule given certain criteria. Some of the most popular sequencing rules used are

1) First-come-first-served (FCFS)
2) Earliest due date (EDD)
3) Shortest processing time (SPT)
4) Critical ratio (CR)
5) Largest dollar value job
6) Largest processing time
7) Random selection
8) Largest number of remaining operations
9) Fewest number of remaining operations
10) Customer oriented priority
11) Shop oriented priority
12) Smallest set-up time

Let us examine some of these sequencing rules by considering five jobs that need to be scheduled on one machine. These jobs, their processing times, and their due dates are shown in Table 12.1.

Table 12.1: Jobs Queuing for Machine I		
Jobs	**Processing Time (hours)**	**Due Dates (hours)**
A	11	15
B	12	22
C	15	30
D	10	15
E	8	40

After scheduling these jobs, the sequencing will be evaluated by calculating the average flow time (to determine the amount of inventory tied up in the system), the average job tardiness, the number of tardy jobs (to evaluate customer service), and the average number of jobs in the system (to evaluate shop congestion and inventory level). Flow time is the time that a job leaves the system and therefore reflects on the total amount of time a job has been in the system. A job is tardy when the flow time is larger than its due date.

2.1 The First-Come-First-Served Sequencing Rule (FCFS)

The first-come-first-serve rule is a customer-oriented rule that is often used in the service industry. Customers join the queue lines in banks, service stations, health centers, post offices, etc. as they arrive in the system. The arrival order determines the service order.

Let us assume that jobs arrive into the system in alphabetical order as listed in Table 12.1. Job sequencing and their scheduling characteristics when using this FCFS rule are then as shown in Table 12.2.

Table 12.2: First-Come-First-Served Sequencing Rule				
Job Sequencing	**Processing Time**	**Due Date**	**Flow Time**	**Tardiness**
A	11	15	11	0
B	12	22	23	1
C	15	30	38	8
D	10	15	48	33
E	8	40	56	16
			176	58

Average Flow Time: $\frac{176}{5} = 35.2$ hr.

Average Job Tardiness: $\frac{58}{5} = 11.6$ hr.

Number of Jobs Tardy: 4

Average # of Jobs in System: $\frac{11\times 5+12\times 4+15\times 3+10\times 2+8\times 1}{56} = 3.14$

2.2 The Earliest Due Date Sequencing Rule

With the earliest due date rule, top processing priority is assigned to the job with the earliest due date. This rule is a good rule if we are concerned with reducing the average job tardiness. However, it does not necessarily generate that sequence of jobs that exhibits the smallest possible average job tardiness.

Applying this rule to our example yields the sequencing and data as shown in Table 12.3:

Table 12.3: Earliest Due Date Sequencing Rule

Job Sequencing	Processing Time	Due Date	Flow Time	Tardiness
A	11	15	11	0
D	10	15	21	6
B	12	22	33	11
C	15	30	48	18
E	8	40	56	16
			169	51

Average Flow Time: $\frac{169}{5} = 33.8$ hr.

Average Job Tardiness: $\frac{51}{5} = 10.2$ hr.

Number of Jobs Tardy: 4

Average # of Jobs in System: $\frac{11 \times 5 + 10 \times 4 + 12 \times 3 + 15 \times 2 + 8 \times 1}{56} = 3.02$

2.3 The Shortest Processing Time Sequencing Rule

The shortest processing time rule is a very popular rule applied in industry for sequencing and scheduling jobs. It minimizes the average flow time (or the average time that a job resides in the system). This rule generates less in-process inventory and therefore creates less shop congestion, as can be measured by the average number of jobs in the system. These characteristics can be viewed in Table 12.4, when applying the shortest processing time rule to the data of Table 12.1.

Note that, as compared to the previous two sequencing rules, this system performs well in terms of average flow time and average number of jobs in the system. In other words, the shortest job sequencing rule controls very well the in-process inventory and tends to reduce shop congestion. However, it does not control tardiness as well as the earliest due date rule does. This rule is normally switched to when the queue is congested with many jobs and smaller jobs have been pushed back in the queue. It is a rule that flushes the system faster than any other rule. Research has shown that workers' productivity goes up when they are given smaller jobs first, rather than larger jobs first. This is perhaps due to the fact that they are happy to see the number of jobs in their station diminishing fast.

Table 12.4: Shortest Processing Time Sequencing Rule				
Job Sequencing	**Processing Time**	**Due Date**	**Flow Time**	**Tardiness**
E	8	40	8	0
D	10	15	18	3
A	11	15	29	14
B	12	22	41	19
C	15	30	56	26
			152	62

Average Flow Time: $\frac{152}{5} = 30.4$ hr.

Average Job Tardiness: $\frac{62}{5} = 12.4$ hr.

Number of Jobs Tardy: 4

Average # of Jobs in System: $\frac{8\times5+10\times4+11\times3+12\times2+15\times1}{56} = 2.71$

2.4 The Critical Ratio Sequencing Rule

The **critical ratio (CR) rule** is a priority rule that calculates a critical ratio ***each time the system is ready to select a job for processing***. The critical ratio for each remaining job in the queue is calculated as follows:

$$CR = \frac{\text{Job Processing Time}}{\text{Due Date} - \text{Today's Shop Date}}$$

The higher the critical ratio is, the more critical the job becomes. So the job that exhibits the largest critical ratio must be scheduled next. It is possible, however, that a critical ratio has become negative. This occurs when today's date is past the due date of a job in the queue, waiting to be processed. In this case that job is already late and should be scheduled promptly in order to avoid further delay. If more than one job has a negative critical ratio, then they must be scheduled in order of their processing time (job with shortest processing time first).

An Example: How does the CR Rule Work?

Illustrated here is how this rather complex dynamic rule, CR, has the advantages of both the earliest due date rule and the largest processing time rule, two elements of the CR formula. The critical ratios in Table 12.5 that are calculated as jobs are being sequenced into the system are shown in Table 12.6.:

- At time T=0 all jobs are candidates for scheduling and their critical ratios (CR1) will determine which job must be scheduled first. All critical ratios are positive and Job A has the largest critical ratio (0.73). Therefore job A is scheduled first.
- If we are ready to select the next job for processing as soon as A is processed (at T=11) new critical ratios for the remaining jobs are calculated. At this time job D exhibits the largest critical ratio (CR2 = 2.50) and is therefore scheduled next.
- Job D is completed at time T=21 (11 + 10). If at this time we are ready to select the next job for processing new critical ratios reveal that job B is next in line for processing (CR3 = 12).
- After B is processed the flow time reaches 33 days (21 + 12). At T=33 new critical ratios for the remaining jobs (C and E) are calculated. Note that now the critical ratio for job C becomes negative (CR4 = –5). Therefore, job C must be scheduled before scheduling job E.

The critical ratio rule performs very well. It not only controls shop congestion well, but also shows excellent customer service. The dynamic nature of the critical ratio rule makes this sequencing rule especially attractive for MRP scheduling, where on a weekly basis schedules are being updated.

Table 12.5: Calculation of Critical Ratios

Jobs	Processing Time	Due Date	$T = 0$ CR1	$T = 11$ CR2	$T = 21$ CR3	$T = 33$ CR4
A	11	15	0.73	---	---	---
B	12	22	0.55	1.09	12	---
C	15	30	0.50	0.79	1.67	-5
D	10	15	0.67	2.50	---	---
E	8	40	0.20	0.28	0.42	1.14

Table 12.6: Critical Ratio Sequencing Rule

Job Sequencing	Processing Time	Due Date	Flow Time	Tardiness
A	11	15	11	0
D	10	15	21	6
B	12	22	33	11
C	15	30	48	18
E	8	40	56	16
			169	51

Average Flow Time: $\frac{169}{5} = 33.8$ hr.

Average Job Tardiness: $\frac{51}{5} = 10.2$ hr.

Number of Jobs Tardy: 4

Average # of Jobs in System: $\frac{11 \times 5 + 10 \times 4 + 12 \times 3 + 15 \times 2 + 8 \times 1}{56} = 3.02$

2.5 Job Sequencing over Multiple Machines or Centers

Realistically speaking, jobs are normally processed through several work centers. Algorithms have been developed and queuing theory has been used to best sequence jobs over several work centers. Some of these procedures are rather complex in nature. Because of the complexity of many algorithms, only one such scheduling rule is presented here, whereas some discussion of **queuing theory** is also discussed in this chapter. Here we will examine the algorithm that can be applied to the assignment of jobs to two work stations. **Johnson's algorithm** provides for minimizing the overall throughput or flow time of all jobs in a two-work center system. The procedure using Johnson's algorithm or rule is as follows:

Step 1: List the processing times of all jobs in two columns: the first column is for the processing times in work center I and the second column contains the processing times for work center II.

Step 2: Identify the smallest processing time.

Step 3: If the smallest processing time is for a job in work center I, then that job is scheduled next. If the smallest processing time is for a job in work center II, then that job is scheduled last or before the last scheduled job. Ties in processing times, and thus job order selection, can be resolved by looking at the processing times in the other work center. Remember that the first work center favors smaller times, while the second work center favors larger times.

Step 4: Eliminate the job just scheduled from the listing and return to step 2. Repeat the steps until all jobs have been scheduled.

Table 12.7: Data for the Two Work Centers/Five Jobs Sequencing Example (see Figure 12.1)

Jobs	Processing Time Work Center I	Processing Time Work Center II
A	11	7
B	12	5
C	15	9
D	10	12
E	8	14

An Example: Illustration of Johnson's Scheduling Job Sequence Algorithm or Rule

Our two-work-centers/five-jobs example (Figure 12.1) is used to illustrate Johnson's rule. Table 12.7 summarizes the data needed for this sequencing problem.

Step 1 of the algorithm requires one to list the processing times in two columns. (See Table 12.7).

Step 2 asks for the identification of the smallest time. The smallest time is 5 hours to process job B in work center II. Since this is a processing time in work center II, step 3 calls for assigning job B to the last slot of the sequence, or job B will be fifth in the queue.

After eliminating job B from the list, the next smallest processing time is 7 hours, the processing time for job A in work center II. Therefore, job A will be assigned before the last scheduled job, or it occupies the fourth slot in the queue.

Again that job is eliminated from the list before identifying the next smallest processing time. The next smallest processing time is 8 hours. It belongs to job E for work center I. Because this is a processing time that belongs to work center I, the job will be scheduled next, or Job E takes the first slot in the queue.

Continue with the steps for the two remaining jobs, job C and job D. Job C has the smallest processing time of 9 hrs. This time belongs to processing center II. So job C will be scheduled before the last scheduled job, or it occupies the third slot in the queue.

The last job D will occupy the remaining slot or slot #2.

Therefore the sequencing of these five jobs is as follows:

Position 1: Job E
Position 2: Job D
Position 3: Job C
Position 4: Job A
Position 5: Job B

There are numerous sequencing rules, some simple ones, and some that are very complex. Sequencing rules are not always dependent on processing time, or due dates, or a combination thereof. Consider the following two scenarios:

- If set up cost varies and largely depends on the previous operation performed on the machine, then the sequencing algorithm may consider this variable cost as a viable parameter in determining the next job to be processed.
- As patients are being sequenced from the emergency room to other departments such as X-ray, blood work, and admitting, certain priority rules may apply that pre-empt non-emergency patients. This would require good coordination between various departments in a hospital, a situation that is not always the case.

2.6 Scheduling

After loading and sequencing jobs in work centers, it is time to identify for each job a starting time and a finish time for processing in these work centers. Scheduled jobs can also be shown in a Gantt chart. Reconsider, for example, the two-work-centers/five-jobs sequence as defined in the previous section. A schedule for these jobs is shown in Table 12.8.

Table 12.8: Start/Finish Times for the Two-Work-Centers/Five-Jobs Problem

Job Sequence	Work Center I			Work Center II		
	Processing Time	Start Time	Finish Time	Processing Time	Start Time	Finish Time
E	8	0	8	14	8	22
D	10	8	18	12	22	34
C	15	18	33	9	34	43
A	11	33	44	7	44	51
B	12	44	56	5	56	61

Carefully go through Table 12.8 and you will notice the following:

- Jobs are scheduled based on the sequence developed in the previous section, using Johnson's scheduling job sequence algorithm.
- In work center I, jobs can be scheduled one after the other without delay. In other words, as soon as one job is finished, the next job can be scheduled.
- In work center II, jobs cannot necessarily be scheduled one after the other without delay. For example, when job C is finished in work center II (at 43 hours into the schedule), the next job, job A, starts in work center II an hour later (at 44 hours). This is because work center I releases job A after 44 hours. Thus work center II is not utilized here for the duration of one hour.
- Also, not all jobs arriving in work center II are immediately being processed by work center II. For example job D arrives after 18 hours in work center II and needs to wait for 4 hours in the queue before being processed in work center II (22 hours – 18 hours).

What Johnson's sequencing rule has accomplished are:

- Minimized throughput time; no other sequencing rule could finish this task in less than 61 hours
- Minimized in-process inventory or the time that jobs wait in queue to be processed by work center II
- Minimized underutilization of work center II, when this center is idle, waiting for the next job

A Gantt chart can be developed to show visually what is summarized in Table 12.8. It can then be used on a daily basis to monitor production on the shop floor. The Gantt chart in Figure 12.2 for example shows that work center II is idle during the first 8 hours, for 1 hour between 43 and 44 hours, and for five hours between 51 and 56 hours. As jobs are being processed, the Gantt chart can be viewed to determine whether one is behind or ahead of schedule, so that appropriate action can be taken.

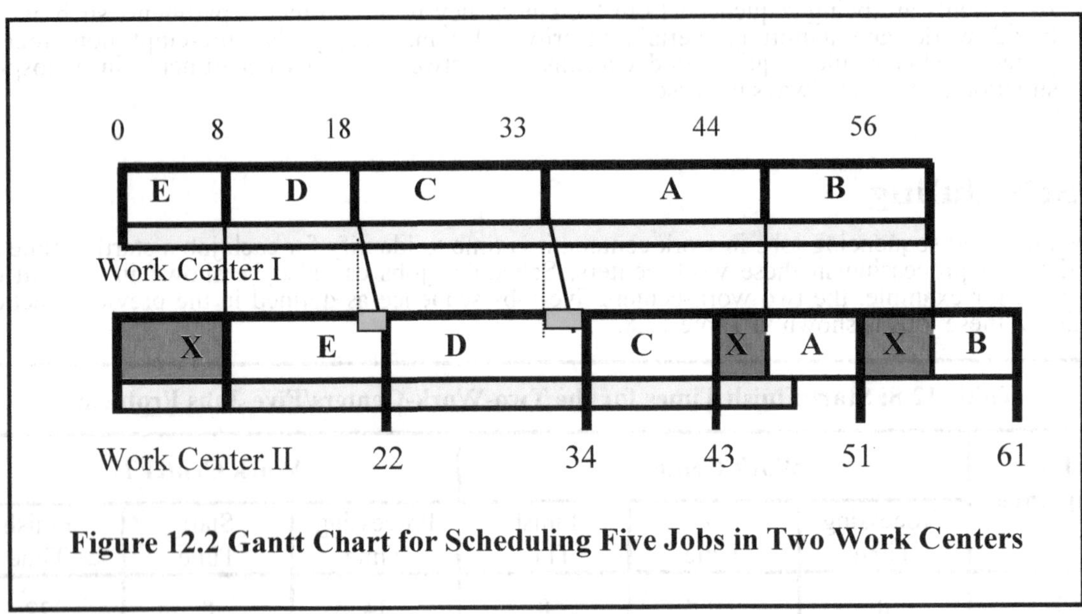

Figure 12.2 Gantt Chart for Scheduling Five Jobs in Two Work Centers

2.6.1 Forward Scheduling

Forward scheduling is a scheduling process that is commonly used in the ***process industries***, the petroleum and chemical industries, and the food processing industry. In this case, a starting date is determined for the first process or operation and all future start times for downstream processes are determined based on capacity availability. In this sense, the due date too is determined by downstream capacity limitations of all future processes or operations.

2.6.2. Backward Scheduling

Backward scheduling is a scheduling technique that is familiar in the ***assembly/subassembly industry***. The scheduling process starts with the expected due date of the product and works back in time to determine the starting times of its subassemblies and in turn the starting times of the parts that go into these subassemblies. This is typically what is done through MRP scheduling. When scheduling jobs, determining their start and finish times for various operations, it is imperative that the system provides for in-between operations allowance time or safety lead time. Computerized material requirement planning systems normally provide for such safety lead times when scheduling jobs.

2.6.3 Expediting/De-expediting

Now that everything is scheduled for processing, one can expect it to happen! But will it happen on time? Perhaps it will; perhaps it will not! Realize that many things can still go wrong. And if things do go wrong, the schedules will be affected likewise. What are the possible problems that may manifest themselves on the production floor? Certain needed materials may not arrive on time, manpower may not be available when needed, machines may break down and need be repaired, priorities may change, orders may get canceled, patients may not arrive on time, doctors may be unexpectedly called for emergencies, etc. Such disruptions call for constantly monitoring the activities. As unexpected disruptions occur, rescheduling of activities will become necessary.

However, as one monitors the status of jobs, it may become apparent that certain jobs need to be expedited. Expediting may occur when the status of a job is not satisfactory. Stock chasers or expediters have the authority to rush certain orders through the system. Such expediting has a significant effect on job schedules, since they delay presently scheduled jobs. It is the objective in business to keep expediting at a very minimum.

De-expediting (or cancelling) occurs when priorities change or when the need for the end job vanishes. It is necessary to de-expedite jobs that presently are not needed any longer. However, industry seems to pay less attention to de-expediting than it does to expediting.

3. *MANAGEMENT OF QUEUING AND WAITING*

Do you recall the last time you went with your family to a fair or an amusement park? You may remember most the frustration of waiting in lines: lines at the entrance, lines at the booths, lines at the rest rooms, lines at the attractions, and even lines at the exits. Perhaps you even left early in the morning, only to discover that many other families had done the same. And there you all were, creeping along in one of several lines that had formed on the tollway to your destination. Inevitably, you wondered whether you had chosen the right lane, since it seemed that all the other lanes were moving faster. Although you would probably describe it in different words, you were in a multiple-server, multiple queue system with apparently unequal rates of service.

Everyone is familiar with waiting lines and situations like the one just described. Waiting lines, or **queues**, consist of "customers" (people in banks, goods on the shop floor, patients in emergency rooms, and so on) who wait for service. They typically arrive in a given queuing system according to a consistent pattern. If a server is available, they need not wait for service. When this is not the case, they must wait their turn, and a queue forms. Queuing management is concerned with the analysis of such waiting lines in an effort to find the best way to manage them so that customers are satisfied and service is rendered at a reasonable cost.

Queues are studied in businesses and organizations in order to define an optimal or satisfactory service level. By optimal service level we mean service that reflects an economic balance between the cost of service and the cost of waiting. However, we often have to be content with a merely satisfactory service level, such as when costs are difficult or impossible to define. What is the cost, for example, of customer's waiting time to a not-for-profit organization? What is the cost of students' waiting time to a university during the purchase of a parking decal? What is the cost of a patient's waiting time in the emergency room of a hospital? In such cases it is more meaningful to develop performance targets.

3.1 Seeking Information about Queues

Consider the general representation of a queuing system shown in Figure 12.3. Customers from a calling population enter the system at a specific rate. Some customers do not enter the system because the system is full and sends customers away (e.g. when emergency rooms are full, patients are sent to other facilities) or because the customer observes a lengthy queue and decides not to wait for service (this type of customer is called a balker). After spending some time in the waiting line a customer may become impatient and leave the system before receiving service (referred to as a renege). The customers who stay in the system are eventually serviced and leave the system.

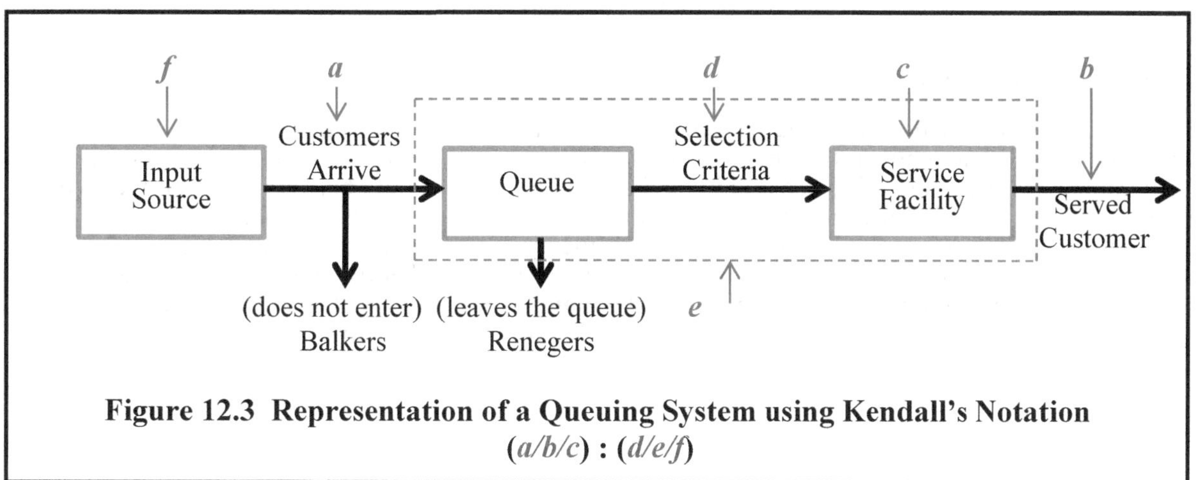

Figure 12.3 Representation of a Queuing System using Kendall's Notation ($a/b/c$) : ($d/e/f$)

Such queuing systems can be studied to answer a range of questions, such as:

- What is the total number of customers/jobs in the system at any one time?
- What is the probability that *n* customers/jobs are in the system at any one time?
- What is the probability that no customer/job is in the system?
- What is the mean arrival rate?
- What is the mean service rate?
- What proportion of time are servers or operators working or what is the utilization factor?
- What is the expected number of customers/jobs in the queuing system?
- What is the expected queue length?
- What is the expected time a customer/job spends in the system?
- What is the expected waiting time a customer/job spends in the queue?

The mathematics behind queuing theory seeks answers to these questions, so that management can design efficient queues. Such designs attempt to reduce the length of time that customers or jobs wait, yet are reasonable in terms of cost for the organization. It is not our intention to present here all the mathematics behind **queuing theory**. However it is important to understand the elements of the system. These will be briefly discussed in what follows.

3.2 Characterization of a Queue

A queuing system can be characterized by the following elements:

a = arrival distribution

b = departure or service distribution

c = number or configuration of servers

d = ervice discipline

e = maximum number of customers allowed in the system

f = *n*umber of possible customers in the calling population

These six characteristics are referred to in Kendall's queuing notation as follows and are identified in Figure 12.3:

$$(a/b/c) : (d/e/f)$$

3.2.1 Arrival Distribution

The **arrival distribution** describes the pattern of customers entering the queuing system. A common assumption about system inputs is that they are Poisson, or random. That is, the number of customers who arrive within a specific time period has a Poisson distribution, and the time between consecutive arrivals (the inter-arrival time) is distributed exponentially. In addition to Poisson arrivals, other arrival distributions that are commonly considered in queuing theory are: deterministic, Erlang (or gamma), and general independent distributions of arrivals. The symbols used to identify specific arrival patterns in Kendall's notation are summarized in Table 12.9. **Balking**, the decision not to join the system due to length of the waiting, line must also be described because it affects the true arrival pattern.

Table 12.9: Arrival and Service Distribution Symbols	
Symbol	**Description**
M	Poisson
D	Deterministic
E_k	Erlang (with parameter k)
GI	General Independent

3.2.2 Service Distribution

The **service distribution** describes the pattern of customer service. As is the case for arrival distributions, many queuing systems are characterized by a service time that is distributed exponentially. Similarly, deterministic, Erlang (gamma), and general distributions of departure are also important service distributions. The symbols used to identify specific service patterns in Kendall's notation are the same as for the arrival patterns and are seen in Figure 12.9.

3.2.3 Number and Configuration of Servers

The number of servers reflects the number of positions from which service is dispensed. Servers can be people (supermarket clerks, bank tellers, doctors, nurses) or machines and equipment (drill presses, airplanes, X-ray machines, beds in a hospital). If there is more than one server in a queuing system, then it is important to know the system configuration, or arrangement, that is, whether they are arranged in parallel or in series. Parallel servers, such as bank tellers, dispense the same type of service at the same time. When servers are in series, then customers must pass by each server in turn. This is the case in a job shop where different machines perform different operations on one part, or in a cafeteria where different foods are served by different servers, or patients who have to be seen by a nurse and a doctor. In Kendall's notation, an integer number (1, 2, 3,..., *n*) is used to identify the number of servers in the system.

3.2.4 Service Discipline

The service discipline describes how customers are selected by the servers from the waiting line. If no priority rules are used, then customers enter the service on a first-come-first-served basis (*FCFS*). Priorities can be preemptive or non-preemptive. Consider the case of a student who calls a professor during office hours by phone. If as a rule, the professor answers incoming phone calls regardless of whether he or she has a student in the office or students waiting outside, then we are dealing with a pre-emptive priority queuing system. Other selection rules are last come first served (*LCFS*), service in random order (*SIRO*), and the general service discipline (*GD*). Typical examples of *LCFS* and *SIRO* selection rules can be found in manufacturing systems where in-process inventories are used by retrieving the goods from the top of the stack (*LCFS*) or are selected from a pool of goods at random (*SIRO*). Some priority rules are based on the size of the job, such as the shortest job first (*SJF*) and the longest job first (*LJF*) rules. Table 12.10 shows some of the most frequently used symbols to identify the service selection discipline in Kendall's notation.

Table 12.10: Service Discipline Symbols	
Symbol	**Description**
FCFS	First-Come-First-Served
LCFS	Last-Come-First-Served
SIRO	Service in Random Order
GD	General Service Discipline
PR	Priority
SJF	Shortest Job First
LJF	Longest Job First

3.2.5 Maximum Number of Customers Allowed in the System

In most cases the number of customers allowed in the system (waiting line plus service facility) is finite because most systems are restricted by size (a doctor's waiting room, a banking area, number of beds in a hospital). Queuing systems that can be very large are often referred to as having infinite (∞) size. For practical purposes, hungry people standing in a food line after a major catastrophe can be seen as having an infinite number.

3.2.6 Size of the Calling Population

The number of potential customers in a queuing system can be finite or infinite. Examples of a finite calling population are machines in a job shop for a maintenance queuing system, potential students for the admissions office queuing system, and the customer base for a dental practice queuing system. When the number of potential customers is very large in relation to the system, then the calling population is infinite.

Some Examples of Queuing Systems Using Kendall's Notation

The notation for the simplest one-server queue stands for Poisson arrivals (M), exponential service time (M), one server, a first-come-first-served discipline (FCFS), and infinite sizes for the maximum number of customers allowed in the system and for the size of the calling population. As an example, consider the arrival of patients at a clinic according to a Poisson process (random arrivals) at an average rate of three patients per hour. At the clinic, patients are seen by one physician according to an exponential service time at an average rate of four patients per hour:

$$(M/M/1) : (FCFS/\infty/\infty)$$

If there are three servers in the system and a maximum of 10 customers are allowed in the system, but everything else remains the same, then the notation becomes:

$$(M/M/3) : (FCFS/10/\infty)$$

Consider a machine shop of 50 machines maintained by four servicers when they break down. Assume that the machines break down according to a completely random process and that the service time is exponentially distributed. A reasonable representation of that system is:

$$(M/M/4) : (FCFS/50/50)$$

A clinic in a major city has 6 doctors who serve walk in patients in the order that they arrive. The system can only hold a maximum of 20 patients at any one time. Patients arrive at random and service time is deterministic. Its representation is as follows:

$$(M/D/6) : (FCFS/20/\infty)$$

3.3 Solving Queuing Problems in Industry

There are four major industries in which queuing theory has been applied: communications, transportation, manufacturing, and service industries. Initially queuing theory was developed for use in the telephone industry. Other communication systems that have employed queuing theory to solve problems are the post office, telegraph, radio, and television systems.

The transportation industry uses queuing theory to solve a variety of problems: for traffic delays at toll booths, for air terminal queues, and air traffic.

The most fertile area for application of queuing theory is no doubt the manufacturing industry. Here, queuing theory is utilized to solve problems of machine interference, maintenance, parts dispensing in tool cribs, assembly line balancing, job shop scheduling, inventory control, and many other applications. Here follow some of the questions answered using queuing theory in manufacturing. How many machines should be placed under the care of one setup worker? How many maintenance people must be assigned for plant maintenance? How many people must operate the tool crib? What is the optimal amount of material handling equipment?

The application of queuing theory in the service industry dates back to the 70s, when applications developed in hospitals, the criminal justice system, banks, and other service centers. Computer scientists, too, are heavy users of queuing theory

One of the most important developments for practitioners, or users, involves the use of simulation to analyze queuing problems. It is often the only method for analyzing waiting line problems when inter-arrival and service times are not uniform or in conformity with standard distributions used in queuing theory.

3.4 The Mathematics of the Most Popular Model

Mathematically, the simplest and most commonly useful arrival pattern is the complete random, or Poisson, arrival pattern. Arrivals are Poisson-distributed if the probability of an arrival in one interval is not affected by arrivals at other times. The mean arrival rate is defined as λ. Furthermore, queuing mathematics can be simplified if the service time can be represented reasonably well by an exponential distribution with a mean service rate of μ. With these distributions, the most popular model is:

$$(M/M/1) : (FCFS/\infty/\infty)$$

It represents the model where customers arrive at random, are served on a first-come-first-served basis by one server with a service time that is exponentially distributed. The queuing system is drawing from an infinite population and accepts all arriving customers in the system.

Rate diagrams are used to analyze steady-state queuing systems with random arrivals and exponential service times. A system is in steady state if, for each state of the system, the mean rate of entering incidence equals the mean rate of leaving incidence. The steady-state relationships for a system can be expressed by the use of a balance equation:

Mean Rate of Entering State n = Mean Rate of Leaving State n

For example, consider the **(M/M/1) : (FCFS/∞/∞)** system that can be represented by the rate diagram as shown in Figure 12.4. This diagram represents all data of the system. It consists of an infinite number of states as represented by the different nodes. The system can be in state zero (as indicated by node 0), meaning that there are no customers in the system. It can be in state one (as indicated by node 1), meaning that there is one customer in the queuing system, and so on. Movements from one state to another are shown by an arrow. Arrivals are normally shown on top, while departures are shown on the bottom.

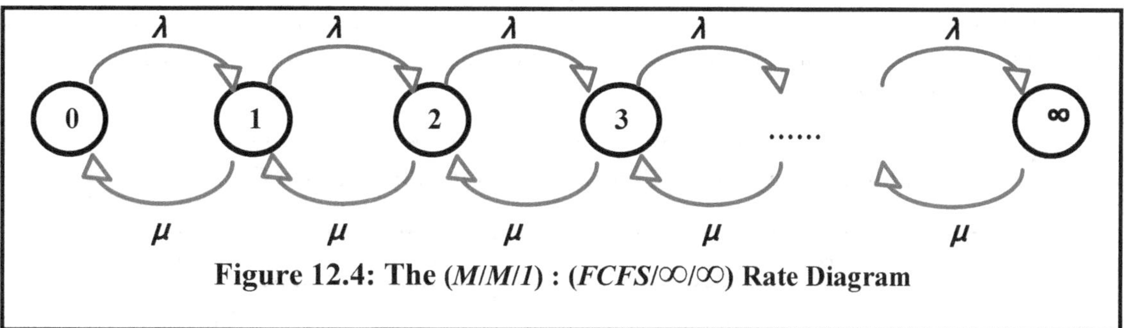

Figure 12.4: The (M/M/1) : (FCFS/∞/∞) Rate Diagram

For each state of the system we can now write the balance equation that shows that the mean rate of entering a state equals the mean rate of leaving the state. For example, consider the construction of the balance equation for node 2 or state 2. The system can go from state 1 (one customer in the system) to state 2 (two customers in the system) at a mean rate of λP_1, and it can go from state 3 (three customers in the system) to state 2 at a mean rate of μP_3. Therefore, the mean rate of entering state 2 is $\lambda P_1 + \mu P_3$. Similarly, the system can go from state 2 to state 1 at a mean rate equal to μP_2, and it can go from state 2 to state 3 at a mean rate equal to λP_2. Consequently the mean rate of leaving state 2 equals $\lambda P_2 + \mu P_2$, and the balance equation for state 2 is therefore:

Mean Rate of Entering State 2 = Mean Rate of Leaving State n

$$\lambda P_1 + \mu P_3 = \lambda P_2 + \mu P_2$$

Balance equations can be established for all states of the system to compute steady-state probabilities. Once steady state probabilities (P_i for $i = 0, 2, 3, \ldots, \infty$) are defined, all other characteristics of interest of the system can be computed. For our popular queuing model these characteristics are listed in table 12.11. Note that for this model they are all expressed in terms of λ (the arrival rate) and μ (the service rate).

Table 12.11: Queuing Characteristics for (*M*/*M*/1) : (*FCFS*/∞/∞)

Description	Formula
Mean arrival rate	λ
Mean service rate	μ
Utilization factor	$\rho = \lambda / \mu$
Probability of no customers in the system*	$P_0 = 1 - \rho$
Probability of *n* customers in the system*	$P_n = \rho^n(1 - \rho)$
Expected number of customers in the system: ($= \sum nP_n$ for n= 0, 2, 3…∞)*	$L = \lambda / (\mu - \lambda)$
Expected waiting time in the system	$W = L / \lambda$
Expected waiting time in the queue only	$W_q = W - (1/\mu)$
Expected queue length	$L_q = \lambda W_q$

* These calculations are shown in Appendix A

An Example: Patients Being Served in a Walk-In Clinic

Let us assume that patients arrive at the clinic according to a Poisson process at an average rate of three patients per hour. At the clinic patients are treated by one physician according to an exponential service time at an average rate of four patients per hour. Table 12.12 summarizes the queuing characteristics of this system.

Table 12.12: Queuing Characteristics for the Walk-In Clinic

Description	Formula	Value
Mean arrival rate	λ	3 per hour
Mean service rate	μ	4 per hour
Utilization factor	$\rho = \lambda / \mu$	0.75
Probability of no customers in the system	$P_0 = 1 - \rho$	0.25
Expected number of customers in the system	$L = \lambda / (\mu - \lambda)$	3 patients
Expected waiting time in the system	$W = L / \lambda$	1 hour
Expected waiting time in the queue only	$W_q = W - (1/\mu)$	0.75 hours
Expected queue length	$L_q = \lambda W_q$	2. 25 patients

3.5 Tools for Reducing Waiting Lines and Improving Flow

5Ss, value stream mapping, kaizen, Six Sigma projects, and other lean tools can be used to reduce waiting lines. Consider the following example, where the problem is complex, yet the approach in finding a solution is rather straight forward.

An Example: The Case of Improving the Patient Flow in the Emergency Department[1]

This example narrates a project a hospital undertook to reduce the wait time and thus improve the flow of patients through its emergency department.

A critical element in the operations of any hospital emergency department (ED) is the efficient flow of patients from the time of entry into the department until final disposition out of the department. There are numerous reasons why this patient flow process is so important not only to the ED, but to the entire hospital operations. Effective patient flow affects the patients' clinical outcomes, the financial health of the institution, the hospital's community relations, and the satisfaction level experienced by the consumers of services rendered. It is therefore important that the hospital leadership supports a project designed to facilitate the effective, timely patient flow process in the ED.

While this patient flow occurs in the ED, it is highly impacted by departments and services outside of the ED. This dependence on other departments is a major challenge in establishing systems and processes to positively impact the ED patient flow. Conducting the improvement project is especially challenging because often the departments and services that impact the ED report structurally via separate clinical and administrative leadership lines.

Therefore, the executive and medical staff leadership team of the institution needs to demonstrate their expectations that the project to improve patient flow in the ED is supported with effective collaboration among their respective directors.

One organization embarked on the goal of improving ED patient flow. The following is a sample of how this organization achieved a more optimal patient flow outcome, using five steps.

Step 1: Defining the Problem and Appointment of a Project Manager and Team Members

Although many individuals were needed to participate in this process improvement project, one person was given the responsibility to support this interdepartmental and interdisciplinary project in order to maximize timely communication, coordinate strategies, and coordinate periodic assessments and progress/outcomes measurement of this complex project.

Since the ED director already had an understanding of the situation, he was chosen to execute this function and was in a position to implement some of the changes that were identified as steps to take. Along with clinical and administrative leadership and selected staff persons from the different selected areas, this person facilitated the group's discussions and understanding of why ED patient flow was so important. The group was then asked to identify observed problems in achieving a smooth, efficient flow. Medical, nursing, other clinical specialties, and support services staff were included in order to have comprehensive input in the definition of the problem and a listing of obstacles/barriers experienced in the delivery of care and procurement of needed services. It is important to include representatives from all relevant areas because these often have very interdependent functions.

In defining the "why" timely flow of the patients is important, several factors were identified. Among these were the following:

Patient Factors:

- The sooner a patient can be seen by the ED provider, the sooner diagnostic work can begin, followed by the initiation of supportive/therapeutic care, such as emergency medications to stop the progression of a sudden illness (post heart attack, stroke), or medications to relieve pain after an injury or internal problem.
- Expedited care allows the provider to start answering the questions that patients and their families have during emergency situations.
- A timely progression through the ED allows the patient to move to a more comfortable location either via discharge to home or admission to a patient room and regular bed.

[1] Contributed by Mrs. Mayble E. Craig, MS, RN.

Hospital Factors:

- Space: It is projected that an ED patient room can accommodate about 1500 patients per year. But if the flow through the ED is protracted, fewer patients can be accommodated in the same space. An inability to fix the flow problem results in patients not being able to be placed in a room in a timely manner. This has caused some EDs to build more beds and add the associated personnel. Some EDs are landlocked in their space so this expansion is not an option.
- Other EDs have simply resorted to diverting ambulances to other hospitals when their capacity is at its maximum. At this institution, one out of every four arriving by ambulances was admitted. Having ambulances diverted for hours or days was causing the loss of potential admissions to the hospital.
- Finances: Both having to add additional resources (space and personnel) or having to divert ambulances and lose the associated patient revenues have an undesirable impact on the hospital's profit margin.

Community Factors:

- Diverting ambulances from the ED also has undesirable consequences for the community. First, if you're the nearest hospital to an ambulance pick up, not being able to stop at your hospital may add several minutes to their emergency trip. This delays patient and keeps the ambulance team longer on the road thus being less available to another emergency.
- The patient's private doctor or usual attending physician may not have privileges at the hospital the patient has been routed to and/or may not wish to travel the longer distance. Thus the patient is now cared for by providers unfamiliar with their care. In situations of chronic problems, the patient's medical records are not readily available at the receiving hospital and continuity of care may be compromised.

Consumer Factor:

- When rerouting occurs, patients and their families may be sent to a hospital farther away from their home, thus potentially posing a hardship on them for visiting, discharge, etc.

Multiple **examples of barriers/obstacles** were generated by the project participants. They grouped them together by similarity in order to prepare for the next step in developing corrective strategies. (It is important to define the barriers in as much detail as possible to assist in root cause analyses.) Among these barriers were:

- Delay in getting the newly arriving patient onto a hospital stretcher because the stretchers are all already occupied with other patients, which in turn causes a delay in the flow process and causes the ambulance attendants delays in unloading their patient
- Delay in getting the patient to X-ray as well as getting the X-ray results afterwards
- Delay in getting laboratory results
- Delay in getting medical specialists consults
- Delay in getting a bed assignment for those patients being admitted
- Delay in getting the receiving unit nurse to take a report on the patient so the necessary equipment and supplies can be at the bedside upon the patient's arrival on the unit

Step 2: Establishing the Organization of Working Groups

This was accomplished by breaking down the larger group into smaller work teams with interdependent functions. Each smaller group tackled a specific barrier/obstacle and members were kept informed of the progress of the other groups in order to avoid duplication of efforts on specific problems. Some examples of problems addressed by the smaller groups are as follows.

Problem A: Delay in getting the newly arriving patient onto a hospital stretcher
Some problems, like this one, were simple to resolve. With a 12% increase in ED visits in each of the preceding three years, the group documented the need for additional hospital stretchers based on increased ED activity. Besides purchasing more stretchers, the transportation department personnel were charged with returning to the ED any unoccupied stretchers they saw throughout the hospital that were labeled as belonging to the ED.

Problem B: Delay in getting prompt X-rays and laboratory results
The leader of this group was the physician director of the ED. This physician worked with the physicians in charge of radiology and laboratory. Together they established systems that would flag requisitions they received from the ED so that they could be prioritized.

Problem C: Delay in getting a bed assignment for patients being admitted
This group needed a number of departments represented because there were several root causes for this delay that crossed departments. These root causes were examined and corrective strategies were implemented across these departments. Some of the root causes of the delays were as follows:

- Bed control would not assign a bed until the room had been given a "terminal" cleaning. Environmental Services/Housekeeping (EVS) could not begin a terminal cleaning—until the previous patient had been discharged and had left the room.
- Some patients were discharged earlier in the day but had to wait for their families to come for them and they consequently remained in the room oftentimes for hours after the discharge orders had been written.
- The EVS bed cleaning team often received multiple requests for bed cleaning- all with a request for a high priority. Prioritizing the requests was difficult for EVS.

The following initiatives were implemented to alleviate the problems:

- A discharge lounge was established on the first floor. Patients who had been discharged but needed to wait an extended time for their ride home were escorted to this lounge to wait in comfort. The patients rested in large recliners instead of beds. Meals were provided and access to a free hospital phone was available so they could call their families. This lounge was staffed with a nurse from the nursing department.
- Timely vacating of the bed allowed EVS to complete the room's cleaning process and thus make the bed available for another admission in a timelier manner.
- Determining the priorities of bed cleaning was assigned to the nursing supervisor on duty. Not only were ED admissions a priority, but also patients coming out of the post anesthesia care unit (recovery after surgery) were another priority as a backup in this area could impact the patient flow in the operating rooms. Likewise beds were also needed for patients who had presented themselves at the admissions department with their private physician's request that they be readily admitted to their service. The nursing supervisor was in a better position to quickly determine the priority bed assignments for these patient groups.

Problem D: Delay in getting the receiving unit nurse to take a report on the patient who is waiting to come up from the ED
Nurses working in the ED and on the various units are oftentimes extremely busy and trying to coordinate their time. The work on the units was realigned so that one nurse was assigned "admissions" for the shift. Thus this nurse's priority was to get a report from the ED and if needed, go to the ED and assist in bringing the patient up to the unit. This solved the problem of the ED nurse not connecting with a unit based nurse in a timely way to give the unit the patient's report. This process was piloted on five units with positive feedback from the ED and the test units. It became a permanent component of the daily assignments.

Step 3: Implementing Change

Chosen changes were reviewed and process changes were finalized, written up, and distributed to all affected departments/disciplines and measurement tools were developed. Changes were implemented.

Step 4: Training, Updating Procedures, and Sharing Results

Ongoing training was done for existing staff and newly hired orienteers. Departmental policies and procedures manuals were updated with the changes. Results of improved patient flow through the ED were widely shared with the hospital board, the leadership, and the staff.

Step 5: Sustaining the System Implementation

Ongoing measurements of outcomes are being reviewed on a quarterly basis. The director of the ED is charged with continuing periodic status evaluation and processes refinement meetings with key designees from the departments involved in the change process. The goal is to continue supporting ongoing processes improvements and avoid reverting back to previous behaviors of working in "silos" with the associated negative impact on ED patient flow.

A measure of success is the numbers:

- Patient drop time (the time an ambulance patient waits to be transferred to a hospital stretcher) was decreased by 40%.
- Rerouting or ambulance diversion which had been a weekly occurrence has not happened since the improvements were done .This is now the third year without a diversion.
- The overall patient length of stay (LOS) in the ED has been reduced by 50%.

4. OPTIMIZED PRODUCTION TECHNOLOGY SYSTEM (OPT)

4.1 The OPT System

A revolutionary manufacturing control system that has gained significant popularity in the U.S. and Western European countries is optimized production technology (OPT), developed by Moshe Eliyahu Goldratt, an Israeli physicist, and marketed by Creative Output, Inc. OPT is a procedure that schedules work centers based on the finite loading principle. It is a two-part package with a simulated manufacturing program and a set of radical shop-floor management rules. When properly implemented it enables a company to increase output while lowering inventories and expenses.

The simulated manufacturing program in OPT has four basic modules:

1. **Buildnet** – a module that uses the network of all the plant's raw materials, resources, products, and customer orders to create the master production schedule (MPS)
2. **Serve** – a module that locates bottlenecks in the system by running load profiles for each machine and resource
3. **Split** – a module that divides the network into two parts: the non-critical portion and the critical portion that contains the bottlenecks, assemblies, and sub-assemblies
4. **Brain** – a module that contains a proprietary set of algorithms used to schedule the workers, machines, or tools at the bottleneck operations

OPT forces production managers and workers alike to coordinate their work of moving parts through a system with one thing in mind: bottlenecks are what ultimately constrain manufacturing output. By identifying bottlenecks in advance and then scheduling all manufacturing activities with these bottlenecks in mind, productivity can be substantially increased. After all, in any system, the bottlenecks determine what can be produced and when it can be produced.

But, as mentioned above, OPT is a two-part package. The manufacturing simulation is just a tool that can be used by managers to see where bottlenecks occur and how to schedule around them. The other part of OPT, and the more important part, is the actual management philosophy. This philosophy goes against the traditional one which says that productivity is highest when all workers and machines are going full tilt at all times. Traditional accounting methods hold that, from a cost standpoint, it is always better to run a batch of 1,000 parts through a machine than it is to run 100 parts. But if 900 parts are just sitting idle in inventory, then that is not really correct. OPT's philosophy is to process only what can be absorbed by bottleneck machines within a reasonable time period, so as not to build excessive inventory or not to idle bottleneck equipment.

Figure 12.5 illustrates an OPT network manufacturing model. Serve has been run and has identified Machine Center A as a bottleneck. All other machines, shown in blue, are non-bottleneck machines. The Split module then divided the network into critical and non-critical segments. The critical segment contains all bottlenecks, sub-assemblies, and assemblies into which bottleneck parts flow. The brain module used algorithms to determine job sequence, as well as process and transfer batch sizes. Machine center A will be scheduled at 100% utilization with enough inventories stationed by it to ensure that there is always enough work to be done. The rate of production for non-bottleneck machines is determined by the rate the bottleneck machine needs the parts for further processing or the rate the parts of the bottleneck machine needs their parts in sub-assemblies and final assembly.

Of course, the subassemblies will be able to handle the output from machine center A without delay because they are not bottlenecks. However, extra inventories must be placed at these areas to ensure that the product can be rushed through to finished inventory as soon as its parts come off machine center A. In other words, inventory must always be placed before bottleneck operations and between the non-bottleneck operations and assemblies/subassemblies that are fed by the bottleneck operation.

Once the bottleneck machines are identified, production managers can seek to improve the output of these machines. One way of doing this is by decreasing the number of set-ups of these bottleneck machines, thus running larger batch sizes and allowing for more productive time on the bottleneck machines. In-process inventory, however, can be reduced for the whole system by significantly reducing the batch sizes of the non-bottleneck machines. If managed properly, the OPT system is superior to the Japanese just-in-time system, because it focusses on improving throughput, while driving in-process inventory to a very low level.

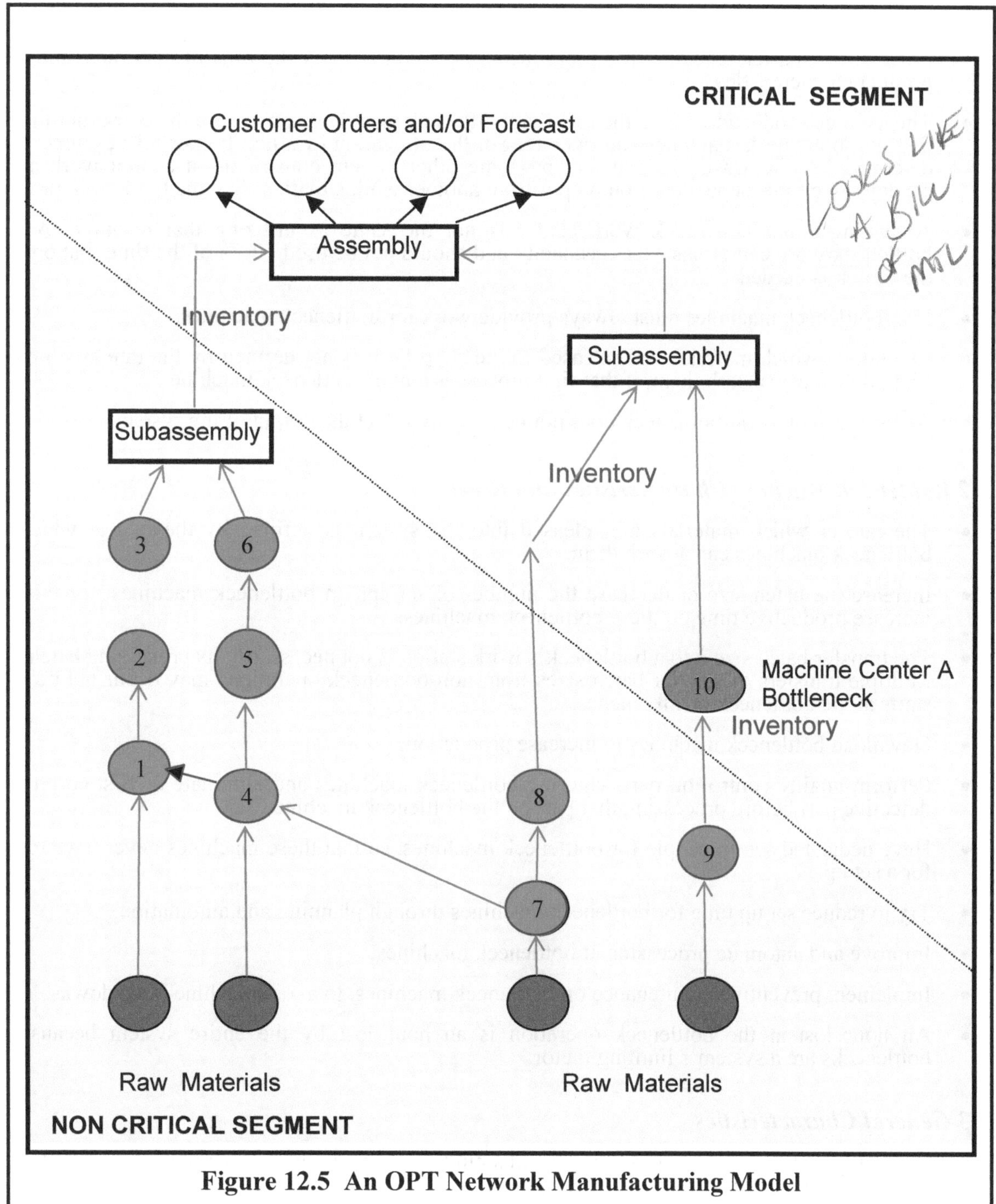

Figure 12.5 An OPT Network Manufacturing Model

4.2 System Characteristics and Summary of Rules

OPT suggests three sets of productivity rules when implementing this finite loading pull system: one set for non-bottleneck machines, another set for bottleneck machines, and a set of general rules governing the system as a whole. These rules can be summarized as follows:

4.2.1 Non-Bottleneck Machine Characteristics and Rules

- Significant reduction in batch size for non-bottleneck machines decreases in-process inventory.
- The process batch size that will change throughout the system is a variable that depends on the process, the master schedule of the products, the complexity of the bills of materials, and other product characteristics.
- The average production rate is the rate that bottleneck machines can absorb the work; not the rate that non-bottleneck machines can operate. So, the utilization of a non-bottleneck resource is not determined by its own potential, but by some other system constraint—it cannot work at full capacity due to its dependence on output from another work situation, like the bottleneck process.
- Activating a non-bottleneck work center is not the same as utilizing that resource. A non-bottleneck work center has excess capacity and should not be used 100% of the time, but only for the time it is needed.
- Non-bottleneck machines must always provide work for bottleneck machines.
- The rate at which materials are released to the shop floor is not defined by the rate at which the first process can absorb them, if that first process is a non- bottleneck machine.
- An hour lost at a non-bottleneck does not necessarily affect the output of the system.

4.2.2 Bottleneck Machine Characteristics and Rules

- The rate at which materials are released into the system is defined by the rate at which the bottleneck machines can absorb them.
- Increase the batch size or decrease the number of set-ups on bottleneck machines, for this will increase productive time on these bottleneck machines.
- The transfer batch size into a bottleneck's work station is not necessarily its processing batch size. Multiple transfers of smaller batch sizes from non-bottleneck operations may occur before work starts at the bottleneck on all batches.
- Download bottleneck machines to increase production.
- Perform quality control on parts entering bottleneck machines and eliminate or first correct any defective part before processing that part on the bottleneck machine.
- Have dedicated set up people for bottleneck machines, so that these machines never have to wait for a set up.
- Try to reduce set up time for bottleneck machines through planning and automation.
- Improve and automate processing at bottleneck machines.
- Implement preventive maintenance on bottleneck machines, to avoid machine breakdowns.
- An hour lost at the bottleneck operation is an hour lost by the entire system because the bottlenecks are a system's limiting factor.

4.2.3 General Characteristics

- Capacity and priority need to be considered simultaneously and not sequentially——output of the entire system must be considered when prioritizing jobs at work centers.
- Murphy is not an unknown and his damage can be isolated and minimized—potential problems can be identified in advance and appropriate actions taken.
- Plant capacity should not be balanced—a balanced plant is theoretically impossible, unless output at each stage is always in the exact same cycle.
- The sum of local optima is not equal to the optimum of the whole. Optimizing throughout at each work center would be sub-optimization on the whole because of bottlenecks. In order to optimize the entire system, it is necessary to sub-optimize some work stations.

An Example: The Two-Products/Four-Operations Manufacturing System

Let us study a simple production system in order to determine for each product the quantities that should be made based on that system's constraints. Consider the manufacturing of two products, product #1 and product #2. Product #1 is an assembly that consists of three parts: W, X, and Y. Part W is a purchased part that costs the company $5 per unit. Part X is a manufactured part. The raw materials cost to manufacture this part is $20. Two machines are used to manufacture X. It takes machine A 15 minutes of processing time, followed by machine C that takes another 10 minutes. Part Y is another manufactured part. Its raw materials cost the company $20 per unit. Two machines are involved in processing this part: it takes machine B 15 minutes per unit, followed by machine C that takes 5 minutes to process it. Assembling all three parts (W, X, and Y) into product #1 takes 15 minutes. The selling price of this product is $90 per unit and the market cannot take more than 100 units per week.

Product #2 is made up of two parts: part Y and part Z. Raw materials of part Y cost $20 per unit. It is processed for 15 minutes on machine B and 5 minutes on machine C. Part Z costs $20 per unit in raw materials and spends 10 minutes on machine A and 15 minutes on machine B. It takes 15 minutes to assemble Y and Z into one unit of product #2. Product #2 sells for $100 and the market cannot take more than 50 units per week.

There are 2400 minutes of production time available per week (5 days, 8 hr. per day, 60 min. per hour) and the company pays $5,000 per week in fixed operating cost. All of the above production data are summarized in Table 12.13.

Table 12.13: Data for the Two Products/Four Operations Manufacturing System

Products:	**Product #1**			**Product #2**	
Selling Price:	$90/unit			$100/unit	
Demand:	100 units/week			50 units/week	
Assembly:	15 minutes/unit			15 minutes/unit	
Operations:	**W**	**X**	**Y**	**Y**	**Z**
Machine C		10 min	5 min	5 min	
Machine B			15 min	15 min	15 min
Machine A		15 min			10 min
Part Cost:	$5/unit (W)	$20/unit (X)	$20/unit (Y)	$20/unit (Y)	$20/unit (Z)

In viewing the data of Table 12.13 we may be tempted to produce as much as we can of product #2, because it yields the largest profit per unit. Unit profit for product #2 is $60 ($100 – $20 – $20), as compared to $45 for product #1 ($90 – $5 – $20 – $20). However, it takes twice as much time to produce product #2 as compared to product #1. The production rate or throughput rate is defined by the slowest operation or the bottleneck operation. On the one hand, all operations for product #1 are balanced: parts are processed and assembled at a rate of one unit every 15 minutes. On the other hand, capacity is not balanced in the manufacturing of product #2: operation B is a bottleneck operation in the processing of parts Y and Z. It is this bottleneck operation that determines the production rate for product #2 at one unit every 30 minutes.

Given an overall production period of one week or 2400 minutes and given the above production rates, 160 units (2400 min./15 min. per unit) of product #1 or 80 units (2400 min./30 min. per unit) of product #2 can be produced or a combination thereof. However, what is the combination that will maximize profits, given the maximum demand constraints of 100 units for product #1 and 50 units for product #2?

A combination of per-unit profit and production rate will determine what and how much to produce, as outlined in the following procedure:

Step 1: Calculate for each product the following ratios:

$$R = \frac{\text{Selling Price} - \text{Variable Unit Cost}}{\text{Constraint units}}$$

Where: Constraint units is the unit production time at the bottleneck operation

Step 2: Produce as much as possible of that product that has the largest ratio; however, do not produce more than its market demand. Thus the quantity that can be produced is equal to the smallest of the following:

1. Weekly demand for that product, or
2. Available production minutes/constraint units

Step 3: If not all available production minutes are allocated in step 2, then the remaining minutes can be used to produce as much as possible of the other product, not to exceed the demand for that product. This procedure can be extended for any number of products and operations.

Applying these three steps to our example we get:

Step 1: The ratios for each of the two products are:

$$R(\text{product } \#1) = \frac{90-45}{15} = 3 \qquad R(\text{product } \#2) = \frac{100-40}{30} = 2$$

Step 2: Product #1 has the largest ratio.

Produce 100 units of product # 1, because it is the smaller of the following two:

1. The weekly demand of 100 units, or
2. The largest amount that the system can produce: 2400/15 = 160 units

Step 3: There is still production capacity left when producing 100 units of product #1. One hundred units use up 1500 minutes (100x15) of the weekly capacity of 2400 minutes. Therefore, there are 900 minutes (2400 – 1500) left. These 900 minutes can be used to manufacture product #2 for a total amount of:

$$\frac{900 \text{ min}}{30 \text{ min (Product 2 constraint units)}} = 30 \text{ units}$$

Now that the optimal production mix is determined, the overall net profit can be figured:

100 units of product #1: 100(90 – 45)	=	$4,500
+ 30 units of product #2: 30(100 – 40)	=	+ $1,800
– operating expenses	=	– $5,000
net profit	=	$1,300

The above profit can only be realized if operation B is 100% utilized, because it is the bottleneck operation of this manufacturing system. Any minute lost on that machine is a minute's worth of production lost that can never be recuperated. This example assumed that the set-up time of any operation, when switching from product #1 to product #2, is zero. Calculations must be adjusted if this is not the case.

5. REPETITIVE MANUFACTURING

Repetitive manufacturing is quite different from job shop manufacturing and processing industries. Repetitive manufacturing deals with ***high volume, standard parts, and relatively short lead times and exhibits repeated production of large run sizes***. Repetitive manufacturing occurs in the automotive industry, the appliance industry, and similar high volume standard manufacturing industries. Some of the basic characteristics of repetitive manufacturing can be summed up as follows:

1. Goods are produced in very large volume
2. Products are highly standardized and have very few options
3. Products produced in a repetitive environment often become the components for other repetitive manufactured products, such as engines for cars, tires and wheels for cars, and condensers for refrigerators
4. Relative to large production times, set up times are small or negligible
5. Relative to large production runs, production queues are small
6. Production over-runs and under-runs are common
7. There is a need to level production loads
8. There is normally more concern for capacity constraints than for material constraints
9. When there is a change in the demand it normally comes with a short lead time
10. Prompt production and delivery are important in order to avoid lost sales
11. Customers usually release orders periodically, but quantities may change from period to period
12. Production operations are often overlapping
13. Production operations often reflect multiple operators per machine, or multiple machines per operator
14. There usually occurs “lot for lot" lot sizing of operations
15. Component materials are normally issued on a regular and repetitive basis

In the 70s, in the U.S.A., MRP was used to plan and control repetitive manufacturing. Presently American industry is paying a great deal of attention to Japanese methods for controlling production. One such method, just-in-time (JIT) manufacturing, has become very popular here. However, major manufacturing companies firmly believe that all major planning and control methods, such as MRP, JIT, and OPT or similar types of capacity optimization techniques, are not mutually exclusive, but rather are complementary techniques. This is why we may find some combination of these techniques implemented in our manufacturing firms. In the next section we will study the characteristics of the Japanese just-in-time manufacturing system.

6. THE JAPANESE JUST-IN-TIME SYSTEM

Philosophically speaking, a just-in-time production system is an integrated manufacturing and supply system aimed at producing the highest quality, and, at the same time, the lowest cost products through the elimination of waste. Waste is here defined as anything that does not add value to the product; it is anything other than the minimum amount of materials, equipment, or workers. The wastes incurred in a production process include: overproduction, wasted time spent at machines, waste involved at the transportation of parts and goods, waste in processing, waste taking inventory, waste of motion, and waste in the form of defective units.

A **just-in-time system** is a system that integrates and controls the entire process. It specifies what should be stored, moved, operated on, inspected, and precisely when it should be done. Just-in-time production continuously strives to improve production processes and methods. It attempts to reduce, and ultimately to eliminate, inventories because high inventories tend to cover up production problems.

One of the most popular just-in-time systems is Toyota's kanban system. Mr. Tahichi Ohno, who felt that overproduction was the central evil that led to waste, developed it. To eliminate the problem of waste, Mr. Ohno devised a production system based on two main structural features: the just-in-time concept and automation. The just-in-time concept implies that the exact number of required units is brought to each successive stage of production at the appropriate time. This meant a reversal of the normal thinking process. Ordinarily, units are transported to the next production stage as soon as they are ready. Mr. Ohno, however, reversed this. Now, each stage is required to go back to the previous stage to pick up the exact number of units needed. When implemented at Toyota Inc., this resulted in a significant decline in in-process inventory levels.

In the Toyota system an order card, called **kanban**, affects the order release mechanism. Kanban means 'sign post' or 'label' and is used as a communication tool between two stages of production. There are two types of kanban cards: the conveyance card and the production card. Production quantities of an item are conveyed from one process to the previous process in containers equal to approximately 10% of the daily demand for that item as follows. When the content of a container has been processed at any given stage, and when there is a production order for processing, the conveyance kanban is removed from the container by the worker and taken to the previous production stage. Here this conveyance kanban is attached to the new container and its production kanban is removed and becomes the order for the previous production stage to produce another container of parts.

This cycle is repeated from the final assembly to all upstream processes, including subcontractors and raw material suppliers. This just-in-time production system results in a system that keeps work-in-process inventory to a bare minimum. It has the advantage of shortening lead time, of reducing time spent on non-processing work, of better balancing all processes, and of reducing poor quality products. In the kanban system no defective parts can be sent to downstream manufacturing stages and upstream manufacturing stages produce only the quantity taken by downstream production stages. Changes in production rates are only possible by changing the kanbans in process or, in case of rate increases, going into overtime production.

Just-in-time production necessitates certain changes in the factory and the way in which it is managed. Changes must occur in supplier selection, plant layout, production equipment, scheduling methods, material handling methods, maintenance control, quality control, and worker training.

The Japanese have worked very hard to overcome a variety of problems inherent to any production system, and especially to the just-in-time system. Some of these problems are: stock-out and component shortages, high set-up costs, idle resources and capacity imbalances, worker resistance and motivation, vendor reliability, inventory imbalances, quality losses, maintenance downtime, and all sorts of productivity losses.

The tools used by the Japanese to combat these problems and to make just-in-time possible are numerous: a stable monthly master production schedule, a stable bill of materials, small end item lot sizes, high volume production, focused factories and group technology, avoiding stock-outs and component shortages, single-digit set-up time that reduces high set-up costs, company unions that allow for a flexible workforce, and careful monthly capacity planning that reduces idle resources and capacity imbalances. Worker resistance is minimized because, together with the foreman, the workers act as middle management and enjoy lifetime employment. Subcontractor networks ensure vendor reliability, and quality circles reduce quality losses. Maintenance downtime is combatted through the introduction of preventive maintenance, quick maintenance response, and a variety of visual displays. Productivity is constantly improved because of continuous improvement of the production system through automation and workforce participation.

The just-in-time system goes beyond the shop floor. It also includes shipments of purchased goods. Suppliers who use small standard-sized containers to replenish shipments several times a day use the replacement principle of kanban. Suppliers, too, avail themselves of kanban cards for authorization of the movement of these containers. This system can only work if suppliers are located relatively close to their customers. In this way, in addition to low in-process inventory, companies stock relatively small amounts of raw materials and purchased parts.

Here, the just-in-time system starts with the just-in-time demand for materials and parts. Since final assembly best and most accurately knows the timing and quantity of parts, this is where the just-in-time system will start. Final assembly goes to its suppliers and brings back only the necessary parts at the necessary time. Suppliers produce exactly the kinds and quantity of parts necessary to replace those taken by the assembly line. Since assembly lines generate products at a fairly steady output rate, frequent deliveries of slightly variable quantities are made. Customers will only accept minimal or no overage or underage in delivered goods. To produce these parts, suppliers go to their own suppliers and get only the necessary parts. Thus, the entire chain reacts very quickly to the actual assembly, and just-in-time production is achieved with minimum inventory throughout the supply chain.

In order to avoid poor-quality parts, customers help suppliers to meet necessary quality specifications through encouraging them to use process control, rather than inspection of finished goods. In order to maintain good quality levels, they encourage a good working relationship amongst suppliers' and buyers' quality control people. Customers' design engineers also work very closely with suppliers' design engineers to ensure proper parts design for future products, and to monitor value analysis of these parts so that suppliers stay price competitive.

Realize, though, that this system does not call for suppliers to carry large inventories. As a matter of fact, the goal is for the suppliers to carry lower inventories than is the traditional practice. Instead, they stay in tune with the production rates of their customers. These suppliers have long-term contracts with their customers and these customers communicate with them with a minimal amount of release papers.

An Example: The Case where Timing is Key in a Just-In-Time Service by a 3PL

Let us look at an example that involves a service provided by a third party logistics (3PL), a warehousing supplier who makes a milk run every Monday morning at 10 a.m., picking up products from its customer, a manufacturing supplier. The 3PL transports the product via airplane and truck, and stores it in a warehouse in another country. The product then waits for pickup by a milk run from the Original Equipment Manufacturing (OEM) customer's supplier for ultimate delivery to the OEM customer's plant. This service is paid for by the OEM customer as part of its contract with the manufacturing supplier to support its just-in-time requirements.

If the manufacturing supplier is unable to meet the scheduled delivery due to problems that cause a delay, missing the pickup time, he then has to expedite shipping another way or pay extra for 3PL to make a second milk run. Either way, this costs additional money to the manufacturing supplier for which he cannot bill the customer.

Likewise, the 3PL must ensure that the milk run happens as required at the manufacturing supplier's plant and that he has sufficient product on hand in the warehouse when the OEM customer's supplier milk run happens. The 3PL may also make deliveries to the OEM customer for engineering test units, send advance shipping notices, and get the receiving department's signature when delivering. Timing is everything to make this service work and make a profit for the manufacturing and 3PL suppliers.

7. LEAN SHOP FLOOR CONTROL

7.1 Principles of Push versus Pull Systems

Figure 12.6 compares the push system to the just-in-time pull system. Push systems are the traditional systems where products are provided to the customer based on forecasts or schedules and where materials are ordered based on the best guess of what the customers need in the future. These materials come in the back door and are pushed from operation to operation, until they are ready to be shipped, if the customer still needs them. In a push system there are more variations in schedules and more in-process inventory at the up-stream processes than at the down-stream processes.

When materials are pulled through the system, the flow of materials is controlled by replacing only what has been consumed. It is a just-in-time system where production and inventory are pulled just in time to meet the customers' demand. In this system there is less in-process inventory at the up-stream processes than at the down-stream processes

As discussed earlier, a just-in-time system is a system that integrates and controls the entire process. It specifies what should be stored, moved, operated on, or inspected and precisely when it should be done. Just-in-time production continuously strives to improve production processes and methods. It attempts to reduce, and ultimately to eliminate, inventories because high inventories tend to cover up production problems.

The Toyota's kanban system, developed by Mr. Tahichi Ohno, is the most popular pull system. Another very popular just-in-time system is the OPT system developed by Moshe Eliyahu Goldratt, an Israeli physicist, and originally marketed by Creative Output. Because the OPT system calls for variable batch sizes (significantly smaller batch sizes for non-bottleneck operations and higher batch sizes for the bottleneck operation) it is often a better system than the Japanese just-in-time system in terms of overall in-process inventory.

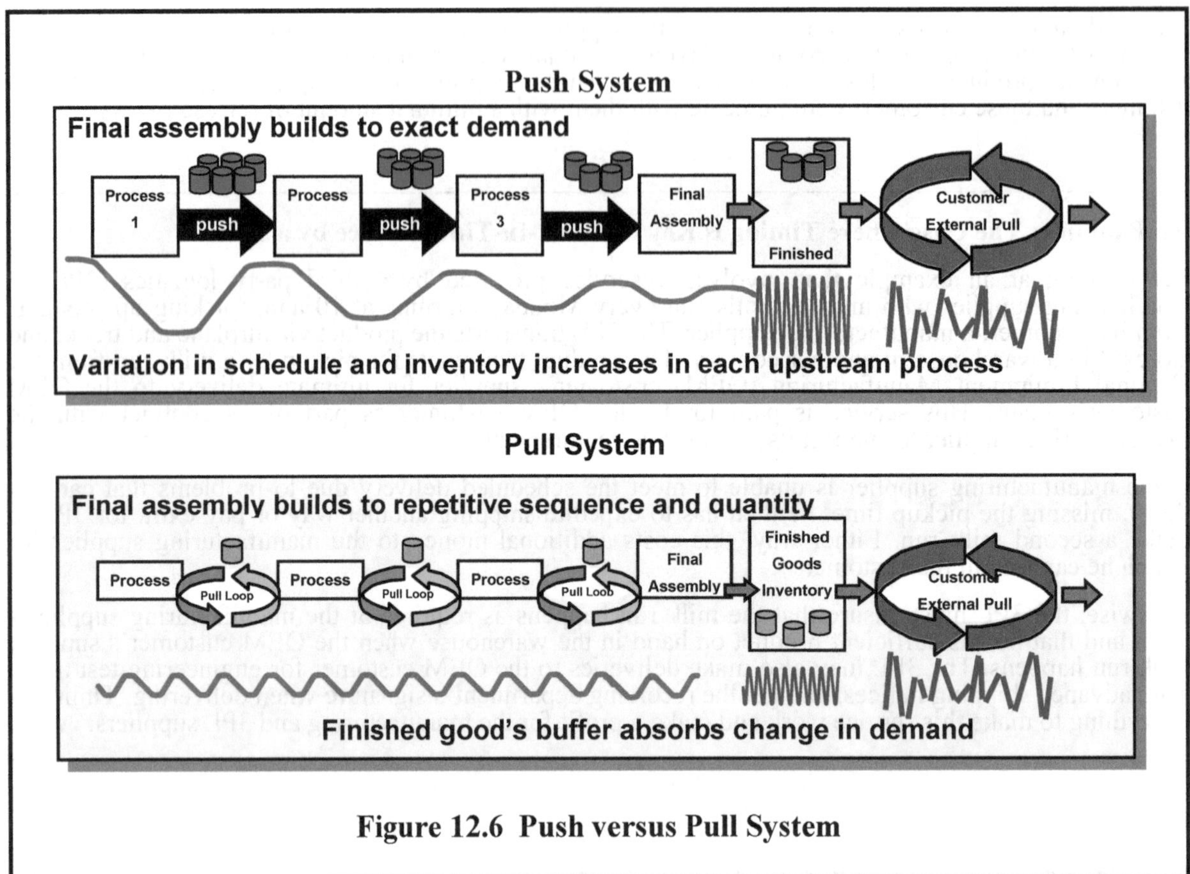

Figure 12.6 Push versus Pull System

7.2 The One-Piece Flow

The ultimate pull system is a one-piece flow. This is a system where products are made in a batch, but one unit at a time is pulled through the operation from one process to the other. A one-piece flow operation eliminates non-added-value activities such as obsolescence, repair, rework, excess inventory, expediting, and other wastes.

While it may not be feasible to utilize a one-piece flow operation, the closer you get to this goal, the better off the company is.

This one-piece flow for a batch size of ten units is illustrated in Figure 12.7.

Assume that the cycle time per process step is 1 minute and one currently produces everything in batches of ten before moving the batch to the next process. There are three processes each batch of ten goes through. It will take ten minutes before the total batch of ten items will be finished in the first processing center. It then will move on to the next processing center. Again another ten minutes of processing occurs in the second processing center and a final ten minutes in the third processing center. This adds up to a total production throughput time of 30 minutes. The first part leaves the system when it has been processed in the third processing center, or after 21 minutes in the system (10 minutes in process one, plus 10 minutes in process two, plus its processing time of 1 minute in process three).

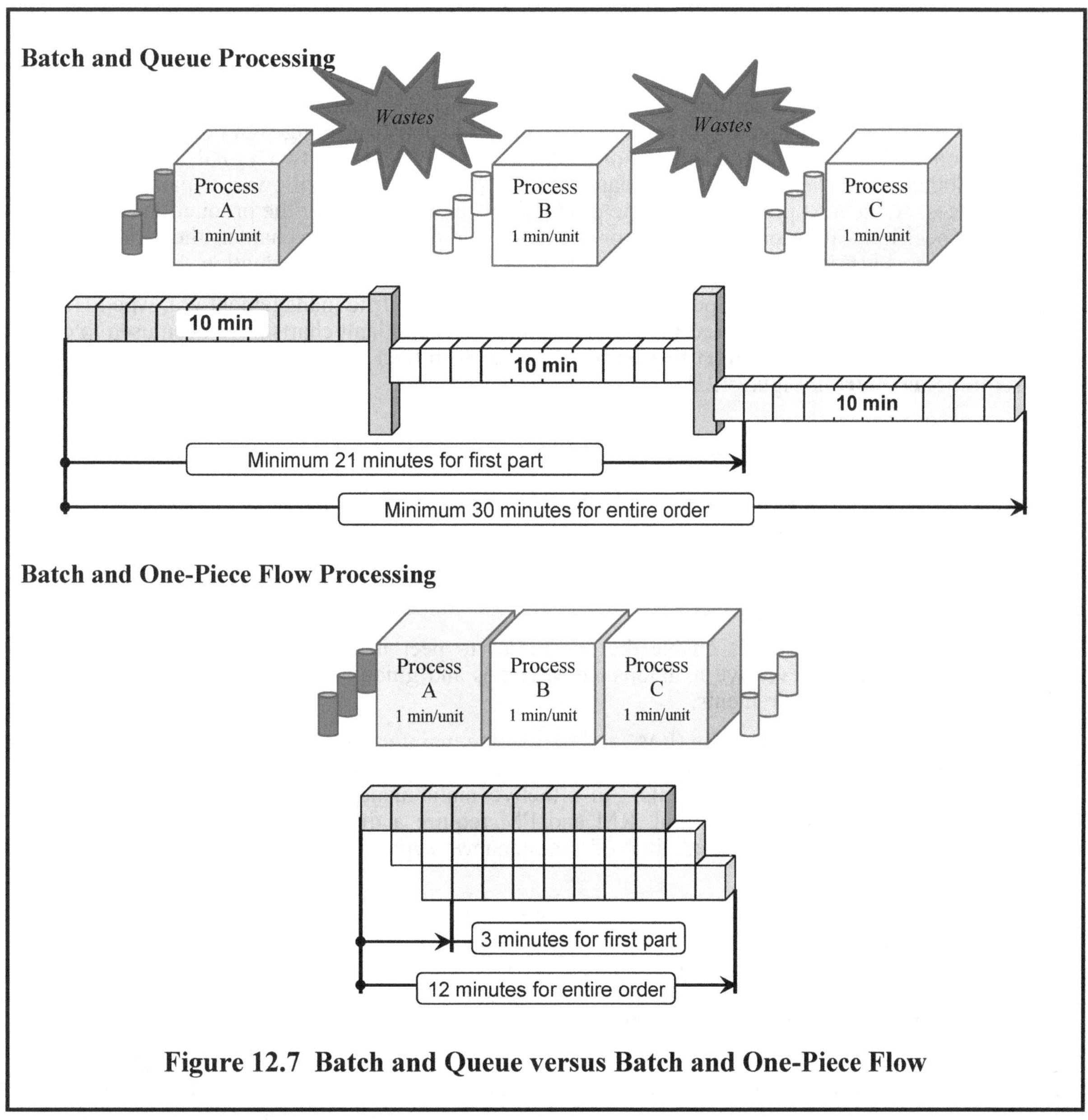

Figure 12.7 Batch and Queue versus Batch and One-Piece Flow

If one goes to a batch and one-piece flow (continuous flow) type of a system, then the first piece moves to processing center two as soon as it is processed in center one, and moves to the third center as soon as it is processed in center two. This yields a reduction in total production lead time from 30 minutes to 12 minutes and in a production lead time reduction for the first piece from 21 minutes to 3 minutes (its actual production time).

7.3 Visual Controls

Lean systems use both visual and computer controls. Visual controls are a system of symbols that conveys the right information to the right person in a timely manner. The objective of visual controls is to achieve management by sight. Often-used visual controls are: kanbans, Gantt charts, andons, color-coded tools and tool holders, labeled tool storage, taped off space on the floor for inventory storage, maintenance load charts, quality control charts, and office pitch boards.

7.3.1 Visual Production Controls

Initially, the most popular just-in-time system, Toyota's kanban system, is a visual control system. Its order release mechanism is triggered by an order card called kanban (meaning sign post or label). It is the communication tool between two stages of production. This system has two visual control cards: the conveyance kanban and the production kanban. The conveyance kanban allows for parts to be moved from one process to the next process, while the production kanban allows for the production or processing of parts at a specific location on the plant floor. As discussed earlier in this chapter, the ultimate goal of this visual system is just-in-time production that prevents the waste of over-production.

Visual controls for production and operations date back to the scientific management era, when Henry L. Gantt introduced the **Gantt chart**, used for scheduling and control. Gantt charts have been used to capture work load, like the **Gantt load chart** in Figure 12.1, and to reflect schedules and sequencing, like the **Gantt sequencing chart** in Figure 12.2.

7.3.2 Visual Maintenance Controls

Andons are visual signals, often color-coded lights, at machines and operations to flag machine stoppage that need maintenance support. There are manual and automatic andons. Personnel operating equipment who notice problems can manually trigger andons. Automated equipment can have built in andons that can be triggered when equipment is not performing according to specifications or when the number of output cycles is reached that trequires tool change or routine maintenance.

Other visual maintenance controls enable the supervisor to peer into the future need for inspections, routine maintenance, and preventive maintenance activities and guide him towards the timely execution of all future maintenance requirements.

A total productive routine maintenance (RM) and preventive maintenance (PM) system is a system that is both efficient and effective. An efficient maintenance system is one that has all the proper tools for timely execution of all maintenance requirements. An effective maintenance system is a system that can be managed with minimum effort of control. RM and PM require a timely execution of inspections, the generation of work orders, the scheduling of maintenance activities, and the timely control of its execution.

In developing a productive maintenance system, one must aim at minimizing paperwork and at generating visual controls. The paperwork and visual controls are part of the communication system of a total productive maintenance system. Effective inspection forms are compact, yet comprehensive forms that use a coding system to communicate work to be scheduled. Do not create these files to be filed for a long period of time, rather they are created to be used to generate work schedules.

Routine and preventive maintenance systems with visual controls significantly improve the scheduling and the control of routine inspections, routine maintenance, and preventive maintenance work. Without the presence of visual controls, a maintenance supervisor spends an enormous amount of time going through files, data forms, past work done, and other documents to ensure the timely execution of all future inspections, PM, and RM activities. This wasted time can better be spent supervising and improving the maintenance department.

An example of such a visual control chart, **the maintenance load chart**, is shown in Figure 12.8. It was developed for a small Mexican resort of an American Time Share Company. The shaded bars in the chart prompt the timely execution of routine inspections and preventive maintenance that need to be performed during a calendar year on all hot water heaters at the resort. As the maintenance activity is performed the supervisor will mark it with an X-mark in the appropriate month/week of the chart. If maintenance is performed in a timely fashion, then each colored strip ought to have an X-mark. If, due to breakdowns, additional work is performed, then a star (*) is marked on the chart. At the end of the calendar year the charts can be reviewed to evaluate the need for increasing or decreasing the amount of preventive or routine maintenance work, or the need for replacement of the equipment, etc.

Here the visual control reflects when maintenance needs to be done and when work is done. It also provides valuable information for future lean maintenance management.

Mar Azul	INSPECCION Y LAVADO/INSPECCION DE CALENTADORES DE AGUA												
Year:	I	II	III	IV	V	VI	VII	VIII	IX	X	XI	XII	
CONDO 10													3 meses
CONDO 11													3 meses
CONDO 20													3 meses
CONDO 21													3 meses
CONDO 30													3 meses
CONDO 31													3 meses
CONDO 40													3 meses
CONDO 41													3 meses
CONDO 50													3 meses
CONDO 51													3 meses
CONDO 60													3 meses
CONDO 61													3 meses
CONDO62/72/82/92													3 meses
CONDO 70													3 meses
CONDO 71													3 meses
CONDO 80													3 meses
CONDO 81													3 meses
CONDO 90													3 meses
CONDO 91													3 meses
PH1													3 meses
PH2													3 meses
	I	II	III	IV	V	VI	VII	VIII	IX	X	XI	XII	

Figure 12.8 Maintenance Load Chart for Hot Water Heaters for a Mexican Resort

7.3.3 Visual Quality Control

Visual quality control charts, such as X-bar charts, R-charts, and p-charts are introduced in Chapter 13. These charts are developed to observe and control the variation in produced parts and products.

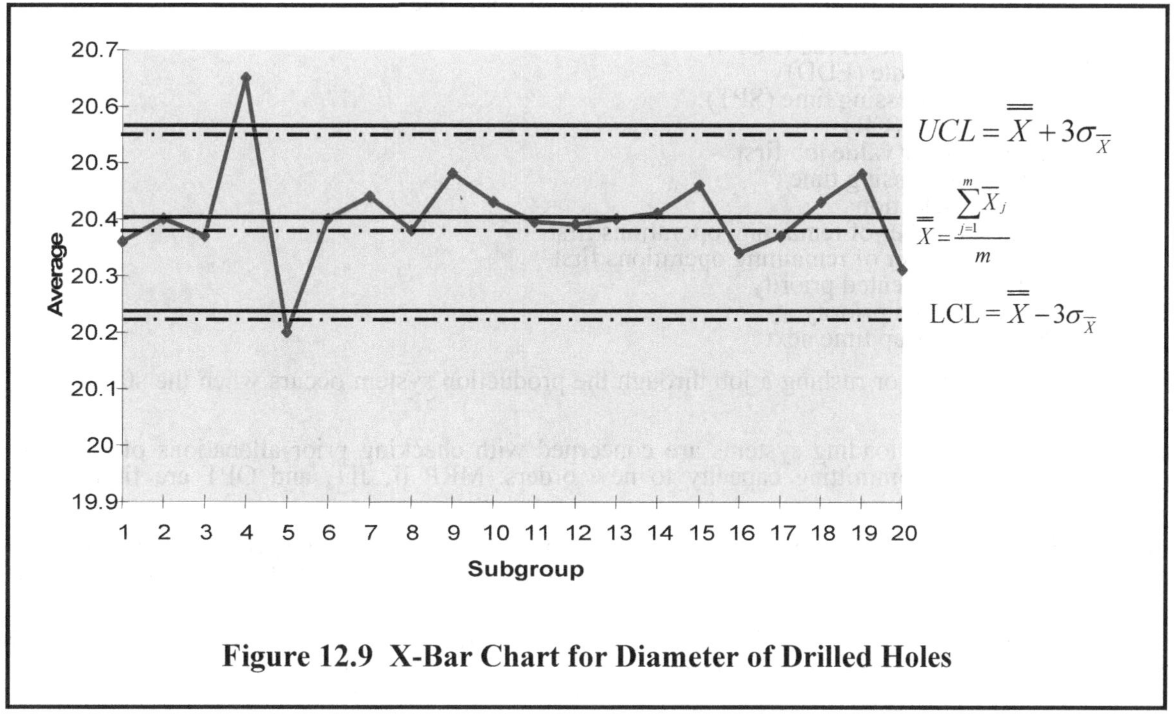

Figure 12.9 X-Bar Chart for Diameter of Drilled Holes

These charts reflect the limits of acceptable variability levels and picture how a product or process conforms to these levels. Many companies post these charts to alert both production supervisors and maintenance people about variation in production. Some causes of such variation could be:

- Improperly maintained equipment
- Tool wear
- Machine vibration
- Poor material quality
- Poorly calibrated equipment
- Sloppy work

7.3.4 Visual Office Control

Visual office control charts must communicate on a daily basis the work that needs to be done. It can be reflected in a visual pitch board. A **pitch board** is a physical device that communicates in a visual way the work that is required throughout the day, or can be used for something as simple as who is in the office and who is out. Specific times show the commencement of various activities. A visual pitch board prompts the start of work and gets it off a worker's desk into a common process. It creates a visual to control of whether work is done in a timely fashion, in so-called pitch increments, rather than rushed towards the end of the day. If a worker gets behind, it steers towards immediate problem resolution.

8. GLOSSARY AND SUMMARY OF METHODS

Brain – Brain is an OPT module that contains a proprietary set of algorithms used to schedule the workers, machines, or tools at the bottleneck operations.

Buildnet – Buildnet is an OPT module that uses the network of all the plant's raw materials, resources, products, and customer orders to create the master production schedule (MPS).

De-expediting – De-expediting occurs when priorities change or the product is no longer wanted.

Dispatching Rules – Some of the most popular dispatching rules are:

1. First-come-first-served (FCFS)
2. Earliest due date (EDD)
3. Shortest processing time (SPT)
4. Critical ratio (CR)
5. Largest dollar value job first
6. Largest processing time
7. Random selection
8. Largest number of remaining operations first
9. Fewest number of remaining operations first
10. Customer oriented priority
11. Shop oriented priority
12. Smallest set-up time next

Expediting – Expediting or rushing a job through the production system occurs when the status of a job is not satisfactory.

Finite Loading – Finite loading systems are concerned with checking prior allocations of capacity to orders, before committing capacity to new orders. MRP II, JIT, and OPT are finite loading systems.

Gantt Load Chart – A Gantt load chart exhibits valuable information with respect to relative workloads of the productive system. They are drawn for work centers, departments, and machines to monitor production on the shop floor.

Infinite Loading – Infinite loading is the assignment of work to workstations regardless of available capacity. Now work orders released to the shop floor exhibit what needs to be done, not necessarily what can be done, under normal production circumstances. The MRP is a finite loading system.

Johnson's Scheduling Algorithm – Johnson's scheduling algorithm for scheduling jobs over two work centers is as follows:

1. List processing times of all jobs in two columns; the first column is for the processing times in the first work center and the second column is for the processing times of the second work center
2. Identify the smallest remaining processing time
3. If this number is for a job in the first work center, then assign that job as early as possible, considering the assignments to date; otherwise assign it as late as possible
4. Eliminate the job just scheduled and return to Step 2

Just-In-Time Production System (JIT) – The JIT production system is an integrated manufacturing and supply system aimed at producing the highest quality and the lowest cost products through the elimination of waste (overproduction, wasted time spent at machines, wasted movement of parts and goods, waste in processing, waste taking inventory, waste of motion, waste through defective units, etc.). The just-in-time concept implies that the exact number of required units is brought to each successive stage of production at the appropriate time.

Kanban – Kanban means signboard or label and is used as a communication tool between two stages of production in a just- in-time production system. There are two types of kanbans: the conveyance card and the production card. The conveyance kanban conveys the need of a production order to the previous process, whereas the production kanban is the actual order to produce a container (approximately 10% of the daily demand).

Kendall's Queuing Notation – A queuing system can be characterized by the following elements:

a = Arrival distribution
b = Departure or service distribution
c = Number or configuration of servers
d = Service discipline
e = Maximum number of customers allowed in the system
f = Number of possible customers in the calling population

These six characteristics are referred to in Kendall's queuing notation as follows:

$$(a/b/c) : (d/e/f)$$

Loading (Machine Loading) – Loading (machine loading) is the allocation of jobs to work centers and the commitment of machine time to jobs. Loads are normally expressed in time units.

Master Route Sheet – A master route sheet is developed for each part of a product that is planned to be manufactured. It shows the sequence of operations, the operation numbers, the departments where operations are to be performed, the set up times, the per unit production time or production rate, the normal or acceptable between-operation dead or idle time, types of raw materials needed, the amount of raw materials needed for one unit's production, worker classification, and acceptable piece rate.

OPT –Algorithm for Determining Optimal Production. The OPT algorithm for a two-product system consists of the following three steps:

Step 1: For each product compute: $R = \dfrac{\textit{Unit Selling}\text{ Price} - \text{Variable Unit Cost}}{\text{Unit Production Time at the Bottleneck}}$

Step 2: Of that product that has the largest ratio, produce as much as possible. In other words, produce the smallest amount of: the weekly demand for that product or the available production minutes divided by the per-unit production minutes at the bottleneck.

Step 3: If not all available production minutes are allocated in Step 2, then the remaining minutes can be used to produce as much as possible of the product with the next largest R.

This algorithm can easily be extended to more than two products and can also consider set-up time when switching from one product to the other.

Optimized Production Technology (OPT) – OPT is a procedure that schedules work centers based on the finite loading principle. It is a two-part package with a simulated manufacturing program and a set of radical shop-floor management rules. The simulated manufacturing program consists of four modules: Buildnet, Serve, Split, and Brain.

Sequencing – Sequencing jobs is defining the order in which jobs will be performed in the various work centers.

Serve – Serve is an OPT module that locates bottlenecks in the system by running load profiles for each machine and resource.

Split – Split is an OPT module that divides the network into two parts: the non-critical portion and the critical portion, which contains the bottlenecks, assemblies, and sub-assemblies.

Takt Time – Takt time, or demand rate, is the ratio of the available work time to the customer demand.

9. ACRONYMS

CR Critical Ratio

EDD Earliest Due Date

FCFS First-Come-First-Served

JIT Just-InTime

OPT Optimized Production Technology

SPT Shortest Processing Time

10. REFERENCES

Conway, R. W., Maxwell, W. L., and Miller, L.W. *Theory of Scheduling*. Reading, MA: Addison-Wesley Publishing Company, 1967.

Fogarty, D. W., Blackstone, J. H., and T. R. Hoffmann, T. R. *Production and Inventory Management.* Cincinnati, OH: South-Western Publishing Co, 1991.

Fogarty, D. W., Hoffmann, T. R., and P. W. Stonebraker. *Production and Operations Management.* Cincinnati, OH: South-Western Publishing Co, 1989.

Goddard, Walter E. *Just-In-Time, Surviving by Breaking Tradition*. Essex Junction, VT: Oliver Wight Ltd Publications, Inc., 1986.

Goldratt, Eliyahu M. and Jeff Cox. *The Goal, Excellence In Manufacturing*, North River Press, Inc., 1984.

Imai, Masaaki, Kaizen. *The Key to Japan's Competitive Success*. New York: McGraw-Hill Publishing Company, 1986.

Lubben Hall, Robert W., Zero Inventories, Dow Jones-Irwin, Homewood, IL, 1983.

Melnyk, Steven A. and Carter, Phillip L., Production Activity Control, Dow Jones-Irwin, Homewood, IL, 1987.

Monden, Yasuhiro. *Toyota Production System, Practical Approach to Production Management*, Industrial Engineering and Management Press, Institute of Industrial Engineers, 1983.

Parrinder, Joann O. "Lean Thinking Applied to Your Idea Development Lifecycle." *Driving Operational Excellence: Successful Lean Six Sigma Secrets to Improve the Bottom Line,* Ron Crabtree, editor. MetaOps Publishing LLC, 2010, pp. 237–250.

Peterson, Rein and Edward A. Silver. *Decision Systems for Inventory Management and Production Planning*. New York: John Wiley and Sons, 1979.

Sandras Jr., William A. *Just-In-Time: Making it Happen, Unleashing the Power of Continuous Improvement*. Essex Junction, VT: Oliver Wight Ltd. Publications, Inc., 1989.

Schonberger, Richard J. *Japanese Manufacturing Technique, Nine Hidden Lessons in Simplicity*. New York: The Free Press, Macmillan Publishing Co., Inc., 1982.

Sekine, K., and K. Arai. *TPM for the Lean Factory: Innovative Methods and Worksheets for Equipment Management.* Productivity Press Inc., October 1998.

Timmons, A. *Six Steps for Implementing Lean Manufacturing*. BHASS Publishing, January 1999.

Vollman T. E, Berry, W. L., and D. C. Whybark. *Manufacturing Planning and Control Systems*. Homewood, IL: Business One Irwin, 1988.

Wight, Oliver W. *Production and Inventory Management in the Computer Age*. New York: Van Nostrand Reinhold Company, 1984.

11. REVIEW QUESTIONS

1. Describe a master route sheet. Why is it needed?
2. Differentiate between finite and infinite loading. Name one production control system that considers finite loading of production orders and one that considers infinite loading of production orders.
3. What is a Gantt chart? What is it used for?
4. Name some of the most commonly used sequencing rules for dispatching production orders.
5. Briefly discuss the first-come-first-serve rule (FCFS).
6. Briefly discuss the earliest due date rule (EDD). Does it always generate a sequence of jobs that exhibits the smallest possible average job tardiness?
7. Briefly discuss the critical ratio rule (CR). What are its advantages?
8. What is Johnson's algorithm for scheduling jobs over two work centers?
9. Distinguish between forward and backward scheduling. Which type of companies use forward scheduling? Which type of companies use backward scheduling? What type of scheduling is done with the MRP system?
10. What do expediting and de-expediting mean?
11. What is meant by queuing?
12. What questions does one wish to answer when studying queuing systems?
13. What is meant by Kendall's notation? Describe the notation.
14. Name some queuing systems using Kendall's notation.
15. What does OPT stand for? Who developed OPT?
16. Name and briefly describe the four basic modules of the simulated manufacturing program of OPT.
17. In the OPT system what are the non-bottleneck machine characteristics and rules? In the OPT system what are the bottleneck machine characteristics and rules? What are the other system characteristics?
18. What is a repetitive manufacturing system? Name some of its characteristics.
19. What is the just-in-time production system? Name the most popular JIT system. Who invented it?
20. What is a kanban? What types of kanbans exist? What are they used for?
21. What are the principles of push versus pull in a lean manufacturing environment?
22. What is meant by takt time?
23. Compare and contrast the batch/one-piece flow processing system to the batch/queuing processing system.
24. Discuss the use of visual controls for production control, maintenance control, quality control, and office control.

12. PROBLEMS

Problem #1

Jobcorp, Inc. has obtained orders for four jobs: I, II, III, and IV. These jobs will be processed through various operations. The sequencing of these jobs, their operation times, and due dates are summarized in the following table.

Job Sequence, Process Time (hours) & Due Dates							
Job	Process 1	Time	Process 2	Time	Process 3	Time	Due Date
I	Lathe	6	Drill	4	Mill	8	48
II	Mill	8	Drill	6			32
III	Lathe	4	Mill	6	Drill	8	48
IV	Drill	10	Lathe	8			32

a) Use the infinite loading principle and the forward scheduling procedure to schedule the jobs/processes as early as possible.

b) Are there any conflicts?

Problem #2

Redo Problem #1 using the forward finite loading scheduling technique.

How does that resolve the conflicts of Problem #1a)?

Problem #3

Reconsider the data of Problem #1 using the backward scheduling technique.

a) Are there any conflicts when using infinite loading?

b) How are the conflicts resolved using finite loading?

Problem #4

Consider ten jobs to be scheduled for two processes (A and B). Their processing times are in the table below. Use Johnson's rule to schedule these jobs so that overall throughput or flow time is minimized.

Processing Time		
Jobs	Process A	Process B
Job #1	6	2
Job #2	8	10
Job #3	10	12
Job #4	18	8
Job #5	7	5
Job #6	9	3
Job #7	15	17
Job #8	10	11
Job #9	9	12
Job #10	12	8

Problem #5

The following table shows the jobs in the order in which they arrived at work center 1 (WC 1).

Jobs	WC 1 Time	WC 2 Time
A	12	5
B	3	2
C	3	5
D	6	16
E	17	9

a) For the FCFS order (as listed above), what is the total throughput time for these jobs?

b) Which order of these jobs will guarantee that the total throughput time is as small as it can be?

c) What will be the throughput time for your answer to b)?

Problem #6

Assume that trucks arrive at a loading dock according to a Poisson process at an average rate of 4 trucks per hour. At the loading dock, the trucks are unloaded by one crew member according to an exponential service time at a rate of 5 trucks per hour.

Use the formulas presented in the text to calculate:

a) Utilization factor

b) Probability of no customers in the system

c) Probability of *n* customers in the system

d) Expected number of customers in the system

e) Expected waiting time in the system

f) Expected waiting time in the queue only

Problem #7

The table below contains information about five jobs waiting to be processed at a work center. The jobs are shown in the order they arrived in the shop. Today is shop date 386.

Jobs	Processing Time	Due Date
A	14	401
B	10	406
C	18	404
D	2	402
E	4	407

a) What would be the sequence using the SPT rule?

b) What is the Critical Ratio for job D?

Problem #8

Consider for machine I the following ten jobs, their processing times, and their due dates

Jobs	Time (hours)	Due Dates (hours)
Job A	14	20
Job B	7	20
Job C	12	20
Job D	8	46
Job E	12	42
Job F	5	55
Job G	12	75
Job H	10	75
Job I	8	80
Job J	2	25

Evaluate the schedules (average flow time, average job tardiness, number of jobs tardy, average # of jobs in the system) using the following scheduling rules:

a) First-come-first-served rule

b) Earliest due date rule

c) Shortest processing time rule

d) Critical ratio rule

e) Largest processing time

Problem #9

Customers arrive at a drive-up bank at a rate of 15 customers per hour. Due to limited space, the system cannot hold more than four cars. The service time is distributed exponentially with an expected service rate of 20 customers per hour.

a) Draw the rate diagram for this system.

b) Write the various balance equations for each state (state 0, state 1, state 2, state 3, and state 4).

c) Use these balance equations to calculate the probability of having 0, 1, 2, 3, or 4 cars in the system.

d) Calculate the expected number of cars in the system, using the following formulas:

$$L = \sum nP_n \textit{for } n=0,\ 1,\ 2,\ 3, \textit{ and } 4)$$

e) Calculate the expected arrival rate: expected $\lambda = \lambda P_0 + \lambda P_1 + \lambda P_2 + \lambda P_3 = \lambda\ (P_0 + P_1 + P_2 + P_3)$, or

$$\text{expected } \lambda = \lambda\ (1 - P_4)$$

f) Calculate expected waiting time in the system: ($W = L/expected\ \lambda$).

Problem #10

Based on the narrative of the Emergency Room case answer the following questions:

a) What are the various processes a patient goes through (from arrival in the ambulance at the hospital, until moved into a hospital room after admitting)?

b) Where can queues form if the process is not well managed?

c) What was done to reduce the queue length and get the patient admitted and in a hospital bed quicker?

d) How could value stream mapping be useful to re-engineer this entire process?

CHAPTER 13

QUALITY MANAGEMENT

The **quality** of a product is often measured by its ***performance quality***, or how well the product performs its function. How the product performs depends on both the quality of design and the quality of conformance. From a manufacturer's or a service provider's point of view, it is important to distinguish these two elements of quality.

The **design quality** (quality specifications) is concerned with the ***stringency*** of the specifications for manufacturing the product. These quality specifications are used to describe the designer's view of a series of quality characteristics, such as a physical or chemical property, a dimension, a surface condition, and others. In general, the greater the requirement for strength, fatigue resistance, weathering, chemical composition, interchangeability, service life and maintainability, the better the quality of design.

The **production quality** (workmanship), or, more precisely speaking, the quality of ***conformance to design*** is concerned with how well the manufactured product conforms to the original design requirements. The higher the design quality is, the more costly and difficult it is to achieve production quality.

Quality control is a system for coordinating group activities in an organization such that quality is designed, built in, and maintained for full customer satisfaction in the most economical way. Quality control not only covers the quality of design but also stresses production quality. While design quality is a ***one-shot deal***, quality control for production quality is a ***continuous, ongoing activity***. Production quality control consists of two primary functions: it detects and segregates the defective parts from the good parts, and it reduces and avoids producing defective parts. Before the 1980s, we were more involved in detecting and segregating defectives from good parts, whereas, more recently, systems have been devised to avoid producing defective parts.

Control charts are used to observe and control the variation in produced parts and products. They reflect the limits of acceptable variability levels and picture how a product or process conforms to these levels. Variations in parts can be accredited to variations in the process, the material, the machine operator, or other external factors such as humidity, temperature, vibration, and others.

Process variability occurs because of improperly maintained equipment, tool wear, and machine vibrations. This is the reason why preventive maintenance of industrial equipment is an important activity in our industry. It helps monitor process variability and controls it within acceptable limits. Tool use of equipment is recorded and tools are regularly replaced to avoid poor production output. Materials too can contribute to poor products. Variability in the quality of materials may result in unacceptable output. This is why raw materials and purchased parts must be evaluated for conformance to set standards. As our manufacturing systems are becoming more and more automated, operator variability is becoming a lesser concern in our industry. This is, however, not the case for the service industry, where quality of service perhaps solely depends on how people perform their duties.

In this chapter we will examine why quality control must be a companywide commitment in both the manufacturing and the service industries. Statistical tools for the recording and control of quality, or statistical quality control, will be covered briefly in this chapter. Here we will cover sampling of production output, control charts, acceptance sampling, various sampling plans, and operating characteristic curves. There are differences worldwide on how the quality control function is performed in industry. Therefore, we will look at Japanese and American quality control and the worldwide implementation of **total quality control (TQC)** and **company-wide quality control (CWQC).**

1. QUALITY CONTROL: A COMPANY-WIDE COMMITMENT

The whole company must be involved in quality management. This includes the production worker up to the company's president. All functions of the organization must strive towards the improvement and maintenance of product standards.

1.1. The Marketing Function

The marketing function must be concerned with the evaluation of product quality as defined by the customer. Market surveys, customers' complaints, field reports, product maintenance reports, product liability cases, and general customer opinions are all valuable data that marketing can use to define proper quality standards for consumer goods. These **quality standards** are part of the general specifications or baseline requirements that are submitted to the design department, where they will be translated into technical product specifications necessary for design and redesign purposes.

1.2. The Design Function

Quality standards, as defined by the marketing department, must be considered by the design function. It is the responsibility of the product engineer to translate the general customer quality requirements into technical product specifications and acceptable product tolerances. Value engineers evaluate design possibilities and identify the design that meets the customers' quality requirements at the least possible cost. The quality of a product is related to the complexity of a product, the number of standard components that make up a product, the number of functions and features, and the allowable production tolerances. The more complex a product is and the more non-standard components it has, the less reliable the product will be, thus affecting its quality. Therefore, industry is encouraged to utilize previously quality designed parts when designing new products and redesigning old ones. Allowable variation in dimensions and other product characteristics is called **product tolerance**. The tighter these tolerances are, the higher the quality of the product is. However, the cost for manufacturing a part or product increases as tolerances tighten.

An Example: Customer-Specified Dimensions with Product Tolerances

A customer specified dimensions of a product's height, length, and width in millimeters (mm) and with an expected tolerance of +/- 0.0001 mm. So, if the height is 2 mm, the length is 4.5 mm, and the width is 1 mm, then the tolerance range for the height is 1.9999 mm to 2.0001 mm, for the length is 4.4999 mm to 4.5001 mm, and for the width is 0.9999 mm to 1.0001 mm. If any measurement is outside these ranges, then the product will not fit properly or may be perceived as poor quality by the customer.

1.3. The Process Planning Function

The process planning function is responsible for selecting or developing appropriate processes and production planning procedures to manufacture a quality product. In doing so, manufacturing engineers are concerned with production cost, product quality, proposed design tolerances, startup cost, and manufacturing productivity. Process planning also gets involved in developing and designing production equipment, in developing maintenance procedures, in designing inspection devices, and in setting up procedures for product quality and process control.

1.4. The Purchasing Function

The purchasing function has the responsibility for procuring quality materials and parts that will be used in the manufacturing of goods. They are responsible for inspecting and evaluating the quality of incoming raw materials and parts. Purchasers must work closely with their vendors to define appropriate acceptance test plans and processes for their products. When quality problems occur, purchasers may wish to visit vendors' plants to survey inspection records, evaluate quality control procedures, and start a dialogue towards improving product quality. A good working relationship between suppliers and buyers is necessary to maintain good quality levels of purchased parts. The company's design engineers may wish to work together with suppliers' design engineers to ensure quality parts design for future products.

1.5. The Manufacturing Function

The manufacturing function is responsible for the production quality or the quality of product workmanship. Production quality must conform to design quality, within specified product tolerances. Production supervisors can be helpful in encouraging quality production. They must provide proper tools and a proper work environment, they instruct workers on how to perform a quality job, and they must get involved in training sessions to help workers maintain set quality levels.

1.6. The Maintenance Function

Proper maintenance of equipment and processes reduces malfunctioning of machines, thus generating quality products. Preventive and routine maintenance activities help identify potential future equipment failures that can be corrected before they generate poor quality products. Production workers should be encouraged to help maintain their equipment and to make appropriate adjustments to their machines in order to control its processing and product quality.

1.7. The Process and Quality Control Function

This function has the responsibility to inspect and test processes and products to judge their conformity to set quality standards. Though quality cannot be inspected into a product, the process and quality control function helps the organization in identifying poor processes and products, so that corrective action can be taken. This function uses a variety of instruments to monitor the output quality of the manufacturing function. Automated equipment can also be installed to evaluate processes on a continuous basis. Unlike the manufacturing function, the quality control function cannot be held responsible for poor quality production, but is responsible for identifying poor quality production. The process and quality control function must work closely with the manufacturing function of the organization to identify production problems that may lead to poor quality products. They must also assist manufacturing in finding ways to overcome production problems resulting in unacceptable quality levels.

1.8. The Customer Help Support Function

This function has the responsibility to provide on-demand help or assistance to the customer who received the product, but may have questions or difficulty in using the product properly. This service is needed especially when the product requires some assembly or implementing software. Even though documentation in the form of instructions and pictures to guide the customer is provided with the delivery of each product unit, the customer may not necessarily grasp the content accurately without human assistance. This function can improve the customer's perception of the product's quality because without it, the customer will think the product is broken or defective and return it for another product or a refund.

An Example: Why a Company needs a Customer Help Support

A customer bought and received a printer to hook up to his new desktop computer. After following all of the directions to set it up, it still would not work. So the customer determined that it was broken and returned it for another one. When the second one arrived, the customer discovered a similar problem. Having some technical knowledge, he decided to diagnose the problem himself by using a different instruction than what was in the documentation before returning this one as defective. The customer's diagnosis was correct and the printer began functioning properly. When the customer got to filling out the customer satisfaction card, he noted that the error in the documentation had caused him several days of delay in getting the printer working because he had returned the first one as broken. He recommended that a customer help support service would have been helpful to determine this error quickly and avoid having him consider the product defective when, in fact, it was not.

2. *QUALITY CONTROL AND THE SERVICE INDUSTRY*

Product quality in our automated manufacturing industry heavily depends on the quality of the equipment, the machines, and the processes. It also depends on the maintenance system that supports that production system, and less on the workers monitoring and operating the equipment. However, in the service industry, quality service very much depends on the people providing these services. Therefore, proper training of employees and retaining of quality personnel are key ingredients that lead to the success of the service industry.

Poor service is equivalent to a poor quality product in the manufacturing industry. Quality standards in the service industry are not defined in terms of measurements and tolerances, but rather, in terms of how people must behave, how they handle themselves, how they address customers, how they perform a job, etc. These quality standards are normally defined in manuals, such as the "switchboard operator's manual," the "wait person's manual," the "housekeeper's manual," the "receptionist's manual," etc. The "switchboard operator's manual", for example, may instruct the operator how to speak to hotel guests, how to deal with emergency situations, how to deal with prank calls, and how to handle any variety of situations that may occur. The "housekeeper's manual" may tell the housekeeper exactly how to tidy up a room, how to change the bed linen, how to clean the bathroom, and how to vacuum. Often audio-visual aids are available to communicate expected quality service standards to employees in the service industry.

In order to ensure that service personnel live up to the standards that are expected from them, industry periodically sends out teams of inspectors to follow up. These teams of inspectors represent all key job skills for that industry. Workers are normally notified when such teams will be arriving. During their visits teams address the workers and evaluate and counsel each worker based on their performance quality. Each worker can then be rated as to their technical proficiency, work attitude, and general performance. Any deficiency in quality job performance will be corrected through additional proper training, because training programs at all levels in a service company is the only way to improve and maintain the valuable quality that customers demand.

As part of a company's quality control program and with the availability of the intranet and internet, a company may provide on-demand training for its employees with computer-based training. This training may be presentation slides and small videos instructing on how to do something including lots of pictures from various angles and viewpoints. Some of this training may also be available to the consumer who buys a product and needs additional instruction on how to assemble and use the many functions and features of the product. The company's website may also have a list of frequently asked questions with answers and gives the opportunity for other product users to discuss how they were able to use the product with satisfaction.

An Example: Quality of the Health Care Industry

High quality health care is delivered when the patients are being properly diagnosed, receiving the best care possible, being discharged promptly and according to schedule, receiving a correct financial statement, and given correct and explicit instructions on at-home care.

Patients who flow through a health care facility in a minimum amount of time, with insignificant waits, and proper treatment will perceive the system to be of high quality.

Unfortunately, errors occur in health care organizations that need to be addressed. Some of these are incorrect diagnosis, wrong medication given to a patient, delayed discharge, errors in a patient's record, inappropriate treatment, error in a patient's financial statement, etc. Such errors are the direct result of inefficiencies or ineffective processes in the healthcare industry. They need to be identified if one wishes to improve the quality of health care delivery. Value stream mapping and lean Six Sigma provide a structured approach as they use process information to solve many problems of the system (Six Sigma will be discussed later in this chapter).

3. *ATTRIBUTE AND VARIABLE CONTROL*

A **defective** is an unacceptable part (or product), because one or more of its quality characteristics deviate from their specified design limits. Quality characteristics may be of two types:

- A **variable** is an actual value, such as a micrometer reading, a dimension, the weight, the tensile strength, and electric conductivity.
- An **attribute** relates to conformance or non-conformance of a product based on non-measurable characteristics. In this case an inspector will look at a product and, based on its appearance, pass it or reject it. Attribute inspection is used when items are obviously good or bad (surface scratches), or when characteristics cannot be easily measured (surface finish or color), or when a characteristic can be measured but the exact amount is not needed (a go/no-go gauge can be used to inspect for conformance to a certain size).

In **statistical quality control (SQC)**, where statistical data are collected, analyzed, and interpreted to solve problems, the distinction between attributes and variables is important because they require different statistical evaluation procedures. Percentages of rejects are normally calculated with attributes, whereas averages or mean values are figured for variables.

4. *SAMPLING PRODUCTION OUTCOME*

Economically speaking, it is not reasonable to evaluate all manufactured parts or products for conformity to standards. A production run can be evaluated properly by analyzing a ***representative sample*** of that run. A representative sample is a collection of parts, selected from all parts, that represents the quality level of the total production run. This means that the sample must be selected at random. In other words, the sample cannot only consist of parts taken from the beginning or the end of the production run. It must include parts taken throughout the production run. A random sample can, for example, be obtained by pulling every 10th or nth item from the production run. In this sense, parts are evaluated throughout the production period.

Samples are normally taken throughout the production period. The size of each sample very much depends on the accuracy that one desires, on the cost of inspection, and on whether the products get destroyed or not as a result of the inspection. Obviously, larger samples are more reliable than smaller samples; however, the reliability does not double as the sample size doubles. Given the desired reliability and variability of the sample data, industry can fairly accurately define the appropriate sample size for a given production run. Tables have been developed by individual companies to establish these sample sizes.

Table 13.1 (based on MIL-STD-105A, Table III -Military Standards Table-) gives the sample sizes for single attribute sampling for three different levels of inspection and for specified lot or production run sizes. Note that more samples are required as the level of inspection increases. The inspection level will increase as the customer requires more stringent protection.

Example 1: Sample Size for a Production Run of 1,000 Units and Inspection Level I

Based on Table 13.1, a lot size or production run of 1,000 units falls in the range of 801 to 1300 units and the sample size for a level I inspection is 50. This means that a total of 50 units will be sampled during this product's production run of 1,000 units. These 50 units are not collected all at once, but are collected in subgroups of specific size. Each subgroup is of equal size. For example, the company may decide to form subgroups of, say, five each. In this case there will be 10 subgroups formed. Quality control then evaluates the data of each subgroup, by comparing subgroup statistics to set norms, as will be discussed later in this chapter.

Table 13.1: Sample Size Table for Single Sampling Plan
(based on Military Standards – 105A, Table III)

Lot Sizes	Inspection Levels I	II	III
2-8	2	2	5
9-15	2	3	7
16-25	3	5	10
26-40	3	7	15
41-65	5	10	25
66-110	7	15	35
111-180	10	25	50
181-300	15	35	75
301-500	25	50	110
501-800	35	75	150
801-1,300	50	110	150
1,301-3,200	75	150	225
3,201-8,000	150	225	300
8,001-22,000	225	300	450
22,001-110,000	300	450	750
110,001-550,000	450	750	1,500
550,001 & over	750	500	1,500

Example 2: Sample Size for a Production Run of 15,000 Units and Inspection Level II

Based on Table 13.1, a lot size or production run of 15,000 units falls in the range of 8001 to 22000 units and the sample size for a level II inspection is 300. This means that a total of 300 units will be sampled during this product's production run of 15,000 units. As we stated in Example 1, these 300 sample units will be collected in subgroups of specific size that is determined ahead of time, such as 5 units, 10 units, or 15 units.

Example 3: Sample Size for a Production Run of 5,000 Units and Inspection Level III

Based on Table 13.1, a lot size or production run of 5000 units falls in the range of 320 to 8000 units and the sample size for a Level III inspection is 300. This means that a total of 300 units will be sampled during this product's production run of 5,000 units. As we suggested in Example 2, these 300 sample units will be collected in subgroups of specific size that is determined ahead of time, such as 5 units, 10 units, or 15 units. Notice that we are using the same sample size as defined in Example 2 in order to evaluate for an inspection level III! This, however, is adequate and satisfactory because the production run is smaller than the one in Example 2.

5. CONTROL CHARTS FOR VARIABLE CONTROL

In the 1920s, Walter A. Shewhart, H. F. Dodge, and H. G. Romig of Bell Telephone Laboratories developed statistical control charts and acceptance sampling charts for statistical quality control. Some of these charts are discussed here.

Control charts are used to make decisions with respect to produced parts and products before releasing them to the customers. Only acceptable production output can be shipped to customers. This output can be evaluated by the use of statistical quality control, whereby samples of the production are plotted and analyzed. In the case of variable sampling, the *X* and *R* charts can be used. The development of these charts depends on sampling data. Therefore, since no two products or processes are the same, control charts vary.

5.1. X-Bar Chart

An X-bar chart is used to observe variations in measurements. Since nothing is perfect, measurements may slightly vary. However, when these variations become too large, then the quality of the product becomes unacceptable. When properly set up, the X-bar chart exhibits the normal and abnormal variations in the mean. Abnormal variations are variations that are too large and that cannot be explained through chance. Any product with abnormal variations cannot be shipped to customers, they must be fully inspected, and all poor parts must be replaced with good ones.

The procedure for setting up an X-bar chart is as follows:

Step 1: Select a quality characteristic. A quality characteristic for an X-bar chart is something that is measurable. It is anything that can be expressed in terms of length, time, mass, temperature, substance, electrical current, luminous intensity, or any unit derived from these.

Step 2: Define the appropriate sample size for the production run and choose a rational subgroup. Data for each subgroup is normally collected one after the other.

Step 3: Collect the data for all subgroups. Special data sheets are designed to record this information. Each line of these data sheets represents data for a subgroup and typically consists of subgroup number, date, time, measurements, average, and relevant comments.

Step 4: Calculate the trial control limits. These are the overall average of the subgroup averages, called "X-double-bar", the upper control limit (UCL), and the lower control limit (LCL).

These control limits are figured as follows:

$$\overline{\overline{X}} = \frac{\sum_{j=1}^{m} \overline{X}_j}{m}$$

$$UCL = \overline{\overline{X}} + 3\sigma_{\overline{X}} \quad \text{and} \quad \text{UCL} = \overline{\overline{X}} - 3\sigma_{\overline{X}}$$

Where: $\overline{X}_j$ is the mean of subgroup *j*

m is the number of subgroups

$\sigma_{\overline{X}}$ is the standard deviation of the subgroup means (in practice the calculations are simplified by using the range of the subgroup means)

Step 5: Plot the subgroup means and trial control limits.

Step 6: Establish revised control limits. Initially, control limits are established based on the data of subgroups. According to Step 4, some of these subgroups may be out of control. If this is the case, then they need to be eliminated and new control limits are calculated based on data that is in control. These new control limits are then used for future quality control analysis.

An example: The X-Bar Chart for the Diameter of Drilled Holes

Twenty samples (m=20) of equal size are selected from a production run and their averages are calculated and plotted as shown in Figure 13.1. Initial control limits are calculated using these 20 samples: the overall average of the sample averages is 20.4 and the standard deviation of the subgroup means is 0.06. Therefore, the upper control limit is 20.58 (20.4 + 3x0.06), and the lower control limit is 20.22 (20.4 – 3x0.06).

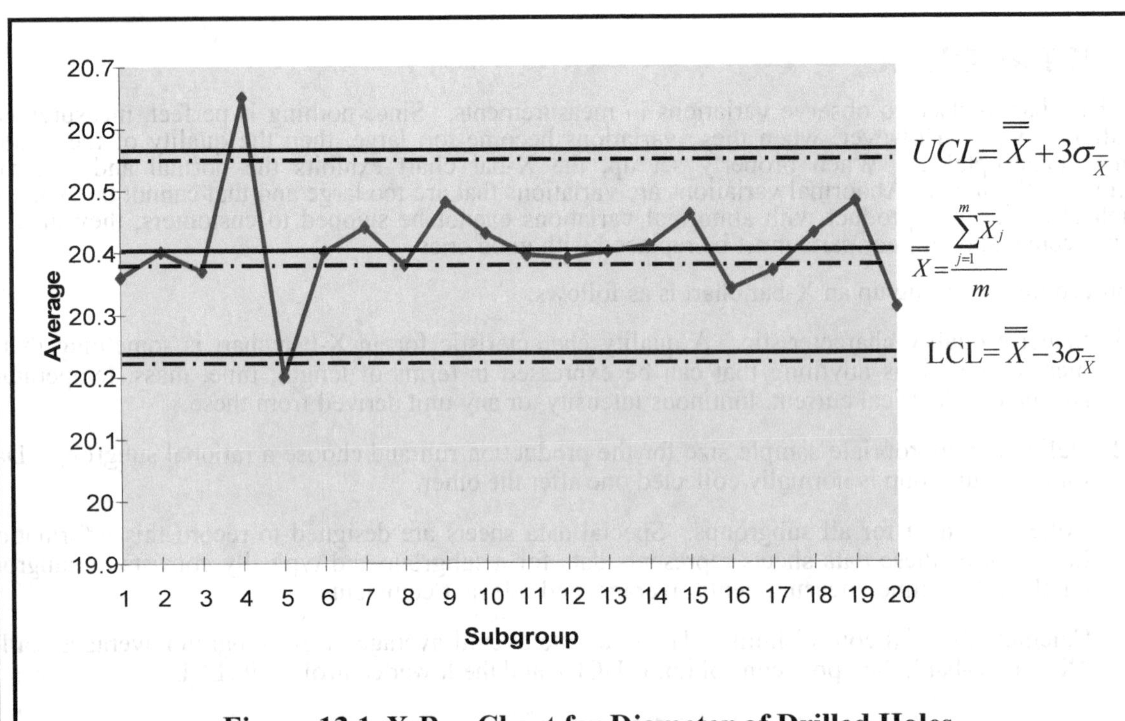

Figure 13.1 X-Bar Chart for Diameter of Drilled Holes

The X-bar chart of Figure 13.1 shows two points outside of the control limits. They are the averages of subgroups 4 and 5. Because points are outside of the control limits, the production batch from which these subgroups came needs to be evaluated before shipping the products to the customer. Furthermore, the cause of the poor production must be determined and appropriate action taken to correct it.

Because the initial control limits were established based on the data of all 20 subgroups and because two such subgroups are out of control, new limits need be calculated. These new control limits are also shown in Figure 13.1 and will now be used for future quality control analysis.

5.2. R-Chart

The R-chart (or range-chart) is similar to the X-bar chart. Rather than plotting the average value of each subgroup, the R-chart shows the range of each subgroup (i.e., the difference between the largest and the smallest value in each subgroup). Figure 13.2 is the R-chart for the diameter of drilled holes.

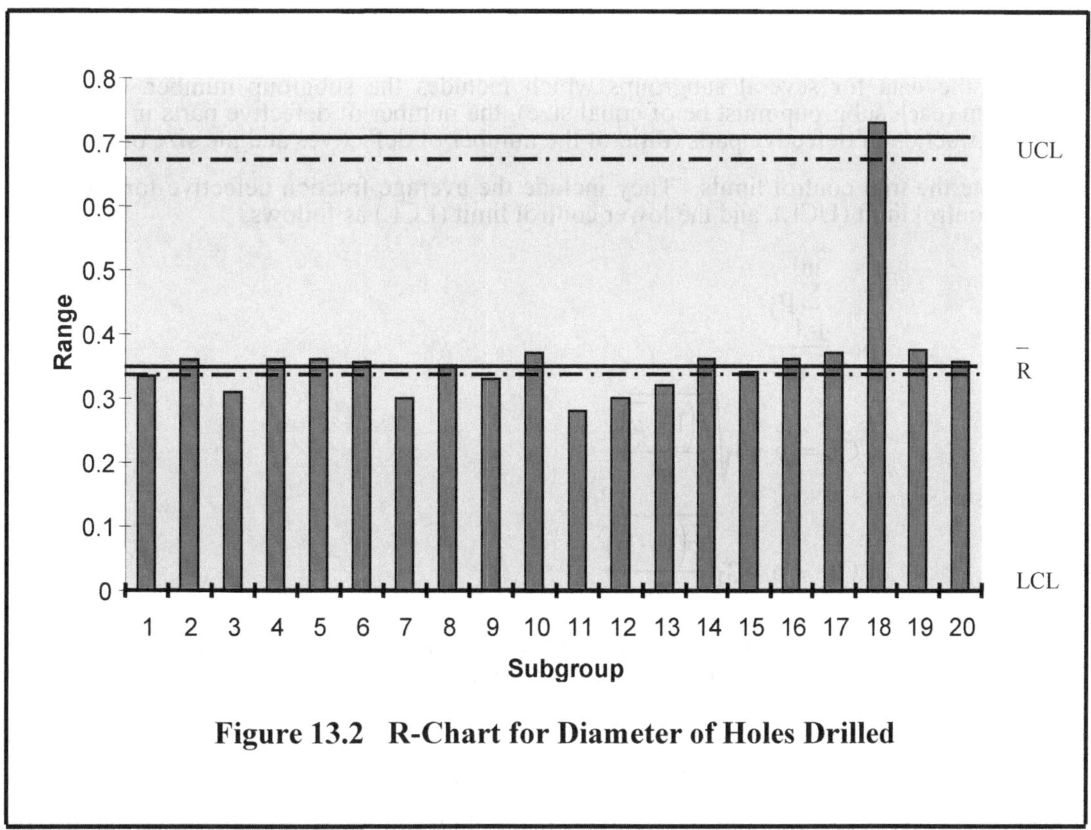

Figure 13.2 R-Chart for Diameter of Holes Drilled

Both the X-bar chart and the R-chart normally hang close to the machine where the parts are produced. The operator or inspector will enter the data as units are produced and samples are measured for the purpose of quality control. The quality of the product often determines the frequency that the inspector will inspect the product. If a machine is producing well, then fewer inspections are required. However, when there are problems, more frequent inspections are called for.

6. CONTROL CHARTS FOR ATTRIBUTE SAMPLING

As defined earlier, an attribute relates to conformance or non-conformance of a product based on non-measurable characteristics. So, an inspector will look at a product and pass it or not, depending on its appearance. If the product is not passed, then it is labeled a defective product. A defective product may have more than one defect or more than one characteristic that does not conform to set standards. It is not the number of defects in a product, but rather the number of defective parts in a sample taken from a production run, that we are concerned about in attribute sampling.

There are basically two types of control charts for attributes, the **p-chart** and the **c-chart**. The p-chart exhibits the fractions of defective parts in sample subgroups taken from various production runs or batches, while the c-chart shows the number of defective parts in sample subgroups. The procedure used in constructing these charts is very similar to the one explained for the X-bar chart.

The procedure to construct a p-chart is as follows:

Step 1: Define the attribute characteristic. An attribute characteristic could be acceptable color, no scratches, properly made-up bed, anything that falls under either conformance or non-conformance of set specifications.

Step 2: Define the appropriate sample size. The sample size of each subgroup in attribute sampling is considerably larger than for variable sampling and very much depends on the acceptable average p value (fraction of defectives). For example, if the acceptable average p equals 0.01, then a sample size of 100 would allow for one defective on the average to occur. This is rather small, because it would require many zeros to be recorded on a chart. A better sample size would be 500 or more. With a sample size of 500, the average number of defectives allowed is 5.

Step 3: Collect the data for several subgroups which includes the subgroup number, the size of the subgroup (each subgroup must be of equal size), the number of defective parts in each subgroup, and the fraction of defective parts (ratio of the number of defectives and the size of the subgroup).

Step 4: Calculate the trial control limits. They include the average fraction defective for all groups, the upper control limit (UCL), and the lower control limit (LCL) as follows:

$$\bar{p} = \frac{\sum_{j=1}^{m} p_j}{m}$$

$$UCL = \bar{p} + 3\sqrt{\frac{\bar{p}(1-\bar{p})}{n}}$$

$$LCL = \bar{p} - 3\sqrt{\frac{\bar{p}(1-\bar{p})}{n}}$$

Where: $\bar{p}$ is the average of the subgroup proportions of defectives
p_j is the proportion of defectives in subgroup j
n is the size of each subgroup
m is the number of subgroups

Step 5: Plot the values of the proportion defectives, p_j, and the trial control limits for each subgroup j.

Step 6: Establish revised control limits. Realize that initial control limits are based on the data of subgroups. Any subgroup that is out of control (using the original control limits) must be eliminated and new control limits determined based on data that is in control. These revised control limits are then used for future quality control analysis.

An Example: p-Charts for Defective Artificial Pearls

Using the first 10 subgroups of the sampling data of 20 subgroups shown in Table 13.2, initial control limits are calculated as follows:

$$\bar{p} = \frac{\sum_{j=1}^{10} p_j}{10} = \frac{0.66}{10} = 0.066 \ (6.6\%)$$

$$UCL1 = 0.066 + 3\sqrt{\frac{0.066(1-0.066)}{100}} = 0.066 + 0.074 = 0.140$$

$$LCL1 = 0.066 - 3\sqrt{\frac{0.066(1-0.066)}{100}} = 0.066 - 0.074 = -0.008 \Rightarrow \text{change to } 0$$

Table 13.2: Quality Control Data for Artificial Pearls			
Subgroup #	Sample Size	# of Defectives	Fraction Defective
1	100	8	0.08
2	100	16	0.16
3	100	8	0.08
4	100	2	0.02
5	100	6	0.06
6	100	2	0.02
7	100	8	0.08
8	100	6	0.06
9	100	4	0.04
10	100	6	0.06
11	100	4	0.04
12	100	8	0.08
13	100	12	0.12
14	100	8	0.08
15	100	4	0.04
16	100	6	0.06
17	100	4	0.04
18	100	5	0.05
19	100	8	0.08
20	100	3	0.03

Figure 13.3 is the p-chart for this example. Note that one of the first ten p-values in the p-chart shows lack of control in sample #2. This point can now be eliminated and new control limits calculated as follows:

$$\bar{p} = \frac{0.66 - 0.16}{9} = 0.056$$

$$UCL = 0.056 + 3\sqrt{\frac{0.056 \times 0.944}{100}} = 0.056 + 0.069 = 0.125$$

$$LCL = 0.056 - 0.069 = -0.013 \Rightarrow \text{change to } 0$$

These new control limits are also entered in Figure 13.3 and future p-values, from sample 11 through 20, are compared to these new control limits.

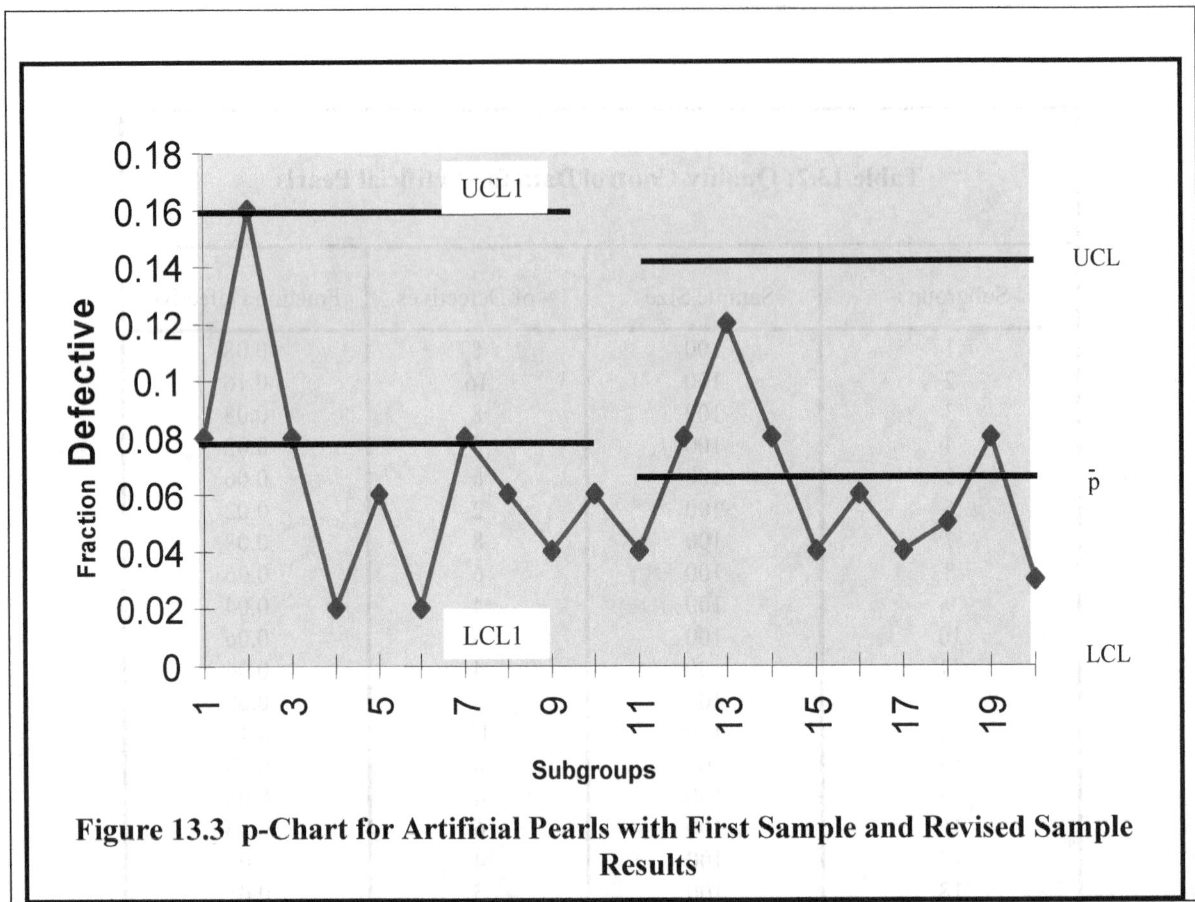

Figure 13.3 p-Chart for Artificial Pearls with First Sample and Revised Sample Results

7. ACCEPTANCE SAMPLING

When shipping goods to customers it is paramount that these goods are "free of defects." "Free of defects" does not mean that every single part or product in the lot must be perfect. Customers normally accept a certain small percentage of defective parts in a large lot of goods. After all, they understand that it is neither possible nor practical to produce nothing but perfect goods at all times, nor is it possible or cost effective to screen all produced items for imperfections. Acceptance sampling can be used to evaluate production runs before shipping them to the customers. Acceptance sampling is the abstraction of a sample from the whole lot, the evaluation of that sample, and the determination of acceptability or non-acceptability of the total lot based on that sample. If acceptance sampling indicates that there are too many defective parts in the sample, then it becomes mandatory to evaluate the whole lot and to replace all defective parts with good ones before shipping it to the customer. However, if the number of defects in the sample is small enough to accept the total lot, then only the defective items in the sample will be replaced by good ones before shipping the whole lot to the customer.

Acceptance sampling for attributes is commonly used in industry and is based on the concept that one can evaluate the content of a large lot by looking at a small percentage of randomly selected items of the lot. With acceptance sampling we can make two types of errors. We can accept a poor lot or we may reject a good lot. In what follows we will see how an operating characteristic curve reflects the probability of accepting a lot, based on the fraction of defectives in the lot.

Sampling plans can be designed and their quality can be evaluated by determining their operating characteristic curves. In general, there are four ways acceptance sampling can be done in order to evaluate lots: single sampling, double sampling, sequential sampling, or continuous sampling.

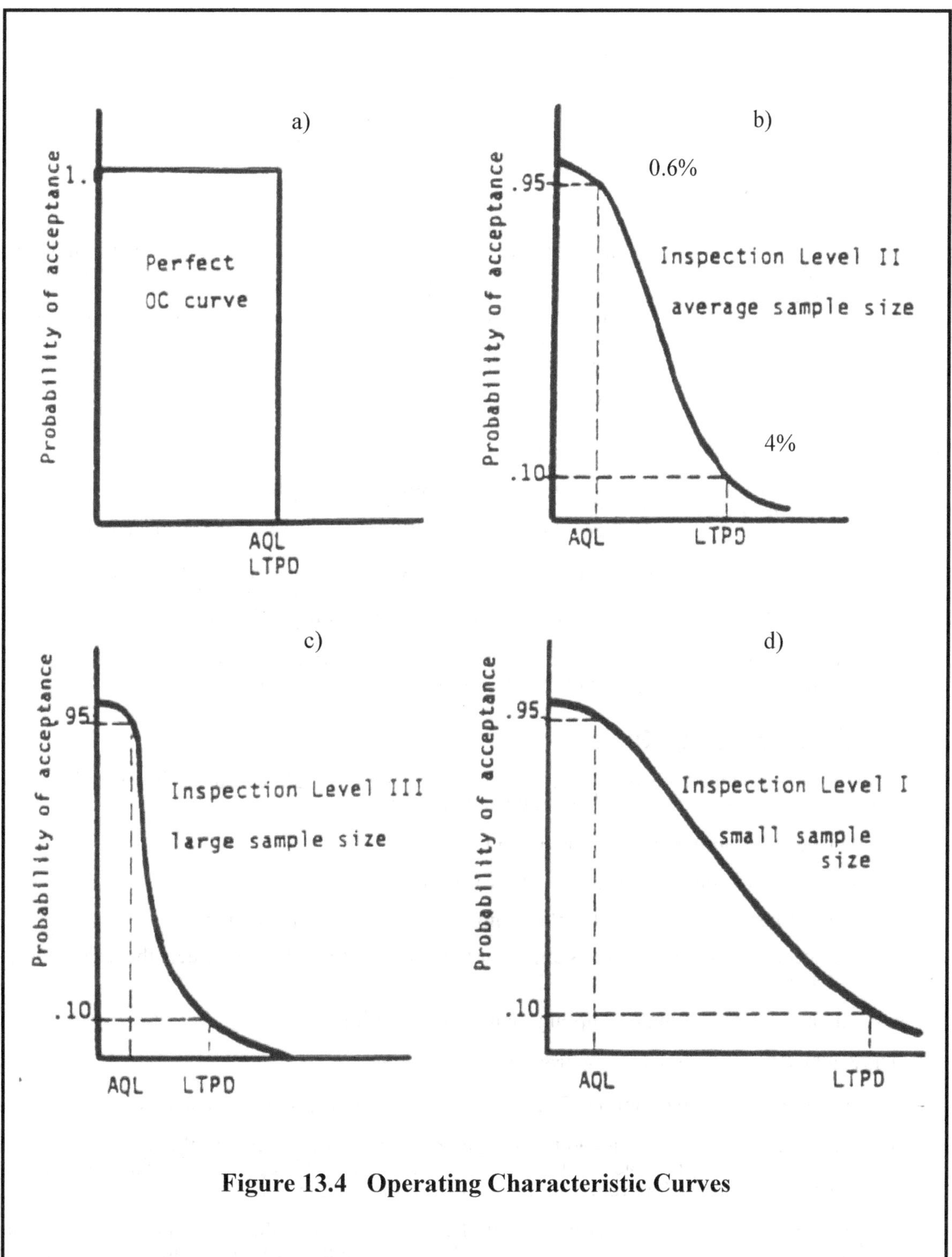

Figure 13.4 Operating Characteristic Curves

7.1. Operating Characteristics Curves

There is a conflict of interest between the producer and the consumer when acceptance sampling is used. A producer wishes that all good lots would be accepted, whereas the consumer does not wish to receive a bad lot. Both producer and customer can be satisfied if 100% inspection of the lot occurs. In this case the operating characteristic curve that reflects the probability of accepting a lot, based on the fraction of defectives in the lot, is as shown in Figure 13.4a. However, as indicated earlier, this exhaustive quality control of parts is neither practical, nor economical. Therefore, both producers and customers have to be willing to take a risk associated with sampling.

The producer has to take the risk of rejecting a good lot. In quality control, the producer's risk is called the **alpha error (α)**. It represents the probability of rejecting a good lot. This risk normally varies between 0.01 and 0.10, with 0.05 being the most frequently used probability value. Its **acceptable quality level (AQL)**, normally defines a good lot. The acceptable quality level is the maximum fraction of defective parts that is satisfactory. The producer desires that lots with the acceptable quality level will be accepted with a high probability, that is, equal to $(1 - \alpha)$. In this sense, there is a close association between the producer's risk, α, and the acceptable quality level, AQL.

The consumer's risk is the probability of accepting a bad lot, as a result of sampling, and is called the **beta error (β)**. This error is normally put at $\beta = 0.10$. "Consumer's risk" implies that there must be a numerically defined value that is equivalent to "bad" quality.

The value associated with bad quality, is known as **lot tolerance percent defective (LTPD)**. LTPD is the maximum percent of defectives in the lot that the customer is willing to tolerate. Figure 13.4b is an operating characteristic curve, OC, where AQL = 0.6% with $\alpha = 0.05$, and LTPD = 4.0% with $\beta = 0.10$.

If we wish to bring the LTPD percentage closer to the AQL percentage, then it will be necessary to increase the sample size. This OC curve is a lot steeper, as shown in Figure 13.4c, and is noticeably better for the customer because the maximum percent of defectives in the lot that the customer will have to tolerate is smaller. Figure 13.4d is the OC curve of a poor sampling plan. It exhibits a large LTPD percentage as compared to the AQL percentage. It is also an OC curve of a sampling plan that requires a relatively small sample size as compared to the OC curves in Figures 13.4b and c.

7.2 Single Sampling Plan

The sampling procedure and decision process used for the single sampling plan is shown in Figure 13.5. This sampling plan is defined by the following characteristics:

N identifies the number of the items in the lot

n is the size of the sample that will be drawn from the lot

d is the number of defects found in the sample of *n* items drawn from the lot

c is the acceptance number of the sample, or the maximum number of defects that are allowed in the sample for acceptance.

Using these characteristic, the single sampling plan is then as follows.

Step 1: Draw a random sample of *n* items from a lot of *N* items.

Step 2: Inspect all n items in that sample. This will reveal *d* defective items in that sample.

Step 3: If the number of defective items in the sample, *d*, is less than or equal to the maximum allowable number of defects, *c*, then accept the lot of $(N - n)$ items and replace all defective items in the sample by good ones before returning the sample to the original lot.

If the number of defective items in the sample, *d*, is larger than the maximum allowable number of defectives, *c*, then the lot must be inspected 100%. All defective items in the lot must now be replaced.

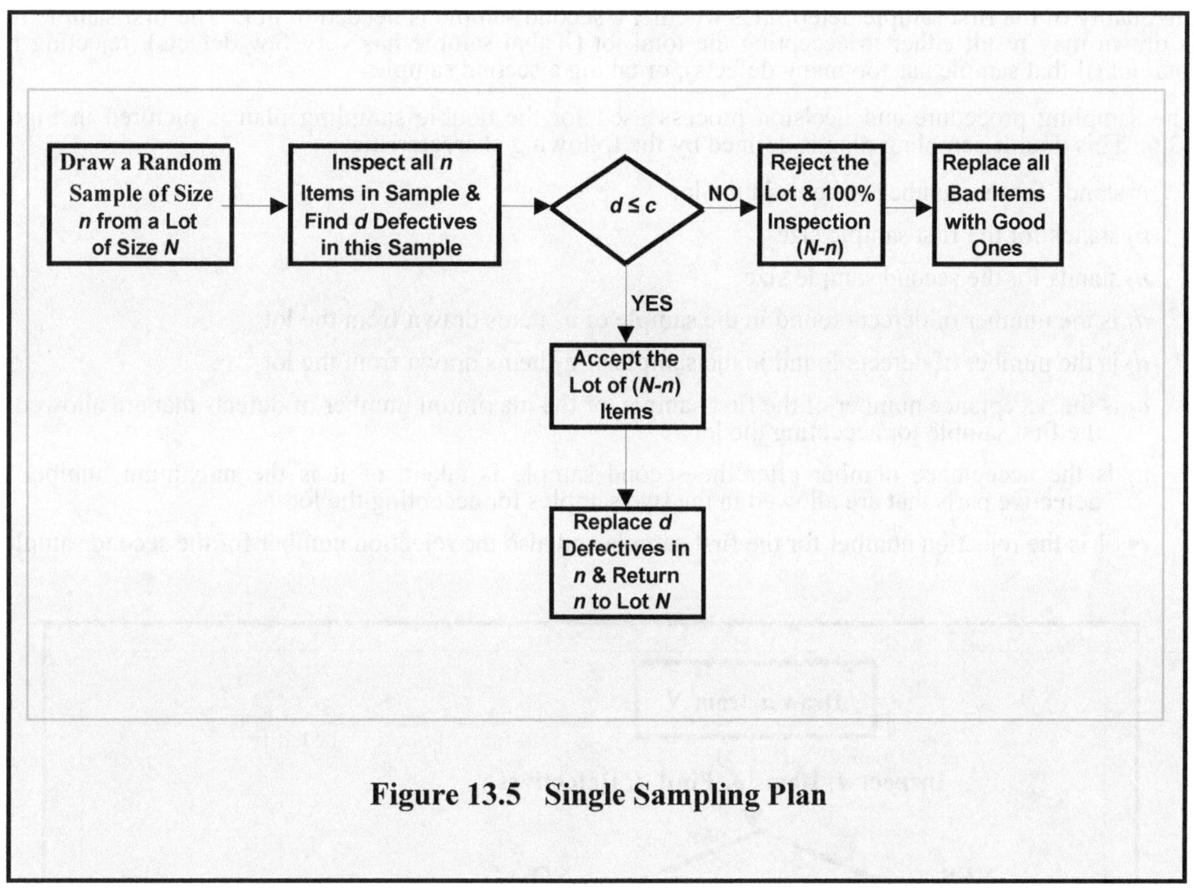

Figure 13.5 Single Sampling Plan

Companies have developed tables that can be used to design an appropriate single sampling plan for a specific production lot size, a defined AQL level, an approximate OC curve, and specified inspection conditions. For example, Table 13.1 can be used to determine the appropriate sample size code. The three inspection levels shown in Table 13.1 determine the shape of the OC curve. So, the inspection level will determine the protection given to the consumer. Level II reflects an average protection level (similar to the one exhibited in the OC curve of Figure 13.4b), level I requires approximately half the sample size as needed for level II, but gives the least protection to the consumer (similar to the OC curve pictured in Figure 13.4d), and level III gives the highest protection with the steepest OC curve (as shown in Figure 13.4c) and requires a sample size that is approximately twice as large as the one needed for level II.

Inspections are usually carried out under normal inspection conditions. However, these conditions can be tightened or reduced depending on previous sample results. Tightened inspection in general starts when the past process average is significantly above AQL. Business uses well defined switching rules that guide them to switch from normal to tightened inspection, from tightened to normal inspection, from normal to reduced inspection, and from reduced to normal inspection. The switching rules between normal and tightened inspection are:

- When normal inspection is being used, one will switch to tightened inspection when two out of five consecutive lots or batches have been rejected.
- When tightened inspection is being used, one will switch to normal inspection when five consecutive lots or batches have been accepted.

7.3 Double Sampling Plan

The double sampling plan requires the sampling of one or two samples of parts from a lot. In this plan the quality of the first sample determines whether a second sample is needed or not. The first sample that is drawn may result either in accepting the total lot (if that sample has very few defects), rejecting the total lot (if that sample has too many defects), or taking a second sample.

The sampling procedure and decision process used for the double sampling plan is pictured in Figure 13.6. This double sampling plan is defined by the following characteristics:

N stands for the number of items in the lot

n_1 stands for the first sample size

n_2 stands for the second sample size

d_1 is the number of defects found in the sample of n_1 items drawn from the lot

d_2 is the number of defects found in the sample of n_2 items drawn from the lot

c_1 is the acceptance number of the first sample, or the maximum number of defects that are allowed in the first sample for accepting the lot

c_2 is the acceptance number after the second sample is taken, or it is the maximum number of defective parts that are allowed in the two samples for accepting the lot

c_2+1 is the rejection number for the first sample and also the rejection number for the second sample.

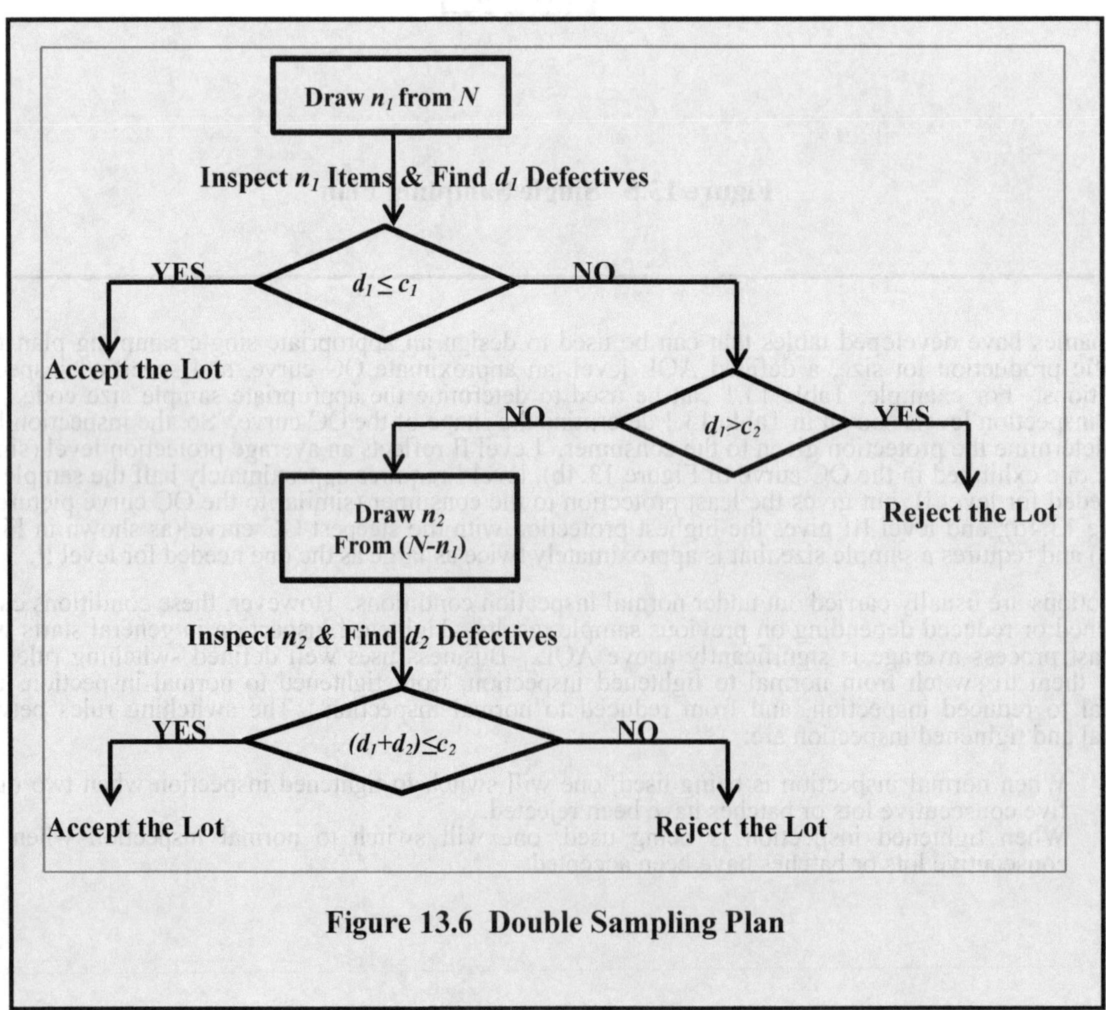

Figure 13.6 Double Sampling Plan

Using these characteristics, the double sampling plan is as follows:

Step 1: Draw a *random sample of n_1 from a lot of N items.*

Step 2: Inspect all n_1 items in the sample that was drawn from the lot. This will reveal d_1 defective items in that sample.

Step 3: If the number of defective items in the sample, d_1, is less than or equal to the acceptance number of the first sample, c_1, then accept the lot of $(N-n_1)$ items and replace all defective items in the sample by good ones before returning the sample to the original lot.

If the number of defective items in the sample, d_1, is larger than the acceptance number of both lots together, c_2, then the lot must be inspected 100%. Good ones must now replace all defective items in the lot.

If none of the above is the case, then a second sample of size n_2 must be drawn from the remaining lot of size $(N - n_1)$. Proceed now to step 4.

Step 4: Inspect all n_2 items in the second sample that was drawn. This will reveal d_2 defective items in that sample.

Step 5: If the accumulated number of defective items in both samples, $(d_1 + d_2)$, is less than or equal to the maximum allowable total number of defectives in both samples, c_2, then accept the lot of $(N - n_1 - n_2)$ items and replace all defective items found in both samples by good ones before returning the samples to the original lot.

If, however, the sum of defective items in the two samples, $(d_1 + d_2)$, is larger than the maximum allowable total number of defects, c_2, then the lot must be inspected 100%. Good ones must now replace all bad items in the lot.

So, double sampling suggests taking a small sample first. If that small sample turns out to be very good or very bad, conclusions can be drawn and no further sampling is needed. This significantly reduces inspection cost for lots that are well or poorly under control. Only for borderline cases must the inspector take another sample.

Company tables are used to design an appropriate sampling plan for a specific production lot size, a defined AQL level, an appropriate OC curve, and a specified inspection level.

7.4. Sequential Sampling Plan

With sequential sampling, very small (much smaller than in double sampling) samples are taken and evaluated. Each time a sample is taken and analyzed the decision is made to accept the lot, to reject it, or to continue sampling. Just like the double sampling plan, sequential sampling has the advantage of significantly reducing the amount of inspection effort. Figure 13.7 pictures what can happen when using sequential sampling. In this example, very small samples of five items are drawn from the lot that is being inspected. As samples are drawn, the accumulated number of defects are figured and plotted. As long as these points are between the rejection and acceptance region, sampling will continue. Therefore, in our example, sampling stops after 30 items have been inspected (or 6 small samples have been evaluated). At that point an accumulated number of five defects were encountered, resulting in the rejection of the total lot.

Industrial tables are used to design an appropriate sequential sampling plan for a specific production lot size, a defined AQL level, an approximate OC curve, and a specified inspection condition.

As discussed, inspection efforts vary depending on the quality of the product and the sampling plan used. For example, a single sampling plan may call for a sample size of 110 units. For the same accuracy, a double sampling plan may require an initial sample size of 75 units and a second sample size of 75 units, while the sequential plan may use a maximum of 7 sub-samples of 30 units each. On the one hand, it is obvious that if production lots are very good or very poor, less sampling is needed with double or sequential sampling. On the other hand, borderline lots require less inspection efforts when single sampling plans are used.

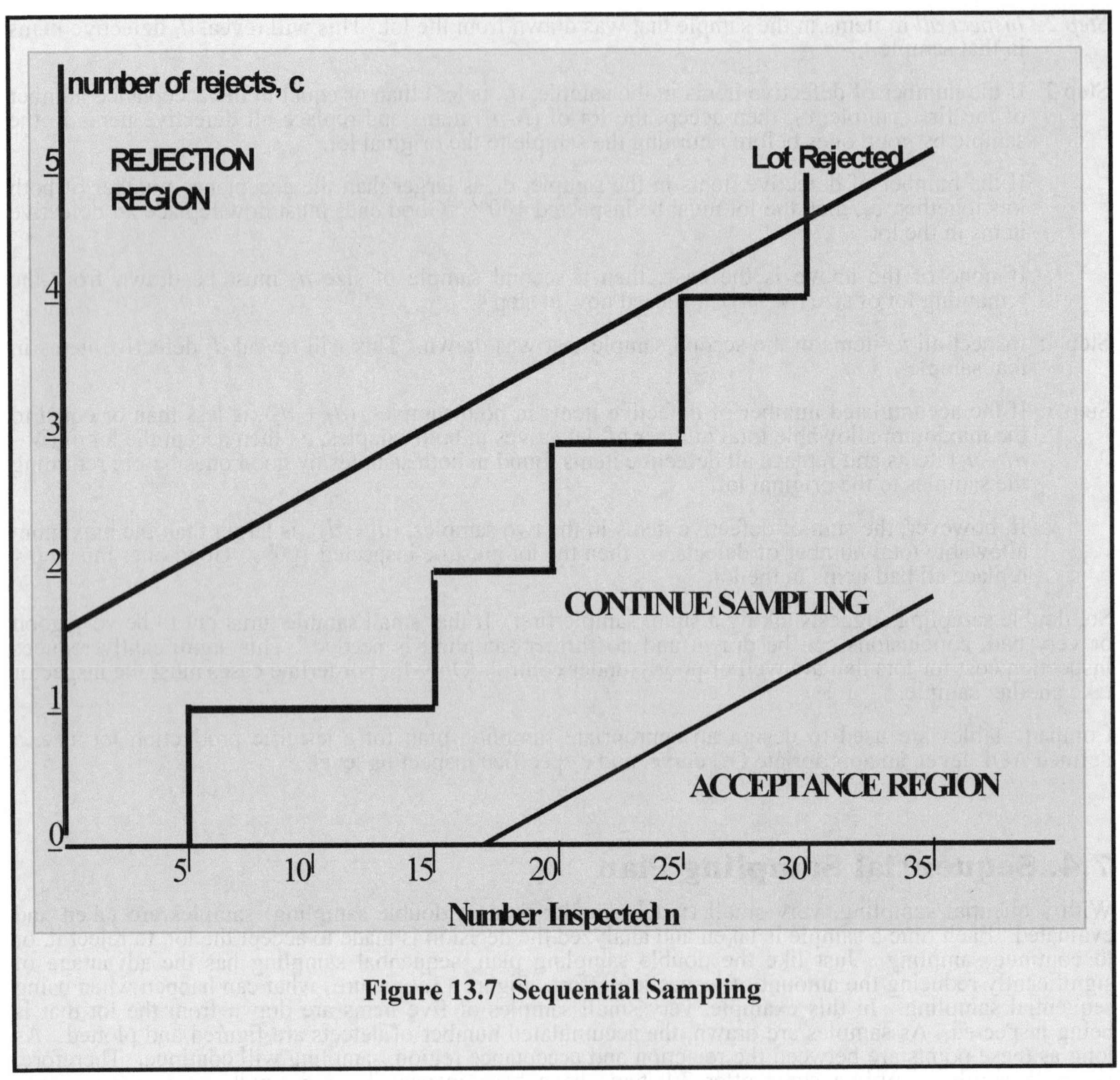

Figure 13.7 Sequential Sampling

7.5. Continuous Sampling Plan

The continuous sampling method can be used for evaluating production when products are produced continuously, like on an assembly line. In this case every *n*th product is inspected, until a defective item is encountered. At that time a large consecutive number of *m* items are inspected and after none of these *m* items are found defective, the inspector returns to inspecting every *n*th item.

8. JAPANESE AND AMERICAN QUALITY CONTROL

After World War II, industrial Japan was plagued with quality problems; they had the reputation being one of the lowest quality producers. Under pressure to improve, industry leaders turned to Dr. W. Edward Deming for aid in boosting quality. Dr. Deming's approach to quality control focuses on management's involvement, continuous improvement, statistical analysis, goal setting, communications, and control of processes. History shows that the Japanese, through careful application of **statistical quality control** (**SQC**) and other programs, have been able to maintain and improve the performance of their manufacturing processes.

While the American companies were more concerned about detecting and segregating defectives from good parts, the Japanese companies were devising systems to reduce and avoid producing defective parts. Statistical quality control (SQC) or statistical process control (SPC) was the key to the Japanese success in controlling quality. **Statistical process control** (**SPC**) is a technique that is used to monitor, evaluate, and analyze a manufacturing process. The operating characteristics of the process determine the quality of its product. Therefore, in order to control and improve quality, it is necessary to control and improve the process. It was only towards the mid- and late-70s that American firms became interested in applying some of these concepts of SQC or SPC.

Quality control standards in Japanese firms are very stringent, with a large number of companies reporting in the late 70s less than five-percent defect rates, and quite a few firms exhibiting a less than one-half-of-one-percent (0.5%) defect rate. Indeed, Japanese companies not only emphasized preventive maintenance, but also quality control, with employees being instructed that zero defects are paramount. The following examples, as reported by various people in the early 80s, illustrate the Japanese success with quality control:

S. C. Wheelwright, in "Japan - Where Operations Really Are Strategic," *Harvard Business Review*, July-August, 1981, pp. 67–74, noted that Motorola Corp. had a very poor productivity and quality record at its Franklin, Illinois television assembly plant. Its records showed 150 defects per 100 completed production sets. However, this changed when the Japanese company Matsushita bought the plant and improved its productivity tremendously with a 30 percent increase and a reduction in the number of defects to less than 4 per completed production sets. While this remarkable achievement was well received, it still was not less than the 0.5% quality standards of other Japanese plants.

Y. Tsurumi, in "Productivity: The Japanese Approach," *Pacific Basin Quarterly,* Summer, 1981, p. 8, commented that 80 percent of Warwick's television assembly plant capacity was closed because its quality was so bad when Japanese manufacturer, Sanyo, bought the plant in Forest City, Arkansas. Even Sears, which had owned 25 percent of the Warwick stock, had stopped buying its inventory for its own label and turned to Japanese manufacturers. However, once Sanyo took control, in a few months its line productivity had improved substantially. The quality of its plant's television sets began to improve from a 30 percent defect rate to less than 5 percent.

David A. Garvin, in "Quality On The Line," *Harvard Business Review*, September-October, 1983, drew some conclusions after his study of manufacturers of room air conditioners in both the United States and Japan. He found that the worst producers (American companies), had air-conditioner failure rates between 500 and1000 times greater than those made by the best producers (Japanese companies). His study further showed that the average number of defects on the assembly line were 70 times worse for an American manufacturer than for a Japanese one. This, of course, translated into 17 times more service calls following the sale during the first service year by the American companies compared to their Japanese counterparts. Even the air conditioners produced by the worst Japanese manufacturers had defect percentages that were less than half of those made by the best American ones. Furthermore, he found that the extra cost spent by Japanese manufacturers to make higher quality products was about half the cost of what American manufacturers were spending to fix defective ones. Thus Garvin concluded that companies with the better quality records also would have the higher labor productivity.

Small-lot production, just-in-time inventory and production control, just-in-time purchasing, extensive preventive maintenance programs, automated equipment and robots, together with worker involvement and responsibility all favor a high quality product in Japanese firms.

In the 80s small-lot production was an industrial advantage Japan enjoyed over manufacturers in the United States. If you produce products in large quantity, you cannot detect quality problems immediately. However, if a quality problem occurs in a small lot production, the problem is noted and corrected sooner at considerable savings. Also, just-in-time production and inventory control call for the need to draw everybody's attention to solve quality problems swiftly. Indeed, when quality problems occur, production is stopped until the problem is corrected. Just like the in-house workers do, just-in-time purchasing tends to develop suppliers that deliver parts of perfect quality. Careful checking of equipment (before the start of each shift) and their extensive preventive maintenance programs guarantee quality production. Furthermore, workers are instructed not to pass defective parts on to the next production operation. In this sense, the workers are responsible for producing parts of perfect quality, or with zero defects, before releasing them to the next station.

9. TOTAL QUALITY CONTROL (TQC) AND COMPANY-WIDE QUALITY CONTROL (CWQC)

9.1 Definition of TQC and CWQC

Total quality control (TQC) and **company-wide quality control** (CWQC) form a revolutionary breakthrough in management philosophy that was coined from Japanese factories. They touch all facets of the organization from shop floor to the boardroom. Quality means excellence. It includes excellence of the product, excellence of management, excellence of community relations, excellence of company performance, excellence of company image in society, and excellence of work environment. In this sense, TQC and CWQC refer to the concept of building quality or excellence into the total corporate structure, and of continuously striving to improve it.

9.2 Implementing TQC and CWQC in Japan

The efforts to study quality control in Japan started in 1949, when a special group was organized in the Union of Japanese Scientists and Engineers (JUSE). This group mainly consisted of professors, governmental officials, and engineers from private companies. The major purpose of this group was to provide educational programs in an effort to promote quality control in Japanese firms.

Dr. W. Edwards Deming from the United States was invited in 1950 to deliver a lecture on **statistical quality control, SQC**. The period of 1946 to 1950 was declared to be the SQC period in Japan. During this period Japan's quality blossomed, statistical philosophy and techniques were spread widely throughout the industry, industrial education systems were established, and the motivation for introducing quality control into Japan's industry became stronger, day-by-day. However, top management was far from being quality control conscious during this period. Therefore, few concrete results were obtained, in spite of active application of statistical techniques in Japanese industry.

All this changed in 1954, after **Dr. J.M. Juran's** lecture on "Planning and Practice in Quality Control." True quality control was launched and promoted throughout Japanese industry, and was backed by all of management. **Company-wide quality control (CWQC)** was indeed born in Japan. The period of time between 1955 and 1960 was designated as the "Years of TQC." During that time period, all company members, from top management down to rank-and-file workers, studied statistical quality control, and jointly participated in the upgrading of company-wide quality control practices.

Quality control in Japan has progressed from inspection-oriented quality assurance, to production-process-oriented quality assurance, to, finally, new-product-development-oriented quality assurance.

In Japan, the producer is responsible for quality assurance. In this sense, the vendors and sub-contractors, too, are fully responsible for quality assurance. Therefore, when the purchaser can trust the vendor, there is no need to inspect the vendor's product, and one has created the so-called **quality assurance purchasing system**. This system works very well in Japan.

Inspecting products presents a great number of problems. Therefore, Japanese companies introduced production process-oriented quality control. Typical features of production process-oriented quality control urge one to:

1. Place emphasis on the usage of process analysis, process control, and process control charts, rather than sampling inspection. In other words, one must build the quality in the product, while still in the manufacturing process, rather than correcting mistakes after the product is manufactured.

2. Improve process capability in order to produce the most reliable and cheapest parts.

3. Get participation of not only the inspection department, but also of such departments as sales, purchasing, production engineering, manufacturing, maintenance, subcontractors, foremen, and workshop people.

However, process control alone cannot accomplish quality assurance. For example, if there is something wrong with the design or product development or selection of the materials, process control will not detect it. For this reason, new-product-development-oriented quality assurance was started in Japan in 1960. It was then that they decided to build quality and reliability into the product during the new-product development phase, starting with new-product planning, design, trial production, and evaluation, and on to mass production design, trial mass production, production, sales, and flow control. In this sense, the Japanese not only built quality into their manufacturing processes, but also into their product during the design phase.

Some of the more important considerations in implementing successful company-wide quality control programs in Japanese companies are top management involvement, emphasis on training, a formal organization, the use of informal quality control circles, giving awards, and lots of patience.

There is a firm commitment from top management in Japanese companies to implementing quality control programs. Top management always initiates and supports, through budget and time, company-wide and total quality control. Their involvement goes beyond monetary commitment. They also get involved with quality control programs, attend quality control seminars, and give awards to employees who have made outstanding contributions to quality improvement.

Training for quality performance is provided to everybody on all levels, from top management and middle management to supervisors, foremen, and workers.

Besides a formal organizational structure that controls quality, namely, the quality control and/or quality assurance department, there is also an informal structure that aids in the control of quality. This structure is called the quality control circle. Most companies will install quality control circles only after management has a well-coordinated program of company-wide quality control.

Even though awards are given for certain quality achievements, it should be noted that employees in Japanese firms do not engage in quality control circle activities for the sake of money alone. They do so because it is satisfying and self-fulfilling to them. The Deming Prize was established in 1951, on behalf of the merits of Dr. W. E. Deming's work, and in an effort to promote the quality control movement in Japan. Initially, the prize was divided into the Deming Prize proper, and the Deming Application Prize. Recently, the Deming Application Prize was again divided into three prizes, namely, the Deming Application Prize proper, the Prize for Small/Medium Enterprise, and the Prize for a Particular Division of a company. In Japan, companies compete fiercely to obtain these prizes.

Other advocates of total quality control are:

- **Dr. Armand Feigenbaum** is considered to be the originator of the total quality movement.
- **Philip Crosby** defined quality management through four absolutes. These absolutes include a quality definition (conformance to requirements), a quality system (prevention of defects), a quality performance standard (zero defects), and a quality measurement (costs of quality).
- **Dr. Kaoru Ishikawa** advocated the use of seven quality tools: histograms (example is Figure 13.2), check sheets, flowcharts (Figures 13.5 and 13.6), control charts (Figures 13.1 and 13.3), Pareto charts (Figure 13.8), scatter plots or diagrams (Figure 13.9), and cause-and-effect or fish-bone diagrams (Figure 13.10).
- **Dr. Genichi Taguchi** introduced experimental design to identify the settings of product and process parameters to reduce performance variation.

9.2.1 Pareto Chart

Vilfredo Pareto, an Italian economist, said that a small percentage of a group accounts for the largest inpact. A Pareto chart graphically exhibits this concept, by ranking causes from most significant to least significant. When applied to quality problems a Pareto chart helps to break a problem down into its various components and is used to help focus on the most significant causes of defects, rather than all causes of defects. Figure 13.8 shows a Pareto chart that has defective type D1, which occurs in most of the samples, upfront in the chart. The focus here is to draw attention to that problem first and resolve it before addressing the other defect types.

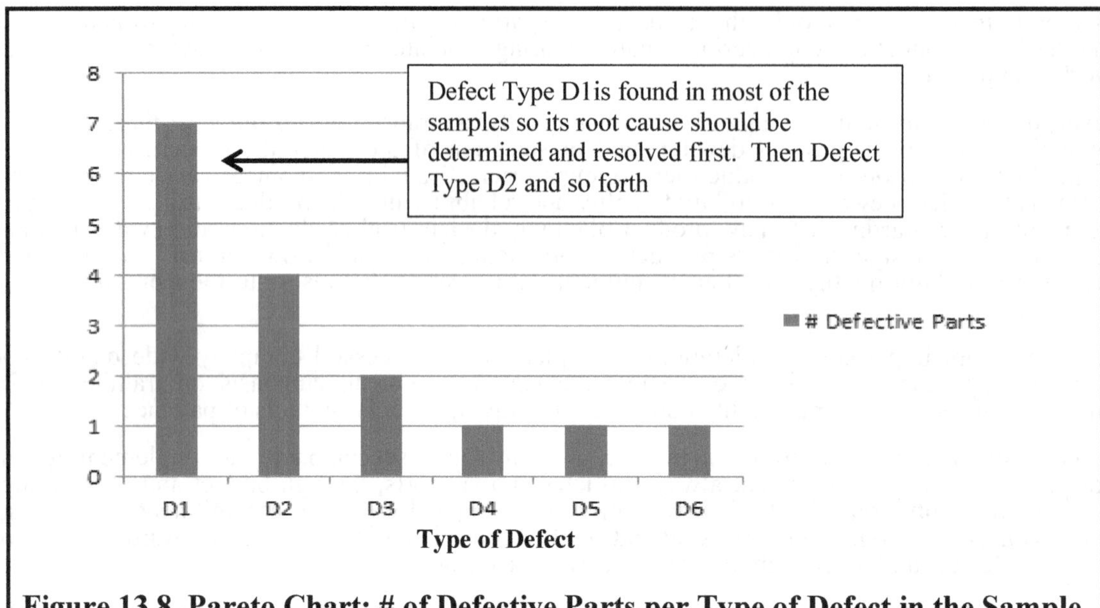

Figure 13.8 Pareto Chart: # of Defective Parts per Type of Defect in the Sample

9.2.2 Scatter Plot

A scatter diagram or plot, when used for quality control, is a graphical technique to analyze measurements of a certain characteristic in samples. The scatter plot shown in Figure 13.9 identifies three samples where the length of wire is significantly different from the other samples. These outlier samples need to be investigated as to why they are so different from the majority.

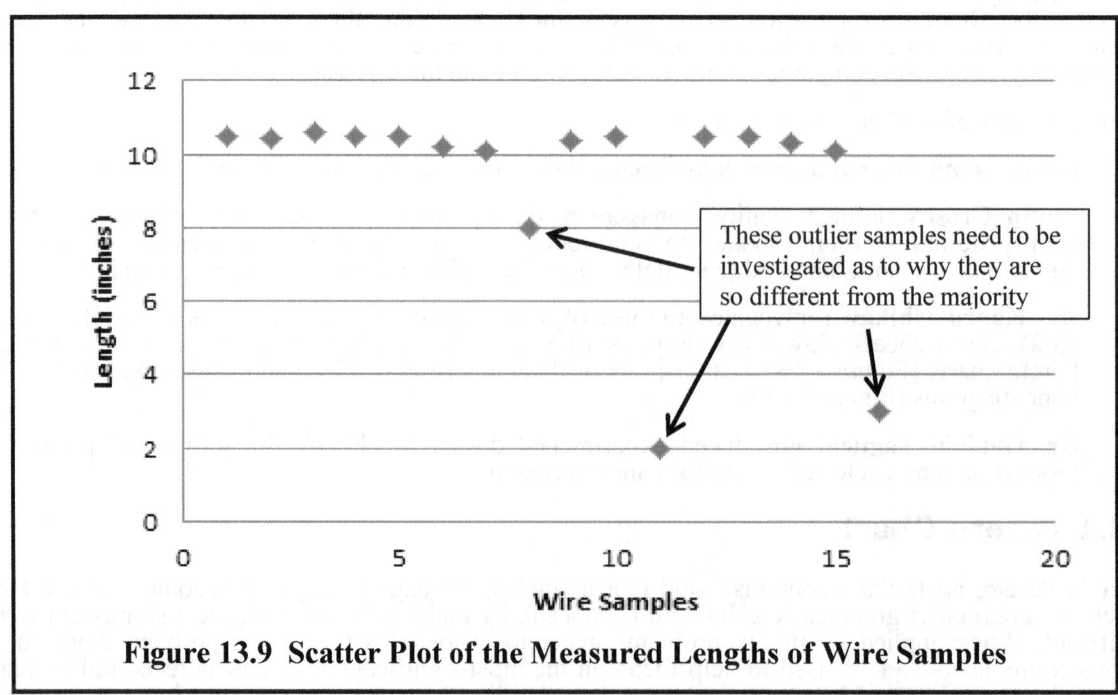

Figure 13.9 Scatter Plot of the Measured Lengths of Wire Samples

9.2.3 Cause-and-Effect or Fish-Bone Diagram

Dr. Kaoru Ishikawa developed the cause-and-effect diagram, a tool for identifying causes related to a quality problem. It is also called the fish-bone diagram because, when drawn correctly, it resembles a fish bone. At the head of the fish bone, on the extreme right of the fish bone, appears the quality problem. Alongside the spine, where the bones of the fish are, the main categories of causes of the quality problem are listed. These causes can be further detailed, creating more bones on the fish. Figure 13.10 illustrates this diagram concept.

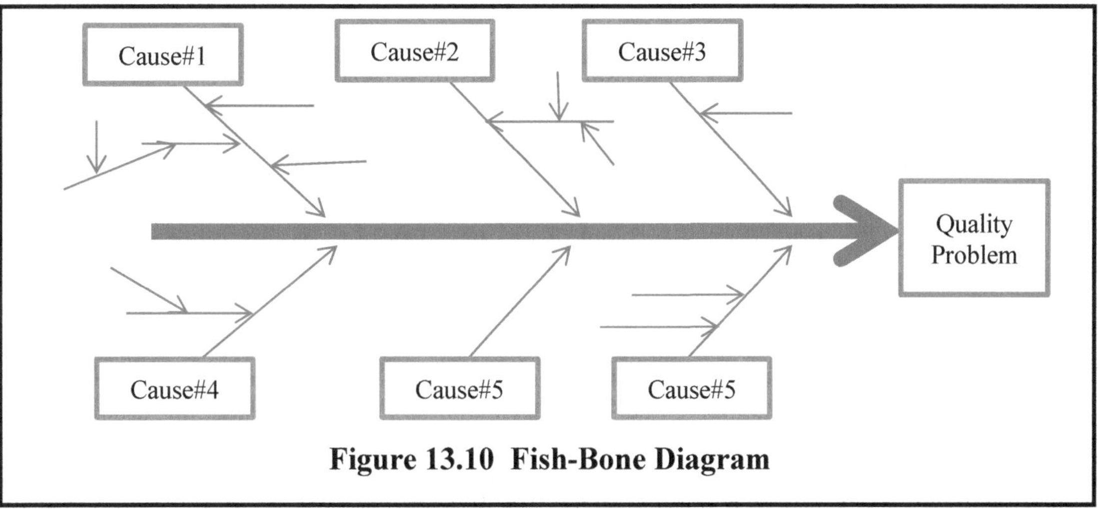

Figure 13.10 Fish-Bone Diagram

An Example: A Health Care Example Revisited
Let us revisit the timeliness of patient transfer from an acute medical service to the rehabilitation service as presented in Chapter 4, section 8.3. This transfer requires coordination between both physicians and nurses on the sending and the receiving services, housekeeping to prepare the beds, transport, multiple steps to obtain insurance approval, and others. The fish-bone diagram for a delay in patient transfer could look as shown in Figure 13.11.

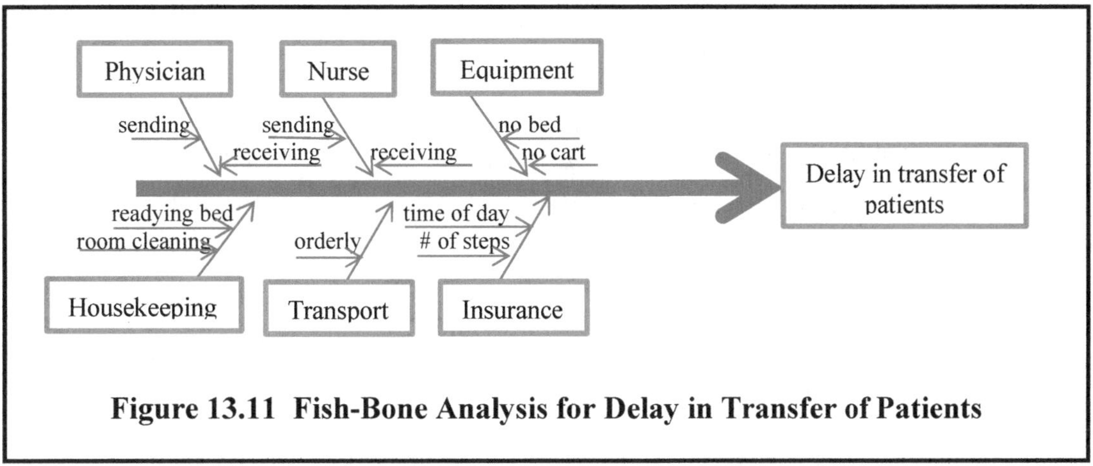

Figure 13.11 Fish-Bone Analysis for Delay in Transfer of Patients

9.3 Considerations When Implementing TQC & CWQC

When attempting to implement total quality control, or company-wide quality control in other countries, one must do so within a given cultural and social heritage. The Japanese quality control programs have been successful within their given cultural and social framework, such as lifetime employment; homogeneity of Japanese people; the paternalistic and collective nature of the Japanese; their labor-management relationship; and management's concern with long-term objectives of the company, rather than being overly concerned with quarterly profit standing.

The above-mentioned cultural and social framework existing in Japan did not stand in the way of implementing similar quality control techniques in the U.S.A. Repeatedly, the Japanese have shown that their quality control techniques work within our culture, as long as they are properly adapted and implemented. In his presentation on "TQC at Tennessee Plant of Toshiba America, Inc." (published in *Three-Day Seminar on Kanban, Quality Control and Quality Management*, by the Cambridge Corporation, April 25–27, 1983, p. 48), Robert H. Traeger illustrated how Toshiba was able to introduce total quality control (TQC) in its Tennessee plant of Toshiba America, Inc. by transplanting as much as possible of the known SQC systems being used in Japan for TV and microwave oven manufacturing plants.

Traeger indicated that when they started production at this Tennessee plant, they found that most of the quality problems were with the U.S. suppliers. So they found it necessary to change the normal U.S. customer-supplier relationship in order to be successful. They invited their suppliers to participate in joint evaluation and frank discussions on quality issues. Together they developed and agreed to effective quality standards and measurement methods and even the subjective ones that were the most difficult to define. The Tennessee plant developed credibility with its suppliers because when a part was declared out-of-specification, it really was the case. This led to a willingness to work together and share information to eliminate future problems. The results of this change in the relationship was dramatic, with not only experiencing fewer defects, but also having suppliers that had become real working partners. So not only had the suppliers' production yields increased, but they had gained a reputation for providing superior quality products which improved their profit and loss, bottom line.

When implementing TQC or CWQC in the Western world, following general considerations are vital for its success:

- Top management has to get involved and be totally committed to producing superior top-quality products and services.
- Top quality has to become an integral part of the organization's business strategies.
- Quality has to be built into the product or service during its product development stage. This demands product standardization, proper engineering design with high product reliability, and proper materials requirements to facilitate processing.
- Production facilities and processes have to be geared towards producing perfect, high-quality products and services. Workers who produce goods and services must become responsible for generating defect-free goods. No poor-quality parts are allowed to proceed from one process to the next process. In this sense, quality control becomes a line function, rather than the responsibility of a quality control department. Workers become responsible for only passing on high-quality products to the next operation, drastically reducing the size of the quality control department and its inspection personnel.
- Quality commitment must go beyond product development and processing. It also becomes the responsibility of warehousing, packaging, marketing, and the distribution system, in general. This aspect of quality control also relates to damaged parts and goods resulting from poor handling during shipping or improper installation.

10. BEYOND LEAN QUALITY MANAGEMENT: SIX SIGMA AND DESIGNING FOR SIX SIGMA

10.1 The Six Sigma Concept

In the early 1950s, as W. Edwards Deming shifted the focus of mass production from quantity to quality he was regarded as the father of total quality management. Throughout the 80s the effectiveness of TQM was improved upon through the implementation of the Six Sigma (SS) process that was created by Dr. Mikel Harry. This Six Sigma process is a disciplined application of statistical problem solving tools that points towards wasteful costs and provides for precise steps for improvement. The Six Sigma process is designed to reduce costs that are associated with waste and defects in product or processes. Cost reduction is achieved by quantifiably identifying all factors that lead to defects, so that they can be adjusted and a perfect level of quality can be achieved. Thus Six Sigma is a management method that focusses on defect or error prevention, through problem detection and solving techniques.

Six Sigma represents an extreme level of high quality. It aims at virtually eliminating defects from every product and process within an organization. Six Sigma (6σ) stands for optimal quality, such as 3.4 defects per million. The Greek symbol "σ" represents the variation, or the number of standard deviations, from the specification limits to the mean of a process. The number of defects per million decreases, as the number of sigmas increases.

Control charts for variable and attribute control, as presented in sections 5 and 6 of this chapter, are based on the concept that customers' specifications are within three standard deviations of the mean. In other words, variation in production is controlled within 3 standard deviations (3σ) of the mean. For attribute sampling this means that approximately 668,076 defects are acceptable in one million parts. In the 80s, so called "average" companies started to operate at about four sigma (4σ), or approximately at 6,210 defects per million. The level of improvement that occurs between the "average" company of the 80s and the company that is at Six Sigma is astounding, or 3.4 defects versus 6,210 defects per million. Now customers' specifications are within six sigma deviations of the mean. To accomplish this company must strive towards a significant reduction in the variability of the process that generates the part.

Six Sigma was first implemented in the early 1980s at Motorola. With an amazing return on investment Motorola claimed that Six Sigma reduced in-process defect levels by a factor of 200 and that it reduced manufacturing costs by 1.4 billion dollars. The stockholders saw a fourfold increase in their share value. Other companies, such as Texas Instruments, Nokia, General Electric, Allied Signal, Dupont, and Sony, soon recognized Motorola's success and they too started to implement Six Sigma with amazing returns on investment.

Quality at the Six Sigma level, together with streamlined processes equal improved yield, decreased operating expenses, and increased market share. The Six Sigma process provides for constantly measuring, continuously reducing defect levels, enhancing process capabilities, and thus ensuring continuous improvement. The ultimate benefit of the Six Sigma methodology is increased customer satisfaction. For the company it fuels company growth, increases operating margins, expands cash flow, and reduces working capital requirements. It also frees up production capacity and enhances growth when the economy is not doing well.

10.2 The Six Sigma Support Group

Companies use a variety of tools to implement Six Sigma. The Six Sigma support group of an organization is trained to use these tools. The support groups are employees who are selected based on a variety of characteristics that include motivation, process and product knowledge, organizational knowledge, communication skills, and team facilitating skills. Amongst the support group, various roles are created within the organization. The main players of any Six Sigma initiative are: consultants, executives, functional managers, support teams, Champions, Master Black Belts, Black Belts, and Green Belts.

All players determine the success of the Six Sigma process. External involvement through consultants is minimized because the hierarchy of the support group allows for further internal training and expansion of the team.

Consultants are individuals who are trained and certified to present Six Sigma to the organization and begin its integration into the culture of the firm. Through collaborative efforts with executive management they support the transition towards Six Sigma by transferring knowledge, ensuring sustainability, and eliminating all barriers.

Executives make the decision to implement the Six Sigma program. They set the meaningful goals for the corporation, define all expectations, commit themselves to ensure continuous improvement, and eliminate all barriers.

Functional Managers, together with the company controller, identify and approve all projects and figure their potential savings. They are also involved in the selection of Black Belt candidates. These functional managers also ensure that all necessary training is done and participate in all Six Sigma reviews.

Champions are individuals that select projects that need improvement. They are responsible for removing any roadblocks that may inhibit or slow down the Six sSgma process. They are the support for the Master Black Belts and all Black Belts.

Master Black Belts are certified Black Belts. They have advanced training that allows them to serve as internal consultants to the corporation. They seem to be one of the most empowered groups of individuals in the organization they serve. They devote all their efforts and time leading and guiding teams in cost reduction projects. They support the Green Belts. The Black Belts are the project leaders: they facilitate the teams in applying Six Sigma methodologies, they spread the use of the methodologies across all functions of the organization, and challenge conventional wisdom by demonstrating the successful application of Six Sigma.

Support Teams own the projects with the Black Belts and the Champions. Once the project is solved they are stakeholders of its solution, thus giving them a sense of employee ownership.

Green Belts are trained to apply Six Sigma tools to improve processes and products. Though they report to their respective supervisors, they continuously interact with their corresponding Black Belt leaders.

10.3 The Six Sigma Model

Six Sigma follows a general problem-solving model that is based on techniques that use quantitative data to produce results. Therefore, the projects that the Champions, Master Black Belts, and Black Belts chose to work on must be definable and measurable.

Each project flows through five phases that General Electric Corporation referred to as the **D-M-A-I-C** five-step process: **D** for definition phase, **M** for measurement phase, **A** for analysis phase, **I** for improvement phase, and **C** for control phase.

D-Definition Phase:

Define what the problem is and how to measure it. Defining which customers are served with the project is essential to the success of the project because Six Sigma is customer driven. This phase leads to the creation of a set of performance measures as defined by critical or important customers. Some of these performance measures for processes and products could be cost of quality, timely delivery, level of customer satisfaction, and others.

M-Measurement Phase:

Measure or collect data on the current problem state. Measurement of the project includes: problem statement, system measurement, capability analysis, and process characterization. While basic statistical analysis provides baseline data, process mapping provides for process characterization. A process map is a graphical representation of how a process is actually performed. It is dynamic and as parameters change it must be constantly updated. Commonly used maps are fish-bone diagrams that easily show all inputs and outputs, referred to as the Xs and the Ys of the project. Measurements must also reflect the cost and waste that are associated with any process. The Black Belt normally creates the process map. He receives input from the support team representatives who ensure that all disciplines provide the necessary input (design, manufacturing, operations, internal and external customer input). After the completion of the process map, an Y-X diagram is constructed showing potential input (Xs)/output (Ys) correlations. It explains which inputs (Xs) have the greatest impact on customer-focused outputs (Ys). This information is placed in a two-level Pareto chart that identifies and quantifies categories of defects or waste.

A-Analysis Phase:

Analyze data and determine better future state. The analysis phase aims at reducing the number of input variables (Xs) from the list identified in the measurement phase, thus narrowing down the vital few variables that are critical to a successful process or product. Tools utilized to analyze the data include the metric graph, a Design of Experiments model, a three-level Pareto analysis, and others. At this phase we identify major sources that cause unwanted variability in processes or products.

I-Improvement Phase:

Improve by implementing the future state solution. During the improvement phase the input variables that have the greatest and most significant positive impact on the outcomes are experimented with and a plan of action is designed and installed that will correct existing waste problems to improve the performance and the outcome of the processes. The following are some of the tools that can be utilized in this phase: Chi-square test, T-test, ANOVA, three-level Pareto analysis, fish-bone analysis and others.

C-Control Phase:

Control by measuring to verify that the problem is fixed permanently. The control phase is the most critical phase of the Six Sigma process. The objective of this phase is that the processes are corrected and that the corrections are lasting. This implies that all the changes in processes are properly documented and are monitored with appropriate process controls. All parties involved must understand that all gains and improvements must be sustained. At some point in the future it is necessary to re-evaluate the project to make sure that improvements are maintained.

The Six Sigma model has been well received by many companies. Its continuous improvement perspective has motivated many companies to see its value as their way to initiate change. So they have therefore incorporated its key principles in their change management process.

10.4 Designing for Six Sigma (DFSS)

In order to improve financially and reward investors with a larger return on investment, companies around the world have introduced Six Sigma and ***Designing for Six Sigma***. When implemented correctly companies have reported savings of 25% of total sales.

Delighted customers equate to happy consumers and designing for six sigma is the initiative that allows companies to develop the right product for their target consumers. To achieve long-term success all new product decisions must be driven by incorporating the Voice of the Consumer (VOC). DFSS moved the initial efforts of the Six Sigma quality movement from the manufacturing function into the design function. It uses specific tools and methodologies to conform products to Six Sigma standards. One such methodology is called ***Knowledge Transfer Process*** **(KTP)**. This methodology starts with a complete gap analysis of the product development system and involves the Six Sigma consultants who represent all cross-functional teams as new products are developed.

There are five phases to Designing for Six Sigma: the planning phase, the identification phase, the design phase, the optimization phase, and the validation phase.

The Planning Phase:

The planning phase is when the design team is empowered to take on the design project, while management focuses on removing all roadblocks that may interfere with the success of the project.

The Identification Phase:

The identification phase is when project concepts are reviewed and the voice of the customer (VOC) is presented to the team. As discussed in Chapter 3, an effective QFD (quality function deployment) process will enable the organization to identify the qualities customers desire to have in the products or processes that will be designed. It will also identify what functions of the organization must be engaged to provide the customers with the correct products and processes. Additionally QFD will identify what available resources best provide the customers with their desired products and processes. This phase is the most critical phase of Designing for Six Sigma, as this is the phase where all variables concerning the customers are identified and quantified.

The Design Phase:

The design phase is when the knowledge of the products or processes is expanded upon. It is also referred to as the build phase.

The Optimization Phase:

During the optimization phase we carefully balance cost, quality, time to market, and the position of the products and processes with respect to the firm's portfolio, without compromising customers' requirements.

The Validation Phase:

During the validation phase the design team is required to demonstrate that the products or processes satisfy the customers' requirements, as originally stipulated and defined through the voice of the customer (VOC). It ensures that the new products that go to the customers will not only please them, but may also exceed their expectations in terms of quality and reasonable cost.

11. CONCLUDING REMARKS

Having determined your method to manage, monitor, and control the quality of your product (or service), you now must show the results in a report comparing them to the customer's requirements to demonstrate that your quality processes are truly meeting your customer's expectations as documented. With this proof, your customer will review and approve, thus granting your company the authorization to proceed into production. That means your company can now start making production products or providing production services and deliver to the customer for payment. Recall we referred to this as "Start of Production" or SOP. Of course, the production operations will continue and be managed until the time your customer or your company, the supplier, decides that the product (or service) life has come to an end or has been replaced (or changed) by another product (or service). And the fun just keeps on coming!

You have now reached the end of your idea's development lifecycle process! Hooray! We hope you have enjoyed this journey as you received a glimpse into each stage of what it takes to get a product (or service) into production. Of course, we have just skimmed the surface here in this text. There is much, much more to learn about business operations and how to manage them well along with your supply chain. But it is for you to decide where you go next to learn more about it: whether it is taking more college courses or attaining certifications like the ones professional organizations (e.g., APICS) have to offer. It does not matter what role you play (e.g., designer, engineer, software developer, human resource manager, recruiter, sales representative, program manager, tester, and so on). What matters is that you know how it is all connected and where your role fits in to make every product, and every service, meet your customers' expectations in order for them to be satisfied and willing to come back with more orders! Remember, you may also be that satisfied customer. *Good Luck!*

12. GLOSSARY AND SUMMARY OF METHODS

Acceptance Sampling – Acceptance sampling is the abstraction of a sample from the whole lot, the evaluation of that sample, and the determination of acceptability or non-acceptability of the total lot based on that sample.

C-Chart – The c-chart exhibits the number of defective parts in sample subgroups taken from various production runs.

Consumer's Risk – The consumer's risk is the probability of accepting a bad lot, as a result of sampling, and is called the beta error.

Continuous Sampling Plan – In the continuous sampling plan every *n*th product is inspected, until a defective item is encountered. At that time a large consecutive number of *m* items are inspected and after none of these *m* items are found defective, the inspector returns to inspecting every *n*th item.

Control Charts – Control charts are charts that reflect the limits of acceptability levels and picture how a product or process conforms to these levels.

Defective – A defective is an unacceptable part (or product), deemed so because one or more of its quality characteristics deviate from their specified design limits.

Design Quality – Design quality is concerned with the stringency of the specifications for manufacturing the product.

Designing For Six Sigma – Designing for Six Sigma is the initiative that allows companies to develop the right product for their target consumers. Incorporating the Voice of the Consumer (VOC) through quality function deployment (QFD) drives it.

Double Sampling Plan – The double sampling plan consists of the following procedure:

Step 1: Draw a random sample of n_1 from a lot of N items.

Step 2: Inspect all n_1 items in the sample. This will reveal d_1 defective items in that sample.

Step 3: If the number of defective items in the sample, d_1, is less than or equal to the acceptance number of the first sample, c_1, then accept the lot of $(N\!-\!n_1)$ items and replace all defective items in the sample before returning the sample to the original lot.

If $d_1 > c_2$, then the lot must be inspected 100%. All defective items in the lot must be replaced.

If none of the above is the case, then a second sample of size n_2 must be drawn from the remaining lot of size $(N\!-\!n_1)$. Proceed now to Step 4.

Step 4: Inspect all n_2 items in the second sample that was drawn. This will reveal d_2 defective items in that sample.

Step 5: If the accumulated number of defective items in both samples, (d_1+d_2), is less than or equal to the maximum allowable total number of defectives in both samples, c_2, then accept the lot of $(N\!-\!n_1\!-\!n_2)$ items and replace all defective items found in both samples before returning the samples to the original lot.

If, however, $(d_1+d_2)>c_2$, then the lot must be inspected 100%. All bad items in the lot must now be replaced.

Fish-Bone or Cause-and-Effect Diagram – The fish-bone or cause-and-effect diagram is a tool for identifying causes related to a quality problem. It is also called the fish-bone diagram because when drawn correctly it resembles a fish bone. At the head of the fish bone appears the quality problem. Alongside the spine, where the bones of the fish are, the main categories of causes of the quality problem are listed. These causes can be further detailed, creating more bones on the fish, and then assist the team in determining which ones to investigate first.

P-Chart – The p-chart exhibits the fraction of defective parts in sample subgroups taken from various production runs.

Pareto Chart – A Pareto chart graphically exhibits the concept, that a small percentage of a group accounts for the largest inpact, by ranking causes from most significant to least significant. When applied to quality problems a Pareto chart helps to break a problems down into its various components and is used to help focus on the most significant causes of defects, rather than all causes of defects.

Performance Quality – Performance quality relates to how well the product performs its function.

Producer's Risk – The producer's risk is the probability of rejecting a good lot, as a result of sampling, and is called the alpha error.

Production Quality – Production quality is concerned with how well the manufactured product conforms to the original design requirements.

Quality Control – Quality control is a system for coordinating group activities in an organization such that quality is designed, built in, and maintained for full customer satisfaction in the most economical way.

R-Chart – The R-chart shows the ranges between the largest and the smallest values of sample data.

Scatter Plot or Diagram – A scatter plot or diagram, when used for quality control, is a graphical technique to analyze measurements of a certain characteristic in samples. It helps to identify the outliers for further investigation as to why they are so different from the majority.

Sequential Sampling Plan – With sequential sampling very small samples are taken and evaluated. Each time a sample is taken and analyzed the decision is made to accept the lot, to reject it, or to continue sampling.

Single Sampling Plan – The single sampling plan consists of the following procedure:

Step 1: Draw a random sample of *n* items from a lot of *N* items.
Step 2: Inspect all n items in the sample that was drawn from the lot. This will reveal d defective items in that sample.
Step 3: If the number of defective items in the sample, d, is less than or equal to the maximum allowable number of defects, *c*, then accept the lot of $(N–n)$ items and replace all defective items in the sample before returning the sample to the original lot. If $d > c$, then the lot must be inspected 100%. All defective items in the lot must now be replaced.

Six Sigma – Six Sigma represents an extreme level of high quality. It aims at virtually eliminating defects from every product and process within an organization. Six Sigma (6σ) stands for optimal quality, such as 3.4 defects per million

TQC and CWQC – Total quality control (TQC) and company-wide quality control (CWQC) means excellence. It includes excellence of the product, excellence of management, excellence of community relations, excellence of company performance, excellence of company image in society, and excellence of work environment. In this sense, TQC and CWQC refer to the concept of building quality or excellence into the total corporate structure, and of continuously striving to improve it.

X-Bar Chart – The X-bar chart is a control chart that exhibits the normal and abnormal variations in the means of measurements in a sample.

13. ACRONYMS

AQL Acceptable Quality Level

COPQ Cost of Poor Quality

CWQC Company Wide-Quality Control

DFSS Design For Six Sigma

KTP Knowledge Transfer Process

LCL Lower Control Limit

LTPD Lot Tolerance Percent Defective

OC Operating Characteristic

SOP Start of Production

SPC Statistical Process Control

SQC Statistical Quality Control

SS Six Sigma

TQC Total Quality Control

UCL Upper Control Limit

VOC Voice of the Customer

14. REFERENCES

Barry, Robert, A. Murcko, and C. Brubaker. *The Six Sigma Book for Healthcare*. Chicago, IL: Health Administration Press, 2002.

Besterfield, Dale H. *Quality Control*. Englewood Cliffs, NJ: Prentice Hall, 1990.

Brue, Greg. *Six Sigma for Leadership: Seven Principles of Problem-Solving Technology To Achieve Significant Financial Results*. Albuquerque: Creative Designs, Inc., 2000.

Evans, James R. *Statistical Process Control for Quality Improvement*. Englewood Cliffs, NJ: Prentice Hall, 1991.

Hall, Robert W. "Chapter 7: Quality Systems in Stockless Production." *Zero Inventories*. Homewood, IL: Dow Jones-Irwin, 1983.

Sandras Jr., William A. "Chapter 11: Solving Problems Using Total Quality Control." *Just-In-Time: Making it Happen, Unleashing the Power of Continuous Improvement*. Essex Junction, VT: Oliver Wight Ltd., 1989.

The Cambridge Corporation. *The Cambridge Report #1: TQC and Quality Circles*. Tokyo: The Cambridge Corporation, 1982.

The Cambridge Corporation. *Three-Day Seminar on Kanban, Quality Control and Quality Management*. The Cambridge Corporation, Tokyo, April 25–27, 1983.

Wu, Nesa L. "Philosophy, Development & Worldwide Adaptation of Total Quality Management." *Productivity Quarterly Journal*. (Vol. 32(3), 1991).

Wu, Nesa L. "Quality Function Deployment and the Migration to Activity Based Cost Accounting." *Productivity Quarterly Journal*. (Vol. 40(3), 1999).

15. REVIEW QUESTIONS

1. Explain the concept of design quality and production quality.
2. What is meant by quality control?
3. Why are control charts used and what do they reflect?
4. Briefly explain what functions are involved in quality control.
5. Differentiate between attribute and variable control.
6. Explain the relationship between sample size, inspection levels, and operating characteristic curve.
7. What control charts are used for variable control? What do they convey?
8. What control charts are used for attribute control? What do they convey?
9. What is the procedure for setting up an X-bar chart?
10. What is the procedure for setting up a p-chart?
11. What is the producer's risk? What is the consumer's risk?
12. What is the meaning of the AQL and the LTPD level on the OC curve?
13. How does the single sampling plan work?
14. How does the double sampling plan work?
15. How does the sequential sampling plan work?

16. How does the continuous sampling plan work?
17. What do TQC and CWQC stand for?
18. What are the seven quality tools and give an example of each?
19. What are the typical features of production process-oriented quality control?
20. What is Six Sigma?
21. What is Designing for Six Sigma?
22. Explain the D-M-A-I-C phases of Six Sigma.
23. What are the five phases of Designing for Six Sigma? Explain.

16. PROBLEMS

Problem #1

For single attribute sampling determine the appropriate sample sizes for the following lot sizes and inspection levels:

a) An average inspection level and a lot size of 3,000 units.

b) An inspection level that gives the least protection to the consumer for a lot size of 500 units.

c) An inspection level that gives the highest protection to the consumer for a lot size of 1,000 units.

Problem #2 (Excel)

Rosewood Farms, a local Tofu manufacturer, sells its products in packages of 1 lb. (454 grams). Sample checks of the inventory reveal that some of the packages weigh more than 454 g. Therefore, Mr. Rose suspects that they may be losing significant amounts of money because of overfill of the containers. He wishes to evaluate this by sampling four units at a time for each production run of 40 containers. He allows a minimum weight of 430 g (to ensure customer satisfaction) and a maximum weight of 480 g (to minimize cost).

The following data was collected to set the initial standards for control.

Sample #	Observed Weights			
1	476	479	472	459
2	482	457	452	458
3	453	451	490	470
4	456	458	440	447
5	459	480	452	460
6	443	454	456	458
7	427	445	455	484
8	477	512	496	505
9	443	462	460	478
10	458	437	450	445

Set up the control chart for the above data using the following formulas:

$$\overline{\overline{X}} = \frac{\sum_{j=1}^{m} \overline{X}_j}{m} \qquad \text{UCL} = \overline{\overline{X}} + 3S_{\overline{X}} \ \& \ \text{LCL} = \overline{\overline{X}} - 3S_{\overline{X}}$$

$$S_{\overline{X}} = \frac{S_X}{\sqrt{n}}$$ (use sample standard deviation in Excel to calculate S_X of all 40 sample data)

$n = 4$

Problem #3 (Excel)

If any of the sample means in Problem #2 is out of control, recalculate the control limits without that sample mean before proceeding to Problem #4.

Problem #4 (Excel)

Consider the new control limits as set in problem #3 to evaluate the following sample results:

Sample #	Observed Weights			
1	455	457	455	463
2	447	449	435	437
3	480	473	475	479
4	454	457	467	447
5	459	457	467	447
6	434	425	427	435
7	471	473	474	480
8	443	460	463	478
9	457	493	461	460
10	461	455	467	453

a) Plot the mean values for each of the above samples.

b) Are any of these samples out of control?

Problem #5 (Excel)

The following data reflect the results of sampling production from an automatic punching machine that punches holes in the plate of a three-hole puncher. The sample size of each of the following 10 samples equals 100.

The engineer believes that the below data reflect normal operation of the automatic punch machine. Use the data below to construct the p-chart.

Does the machine seem to be in control?

Sample #	No. of Defectives	Fraction of Defective
1	0	0.00
2	2	0.02
3	3	0.03
4	4	0.04
5	1	0.01
6	0	0.00
7	0	0.00
8	0	0.00
9	0	0.00
10	1	0.01

Problem #6

After receiving complaints from the assembly department that assembles the three-hole punch (see Problem #5) the engineer wishes to control production over the next 20 runs. The following defects were detected in samples of one hundred units

Sample #	No of Defectives	Fraction Defectives
1	4	0.04
2	5	0.05
3	0	0.00
4	1	0.01
5	3	0.03
6	2	0.02
7	4	0.04
8	4	0.04
9	2	0.02
10	1	0.01
11	4	0.04
12	3	0.03
13	1	0.01
14	4	0.04
15	1	0.01
16	6	0.06
17	3	0.03
18	2	0.02
19	5	0.05
20	1	0.01

a) Use the controls as established in Problem #5 and plot the results of the above samples.

b) Is the assembly department justified to complain about the punches in the three-hole punch? Explain your answer.

Appendix A
Derivation of Some Queuing Characteristics

The (M/M/1) : (FCFS/∞/∞)

The Rate Diagram

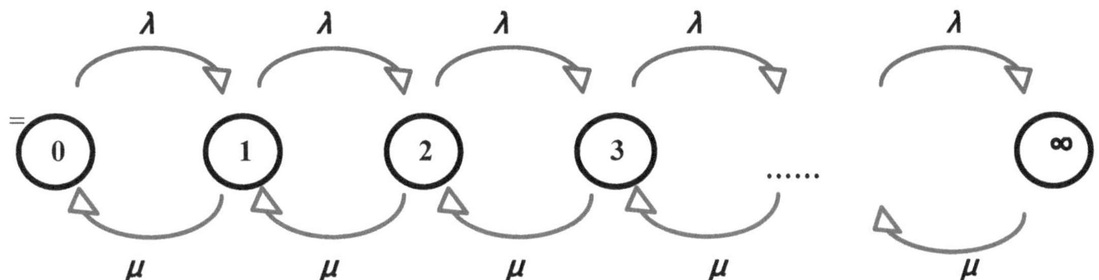

The Balance Equations

Balance equation at state 0: $\mu P_1 = \lambda P_0$ (1)

Balance equation at state 1: $\lambda P_0 + \mu P_2 = \mu P_1 + \lambda P_1$ (2)

Balance equation at state 2: $\lambda P_1 + \mu P_3 = \mu P_2 + \lambda P_2$ (3)

Balance equation at state n-1: $\lambda P_{n-2} + \mu P_n = \mu P_{n-1} + \lambda P_{n-1}$ (4)

Calculation of Steady-State Probabilities

The above balance equations can be used to calculate these probabilities

The first balance equation (1) can be used to calculate P_1:

$$\mu P_1 = \lambda P_0$$

$$P_1 = (\lambda/\mu)\, P_0$$

Similarly, the second balance equation (2) can be used to define probability P_2

$$\lambda P_0 + \mu P_2 = \mu P_1 + \lambda P_1$$

$$\mu P_2 = \mu P_1 + \lambda P_1 - \lambda P_0$$

Substituting $P_1 = (\lambda/\mu)\, P_0$ in the equation we get

$$\mu P_2 = \mu\, (\lambda/\mu)\, P_0 + \lambda(\lambda/\mu)\, P_0 - \lambda P_0$$

Or $$\mu P_2 = \lambda\, P_0 + (\lambda^2/\mu)\, P_0 - \lambda P_0$$

Or $$\mu P_2 = (\lambda^2/\mu)\, P_0$$

Or $$P_2 = (\lambda\, /\mu)^2\, P_0$$

By the same procedure we can define $P_3, P_4, \ldots\ldots, P_n$ as a function of P_0, λ, and μ:

$$P_n = (\lambda/\mu)^n P_0 = \rho^n P_0 \quad (5)$$

The value of P_0 (probability that no customers are in the system) can be defined based on the fundamental probability law that

$$\sum P_i = P_o + P_1 + P_2 + P_3 + \ldots\ldots\ldots + P_n \ldots\ldots\ldots P_\infty = 1 \quad (6)$$

Based on equation (5) and equation (6), we can rewrite equation (6) as follows:

$$\sum P_i = \sum (\lambda/\mu)^i P_0 = 1 \quad for\ i = 0, 1, 2, \ldots\ldots, n-1, n, \ldots\infty$$

Or

$$P_0 \sum (\lambda/\mu)^i = 1 \quad for\ i = 0, 1, 2, \ldots\ldots, n-1, n, \ldots\infty \quad (7)$$

The geometric progression of equation (7) can be rewritten as follows:

$$P_0 [1 - (\lambda/\mu)^\infty] / [1 - (\lambda/\mu)] = 1 \quad (8)$$

Since the utilization factor (λ/μ) must be less than one (1) for steady state to exist, $(\lambda/\mu)^\infty$ converges to zero (0). Therefore equation (8) becomes:

$$P_0 / [1 - (\lambda/\mu)] = 1 \quad (9)$$

Solving for P_0 we get:

$$P_0 = 1 - (\lambda/\mu) = 1 - \rho \quad where\ \rho\ is\ the\ utilization\ factor \quad (10)$$

Derivation of the Expected Number of Customers in the System

The expected number of customers in the queuing system is defined by the following equation:

$$L = \sum n P_n \quad for\ n = 0, 1, 2, \ldots\ldots, \infty$$

Using equations (5) and (10) we get:

$$L = \sum n \rho^n (1 - \rho) \quad for\ n = 0, 1, 2, \ldots\ldots, \infty$$

This can be reduced to:

$$L = (1 - \rho) \rho \sum n \rho^{n-1} \quad for\ n = 0, 1, 2, \ldots, \infty \quad (11)$$

Because $n \rho^{n-1} = \frac{d}{d\rho}(\rho^n)$ equation (11) can be rewritten as follows:

$$L = (1 - \rho) \rho \frac{d}{d\rho} \sum \rho^n \quad for\ n = 0, 1, 2, \ldots, \infty \quad (12)$$

Recall that since ρ is less than 1, the infinite sum of ρ^n equals $1/(1 - \rho)$; therefore:

$$L = (1 - \rho) \rho \frac{d}{d\rho} (1/(1 - \rho)$$

$$= (1 - \rho) \rho [1/(1 - \rho)^2]$$

$$= \rho / (1 - \rho)$$

$$= (\lambda/\mu) / [1 - (\lambda/\mu)]$$

$$L = \lambda / (\mu - \lambda)$$

Appendix B
Answers to Selected Problems

Chapter 2

Problem #1

Year	P	I	P_L	I_L	P_M	I_M	P_C	I_C
1985	1.333	1	2.667	1	6.667	1	5.333	1
1986	1.413	1.06	3.533	1.32	3.926	0.59	7.067	1.325
1987	1.507	1.13	3.758	1.41	4.203	0.63	7.515	1.409
1988	1.455	1.09	3.629	1.36	4.059	0.61	7.258	1.361
1989	1.447	1.09	3.795	1.42	4.246	0.64	6.036	1.132

Problem #2

Output value base year: $30,550; Output value last year: $37,120
Input value base year: $19,363; Input value last year: $22,067

Period	P	I	P_E	I_E	P_L	I_L	P_M	I_M	P_C	I_C
Base Y	1.578	1	16.62	1	13.68	1	13.70	1	3.48	1
Last Y	1.682	1.07	16.44	0.99	15.10	1.10	15.09	1.10	4.38	1.26

Problem #3

	Value Base Month	Value Last Month
Input		
Labor	62,230	64,770
Short Term Capital	10,900.8	11,610.57
Rent/Supplies	3,260	3,653.85
Net Output	100,000	120,000

Period	a)		b)	c)	d)	
	Input	Output	P	I	P_L	I_L
Base month	76,390.8	100,000	1.31	1	1.61	1
Last Month	80,034.42	120,000	1.50	1.14	1.85	1.15

Chapter 3

Problem #1: $R = 0.982$

Problem #2: $R = 0.8955$

Problem #3: a) $R = 0.974$ b) increase in reliability = 0.254

Problem #4: Both systems have the same reliability: $R = 0.882$

Chapter 4

Problem #1

a) Fill out on attached form (each step is one line), summarize results.
b) Exclude wasted elements (steps 3: inspection; step 4: avoidable delay; and step 9: inspection)
Value-added time: 21.8 minutes
c) Production throughput time: 27.8
d) Efficiency: 78%

Problem #2

a) Value-added Time: 13.25 (operation) + 4.90(most transport is not avoidable) – 1.70 (from steps 11 and 13) = 16.45 minutes
b) Throughput time = 48.65
c) Efficiency = 34%
d) Place all tools together, so they can all be retrieved at once. Sprinkle grass and water flowers simultaneously or find work that needs to be done during the delay.

Chapter 5

Problem #2: answer can be found in paragraphs #2 and #3 (inventory accuracy of 80%, parts inventory is very questionable, need to take physical inventory, etc.)

Problem #3: answer can be found in the last two paragraphs: 40% of floor space is occupied by inventory, accuracy is low in tool crib, inventory turns are 40, etc.

Chapter 6

Problem #1: Average time = 2.5 minutes; Normal time = 2.25 minutes; Standard time = 2.647 minutes

Problem #2: a) Normal time = 36.14 seconds; b) Allowance = 0.125; Standard time = 41.30 seconds
c) Pieces per standard hour: 87.161 units/hour

Problem #3: a) Normal time = 9.257 minutes; idle time = 480 minutes; Standard time = 10.286 minutes

Problem #4: a) Normal time = 0.725 minutes; Standard time = 0.853 minutes

Problem #5: a) Normal time = 1.926 minutes; Standard time = 2.140 minutes
b) Required sample size is 19 (calculated value is 18.51) for element I and 9 for element II
c) Normal time = 1.951 minutes; Standard time = 2.168 minutes

Problem #6: a) Normal time = 9.377 minutes; Standard time = 10.778 minutes

Problem #7: a) Normal time = 67.93 seconds;
b) Reasonable allowance is 15% (5% personal, 55 very exacting work, and 5% very tedious work); Standard time = 79.918 seconds

Chapter 7

Problem #1: Score location A = 6; Score location B = 7.5; Score location C = 10

Problem #2: Score using absolute weights = 424; Score using relative weights = 6.95

Problem #3: Using absolute weights: Score for location A =104 and for location B = 118.32.
These values are significantly different, so B is a better location.

Problem #4: Note that the weights for tangible factors are correct!
Using the absolute weights: Score for location A = 420.10 and for location B = 535.97. These values are significantly different, so location B is a better location.

Problem #5: For this problem you have to calculate the weights for the tangible factors and assign an equal weight to each of the intangible factors. It is best to calculate relative weights before calculating the scores. Good luck!

Problem #6: a) The weights (rounded to an integer value) for the tangible factors are correct
b) Using the absolute weights: Score for city A = 703.30 and for city B = 787.03. These values are significantly different, so location B is a better location.

Problem #8:

a)

	F1	F2	F3	F4	F5	Demand
W1	0	10	30	0	0	40
W2	0	0	0	20	0	20
W3	0	0	0	0	55	55
W4	0	0	0	30	0	30
W5	5	35	0	0	0	40
W6	50	0	0	0	0	50
Capacity	55	45	30	50	55	2015

b) No change in allocation because capacity of F3 was already fully utilized. The overall cost reduces by $3(30).

	F1	F2	F3	F4	F5	Demand
W1	0	10	30	0	0	40
W2	0	0	0	20	0	20
W3	0	0	0	0	55	55
W4	0	0	0	30	0	30
W5	5	35	0	0	0	40
W6	50	0	0	0	0	50
Capacity	55	45	30	50	55	1925

c) There is potential change because this higher cost may reduce allocation

	F1	F2	F3	F4	F5	Demand
W1	0	10	30	0	0	40
W2	0	0	0	20	0	20
W3	0	0	0	0	55	55
W4	0	0	0	30	0	30
W5	25	15	0	0	0	40
W6	50	0	0	0	0	50
Capacity	75	25	30	50	55	2065

Problem #9

a) Indianapolis is the preferred one:

	Fort Wayne	Dayton	Evansville	Capacity:
Chicago	160	0	90	250
Detroit	130	0	0	130
Louisville	0	110	70	180
Saint Louis	0	100	0	100
Demand:	290	210	160	4750

	Fort Wayne	Dayton	Evansville	Capacity:
Chicago	190	0	60	250
Detroit	100	30	0	130
Louisville	0	180	0	180
Indianapolis	0	0	100	100
Demand:	290	210	160	4480

b) Saint Louis is the preferred one:

	Fort Wayne	Dayton	Evansville	Capacity:
Chicago	160	0	90	250
Detroit	130	0	0	130
Louisville	0	110	70	180
Saint Louis	0	100	0	100
Demand:	290	210	160	77100

	Fort Wayne	Dayton	Evansville	Capacity:
Chicago	190	0	60	250
Detroit	100	30	0	130
Louisville	0	180	0	180
Indianapolis	0	0	100	100
Demand:	290	210	160	79830

c) Total cost with Saint Louis as a new plant: $8,550+$13,550+$11,550+$22,550+$77,100 = $133,300
Total cost with Indianapolis as a new plant: $8,550+$13,550+$11,550+$19,050+$79,830 = $132,530
Indianapolis is preferred. Assignment can be seen in the last table above.

Problem #11

a) Ambulance should take the country road; if the 1st bridge is closed he should continue to the second bridge; if this is closed he should return and take the highway: Expected time of travel: 1.07hrs

b) Same answer as above (take country road): expected miles to travel: 56 miles

Chapter 8

Problem #1: Minimum number of stations = 19

Problem #2: Cycle time = 6 minutes Minimum number of stations = 9

Problem #3: a) max cycle time = 48 seconds; b) optimal cycle time = 47 seconds;
c) maximum rate of production = 76.6 units/hour; d) total slack time = 30 seconds;
d) balance delay = 6.62%

Problem #4: a) 0.70 minutes

b)

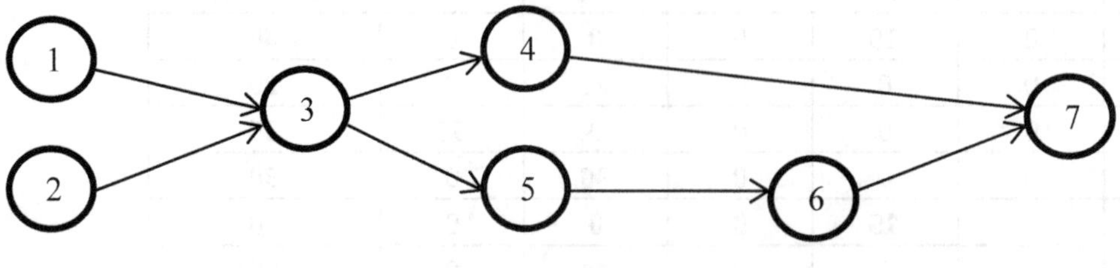

1 2 3 4 5 6 7

c)

Station #	Work Element #	E_i	$Sum\ E_i$	*Slack time*
1	1	0.66	0.66	0.02
2	2 3	0.35 0.30	0.35 0.65	0.03
3	4 5	0.32 0.31	0.32 0.63	0.05
4	6 7	0.35 0.33	0.35 0.68	0

d) Optimal cycle time = 0.68 minutes (slowest station or station with largest station time)
e) Hourly production rate = 88.24
f) Balance delay = 3.82%

Problem #5

a)

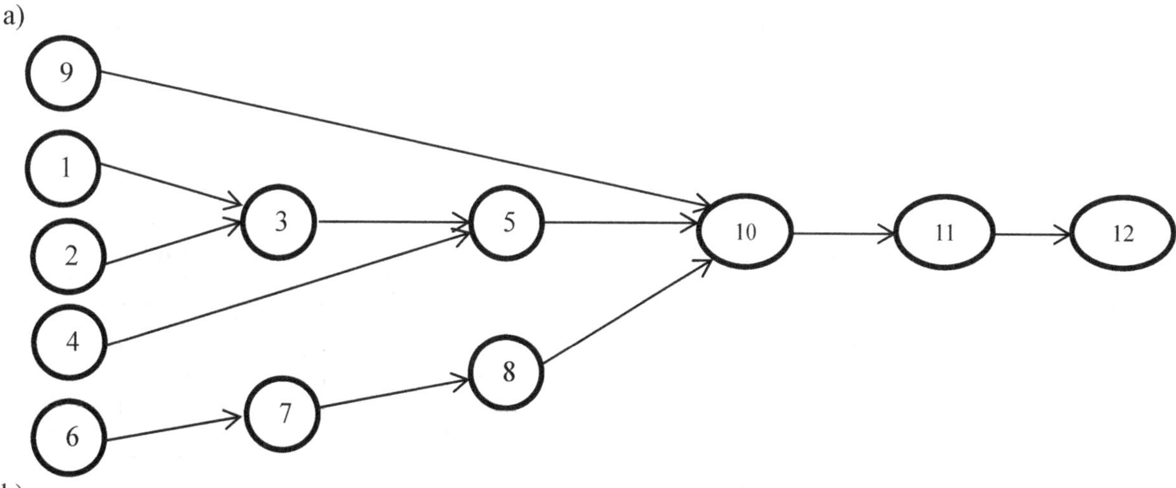

b)

Demand:	1,500	3,000	4,500	6,000	7,500	9,000
Cycle Time:	60 min.	30 min.	20 min.	15 min.	12 min.	10 min.
Min # stations: ($\sum E_i$ = 62 min)	2	3	4	5	6	7

Problems #6 #7

These problems are for class discussion. Think in terms of large amount of WIP and finished inventory on shop floor, consider changing part of this process layout to a GT layout, JIT customer and smaller lot sizes, use of spaghetti diagrams, etc.

Problem #8

Capacity Type	Minutes/shift	Production output/shift	Production output/hour
a) Design Capacity:	480 minutes	25,600 boxes	3,200 boxes
b) Effective Capacity:	450 minutes	24,000 boxes	3,000 boxes
c) Achieved Capacity	430 minutes	22,933.33 boxes	2,866.67 boxes

d) Machine Utilization = 90%
e) Machine Efficiency = 96%
f) Overall Machine Effectiveness = 82.62%

Chapter 9

Problem #1: b) There is a trend and seasonality

Problem #2: Estimated demand = 25.91 + 2.06T

Problem #3: a) Correlation coefficient R = 0.7016; b) no, it should only be used to understand the trend
c) June 2008 = period 30, estimated demand for T = 30: 87.62174
December 2008 = period 36, estimated demand for T = 36: 99.96348

Problem #4: For all calculations use Excel and "Data Analysis" for a) through d)
b) Sum of absolute error for 2007 = 213.2 for simple moving average technique
d) Sum of absolute error for 2007 = 190.8 for adjusted weighted moving average technique
e) The adjusted weighted moving average technique seems to be better (based on errors)

Problem #5:

b)	α=0.1	α=0.3	α=0.5	α=0.7	α=0.9
Accumulated absolute error	401.7975	257.9855	223.4922	193.08414	171.10383

c) α = 0.9 gives the best results. The data is unstable

Problem #6:

a) One worked out example for α=0.1 is shown here:

Period	Demand	Exp. Smoothing α = 0.1	Trend Estimate	Smoothed Slope Estimate	Predicted Demand	Absolute Error
1	18	#N/A				
2	24	18.00	0.00	0.00	18.00	6.00
3	34	18.60	0.60	0.06	19.14	14.86
4	41	20.14	1.54	0.21	22.01	18.99
5	45	22.23	2.09	0.40	25.79	19.21
6	38	24.50	2.28	0.58	29.76	8.24
7	40	25.85	1.35	0.66	31.80	8.20
8	39	27.27	1.41	0.74	33.89	5.11
9	41	28.44	1.17	0.78	35.46	5.54
10	37	29.70	1.26	0.83	37.14	0.14
11	34	30.43	0.73	0.82	37.79	3.79
12	32	30.78	0.36	0.77	37.73	5.73
13	41	30.91	0.12	0.71	37.27	3.73
14	58	31.92	1.01	0.74	38.55	19.45
15	79	34.52	2.61	0.92	42.84	36.16
16	92	38.97	4.45	1.28	50.46	41.54
17	93	44.27	5.30	1.68	59.39	33.61
18	71	49.15	4.87	2.00	67.13	3.87
19	76	51.33	2.19	2.02	69.49	6.51
20	72	53.80	2.47	2.06	72.36	0.36
21	68	55.62	1.82	2.04	73.96	5.96
22	60	56.86	1.24	1.96	74.48	14.48
23	58	57.17	0.31	1.79	73.31	15.31
	48	57.25	0.08	1.62	71.86	23.86
					Total:	300.66
					Average:	13.07

α	Sum Absolute Error	Average Error
0.1	300.66	13.07
0.3	250.43	10.89
0.5	190.53	8.28
0.7	165.71	7.20
0.9	163.87	7.12

b) the higher α, the better the results are

Problem #7: For all α values the model that includes trend is better

Problem #8: a) Y(t+2) = 279.398 + 2.347X(t) b) R = 0.753023 c) Y(13) = 377.972, Y(14) = 373.278

Problem #9: a) Estimates # of Lubes = 723.75 + (180.2206) T
b) May: 3787.5; June: 3967.72; July: 4147.941

Problem #10:

Period	# of Lubes	MA	Trend Factor	AMA	ABS Error
1	660				
2	1120	#N/A			
3	1550	#N/A			
4	1500	#N/A			
5	1400	#N/A			
6	1660	1246	558	1804	144
7	1860	1446	279	1725	135
8	2240	1594	234	1828	412
9	2600	1732	582	2314	286
10	2730	1952	894	2846	116
11	2900	2218	864	3082	182
12	2890	2466	771	3237	347
13	2900	2672	480	3152	252
14	3160	2804	228	3032	128
15	3350	2916	258	3174	176
16	3570	3040	351	3391	179
				Total	2357
				Average	214.2727

Problem #11:

Period	Demand	Exp. Smoothing α = 0.2	Trend Estimate	Smoothed Slope Estimate	Predicted Demand	Absolute Error
1	660	#N/A				
2	1120	660.00	0.00	0.00	660.00	460.00
3	1550	936.00	276.00	165.60	1046.40	503.60
4	1500	1304.40	368.40	287.28	1495.92	4.08
5	1400	1421.76	117.36	185.33	1545.31	145.31
6	1660	1408.70	-13.06	66.30	1452.90	207.10
7	1860	1559.48	150.78	116.99	1637.47	222.53
8	2240	1739.79	180.31	154.98	1843.11	396.89
9	2600	2039.92	300.12	242.07	2201.30	398.70
10	2730	2375.97	336.05	298.46	2574.94	155.06
11	2900	2588.39	212.42	246.83	2752.94	147.06
12	2890	2775.35	186.97	210.91	2915.96	25.96
13	2900	2844.14	68.79	125.64	2927.90	27.90
14	3160	2877.66	33.51	70.36	2924.57	235.43
15	3350	3047.06	169.41	129.79	3133.59	216.41
16	3570	3228.83	181.76	160.97	3336.14	233.86
					Total	3379.90
					Average	225.33

Problem #12: Adjusted Moving Average is better than exponential smoothing, based on average ABS error

Chapter 10

Problem #1:

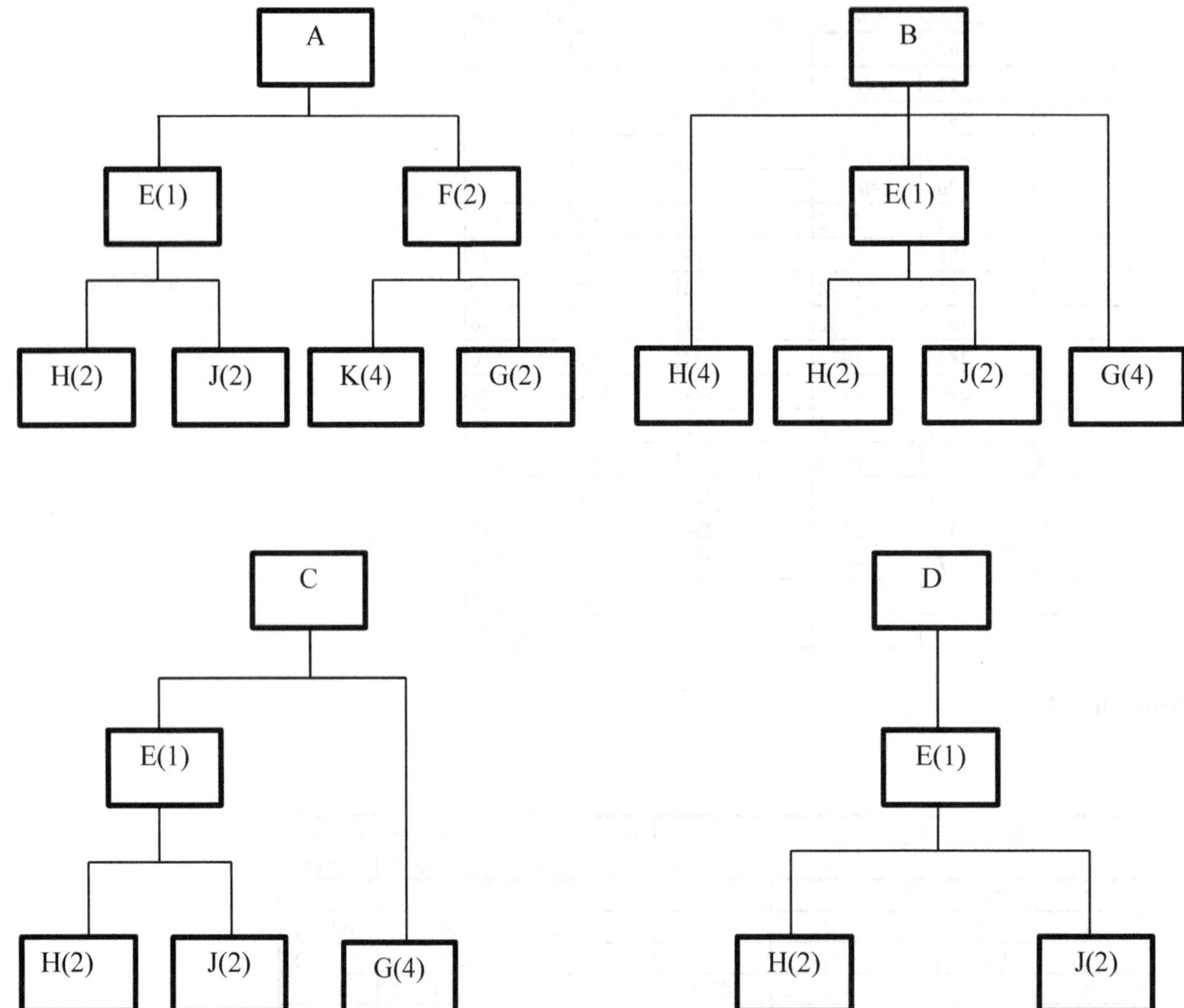

Problem #2: Working through the trees, starting with level 0, the following accumulated totals result:
E: 450; F: 600; G: 1760; H: 1100; J: 900; K: 2400

Problem #3: Working through the trees, starting with level 0 and adjusting for inventory, the following accumulated totals result:
A: 280; B: 50; C: 80; D: 10; E: 369 ; F: 460; G: 1240; H: 900; J: 720; K: 1340

Problem #5:

Production Requirements							
	January	February	March	April	May	June	Total
Beginning Inventory	20	45	25	25	30	40	185
Forecasted Demand	450	250	250	300	400	450	2,100
Safety Stock (10%)	45	25	25	30	40	45	210
Production Request	475	230	250	305	410	455	2,125
Productions Hours Req'd	16,625	8,050	8,750	10,675	14,350	15,925	74,375
Operating Days	22	20	22	21	22	22	129
Regular Hours	176	160	176	168	176	176	1,032
Cumulative							
Forecasted Demand	450	700	950	1,250	1,650	2,100	
Production Request	475	705	955	1,260	1,670	2,125	
Production Hours Req'd	16,625	24,675	33,425	44,100	58,450	74,375	
Regular Hours	176	336	512	680	856	1,032	

Problem #6: Starting with 80 workers and adjusting through hiring and layoff results in an adjustment cost of $191,000

Problem #7: Simulated optimal manpower level is 64 workers with an overall capacity adjustment cost of $229,360

Problem #8: With 64 workers the cost is $63,544.00
Optimal level is 80 workers with a cost of $23,678.00

Problem #9: Optimal level is 80 workers with a cost of $ 29,713.00

Problem #10: Disaggregating the aggregate plan, the production requirements are as follows:

	WK1	WK2	WK3	WK4	WK5	WK6	WK7	WK8
Product A	155	0	0	0	135	0	0	0
Product B	154	0	0	0	155	0	0	0
Product C	160	0	0	0	71	0	0	0
Product D	6	0	0	0	16	0	0	0
Total Production:	475	0	0	0	377	0	0	0

Considering the economical lot sizes the production requirements are as follows:

	WK1	WK2	WK3	WK4	WK5	WK6	WK7	WK8
Product A	160	0	0	0	140	0	0	0
Product B	155	0	0	0	155	0	0	0
Product C	160	0	0	0	75	0	0	0
Product D	6	0	0	0	16	0	0	0
Total Production:	481	0	0	0	386	0	0	0

Problem #11: Use the production requirements generated in Problem #10 and try to schedule the requirements over the 8 weeks in such a way that the **production hours** reflect a relatively low variability. There are several acceptable master production schedules possible.

Chapter 11

Problem #1: a) 14,852 units (rounded); b) $4,038 (approximately); c) every 18 to 19 days

Problem #2: a) $EOQ = Q = \sqrt{\dfrac{2 \times D \times c_o}{c(h1) + 2 \times c(h2)}}$

b) 13,056 units (rounded); c) $2,297.79, $2,297.85, $4,595.64; d) ROP = 3,200 units

Problem #3: $EPQ > EOQ$ because the denominator of the EPQ is less than the denominator of EOQ.

Problem #4: 150 pcs is fairly close (calculated amount is 149 rounded)

Problem #5: a) Total yearly cost at price break of $1.15 and for order quantity 2,000 = $14,270;
for this price break the EOQ = 1,575 units < 2,000 units
Total yearly cost for EOQ of 1,732 (no discount) = $14,815.69
Therefore orders for 2,000 units ought to be placed: $14,270 < $14,815.69
b) Proceed in same way as for a)

Problem #6: a) *EOQ* = 4,470 units; b) 8.05 orders/year; *ROP* = 3,000units; Inventory cost = $1,788

Problem #7:

c)

Lot size:	10	20	50	100	200
Average inventory Average inv. value	5 600	10 1200	25 3,000	50 6,000	100 12,000

b)

Lot size:	10	20	50	100	200
c_h Total yearly cost	24 103,032	23.5 97,921	23 94,321.40	22.5 92,218.2	22 90,961.60

c) *ROP* = 87.1 units (26 days of inventory)

Problem #8:

EOQ (buy) = 3,000 units; Total yearly cost (buy) = $81,200
EPQ (produce) = 4,000 units; Total yearly cost (produce) = 40,720
Savings over 8 years (life of the machine) = $323,840
Maximum cost the company is willing to pay for the machine = $971,520

Chapter 12

Problem #1:

a)

Time (hrs)	**1**				5					1 0					1 5			**1 8**											
Job I	L	L	L	L	L	L	D	D	D	D	M	M	M	M	M	M	M	M											
Job II	M	M	M	M	M	M	M	M	D	D	D	D	D	D															
JobIII	L	L	L	L	M	M	M	M	M	M	D	D	D	D	D	D	D	D											
JobIV	D	D	D	D	D	D	D	D	D	D	L	L	L	L	L	L	L	L											

b) There are conflicts, as are obvious using the colored coding of equipment. For example: at time 7 hrs. the drill is scheduled for Job I and Job IV, at time 6 hrs.the milling machine is scheduled to work on Job II and Job III, etc.

Problem #2:

Time (hrs)	**1**				5					1 0					1 5					2 0					2 5			**2 8**	
Job I	L	L	L	L	L	L					D	D	D	D			M	M	M	M	M	M	M	M					
Jəb II	M	M	M	M	M	M	M	M							D	D	D	D	D	D									
JobIII							L	L	L	L	M	M	M	M	M	M					D	D	D	D	D	D	D	D	
JobIV	D	D	D	D	D	D	D	D	D	D	L	L	L	L	L	L	L	L											

Note that conflicts are resolved. Job IV goes through the system without queuing or delay. All other jobs need to queue in between some of their processes.

Problem #3:

a) Perform the scheduling backwards from their due dates: there are conflicts on the lathe only.

T	**14**	15					20				25					30		**32**			35					40					45			**48**
I																	L	L	L	L	L	L	D	D	D	D	M	M	M	M	M	M	M	M
II					M	M	M	M	M	M	M	M	D	D	D	D	D	D																
III																	L	L	L	L	M	M	M	M	M	M	D	D	D	D	D	D	D	D
IV	D	D	D	D	D	D	D	D	D	D	L	L	L	L	L	L	L	L																

b) Perform the scheduling backwards from their due dates, making sure that each job is done exactly by its due date: there are no conflicts.

T	**14**	15					20				25					30		**32**			35					40					45			**48**
I					L	L	L	L	L	L													D	D	D	D	M	M	M	M	M	M	M	M
II					M	M	M	M	M	M	M	M	D	D	D	D	D	D																
III	L	L	L	L																	M	M	M	M	M	M	D	D	D	D	D	D	D	D
IV	D	D	D	D	D	D	D	D	D	D	L	L	L	L	L	L	L	L																

Problem #4:
Correct scheduling sequence: Job#2, #9, #3, #8, #7, #10, #4, #5, #6, and #1.
Use table format or a Gantt chart to schedule the jobs in this order.

Problem #5: a) 50 hours; b) correct sequence of jobs: C, D, E, A, and B; c) 45 hours

Problem #6: a) 0.8; b) 0.2; c) $(0.8)^n(0.2)$; d) 4; e) 1; f) 0.8

Problem #7: a) Correct sequence for SPT: D, E, B, A, and C; b) $CR_D = 2/16 = 0.125$

Problem #8:

Rule	Average Flow Time	Average Job Tardiness	# of Jobs Tardy	Average # of Jobs in System
First-come-first-served	54.8	10.6	7	6.09
Earliest due date	50.9	6	8	5.66
Shortest processing time	39.7	12.5	4	4.41
Critical ratio	50.9	6	8	5.66
Largest processing time	59.3	18.9	5	6.59

Chapter 13

Problem #1: a) 150; b) 25; c) 150

Problem #2:

Sample #	Ob served Weights				Sample Average
1	476	479	472	459	471.50
2	482	457	452	458	462.25
3	453	451	490	470	466.00
4	456	458	440	447	450.25
5	459	480	452	460	462.75
6	443	454	456	458	452.75
7	427	445	455	484	452.75
8	477	512	496	505	497.50
9	443	462	460	478	460.75
10	458	437	450	445	447.50
		Average of Sample Averages			462.40

standard deviation sample : 18.48464

standard deviation sample means: 9.242322

UCL :	490.127
LCL:	434.673

one average out of control

Problem # 3:

Sample #	Ob served Weights				Sample Average
1	476	479	472	459	471.50
2	482	457	452	458	462.25
3	453	451	490	470	466.00
4	456	458	440	447	450.25
5	459	480	452	460	462.75
6	443	454	456	458	452.75
7	427	445	455	484	452.75
9	443	462	460	478	460.75
10	458	437	450	445	447.50
		Average of Sample Averages			458.50

standard deviation sample: 14.30385

standard deviation sample mean: 7.151923

new UCL: 479.9558

new LCL: 437.0442

Problem #4:

new UCL: 479.9558
new LCL: 437.0442

Sample#	Observed Weights				Sample Average	
1	455	457	455	463	457.50	
2	447	449	435	437	442.00	
3	480	473	475	479	476.75	
4	454	457	467	447	456.25	
5	459	457	467	447	457.50	
6	434	425	427	435	430.25	out of control
7	471	473	474	480	474.50	
8	443	460	463	478	461.00	
9	457	493	461	460	467.75	
10	461	455	467	453	459.00	

Problem #5:

Sample #	# Defects	p	
1	0	0.00	
2	2	0.02	
3	3	0.03	
4	4	0.04	
5	1	0.01	
6	0	0.00	
7	0	0.00	
8	0	0.00	
9	0	0.00	
10	1	0.01	
	average p:	0.011	1.10%

UCL =	0.042291	
LCL=	-0.02029	:set at 0

Problem #6:

b) The following samples are out of control:

#2, #16, and #19

INDEX

CPSIA information can be obtained at www.ICGtesting.com
Printed in the USA
LVOW01s0343200815

450657LV00002B/2/P